For Bobbie —

With thanks for
your loving support
during a trying time
for both of us.

Harold
March 3, 2002

The Gold and the Blue

VOLUME ONE

CLARK KERR

THE GOLD
AND THE BLUE

A Personal Memoir of the University of California, 1949–1967

VOLUME ONE

Academic Triumphs

WITH A FOREWORD BY NEIL J. SMELSER

UNIVERSITY OF CALIFORNIA PRESS

BERKELEY · LOS ANGELES · LONDON

Frontispiece: Clark Kerr, chancellor, Berkeley campus, 1952–58; president, University of California, 1958–67. Photo: Jack Fields.

University of California Press
Berkeley and Los Angeles, California

University of California Press, Ltd.
London, England

Library of Congress Cataloging-in-Publication Data

Kerr, Clark, 1911–
    The gold and the blue : a personal memoir of the
University of California, 1949–1967 / Clark Kerr ;
with a foreword by Neil J. Smelser.
        p.   cm.
    Includes bibliographical references and index.
    Contents: v. 1. Academic triumphs
    ISBN 0-520-22367-5 (cloth : alk. paper : v. 1)
    1. Kerr, Clark, 1911–.   2. University of California,
Berkeley—Presidents—Biography.   3. University
of California—History.   I. Title.
LD755.K47 A3   2001
378.794'67—dc21   2001027243

Printed in Canada
09 08 07 06 05 04 03 02 01
10 9 8 7 6 5 4 3 2 1

The paper used in this publication meets the
minimum requirements of ANSI / NISO
Z39 0.48-1992(R 1997) (Permanence of Paper).♾

TO MY WIFE, KAY, who worked so hard and effectively to further the welfare of the University of California and that of our whole family and, at the same time, to "Save San Francisco Bay—now and forever."

TO THE ACADEMIC SENATE OF THE UNIVERSITY OF CALIFORNIA, which, for the past seventy-five years, has wielded such great influence over the most essential endeavors of the university and, with a few exceptions, has done so with high expectations matched by outstanding results.

TO THE BOARD OF REGENTS OF THE UNIVERSITY OF CALIFORNIA, which has the supreme authority over the University of California and, again with a few exceptions, has exercised that authority with devotion and wisdom.

The credit belongs to the man who is actually in the arena . . . that his place shall never be with those cold and timid souls who know neither defeat nor victory.

THEODORE ROOSEVELT

Contents

Part I. Introduction

Part II. The First Chancellor at Berkeley, 1952–58

Part III. The Presidency of the University: Overarching Issues, 1958–67

and a "Summit" · What the Master Plan Did · The Plan in Operation ·
Resources · *Process* · The Vision · The Master Plan Forty Years Later

Part IV. Nine Campuses

strength • *Other comparisons* • Rankings by Test Scores and by Persistence Rates • *A summary* • Conclusion • *The best tempered by the worst* • *Paradise lost: Is the view of gold coming to an end?* • Addendum: Excerpts from David S. Webster and Tad Skinner's Report on the University's Outstanding Rankings

Figures and Tables

Figures

Tables

Foreword

In the late 1960s, after I had been on the faculty of the University of California at Berkeley for about a decade, I posed a riddle to myself: How could my institution, beset with destructive conflict generated from without and within, ever have achieved its eminence and emulation in the world of higher education? This riddle has come back again and again to my mind ever since, and I have never been able to figure it out, even though I continued to deepen my knowledge of the institution over the years and conducted research on conflict in California higher education.

The appearance of Clark Kerr's two volumes of memoirs helps me greatly in struggling with this riddle and will help all other readers as well. Volume I, *Academic Triumphs,* deals mainly with the greatness, and Volume II, *Political Turmoil,* deals mainly with the conflict. Reading them together, moreover, reveals that the greatness and the conflict do not, as my riddle would have it, stand in contradiction to one another. Rather, they are two interlaced—perhaps even necessary—aspects of the single, remarkable institutional history of the University of California.

Clark Kerr stood at the center of both the greatness and the conflict. His years at the helm—from 1952 to 1958 as chancellor of the Berkeley campus and from 1958 to 1967 as the university's president—were the golden years. Berkeley rose to the peak of scientific and scholarly stature during this period, and the contours for the rise of the University of California system to its preeminent place were laid with the invention and consolidation of the 1960 California Master Plan for Higher Education. As the university's visionary, architect, leader, entrepreneur, fighter, and implementer in these years, Kerr established his deserved reputation as one of the century's great figures in higher education. These were also the years of greatest conflict. In 1952 Berkeley was reeling from the trauma of the loyalty oath controversy, and from 1964 through 1970 the entire university—Berkeley mainly, but the other campuses as well—was embroiled in conflicts arising from student activism, the Vietnam war, and Ronald Reagan's first term as governor of California. Kerr was always in the middle of these storms as well.

In these volumes Kerr tells his story of these years. He calls the works "personal memoirs," conveying that his is a partisan and therefore a partial view (p. xxx). This disclaimer on his part is fair enough, but it is too modest and therefore mistaken. To be accurate, we would have to say (in an ungainly phrasing) that his is simultaneously an intellectual, analytic, institutional, political, and autobiographical account of the university in those critical years, replete with more general observations and reflections. The reader will find all these aspects surfacing and resurfacing throughout the volumes.

In this foreword to the first volume, I will touch only three of the scores of possible dimensions these memoirs manifest—first, the historical situation Kerr faced at the University of California in the 1950s and 1960s; second, Kerr the leader and person; and third, Kerr the author of these volumes.

Before beginning, I might mention my own intersection with Kerr's years. I was recruited as a faculty member in the sociology department at Berkeley in 1958, the first year of Kerr's presidency. I was one of the 1,000 "new faculty appointments to tenure at Berkeley" between 1952 and 1963 (p. 62). (I suppose there was additional symbolism in my appointment because I was a "theft" from Harvard—Berkeley's greatest competitor in those years—which had offered me a similar position in the same year.) Between 1958 and 1964 I experienced, with great intellectual and personal excitement, the greatness of the golden age, both for sociology and for the Berkeley campus as a whole. In the troubled years of the 1960s I was drawn into the heart of turmoil, serving in 1965 as Acting Chancellor Martin Meyerson's main assistant for student political activities and in 1966–1968 as Chancellor Roger Heyns's Assistant Chancellor for Educational Development. After Kerr was dismissed as president in 1967, he asked me to join his Technical Advisory Committee for the Carnegie Commission on Higher Education, and I served as a member of that committee during its entire existence. Kerr did not know me well during his years of university leadership, but afterward we developed a friendship that has continued to the present.

The University in the Kerr Years

Readers of these pages will learn that ten years after World War II the University of California faced a situation it had never experienced before and will never experience again. The state's higher education apparatus, having been strained to accommodate the flood of World War II veterans, was about to be overwhelmed by the massive cohort produced by the baby boom that began in World War II as well as migration into the state. The system's existing facilities simply could not accommodate the numbers. This situation was made more extreme by the fact that California had long been committed to a mission of *mass* education, and it could not solve the problem by turning the clock back and admitting smaller proportions of the age cohort.

It was fortunate that the state was wealthy, enjoying a rapid rate of economic growth at the time, that the prospect of massive support for research from the federal government was coming into view in the 1950s, and that foundations would supplement the federal dollars. It was also fortunate that California's educators and politicians were proud of the state's educational system and were committed to a competitive, "we-want-to-be-number-one" mentality consistent with the state's fierce chauvinism. It was also true, however, that the state did not know much about how to expand its system of higher education, because it did not possess orderly institutional mechanisms to do so. In the 1950s a swelling chorus of voices from all regions of California clamored to establish, expand, and upgrade junior colleges and four-year colleges, and the state's traditional political means of responding to these voices through ad hoc legislative approvals or denials was being overwhelmed (Coons, 1968).

On an earlier occasion I tried to summarize this situation by saying that the impetus to growth in the 1950s was "overdetermined":

> By virtue of their commitment to the values of competitive excellence and egalitarianism, the leaders and citizens of the state *wanted* the system to grow; because of great demographic and economic pressures, it *had* to grow; because of the availability of substantial financial resources from many quarters, it *could* grow; and because the political forces regulating the growth were found, in the long run, in the state's representative bodies, the state was not very well equipped to *prevent* the system from growing (Smelser, 1974, p. 33).

So, at that time, the pressures to grow were powerful and irresistible. But to grasp that fact was only to begin to understand its implications. Whatever growth was to occur had to be realized in the context of the *inherited structure* of higher education in the state. The university was a constitutionally established entity; the state college system had a statutory base; the already vast system of community colleges had not yet formally joined the state's higher-education system, being tied to local school districts. The critical questions were where and how much to concentrate the growth in this array of institutions, and no systematic answers were available. At the level of the University of California itself, similar problems emerged. Here the central questions were also where to accommodate growth in the university and what structural changes might be necessary; no ready answers were available there, either. To aggravate matters, the entire structure of higher education was honeycombed with vested interests, all poised to fight for their share of the growth and prosperity.

Furthermore, because the segments of higher education stood in *systemic* relation to one another (and the same could be said for units within the university), changes could not be carried out piecemeal. Change in any part of the system would excite pressures to change (and political conflicts) throughout the system. To demonstrate this connection, let me take as a hypothetical and analytic starting point the decision to cap enrollment at the Berkeley and UCLA campuses. This is not so hypothetical, of course—it actually was done in 1960. I am using this action as a foil for demonstrating the "systemness" of the system. The decision was not without its paradoxes. For example, it seemed to fly in the face of the intense pressures to increase enrollment in the university. But for various reasons, Kerr and others felt it would not be wise to expand campus numbers, as the University of Minnesota, Ohio State University, and others were doing.

In all events, this capping action could not be taken without necessarily raising an immediate question: if not at Berkeley and UCLA, where would the new students be accommodated? By expanding units, by developing new campuses, or both? If new campuses, then how many and where?

A further question occurs immediately in considering expansion or addition: where would the resources come from? This question activated the relationship between the university and the state of California. Assuming resources were available and the requisite expansion was possible, another range of questions arises. What were the implications for academic programs and physical plant? Could the expanded or new units be accommodated in the existing system of governance, or was some new system required (the balance of centralization and decentralization of authority)? How could the academic quality of the expanding and new units be ensured? How could competition among them be managed? What would be the effect on university "communities" as they expanded or were created? How would new constituencies (faculty, students, and staff) in them fare and be accommodated? And in connection with all these questions a further, political query arises: what vested interests would want no change at all or changes different from those envisioned?

These are some of the systemic complications that arose for the university itself. It would be unrealistic to believe, moreover, that even if changes in all these areas could take place in an orderly way, the rest of higher education and the state would not be affected. The state college system was in a restless state and in high competition for expanding its base and upgrading its institutions to university status, and thus was poised to come into conflict with the university at every stage. The community colleges and the private institutions were also important political constituencies, though not quite so immediately preoccupied with the university. The fact that these constituencies were linked to the state's political system in various ways meant that the state's political apparatus was involved, too.

The bottom line was that the state's institutions of higher education had to grow and grow rapidly, and their structures had to be fundamentally rearranged. There was no necessarily right format for this growth and restructuring. Changes might generate leads and lags, meet stiff opposition, and create moans and groans throughout the system, but pervasive change was on the way.

Kerr the Leader and Kerr the Person

One of my purposes in developing the foregoing line of reasoning is to set the stage for understanding Kerr's leadership in engineering the headlong changes of the 1950s and the 1960s. Put in a nutshell, his leadership rested on a *combination* of personal qualities:

- He had an ability always to grasp the *big picture,* no matter what issue he was pursuing. We cannot know precisely where it came from, but his training in and research on economic systems must have helped. That ability certainly appears in the pages of these volumes. Whenever Kerr casts his analytic net and lists the six (or five, or eight) historical trends or forces at work in a given situation, we can rest assured that his diagnosis has nailed down the main ones and that other factors are secondary. We also see his capacity for embracing the large context in his work on the dynamics of industrial societies (Kerr et al., 1964; Kerr, 1983) and in his enormously influential work on higher education developed in the Godkin lectures (Kerr, 1963).

- Kerr's talent for grasping the big picture served him well in comprehending the "systemness" of California higher education to which I referred. True, he was involved in some immediate and transparent situations that sensitized him to the need for changes. His poignant account of how hemmed in and powerless he found himself in the first days of the Berkeley chancellorship (pp. 39–55) certainly alerted him in a dramatic way to the issue of decentralization. But his gaze constantly went beyond his own situation and scanned the broader horizon. Readers who turn to the table of contents of *Academic Triumphs* will discover that the chapter headings correspond almost point by point to all the interrelated structures mentioned above. Those structures were where the action was in Kerr's years, and where he was most active.

· He had the ability to translate his grasp of the big picture into a *vision.* Most scholars cannot or do not take this step. Kerr, identified with and loyal to the University of California, was able to conceive—not always in a completely conscious way, no doubt—a view of the future and the general directions that had to be followed to move toward that vision. In Kerr's case the vision was a timely one for the culture of California—a university that would simultaneously lead the world in quality and serve the people of California as a mass institution with full opportunities for qualified students.

· He had the further ability to ground his understanding and vision in the *realities of social, political, and economic life.* He combined pragmatism with his idealism, and he could discern, in concrete ways, organizational and structural scenarios necessary to realize ambitious goals. No doubt he was helped in this capacity by his work in labor economics, which calls for, above all, an understanding of the institutional embeddedness of work and markets. Kerr also understood the fundamental messiness of institutions—their imperfections as well as the nonrationalities and irrationalities of those who inhabit them—despite his unwavering, self-professed philosophy of rational optimism and trust in others.

· He possessed an exceptional power to *persuade and influence,* augmented by his open, modest personal style, which gave no hint of calculation or manipulation. We cannot know the origins of this power either, but it is consistent with the style of conflict solving that his Quakerism embraces and certainly consistent with his experience in labor mediation and arbitration. His ability to influence was a great asset for him in the world of academic administrators and faculty, where consensus building through persuasion—not the straightforward exercise of power and authority—is the name of the institutional game. It was also evident in Kerr's participation in the loyalty oath controversy, in which he played a conciliatory role that brought him—at a very young age— to the attention of those who were seeking leaders for the campus. Perhaps the most dramatic example of his powers of persuasion appeared in the design of the Master Plan, in which he played a pivotal role. This plan was fashioned, in the first instance, as a political strategy to contain the unbridled forces of competition among the various segments of higher education. At the same time it turned out to be an institutional coup, containing something for all parties and gaining full consensus, as well as a singularly stable institutional framework for the system's future growth.

I experienced Kerr's power to influence in a couple of minor ways. When I was a member of the Technical Advisory Committee of his Carnegie Commission, he would occasionally ask me to join him for a few minutes after a meeting of the committee. We would talk about matters facing the commission, and he would seek my advice on various projects he had in mind. On these occasions I would usually spend the following few days becoming aware of and counting up exactly how many things I had promised to do for him—without realizing it—in those meetings. Clark also asked me to write the introduction to these memoirs after he had finished them. In this case, no persuasion was necessary, because I was honored to be asked. But by the time he got around to asking the question, my full agreement, if conceivably in doubt, was completely in the bag.

· He possessed a unique *dedication, energy, and doggedness.* No doubt the early influence of Franklinian Protestantism, with its compulsive and never-realized pursuit of perfection, must have had its impact. These characteristics were what made Kerr into a determined fighter for his goals, even though he always fought in a nonfighting manner.

Not many people in this world possess this mix of characteristics, and of those who do, very few confront unique historical situations that demand them in the way that the situation of the University of California made demands on Kerr in the 1950s and 1960s. It was that mix, matched with those times, that assured Kerr a unique leadership position and helped the university evolve— in the complex, multifaceted way that it did—into the institution it became.

Kerr the Author

In these volumes Kerr gives us his own story of himself and his historical circumstances. It is certainly a service to the world that he has done so, because no one else could offer his perspective and these accounts.

He acknowledges that there will be other accounts, and many of them will be counteraccounts developed in response to his. There is a certain necessity about all this. Any era that is simultaneously as dynamic, as glorious, as conflict-ridden, and as traumatic as the 1950s and 1960s were will have many rememberers. Moreover, their diverse memories will be or will become matters of contestation. In fact, the memories of such eras constitute not only a microcosm of different perspectives embraced at the time the events occurred but also a reflection of how subsequent generations *want* to remember them. Because Kerr was at the center of things during that era, his own accounts and memories assume a valence that is all the greater, and his memories will be a special object of interest for all other rememberers, both sympathetic and unsympathetic.

Those who read these memoirs will notice that Kerr has a distinct expository style. He speaks in short, direct, declarative sentences. The style is almost telegraphic at times. Readers should not be misled by his style, which is deceptive in its simplicity. It should not obscure either the depth or subtlety of his grasp of his times or the profundity of his analyses and interpretations. Kerr the scholar is always present in these pages, and scholars will return to them repeatedly in the future, whether to learn from them or to contest them.

One of the most striking features of Kerr's story is his power of objectification. By this I mean his ability to step back from the events and situations in which he was a principal—and often controversial—actor and to describe and interpret them with a remove and dispassion that are almost incredible. This power permitted Kerr to develop, for example, a balanced and believable account of his greatest institutional lament—the failure of the Santa Cruz campus to live up to its promise and design. It also permitted him to shed light on the complex history of the Berkeley campus, which was perhaps the object of his greatest love but also of his greatest disappointments.

To be sure, an elapse of time does give one the power to distance oneself from events. Nevertheless, we must wonder how many institutional leaders, when in the trenches of social change—many aspects of which they themselves are engineering—can maintain the kind of distance we observe in Kerr's accounts? Perhaps more aptly, we must ask how many people who have been severely scapegoated—as Kerr was continually, from both the left and the right—can produce an intelligible account of the causes and dynamics of that scapegoating process, even with the passage of time? In reading these memoirs *in toto* before writing this foreword, I found this aspect of Kerr's mind and style to be the most intriguing.

One of the by-products of the capacity for objectification is self-objectification—the power to develop a sense of self-criticism. In many places in his memoirs Kerr grades himself harshly and frankly acknowledges grave mistakes that had serious negative consequences. At the same time, he sometimes criticizes the mistakes, unguided or misguided behavior, and wrongdoings of others—Robert Gordon Sproul, James Corley, Franklin Murphy, the radical left, the Reagan right—though he is careful to balance these criticisms with positive assessments, and he scrupulously avoids *ad hominem* attacks. Probably no single interested reader of these memoirs will agree completely with Kerr's balance of identifying problems and assigning responsibility. But to find such a balance in any person's memoirs is rare.

A Note in Conclusion

In these memoirs we find both vintage Clark Kerr and a great deal of what we have not seen before. The vintage Kerr is the social scientist, the analyst, the comprehender of macroscopic institutions and social change, and the master interpreter of them. What is new is of a more personal nature. We learn much about the parts of his background that are important to him, his working philosophy, and his personal assessment of and reactions to many who acted with him on the same stage during his eventful career. In addition, we are able to see coming through the down-to-earth, unassuming prose, the deeper feelings as well—his hopes and ambitions, his disappointments, his nostalgia, his regrets, and his pride in things accomplished.

Neil J. Smelser
Center for Advanced Study in the Behavioral Sciences

REFERENCES TO THE FOREWORD

Coons, Arthur. 1968. *Crises in California Higher Education.* Los Angeles: Ward Ritchie Press.

Kerr, Clark. 1963. *The Uses of the University.* Cambridge. Mass.: Harvard University Press.

Kerr, Clark. 1983. *Industrialism and Industrial Man: Convergence or Continuing Diversity?* Cambridge, Mass.: Harvard University Press.

Kerr, Clark, John T. Dunlop, Frederick Harbison, and Charles A. Meyers. 1964. *Industrialism and Industrial Man: The Problems of Labor and Management in Economic Growth.* New York: Oxford University Press.

Smelser, Neil J. 1974. "Growth, Structural Change, and Conflict in California Public Higher Education," in Gabriel Almond and Neil J. Smelser (eds.), *Public Higher Education in California.* Berkeley and Los Angeles: University of California Press. Pp. 9–141.

Preface

Gold and blue are the colors of the University of California. The gold is the gold in California's hills and the golden color of those hills in summer. The gold also represents the wealth created in the valleys and the cities of California that made possible the development of a great public university on the West Coast that became the greatest state university system in the United States. The blue is the blue of Yale. Yale alumni initiated the university. Yale blue also represents the long history of evolution of universities in the western world since 1100 when the University of Bologna began. The University of California has inherited that long tradition and built upon it. Gold and blue, blue and gold: in another sense the blue stands for the difficulties and the gold for the triumphs in building this system to its present levels of distinction.

The university's academic and administrative affairs make up its "private" life; the internal and external political contexts that condition so much of its environment are the university's "public" life. The two are generally separate. The private life unfolds largely in silence and most directly affects members of the university community. The public life takes place in the open, through the media, and also involves interested persons among the general citizenry. This public life is the primary view of the university by the outside audiences.

These two lives are mostly subject to their separate sources of initiation, their disparate casts of characters, their divergent paces of development, their distinctive internal dynamics, their contrary sets of motives—during the 1950s and 1960s, for example, the inquiries of the California legislative Committee on Un-American Activities were hardly noticed internally. But the two lives are to varying degrees intertwined—most intimately in the loyalty oath controversy after World War II, the student revolts of the mid-1960s, and the intervention of Governor Ronald Reagan in the late 1960s.

The private life has been mostly calm, measured, and based on reason. The public life, on the contrary, has been often turbulent, disjointed, and based on passion and ignorance. The big mystery has been this:

xxix

How could the University of California be so much more successful in its private life of academic accomplishments than most other research universities while, comparatively, so much more tossed and tortured in its public life? How did it avoid being destroyed?

∎

To recount my part in each of these partially self-contained worlds, I separate my memoirs into two volumes. The first, *Academic Triumphs,* is mostly concerned with the private life of the University of California, which has been one of the centers of my life for over sixty-five years. By way of introduction to part I, chapter 1 sets out how I came to know Berkeley as a graduate student and young faculty member. Chapter 2 is a retrospective on Robert Gordon Sproul, president of the university from 1930 to 1958, and the administrative structure he had created by 1952, when I became the first chancellor at Berkeley. Chapters 3 through 10 form part II, relating to my years as chancellor. The book's part III takes up the years of my presidency of the university, which in 1958 had six campuses and, by 1967, had nine.

The second volume, *Political Turmoil,* covers the political contexts, both external and internal, of my years as chancellor and president within which the university had to function, from the oath controversy through the student revolts to the reaction of the Reagan administration. This book ends in 1967, when my presidency of the university ended.

I identify the memoirs as "personal"—even very personal. They are not a formal record of these years. They are, rather, my perceptions, as a participant and observer, of what was going on. I saw some, but not all, of what was happening, and what I saw was from the point of view of an interested partisan.

I write these memoirs for the possible interest of those fellow participants in the great transformation in the University of California's life from 1952 to 1967—faculty members, staff members, alumni—who may still be interested in the development of that history of which they were a part. I also write for current faculty, staff members, and alumni, and for those students who may be curious about what went before. I realize, of course, that the 1950s are as long ago now as the 1910s were when I became chancellor. At that time I had only some idle curiosity about Benjamin Ide Wheeler's presidency as a crucial background to the 1950s. Ancient history! The 1950s are only yesterday for me, but ancient history for the students of the 1990s.

As I record my perceptions of one period in the life of a single institution, I hope also to contribute to the broader history of higher education in the United States during the years 1950–70. What was happening in California was also happening to American higher education generally, but often sooner and more dramatically here. The University of California has been and is today an avant-garde segment of the larger national entity. To look at the University of California is to look at some aspects of the nationwide transformation writ large.

In order to provide some information on what was happening inside the university and within the larger context, I have included a number of tables, charts, and appendices. These in no way set forth a complete picture of the University of California or of higher education during the years in question, but they do reproduce information and pull together relevant data that are not now readily available elsewhere.

I also write these memoirs as a devoted University of California faculty member of more than fifty years' duration who was, once upon a time, otherwise engaged.

What follows, then, is an insider's account of how Berkeley and the whole University of California responded to the McCarthy period of political life in the United States, to changing labor markets, to the advanced role of research on campus energized by the Cold War and the influx of federal dollars, to the oncoming tidal wave of students requiring new academic and physical plans, to the student revolts of the mid-1960s, and, perhaps above all, to the need for new visions of the future. The results were both turmoil and triumph.

■

These two volumes each have an appended list of acknowledgments of persons who so kindly helped search for information, who granted interviews, and who read parts of the manuscripts. Here I would like to acknowledge only my greatest debts of gratitude:

> To the University of California Press, which accepted these manuscripts for publication and particularly to its director, James Clark, for his encouragement and good advice; and to the project editor and copyeditor, Suzanne Knott and Edith Gladstone.

> To Maureen Kawaoka, my incomparably skilled and devoted secretary and administrative assistant, who has managed all of my many manuscripts for

over thirty years. She has taken my chicken-feet scratches in the barnyard dust and turned them into readable prose, as an alchemist turns lead into something of greater value, with patience and a sixth sense that passeth all understanding. Eric Ashby, then vice-chancellor of Cambridge University, once wrote to me that my handwriting looked to him like the recording of a seismograph tracking a minor earthquake in a far corner of the planet.

To Marian Gade, my research associate and occasional coauthor, also for over thirty years, who has pulled together documentation and statistical data, edited my prose, corrected my errors, and added to my understanding with her comments, all with endurance and goodwill and intellectual talent that no one else in my long experience could have matched. In the course of this, she has become, in her own right, an authority on American higher education sought after and admired around the nation and around the world. She has accepted my endless requests for information with the calm of a Stoic and the understanding of a Swarthmore honors student, as she once was.

To Sangwan Zimmerman, who assisted Marian Gade for seven years, surviving the frustrations of searching for so many items that could not be found, who charmed so many keepers of records to uncover items they did not even know they had, and who, along the way, found some gems I did not know existed.

To William M. Roberts, the archivist of the University of California, Berkeley, who provided exceptional, irreplaceable aid to me and my staff over a period of years. Bill retrieved documents, often obscure, from at least fifty different archive collections, covering issues and events in university and Berkeley campus history from the 1940s to the 1970s. His knowledge of the collections, where guides are sometimes incomplete, is legendary, and his ability to appear suddenly with just the right document in his hands was uncanny. Throughout, he responded with a constant spirit of friendly cooperation and real interest in the project.

These two volumes do not stand alone. The Institute of Governmental Studies (IGS) at Berkeley will be publishing a combined supplement of documents to inform and expand the text of each volume (referred to by IGS Documentary Supplement + number and listed in Appendix 4 of each volume). The IGS is also publishing a series of essays that I initiated, the Clark Kerr

Memoirs Project. Each of these essays will go beyond my own knowledge to set forth an important aspect of University of California history. The first is by Angus Taylor, formerly vice president–academic affairs for the University of California and chair of the universitywide Academic Council of the Academic Senate, and has already been published. It is entitled *The Academic Senate of the University of California: Its Role in the Shared Governance and Operation of the University of California.*

The other tentatively titled essays associated with this volume will be "An Abridged History of the University of California, 1868–1952," by Verne Stadtman; "The Physical Evolution of the Berkeley Campus, 1868–1956," by Sally Woodbridge; "Strengthening Letters and Science at Berkeley," by Lincoln Constance; "Strengthening Engineering at Berkeley," by John Whinnery; "A Place for the Arts on Campus," by Travis Bogard, Betty Connors, Jacquelynn Baas, Robert W. Cole, and David Littlejohn; and "Budget Policies and Their Reform at UC" and "Decentralization of Administrative and Business Affairs at the University of California," by Loren Furtado; "The Rise and Demise of the UCSC Colleges," by Carlos G. Noreña; and "A Global Campus: The University of California's Education Abroad Program," by William Allaway

Now that the University of California has advanced to a position of leadership in the intellectual world, it deserves more attention to its history. This neglect, fortunately, is being corrected by the efforts of Carroll Brentano and her associates in publishing a new periodical, *The Chronicle of the University of California.* In addition, the recently published series "Chapters in the History of the University of California" has helped fill in some of the blanks.[1]

PART I

Introduction

Getting to Know Berkeley

My first visual contact with Berkeley was the sight of the Campanile looming up at the end of Telegraph Avenue. The Campanile remains my favorite view off and on the campus, and I was so fortunate that the window of my office, many years later when I became president of the university, looked straight at it with the Big C beyond on the Berkeley hills.[1]

It was the fall of 1932. I had driven the 40 miles north from Stanford across the Dumbarton Bridge and past the tomato fields and canneries of southern Alameda County, then almost entirely rural. I was driving my 1928 Model A Ford—a convertible coupe—on my way to International House to visit a friend. There I made my first contact with life at Berkeley.

My friend and I were having a snack in the coffee shop when in burst a small mob of people shaking their fists and screaming slogans. We were asked to join the mob. We refused. It was led by a red-haired young man of great dynamism—Lou Goldblatt. I later came to know Lou well when, as Impartial Chairman for the West Coast Waterfront, I arbitrated disputes between the International Long-shoremen's and Warehousemen's Union (ILWU) of Harry Bridges and the Waterfront Employers' Association of Frank Foisie; Lou was vice president of the ILWU. I last saw Lou at a reception in San Francisco in the 1970s. I had met Harry Bridges at the door and—forgetting for a moment that the two had parted company—asked him whether Lou was there. He pointed across the room and said, "There he is—that Maoist." When the Bancroft Library needed an introduction to Lou's oral history (others being hesitant to be associated with him), I wrote one, noting our profound political disagreements but acknowledging him as an important figure in the history of the West Coast and Hawaii—one of many Berkeley graduates who became important figures in many ways in many parts of the world.

So my first two impressions were of the physical beauty of Berkeley centering on the Campanile and of its avant-garde political ambience—the former has always been one of the great pleasures of my life and the latter, from time to time, one of the sources of greatest challenge.

■

How I Got Started at Berkeley

In the fall of 1932 I had enrolled as a graduate student at Stanford on the spur of the moment; I had been in California that summer as a "peace caravaner" for the American Friends Service Committee (the AFSC, the Quaker service organization). We were advocating before church groups and businessmen's luncheon clubs for the United States to join the League of Nations and the World Court in those fiercely isolationist days. I was planning to enter Columbia Law School that fall but had a few free days before I needed to start back East. So I took a fling at entering Stanford for one year before Columbia. I went to the registration line with my college transcript from Swarthmore College in my hand. I had never submitted an application. When I reached the head of the line, I was referred to the registrar sitting under an oak tree. He looked at my Swarthmore transcript, and I was accepted on the spot.

I stayed the year at Stanford but soon decided to go on to Berkeley. First, because my major professor (Clair Wilcox) at Swarthmore had immediately replied to my note telling him where I had ended up. I was making, he wrote, a terrible mistake; if I were foolish enough to be in California at all, I should transfer as quickly as possible to Berkeley, which was much the better university. Second, because I had become interested in the self-help cooperatives of the unemployed and wanted to write a thesis about them. My faculty friends at Stanford were politely supportive but not really interested. They had read about unemployment but none of them had ever met an unemployed person and, according to the economic textbooks of that day, unemployment was in any event bound to cure itself. I heard that a professor at Berkeley was interested in my topic and was out in the field on his own investigations. I went to see him and he offered me a research assistantship at $400 per year. This led to my third great impression of Berkeley. I quickly discovered that Berkeley was much more a part of the real world than Stanford then was.

Paul Taylor, my professor at Berkeley, was a great expert on farm labor. I had barely registered for my seminars when the cotton pickers' strike of 1933 in the San Joaquin Valley broke out. It was the biggest and bloodiest rural strike in American history. Taylor sent me out into the field to talk with farmers, sheriffs, strikers. Here was life in the raw as I had never seen it. There had been vigilante massacres in Pixley and Arvin at the southern end of the great valley. Strikers were living on the banks of irrigation ditches that were both sources of water and receptacles of sewage. There was hunger. There was violence as strikers entered the fields with sticks and stones to drive out nonstrikers. There was hatred, not only between strikers and farmers but among the strikers: between the "Okies," led by their politically conservative lay preachers, and the "Mexicans," led by Communist Party officials. It was a long way from the peaceful Oley Valley in eastern Pennsylvania where I had been raised on a family farm. A long way also from the Quaker atmosphere of Swarthmore. And a long way from the isolation of the Stanford campus. A great big dose of reality.

Through Paul Taylor I met his second wife, Dorothea Lange, the acclaimed photographer.[2] Paul wrote about and Dorothea took pictures of America during the Great Depression that will stand forever as records of that tragic time. To be in the fields with Paul was a wonderful experience for a young graduate student at Berkeley. And through Paul I first got to know the formidable economics professor Ira B. ("Doc") Cross. Doc was one of the great lecturers in Berkeley history. Every undergraduate knew him or knew about him. He fell in rank just below Henry Morse Stephens (1900 to 1919) in modern European history and Charles Mills Gayley (1889 to 1923), who lectured on Shakespeare in the Hearst Greek Theatre. Doc held forth in Wheeler Auditorium, and with total discipline—"What is it that the male student in the twelfth row, three seats in from the aisle, finds so much more interesting in the *Daily Cal* than my lecture? Please stand up and tell us."

Doc was an iconoclast and had many prejudices—all held with absolute assurance. One was that married graduate students were not serious scholars, a waste of his time. He would never have one as a teaching assistant—never! But once he did. One afternoon just as the term was under way, I heard someone pounding up the steps to the small upstairs apartment my wife, Kay, and I had in an old house on College Avenue. Then came a heavy knocking on the door. I opened it. There was the legendary Doc. He said, "If I am willing to forget my principles, I expect you to forget that I did not ask you earlier. My course is oversubscribed. I need another T.A. I expect you to be there tomorrow morning." And so I was. Shortly he gave me about my only and certainly my best advice on teaching. The economics department then had a "bullpen" on the first floor of South Hall. All the professors were there for an hour or two after lunch each day seeing students and one another. Doc saw me come in the door and yelled at me, attracting the attention of all in the room: "Speak up, Kerr, speak up—the girls in your classes tell me they have to hug you to hear you!"

Cross had once been known as the Stormy Petrel of the Berkeley City Council and of the Academic Senate. He had calmed down somewhat and now gave seminars for San Francisco bankers. One day, Paul Taylor and I were working over a manuscript at the table in Paul's kitchen. In came Doc. He had in his hand a copy of a populist weekly (*The Guardian* from someplace in Oklahoma). He read a column about a farmyard and how twice a year, when the wild geese flew overhead on their migrations, the fat tame geese on the farm below would try their wings unsuccessfully a few times and return some feeble cries, as the wild geese above flew freely overhead, proud and undaunted. Then Doc walked out. He had become a tame goose and he knew it; Paul and I were still flying freely in the air.

Doc later took very good care of me. He gave me the Newton Booth Fellowship, which the economics department conferred each year on a chosen student. Later he gave me his precious card file of set jokes for use in my classes, but his style and mine were too different. Later still, after I became chancellor, he passed on to me his academic gown, just as President Sproul some years later gave me his presidential gown to wear. I felt greatly honored on each occasion.

Doc was not a great scholar but he was a great character. Berkeley now has many more great scholars than then but many fewer great characters.

How I Got Committed to Industrial Relations

As World War II was coming to an end, Governor Earl Warren (Berkeley class of 1912) was worried about disruptions in labor relations resuming from the turbulent thirties. He proposed, and the university accepted, the idea of an Institute of Industrial Relations to work with both industry and labor and to make studies in the area. Dean E. T. ("Greth") Grether, on behalf of the School of Business Administration and the Department of Economics (for I was given a joint appointment), asked me to be the first director. I was then at the University of Washington. The University of California at Berkeley in those days preferred Ph.D.'s from other universities (no "in-breeding"). As graduate students we had all come to know that policy, and to respect it. Kay and I would drive around the Berkeley hills looking at the houses and the views—our favorite views came when the morning fogs were rising through and above the eucalyptus trees—but knowing how unlikely it was that we would ever be back. I even thought that perhaps I could get a job in the "City" (as San Francisco is known in the Bay Area) and perhaps teach an occasional course in University Extension—we might possibly get that close to our Shangri-la. Then came Greth's unexpected letter. It was an impossible dream come true.

My fourth impression of Berkeley was of a great postwar door to opportunity. The GIs came flooding in and enrollment jumped by nearly 50 percent—25,000 instead of the pre-war 15,000.[3] Less interested in "liberal education" than in professional courses—business administration and engineering—they sat in the aisles of our classes and stood along the walls. They were the best students we ever had, and that made us better teachers. My big lecture course was in labor economics and held in 101 California Hall—then an amphitheater holding (nominally) 400 students. My topic was a hot one in the daily headlines, and the College of Letters and Science had made my course one of the select ones to fulfill its breadth requirements. So I had a full house, including standees. Among other things, I brought in guest lecturers from industry and labor to present their views directly. The students were tough in their questions, and industry leaders would tell me how anti-industry they were and labor leaders how anti-labor. I would tell them both that the students had sharp, inquiring minds and were fearless in asking questions even in such a large class. And they were.

One of those outside lecturers was Boris Shiskin, the nationwide research director for the AFL-CIO. I would leave the back doors into the amphitheater open to let fresh air circulate to all those students, and a whole pack of the many campus dogs shared the platform with me. They were all very well behaved. Except once. The AFL-CIO speaker was attacking the National Association of Manufacturers (NAM). After one very critical comment, one of the dogs let out a loud yelp and tore up the stairs and out of the upper entrance and the others, also yelping, all followed him. The speaker turned to me and said, "Professor, you did not tell me your class had so many representatives of the NAM!" The students applauded wildly.

The GIs

The GIs who came back from the military were far more mature than earlier students, more determined to get their degrees and to start making their ways in the world (and they had no taste for supervision in *loco parentis*). Some had already taken more life-and-death responsibility than the average professor would in a whole career. They were a joy to teach. Even to grade. One student, on a one-question exam that asked what he would do if faced with a very difficult problem, simply wrote, "Hire Professor Kerr as my consultant and do exactly as he told me." He turned in his blue book and, smiling smugly, left the room. He must have made millions later in life.

The GIs were also the wave of the future. The land-grant universities created after the Civil War (UC being one—1868) had welcomed the children of farmers. The GI Bill of Rights welcomed everyone regardless of family background or race. And many came. We were moving toward universal access. Later, when I was involved in developing the Master Plan for Higher Education in California, I thought back to the GIs' arrival and hoped for such opportunity always. California became the first state in the nation and the first political entity in the world to guarantee access to higher education to all qualified persons, which meant all high school graduates.

The Loyalty Oath

The other great postwar development, beyond the avalanche of GIs, was the oath controversy. This demonstrated another outstanding aspect of Berkeley—a proud faculty protective of its rights. Here was my fifth great experience in getting to know Berkeley. U.S. Senator Joseph McCarthy was dominating the headlines and the air waves. There was fear among intellectuals across the nation. Into this atmosphere was introduced the loyalty oath, proposed most specifically by U.C. president Robert Gordon Sproul, in part as an answer to problems in Sacramento in the 1949 session of the legislature but without prior consultation with the Academic Senate. The regents adopted the proposal initially with some hesitation and never with the full consent of all the regents (one of its opponents was Governor Earl Warren, a Berkeley graduate). The faculty slowly rose in what became increasing opposition.

The issue was never only communism, much as it may have appeared that way to some in the public. What was really at issue was that the regents seemed to identify the members of the university faculty as particularly suspect among all citizens in the state. Faculty members had already signed, without objection, an oath of allegiance to the Constitution. Why should they also have to sign a special political oath denying any Communist beliefs or affiliations? Why was the Academic Senate not consulted in advance? Berkeley had then, and still has, the most powerful senate among all American universities, largely as the result of the "revolution" of 1919–20 led, among others, by the then young Joel Hildebrand of great subsequent scholarly fame.

I saw the oath battle at firsthand. As a young faculty member, I served as a member of the Committee of Five selected at one point to lead the opposition to the oath (I was myself a signer, as were over 95 percent of the faculty). I subsequently served as a member of the Committee on Privilege and Tenure in trying to carry out a compromise accepted by the regents that those who refused to sign could go before the Committee on Privilege and Tenure as an alternative. With my Quaker background, I was particularly sympathetic to reasons of conscience for not signing an oath, and particularly a political oath. But a majority of regents, after having agreed to this alternative, then rejected our report on August 25, 1950, and fired *all* the nonsigners—even those whom the committee had "cleared"—thirty-one in total! I thought this was a terrible breach of faith. In the end, however, the State Supreme Court declared the special oath null and void; the nonsigners were subsequently invited back, and a few accepted. Later a Berkeley faculty committee nominated me to become the first chancellor in the history of the campus, mostly because of my role in the loyalty oath controversy, which was the only way they then knew me. The wounds were healing—the regents accepted the nomination.

■

These are some of the ways that I got to know and develop great affection for and devotion to the Berkeley campus—as a place of great beauty, of an avant-garde political ambience, of active participation in the life of society, of opportunity for the GIs to advance on ability and motivation into positions of leadership in the American community, of a faculty marked by pride and high spirit.

My Life before Berkeley

While most of my professional life has been centered on Berkeley and the University of California, my interests and convictions were well established before I came to Berkeley as a graduate student in the fall of 1933. These interests and convictions have had major impacts on my subsequent conduct.

HARD WORK AND A CARING COMMUNITY

I was born into a hard-working family. My father was a combination school-teacher and farmer. Our first farm was a 3-acre piece of land on a hillside near the village of Stony Creek on the outskirts of the city of Reading, Pennsylvania. We raised fruits, grapes, berries, and vegetables, and we had a henhouse with about 100 chickens. The products were for our own use and, in addition, my father would take some items in a big basket by trolley car to a general store in Reading, where he was given credit that applied against what he bought there. He also taught in Reading High School—Latin, mathematics, and history. My mother made all the clothes for my three sisters and for me. She also did a lot of canning and baked our bread. I remember no times when we children had no chores to do, beginning at age three or four with cleaning eggs for market—a messy job.

When I was ten years old, we moved to a 140-acre farm in the nearby Oley Valley, which was on the same trolley car line as Stony Creek. This was a general-purpose farm with horses, sheep, cows, hogs, chickens, ducks, geese, guinea hens, two apple orchards, a long meadow on a creek, and a big barn. It was a four- to five-horse farm. I had my own team of horses when I was fourteen, and they were my best friends—Maud and Kate. We were at least half self-sufficient on that farm with much of the rest of our needs met by the local community—a grist mill to grind our corn, wheat, and oats; a big cider press; a neighbor who helped us turn our hogs into many useful products— a highly specialized skill. We had our own wood lot and did our cooking and heated the two central rooms of our house (the kitchen and the dining room) with an old-fashioned Majestic wood-burning stove. One of my tasks was to collect, saw, split, and then pile on the back porch enough wood each summer and fall to see us through the winter. My many chores took me home from school each afternoon with no time for sports or other activities and kept me busy on Saturdays and most of Sundays, and all holidays; and no vacations. There was no time for "lives of idleness." My father quoted to me a thousand times or more these proverbs:

Hard work never hurt anyone.

One thing at a time,
and that done well,
is a very good rule,
as many can tell.

Early to bed
and early to rise
makes a man
healthy, wealthy, and wise.

Work was at the constant center of our lives. All my life I have asked nightly as I go to bed, "What did I accomplish today?" And I remind myself, "Lost time is never found again." *Poor Richard's Almanac* of Benjamin Franklin and the Bible were our chief guides to lifestyle.

Another lesson learned from rural life in Pennsylvania was the importance of concern for the welfare of others, of helping others when they needed it— when a horse had run away, when a spouse had died, when a child was sick. The whole valley went quiet when the church bell tolled a few times, then began to count the years someone had lived: seventy-one meant old Mr. Knab's wife; one meant Leah Yoder's little baby. And women would start cooking food to take, and men would offer to care for the place for a few days.

EDUCATION

Both my father and my mother were committed to education. My paternal grandfather was a farmer who had been elected superintendent of schools for Perry County, Pennsylvania, in an eastern ridge of the Appalachian mountains, just west of the Susquehanna River. An earlier ancestor had come from the borders of Scotland where chiefs of the family of Norwegian ancestry (Kjarr or Kjaerr) had served as wardens of the Middle Marches. He had arrived in the Cumberland Valley in 1759 and seven years later, after the Indian Wars (1763–65), had crossed the mountains into Perry County with his wife (her family name was Harbison), one horse, one cow, and three sheep. By 1780 they had two horses, six cows, and 50 acres, according to the county assessors' records.

My father's generation consisted of six children. The two eldest went to Shippensburg Normal School (now University). They then became teachers and helped finance the younger children in their higher education. My father, Samuel William, thus graduated from Franklin and Marshall College. The youngest, Mina, later obtained a Ph.D. from the University of Pennsylvania and eventually became the executive secretary of the American Association of University Women (AAUW). My father founded the Reading Classical School before public high schools concentrated on college preparatory instruction. When the local high school took on such instruction, the Classical School failed and he transferred to Reading High School, where he taught for many years.

While he was still head of the Reading Classical School, my father met my mother, who was working as a milliner for one of the local department stores. She made fancy hats with flowers on order for local women. She would sit in a front window of Whitners on Penn Street, making these hats for customers, and people would stop and watch and some would then enter the store. Apparently she was quite expert and had traveled at least as far west as Milwaukee displaying her talents. She came from an English background (her family name was Clark). The family had first settled in Connecticut and then in the area around Wilkes-Barre, Pennsylvania. Her father and mother ran a country store in the small town of Beaumont as well as a hillside farm behind the store, with a horse and a cow.

My mother had only a sixth-grade education, but she was determined that her children would go to college. She refused to marry my father until she had saved enough money to be able to send any daughter or son of hers to college. As a result, my three sisters went to Oberlin and I to Swarthmore. Mother's best friend in our neighborhood was the local schoolteacher, Miss Elba. The school was the traditional one-room brick schoolhouse at the end of a lane leading up the side of Mt. Penn and covered by a canopy of trees that admitted no sunlight—scary to a child and thus given the name Spook Lane. Miss Elba taught us from the final edition of McGuffy's Readers—the best textbooks ever. It was hard not to skip the fifth grade, because by that time we had already sat there listening to that year's assignments four times over. Miss Elba tried to teach me the Palmer method of writing. I rebelled and went back to the scribble my mother had already taught me (and which I inflicted on others and myself all my life). Miss Elba would tell me, "Unless you learn to write (the Palmer method), you will never amount to anything."

My father recommended four colleges to me: Oberlin (but my two older sisters were going there and I did not want to continue under their supervision as I had been since our mother died), Rollins College in Florida (too far away), Antioch (then being renovated by Arthur Morgan), and Swarthmore. Swarthmore was nearest, and President Frank Aydelotte's "honors" plan attracted me.

Swarthmore College, which I entered in the fall of 1928, was the greatest transformational experience of my life. It was so beautiful—even more now, because of the inspired care of the Scott Arboretum. It was small, so I could participate in all those activities I had missed in high school without being very good at any of them—sports (soccer, basketball, track), the weekly newspaper (Jim Michener was editor my freshman year), the yearbook, debating (I was captain of the team), student government (I was president of men's student government), and much else. I was trying to follow the Aydelotte ideal of the all-around student.

Swarthmore had so many bright and well-educated students and such excellent teachers. A whole world of intellectual discourse opened up to me. I took "honors work" under the Aydelotte plan, which involved small seminars and the writing of many papers, and then examinations by outside examiners from other colleges and universities. I started with rather low grades in my first two years but ended up with "high honors." A review of my notes for the junior year seminar in history of political thought (under Roland Pennock) got me through that area of my outside field exam for the Ph.D. at Berkeley.

Swarthmore introduced me to its silent Quaker meeting and to the American Friends Service Committee. My father and mother were not Quakers. But about a mile away from our farm there was a Quaker meeting that had been founded by members of the Abraham Lincoln and Daniel Boone families, so I knew about the Quakers and thought of them in a respectful way. While I was a student at Swarthmore, I became a member of the Swarthmore meeting as a "convinced friend," not a "birthright friend." I spent three summers as a peace caravaner for the AFSC in New England, Virginia, North Carolina, and California, arguing for means to assure world peace. I became a pacifist, at least in relation to World War I. I later found I was not a pacifist in relation to World War II. But I remained an opponent of the use of force as a means of settling disputes, if there were any peaceful alternative, which I then thought, and still think, there usually is. Also through the AFSC, I helped prepare and serve breakfasts of donated bread, milk, and apple butter to famished children in the black ghetto of north Philadelphia. I also accompanied "Ruff," the black trainer of athletic teams at Swarthmore, to black churches in the Philadelphia area. Ruff was a lay preacher and I went along carrying the message of world peace. I saw at these churches the same spirit of goodness expressed in a more vocal way than in the silent meeting at Swarthmore.

The Swarthmore Meeting was "Hicksite," which meant liberal. Instead of saying "there is that of God in every man," the Swarthmore version I came away with was "there is that of good in every person." I have kept that message all my life, but not without some disappointments. After my later experience with industrial relations, I came to add "but it takes me longer to find it in some people than in others." After experiencing academic administration in-fighting, I came to add, "and with some people I am still looking." But that Hicksite message still guides my life.

James Conant, longtime president of Harvard (1933–53) and a friend of mine, wrote that he followed a different course and called it a more realistic one. Conant said, "My tendency to expect the worst when dealing with other people may well be traced to a prolonged self-inflicted dose of British seventeenth-century history. One might well say that a future college president in a turbulent period required no such lesson. He would face, soon enough, the liar, the 'double-crosser' and the intriguer." But he added: "It might have been better if he had not already acquired a drab view of human nature by the vicarious experiences provided by studying history. He should have started out with the almost naive optimism of one who had lived in a strife-free college—the twentieth-century equivalent of an ivory tower."[4] And, as I recall my many disappointments as an administrator, I now question whether—*pace* Conant— I would not have been better off to doubt more and read well of the history of England in the seventeenth century, as he did.

Peaceful Solutions

When I entered the field of industrial relations, I had a chance to practice the art of peaceful solutions. My first experience in the field was in the fall of 1933 during the bloody cotton pickers' strike in the great Central Valley of California. Then later, while teaching at the University of Washington, from 1940 to 1945, I became the leading arbitrator of industrial disputes in the Seattle region. This led to my participation during World War II in the work of the regional War Labor Board stabilizing wages and settling labor disputes, hundreds of them. After the war, I continued in arbitration and became a leading arbitrator on the West Coast. I saw how violence once unleashed came to lead an uncontrolled life of its own. I saw how patience and reason led to less costly processes and better solutions than did passion and violence. Later in life, I served as national chairperson of a pro-peace and pro-American moderate group called Negotiation Now (it later became Committee for a Political Settlement in Vietnam); and as chair of the Land Council that helped incorporate land reforms in El Salvador, and as a member of the U.S. delegation led by Senator Nancy Kassebaum of Kansas to help assure honest elections in El Salvador, as an alternative to violence. "Blessed are the peacemakers."

These thus became central facets of my life: hard work and support from caring communities, advancement through education, the belief that "there was that of good in every person," pursuit of peaceful solutions in a world of conflict. I have lived my life with two great illusions and misperceptions of reality, as my wife has often reminded me. Intellectually I have known that there is *not* that of good in every person, and that all problems do *not* have reasonable and peaceful solutions I can find. Yet I would rather live with these operational beliefs (or misbeliefs) than with their opposites, and I had been brought up to reject the alternatives: distrust of others and expectations of failure.[5]

A Giant Astride
the University

An Appreciation of Robert Gordon Sproul

The University of California in 1952 could celebrate two recent triumphs: the success at Berkeley in helping to release the power of the atom, and its very effective handling of the rush of GI students after World War II. Also, however, it was in the midst of two substantial controversies: one over the loyalty oath, another over decentralization of the administration. The triumphs must be celebrated, even as the controversies must be examined (unfortunately, I saw more than my share of the latter).

Most of all, in 1952 it was the university of Robert Gordon Sproul. He was one of the outstanding university presidents in American history and served from 1930 to 1958. Earlier, as comptroller from 1920 to 1930, he filled one-half of a bifurcated presidency, as it was then constituted, the president handling academic matters and the comptroller the administrative side of the university. The university was well administered—efficiently and with fiscal integrity—and was excellently represented in Sacramento and to the people of the state. Berkeley advanced steadily in the university world and UCLA began its spectacular climb up the academic ladder. But because two major controversies occurred in what were otherwise Sproul's thirty-eight glorious years of immense accomplishments, and because I treat with them later in detail, I start with an appreciation of him that encompasses all the endeavors during these years.

■

I have always admired Bob Sproul. He had an enormous public personality with a fabulous voice, a hearty manner, and a genius for remembering names. He also had enormous vitality and the fathomless ability to recuperate from setbacks.

Additionally, he had a capacity to handle detail that was astounding. Longtime UCLA faculty member Paul Dodd, in an interview for the Robert Gordon Sproul oral history project, tells about an occasion when he was director of the Institute of Industrial Relations–south and I was director-north.[1] In the course of a conversation on other matters, I said that I had just had a call from Bob Sproul about my application for a file cabinet and, before approving it, he wanted to know where I was going to place it in my office (actually I was not quite sure). Paul also told me later that, one year when he was dean of letters and science at UCLA, he had counted the number of changes, most of them small, made by Sproul in Paul's line-item budget request, and they added up to one-third of all those hundreds and hundreds of items—usually $10 to $50 each up or down. My own experience of budget changes when I was chancellor at Berkeley, however, did not come near the level Paul claimed.

First as assistant comptroller of the university (1918 to 1920) and then as comptroller (1920 to 1930), Sproul had dealt in the utmost budgetary and administrative detail. He continued these micromanagement practices as president. It was clear throughout the university, to all employees at all times, who was the one and only president. Almost everybody experienced waiting for a presidential decision at one time or another.

In terms of the daily operations of the university, Sproul was actually the "operational president" from 1920 to 1958. In addition to becoming comptroller in 1920 and reporting directly to the regents, he also became secretary to the board and land agent. In 1925, on top of these positions, he was made vice president of business and financial affairs and held all four titles until he became president in 1930. In addition, he represented the university in Sacramento. During these years the two presidents, David Prescott Barrows and William Wallace Campbell, were involved only in strictly academic affairs. Sproul was more nearly the operational president than they were. After Sproul was appointed president in 1930, James Corley became variously assistant comptroller, comptroller, university representative in Sacramento, and vice president–business affairs. Sproul and Corley were close friends and they worked together amicably on an informal basis although Corley was an officer of the regents also reporting directly to them. This is why I think of Sproul as actually running the university for thirty-eight years (see chapter 4, which sketches the university's history before 1952).

Standing along with Benjamin Ide Wheeler (1899–1919) as dominant in university history, Sproul presided over the university officially during a period of considerable quantitative growth (from 20,000 students in 1930 to 48,000 in 1958) and very considerable qualitative advancement. By 1952, Berkeley was and had long been ranked as one of the "Big Six" research universities in the United States (along with Harvard, Yale, Columbia, Chicago, and Michigan). UCLA, once a teachers' college and part of the university since 1919, had 15,000 students, was rising rapidly in academic distinction, and had given its first Ph.D. in 1938. Davis, started as a "farm school" in 1905, still concentrated on agriculture but had added a college of letters and science (in 1951); it had 1,500 students. Santa Barbara, a former teachers' college, had been attached to the UC system by legislative fiat in 1944 and had 1,700 students in 1952; it still concentrated on teachers' education.

There were, in addition, a medical center in San Francisco, the Lick Observatory near San Jose, the Scripps Institution of Oceanography in La Jolla, and the Citrus Experiment Station in Riverside. Each was then identified as a "campus." Thus on the university's eight so-called campuses, the total number of students in 1952 was 34,000—the size of UCLA in the 1990s.

Sproul took particular interest in the sciences at a time when physics and chemistry were the stars of the intellectual world. Six faculty members were named winners of the Nobel Prize while he was president, as were five more later who had been appointed to the faculty while he was president—eleven in all. I particularly admired Sproul's concern for the quality of each new professorial appointment or promotion to tenure, and what I considered his excellent judgment in deciding on them. This was especially remarkable because he was never a faculty member and his undergraduate training had been as an engineer (class of 1913). In my six years as chancellor, he turned back only four of my recommendations for promotions to tenure or new appointments at tenure level, and they would have been the marginal four if I had been a little tougher. He also approved only four promotions to tenure that I had turned down, but, if I had then given more credit to "university service" (which I now wish I had done), these are the four I would have chosen.

As a graduate student in the 1930s, I had seen Sproul from afar and had marveled at his public personality. As a young faculty member and director of a new institute beginning in 1945, I had greatly appreciated his support and the personal interest he had shown in my efforts. I still marvel at how effective he was externally in public relations and, at the same time, internally at detailed decision-making. I have never worked with anyone who was so talented at both of these quite disparate capacities. Sproul had great strengths in his relations with Berkeley alumni, for many of whom he was and always would be *the* university, and also among longer-term legislators in Sacramento where he had, as noted above, represented the university from 1920 to 1930 before becoming president. He had many longtime friends in the faculty. The members of his administrative staff were devoted to him, with only one major exception to be noted later.

Along with Sproul's formidable strengths, however, there were also certain tendencies that became handicaps as the university grew in size and complexity, and particularly as it faced enormous further expansion and changes in emphases, and as it faced new political pressures.

The latter tendency was to allow the state's political climate to influence his decisions (as encouraged by Jim Corley), particularly in proposing the loyalty oath for faculty members in 1949 and in agreeing to appoint a "contact man" on each campus to work with the Senate Committee on Un-American Activities (the Burns committee) in 1952—each of which I shall discuss in *Political Turmoil.* By the end of World War II, Sproul was already opposing efforts of southern regents, urged on by UCLA alumni and deans, to decentralize the university and to assure more generous treatment of UCLA. Then, beginning in 1949, came the devastating oath controversy. I saw him in some of his most difficult years and felt very sympathetic when I observed the hostile and, I thought, disgraceful way in which some regents treated him.

Sproul's tendency was to concentrate rather than share governance with other administrators. He had a large presidential staff for decision-making but little organized administrative machinery for consultation. Such consultation as existed he generally carried out on a one-to-one basis with faculty members and subordinate administrators. This tendency led him to neglect macroplanning. Thus in 1952, there never had been an academic plan at Berkeley and the physical development plan was out of date. Not so incidentally, these were the areas into which I moved. Actually, we complemented each other quite well—he and Corley handled the daily administration of the Berkeley campus and I, as chancellor, worked hard on anticipating and preparing for the future.

His administrative tendency also led to the one basic disagreement Sproul and I had over the development of the chancellorship. It was not a contest I initiated. The deans and some regents, not I, were Sproul's longer term opponents in this dispute. But I did become a central participant, necessarily and reluctantly, without ever losing my admiration for and wonderment at Bob Sproul.

We disagreed in the area of administrative structure, which was immensely important to him. I turned out to be Sproul's toughest opponent ever inside the university administration. On occasion, he became quite exasperated with me—understandably so. I did not then realize why keeping the detailed administration of the Berkeley campus in his hands meant so much to him. Only slowly did I come to realize how this campus was most of what he had left to administer. Davis and Riverside reported to the vice president–agriculture. UCLA was increasingly dominated by southern regents, who tried to recruit a chancellor there without even informing the president (see chapter 23).

Why I became such an opponent of Sproul on decentralization, I still only partially understand. I was only forty years old at the time of my appointment as chancellor, the head of a small institute in an area of no campus prestige, and in that position had liked dealing directly with President Sproul. I had little campus standing. I had never been a department chair or dean, had never been the chair or even member of one of the long-term basic committees of the Academic Senate. Despite having spent a professional life in industrial relations, an area marked by controversy, I still did not like controversies. That, perhaps, is one reason I always worked so hard to resolve them. Yet here was a confrontation that went on for six years with a person I held in high esteem, and a controversy over centralization versus decentralization of the administration of the university about whose history and merits I started out being almost totally ignorant, and about which I had once cared even less. This turned me into an opponent of President Sproul in this one area of central importance to him, but an opponent who admired him as a person and who greatly respected the many contributions he made to the advancement of the university. His total record was overwhelmingly positive.

When Sproul left the university in 1958, it enjoyed a higher level of public approval than ever before or ever after. This was, of course, a national era of good feeling under President Dwight D. Eisenhower. All institutions were at their peaks of public confidence. Yet auspicious as the times were, the special public luster of the University of California owed particularly to the thirty-eight years of leadership by Robert Gordon Sproul.

PART II

The First Chancellor at Berkeley, 1952–58

3

Answering the Big Question: Who Will Take Berkeley's Place in the Academic Big Six?

In 1952 the Berkeley campus had already met its goal of becoming the best of the great public universities, along with the University of Michigan. There were 12,000 undergraduate students, 8,600 of them in letters and sciences, and 4,000 graduate students. The total enrollment was about the same as it was just before World War II. A new enrollment tidal wave, however, was beginning to loom ahead. How could the Berkeley campus within the University of California make good use of the lull between two storms?

The campus was administered directly by the president of the university, who lived in a well-appointed house on campus. And as the campus recovered from the destructive effects of the oath controversy, the Academic Senate was very powerful and had strong faculty leadership. Yet a sense of apprehension remained. There was little planning for the future. And the position of provost—which had been mostly that of a very high-level assistant to President Sproul, with ad hoc assignments—had been vacant for six years (the provost from 1931 to 1947 was Monroe Deutsch, a professor of classics).

On March 30, 1951, the regents decided to create chancellorships at Berkeley and UCLA. The chancellors were to be the "executive heads" of their campuses. In reality, President Sproul strongly preferred the old system, particularly at Berkeley. What was worked out over the years was an understanding under which Sproul and Corley continued to administer the Berkeley campus, and I took the opportunity to establish a role of what amounted to academic provost engaged in what became substantial accomplishments.

The big question, after the devastation of the oath controversy, was whether or not Berkeley would fall out of the academic Big Six, then defined as Harvard, Yale, Columbia, Chicago, Michigan, and Berkeley. It was widely assumed in university circles that Berkeley was on the way down and out. It was widely feared at Berkeley that this might be the future fate of the campus. Other universities were eagerly waiting to take Berkeley's place. The fate of Berkeley was at stake. This fate was placed, in small part, in the hands of whoever would become the first chancellor in the history of the Berkeley campus. Could Berkeley rise up to take charge of its own fate?

■

My first intimation of a new assignment came in August 1951 when President Sproul told me that I was on a list of possible chancellors at Berkeley presented by a faculty committee. I paid no attention to this listing. There were so many more experienced faculty members at Berkeley than I. And I presumed that a national search was also being made.

My second warning that something might be about to happen came in January 1952 when I was asked to attend a luncheon at the President's House. When I got there, I found I was in company with most of the members of the Board of Regents. I was seated at the far end of the table to the right of Sidney Ehrman, a longtime regent and a leading lawyer and citizen of San Francisco when the City still had a recognized "establishment." He was chair of the powerful Committee on Finance. This committee routinely met at each regents' meeting (eleven meetings per year) and also once monthly in between (twelve per year). The committee had authority to act when necessary on all issues on behalf of the full Board of Regents. To be chair of finance at that time was more important than being chair of the board. At the end of the luncheon, Ehrman announced to the table at large, in his authoritative style, "I like the cut of this young man's jib." What could be the point of that remark?

I got the point a few days later when a newspaper reporter phoned to talk with me as the newly appointed chancellor, and to tell me of the action of the board on January 25, 1952. By then I had known the Berkeley campus for nearly two decades as student and faculty member, and I was devoted to it. To be asked to participate in its leadership was the greatest of honors—even though the chancellorship was ill defined. I was often asked, in the early days, what the chancellor really did. In public situations, I took to saying that the position was totally new within the university but was an ancient title in Great Britain. The *Oxford English Dictionary* called it an "honorary" position and said that the chancellor, among other things, was "Keeper of His Majesty's conscience" and "guardian of infants, lunatics, and idiots." Not a very helpful answer but a diverting one. What the chancellor actually did was still to be created.

From my point of view, the position's opportunities came gradually to over-balance the great uncertainties. I did not care much about assigning office space or undertaking many of the other administrative duties performed by President Sproul and Vice President Corley and their assistants. Nor did "total control" to match "total responsibility" ever appeal to me, either as chancellor or as president. I believed in shared consultative governance.

Nor did I care much—or, on reflection, as much as I should have—about the position's regal aspects: a large office (both as chancellor and president I worked in a rather small office and with a round table instead of a desk so that those talking with me could also use the table for their papers and have a comfortable place to put their legs); a big car and a driver (I mostly drove myself); an elaborate mansion to live in (I lived in my own house); presiding at all official affairs; active participation in the "best" clubs or on corporate boards; the services of a personal press officer, and so forth. Some regents came to think, and to tell me, that as chancellor and later as president I was not "living up to" my position. In exasperation one very influential regent told me that for the chancellor to have, as I did, a combination receptionist and typist who was an African-American (when I finally got presidential approval for a receptionist) did not "show respect for [my] position."

Yet the position of chancellor was not entirely weak even before it was delegated the final power to say "yes" on anything. One strength was the power to say "no" within the chain of command. Robert Brode of physics, a wise and devoted faculty leader, once told me that in academic life the power to say "no" and the judgment to say it judiciously was much more important to the long-run quality of the endeavor than the power to say "yes." I came to agree that it was the easy "yes" that led to perdition, and the hard "no" to distinction.

My first "no" came about this way. Shortly after I at last had an office of my own as chancellor in October 1952, a proposal came to my desk on taking over the entrance to Strawberry Canyon above Memorial Stadium for a new center for the shops and storage sheds of the Grounds and Buildings operations—a "corporation yard." It seemed to me too beautiful a location for this purpose, and we later used the area for the Haas Recreation Center with a swimming pool and playing fields, including a field for rugby. Also, all the accompanying traffic for Grounds and Buildings vehicles would have had to make its way on the narrow and twisting streets around the stadium and into the canyon. I found myself writing the word "Never." I remember how startled I was when my "never" stood up without a challenge! We actually located the shops for Grounds and Buildings in downtown Berkeley, which had easier access and was closer to sources of supply and specialized craft skills.

I thought that each piece of land should be reserved for its best possible use. The site above the stadium figures in an account by the famous Harvard economist John Kenneth Galbraith, M.S. and Ph.D. at Berkeley in the early 1930s. He tells of wandering around this particular spot with a beautiful and sophisticated fellow student who finally turned around and confronted him. "She asked me if I thought it right, as an economist, to be wasting both her time and mine" walking about aimlessly kicking up dust when the two of them might be doing something else.[1]

A second early "no" was on a proposal to tear down South Hall, built in 1873—the remaining one of the two original buildings on campus (North Hall had been razed earlier). It was less costly to tear down South Hall and rebuild than to renovate it, and the site could accommodate more usable square feet. But South Hall was part of history and a history I valued personally, as many others also did for their own reasons. I had been a teaching assistant in the basement of the building under Professor Cross of economics. For this reason, I feared a charge of prejudice when I said "no" but, as far as I know, it never came.

I later resorted to the use of "no" on so many nominations for tenure and on so many departmental first choices for chairs that the rising academic distinction of Berkeley could be said to be built, in no small part, on that word "no." My personal distaste for saying "no" gave way to a more reasoned acceptance of its values. A familiar phrase among the deans, who had been accustomed to long waits for answers, was that "the new chancellor has the fastest 'no' in the West." But it was not easy for me. I wanted to accept every invitation to speak, to grant every request for money, never to make an enemy—like the unfortunate major character in Osamu Dazai's *No Longer Human* (as translated by Donald Keene): "My unhappiness was the unhappiness of a person who could not say no. I had been intimidated by the fear that if I declined something offered to me, a yawning crevice would open between the other person's heart and myself which could never be mended through all eternity." There's some truth in that.

A very efficient secretary of mine, Florence Eisemann, once said to me when I asked her to add something to my calendar when it was already full and overflowing: "Dr. Kerr, do you know what is wrong with you? You can't say no." And then, in exasperation, she added, "It is a good thing you are not a woman!" and slammed her pencil and pad on the table.

Support for the Chancellorship and the Agenda

There were other strengths to the position of Berkeley chancellor beyond taking blocking actions on a selective basis. The regents hoped to have an effective chancellorship at Berkeley as well as at Los Angeles. They gave me all that I ever asked for and would have given me more if I had requested it. Among the northern regents, Bob Sproul's longtime friends, particularly Gerald Hagar, Edward Heller, Donald McLaughlin, and Jesse Steinhart, gave their full support and even offered it by inquiring how things were going. They helped me get a copy of the budget I was supposed to be administering, the open-session minutes of the Board of Regents as they related to Berkeley, a standing invitation to attend the open meetings of the Board of Regents, the opportunity to receive in advance materials relating to Berkeley sent to the regents, and a staff of modest size.

Although they had been appointed by Sproul, the academic deans at Berkeley were also fully supportive. The new Council of Deans brought them into more contact with developments on the campus at large and invited them into the processes of making major decisions. They got quicker answers than in the past. And they had more personal contact with higher authority. To my knowledge, only one dean (engineering) and one department chair (physics) kept open a direct channel to the president while also reporting to the chancellor. Both were continuations of long-term relationships. One nonacademic dean (student affairs) and the in-place business manager when I became chancellor reported exclusively to the universitywide level of administration.

"WHO WILL TAKE BERKELEY'S PLACE?"

Berkeley had gone through the devastation of the loyalty oath controversy. As a consequence, the University of California had been "censured" by the American Association of University Professors (April 5, 1956) and by other academic associations. For onlookers and most members of Berkeley's faculty, students, and alumni, the Berkeley campus *was* the university, and many feared that Berkeley was on the way down the academic ladder it had already climbed so high. To illustrate the climate of opinion, one day at a board meeting of the Center for Advanced Study in the Behavioral Sciences at Stanford, Paul Buck announced an engrossing topic for our discussion. Paul was the provost at Harvard, initiator of the "Red Book" curricular reforms there, and the greatest guru of American higher education at that time. He was also our academic chair, and the board members came from leading universities of the nation. Paul liked substantive discussions at our lunches and dinners. That day he said that the most interesting question currently in the academic world was "Who will take Berkeley's place" in the Big Six? Several institutions were nominated as the argument advanced. As a founding member of the board I sat there, facing the accepted assumption of the inevitable decline of Berkeley burning into my soul as though it were a red-hot poker. My answer to Paul's question was "No one." That answer stood up to the test of time.

The answer of "no one" was also the widespread conviction within the Berkeley faculty. Its members rallied round. The senate committees and the administratively appointed faculty advisory committees along with the deans and the department chairs responded aggressively to the challenge of preserving and advancing the status and prestige of Berkeley. There were at that time exceptionally competent and loyal leaders of the Academic Senate and administrative committees at Berkeley. To serve in academic governance was then still more of an honor and expression of trust than an unrewarded obligation or "chore." Berkeley would never have held its place (or advanced it) without the quiet and effective determination of Berkeley faculty leaders.

Many people had built Berkeley over prior years to its position in the Big Six. Many more built Berkeley over the decade that lay ahead into the "best balanced distinguished university" in the United States, as it came to be rated. I shall note some of these individuals in the pages that follow. Any account of the advancement of Berkeley is, in very large part, a record of what they accomplished. The most essential Academic Senate committees were the Committee on Budget and Interdepartmental Relations (really on academic personnel, which is the term I shall use) and the one on educational policy. The crucial administratively appointed faculty committee was the Committee on Buildings and Campus Development.

I established and chaired an Academic Advisory Committee that included the top deans (letters and sciences, graduate affairs) and senate leaders, and the Council of Deans, which the regents had provided for in 1951 when they established the chancellorship. Each of these bodies considered all important developments. I also established and chaired a committee on student affairs that included student leaders, personnel from the Dean of Students' office, and selected faculty members most engaged in student affairs. A substantial consultative framework was thus established with very active participation; and there was much to consult about.

AN AGENDA FOR ADVANCING THE ANSWER, "NO ONE"

An agenda of necessary and possible projects gradually fell into place. It filled the wide open spaces beyond what was continuing to be done administratively at the universitywide level. In broad outline, the projects aimed to

create a viable position of chancellor-provost,

keep Berkeley in the Big Six,

develop an academic plan for the future,

improve facilities for the quality of undergraduate life,

set up a physical development plan that followed the academic plan and the student affairs plan,

develop a plan to improve facilities for cultural life on campus, and

restore confidence in academic freedom at Berkeley.

I chart the process of developing and carrying out this agenda in the next five chapters. As it progressed, I was de jure—by action of the regents—the first chancellor at Berkeley with responsibility for all campus operations, academic and administrative, but de facto—by my own actions and facing the resistance of Sproul and Corley—the first academic provost with significant influence. As de facto provost, I was internally and academically oriented, with the external and the nonacademic outside the orbit of my permitted and accepted concerns.

The Chancellor's Office

The staff was small. It started out at three and rose to nineteen over the six years. In October 1952 the chancellor's office was established on the ground floor of Dwinelle Hall in an area once reserved for the history department's teaching assistants. We had no proper reception room—only the end of a corridor with a door that closed it off and, until 1956–57, no receptionist. A modest-sized office held my round conference table, and the adjoining conference room was large enough to accommodate the Council of Deans. And then there was a small but growing series of staff offices.

Aside from me, the first employee was Barbara Annis, who had been working for the dean of letters and science. She knew everybody and was very sweet and pleasant but too restrained to speak her mind. She had also served as secretary to Provost Monroe Deutsch (he had a staff of four) and saw the chancellor's office as no more than a continuation of the provost's responsibilities: he had mostly done odd jobs on assignment and had few fixed responsibilities. Because I wanted an administrative assistant with independent judgment and the willingness to say what she thought, I arranged to secure Gloria Copeland from the dean of the College of Letters and Science in Barbara's place. She was perfect and worked with me right on through to the end of my presidency.

I had a number of other key assistants. Frances Essig was my first secretary—bright, sharp, efficient, and with a mind of her own that she was ready to share with others; and then later Florence Eisemann and Katrine ("Kitty") Stephenson, each highly talented. Dorothy Gardner (later Powell), recommended to me by the chair of the Department of English, kept the minutes of the major advisory committees and did general research and reading for me. Maggie Johnston, full of enthusiasm and good ideas, was administrative assistant to Kay, my wife. Both had been student leaders (Maggie at Berkeley, Kay at Stanford) and took pains to arrange social events that would include student leaders at Berkeley. Maggie was in charge of our social calendar, which was always very heavy except on Sunday (our only unscheduled time, kept as a family day with our three children). Kay's schedule later included meetings of Save San Francisco Bay, which she began in 1961 with Sylvia McLaughlin (wife of Regent Donald McLaughlin) and Esther Gulick, a faculty wife.[2] Maggie later became a universitywide source of advice on social affairs when I was president. She continued on to assist Mrs. Hitch, Mrs. Saxon, and Mrs. Gardner, the wives of my successors.

Two other key assistants were Eugene C. Lee and Virginia Taylor (later Norris). Gene was a graduate of UCLA (B.A., 1946) and Berkeley (Ph.D., 1957), had been president of the associated students (ASUCLA), and lettered in football. He became a longtime member of the political science department at Berkeley and director of the Institute of Governmental Studies. While a graduate student, Gene had participated in the 1948 Public Administration Service report[3] on the governance of the University of California and continued following its development clear through my presidency when he served as vice president–executive assistant. Gene was chief budget officer in the chancellor's office and advisor on administrative relationships. Virginia had been a student of mine and president of the student body at the University of Washington and then worked with me at the Institute of Industrial Relations. She had a very quick and precise mind, was a superb policy analyst, and gave me excellent assistance in drafting speeches and memos; and she was the best editor with whom I ever worked.

I had a special arrangement for "faculty assistants." These faculty members, mostly younger, took on a series of specific assignments, always working part-time. They augmented my staff at little cost. They had eleven- instead of nine-month appointments and carried reduced teaching assignments. They gave me more direct contact with faculty interests and attitudes while they learned about academic administration. Some of these assistants were quite influential, and several went on to higher executive positions. Edward Barrett of the law school gave general advice, particularly on matters with a legal aspect, later working with Bob Brode to loosen Rule 17's restraints on political activity on campus and going on to become the founding dean of the law school at Davis. Robert Brode of the physics department brought wisdom, loyalty, and the best of advice, serving in a similar position when I became president. In particular, he was instrumental in developing policies for voluntary ROTC and for relaxing Rule 17, serving also as chair of the Berkeley chapter of the American Association of University Professors. Eugene Burdick of the political science department and a winner of the Pulitzer Prize for Literature *(The Ugly American)* was full of zest and initiative, especially in helping prepare the physical development plan for the Berkeley campus and in renewing the university's relations with the city of Berkeley. John E. Kelley of mathematics was a nonsigner who resigned rather than be fired by the regents during the oath controversy; his attachment to the chancellor's office and later his chairship of mathematics, among other things, were proof that the nonsigners were welcomed back in full. John Oswald of agriculture worked at all trades in the chancellor's office with energy and enthusiasm, but particularly on the establishment of the Bodega Bay Marine Laboratory and the Hat Creek Radio Astronomy Project; he became vice president–administration for the university and, still later, president of the University of Kentucky and of Pennsylvania

State University, and chair of the Association of American Universities. Alex C. Sherriffs of psychology was a major contact with student leaders, one of the most popular lecturers on the Berkeley campus, and a favorite invitee to fraternity and sorority lunches and dinners, providing a warmer approach to students than that offered by the dean of students, Hurford Stone; after my chancellorship, he was appointed vice-chancellor–student affairs and, as such, became an opponent of student activists and they of him; still later he became education adviser to Governor Reagan.

The ad hoc position of vice-chancellor was out of the general line of decision-making but gave its holder greater leverage in accomplishing specific goals: for Donald Coney (librarian), that of building the cultural programs of the campus; and for James D. Hart (member of the English department and later head of the Bancroft Library), of planning for the undergraduate library and the art museum, both projects I would have liked to follow more directly if I had had the time. For A. R. ("Sailor") Davis (dean of letters and science), the title was purely honorary since he was the faculty member, I thought, most in line for being chancellor, a position I thought he had well earned.

At the level of general advice, I relied very heavily on the Council of Deans and the Academic Advisory Committee, and also on the vice chairs of the Academic Senate (the university's president was the chair). A frequent saying at the time—I had arranged for the office of the senate to be located on the same floor of Dwinelle Hall and in the same general area as the chancellor's office— was, "It's hard to tell where the chancellor's office ends and the senate's office begins." For example, the Committee on Committees appointed all senate committees, and I asked it for advice (this had never happened before) on all major administrative committees that, in effect, it also came to appoint. Incidentally, I stopped the practice of having the provost or president attend all meetings of the Committee on Committees in order to keep the committee's choice of senate and faculty committee members free of administrative influence.

At a more informal level, I relied for general advice most heavily on Gloria Copeland and Virginia Norris, on Robert Brode and Eugene Lee and Jack Oswald, on A. R. Davis and Lincoln Constance, his successor as dean of letters and science. Among the deans of professional schools, I had the most help from Milton Chernin of social welfare, whom I came to know when we were fellow graduate students playing handball, and E. T. Grether of business administration. Greth, in particular, was my closest longtime advisor. As dean, he had brought me back to Berkeley and helped me establish the Institute of Industrial Relations. He gave me strong support both as chancellor and president. I found one sympathetic friend at the universitywide level in Harry R. Wellman, vice president–agricultural sciences, who had been one of the examiners for my Ph.D. in economics. (For my memorial tributes to Gloria, Greth, Milton, and Harry, see IGS Documentary Supplements 1.1 through 1.4.)[4]

These were the principal people who worked most closely together in the recovery of Berkeley from the devastation of the loyalty oath controversy, in making the chancellor's office an effective aspect of campus governance, and in advancing Berkeley in the academic world. I was very fortunate to have these colleagues.

My Approach to the Chancellorship

My tenure in the position of chancellor, particularly in the early years, was insecure both because of the conflict over the role of the chancellor and the legacies of the oath controversy. Consequently I wanted my sense of independence. I kept on teaching. I continued publishing in my fields of specialization. I lived in my own house; no other alternative was available to the chancellor. But in any case, even though provision of a house and its full maintenance would have added substantially to the material rewards of the position, I would have rejected it. I wanted my salary kept low out of deference to faculty salary levels (my highest salary as chancellor was $24,000). And, after I became president, because of comparison with the governor's salary I kept the same policy. For example, the minutes of the executive session of the Board of Regents for July 24, 1964, say that, while Chairman Edward Carter "favored increasing the president's salary by the recommended increase in academic rate, he said that the president preferred that his total salary not be raised." Thus my highest salary as president was $45,000 and without the provision of a university-owned residence. The governor's salary was $47,000, but with a very liberal allowance for retirement, which I did not receive and did not want. I preferred to be part of the same retirement plan as other faculty members.

I did not want to become too attached to any perquisites of the office. I never wanted to feel compelled to conform against my will. I wanted to feel independent, to be able to say "no" as well as "yes." I wanted to be willing to mow my own lawn and to enjoy it, to be able to teach my classes, to write my articles, to preside over industrial relations arbitrations—which I continued to do albeit on a very reduced basis. I did not want to build prison walls around myself. Being aware of the perils of the position, I took precautions to anticipate possible eventualities and looked upon myself as a faculty member otherwise engaged for an uncertain period of time.

In terms of impacts on my life, I would add that the chancellorship gave me an opportunity to learn a great deal about the university system while sitting on the sidelines, and this turned out to be very helpful to me when I became president.

Did Sproul Make a Mistake?

More than once Greth—who joined the faculty in 1922, was my friend and mentor since my days as a graduate student in the 1930s, the dean of business administration from 1941 to 1961—raised this question with me: did Sproul make a mistake in recommending to the regents my appointment as chancellor? Greth had known the Deutsch-model provostship and seen Sproul's fantastic ability to administer infinite details and his commitment to doing so. And Greth knew my personality. He knew that I had stood the test of being under fire in many industrial relations battles, for he had researched my career meticulously before inviting me to join his faculty in 1945. (A report many years later in connection with the largest labor arbitration in U.S. history involving 700,000 employees and $14 billion in dispute stated, "the neutral chairman, Clark Kerr, was one of the most experienced labor arbitrators and mediators in the country. He was unlikely to be swayed by emotional appeals or aggressive language and could not be threatened.")[5] Incidentally Greth, with his understanding of the situation, served as acting director of the Institute of Industrial Relations for two years after I became chancellor, thus holding the position open for my possible return.

Given the Deutsch model, I can see why—mistake or not—Sproul chose me. Of those under consideration to be Berkeley's first chancellor, I was the youngest, the least experienced and established on campus, and the most liberal and thus the most subject to the potential opposition of the pro-oath regents and right-wing elements external to the university. I constituted the least potential threat in an unwanted position.

Sproul and I had had good relations when I was director of the Institute of

Industrial Relations–north, and I had been a loyal supporter of his. For example, at an all-university faculty conference at Davis in 1947, President Sproul was accused of having ordered Provost Clarence Dykstra at UCLA to withdraw an invitation to lecture extended by the Institute of Industrial Relations–south. The invitation was to Harold Laski of the London School of Economics and an active leftist member of the British Labor Party. (I had audited Laski's famous course on "theory of the state" when a student at the London School of Economics.) I stood up to say that I, as director of the Institute of Industrial Relations–north, had also invited Laski to Berkeley when I had heard he was to be at UCLA, and that I had never received an order or any advice at all to withdraw the invitation. What had happened at UCLA, however, I did not know. This greatly dampened the attack on Sproul.

A second, more significant, incident took place at a meeting of the Board of Regents in San Francisco on July 21, 1950, to consider a report of the senate Committee on Privilege and Tenure. I was the committee's most junior member and spoke up in direct opposition to Regent John Francis Neylan, who by then was the leader of the pro-oath faction and of the anti-Sproul regents, and was the longtime attorney for William Randolph Hearst. As a compromise, the regents had agreed that nonsigners of the oath could appear before the Committee on Privilege and Tenure to explain their beliefs as an alternative to signing the oath. We cleared all of those who appeared before us and were willing to discuss their views. Neylan introduced a motion to fire all these faculty members anyway. I stood up. (Incidentally, the act of getting to my feet was not so easy to manage because a conservative faculty member, William Prosser, dean of the School of Law and a senior member of that same committee, was seated directly behind me. He seized my coattails and tried to pull me back into my seat. I grabbed the back of the chair in front of me. It, fortunately, held a heavy person and so I maintained my balance. I assumed Prosser acted as he did because he thought the most junior member of the committee and its most liberal member should not presume to speak.) I said as my opening sentence: "Regent Neylan, no one in good faith could possibly vote for your proposal." I went on to explain that the regents themselves had voted for this alternative to signing the oath and that the Committee on Privilege and Tenure had proceeded with its hearings in good faith. That evening Miss Robb (President Sproul's secretary), who was in attendance, wrote me in longhand one of the nicest letters I ever received.

What was at work within me that Sproul could not know when he recommended my appointment as chancellor? Perhaps, but only perhaps, a Quakerly inspired belief that you do not bend the knee or tip the hat to power—it worked within me in all directions: in the direction of John Francis Neylan in trying to dismiss the nonsigners but also in the direction of Robert Gordon Sproul in trying to hold onto control that the regents intended to give to the chancellor; and later, also, in the direction of Governor Reagan. Earlier this tendency had helped me gain a reputation for independence under severe pressures in many industrial relations disputes, and this reputation is basic to the mutual acceptance of an arbitrator by opposed parties.

Ida Sproul, Bob Sproul's friendly, efficient, perceptive, and all-around lovely wife, said several times, aware of my presence, "Bob, you must reconcile yourself to the fact that you cannot be the baby at every christening, the groom at every wedding, the corpse at every funeral." I, without ever originally intending to, became Sproul's challenger for participation in areas of great importance to him; and neither of us, by temperament, was inclined to withdraw from combat. Just before he retired on June 30, 1958, Sproul called me to his office. He was in a retrospective mood. He said, among other things, that he regretted that I had not seen him closely in his "best years" (the 1930s to the end of World War II). I regretted that too. And I also now regret that I made his later years somewhat less pleasant than they otherwise might have been. Overall, during his twenty-eight years as president, the university became more famous academically than it had ever been before, and that is the ultimate test. But times were changing.

Times were changing. The university was becoming larger and much more complex. This was sad for Bob Sproul. Once upon a time, as in my days as a graduate student, he was known by face and by voice to every student at Berkeley including graduate students, and even by many on the other campuses. At the last university meeting over which he presided in the late spring of 1958, he told the following story. He was walking one evening across the campus from his office in the administration building to the president's house and was wondering whether students knew him anymore. He fell in step with a male student and asked him, "Do you know who I am?" The student replied, looking him up and down, "No sir, I do not." Then, after a pause, the student added, "But if you have any idea of where you might live, I would be glad to help you find your way home." The day of the president knowing all, being known by all, and deciding all was gone forever.

Sproul and I had only two areas of sustained disagreement, and the one over our respective roles in governance was the major one. We did not disagree over what should be done but rather over who should do it and how. (For the other area, see *Political Turmoil* concerning the "contact man.") Tradition, his strong personality and great competence, and a staff of 1,000 were on Sproul's side. On mine were the regents, the deans, and the growth in size and complexity of the university. The ultimate result was, in any event, decreed by the passage of time itself. A great past was the result of the one approach; a greater future of the other.

In retracing this account, I recognize the importance of perspective. Bertrand Russell once emphasized the difference that perspective can make by giving the following illustration:

I am resolute.
You are stubborn.
He is pig-headed.

And various people did use a variety of adjectives to describe both Robert Gordon Sproul and me.

So my overall approach to the chancellorship became one of accepting past administrative practices, with a few essential changes, and of developing areas of past neglect into a solid and distinguished force for progress.

The "x" Factor

The most important force for progress, during the period after the loyalty oath controversy, was the spirit and determination of the members and leaders of the Berkeley faculty that they made effective through the committees of the Academic Senate and through the administrative committees on which they sat. Tolstoy, in *War and Peace* (part 3, ch. 2), describes how the Russian army held together and recovered after defeat in the battles of Smolensk and Borodin in the face of superior forces. There was what he called an "x" factor at work that went beyond the number of troops and quality of equipment or the experience of top leaders, in each of which the French and their allies were clearly superior. That factor was the indomitable morale and cohesion of the small units and their individual participants—"the spirit of the army." The Russian army retreated but in good order and then later decimated Napoleon's forces in their withdrawal from Moscow. I saw that same "x" factor at work at Berkeley after the loyalty oath controversy in individual departments led by their chairs and in faculty committees across the campus. The Berkeley faculty had "velocity," in the term used by Tolstoy. And Berkeley rose from threatened disaster to greater academic heights. The "x" factor in the soul of the Berkeley faculty did it above all else—the "spirit of the faculty." The same resiliency reappeared in the fast recovery from the events of the 1960s.

I once said to Professor Sanford ("Sandy") Elberg, who later became graduate dean, "I asked you to take on too many assignments and I should like to thank you and also apologize." He replied, "If you had not asked me, I would have been devastated." There were many others just like Sandy Elberg. Here was the "spirit" of the Berkeley faculty at work.

I have never seen any group of people respond so gallantly and determinedly to possible catastrophe as the Berkeley faculty after the oath controversy. In the long history of the University of California, the glorious recovery of the Berkeley faculty should never be forgotten. (See Appendix 1 sections A–E, for lists of its distinguished members.)

And "no one" took the place of Berkeley.

4

Defining a Chancellor's
Sphere of Action

I was the first chancellor at Berkeley. But what did this title mean? I had a title in search of a job.

The regents had said in the reorganization plan that the chancellor was to be the "executive head of all activities" on the campus. This I never was.

In explaining the plan, President Sproul said that the "duties of the President are essentially the same as they have been for many years . . . he is executive head of the University of California." To him these words meant that I was to be an assistant to the president, as the provost from 1931 to 1947 had been. This was not acceptable to me.

A third possibility was that, as chancellor, I would in reality become an active, if unwanted, academic provost. And this is the way my chancellorship worked out. The period from July 1, 1952, to July 1, 1958, was the third act in what turned out to be a four-act play with many scenes. The fourth act came after I was appointed president and the chancellors, in fact, did become the "executive head[s] of all activities" on the campuses.

From its founding in 1868 until 1952, the University of California was a highly centralized institution. At first, all control resided with the regents. The first decentralization came reluctantly in 1891 when the regents gave President Kellogg the authority "to employ, dismiss, and regulate the duties of janitors . . . [provided he] promptly reported his action to the Board." This was toward the end of act 1—1868–99.

President Benjamin Ide Wheeler (1899–1919) wrested from the regents substantial influence and, in particular, the policy that all faculty contacts should be with him and through him, and not directly with the regents—a policy subsequently not always followed fully in practice. In 1918, for the first time, the university budget became a presidential budget and not a regental budget prepared under the regents' direct supervision. The Wheeler-regents' power-sharing arrangements (academic affairs by and through Wheeler and business affairs by the regents through the comptroller) continued unchanged until 1951, when the regents voted to establish chancellorships at Berkeley and UCLA. This was the climax of act 2's final scene.

Act 2, scene 1: Wheeler reigned almost supreme over academic affairs for twenty years, ending in 1919. Act 2, scene 2: in the "revolution" of 1919–20 the Academic Senate assumed substantial influence over academic affairs, particularly academic appointments, courses of instruction, granting of degrees, and admissions. Act 2, scene 3: Robert Gordon Sproul, who had been comptroller, became president in 1930. He and the new comptroller, James Corley, who still reported directly to the regents, were working closely together as friends instead of as checks and balances on each other. Act 2, scene 4: in 1948 UCLA and the southern regents in particular, but also academic leaders of Berkeley, began to agitate for more campus autonomy (see Eugene Lee's excellent description of the scene).[1]

As it turned out, however, the regents' new plan for chancellors was not fully acceptable to President Sproul. His insistence on acting as campus head at Berkeley as well as president of the university put him and the new chancellor into conflict. This was act 3, which I discuss below.

A new structure was developed under my leadership (1958–66) and maintained, although changed in major aspects, for nearly forty years. It becomes act 4 (the subject of this book's part III).

I realize that the evolution of the chancellorship from 1952 to 1958 is of least general interest in a narrative of the Berkeley campus, and it may look to some like just a series of internal quarrels. The six years' developments did have many costs in personal relations and time spent, as I shall describe below. They also led to major positive consequences for the Berkeley campus.

▪

My first days as the chancellor-in-waiting were very nearly the last days. On a few occasions later on I wished they had been. The regents had voted on January 25, 1952, to appoint me as the first chancellor at Berkeley, and the duties were to begin on July 1, 1952. But a few days after the action of the regents, Bob Sproul phoned to say he would like me to start "learning the ropes right away"—which meant the following Monday. I did not know what to expect. And all my wild guesses were wrong. I thought I might be asked to take care of some of the president's pending appointments and correspondence (both of which were always substantial), and to sit in on staff discussions. Not at all.

I showed up on Monday morning at eight o'clock outside the president's suite of offices in the central administration building. (When Sproul retired, the regents named this building after him—at my request—and awarded him an honorary degree.) Jeanie, the very pleasant receptionist, showed me to a small office on the hallway that led to the president's office. This office had a yellow oak, general-issue desk accompanied by two small yellow oak straight-back chairs; no carpet on the floor, no paper or paper clips in the drawers, nothing but vacant walls. Nothing happened all morning. I just sat there. After lunch I asked the receptionist how I could get any secretarial assistance when I needed it. She smiled enigmatically and replied, "You won't need any," but said she would check and then later informed me that if I ever needed any help, I should ask the supervisor of the stenographic pool whether anyone was free to help me. As it turned out, I never had any reason to try to find out.

The next day I went to Agnes Robb, the president's extremely able and totally loyal administrative secretary. I admired her greatly both then and later. Miss Robb knew everybody and everything. I asked her whether there was anything I could do to help. On earlier visits to her office I had seen the stacks of pending folders from floor to ceiling (she knew what was in every one!). I'd worried each time I was there about what would happen if an earthquake occurred as she sat there surrounded by all those piles of folders. Somewhere, I suggested, there must be something in those piles I could work on. Several days later I got three ancient folders with scores of initials of staff members lining each side of each folder but no indications of any action.

The first was a complaint from women secretarial employees in the then still-standing Decorative Arts building: fleas, ticks, and lice from the wild animals living below the wooden floors were climbing up their feet and legs and causing them more discomfort the higher they went (apparently the insects recognized no limits to their endeavors).

The second was a petition to ban dogs from the campus. The campus had a sizable canine population, and I had taken it as part of the ambience of Berkeley ever since I had first known the area as a graduate student in 1933.

The third was a demand (dated about three years earlier) to put an immediate stop to a certain practice on campus. There was a big dog who stood beside a drinking water fountain in the Doe Library. Student friends would turn on the fountain and the dog would lap at the water—obviously unsanitary.

My first reaction was that I was not the best person to handle these problems. On the all-purpose family farm in rural Pennsylvania where I was raised, fleas, ticks, lice, and other insects were not considered as much of a menace to life and limb as the petitioners claimed. I also liked dogs and thought they had a right to life, liberty, and a drink of water. I had always welcomed them on campus.

What, then, to do with these folders Agnes Robb had given me? As so many had done before me, I added my initials (but in green ink) and sent them back. I got no acknowledgment and received no new folders. Incidentally, I started my use of green ink so that the president could, if he wished, more easily identify my initials among the long list of initials on the long line of folders he circulated so widely among his top staff.

My second reaction to the episode of the three folders was to recognize that my job as chancellor had already been precisely defined for me: I had already learned "the ropes" and would be in charge of whatever nobody else wanted. I was slated to be a garbage can.

The Old Provostship

The office that was given to me that first day in late January 1952 was one that I had been in before, when it was occupied by Monroe Deutsch, the provost at Berkeley from 1931 to 1947. It had been vacant for five years because the position of provost had not been filled after Deutsch's retirement (the president had acted as provost as well). Deutsch was a dignified and courtly gentleman, a classical scholar who had taught Bob Sproul Latin in the public high schools of San Francisco. When provost, he had once asked me to drop by for a chat, and a friendly and pleasant one it was. Deutsch said he was curious to know what we were doing at the Institute of Industrial Relations, and I told him. I never went to see him again because he was in no way a part of the decision-making process above me. I always dealt directly with President Sproul.

So I sat there in Deutsch's office from eight to five each day for three weeks, with time out for lunch alone at one or another of the several hole-in-the-wall eating places along Telegraph Avenue. In addition to the three folders, I had one visit from a faculty member whose initiative I greatly appreciated. It was Garff Wilson, professor of rhetoric, and the very gifted director of public ceremonies—the best of any I have ever seen anywhere. He handled all public ceremonies to perfection, including the most spectacular in university history—the address in 1962 by the president of the United States, John F. Kennedy, before 90,000 people in the stands and on the field of Memorial Stadium. Garff wanted to know what ideas I had about my inauguration. At that point, I had none.

Sproul went by my open door several times a day but never said "hello" (I waved but got no response), and he never invited me into his office. And I was too timid to demand an appointment. Not one of the thousand people who then worked for the universitywide administration, including vice presidents and directors, ever dropped by to welcome me. No phone calls. No mail.

I was being treated as the new Provost Deutsch and not as the chancellor and "executive head" of all activities on the campus as the regents had specified, and I knew what that meant. But it turned out that I was not Monroe Deutsch.

The New Context

The administrative context of the chancellor's position was not identical with that of the provostship Deutsch accepted in 1931. The university was by 1952 both much larger and more complex, less easy for one man to administer in great detail. Also, a rising attack had been under way on the high degree of centralization of administration initiated by some powerful deans at UCLA, then by some of the southern regents, and also later by Berkeley deans. (For Joel Hildebrand's 1943 remarks to the Academic Senate at Berkeley on university and faculty welfare, see Appendix 2 section B. A participant in the faculty's 1919–20 revolt and one of the senate's greatest leaders, Hildebrand served variously as dean of men, dean of letters and science, and dean of the College of Chemistry.) All this led, in 1946, to the university's commissioning a management consulting firm to study the university's organization and to recommend changes. The firm's report (1948) advised a decentralization of operations to the campuses as much as was possible along with maintenance of unity within the university system. Nothing was done about the report until 1951, when the two chancellorships were established.

As an indication of the long-standing difficulties, a committee of southern regents was established in 1920, the Committee on Southern California Schools, Colleges, and Institutions, led for many years by the powerful Edward A. Dickson (the "father" of UCLA and, in 1952, also chair of the regents). The committee was instrumental in drawing up the 1951 reorganization plan (see Appendix 2 section A). It had earlier been involved in establishing professional schools and the graduate division at UCLA. The deans at UCLA, and some individual faculty members, used this committee to air their grievances and kept this route of contact, and particularly to its chair, as long as the committee continued (until 1958).

The Committee on Southern California Schools, Colleges, and Institutions set up a subcommittee to advise the regents on a replacement for Provost Dykstra at UCLA following his sudden heart attack and death in 1950. The subcommittee was chaired by Regent John Canaday, a vice president of Lockheed and a former executive secretary of the California Alumni Association at UCLA. The other members were Brodie Ahlport and Victor Hansen. The subcommittee rendered its report on October 11, 1950. It fully endorsed the recommendations of the Public Administration Service report of 1948. But then the subcommittee went beyond that report in two respects: it said that the provost title should be replaced by that of president and that the president should be called chancellor; and it stated that universitywide headquarters should be moved away from Berkeley.

Sproul replied on October 26, 1950, in strong disagreement.[2] He said that these recommendations would "set the stage for conversion of the University of California from a strong, statewide institution, under unified administration, to a loosely knit federation of institutions without strong leadership." He added that there must be a "single head—not on paper but in fact," and he feared the development of a "Provost-Regents relationship" instead of a president-regents relationship. Here was an important warning, and one I always had in mind: decentralization could go too far in the direction of a "confederation." Later, as president, I opposed a proposal to do just this. But the issue still remains open: how to maintain the essential unity of the university while advancing the decentralization of operations? In retrospect, I have concluded that President Sproul was more nearly prescient in his fears than I thought at the time.

Sproul, of course, was supported against decentralization by the 1,000-person universitywide staff, and he also had the very loyal support of Berkeley alumni in anything he wanted to do.

Thrusts and Parries

I came to the conclusion that I would be better off doing something rather than nothing, so I went back to the Institute of Industrial Relations. I was still its director and had my spartan "office"—a chair at the end of the table in the institute's conference room—as well as an ongoing research program and teaching. I remained in my institute office until the end of October (nine months later) when a universitywide staff member finally assigned me some minimal office space in Dwinelle Hall. As the new chancellor, I did not have the authority to assign any space at all on the Berkeley campus and never did have such authority in the six years I served in that position. One of my first acts as president was to delegate such authority to my successor as chancellor—Glenn Seaborg. (I also made sure my predecessor as president had a large office and a reserved parking space; I continued his administrative secretary's job and always placed him as one of the leaders of the presidential party in all academic processions, as with the great convocation for President Kennedy in 1962.)

I managed to find other things to do—some of them quite important. And I did not, at first, take my antagonistic introduction to the chancellorship personally. An active life in the contentious world of industrial relations had taught me that there were many sources of action other than personal feelings. For example, John L. Lewis of the United Mine Workers and founder of the CIO once had the following encounter with Donald Richberg, who had been a lawyer for labor unions and then switched to the employer side. The first time Lewis and Richberg met across the bargaining table, Lewis attacked Richberg saying, "There you sit, born of the womb of Labor, suckled at the breast of Labor, taught in the lap of Labor, and now, for filthy lucre, you represent the greedy exploiters of Labor." At a recess, Richberg went up to Lewis and said, "You were a little rough on me, John," and Lewis replied, "Nothing personal, Don, nothing personal."

"Nothing personal." I did not think that Bob Sproul had taken a sudden personal dislike for me. I did know that Deutsch had been confined to doing nothing of importance for sixteen years. I did know that Sproul had earlier opposed creation of the chancellorship. But I also knew of Sproul's affirmative vote in the Board of Regents (he actually introduced the motion) on the implementing action to create chancellorships at UCLA and Berkeley. It was also Sproul who afterward announced that the "reorganization" was "designed to do three things: (1) to streamline the administrative machinery of the enlarged University of California; (2) to define clearly the duties of the various university offices; and (3) to give each of the eight campuses within the statewide university the maximum degree of autonomy consistent with unity."

I took this to be the definitive statement of what was being done and believed that Sproul fully supported it. A new day had dawned!

What I did not know was that Sproul had not really accepted the decision of the regents to "streamline the administrative machinery" through giving chancellors a "maximum degree of autonomy" at the campus level. Sproul's opposition, it turned out, was just taking a different form at a different level: quiet opposition in practice at the level of relations between the president and the chancellors instead of open confrontation over a policy of decentralization with the deans and some of the regents. But I still accepted that what was happening was "nothing personal," which I am sure was true at that time. I also, quite naively, expected that the regents' official vote had set the course of subsequent actions and would come to prevail in an amicable fashion.

Bob Sproul was far from ready to accept such a course of developments. He was experienced, determined, and very adroit; and I was young and greatly in awe of President Sproul. My job had a name but nothing to "define clearly the duties." Sproul was fighting with all his great ability and his total conviction of the importance of preserving a unitary administration for the sake of preserving a single university. He kept the vision of the presidency he had known as a student (class of 1913) and young staff member when Wheeler was president, and he put it into effect in his own presidency. It was a status he greatly enjoyed (as one of his close associates later told me, he "loves being the one and only boss"). But now there were two chancellors, and one of them was at Berkeley.

From the beginning, much was at stake. On one side, the belief that the University of California could best (or only) be held together by a single personality and by highly centralized decision-making processes; on the other, that the university in the long run would be held together best (or at least better) by mutual advantages of association and would be managed better with detailed decision-making closer to the origins of problems in time and in place. Both sides wanted a single university and one of high distinction but disagreed on how best to preserve this.

At stake too were jobs and power. The huge staff of universitywide administrators and their assistants abhorred decentralization to the campuses for both reasons. The campuses, on the other side, and with increasing regental support, wanted more local responsibility and faster actions. The opposed alternatives were one "unitary campus," under highly centralized control, with several physical locations (such as the "Southern Branch," which was the early name for what became UCLA) *versus* several independently administered campuses coordinated in their general policies and their representation in Sacramento. Also at stake, more personally, was Sproul's traditional mode of operation *versus* my resistance to holding a fake position instead of actually serving as executive head of the Berkeley campus.

As 1952 came toward a close, I continued to evaluate the situation as it unfolded. I still thought of withdrawing. I had been happy in what I had been doing as a faculty member. I liked my teaching. I had a research program planned ten years ahead. I had a good income from arbitration ($40,000 a year) but was taking a cut (to $15,000 a year, the chancellor's original salary) because I thought it unwise to continue with my arbitration except for one long-standing occasional obligation in the national meat-packing industry. I had become the leading arbitrator on the Pacific Coast, but on a very part-time basis, and sufficiently recognized nationally so that I was selected as a founding vice president when the National Academy of Arbitrators was started in 1947. I had never thought, as is true of many young faculty members, that an administrative career was attractive. I later found that, under favorable circumstances, it could have its challenges and rewards.

But I hesitated. My faculty friends told me that, after the very divisive oath controversy, any one nominated by the Berkeley faculty who was also acceptable to the Board of Regents had an obligation to serve. Also, it would be potentially very difficult to open up the selection process a second time—difficult particularly for the president, who would be charged with impeding the agreed-upon decentralization. The board, following the oath controversy and other disagreements (including over the reorganization of the university), was split almost in half over Sproul's administration, with the opposition group constituting the "almost" one-half.

Battles over Decentralization

So I talked several times with Raymond Allen. Ray had been appointed chancellor at UCLA at about the same time I was appointed at Berkeley. The position of provost there had been vacant for two years, since Provost Dykstra's death. Dykstra, former president of the University of Wisconsin, had been a disappointed provost since 1945. A committee of three deans then exercised such authority as was delegated to the campus, which was a little more than at Berkeley—but not much. The pressure for the creation of chancellorships came more from the south than from the north. The very influential UCLA Alumni Association and the increasingly powerful southern regents were the primary leaders. But the deans of colleges and schools throughout the university also joined in. They felt that they not only were given too little authority but also that they were never consulted on policy and never properly informed about on-going developments. One response to their complaints was the provision by the regents, when they created the chancellorships, that each campus should have a council of deans with which the chancellor should meet regularly. The deans at Berkeley told me of their pleasure when the council was started at Berkeley and noted how the regents had at last responded to their requests. They seemed more impressed with their own new position of influence in governance than with the establishment of the office of campus chancellor. This new council was their triumph. I got the same impression from several of the deans at UCLA whom I already knew or with whom I shortly became acquainted.

Ray Allen's situation differed from mine in several respects, in addition to the UCLA attitude of separatism from Berkeley. He had been president of the University of Washington from 1946 to 1952. There he had had an effective career, including building a medical school (he was himself a physician). UCLA too was still building its medical school. At Washington, Ray had publicly fired three alleged "Communists" from the faculty. This made him additionally attractive to those regents who had been pro-oath. Hansena Frederickson, the immensely competent secretary to provosts, administrative committees, and chancellors at UCLA from 1936 to 1966, says in her oral history, "I saw this editorial about Raymond B. Allen taking a strong stand about Communism and praising him. So I realized that he was going to be our new chancellor."[3] The editorial appeared in a newspaper owned by Regent Dickson.

Most observers in 1952 assumed, as Ray and I did, that he was the president-in-waiting at the University of California (Sproul was then widely expected to retire in four years, at age sixty-five). Allen had stronger potential support for his position on decentralization of the administration, by UCLA deans, by UCLA alumni, and by southern regents, than did I in the north. On the other hand, he had already resigned his position at the University of Washington and was otherwise unemployed. I was not.

Had Ray not also been involved and the more motivated to hang on, I would not have entered the chancellorship on July 1, 1952. On my own I would have withdrawn my name. Ray needed the chancellorship at UCLA; and he needed my support in the north to help make the chancellorship minimally acceptable.

THE CAMPUS BUSINESS MANAGER

Ray and I, despite the dissimilarities in our situations, agreed to fight together for some initial decentralization before July 1, 1952, when our chancellorships were scheduled to start. We chose as our number one issue the question of to whom the campus business manager would report. It was crucial. Each campus business manager then reported directly to the universitywide vice president–business, James Corley. Each had far more authority and influence over daily operations than anyone else on campus. The business manager ran everything except strictly academic matters, which were, through other channels, also largely determined universitywide. Such a prominent role was then not unique to the University of California's business managers. It was widespread, particularly in the Big Ten universities and especially so at Michigan and Minnesota.

July 1 was approaching, and Ray and I became anxious. Only at the last minute (June 22) did we receive word from President Sproul that a solution was possible, and a few days later we each entered office. Sproul said he would seek an agreement between us and Jim Corley, and, if there remained any open issues, they would be referred to the Board of Regents for settlement. Sproul noted that Corley, as vice president–business, had a direct reporting line to the board and thus that the board had responsibility for conduct of that position. Corley quickly noted, on June 27, that the same person should not "assume the responsibility as business manager and chancellor at the same time." This would be too great a burden. He said, however, that the business manager, while reporting to him, should keep the chancellor "informed."

Deutsch sent me a longhand letter dated July 11, 1952, which said in part: "You are right in insisting that the business situation be cleared up . . . your position is absolutely sound." On January 27 he had written me that "the group of pygmies and/or clerks surrounding the president has had altogether too much to say; their influence must be broken." He also warned me about certain named individuals on the president's personal staff—with some, to me, surprising names of those not to trust.

The situation, however, never was "cleared up." Allen and I never did take the problem formally to the board for a final settlement. The understanding about keeping the chancellor "informed" did actually come to mean something at UCLA but meant nothing at Berkeley. The business manager at Berkeley, William Norton, kept on reporting solely universitywide. He never came to my office. He never asked me for advice. He never reported to me on any single development. I accepted this as a continuation of a long-standing relationship not subject to change while Norton was still in office. When he retired, Corley proposed a replacement with which I agreed. It was William Monahan of the class of 1924. Bill, as a Berkeley student, had been president of the Associated Students of the University of California (ASUC) and later, as an alumnus, its manager and thus also director of athletics. He had many friends among the alumni. He was the bluest of the "Old Blues." Bill accepted decentralization and personally was entirely loyal to me, as I was to him. But Vice President Corley selected an associate business manager (Robert Kerley) who, in private, reported directly to the vice president and not to me. Bill was thus business manager mostly in name, and he was personally given a bad time of it. His health and enjoyment of life greatly suffered. He was the greatest single personal casualty of the contest over decentralization. I shall always regret that I could not help him more. I did later take him onto my staff when I became president of the university.

In any event, I rode along with the historic reality at Berkeley, in part because I knew that the policy record was not all that clear: in establishing the chancellorships, the regents had exempted the areas under the vice president–business affairs from the chancellor's control but insisted on the chancellor's "administrative authority" over "all matters relating to business operations on his campus"—an impossible mandate. Also, Corley had great strength in Sacramento, among Berkeley alumni, and within his staff. Additionally, I did not care that much about his areas of responsibility. In effect, I lost that battle—until I became president when I won it for my successors as chancellors.

DEPARTMENT CHAIRS

That contest over business affairs was not the last battle, but it was the last in which Ray Allen and I supported each other. Why he withdrew from the warfare I never knew, but I suspected that it might have something to do with the fact that he was the president-in-waiting and I was not; and that, as president-in-waiting, he did not want to incur the wrath of the president-in-place and his supporters among the regents.

The next major battle was over who would appoint department "chairmen" (as then designated). These were crucial appointments, particularly when we needed so desperately to recover from the loyalty oath controversy and so hoped to raise our standing in the academic world. Campuses improve or deteriorate one department at a time, and recruitments and retentions are at the core of faculty quality and at the core of the responsibilities of department chairs. It is seldom fully recognized how important these positions are, particularly in recruiting new faculty members—and we faced heavy recruitment.

Ray Allen and I were to meet at UCLA with President Sproul (February 26, 1953), after the issue had been in contention for nearly a year. I could not find Ray in advance, as we had arranged, so I went alone into the meeting. Ray and Sproul and Harry Wellman, the vice president–agricultural sciences, were there sitting on one side of a table and a chair was placed for me on the other side facing them. President Sproul said that Ray Allen, who had already been meeting with them, had withdrawn his request to appoint department chairs. Ray nodded in agreement. Harry explained why, in agriculture, it was best to have department chairs appointed universitywide but that he would consult me in advance. I agreed because many of the agricultural departments had universitywide service responsibilities to elements of California agriculture. Also, I had full confidence that Harry would do whatever he promised. President Sproul asked if I would like to withdraw my request. I said no and gave my reasons. He then told me that the three of them agreed that my request should be denied, and he was denying it. I replied, "Mr. President, that is not a decision that I can accept." To my utmost surprise, a week or so later I received a letter from the president (March 5, 1953) saying that he had "reconsidered" and was giving me the authority to appoint department chairs at Berkeley. The same authority was given to the chancellor at UCLA.

INFORMATION AND PARTICIPATION

An additional battle, and one that took almost two years to conclude, was over a series of individually minor matters in which I made no attempt to elicit the support of Ray Allen. As of the summer and early fall of 1952, I made several requests:

To obtain a copy of the budget for the Berkeley campus.

To receive the minutes of the Board of Regents in open session that involved decisions directly affecting the Berkeley campus.

To be allowed to attend open sessions of the board without having to secure special permission in advance each time (the fact that they were "open" meant that any member of the public could drop in).

To receive materials sent to the regents on Berkeley matters that were to be considered in open session.

Decisions on these matters were subject to controversy into early 1954. At that point Regent Gerald Hagar, who was a longtime friend of Bob Sproul, intervened informally to bring about a full granting of these requests.

The list of requests I never made is longer:

To be given authority over architects and engineers, or over nonacademic personnel, although I did ask at one point for control over space assignment, which was refused, and I did inquire about the campus police force and was told "No." Berkeley had a designated public information officer. The universitywide person assigned to Berkeley affairs was in my office only once—on a Saturday morning asking me to sign a press release prepared universitywide that no one at that level wanted to have his or her name associated with. It had to do with some scandals in intercollegiate athletics. I signed. I never asked to have that officer report to me.

To have the dean of students I inherited (Hurford Stone) report to me in actuality. He chose to report universitywide. I accepted that. Stone and I totally disagreed on the conduct of student affairs.

To be allowed to plan and take charge of public ceremonies on the campus, or the meetings of the Academic Senate—the president handled both of these although I technically presided, as the regents had provided, over public ceremonies. Garff Wilson on the president's staff was in charge of public ceremonies. He was, fortunately, one of a handful of cooperative and cordial individuals on the 1,000-member presidential staff.

To make any, except informal, contacts with the California Alumni Association at Berkeley. It directly related to President Sproul through Vice President Stanley McCaffrey.

To have a university-provided residence. I enlarged my own house for university functions totally at my own expense. I later received a rent rising from $2,000 to $4,000 per year (when I was president) for the use of our house for the many university dinners and receptions held there, for an office for the use of the part-time social secretary working for my wife, and for the use (after our own enlargements) of our collections of silverware and china and of much else—the net cost to us was substantial. Provision along the way, however, was made for a housekeeper and gardening assistance.

Delegation of all the above excluded areas to the chancellors took place immediately after I became president, along with the provision of an official university residence fully maintained (and tax free).

THE CHANCELLOR'S STAFF

One further climactic event led me later to place my resignation confidentially and quietly before President Sproul as of early 1956, and it lay there until June. The delays in getting decisions and infrequent consultation on matters affecting Berkeley were problems in the background. The big open issue was the organization and staffing of the chancellor's office. As of June 25, 1952, I had been given a staff of three persons for the year 1952–53: two administrative assistants and one secretary. Deutsch as of 1947 had a staff of four full-time equivalent (FTE) positions. My staff had grown by the 1955–56 academic year to sixteen FTEs. I was asking for three more positions.

There was also a specific disagreement over the position of vice-chancellor. First I had arranged an honorary vice-chancellorship for Sailor Davis without stipend or assignment. (Sailor was the longtime and powerful dean of letters of science and had been terribly disappointed when he was not named chancellor.) I then secured the appointment of Donald Coney, the librarian, as the very part-time vice-chancellor for 1955–56 and 1956–57 with one specific assignment. I was going all-out for an augmentation of the cultural programs on the Berkeley campus, and, in particular, wanted to enhance all kinds of invited performances—dance, music, singing, lectures—through a committee on drama, lectures, and music (later called Committee for Arts and Lectures and then Cal Performances). Coney was ideal for this and terrific at it. The title of vice-chancellor gave him additional incentive and clout. Then I arranged to add, for 1956–57, a second very part-time vice-chancellor, James

D. Hart, a highly distinguished professor of English and later director of the Bancroft Library. Jim had two specific assignments that were also projects in which I took great personal interest: creating an art museum and building a library for undergraduate use (the Moffitt Library). I was to be limited, for 1956–57, however, to only one of these positions—the word on campus was that I had been "limited to one vice."

In the course of the budget hearing for the 1956–57 budget with President Sproul in late fall 1955, he told me that he thought reorganization had gone too far, particularly at Berkeley, and had to be restudied. His words alarmed me. I became even more alarmed when I saw a copy of the 1956–57 budget presented to the regents in December. Without further consultation with me, the budget cut four positions from my staff, one-quarter of the total. Each had an incumbent in place: I would have to fire four people. I then made my one and only protest to the Board of Regents. I was fed up with the nearly four years of continuing guerrilla warfare.

On March 5, 1956, I wrote Sproul that I thought there "should either be willing acceptance or explicit rejection of the reorganization as it affects Berkeley." Four regents, Edwin Pauley, Jesse Steinhart, Edward Heller, and Gerald Hagar, quietly intervened and helped solve some problems and change some attitudes. Jerry Hagar was particularly helpful. Sproul argued with Hagar that he was fighting for the dignity, prestige, and power of the presidency. He noted that he had never permitted dissension on his staff and never would, but that he had not yet made up his mind about my future. The regents, however, argued for a more generous attitude toward the chancellorship. They were persuasive as far as the president was concerned, and the situation greatly improved. Basically, Sproul dropped his contention that reorganization at Berkeley had gone too far. The staff positions were restored for 1956–57 and subsequently, for one year only (1956–57), two part-time vice-chancellors were still permitted.

How It Turned Out

In the last two years of my chancellorship, relations with the president's office went along much more smoothly. My assumption was that Sproul questioned the extent of reorganization in fall 1955 because the regents' postponement of his retirement from age sixty-five to sixty-seven had given him a longer time horizon. Over the six years, Sproul slowly and reluctantly conceded the minimum I thought essential. Corley, however, never gave an inch. In effect, the president managed (with Corley) the nonacademic operations on the campus and its public relations, and I handled academic decisions and long-range planning. In each case, we were in charge of what most interested us; and the campus prospered.

I found this eventual arrangement acceptable and even agreeable. It made it possible for me to spend additional time on academic matters and on campus plans that I considered more important. Additionally, the decisions made universitywide in the excluded areas were, in my judgment, generally competently made even though usually with long delays; and I had no great interest in the details of daily bureaucratic administration.

End of act 3 in the reorganization of the university.

"The Best Balanced Distinguished University"

By 1906, some forty years after its founding—and despite its contentious origins and location on the West Coast— Berkeley was considered to be one of the Big Six research universities in the United States. In 1934, in the last national ranking before I became chancellor, Berkeley was tied with Chicago and Columbia for second place after Harvard, according to the number of distinguished departments.

Its rank within the Big Six rose during World War II and the years afterward, particularly in science: the Keniston ranking survey[1] of 1957 placed Berkeley first in the physical sciences and second overall to Harvard. From 1934 to 1957, Berkeley had risen from a tie with Chicago and Columbia to be rated above both of them. The other members of the Big Six at that time went in this order: Columbia, Yale, Michigan, Chicago.

The account below covers developments from 1952 to 1962, the central period of one of the golden ages in the academic life of the Berkeley campus that led up to its 1964 ranking as the country's "best balanced distinguished university." These ten years covered my chancellorship and that of Glenn Seaborg; they included the years of A. R. Davis and Lincoln Constance as deans of letters and science, of Morrough P. O'Brien and John Whinnery as deans of engineering, and of many other deans, department chairs, and members of senate committees, and the years of a remarkable spirit of determination to recover and to advance on the part of the Berkeley faculty as a whole. It was also a period of prosperity in California and of strong gubernatorial support particularly from Earl Warren and Edmund G. ("Pat") Brown. The spirit was there and also the resources—a happy combination with spectacular results.

The basic Berkeley strategy was one of selective attention, not equal across-the-board distribution of efforts and resources, and aimed at the best investments of administrative talent (department chairs) and intellectual resources (faculty positions) for advancing academic performance. The overall picture was that of quality rising in the physical sciences, and of quantity and quality rising in the social sciences (including history and business administration), mathematics (and statistics), engineering, and environmental design including architecture. The creative arts gained greatly in the facilities for their efforts. The biological sciences (and psychology) and the humanities (other than English and philosophy) and professional schools (other than engineering, business administration, and environmental design) were less affected. Mathematics and statistics composed the area of greatest advances; and mathematics is now as central a department to intellectual endeavors as philosophy was a century ago. Griffith Evans (mathematics) and Jerzy Neyman (statistics) were the two chairs primarily responsible, replicating the historic places of G. N. Lewis in chemistry, and Ernest Lawrence and Raymond Birge in physics.

▪

To decline, restabilize, or possibly even rise were the alternatives before Berkeley after the devastating loyalty oath controversy. In a time of great uncertainty and some peril, the apparent likelihood was to decline. The hope was to restabilize. But there was also an off chance to rise. And this last, least likely scenario became the operative one. An American Council on Education study made in spring 1964 ranked Berkeley at the top of the Big Six—not out of the running as some had so confidently predicted a few years earlier.[2] Berkeley was judged to be "the best balanced distinguished university in the country" (see Table 1). As an intended joke, I sent to the president of Harvard an Avis button carrying the message to "try harder" (and credited a lack of reply to a discreet secretary with the good sense to intercept the message).

Actually this ranking was not entirely fair to Harvard. It was fair only within the areas studied: letters and science, and engineering. Harvard was weak in engineering and Berkeley strong by that time—second after Massachusetts Institute of Technology. If some other major professional school had been chosen instead of engineering, or all professional schools had been included, Harvard would have been clearly first. But that a relatively new and public institution on the far West Coast should have come to be rated that high would still have been amazing. What was even more amazing was that this position should have been achieved so soon after such an internal conflagration as the loyalty oath controversy. Berkeley had jumped far ahead in the rankings not only of its historic public competitors (particularly Michigan, Wisconsin, and

TABLE 1
Reputational Rankings as of 1964

Institution	Number of Departments in Top 6 in Each Field (out of 29 rated)
California-Berkeley	28*
Harvard	23
Princeton	13
Yale	13
MIT	10
Stanford	10
Cal Tech	9
Michigan	9
Wisconsin-Madison	9
Chicago	8
Columbia	7
Illinois-Urbana	7
Johns Hopkins	3
Minnesota	3
Pennsylvania	3
Cornell	2
Purdue	2
Washington-Seattle	2

Source: Allan M. Cartter, An Assessment of Quality in Graduate Education (Washington, D.C.: American Council on Education, 1966).

*Berkeley did not have the 29th field. Thus it had 28 out of 28.

Illinois), but also of its historic major private competitors (Harvard, Chicago, Columbia, Cornell, Yale, Princeton, MIT, and Stanford).

Though academic reputations and their rankings may not be "scientific"— they represent the opinions of informed people and lag by at least two or three years behind the actualities—they are very influential in recruiting new faculty members and graduate students (by the early 1960s, only Harvard passed Berkeley in attracting Woodrow Wilson fellows and National Science Foundation fellowship winners as graduate students). And despite the gloom of the early 1950s, Berkeley had two major assets: the strength and support of the Academic Senate, and the solid academic base it had already achieved, particularly in the sciences.

When the first ranking study of reputations appeared in 1906 (see Table 2),

TABLE 2
Reputational Rankings as of 1906

1.	Harvard
2.	Columbia
3.	Chicago
4.	Cornell
5.	Johns Hopkins
6.	California-Berkeley
7.	Yale
8.	Michigan
9.	MIT
10.	Wisconsin-Madison
11.	Pennsylvania
12.	Stanford
13.	Princeton
14.	Minnesota and Ohio State

Source: James McKeen Cattell, "A Statistical Study of American Men of Science," Science, 2d s., 24 (1906): 739.

Berkeley was already one of the Big Six. It followed Harvard, Columbia, Chicago, Cornell, and Johns Hopkins and preceded Yale, Michigan, and seven others.

What Berkeley Had Going for It

Berkeley had several advantages: the climate on the West Coast, the fast grow-ing state of California, the attractiveness of San Francisco in its geography and cultural life, the vision of the early supporters of the university who aimed high—Oakland was to become "the New Haven of the West," the aspirations of a frontier society seeking to match the sophistication of the East (as, for ex-ample, in opera).

Berkeley had gotten off to a difficult start in 1868 with a passionate battle over whether it should emphasize scholarship or service to agriculture and in-dustry: Yale alumni who founded the predecessor College of California in 1855 favored academic excellence, but the legislative action establishing the uni-versity was inspired by the federal Land-Grant Act of 1862. Daniel Coit Gilman had come from Yale but left Berkeley in despair and disgust in 1875, after three years as president, to be the founding president of Johns Hopkins University.

In responding to the invitation from Johns Hopkins, Gilman wrote (November 10, 1874): "The guidance of such a trust as you represent seems to me one of the most important educational responsibilities in our country. . . . My personal inclinations would lead me to resign my position here at once irrespective of any call elsewhere, on the ground that however well we may build up the University of California, its foundations are unstable because dependent on legislative control and popular clamor. These conditions are different from what they were represented to be at the time of my coming here."[3] As Berkeley slowly recovered from this distressing beginning of "unstable foundations," it became a successful combination of Yale and land-grant. By 1900, when the American Association of Universities was started, the University of California was one of fourteen founding members. Only Harvard, Yale, and Columbia surpassed it in numbers of graduate students.

In its early years, Berkeley had drawn heavily on some outstanding faculty members leaving the defeated Confederacy. Eugene Waldemar Hilgard, early professor of agriculture, came from the University of Mississippi, and John LeConte, physics, and his brother Joseph, natural science, from South Carolina College. The first professor of mathematics, William Thomas Welcker, had been a captain in the Confederate Army. Streets near the campus bear the names of the first three of these to this day as do Hilgard Hall and LeConte Hall on the Berkeley campus.

Around 1900 there were two additional favorable developments. The founding of Stanford helped create a larger concentration of academic talent in the area (a critical mass) in a period when it took four days by train to reach colleagues on the East Coast. Many formal and informal contacts between Berkeley and Stanford followed at the faculty level. And the two universities became good friends in Sacramento and elsewhere. No two other universities in the United States, except for Harvard and MIT, have had such a long-term mutually advantageous relationship. In 1993 Berkeley and Stanford were ranked one and two in academic reputations, with Harvard as three and MIT and Princeton tied at number four (see chapter 28) as measured by numbers of fields in the top six. Neither Berkeley nor Stanford would have rated so high without the other.

The other development around 1900 was the appointment (1899) of Benjamin Ide Wheeler as president of the university. Wheeler had studied at Berlin, Leipzig, Jena, and Heidelberg (with a Ph.D.—a Summa—from Heidelberg) and revered the German-model university of that age. He was a dominating president as he rode a horse around campus, stopping to make decisions as petitioners approached him along the way. He was once introduced at Heidelberg University as a "monarch from a democracy visiting a democracy in a monarchy." In particular, Wheeler put emphasis on the sciences and the classics, which were also then the German favorites. The most important faculty appointment he made (among several) was that of G. N. Lewis in chemistry (professor and dean, 1912 to 1946), who, as dean, recruited one of the world's leading faculties in chemistry in the first great academic triumph at Berkeley. Chemistry was a "college," not a department, as it remains to this day (with two departments within it—chemistry and chemical engineering). It has been, and still is, in my judgment, the outstanding unit within the University of California—superb in research, superb in the teaching of both undergraduate and graduate students, and superb in the contributions of its faculty members to university governance.

Wheeler made another great but unintended contribution—negative for him but positive for Berkeley: his authoritarian style (abetted by his alleged pro-German sympathies in World War I) led to a faculty revolt in 1919–20. The result was that a new set of standing orders of the Board of Regents (1920) gave more responsibilities to the faculty senate than any other faculty in the United States enjoyed. In particular, it required the president to consult with the senate on all academic personnel decisions. The senate committees that have exercised these responsibilities have mostly done so with great devotion and good judgment. One of the advantages that Berkeley has had ever since, in the competition with Harvard, has been the existence of a unified strong senate able to support faculty quality across the board, while Harvard has had a series of more or less autonomous faculties.

The next highly effective president was Robert Gordon Sproul (1930–58). He strengthened relations with the state in Sacramento and further encouraged the development of science. The most important faculty appointment around that time, with the essential assistance of Raymond Birge, longtime chair of the physics department, was of Ernest Lawrence (1928) and led to the building of the cyclotron and much else. Sproul, when he became president in 1930, strongly encouraged Lawrence in his exploits, particularly by helping him secure research support. Out of this came directly five Nobel Prize winners on the faculty, and indirectly a general strengthening of the sciences. The great concentration of the highest scientific talent at Berkeley was, particularly, the result of the efforts and good judgment of Wheeler, Sproul, Birge, Lawrence, and G. N. Lewis (see Appendix 1 section F, for Berkeley faculty members holding Nobel Prizes or membership in the National Academy of Sciences).

Out of these and many other developments, Berkeley, by the early 1950s, was ready to challenge Harvard in the rankings. But it was also poised, as an institution "blacklisted" by the American Association of University Professors because of the loyalty oath controversy, to fall out of the Big Six—as external wisdom assumed and internal self-evaluation feared. And since competition at the top of university life in the United States is very intense, you must—as Alice did in *Through the Looking-Glass*—run as fast as you can just to stay even. To get ahead, it is necessary to run twice as fast as you ever had before. So it was with Berkeley.

The Berkeley Campus Takes Charge of Its Future

Two sets of actions were essential.

One action related to the best possible use for every faculty appointment or promotion to tenure. Fortunately, there was a large pool of positions to work with. Some new positions were developed as the student body increased from 16,000 in fall 1952 to 25,000 in fall 1962. Other positions had been held by less qualified members of the faculty appointed so quickly after the close of World War II to teach the GIs. Some members of this group were possibly adequate but certainly not distinguished scholars. They had served usefully during an emergency period. Now, however, they were a potential drag on quality instead of godsends in filling teaching positions. Many of them were my friends, as I belonged to the same age cohort. Mostly the reviews of their dismissals came to my desk just before Christmas, and each year I went through the process of hearing a series of personal appeals—and I hated it. As an aside, I was more impressed with the wives—they usually made a better case than their husbands and spoke more eloquently of the heavy teaching responsibilities, young children, delayed completion and/or publication of research projects—and some of these women were unusually impressive people. I kept an extra handkerchief available to wipe up the tears on my conference table.

Another source of new positions was retirements. In total, from 1952–53 to 1962–63, there were over 1,000 new faculty appointments to tenure at Berkeley. By 1962, two-thirds of the faculty was new. The future of Berkeley, for at least the next generation—including the 1993 ratings, published in 1995—depended on how well those 1,000-plus decisions were made.

Making good use of these open positions was a massive group effort. It started with recommendations for appointments from the departments—a point to which I shall return shortly. All recommendations went from there to an ad hoc review committee of the senate, each committee composed then of five persons from within and outside the department involved, and the opinions of the three "outside" members were of particular importance since they were not so committed to prior departmental action. Next the cases advanced to the Academic Senate Budget Committee (actually, the academic personnel committee), which played the most central role of all. Then followed action by the several deans, and the deans of most importance to the subsequent rankings were those of letters and science and of engineering. At last the cases came to the chancellor, and in my day and in that of Glenn Seaborg (chancellor, July 1958–January 1961), there followed the most careful personal review of each case. If I were negative on a recommendation (and later Glenn also), I wrote a letter to the academic personnel committee explaining why. I never had a single protest from that committee. Importantly, I never recommended an appointment or promotion against the academic personnel committee's advice.

We turned down recommended promotions and new appointments on their individual merits, but we also, in doing so, set our definition of "merit" at a somewhat higher level so that we were also raising the standards for future cases; and the word got around. President Sproul nearly always, and the regents always, accepted my actions. The tough points of review were by the academic personnel committee and at the level of dean-chancellor in consultation. I took the firm position, and so did Glenn, that no department had a right to choose mediocrity over excellence. We, of course, respected the recommendations of high-ranking departments (as, for example, English, physics, chemistry, and mathematics) more than low-ranking ones. Key aspects of the review at my level were a careful reading of academic personnel committee recommendations. Some recommendations were more equivocal than others. Also important was an analysis of the votes within the departments and within the ad hoc committees and, particularly, within ad hoc committees, of those of the outside members. Thus, hesitancies expressed in academic personnel committee recommendations and negative votes of highly respected departmental members and of outside members of the ad hoc committees were the main bases for most negative actions. Attention was also paid to the quality of journals and of publishing houses where works by each person under consideration appeared.

The second set of campus actions that helped secure Berkeley's future was the careful selection of department chairs. These chairs made the nominations for new appointments and did most of the recruiting. Department chairs in 1952 appeared to me to vary greatly in ability, and some had served for very long periods. The first step in improving the overall quality of the chairs was to get the authority to appoint them. This was the only major delegation of authority made to me as chancellor by Robert Gordon Sproul (March 5, 1953; see chapter 4's discussion of the confrontation). The second step was to set a normal period of service as a department chair at three to five years instead of indefinitely, with the possibility of extended years of service after review. This had two major effects. One was to rotate out ineffective chairs. The second was to get some people of high ability to serve on the grounds that it was not a "life sentence" and to establish the principle that all full professors had an obligation to serve if asked. The negative side was that fewer chairs had really long-term personal responsibility for results.

The greatest attention was paid to selection in the College of Letters and Science, where most of the chairs were located. The dean of letters and science and I met once a week and much of our time was spent in selection of chairs, as well as in reviewing promotions and appointments to tenure. Often we would consult the academic personnel committee on appointment of chairs, as always on professorial appointments. Sometimes we would bring in an outside person as chair, and sometimes we would appoint a person from Berkeley but from another department—this was usually a short-term appointment to "clean house." New chairs were often given a substantial number of new appointments to make, including some at the tenure and even "overscale" level. Sometimes new chairs were also given advice (one of my suggestions, to the new chair of psychology, was to stop having those suicidal weekly departmental meetings and, instead, to conduct business in the halls and offices one on one).

The result was that we obtained an outstanding group of chairs, due particularly to the two deans of letters and science who knew the faculty so well and had such good judgment—A. R. Davis (1947 to 1955) and Lincoln Constance (1955 to 1962). We also raised standards for promotions and appointments. Sailor Davis once told me that, during our joint period in office (1952–55), according to his count, 20 percent of all proposed promotions and new appointments to tenure that had been approved before our final reviews were turned down at our levels. That sounded high to me, but there were many turndowns. This was the period, of course, when many hasty recruits during the GI rush were coming up for tenure review. Also, several times resentful chairs charged that Sailor was out to "get" their departments. There was substance to these charges. Sailor had good judgment and, with my backing as chancellor, used it effectively. Both Sailor and Lincoln were greatly advantaged in having been members and chairs of the academic personnel committee. When Sailor was retiring, I asked for and accepted his nomination of his successor, and appreciated it. Sailor was the better of the two deans at tough decisions on tenure; Lincoln was a genius at selecting department chairs; and with each of them, in these areas of action, we always ended up in agreement. These two deans were essential to the academic recovery at Berkeley. It would not have happened without them and the senate academic personnel committee. In his oral history (Regional Oral History Office, UC Berkeley), Lincoln says that Sailor once told him, "Sproul makes great use of the Budget Committee because he thinks it's a good idea. Kerr will, also, because he believes in it." And I did.

There was one organizational disagreement, however, and that was with Lincoln. The consolidated College of Letters and Science did very well with budgets, with selection of chairs, with appointments and promotions; and it was the very best unit to administer a coordinated general education curriculum. However, it did not do so well, I thought, with working out directions of forward movement that involved two or more departments: for example, in planning the biological sciences' modernizing of space and scientific approaches; in handling most of the social sciences' fast emerging international dimensions (anthropology was an exception) or in putting together a new building for several departments; in developing language laboratories and comparative literature; in managing the conflicts between the critical "scholars" and the expressive "creators" in the arts, and in getting new campus-wide physical facilities. As director of the Institute of Industrial Relations, I had had great difficulty in developing a new Center for Survey Research in the absence of a supportive divisional structure within the College of Letters and Science. Lincoln favored the old consolidated structure and I yielded to his judgment and his strong preference. Later on, a divisional structure was introduced.

The dean of engineering, Morrough P. ("Mike") O'Brien (dean from 1943 to 1959), called the 1964 ratings on engineering his "report card." Berkeley stood with MIT at the top of the engineering list. Mike was tough and he could be imperious. He took a good regional school, strong on the applied side, and

TABLE 3

Rankings of Professional Schools in Big Six Universities*

Professional school	Berkeley	Harvard	Princeton	Yale	MIT	Stanford
Architecture	2	3	5	7 (tie)	1	—
Business administration	7	1	—	—	6	2
Education	—	5	—	—	—	1
Forestry	1	—	—	6 (tie)	—	—
Law	7	1	—	2	—	6
Library science	7	—	—	—	—	—
Optometry	1 (tie)	—	—	—	—	—
Public health	3 (tie)	3 (tie)	—	—	—	—
Social work	5	—	—	—	—	—

Source: Peter M. Blau and Rebecca Zames Margulies, "The Reputation of American Professional Schools," Change 6, no. 10 (winter 1974–75): tb. 1 on 42–47.

*Top Six in 1964; see Table 1.

made it into one of the best in the world and at the scientific level. He was, however, very unhappy that I decided to leave chemical engineering in the College of Chemistry where it had an outstanding record and where its faculty members were very satisfied. A hot dispute, but Mike reluctantly accepted my decision. Thus chemistry also deserves some of the credit for the high ranking of engineering at Berkeley, as well as of the campus as a whole.

Mike was often off campus and we relied on the very effective administration of his executive assistant, Frances Woertendyke (later Eberhart), to keep the college running. This was not the only situation at Berkeley where an executive assistant made such a crucial contribution to the advance of a school, college, or department. Deans and chairs come and go and when they come, they are often absent. (The nicest thing about part-time faculty members is that they *are* around at least part of the time.) It was, I often thought, a strong core of executive assistants, as much as anyone, that kept Berkeley running on a daily basis and advancing. Fran was one strong representative of this essential group. She always either had or could get the answers. John Whinnery as dean of engineering, 1959 to 1963, carried on with great distinction the transition from a good regional school to a school with high international distinction. John had earlier led electrical engineering into the front rank.

The 1964 ratings were not only O'Brien's and Whinnery's report card; they

TABLE 4

Individual Faculty Honors at the Big Six Universities, 1962

	*Nobel Prize Winners**	*Members of National Academy of Sciences**	*Guggenheim Fellowships*
	1962–63	*1962–63*	*1960–64*
Berkeley	9	37	76
Harvard	5	53	48
Princeton	2	15	17
Yale	—	20	42
MIT	—	28	32
Stanford	4	19	21

Sources: National Academy of Sciences/National Research Council, Annual Report Fiscal Year 1962–63 *(Washington, D.C.: U.S. Government Printing Office, October 1966); John Simon Guggenheim Memorial Foundation,* Reports of the President and of the Treasurer *(title varies) (New York, 1959 and 1960; 1961 and 1962; 1963 and 1964).*

*Numbers for faculty members in 1962, not for the total of those honored.

also showed the work of all those other deans and department chairs and senate committee members who contributed so much to that great effort.[4] (For rankings in other areas than letters and science and engineering, see Table 3; and, for additional ways of looking at rankings of the faculty as a whole, see Table 4.)

Departmental Life

Much more was going on at the departmental level than changing chairs and adding faculty. The internal life of academic units is often quite lively. Before I became chancellor, I once thought that all departments constituted happy families, except for those that I knew well, which were then three. As I got to know more departments and then later all, I kept to the same observation— all appeared to be happy families until I came to know them. As illustrations, set forth crudely and without all the nuances that brilliant and sensitive minds can conjure up, there were the following:

Physics and to some extent chemistry: fans or critics of Robert Oppenheimer, and the neutrals.

Sociology: centrist versus leftist political theorists.

Political science: the supporters of older "political thought" versus newer "political analysis."

Economics: neoclassicists versus Keynesians, and later broadly oriented real-life observers versus econometricians and mathematical model builders.

Mathematics and statistics: proponents of universal laws versus universal skeptics (I ruled that the two departments should be separate, in part on the grounds of these diverging mentalities).

Biology: proponents of the "old" (horizontal forms of life, e.g., entomology) or the "new" (vertical levels, e.g., cellular) biology.

The arts: the "scholarly" historians (or critics with a theoretical bent) versus the "creative" practitioners.

Philosophy: the "Greeks" versus the logicians and/or the linguists.

Literature: comparativists versus single-language advocates.

International studies: specialists versus generalists (area studies or comparative analysis of systems).

Psychology: experimentalists (on rats) versus observers (of human beings), and social versus clinical researchers, ranging from the softer social sciences to the harder biological sciences.

A campus is a collection of departments, and each department has an external and internal life. I sometimes thought of Selma Lagerlof's description of ancient houses in an old Scandinavian city, so solid looking outside but inside the walls every night the rats fought it out. Ivory towers too have their outer appearances and inner realities. Berkeley is in no way unique among universities. It is and was different only in detail.

In any event, when the 1964 ratings came out, every ranked department at Berkeley (twenty-eight of them—the twenty-ninth rated department, pharmacology, did not exist at Berkeley) was rated in the top six nationwide. That has never happened again at Berkeley or, beginning with the 1964 ratings, at any other institution. One advantage Berkeley had was a close working relationship between the Academic Senate and the administration, and also within the campus administration. An additional advantage over Harvard, beyond having an all-encompassing senate, was that Berkeley had a lump-sum budget to use across the board, while Harvard had a policy of "each tub on its own bottom." Berkeley had the greater fiscal, as well as governance, capacity to pull up weak areas.

The Berkeley faculty in these years accepted more administrative participation in the academic life of the campus than is normal in research universities, particularly in review of professorial appointments and promotions and in appointment of department chairs, as well as in other ways, as the next chapter will note. The explanations are that the faculty faced a clear up or down alternative in direction of development, that it was closely consulted, and that it had the best of senate leadership.

Berkeley rose farther than it ever had before. It had some additional advantages at that time beyond those already noted: relatively attractive and inexpensive homes close to the campus, a good local public school system, and a policy that put assistant professors on the "ladder" with comparatively good prospects for moving up that ladder. But our approach had some costs. An irate department chair once told me that, in following this tough approach, I was putting "my head in a buzz saw"; all departments—he said—had an "unalienable right to be no better than they wanted to be." I accepted that "right" only for departments in the very top rank. That kind of opposition could have been fatal. A faculty member who failed to make "the cut" told me later, "You tried to make us climb a mountain we did not want to climb." The Berkeley faculty, as an entity, however, not only wanted to climb that mountain but did so. Naturally, some resentments accumulated along the way.

In the course of all that competitive recruiting effort, I learned the importance of three sometimes neglected aspects of recruitment, and they guided actions I took then and later: the appeal of good on-campus cultural programs, the drawing power of an excellent retirement system, and the attractiveness of an outstanding library.

The 1964 rankings were the single greatest recognition of Berkeley's new position in the highly competitive environment of American research universities. There were other recognitions. When President Kennedy gave his famous White House dinner for America's Nobel Prize winners on April 29, 1962, he included a few university presidents: Pusey of Harvard, Beadle of Chicago, Bronk of Rockefeller, Killian and Stratton of MIT, DuBridge of Cal Tech, and Kerr of California. Harvard awarded me an honorary degree at its commencement in 1958. I was only the second University of California president (or chancellor) ever so honored—the other was Robert Gordon Sproul. Also,

Harvard asked me to present the Godkin lectures in 1963, part of a series that began in 1903 and is the oldest continuous such series in the history of Harvard, one in which no other university president has participated (my lectures gave rise to *The Uses of the University*, which Harvard University Press has now kept in print for five expanding editions). The recognition was personal, but it belongs also to all of those who had a share in the advance of Berkeley.

Stephen Graubard, longtime editor of *Daedalus*, recently wrote (1994) that "there was no longer any need for the University of California to look at the University of Michigan as a model; it had itself become a model for others"[5]— and not for public research universities alone.

6

Getting Ready
for the Tidal Wave

In 1952, the Berkeley campus still lacked any academic plan. All decisions were ad hoc. In the 1880s the curriculum had emphasized agriculture and then, after the turn of the century and particularly before, during, and after World War II, the physical sciences. Now, in working out a coordinated academic plan, we focused on several questions:

How big should the campus become?

What relative emphases should there be on lower division, upper division, and graduate studies?

What areas should be chosen to expand and/or strengthen?

How would the plan for Berkeley relate to the rest of the university?

The resultant plan, and the discussions during its development, guided assignment of new faculty positions, selection of department chairs, and allocation of new building priorities.

One central decision was to place a limit on campus enrollment.

One evolving goal was to go beyond being a leader among public universities and to become a leader among all universities, public and private.

▪

The central planning decision in the modern history of the University of California took place over what came to be known as the "magic figure" of prospective enrollments. At a meeting of the regents in August 1956, I presented a physical development plan for the Berkeley campus, arguing for a ceiling on prospective enrollments—a "cap"—at 25,000. The regents had never before seriously considered such a possibility for either Berkeley or Los Angeles. Regent Pauley, for openers, asked me what was the enrollment at the University of Rome. I said it was about 65,000 but it was spread all over town in the

71

office buildings of separate professional schools, and I thought he would not like it at all. He then asked me how many people could be seated in the stands in Memorial Stadium. I answered: 75,000. He then suggested that we set a ceiling of 75,000 students for Berkeley on the grounds that every student should be able to attend the football games.

Whatever figure was to be established for Berkeley was likely to be set for UCLA also (excluding its medical center), which is what in fact happened. Two times 75,000 would have provided 150,000 places (plus those for the medical center). That would have taken care of prospective enrollments for many years to come. The 150,000 figure was not actually reached in total university enrollments until 1987, and there was the additional capacity available at the Davis, Santa Barbara, Riverside, and San Francisco campuses.

Other American state universities were growing without caps, including Ohio State, Michigan, Michigan State, Minnesota, Texas (Austin), and Wisconsin (Madison)—some eventually to 40,000 or 50,000 and more. Why could not or should not Berkeley and UCLA follow this pattern? Fifty thousand each at Berkeley and UCLA plus the potential capacity at the other existing campuses would have carried the university to the year 2000. To my knowledge, Berkeley was the first major public research university in the United States to set a specific cap on its enrollment.

Already in 1952, a national tidal wave of students was recognized as inevitable. The birthrate after World War II had risen to 3.6 per woman of child-bearing age (2.1 is the "replacement" rate that maintains a stable population)—the highest in recorded American history. California's prospective net population increase of 500,000 persons per year for the 1960s and 1970s included in-migration. Additionally, during the GI rush after World War II, college enrollment of young adults had become an experience for the first time in the lives of at least a million families, and this had raised expectations for the future. The GI wave had carried total University of California enrollments from 29,500 in 1940 (and 18,800 in 1943) to 49,100 in 1948, and the subsequent demographic tidal wave took the figure to 128,500 in 1975. (See Table 5 and Figure 1 for the enrollment history of the University of California and of the Berkeley campus.)

I began discussions at Berkeley in four forums: the Council of Deans, the faculty Committee on Buildings and Campus Development, the Student Affairs Committee, and the Academic Advisory Committee, each of which was newly established. Of these, the Academic Advisory Committee was the most im-

TABLE 5

Enrollment History of the University of California and Berkeley Campus (based on opening fall enrollment)

Year	University of California	Berkeley
1880	365	245
1890	685	455
1900	2,900	2,000
1910	4,300	3,400
1920	13,900	9,700
1930	19,700	10,600
1940	29,500	15,600
1943	18,800	7,700
1948	49,100	23,100
1952	38,100	16,100
1958	46,900	19,300
1960	55,900	21,900
1962	58,600	25,100
1966	87,100	27,000
1970	109,000	28,500
1975	128,500	30,000
1980	135,800	30,900
1987	157,300	32,100
1990	166,500	30,600
1995	163,700	29,600

portant. It had more significant impacts, perhaps, than almost any other com-mittee in Berkeley history. For me, it was the most interesting and challenging committee over which I ever presided. (A list of its members is in Appendix 1 section E, and that of the senate's Committee on Educational Policy—another group heavily involved in discussions of academic planning—is in section D.)

Berkeley's Historic 27,500 Cap

Our "nostalgic" Berkeley campus wish-fulfillment figure was 15,000—the en-rollment level in the 1930s before World War II. It was possible to have an all-around university of distinction at that level. Harvard then (1950) had 10,500 students. But no one in any of our discussion groups thought we could fight our way back to 15,000. Berkeley had 23,000 students at the peak of the GI rush (1948–49). They had been accommodated and new buildings had been

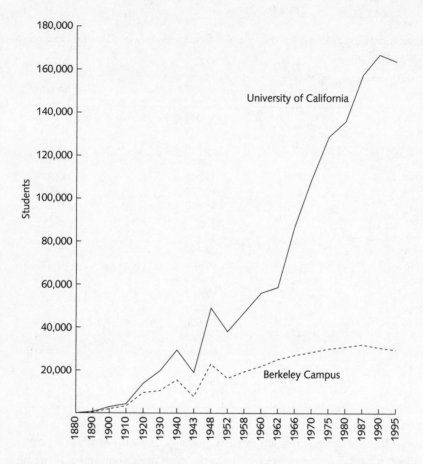

FIGURE I. Enrollment History of the University of California and Berkeley Campus.

added since then, and were still being added. That set a minimum of 25,000 for our discussions. The highest figure suggested, by Sailor Davis, the eminent dean of letters and science, was 28,500. He never said how he got that figure, but it was absolutely fixed in his mind, as was much else including a list of the "good" and the "bad" departments at Berkeley; and I had come to respect greatly his knowledge and his judgment.

We actually settled on our minimum figure of 25,000. It was this figure that was recommended to the regents in August 1956 when we presented the Berkeley Physical Development Plan and again in August 1957 when we presented the Berkeley Academic Plan. We were asked at one point along the way to consider the possibilities for a larger figure, and we prepared a statement on the impacts on the campus of having 35,000 students. We argued that this would lead to unacceptable crowding. The regents agreed. The actual final figure was later set at 27,500 in the 1960 master plan, on the grounds that by that time no adequate facilities elsewhere could be added in time to meet the rush of students.

We looked then and later at many considerations, including these:

- The Berkeley central campus, with its classroom buildings, was located on 300 acres. This was set by history. And, 300 acres, roughly in a square, was about the maximum area within which students could get from one corner to the opposite corner within a ten-minute period—even running all the way; and we did not want to allocate more than ten minutes each hour to class interchange.

- We did not then want our classroom and faculty office buildings to go more than two stories underground and three or four above ground, the latter, in part, for aesthetic reasons. But the main reason was elevators. On campus, almost everybody moves for ten minutes and then almost nobody for fifty minutes. We felt we must rely on walking. I had seen the Cathedral of Learning at the University of Pittsburgh and thought it was a disaster in terms of moving people in short spans of time. Later on, when the mathematics building at Berkeley kept adding floors, with new federal grants and without full consideration of consequences, elevator service was found to be quite inadequate.

- We also wanted to keep building density down to 25 percent of the central campus land, to preserve a parklike environment. We recommended retaining the open spaces of walkways and parks and playing fields—including Faculty Glade, the Campanile Plaza, the banks along the two branches of Strawberry Creek, the Eucalyptus Grove, the grounds around University House, the North Gate area, the West Gate area, the Sather Gate area, the Mining Circle, Observatory Hill, the playing fields around Hearst Gymnasium and Harmon Gym, the central swale in front of Doe library, and other areas.

- Additionally, and much less precisely, we talked about the capacity of the city of Berkeley to provide faculty housing in private homes and student housing in rooming houses and residences within walking distance of the campus.

- Above all, we discussed the maximum effective number of faculty in the big departments, such as English, history, physics, chemistry, mathematics, and

TABLE 6

Departments at Berkeley with More Than 50 Members in Fall 1975
(at 30,000 enrollment)

Department	Budgeted FTE Faculty*
Letters and science	
English	76.03
Mathematics	74.72
Physics	58.83
History	56.92
Professional schools	
Architecture	51.36
Business administration	67.50
Chemistry	54.50
Civil engineering	52.93
Electrical engineering/computer science	63.91

*Total for all ranks budgeted FTE (full-time equivalent) faculty.

political science. We concluded there was some maximum desirable size, however subject to judgment and experience, above which not all senior members could easily know all junior members of the department on whose careers they would pass judgment, and above which not all senior members could even easily know all other senior members as cooperating colleagues—exchanging and reading papers and discussing topics of common intellectual concern. We feared having "too big" departments, and that meant to us over fifty to sixty members (some thought forty). I think that, with all of us on the Academic Advisory Committee, this issue of departmental size came to be the single most central concern. (For sizes of the larger departments in 1975, the year that enrollment first reached 30,000, see Table 6.)

In the 1980s, when the campus temporarily went to 32,000 students, the complaints against massification, impersonality, and crowding increased greatly, and the 1988 long-range academic planning report recommended a cut to about 29,500—difficult as a cut is to carry out. When departments actually reached fifty to sixty members or more, I heard more and more comments of regret that the campus was no longer the "academic community" it once had been.

Berkeley, approaching 27,500 students and then staying at around 30,000, came to be rated the "best balanced distinguished" American research university. Michigan, from 1964 to 1993, fell in the rankings from 7 to 10, Minnesota from 13 to 21, and Wisconsin from 7 to 18. Neither Michigan State, Ohio State, nor Texas (Austin) reached the top 20 with all their size. (Rankings were based on the number of departments in the top six in their field in each year. See chapter 28.) In each case, of course, other factors were also at work. But there is no proof that adding size, above some reasonable level, necessarily adds distinction. Experience is rather to the contrary.

In any event, for the above and other reasons, we proposed 25,000; and the master plan subsequently disposed at 27,500. This 25,000 figure also became the initial figure for UCLA plus 5,000 in the medical center. UCLA has 400 acres, instead of the 300 on Berkeley's central campus, but a medical center, including its parking, eats space as a hyena eats raw meat. The limit of 25,000 students also became the initial planning figure for the new campuses and the maximum figure for planning for the other existing campuses, except for the medical center at UCSF, and the campus at Santa Cruz. In each case this figure was subsequently raised to 27,500; and so we thought we had set in concrete our magic figure.

It should be noted that, along the way to originally settling on 25,000 students at Berkeley, we discussed the possibility of a "satellite campus" perhaps to be located in a renovated area of west Oakland or on university-owned property in the nearby town of Albany. But every group concerned with the decision rejected it. The students and faculty members at the satellite would be second-class citizens; departments would be bifurcated. We thought it better, and no more costly, to have new campuses with their own independent personalities, serving additional areas of the state.

The discussion by the Academic Advisory Committee on the issue of a maximum size for Berkeley began in January 1954 as we examined forecasts of the tidal wave ahead of us—it was then about ten years away. Our solution was based largely on the realities of Berkeley as we saw them. However, we looked around at experience and plans elsewhere. Actually we looked more at private institutions (Harvard, Stanford, Cornell, Chicago, Yale, Princeton, MIT, among others) as our reference group than at public institutions (Michigan, Minnesota, Illinois, Texas, Wisconsin, among others). More of our faculty members came from and knew better the former than the latter group of institutions. From this perspective, 25,000 was certainly more appealing than 50,000.

Reaching Up to the Top

Our perspective and our sights were shifting. Traditionally, Berkeley had compared itself with Michigan and Wisconsin and Illinois—the best of the public universities. We were now setting our sights higher—on the best of both publics and privates. This just happened. We never specifically made that choice. But it was a very major reorientation of our aspirations to watch Harvard and Stanford and Princeton and MIT and Chicago and Yale as much or more than Michigan and Wisconsin and Illinois and Texas. It was a not fully conscious "great leap forward" in our thinking, but it had clear repercussions not only at Berkeley but also elsewhere in the university, particularly at UCLA and at San Diego.

We were moving ourselves out of the "public university" category to that of "all research universities," whether public or private. We were aiming to compete with the best in this expanded category. Regent Carter, then chair of the Committee on Educational Policy, perceived this implication and prophetically commented, at the time the Berkeley academic plan had been presented to the regents (August 15, 1957), "that the whole philosophy of the Berkeley study seemed to be one of critical self-examination, aimed at up-grading the character of the institution." If put into effect, he was sure that the Berkeley campus would be challenging Harvard for first place in ten years. Carter had an M.B.A. from Harvard and his B.A. from UCLA. Actually the successful challenge came in 1964—in just seven years.

This new orientation toward a broader set of comparison institutions for Berkeley and the cap on enrollment were the two most important contributions of the Academic Advisory Committee, concurred in by the Council of Deans and the Academic Senate Committee on Educational Policy.

This new orientation had an impact on our budget requests. The historic student/faculty ratio at Berkeley, prior to 1950, varied in a general range (special circumstances aside) from about 22 to about 25 to 1. When the GI rush was over, it fell to 18 to 1 in 1953, and to 16.5 to 1 in 1962, and to 14.5 in 1966. 1966 was my last full year as president of the university. This 14.5 to 1 ratio brought us much closer to that in the leading private universities. We reached the 14.5 figure, aided by the prosperity of the state and the support of a friendly governor (Pat Brown) and legislature. A lower student/faculty ratio was particularly desired also as Berkeley expected to add to its proportion of graduate students (see Table 7 and Figure 2 for student-faculty ratios in selected years).

TABLE 7

Student/Faculty Ratios at Berkeley, Selected Years

Year	Student/FTE Faculty Ratio
1930	21:1*
1940	26.5:1
1944 (low point of enrollment, WW II)	14.6:1
1948 (high point of enrollment, GI rush)	29:1
1953	17.9:1
1962	16.7:1
1966	14.5:1
1972	17.4:1
1975 (enrollment at 30,000)	18.2:1
1981	17.8:1
1987 (high point of enrollment)	18.1:1
1990	17:1
1994	16.5:1
1997	17.4:1

Faculty FTE data for 1930 are estimates.

In aiming higher, in addition to decreasing the student/faculty ratio, we needed to (and did) raise the competitive level of faculty salaries. In 1960–61, Berkeley stood first at all professorial levels (see Table 8).

For these and other reasons, state support per student in constant (1990) dollars rose from $5,400 in 1950 to $12,000 in 1966, and the University of California's proportion of the state general fund from 6.3 percent to 8.0 percent.

The Berkeley Cap in a Larger Context

We, at Berkeley, were the first to recognize that a limit of 25,000 at Berkeley meant there would need to be new campuses, and we so recommended to the regents. Our August 1956 figure of 25,000 was accepted later that year by the universitywide senate's Committee on Educational Policy and in early 1957 by the *Additional Centers* report[1] of the liaison committee between the Board of Regents and the state Board of Education representing the state colleges. Shortly thereafter it was also accepted by the McHenry report[2] (named after Dean McHenry of UCLA, who was the committee's chair; with Frank Newman of UC Berkeley as vice chair). The regents voted for three new campuses

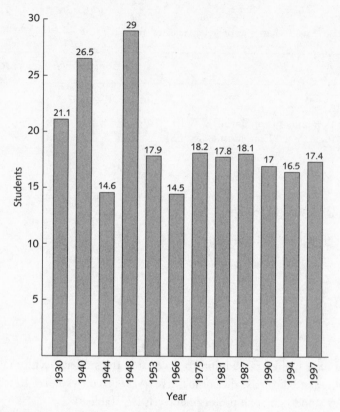

FIGURE 2. University of California Budgeted Student/Faculty Ratios at Berkeley.

and further consideration of a fourth, in October 1957. They were, in effect, accepting the McHenry report. Time was obviously pressing us hard to make fast decisions.

We were reacting, in part, against the mega-campus possibilities of the Mc-Connell report (named after Thomas R. McConnell, former chancellor of the University of Buffalo and later a distinguished member of the Berkeley faculty, who was the chief author of what is more precisely identified as the *Restudy* of 1954 [published in 1955]).[3] This report was extensively discussed by the Board of Regents. McConnell anticipated increasing efficiencies with greater size, and no negative effects on "quality of instruction" or "student welfare." He thus recommended no maximum size for Berkeley and UCLA, and thus also no new campuses at that time. The *Additional Centers* report of early 1957, how-

TABLE 8

Comparative Average Faculty Salaries in College of Letters and Science
at UC-Berkeley and at Other Leading Universities (in dollars)

	1950–51	*1955–56*	*1960–61*
Professor[a]			
UC-Berkeley	8,464	10,459	14,381
4 universities[b]	9,670	11,257	14,166
9 state universities[c]	6,910	8,908	11,620
Assoc. professor[a]			
UC-Berkeley	6,034	7,197	9,643
4 universities	6,224	7,524	9,428
9 state universities	5,404	6,718	8,460
Asst. professor[a]			
UC-Berkeley	4,700	5,610	7,431
4 universities	4,772	5,544	7,231
9 state universities	4,391	5,463	6,907
Instructor[a]			
UC-Berkeley	4,077	4,502	6,090
4 universities	3,523	4,222	5,819
9 state universities	3,458	4,436	5,540

Source: University of California, Berkeley, Progress at Berkeley: A Report on the Past Decade *(1962), 21.*

[a]*On nine-month appointments.*
[b]*Harvard, Yale, Columbia, and Michigan.*
[c]*Illinois, Minnesota, Wisconsin, Ohio State, Michigan State, Indiana, Washington, Oregon, and Purdue.*

ever, cautioned against a campus size that "substantially exceeds 25,000 students." The McHenry report came out flatly against a campus size over 25,000. It argued against "congestion" and unfavorable impacts on "faculty and student welfare," and thus in favor of new campuses to serve other areas of the state in addition to those then served. Both the *Additional Centers* and McHenry reports came to the same conclusion as we had at Berkeley: growth in campus size should be limited.

Major consequences flowed from adoption of a maximum figure on size, first for Berkeley and then for UCLA. The smaller campuses would have to expand, and new campuses would have to be built. The university would have to negotiate with the state colleges over which system got how many new campuses and where, and this was a factor in developing the Master Plan for Higher Education in California. (The university got three new campuses plus a possible fourth, and the state college system got five.) Also, at

Berkeley, we would need a new physical development plan as well as an academic plan—each with repercussions on budgets, on departmental growth, and on much else.

Academic Planning within the 27,500

Academic planning came first (starting January 1954), physical planning next, and budget planning last. (The physical plan reached the regents first although the discussion of a cap was discussed first and settled upon by the Academic Advisory Committee.) Always before, at Berkeley and at many other places also, the revenue plan had come first and actions (not plans) in the other areas followed. The basic law of university and college planning has been to get all the money you can and spend it all as fast as you can through ad hoc decisions. Berkeley was among the first to reverse the traditional order and start with academic planning; and this later became the accepted approach for all planning within the University of California.

There are political problems, of course, with making plans, and this is probably why no academic plans had ever been made before. Plans involve endless consultations. They are subject to possible long-term disappointments if they cannot be carried out. They are also subject, more importantly, to actual short-term disappointments for all those who do not get everything they want, and that is mostly everybody, and these protests can coagulate. The ad hoc approach makes it possible to hold out hope eternally—no doors are ever closed. For administrators, ad hoc decision-making is the easy way out. Every "no" might later become a "yes"—or this is at least implied. "Wait until next year," and "keep on supporting us."

Once we had a total figure for enrollment, the Academic Advisory Committee turned to the question of proportions among lower-division, upper-division, and graduate students. A big debate was over whether we should have any lower-division students or not. Some years earlier it had been suggested by President Sproul that lower division be abandoned and that the university concentrate on upper-division and graduate work, leaving lower-division teaching to the community colleges. We examined this possibility once again very carefully. Many faculty members did not like to teach (and many never did) lower-division courses. But the possibility of concentrating solely on upper-division and graduate studies was rejected unanimously for reasons high and low:

The faculty was unwilling to rely exclusively on community colleges for lower-division training without setting standards through its own lower-division programs.

Graduate students are financed in substantial part by their stipends as teaching assistants in lower-division courses. Also, this is the only supervised teaching experience they will ever have.

The university receives public support substantially because it has undergraduate students. The undergraduate student body "subsidizes" graduate work both economically and politically.

Four-year students are the basis for subsequent leadership in the alumni association.

The University of California could not compete well with Stanford and other private institutions in getting the best undergraduate students if it did not offer a four-year experience.

Additionally, it could not compete at all in intercollegiate athletics.

At the 25,000 figure, we settled on 6,000 (or 24 percent) lower-division students, 11,000 (or 44 percent) upper-division students (in order to allow for about half of the upper-division students to be transfers, particularly from community colleges), and 8,000 (or 32 percent) graduate students. The graduate figure was really determined by how many Ph.D. students individual faculty members wanted to have under their guidance and that averaged out to about 5 per faculty member (see Table 9 for a historic view of these proportions). Along the way we had asked each department for its own academic plan. Thus all faculty members were involved in the planning process, including determining the number of graduate students.

Choosing Academic Priorities

Another issue was which areas to push the hardest among the schools, colleges, and departments. The physical sciences were universally in comparatively good shape at Berkeley as were most of the humanities. The biological sciences were generally well rated academically but were not then willing to agree on the two historic moves that most needed to be made: new and improved physical facilities including for animal care, and a reorientation from an emphasis on horizontal forms of life (entomology, etc.) to vertical levels of

TABLE 9
Percentages of Students in Lower-Division, Upper-Division, and Graduate Studies,
Selected Years

Year	Lower-Division	Upper-Division	Graduate Studies
1930	36	43	21
1940	37	44	18
1944	53	33	14
1948	35	45	20
1952	33	42	25
1962	30	36	33
1971	27	40	33
1975	26	43	31
1981	33	36	30
1990	30	41	29
1995	28	43	29

life (cellular, etc.). The social sciences had not been comparatively heavily emphasized at Berkeley. However, particularly after the New Deal and with new statistical information available, they were a growing area of academic life nationwide. They needed attention generally. Political science and sociology were given special encouragement. The creative aspects of the arts and facilities for display and performance had been almost totally neglected. So the social sciences and the creative arts were chosen for particular efforts at improvement.

My biggest regret at that time was that the biological sciences were so divided among themselves and so influential in opposing the initiatives of others that the needed reforms were not undertaken. It worried me greatly, particularly the inability to agree on new and improved facilities at a time when funds were readily available. Berkeley had begun moving toward the "new biology" with the establishment of the Virus Laboratory under Wendell Stanley, who was its founding director (1948), and the appointment of Horace A. Barker as chair of plant biochemistry (1950) and then of biochemistry (1962)—but very slowly. I wish a smoother and better articulated transition could have taken place instead of the big lurch that later occurred. (Each of the three new campuses did start out on the basis of the new biology.) Sandy Elberg of bacteriology says in his oral history that "we really lost twenty-five years before the biological sciences could have their day in court again."[4]

Several more specific areas were also chosen for particular assistance. One was engineering, which had the possibility of matching the existing distinction in the physical sciences but was then looked upon by the scientists as a poor relation. Engineering was given many new academic positions and a disproportionate share of new building construction.

I had a special interest in those departments that contributed the most to other related departments and decided that they included English in the humanities, history in the humanities and social sciences, chemistry in the physical and biological sciences and engineering, and mathematics across the board.

History was a more central department to both the social sciences and the humanities than any other. It had once been more highly rated than more recently, and it was given the chance to regain and surpass its former high ranking.

Mathematics had quality of faculty under the guidance of Griffith Evans, but not quantity. The sciences and engineering had treated it mostly as a "service" department for training their students. I was convinced, although I was a nonmathematical economist, that mathematics should and would be as central a department in a great research university of the future as philosophy had been in the past. Philosophy, once the "mother" of so many other departments, itself had become one of its own more specialized children. Quantitative methods were rapidly getting more emphasis across the board (as they had been gradually and intermittently since Pythagoras). Thus, I concluded, if a campus were to have one preeminent department in modern times, it should be mathematics. Also, statistics was a new department at Berkeley under the excellent leadership of Jerzy Neyman, and deserving of expansion for related reasons.

On the other side of the balance sheet was agriculture, which was better off gradually moving to Davis, where there was more land and laboratory space, and which was closer to the agricultural industry. The School of Education was of modest quality, but significant improvement seemed at that time to have only modest prospects; and it was neglected. Here was my second area of regret: that greater efforts were not made to energize the field of education. A jump in openings for high school teachers had brought substantial augmentations in the size of the faculty to reflect the then increasing student demand. Improved efforts were surely possible.

Two areas were dropped: home economics, in a very bitter series of battles (we reconfigured it into a Department of Nutritional Sciences);[5] and the area of criminology (mostly police training) merged into law.

The language and literature departments (other than English, which was outstanding) were well rated nationally but not part of the dynamism of the Berkeley campus. Lincoln Constance and I tried to move them toward a more general concern for "culture" in addition to language and literature, to encourage them to participate more in the cultural life of the campus, and to get them to make more contact with interested citizens in the surrounding Bay Area community. Italian showed interest in our ideas. When or if the others followed, they did so with less enthusiasm. Constance and I also encouraged work in comparative literature.

The arts were a special case. They were farther advanced, as in music and the visual arts, in the noncreative spheres (historiography and criticism) than in the creative and/or performance areas. Faculty members in the former constellation considered themselves to be "scholarly" individuals. They viewed the work of practitioners in the creative and performance areas as subject only to tests of personal taste—with no "standards." Generally, this first group opposed the addition of the "creative" types. Scientists, however, were the keenest supporters of adding the more creative types—themselves being of inventive inclinations. I too favored more emphasis on creation and performance. This led to some uneasy situations at first; and, to this day, in art but not in music, there is a separation between "history" and "practice." I also thought this move would add a dynamic element to the campus community and would result in a more balanced and inviting cultural atmosphere. It did both.

Preparatory work was undertaken to add academic aspects of the study of religions to the curriculum and to arrange for cooperative relationships with the Pacific School of Religion and later the evolving Graduate Theological Union, both located just to the north of the campus. The attorney for the regents had objections—on the grounds of separation between church and state—but it seemed to me that religions were as much a proper academic study as nationalisms, since together they supply much of the motive power that makes the societies of the earth go round.

Business administration was a separate situation. It was destined to be Berkeley's second big professional school, along with engineering. Its identity, however, was not predestined. Under the historic leadership of Dean E. T. Grether (1943 to 1961), it sought to make close contact with the other social sciences and even beyond. With this I fully agreed, and I thought it could become a central rallying point for all the social sciences and, in return, could greatly benefit intellectually over time. However, as with almost all schools of business in other universities, it later became increasingly more separatist and more responsive to its related external professions—to the great regret of both Dean Grether and me.

Architecture, under the leadership of Dean William Wurster, was joining with city and regional planning, landscape architecture, and decorative arts (renamed design) to become a College of Environmental Design. For a time, it was the best in the nation along with MIT. This high ranking reflected the inspired leadership of Wurster and his successor, Martin Meyerson, later acting chancellor at Berkeley for the spring 1965 semester. Martin had been director of the Joint Center for Urban Studies at MIT and Harvard and with a chair at Harvard. He had also taught at Chicago and had a worldwide reputation in the area of urban policy and development, as well as broad intellectual interests. Architecture was given very substantial support.

All the above and other changes were undertaken, one at a time, in full consultation with the instrumentalities of the Academic Senate and, particularly, with the academic personnel committee and the Committee on Educational Policy. It was the latter, especially, that brought me briefly into a nationwide conflict with the home economics profession that stood for the home, the family, the American flag, and all things good. I was deluged with protest letters when we considered abandoning home economics. I was told that women live longer than men, are more numerous, and that "We'll get you yet." Actually, the problem with home economics at Berkeley was that it was a miscellany. We took its best part, nutrition, and made that into a high-quality specialty. The most popular home economics course had been "Marriage" with ten lectures, the first on "courtship" and the last on "venereal disease." The students relabeled the course "From Courtship to Venereal Disease in Ten Easy Lessons." It was popular, in part, because there were no reading assignments and nobody flunked; and the subject matter held substantial student interest. But the course was a source of embarrassment to the department and the campus.

A period of growth can be a period of change, and Berkeley changed, and mostly in progressive ways. It became, among other things, better "balanced." (For data on the areas given the most new faculty positions, see Table 10.)

The Revised Academic Plan 1969–75, developed when Roger Heyns was chancellor at Berkeley (1965–71), identified the 1957 plan as "the first Academic Plan for the Berkeley campus." It said that this "remarkable statement . . . was prescient in charting the future lines of the academic development of the

TABLE 10

Most Substantial Departmental Gains in Ladder Faculty,* 1953–54 to 1962–63

School or College and Department	*1953–54 to 1962–63*
School of Business Administration	29
College of Chemistry (includes chemical engineering)	29
College of Environmental Design	21
School of Education	18
College of Engineering	52
Civil engineering	11
Electrical engineering	19
Industrial engineering	12
School of Law	15
College of Letters and Science	337
English	36
History	23
Mathematics and statistics	48
Philosophy	13
Physics	29
Political science	19
Psychology	17
Sociology and social institutions	14
Zoology	12

Professor, associate professor, assistant professor (FTE).

campus. . . . It was also perceptive in outlining the policies necessary to enable it to deal with the problems of rapid growth. . . . [and] the maintenance of intellectual vitality."

Forty Years Later

Carrying the story forward to the turn of the century, I note the further progress of Berkeley's growth in various areas. First, enrollment at Berkeley, which reached 30,000 in 1975 and 32,000 in 1987 (mostly as a means to maintain the level of state support for the total university when the state cut the subsidy per student substantially), has now stabilized at slightly under 30,000. Changes in existing departments included the College of Agriculture, transformed into the College of Natural Resources in 1974 (with the addition of forestry); biology, substantially reorganized in the 1980s and early 1990s with fabulous new facilities and a new orientation under the leadership of Professor Daniel E. Koshland, Jr., and his associates and with the support of Chancellor Ira Michael Heyman and Vice-Chancellor Roderic Park; a great new emphasis on ethnic and women's studies, resulting in an increase of faculty members in these areas from none in 1970 to twenty-three in 1994 (1.4 percent of the faculty), even as the total faculty on campus increased by only twelve; and an unsuccessful effort during the 1980s to reorient the School of Education following a report by Professor Neil Smelser of sociology.[6]

Major additions encompassed a Graduate School of Public Policy (1969); a pre-clinical program in health and medical sciences in conjunction with the University of California, San Francisco (1973); and a joint doctorate in Near Eastern religions in cooperation with the Graduate Theological Union—a consortium of schools of religion adjacent to the Berkeley campus (1972). Also a program was introduced of cross-registration of students between Berkeley and GTU schools (1973) and joint access to libraries.

Improving Facilities for
Student Life at Berkeley

The University of California was the last of the major American land-grant universities to abandon the German model of student life, in which a university provided classrooms and laboratories and a library and a faculty, and students were otherwise on their own. Land-grant universities mostly had begun that way. The first initiatives in the University of California toward what was becoming the dominant American pattern of providing facilities for a fuller student life on campus, as in English universities, were taken by Regent Phoebe Apperson Hearst at the beginning of the century. She was then the university's greatest friend and benefactor.

A renewed movement at Berkeley began in 1944, with limited immediate practical results. Postwar events encouraged this movement, as did particularly the publication, in 1948, of the alumni association's Students at Berkeley[1] *report with its recommendations for more residence halls and other student amenities. However, it took the creation of the chancellorship at Berkeley in 1952 to implement a major transformation that quickly extended to the other campuses of the university. Given the strong student, alumni, and faculty support for a break with the German mode, the resistance was much less than I expected.*

My first effort to pay more attention to student life outside the classroom was a complete failure. But before turning to that I should like to explain why I exclude classroom life. This is territory that belongs to the individual professors and is properly "off limits" to anyone else; but the classroom is the most important aspect of student life. The second most important aspect is student-to-student contacts inside and outside the classroom—which, in turn, belong to them. Yet these contacts can be hindered or aided by what facilities are available.

I have always been impressed with how well classroom life has been and still is handled by faculty members at Berkeley. The circumstances, however, have been and are somewhat difficult. The student/faculty ratio at Berkeley in the 1950s was substantially higher than in comparable private universities—seventeen to one versus eight or ten. Total spending for "education and general" purposes per student per year has generally been less than half as much—$15,000 versus $30,000 to $40,000 (1995 figures. Here and in the next paragraph I use current data for these comparisons because earlier data are not equally available; they are probably fairly indicative of the 1950s situation too. See Table 11). As such discrepancies suggest, the student satisfaction rate, as measured very roughly by the alumni giving rate, has also been lower than in comparable private universities and in some public universities as well, including Michigan and Virginia. The graduation rate too has been comparatively low—80 percent versus 95 percent in the Ivy League. There are, and were, other difficult circumstances.

Academically the Berkeley faculty is of the very highest rank but the undergraduate student body is not. On the average, test scores of entering students have been lower by 100 to 150 SAT points (or about 10 percent) than those of students in private universities with the highest ranked faculties; and the spread from the 25th to the 75th percentiles is larger (250 versus 180 points). The top 10 percent of undergraduate students at Berkeley are at Cal Tech levels, but the others are not. The higher levels and the more equalized scores at the private institutions most comparable in their quality of faculty (Harvard, Yale, MIT, Stanford, and Princeton) make undergraduate teaching potentially somewhat more attractive there than at Berkeley. In competition with graduate teaching, where candidates for the Ph.D. at Berkeley are at about the same level as those at the most distinguished private graduate training and research institutions, undergraduate teaching is comparatively less attractive, and many faculty members at Berkeley quite naturally tend to be more drawn to their outstanding graduate students.

Notwithstanding its more difficult circumstances, most of the undergraduate teaching at Berkeley is excellent. I base this statement on impressions, but these impressions come from many discussions with students—in groups and individually. As chancellor, I held an open office two hours each week, whenever my out-of-town schedule did not interfere, when students could come in without appointments. Many did. Few students commented about their teachers but, when I asked them—which I usually did if they did not volunteer—most responded in very affirmative ways. I would often ask for

TABLE 11
Comparative Student Life Indicators

	S/F ratio	Education and General Expenditure per Student ($)	Graduation Rate (%)	Test Scores (25th–75th percentile)	Spread between Test Scores (25th–75th percentile)	Freshmen in Top 10 Percent of High School Class (%)	Alumni Giving Rate (%)
Berkeley	17/1	15,140	78	1100–1370	260	95	10
Harvard	11/1	39,525	97	1320–1480	160	91	54
MIT	10/1	34,870	91	1290–1470	180	94	38
Michigan	16/1	15,470	85	1060–1300	240	65	14
Princeton	8/1	30,220	95	1280–1470	190	91	56
Stanford	12/1	36,450	93	1270–1450	180	90	28
Virginia	14/1	13,349	92	1110–1340	230	77	25
Yale	11/1	43,514	96	1290–1460	170	95	46

Source: U.S. News and World Report 119, no. 11 (September 18, 1995): 126–27, 129.

student drivers if I did not drive myself to meetings or to the airport, and here again I queried them about their professors with similar results. I also listened to many group discussions at meetings of the Order of the Golden Bear, Cal Club, and elsewhere.

Why were the reports so good when the circumstances were not the best and when the faculty review system, in fact, paid (and pays) limited attention to the quality of undergraduate teaching? Departmental evaluations of individual professors almost universally have said "teaching—above average." When I would ask how *everyone* could be above average, the standard reply was, "We do not know, and that is the politic way to comment—it offends no one." Yet most students judged the teaching to be generally "good" or "excellent." I concluded that high grades for undergraduate teaching reflect the excellent training and deep interest faculty members at this level of competence take in their subjects; also, that persons who could rise to this level of distinction have an intense "instinct of workmanship" and do not like to perform poorly at any task.

Traditions at Berkeley

Outside the classroom, Berkeley has had its own special traditions. The German pattern at Berkeley intensified under the leadership of Benjamin Ide Wheeler (1899–1919)—who had attended several of the leading German universities and greatly admired them—and his next three successors, David Prescott Barrows, William Wallace Campbell, and Robert Gordon Sproul, accepted it.

The historic English tradition of Oxford and Cambridge was quite different. It included residence halls and dining commons living, the provision of sports fields, and opportunities for faculty-to-student contact outside the formal classroom as in tutorials, special lounges, and tea rooms. This was the tradition inherited by the Ivy League and many other private American universities, and nearly all of the most selective liberal arts colleges. The Big Ten, in the Midwest, began shifting toward the British model at the time of World War I, but particularly during the Great Depression, when federal funds were easily available for residence halls and student unions. Other public universities slowly followed. But not Berkeley.

In 1952 Berkeley had no settled plans to provide university-initiated residence halls for undergraduates—Stern Hall and Bowles Hall and International

House were the results of private gifts. The Fernwald-Smythe dorms and Albany Village (the latter for married couples), with their temporary-type construction, were put up on an emergency basis with federal funds to help make room for the veterans returning from World War II. (There had been some student "cottages" on campus in the early years of the university.) There were two buildings for the use of the ASUC (Stephens Union) and for student publications (Eshleman). There were few intramural sports fields or tennis courts. There was a student infirmary and hospital—Cowell, a private gift.

Enrollments at Berkeley had reached 16,000 in 1952, and still more students were coming. Many of the local rooming houses were seriously deteriorating—I had lived in several and had seen them slowly decompose.

Why not more university-owned residence halls at Berkeley? I was told when I became the new chancellor that there was an informal compact with the city of Berkeley not to compete with private boarding houses and restaurants, and that the regents had always been against "socialism." By my time at least, I found no major opposition to my efforts to change the policy from German to English for either of these reasons. In September 1954 Regent John Francis Neylan was still arguing before the regents against "socialist living conditions," but he was clearly in the minority.

As early as November 1944, the regents had accepted a report from a special committee favoring applying for federal funds to build residence halls to accommodate the postwar wave of students—one hall each at Berkeley and UCLA (expanded a year later to include one hall at Davis, where there had already been two historic halls—North Hall and South Hall, for students from rural farms). The one residence unit at Berkeley became Fernwald-Smythe. Not until August 1956 did the regents vote to approve a physical development plan for Berkeley that called for a series of specifically located university residence halls to accommodate 25 percent of all undergraduates. A program to implement this policy quickly followed. Thus twelve years passed between ad hoc acceptance of one residence hall at Berkeley for special reasons (1944) to approval for a general policy and a permanent one for building residence halls (1956). In the meantime, other universities were going ahead vigorously with their programs using federal funds.

As an aside, the idea of a residence hall program at Berkeley had been long discussed in faculty circles. The model was the "houses" at Harvard and Yale—very much in accord with the English model. Shortly after I became chancellor, Stephen Pepper, chair of philosophy, talked with me about the idea and

I indicated my support. Later, on October 16, 1957, after the regents had voted for residence halls, he sent a letter on his own behalf and on behalf of a group of other leading faculty members, proposing a series of small "liberal arts colleges." The colleges were to have "liberal education" academic programs as a basis of intellectual life. Later, when the new residence halls became available, under the leadership of Chancellor Seaborg, a series of "fellows" were appointed to the new units. However, the effort never really took hold with the faculty. A great disappointment! I later transferred the "intensity of my interest" (as I had written Pepper on October 28, 1957) to planning for the new Santa Cruz campus.

In two major ways, however, Berkeley had deviated from the German model. One was in its active participation in intercollegiate sports. Spectator sports, particularly in Memorial Stadium and Harmon Gym, helped build student cohesion and alumni loyalty. These programs, however, were under the direction of the powerful student association—like German student clubs—not the university itself.

The other divergence was in the personalities of two of its presidents, Benjamin Ide Wheeler and Robert Gordon Sproul. Probably no German university rectors ever matched them in their public personalities, their rhetorical abilities, their capacities to draw the interest, the attention, and the devotion of so many thousands of students that carried on in fond memory into their years as alumni. Both presidents attracted a binding personal loyalty that was entirely remarkable. The main opportunity for them to contact the student body at large was at university meetings, originally held by Wheeler every Friday during the school year. The meetings were highlights of each academic year.

Three other important aspects of student life were part of Berkeley's own special character. One was that politics were "off campus." Twice while I was chancellor, I had to tell Adlai Stevenson that he could not come on campus to speak because he was a candidate for the presidency of the United States! University policy barred him. So he spoke from Oxford Street facing the western end of campus. I felt humiliated each time. The basic policy was part of the university's longstanding Rule 17 and regulated who could and could not speak on campus. Here was a dragon I decided I had to confront. I started on it as chancellor, going with some activist student leaders to get some small revisions from President Sproul. Much was done but not quite all that needed to be done. What was not done resulted in a history of some importance that I discuss in the chapters on events at Berkeley in 1964–65 in *Political Turmoil.*

Rule 17, however, for many years gave the University of California the most restrictive policies governing approved on-campus contact with political life of any major university in the United States.

A second aspect was, strangely enough, that Rule 17 existed within one of the most liberal, or even radical, political contexts in the nation. Only City College of New York and the University of Wisconsin in Madison (and thus in the state of the "progressive movement") had as radical a surrounding community of political expression as Berkeley. The Bay Area was a natural habitat for an avant-garde campus—home to Jack London, the socialist; and to Henry George, the single tax proponent; to the San Francisco General Strike of 1934; to the IWW (Industrial Workers of the World) and Harry Bridges and the Longshoremen's Union; and to many other persons and movements weird and wonderful. The Berkeley campus itself was public and thus had a more heterogeneous student body than private universities; it was academically elite in its student composition and thus had many bright and self-confident students. And because the campus was large it provided a "critical mass" for student movements. Rule 17 was originally intended to protect the university from this turbulent political environment. It ended up, however, adding to the turbulence. The ambience of the community and the regulations of the campus were inherently incompatible.

Stiles Hall of the YMCA was the most important off-campus center for student activism in the 1930s, 1940s, and 1950s. The administration informally encouraged it as a safety valve. Campus politics pitted the independents around Stiles Hall against members of the fraternities and sororities, and the latter were always dominant in campus politics. In addition, there was the "Sather Gate tradition"—a place like Hyde Park corner, on city property just outside the main pedestrian entrance to the campus. Many mass meetings and demonstrations were held there.

A third special aspect of student life at Berkeley was the historic strength of the ASUC. It ran, on its own, all intercollegiate sports, which constituted a huge enterprise, and supported all student publications and many special interest clubs. The elected presidents of the ASUC were the biggest men on campus—and they were always men. The general manager of the ASUC had a substantial empire to run on campus but one that was independent in its governance from the administration of the university—and ran on the German model.

So Berkeley was a very special place for student life as the campus entered the 1950s.

My Efforts at Change—German to British

My first attempt to affect student life outside the classroom gave rise to the complete failure mentioned at the start of this chapter. It was November 1952. An alumnus offered a Christmas tree for Dwinelle Plaza and the skilled artisans in Grounds and Buildings offered to make ornaments on their own time. I accepted both offers and in fact had encouraged them. I had always looked at Berkeley as a "cold" place that went "hot" only in anticipation of the "Big Game" with Stanford.

At the Faculty Club, a faculty member from forestry went from table to table with a branch from the tree saying, "Here lie the remains of a once living friend now murdered by the new chancellor." Comments ran along the lines of "How bourgeois can you get—Christmas at Berkeley!" The next Christmas I retreated to the decoration of a growing tree (now deceased) at the corner of Wheeler Hall, which the students came to call "the Sophie Tucker tree" because of its specific ungainly shape. The *Daily Californian* then blasted me. As the new chancellor, I had single-handedly assassinated an ancient and valued tradition at Berkeley—how Scrooge-like can you get? The "ancient" tradition was the prior year's gesture of a Christmas tree.

Fortunately I could turn to a better idea, an idea that had its roots in the return of the GIs from World War II in 1946. They made up one-half of the male student body. Along with their self-confidence went a conviction that a university education was eminently worthwhile. They were excellent students, aggressive in asking questions and challenging ideas about which they had doubts. Many had been students at other colleges and universities before they went into military service. They had seen and liked the better facilities. (For information on Berkeley's comparative deficits in student facilities, see Table 12.)

As a young professor, I heard many complaints and I sympathized with them because I had been a student at Swarthmore and Stanford with their excellent student facilities, as well as at Berkeley. Students here had too few places to live and to eat and to exercise. On top of it all, Berkeley had a losing football team. At the end of one lost Big Game against Stanford, the men's rooting section began burning bonfires in the stands of Memorial Stadium. That drew the attention of the alumni! (I was there at the game in November 1946, as an interested and loyal faculty member.) A direct result was a new football coach, Lynn ("Pappy") Waldorf. Another early result was a new look by the alumni association at the conditions for student life.

TABLE 12 (PART 1)
Berkeley's Comparative Deficits in Student Facilities

University	Students Housed in University-Operated Residence Halls, Fall 1954 (%)
Michigan State	49.4
Stanford	36.0
Michigan	34.0
Washington State	31.3
Purdue	29.7
Indiana	28.0
Iowa	25.0
Oregon State	21.3
Wisconsin	19.0
Oregon	18.9
Ohio State	18.0
Northwestern	16.2
Illinois	11.3
Minnesota	10.8
Washington	9.2
University of Southern California	4.9
UC-Berkeley	**4.8**

Source: University of California Office of the President, Long-Range Development Plan for the Berkeley Campus *(August 1956), Appendix D on 29.*

The California Alumni Association in 1946–48 was headed by Stanley N. Barnes, class of 1922, a member of the famed "Wonder Teams" in football and, by 1946–48, a federal judge. Cort Majors, class of 1921, and a captain of the Wonder Teams and then vice president of Crown Zellerbach, was also a member of the alumni board along with other famous alumni of Berkeley. This influential group was in charge when, on May 28, 1948, the alumni planning project issued a report called *Students at Berkeley,* referred to in the introduction to this chapter. (See a list of California Alumni Association board members and project committee members in Appendix 1 section G.)

I looked on this report as an extension of the residence hall report of 1944 briefly noted above. This 1944 report involved Jean C. Witter of the class of 1916, president of the alumni association (1944–46), and from the famous Witter family of Cal supporters. As an alumni member of the Board of Regents, Witter chaired the Special Committee on Dormitories of which the powerful

TABLE 12 (PART 2)

University	Student Union Space (sq. ft. per student)
Purdue	33.0
Washington State	32.5
Oregon	24.5
Oregon State	15.9
Iowa	15.1
Michigan	14.9
Wisconsin	12.4
Minnesota	12.3
Washington	11.5
Ohio State	11.0
Michigan State	9.1
Indiana	7.9
Stanford	7.6
Illinois	7.2
Northwestern	6.4
Berkeley	**4.5**

Source: Clark Kerr, "The Berkeley Campus and Its Students Now and in 1965," California Monthly 65, no. 5 (January 1955): 10.

Sidney Ehrman was also a member. This committee endorsed to the regents (November 17, 1944) a proposal to consider federal funding for one dormitory (500 students) at Berkeley and one at Los Angeles, as an extension of existing board policy of accepting private donations for construction of dormitories. For one time only, under special circumstances, it was in effect classifying federal funds as private. This report marked the first, and very important, shift in the regents' opposition to "socialism" in university provision of student housing (except for private gifts). It broke the ice. Jean Witter, as a past president, was a member of the alumni board that endorsed *Students at Berkeley;* I thought of the two reports as Witter I and Witter II. When the residence halls were built, I recommended to the regents that one of them be named after Ehrman. No more influential men than these two, pillars of the establishment, could introduce so fundamental a new approach to student life.

The alumni association had appointed, in early 1947, an alumni project committee headed by Fred Stripp, class of 1932, who had been president of the ASUC in his senior year, and was a longtime faculty member in the Depart-

TABLE 12 (PART 3)
Intramural Sports Facilities, Fall 1954

University	Mens Enrollment	Touch Football Fields	Softball Diamonds	Tennis Courts	Volleyball Courts	Basketball Courts	Handball Courts	Bowling Alleys	Golf Courses
Midwestern									
Illinois	10,750	24	24	5	5	10	16	8	2
Indiana	7,494	2	4	31	5	3	3	0	0
Iowa	5,137	2	2	18	0	4	3	16	1
Michigan	10,599	6	7	38	6	4	14	7	1
Michigan State	9,661	3	12	19	0	4	7	16	0
Minnesota	14,240	3	7	21	6	7	10	16	2
Northwestern	5,201	4	6	16	4	2	0	0	1
Ohio State	14,225	20	14	46	5	5	6	16	1
Purdue	8,300	20	21	22	5	4	3	12	2
Wisconsin	8,796	9	14	10	4	3	0	8	0
Pacific Coast									
Idaho	2,056	6	6	8	3	3	0	8	1
Oregon	2,355	4	3	14	2	2	8	4	1
Oregon State	3,500	5	8	17	4	3	4	0	0
Stanford	5,117	7	4	17	5	2	3	0	1
UC Berkeley	9,500	3	4	(9) 18[a]	3	4	0	0	0

	Enrollment							
USC	12,972	0	0	7	0	4	4	0	0
Washington	9,300	5	10	8	2	3	6	12	1
Washington State	3,400	0	8	16	8	4	1	10	1
Others									
Chicago	840[b]	4	6	14	0	2	3	0	0
Colorado	4,500	11	9	14	9	2	2	6	2
Columbia	2,255[c]	0	0	5	2	3	6	4	0
Cornell	5,700	10	0	24	0	10	0	16	1
Harvard	10,153	6	6	49	6	4	0	0	0
North Carolina	4,711	5	6	23	7	7	13	0	1
Princeton	2,900	24	23	32	4	4	0	0	1
Yale	3,910[b]	4	5	24	0	2	8	0	1

Source: Enrollment figures from Blue Book of College Athletics, 1954–55; other data from replies to questionnaire, 1954–55.

[a] *Berkeley would soon lose 9 tennis courts to new construction.*
[b] *Undergraduate.*
[c] *Columbia College only (Columbia University—25,259 men and women).*

ment of Speech (now Rhetoric). John P. Symes, class of 1921, a former captain of the basketball team and later an alumni member of the Board of Regents, was the second of three members. The committee personally listened to students' grievances, and the ASUC conducted a study that included hour-long interviews with more than 2,000 individual students.

The resultant report called for many new facilities for student life. "The University must extend its interest in student well-being, giving attention to many modern problems of student living and activity that have traditionally been considered outside administrative purview. . . . To put it bluntly, the student body is not served outside the classroom in a manner consonant with the size and importance of the University." What was needed was "a more hospitable environment." The final paragraph of the alumni report stated: "The requisite is leadership."

But nothing happened. I read the report and wondered why it was ignored. Why wait?—Sidney Ehrman, Jean Witter, Stan Barnes, Cort Majors, Jack Symes (and many others of importance) had endorsed forward movement, but there was no response from President Sproul or the regents. And there was no action on the report for six years. I took that report as my platform when I became chancellor in 1952. Working with student and alumni leaders and the faculty Committee on Buildings and Campus Development, we turned that report into a list of specific actions. In the end, every recommendation of *Students at Berkeley* was accomplished—a record seldom matched in a long series of reports within the university calling for progress. (A list of leaders of the ASUC who were involved in supporting this report is in Appendix 1 section H.) The class that was most helpful was the class of 1954, the first class with which I had a full opportunity to work. Many years later this same class made a gift that greatly improved the North Gate entrance to the campus— the most beautiful addition to the campus by any class in history. Students in general, via the ASUC, several times voted for an increase in student fees to help finance some of the projects. These votes were very persuasive in my presentations to the Board of Regents.

The top universitywide administration lent no support but it also organized no direct opposition to my efforts. The big breakthrough came in August 1956 with board approval of the plan for campus development, which included several new residence halls. A second breakthrough came at a regents meeting in December 1956 when two powerful regents, with my encouragement, declared their support for a new student union building. Regent Heller pledged $1 million for what became the Heller Lounge, and Regent Pauley pledged $2 million for what became the Pauley Ballroom. And, at that same time, the regents declared their firm support for the student union project. All of a sudden, the gates were open, not only at Berkeley but also on all the campuses. The next month UCLA came in with its own proposal for a modern student union, and new residence halls were subsequently planned on all campuses.

At Berkeley, in addition to the student union and residence halls, we also built more student playing fields and tennis courts. Plans were also made for parking spaces for students, for cultural facilities (Zellerbach Hall and the Playhouse), and for proper paths for students walking across the campus (they had complained in the alumni report about walking in the "mud," so we put in paved paths where the students actually walked); and for more counseling services. Attention was also directed at creating a more park-like campus ("pleasant landscaping"), which involved reducing the large number of formal and informal parking lots within the central campus, and reducing "drastically the extent of automobile circulation on the campus," as the report had recommended. A big message of the GI students had been to get the cars off the campus proper, and we did so but at the cost of many faculty objections at the time. There were faculty members who argued that it was not the cars but the chancellor who should be gotten off campus! Photographs that accompanied the alumni report showed mud and cars and dilapidated boarding houses—a chamber of horrors. Recently, a faculty member who had once fought to keep cars on campus told me he would now "fight to the death" to preserve the current park-like campus and against making it ever again into a great big parking lot. We had to keep it as a park, not a parking lot!

An additional contribution to student and staff life, separate from the facilities recommended in the *Students at Berkeley* report, was the Haas Recreational Center in Strawberry Canyon. It includes two large swimming pools, a clubhouse, and a sports field that later became Witter Field for rugby.

The Haas Center came about in this way. On a warm night in late spring 1956, students from the fraternities went on a "panty raid." The incident now seems innocent enough, but at that time it made headlines around the world. One alumnus sent me a newspaper story from Beirut about how naked women had been carried through the streets of Berkeley on the shoulders of men students on their way to an orgy that would match anything the ancient Romans could have organized. Another sent a story from a USSR Communist Party newspaper that this incident was evidence of the impending "final collapse" of capitalism! I went to Walter Haas of the class of 1910 to ask him whether the answer to a warm night in spring might better be a cold dip in a supervised swimming pool. He answered "yes" and contributed $300,000. He often told me later that this gift, as he saw its many uses, had given him the most personal pleasure of the many gifts he made. In any event, there were no more panty raids. But it was far from the only time that Berkeley students were the subject of headlines.

A further addition to the *Students at Berkeley* report had this origin. Students, at my office hours, in the Student Affairs Advisory Committee, in discussions of the Order of the Golden Bear, and Cal Club, complained that there were too few places for them to sit and study, and that it was too hard to get books out of the library's general stacks, which were closed to them. To obtain books, students had to get in a line to make a request, and then wait in the large reading room until library personnel fetched the books. These complaints gave rise to my efforts to develop what became a beautiful new undergraduate library built with open stacks and 1,500 spaces for student study, named after a former devoted regent and chair of the board, James Kennedy Moffitt. I personally chose the library's name. As an ex-regent, Moffitt had supported before the Board of Regents (July 1949) the efforts of our Academic Senate Committee on Privilege and Tenure to prevent the firing of the nonsigners during the oath controversy. He had also chaired the committee of regents that granted the Academic Senate its enlarged sphere of influence over academic life in 1920.

My concern throughout this long and involved effort was to provide facilities for the "total student," and I spoke about it in many presentations. This concept included more opportunities for a residential experience, for participation in sports, for contacts with an enriched cultural life. One of my inaugural addresses as president was on the "total student."[2] This statement was my formal repudiation in 1958, as the new president of the university, of the German approach and support for the English model.

With this background of concern for student-life facilities, I was particularly pleased when the regents, many years later, accepted the recommendation of Berkeley's chancellor, Ira Michael Heyman, and the university's president, David Pierpont Gardner, that the newly acquired and recently beautifully renovated former School for the Deaf and Blind, a few blocks south of the Berkeley campus, be named the Clark Kerr Campus. Kay and I later provided the rows of flowering crabapple trees lining the main entrance drive-way. It is a joy to drive by there during the spring. The campus includes res-idence halls (800 students), intramural sports facilities, a field for intercolle-giate sports (the Clark Kerr Field), faculty housing, and a conference center. I had begun the process of transferring this facility to the university in con-sultation with Roy Simpson, then state superintendent of public instruction, many years before.

Side Effects

One unintended consequence of improving student facilities was a change in the nature of student political life on campus. Campus politics historically had been organized principally around the fraternities and sororities. As many more students came to be lodged in residence halls and in the student coop-eratives, the fraternities and sororities began to lose their dominance. Inci-dentally, I had played a minor role twice in the development of the co-ops. As a graduate student at Stanford, studying the self-help cooperatives of the unemployed during the Great Depression, I had been asked to go over to Berke-ley to consult at Stiles Hall with the original organizers on how to develop co-operatives. Later, as chancellor, I took the lead among college and university presidents in sponsoring legislation that made co-ops, along with university-owned residence halls, eligible for federal supporting funds. I worked with Harry Kingman, the longtime and venerated head of Stiles Hall, who was the other chief proponent, and years later I was the main speaker when Kingman Hall was dedicated as part of the co-op system.

Student life grew more concentrated around the campus than it had been when more students were commuters. It also became more subject to orga-nized activities, including political demonstrations, than when students liv-ing around the campus were scattered in many separate private rooming houses or in politically conservative fraternities and sororities. We had created an in-residence critical mass for student activism, never known, for example, at com-munity colleges that have only commuter students.

The political life of the city of Berkeley shifted from Chamber of Com-merce conservatism to political liberalism supported by student votes, now extended to include eighteen-year-olds. It became "Berzerkeley." Telegraph Av-enue took on a new flavor, paralleling the variety of activities in the great pub-lic square next to the souk in Marrakech in Morocco—without the monkeys, bears, and snakes but with much else. The city came to be the Berkeley of David Lodge's *Changing Places*—shocking and delightful.

A New Look at Student Affairs

In all my efforts to change the context for student life on campus, I had no support from the longtime dean of students, Hurford Stone (1946–59), who continued to report to the universitywide administration. He was a devotee of Rule 17 and of the university's action in loco parentis on campus and off. He found what little student support he had in the fraternities and sororities. Other students pretended there was a Berlin Wall around the campus, which they called the "Stone Wall" and, on occasion, floated balloons across.

My most bitter argument with Dean Stone was over his suspension of a male student who was reported in a local newspaper as having been arrested for being drunk in a bar in a nearby city. Stone had a staff member who read several local papers looking for such incidents. I overruled him. Stone said that such incidents brought discredit to the university, and that I must be intent on destroying the university's dearly won reputation for clean behavior. I replied that this event had occurred off campus, that it had nothing to do with academic performance and on-campus behavior, and that it was a strange brand of justice if punishment depended on the happenstance of a staff member reading a story in one of the local papers to which his office chanced to subscribe.

A somewhat similar incident, also an indication of the existing campus practice, was the assignment of an F grade in ROTC to an otherwise straight A student for the way he was dressed at a protest demonstration against compulsory ROTC. He was wearing his ROTC uniform. This was the sole basis for the F. There was a request to reverse the grade, which I supported, but the ROTC department appealed to the appropriate Academic Senate committee, which sustained the department on the grounds of departmental autonomy.

I took several actions to offset Dean Stone, who personified a hard line toward students. I set up and chaired the Student Affairs Committee. It included top staff in the Dean of Students office, including the dean, student leaders from across the campus, and faculty members highly regarded for their interest in student welfare. We talked about many matters affecting student life, including the academic and physical plans for the campus. I also appointed students to faculty committees, and the students appointed to the Committee on Buildings and Campus Development were particularly effective in supporting projects related to student life.

I recruited Katherine Towle to be dean of women and a prospective dean of students. She was a former colonel in the U.S. Marines, a dignified lady of great presence and good judgment, a Berkeley graduate (class of 1920; M.A. 1935), and a descendant of a pioneer California family after whom a town was named in the foothills of the Sierra Nevada. I later nominated her to the regents to be Dean of Students, and I think she was the first woman to hold that title in any American research university.

I also had a policy of having a faculty assistant to act as my liaison to students. The most effective of these was Alex Sherriffs, a very popular teacher in the psychology department. Later, when I was no longer chancellor, he was made vice-chancellor of student affairs and then took, so sadly from my point of view and for reasons I never fully understood, an uncompromising stand against the student activists and was a major factor contributing to the development of a new student movement. In the 1950s, however, he was an antidote to Hurford Stone, turning a "human face" to the students from inside the chancellor's office.

Athletics

The 1950s were a golden age for sports at Berkeley—surpassed only by the 1920s. The 1920s saw two Rose Bowl victories, two national championships in track, four gold medals in women's tennis from the 1924 Olympics, a gold medal in Olympic crew in 1928, and much else.

The 1958 football team went to the Rose Bowl on New Year's Day 1959. (The Cal Band, incidentally, took advantage of the opportunity to spell out my name on the floor of the stadium at half time, in recognition, I thought, of my intense interest in student life.) The 1958–59 basketball team won a NCAA championship for the first and only time as did the 1957 baseball team for the second time. There was a fantastic array of coaches: Pappy Waldorf in football with three Rose Bowl teams, Brutus Hamilton in track, Ky Ebright in crew, Doc Hudson in rugby, Pete Newell in basketball, Clint Evans and George Wolfman in baseball. These coaches had been recruited and appointed by the ASUC, and many and perhaps all of them in consultation with President Sproul. I took a particular interest in rugby. I liked the spirit of good sportsmanship that marked it during and after games, and I helped in arranging contacts to schedule famous teams from around the rugby world—from Britain, from New Zealand, from Australia, and Kay and I entertained them in our home with members of the Cal team.

All looked well—but was it? Beneath the surface trouble was rising. Berkeley was still winning on the playing fields but beginning to lose in recruitment of promising new athletes. So also was Stanford. Berkeley and Stanford were willing to accept the handicaps of high student admission standards and the comparatively heavy classroom assignments, but not of under-the-table recruiting practices. Several incidents of rough play against Berkeley athletes were another problem. Wallace Sterling, president at Stanford, and I talked often about the collapse of ethical conduct both off and on the playing field that had occurred at the University of Southern California and then—as UCLA competed in the same geographical area—within the University of California itself. Wally, at one point, even raised the question of how we might have to withdraw from intercollegiate competition altogether. Instead of that, we thought of joining the Ivy League. We divided up Ivy League presidents to sound out the possibility at a meeting of the Association of American Universities. My first two were affirmative and the first one for Wally was also, but his second said absolutely "No," and he represented the institution that above all others had been the leader in creation of the Ivy League.

So we agreed on a frontal attack. That meant both institutions needed the best possible "faculty athletic representative." I thought of only one person— Glenn Seaborg. He attended so many athletic contests anyway and so did his wife, Helen. As a Nobel Prize winner, he carried the ultimate academic prestige. He was also a person of courage, conviction, and determination. I had total confidence in his good judgment. He was startled at first by my suggestion but, on reflection and with Helen's advice, accepted the offer and, I think, never regretted it. Rixford K. ("Rix") Snyder at Stanford was his counterpart, and between them they carried out our efforts to get both more reasonable recruitment rules and more effective enforcement of them. They were successful and the Pacific Coast Conference (now the Pac-Ten) has stayed relatively clean (and fully competitive) ever since.[3]

In the end, we proved that you could have a better sports program while playing within the rules. The prior road led to disintegration of good relationships and of good sportsmanship. Along the way, we regretfully had to take away ownership and control of intercollegiate athletics from the Associated Students at both Berkeley and UCLA so that the university could directly guarantee compliance with the new rules. The regents gave their total support. They were appalled at what had become highly publicized scandals.

My greatest disappointment was to find out how many sports enthusiasts thought that insistence on "clean" competition in recruiting meant bias against sports. I had thought that one of the principal virtues of sports was that it taught the importance of behavior within the rules on a level playing field. My worst experience was at a meeting held in the central dining room of the California Club in Los Angeles with alumni of UCLA just after I had been appointed president. I was placed in the center of the room, where I could best absorb the invective and shouts of outrage. Some of those present thought that my efforts were directly aimed at their very successful football coach, "Red" Sanders, who was as effective off the field in recruiting as on it in coaching. Sanders died shortly thereafter, under special circumstances, and I never had to hear those shouts of outrage again.

Consequences

The six years as chancellor at Berkeley gave me my agenda for student life when I became president: to revise Rule 17, to set up a "Hyde Park corner" on each campus, to make ROTC voluntary, to end discrimination in fraternities and sororities (then nearly total), and to start an "equal opportunity" program for greater minority access to what was then an almost totally "Anglo" student body.

I did accomplish all these self-imposed assignments but the first not fast enough or far enough; and each had its costs. One cost was the support of many conservative alumni. Student leaders might refer to me as the "students' chancellor" (or president), as they did, but I was never the "alumni's chancellor" (or president). Robert Gordon Sproul was rightly the alumni's president after all of his years in office and his constant and effective contact with alumni. When I became president, I delegated alumni relations to the chancellors and, as a consequence, Sproul became the last president to find his strongest support among alumni. One of his vice presidents (later president of Rotary International, Stanley McCaffrey) was a very effective liaison with alumni.

I have always regretted that circumstances led me to have so little close contact with alumni either as chancellor or as president. It was, however, that alumni report of 1948, *Students at Berkeley*, that became my platform for changes at Berkeley. Few reports in university history have been so completely and significantly translated into reality. The Berkeley of today owes so much to the GIs of 1946 and the alumni leaders of 1946–48, as does the whole university as it followed the new Berkeley pattern. When I walk around the Berkeley campus today, I often think of the many changes for the better that came out of the comments and actions of the GIs, and the prompt and progressive response of those committed alumni leaders.

Reprise

There were places for students (as of 1996) in university residence halls at Berkeley numbering 5,000, and universitywide 26,000. Modern student union facilities exist on all nine campuses. All campuses look more Ivy League, more Big Ten, and more like parks and less like parking lots. Looking back at history, I know of no student-initiated reversal of basic campus policies (albeit dramatized by a bonfire) and vigorously endorsed by alumni that so changed the face of a campus as *Students at Berkeley* did—first at Berkeley and then on all campuses within a multicampus university.

The Sears Directors' Cup standings for all-around excellence in intercollegiate sports (22 sports) for 1997 showed 7 of the Pac-Ten schools in the top 25 (Stanford, UCLA, Arizona, Southern California, Washington, Arizona State, and Berkeley) out of over 200 ranked schools. The Big Ten had 5. Fair play and athletic success are compatible.

The 140-acre general-purpose Kerr family farm near Jacksonwald, Pennsylvania (in background). The "old house" (1732) in foreground left; the barn to its rear; two-story Kerr house in the middle; "little old house," which predates the "old house," at right.

"Peace Caravaners" from Friends colleges, assembled at conference at
West Town School, summer 1929. Clark Kerr on top of car.

Swarthmore College Class of 1932.

Catherine (Kay) and Clark Kerr on their wedding day, December 25, 1934, with their 1928 Ford roadster.

Leaving the office of the
Institute of Industrial Relations
after becoming first chancellor
at Berkeley in 1952. Photo: Jon
Brenneis/Cal-Pictures.

First Berkeley Chancellor
Clark Kerr and University of
California President Robert
Gordon Sproul, 1954.
Photo: *Blue and Gold,* 1954.

The Kerr family sit on their patio for a photographer in 1952.
Photo: Jon Brenneis/Cal-Pictures.

Roger Lee, a member of the
Berkeley architecture department, was the architect for
the Kerr home in El Cerrito,
which served as the official
chancellor's and president's
residence from 1952–1967.
Photo: Ernest Braun.

Enjoying garden work, 1957.
Photo: Buck Joseph/
Oakland Tribune. Used with
permission.

Neighborhood touch football team on the Kerr playfield in El Cerrito, 1957.
Photo: Buck Joseph/*Oakland Tribune.* Used with permission.

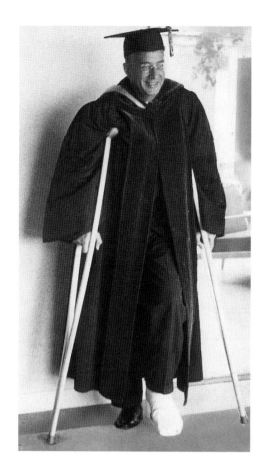

Kerr attended 1958 baccalaureate and honorary degree
ceremonies at Harvard on crutches after breaking his ankle in
a gopher hole during a touch football game.

(Opposite, above) UC Regent Dorothy Chandler joins Kerr in
celebrating a 1958 honorary degree from Occidental College
President Arthur Coons (later chair of the California Master
Plan Survey Team, 1959).

(Opposite, below) Kerr and Stanford President Wallace Sterling
following commencement ceremonies at Stanford, 1953.

Chancellor's office staff, May 1957. Back row from left: Connie Wilson, Dorothy Gardner Powell, Civilla Deming, Eugene Lee, Gloria Copeland, Kitty Molloy, Florence Eisemann, Jeanne Grimm, Carol Blackwell, Gretchen Klug. Seated front: Virginia Taylor Norris, Clara Kisch.

San Francisco Opera Company production of *Turandot* at Berkeley's Greek Theatre, 1957. Other San Francisco Opera productions on the Berkeley campus during Kerr's tenure as Berkeley chancellor and UC president included *Medea, Aida,* and *Elektra*. Photo: Courtesy of University Archives, Bancroft Library, University of California, Berkeley, no. 1:39(a).

His booming voice and hearty laugh were characteristics of President Sproul, shown here in 1957. Photo: Howard Erker/*Oakland Tribune.* Used with permission.

Official portrait as twelfth president of the university, 1958. Photo: Gabriel Moulin Studio.

Members of the Cal Straw Hat Band welcome Chancellor and Mrs. Kerr at their home after news of Kerr's appointment as twelfth president of the university, October 1957. Photo: Roy Williams/ *Oakland Tribune.* Used with permission.

At inauguration ceremonies at Berkeley, President Kerr shows Mrs. Kerr the labels in the historic inaugural gown worn by Presidents Wheeler, Barrows, Campbell, and Sproul, September 29, 1958. Photo: Ted Streshinsky/*California Monthly*.

Professor Garff Wilson, director of public ceremonies at Berkeley, helps robe President Kerr for inaugural ceremonies. Daughter, Carolee, in foreground; Regent Pauley behind her. Photo: Ted Streshinsky.

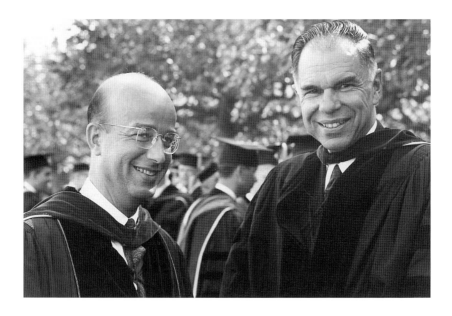

New University of California President Kerr with Glenn Seaborg, who succeeded him as chancellor at Berkeley. Photo: Ted Streshinsky/*California Monthly*.

(Opposite, above) Berkeley inaugural ceremonies for Kerr. At left is Nathan Pusey, president of Harvard University and speaker at the inaugural. He joins Berkeley Chancellor Glenn Seaborg, Kerr, and outgoing UC President Robert Gordon Sproul. Photo: Leo Cohen/*Oakland Tribune*. Used with permission.

(Opposite, below) President Kerr with Regent Don McLaughlin, chair of the Board of Regents, at inaugural ceremonies at UCLA, 1958. Photo: Tommy Amer.

President Kerr greets student leader, Rafer Johnson, at UCLA inaugural reception, 1958. Photo: Tommy Amer/ *California Monthly*.

Chancellor and Mrs. Spieth join the Kerrs in greeting students at the UC Riverside inaugural reception, 1958. Photo courtesy of *California Monthly*.

UC Davis students present President Kerr with a bowl of fruit during inaugural ceremonies at Davis, 1958. Photo: Jon Brenneis.

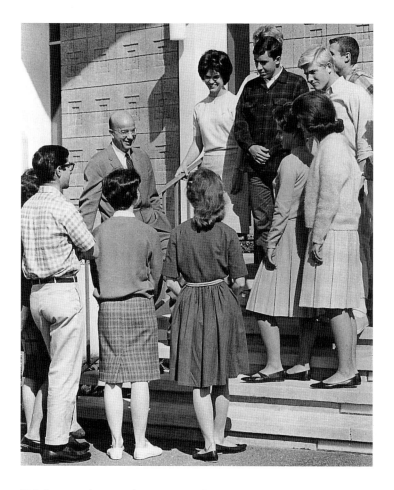

UC Santa Barbara students enjoy a chance to talk to the
new UC president, 1958.

(Opposite, above) Davis Vice Chancellor Vernon Cheadle (later
chancellor at UC Santa Barbara) joins the Kerrs and Chancellor and Mrs. Mrak in welcoming new students to UC Davis.
Photo: University Camera Shop, Davis.

(Opposite, below) Cal Band salutes President Kerr at the 1959
Rose Bowl game.

Kerr escorts U.S. President John F. Kennedy into Berkeley's Memorial Stadium for 1962 Charter Day ceremony where Kennedy spoke to a crowd of 93,000. Following in the procession: Governor Edmund G. (Pat) Brown, former UC President Robert Gordon Sproul, and Berkeley Chancellor Glenn Seaborg. Photo: ASUC Photography.

Kerr welcomes former U.S. President Dwight D. Eisenhower to the 1963 UCLA honorary degree ceremony.

U.S. President Lyndon B. Johnson dedicates the site of Irvine campus, June 20, 1964. From left: Orange County Assemblyman Dick Hanna, Governor Edmund G. (Pat) Brown, President Johnson, Regent Edward Carter, Ivan Hinderaker, Clark Kerr. Photo: Ted Streshinsky.

UCLA Chancellor Franklin Murphy looks on as President Kerr awards
an honorary degree to Mexican President Adolfo López Mateos during
the UCLA Charter Day ceremony, February 21, 1964.

University of Bordeaux Rector Jean Babin greets President Kerr during
an honorary degree ceremony at Bordeaux in 1962. Babin welcomed the
first UC Education Abroad program to his university that fall.

Regent Thomas Storke, Regent Catherine Hearst, Kay Kerr, Regent Elinor Heller, and President Kerr at a dinner party in Santa Barbara, 1963. Photo: Hal Boucher.

Regent Jesse Steinhart celebrates his eightieth birthday in the company of President Kerr and Chief Justice Earl Warren, May 1961. Photo: Jim Mazzuchi.

Regent William Matson Roth.
Photo: Courtesy of University
Archives, Bancroft Library, University of California, Berkeley, no. 1:243.

Regent William K. Coblentz.
Photo: Dan Cheatham/Courtesy
of University Archives, Bancroft
Library, University of California,
Berkeley, no. 1:261.

The Board of Regents, September 1962. Seated from left: Jerd F. Sullivan, Jr., Samuel B. Mosher, G. Norris Nash, Jr., Philip L. Boyd, Glenn Anderson, Clark Kerr, Edwin W. Pauley, Donald H. McLaughlin, Theodore R. Meyer, Edward W. Carter; standing from left: Cornelius J. Haggerty, Catherine C. Hearst, Elinor R. Heller, William M. Roth, Robert E. Alshuler, William E. Forbes, and John S. Watson. Photo: Gilberts of Goleta.

Kerr with Governor Edmund G. (Pat) and Bernice Brown. Photo: Courtesy
of University Archives, Bancroft Library, University of California, Berkeley,
no. 1:387

Council of Chancellors, circa 1962. From left: Dean McHenry (Santa Cruz), Herbert York (San Diego), Franklin Murphy (UCLA), Emil Mrak (Davis), President Kerr, Edward Strong (Berkeley), Vernon Cheadle (Santa Barbara), John Saunders (San Francisco), Daniel G. Aldrich, Jr. (Irvine), Herman Spieth (Riverside). Photo: Jack Fields.

Roger Revelle and Clark Kerr at groundbreaking ceremony for School of Science and Engineering, the first building for UC San Diego, May 18, 1961. Photo: University of California, San Diego, Archives.

Chancellor Daniel Aldrich with the new Irvine campus rising around him, spring 1965. Photo: Beth Koch/Beth Koch Collection, University Archives, UCI Libraries.

Chancellor Dean McHenry in the redwoods at the Santa Cruz campus. Credit: Ansel Adams/University of California, Santa Cruz, Archives.

Santa Cruz Chancellor
McHenry, President Kerr, and
Regent Donald McLaughlin
informally discuss the new
Santa Cruz campus. Photo:
Ted Streshinsky.

UCR Chancellor Ivan
Hinderaker conferring a
degree at commencement
exercises. Photographic image
is used with the permission of
the Special Collections
Department of the University
of California, Riverside.

The grandeur of the Greek Theatre at Berkeley during the 1965 United
Nations Convocation. Photo: Courtesy of University Archives, Bancroft
Library, University of California, Berkeley, no. 1:340.

The Berkeley chancellors at Charter Day, 1981. From left: Clark Kerr, Glenn T. Seaborg, Edward W. Strong, Roger W. Heyns, Albert H. Bowker, and I. Michael Heyman. Photo: Courtesy of University Archives, Bancroft Library, University of California, Berkeley, no. 1:300.

In 1988 four longtime leaders and great builders of Berkeley's academic preeminence during the Kerr years were presented with the Clark Kerr Award by the Berkeley Division of the Academic Senate. From left: Lincoln Constance, former dean of letters and science; E. T. Grether, former dean of business administration; Clark Kerr; Harry R. Wellman, former UC vice president–agriculture and executive vice president; and Morrough (Mike) P. O'Brien, former dean of engineering. Photo: Janice Sheldon.

A New Physical Development Plan for Berkeley

Enrollment at Berkeley in the fall of 1952 was 16,000 students, about the same level as just before World War II. But the national move toward universal access to higher education, and the heavy postwar in-migration to California were beginning to have their impact. Taken with the projections for the enrollment of the GIs' children in about ten years, the three changes were to carry enrollments at Berkeley to 27,500 by 1964.

A new physical plan was necessary to reflect our proposed academic plans and other changes in the composition of the campus. The last prior physical plan, developed by the universitywide staff and adopted in 1951 by the regents "in principle" and without much deliberation, assumed an enrollment of 20,000 students. This plan—prepared under Chief Architect Robert J. Evans as the principal author[1]—became an important building block for the 1956 plan (of McLaughlin, Wurster, and Kerr).

The campus already reflected a series of architectural styles established by supervising architects over the prior half century and by individual building architects.[2] It was a "museum" of many styles. The 1951 plan said the "campus appears disorderly" but was not "forever ruined": it "is truly in a critical stage of development." Earlier campus administrators had not given high priority to physical planning and the faculty was only marginally involved. Students and alumni were not involved at all.

This is where we stood in fall 1952. A new plan, a new approach to planning, and some additional land were needed. All of these were achieved. The campus of 2000 is substantially a product of these achievements, and of the earlier vision of Phoebe Apperson Hearst.

■

A Vision of Greatness—Phoebe Apperson Hearst

Phoebe Apperson Hearst had the first great concept of what the Berkeley campus might become in terms of physical facilities. She was, perhaps, the most influential single regent in Berkeley history. Her origins were humble. She was raised on a hardscrabble farm in the northern reaches of the Ozark Mountains where they extended into Missouri—an area of marginal farms and small lead mines. A neighbor, George Hearst, had gone west from there to begin accumulating a fortune in mining. He became involved with the Comstock Lode in Nevada, the Anaconda in Montana, and the Homestake in South Dakota, as well as properties in Mexico. When he was about forty, he returned to Missouri and married Phoebe Apperson, the daughter of a girl he had courted before going west. They then moved to California. They led compatible but largely separate lives. He was a miner and loved frontier towns and life. He made a huge fortune and at one point owned a million acres in the U.S. and Mexico. Phoebe developed interests in cultural life and in travel to Europe. George's interests ran more to mining, to whiskey, and to poker. They had one son, William Randolph.

Phoebe Hearst was the first woman appointed to the Board of Regents in 1897 and served for twenty-two years. She early showed a special interest in the Berkeley campus by initiating and financing an international competition to develop a physical plan for the campus. This led to the Bénard plan of 1899. It was a grandiose architectural plan with a neoclassical theme. Out of it came the central core of the campus: the Doe Library, Wheeler Hall, California Hall, and Durant Hall. The most important physical development plans for the Berkeley campus were this plan and the 1956 plan developed under the chairmanship of Regent Donald McLaughlin, who was raised in Mrs. Hearst's household. Mrs. Hearst also initiated and helped finance several specific projects: the Hearst Mining Building, Hearst Hall, a gymnasium for women, and the first building on campus to house the anthropological and archaeological collections.

Her other great interest, in addition to the physical development of the campus, was in the cultural life of Berkeley. She saw to it that the Greek Theatre was well utilized for theatrical productions. She developed great anthropological and archaeological collections and gave them to the campus. She financed a professional musical quartet on campus. She had two small "cottages," residence halls for women, and she supported scholarships for women students.

University President William Wallace Campbell called her the "best friend the University of California ever had." But nobody took her place. Physical planning and the cultural life of the campus both suffered. I look on the period of 1920–50 as the "dark ages" following the "classical" period (1897–1919) of Phoebe Apperson Hearst's unfolding vision. The revival that began in the 1950s was, in substantial part, an extension of her interests. She was the "best friend" of and had the greatest vision for the future of the Berkeley campus. The 1956 plan was the 1899 plan redux. First of all, it was a comprehensive plan. Second, it provided for cultural facilities. Third, it called for better student life facilities, including a student union and residence halls. And it was appropriate that Donald McLaughlin should play such a prominent part in advancing what Phoebe Apperson Hearst had started.

A New Approach to Planning—1956

This account of the great transformation in the physical aspects of the Berkeley campus after 1956 sets forth the intermingling of external and internal forces and conditions that had to be brought together in a more or less consistent whole. External forces included the impending avalanche of students, the vast increase in federal research and development funds, and the pronounced shift of student interest toward professional fields, including engineering and business administration. Another external force was intensified competition among research universities for the best scholars and the resultant pressures to make Berkeley as attractive as possible not only in its faculty salaries, but also in the drawing power of its physical and cultural environments. Internal forces and considerations included a strong faculty desire to remain as a top ranked research university after the traumatic experience of the loyalty oath controversy, and the GI students' drive for facilities more comparable to those at competitive private and public universities. Another internal consideration was to accommodate, as best as possible, the automobile.

What were the attempted solutions to the impacts of these forces and desires? And what processes were devised to seek these solutions? How was quantity to be reconciled with quality and beauty?

The Berkeley campus in the early and mid-1950s urgently needed a new physical plan, and such a plan became a high priority of my office. It also required a new approach to planning more related to academic policies and involving all elements of the Berkeley campus community in the process—an end to the separation between physical and academic planning, and an end to regental domination of physical planning.

The new physical plan needed to respond to the new academic situation developing (for a listing of the 1956 plan's major beneficiaries, see Table 13):

We needed to adjust to the new enrollment prospects that envisioned an increase by more than two-thirds over the current and historic level of about 16,000.

We needed to adjust to the higher proportion of graduate students being planned. We expected to more than double graduate enrollment.

We needed more research space with fast increasing federal research funds.

We needed more space—particularly for engineering, mathematics and statistics, and the social sciences (including business administration), to each of which greater attention was being given.

We needed additional cultural facilities.

We needed additional facilities for student life.

We needed more parking space and more of it off campus.

We needed more attention to landscaping and to pedestrian circulation.

We needed to settle some increasingly contentious issues with the city of Berkeley.

The physical plan turned out to be more difficult to put together than the academic plan, although it was presented to the regents one year earlier (August 1956 versus August 1957) because of the urgency of getting under way with the long process of financing and building the necessary facilities. The academic plan involved working mostly with committees of faculty members—and that was pure joy. The physical plan, at the staff level, however, was in a no-man's land contested between the well-established "Corley empire," which included the office of Architects and Engineers, and an emerging "campus empire" of the chancellor's office and the largely faculty-constituted Buildings and Campus Development Committee (BCDC) newly appointed by the chancellor in October 1953. There had been a prior universitywide Committee on Building Needs with campus subcommittees to set priorities for new buildings, which was continued for a time. There was also an existing Committee on Building Locations, which was incorporated into the new BCDC.

TABLE 13

Major Gainers in Space Resulting from the 1956 Plan

Function or Academic Field*	Approximate Square Footage Gained
Student housing and dining	1,250,000
Clark Kerr Campus	415,000
Student union and student services	280,000
Recreational facilities	265,000
Parking structures	820,000
Biological sciences	652,420
Social sciences	397,580
Performing and visual arts	370,000
Chemistry	321,000
Engineering	418,000
Mathematics and statistics	285,000
Physical and earth sciences	265,000
Environmental design	217,000

For the humanities, Dwinelle Hall with 228,000 sq. ft. had been added in 1952.

Who was to be in charge? Fortunately, the staff members of Architects and Engineers, with whom we in the chancellor's office dealt, were very competent and very cooperative (Robert J. Evans, Louis A. DeMonte, and Albert R. Wagner). They acted as dedicated professionals and not as partisans of the universitywide administration versus the chancellor's office, although it took me some time to realize this—I regret to say. But, how to get our plans to the regents promptly, with layers of less interested and less sympathetic decision makers in between? The answer was to go around them.

The McLaughlin-Wurster-Kerr Committee and the BCDC

A new regents' Committee on Campus Planning–Berkeley was appointed and assigned by the board to "perform the duties of supervising architect," with Regent Donald McLaughlin as chair, and myself and Dean William Wurster of architecture as the other members. The most important member was Don. He was a graduate of Berkeley (1914) and a former faculty member at Berkeley as well as at Harvard. He had been raised in Berkeley in the family of Regent Hearst, who had taken (as did Don) the utmost interest in the development of the Berkeley campus. Don was the son of one of Phoebe Hearst's staff members, and she treated him as though he were her own grandson, providing for his education at Berkeley and Harvard and a grand tour of Europe. Don was devoted to Berkeley. His experience in mining in Latin America had convinced him that it was better to look down on red-tile roofs from the Berkeley hills than on asphalt coating. I came to agree with his fervent belief. Don was perfect for the position for an additional reason: he could—as a regent and committee chair appointed by the regents—make sure that the committee's plan would pass without comment to the Board of Regents through Corley's staff and the president's office; and it did. We submitted our plan to President Sproul on August 10, 1956, and it was presented to the regents on August 24, 1956, and adopted unanimously (with two reservations relating to parking and the purchase of additional property). This was unprecedented—and only because of Don and the board's tremendous respect for him. Bill Wurster was also a Berkeley graduate (1919), as was I (1939 Ph.D.). Bill had raised architecture at Berkeley to its number one ranking among American universities. All three of us had been or currently were Berkeley faculty members.

However, it was a very questionable tactic (a tactic to which I confess) to have a regent chair a single-campus committee, and I would not have liked it if I had been president. But we were under great time pressure: to get a plan approved by the regents, to get a priority list within that plan for the most needed new buildings, to get that list accepted by the universitywide administration, by the regents, and in Sacramento, to get our share of the state and federal funds then available, to plan and erect the buildings, to be ready for the tidal wave—and we were. Berkeley was clearly advantaged by the work of the McLaughlin committee.

The first push for a new plan and a new approach to planning had come from the faculty. In March 1949 a memorandum was sent to President Sproul, signed by 150 faculty members (I was one of them), expressing a "grave concern over the functional and aesthetic deterioration of the campus" and stating the need for a "flexible, up-to-date master plan." This memo was prepared by Stephen Pepper (philosophy and art). It noted, among other things, the "chaotic traffic and parking situations." It said there would be "irreparable damage" if there was delay in campus planning. Pepper says in his oral history that the memorandum was written in his dining room with the help of Walter Horn (art) and Jack Kent (city and regional planning). Pepper added that the proposal "fell on deaf ears" at the presidential level but "fortunately, about that time, Kerr became chancellor" and he was not "browbeaten by the president."[3] I remember that, early on when I became chancellor, Pepper and Horn came to see me asking for action on the faculty memo of March 1949, which I came to think of as the "Pepper report." One early result of the report was my appointment of the new administrative Buildings and Campus Development Committee (BCDC), made up of faculty members from many disciplines.

The BCDC, with which I worked so closely, had devoted chairs and members—sometimes too devoted, for they would fight harder over the placement of a tree than their counterpart academic committee did over the allocation of a new faculty position. Altogether, with the faculty members of the full committee (27) and all of its subcommittees, more than 15 percent (one in six) of all faculty members participated in the physical planning process. No planning process at Berkeley, except for the academic plan, ever drew on the participation of such a high number of the faculty. It was a community effort of historic proportions.

Two chairpersons were indispensable: Professors C. W. Brown of psychology and Sanford Elberg of bacteriology and immunology. Six members were students, a new departure in Berkeley practice. I think never before were students so involved in any "faculty committee." Their participation helped incorporate the proposals in the alumni association's report on *Students at Berkeley* into the long-range campus plan, and this was one of my reasons for their appointments. The other reason was to give students more of a voice in campus decision-making. There were also four members from the administration. (For a list of members of the full committee who worked on the 1956 plan, see Appendix 1 section I.)

The New Process and Some Problems

This planning process was unique in campus history. Previously, all plans were made by professional architects appointed by and working directly with the Board of Regents, and not by campus faculty members and administrators and students. And the last "supervising architect," Arthur Brown, had retired in 1948. The campus had never had an academic plan to guide the physical plan, and faculty members had been mostly involved only in plans for the interiors of buildings. Now there was close overall consultation involving the BCDC, the Council of Deans, the Academic Advisory Committee, the Student Affairs Committee, and the Alumni Council—an all-campus effort.

We got an excellent plan out of this process that passed the Board of Regents unanimously and was endorsed by the Academic Senate and by the Alumni Council. Based on this plan, 7,300,000 square feet of building space out of a total of 13,000,000 on the campus in 1994 (over 50 percent) were put in place, and the open spaces and parklike atmosphere we wanted were greatly improved upon. But we had problems. Among them, parking was a hardy perennial.

PARKING SPACE ON CAMPUS

How to add that much building space and not infringe upon open space? The big casualty was parking space on the central campus, and I was at the center of the bitter battles that ensued. It seemed that faculty members thought they had a constitutional right to life, liberty, and a parking space right next to their offices and free of charge! One faculty member had his secretary stand in "his" space until he arrived each day. She served him with religious devotion for many years but one morning came into my office sobbing beyond control. It was a rainy day. Another faculty member had pushed her out of his way with the fender of his car and had taken that sacred parking space. The Herr Professor, when he arrived, had fired her on the spot. She was a temporary casualty, later reinstated with my intervention. That space, incidentally, is now allocated to the department of which he was a member, which means in practice to the department chair.

I was also a casualty (and a more permanent one) because I was held personally responsible for taking much of the parking out of the central campus, replacing it with parking structures off the central campus, and then charging for the new spaces! An atrocity! There was no point in noting that every step of the way was approved by the appropriate faculty committee or committees. I am sure there must have been some kindly faculty member who approved of what was being done, but I never heard from her or him. I did hear from many others. In total, we increased authorized parking spaces from 900 to 6,000. (There had also been many unauthorized spaces on lawns and under trees—300 parking places out of 1,200 in a 1950 survey were identified as "unorganized" although my impression was that it was more like 3,000!) Occasionally to this day, a faculty member will point out to me the cherished space under a tree that I stole from him.

THE CITY OF BERKELEY

How to placate the city that surrounded the university? The new plans took property off the Berkeley tax rolls, particularly to the north across Hearst Avenue and to the south across Bancroft Way. But there were other problems, too.

One day I got a frantic telephone call from George Pettitt in Sacramento. George was a chief assistant to President Sproul. He also held what was then thought of as the "University seat" on the Berkeley City Council. He told me to get over immediately to the Durant Hotel on the other side of Durant Avenue just south of the campus because we had trouble with the Chamber of Commerce whose members were meeting there. And this is how, for the first time, any relations with the city were delegated, however informally, to me as chancellor. I got to the Durant to be shouted at by a group that had voted to fight the university's budget before the legislature (and had been energizing itself for combat in the usual way before I arrived). I listened. There were two main reasons for the revolt. One was that the university would not talk openly about its use of campus property. It owned it and that was that. The other was that it would not talk about its future designs on private property within the city. It had the power of eminent domain and that was that.

I set up, as of 1953, a hard-working liaison committee, chaired first by Dean Wurster and later by Richard Jennings of the law school (see the list in Appendix 1 section J). We agreed to improve traffic movement around campus by opening up Gayley Road below the Hearst Greek Theatre as a public road and by rounding the corners at the edges of the central campus to improve circulation. We also agreed to make firmer our plans for campus intrusion into the city, to announce them publicly, and to abide by these plans. The result was that local owners would be better able to manage their properties— to decide what to build or not build and what to maintain or not maintain. We agreed to buy our designated future property as soon as possible. One happy consequence was that I did not have to hear any more from my dentist about the problem of what he should do or not do with the property he owned next to his office building each time I sat in his chair of pain. A Berkeley city liaison committee report on relations with the Berkeley campus later stated (1957), "the traditional University policy of treating planning matters confidentially was changed to a policy of open discussion." This reversed a policy nearly a century old. It opened up and greatly improved relations with the city of Berkeley and its residents. Not that the university avoided all specific disagreements later.

SACRAMENTO

How to be successful in Sacramento? Our troubles, other than getting the money we wanted from the governor and legislature, centered around these facts of life: (1) There is nothing so permanent as a temporary building. (2) A new building does not have to be cheap. It just has to look cheap. Taxpayers' gothic! (3) All space in a building must be "useful," which meant minimizing opportunities for informal human contact. (4) A community college architectural style ought to be adequate also for a research university. It took endless efforts at persuasion, only partially effective, on each of these points.

My biggest disappointment, after one or two early successes, was to lose requested space for faculty and student lounges in each major new building (point 3 above)—the reviewers in Sacramento caught up with us much too fast. One of the few lounges we got was almost immediately assigned by the faculty involved to some new laboratory machinery—so it was probably a lost cause anyway. I dropped by one day, with great anticipation, to see how faculty and students were making use of the intended lounge. And what I saw was all that machinery and not a soul around. Total defeat. One way or another, there would be no friendly lounges at Berkeley for coffee and tea and an informal chat—the best way to know each other and to get business transacted. I had seen the value of such lounges as a graduate student at the London School of Economics. It was a tragedy that the effort to establish a series of them at Berkeley was killed. Human relations were not considered "useful." (The new [1995] building for the Haas School of Business Administration very fortunately does make such provisions—with private funds. In that and many other ways, it is the best building on the Berkeley campus for academic uses.)

Facilities for Cultural Life—Sparta to Athens

On a comparative basis with other leading universities, Berkeley in 1952 lacked attention to the cultural life of the campus. An abandoned utility building just east of Sather Gate (the old power house) served as an excuse for an art gallery. The large classroom in Wheeler Hall, holding 800 persons, was used for dramatic performances despite a very restricted staging area. Both were very unsatisfactory.

As a graduate student at Berkeley and a young faculty member, I was slightly conscious of the lack of cultural facilities, but then there was always the City (San Francisco) across the bay. However, when I became chancellor and started traveling to other universities, I saw how much better equipped were not only Ivy League institutions but some Big Ten universities, particularly Michigan and Illinois. In fact, I even saw high schools with better facilities than the Berkeley campus.

Then I had a shock. One of the first summers after I became chancellor, as part of a practice of inviting leading visitors on the summer school faculty to drop by for a visit, I met Gerald Holton, a famous professor at Harvard in the history of science. I asked him what he was doing at Berkeley. He replied, "I am from Athens; I thought I better take a look at what Sparta was doing." SPARTA! Was it true? In a way it was—heavy on science including research into the military use of the atom, and weak on cultural facilities. In college, I had gone through Thucydides as pro-Athenian all the way. Athens was the home of civilization! I also found out that, in the recruiting process for new faculty members, I was meeting doubts about the quality of cultural life at Berkeley—from prospects and from their spouses. And then we lost to Indiana University a faculty member we very much wanted to keep. What did Indiana have that we did not? I had never been to Bloomington so I made arrangements to stop by for three days on a trip East. Indiana had a lot, including excellent facilities for operatic and musical and dramatic performances. You could step off your porch in town and be at a world-class concert in five minutes!

What did we need? We needed an art museum, and an auditorium and playhouse. So in making our plans for physical development of the campus, we added some important cultural facilities, particularly the Berkeley Art Museum with an attached movie theater, and Zellerbach Hall for lectures and symphonies and dance performances with an attached playhouse. I had hoped that there might also be a small conference center attached to the art museum, but this never developed. I was successful, however, along with Erle Loran of the art department, in getting a gift of forty-five paintings by Hans Hofmann that became the basis for the permanent collection. Peter Selz, the first director of the museum, and I were not able, unfortunately, to persuade Peggy Guggenheim to give her Venice collection of paintings and other artwork to us. We also renovated the Hearst Greek Theatre, which had become quite dilapidated. This was done with substantial help from the Hearst Foundation. For several years after the renovation, we brought the San Francisco Opera annually to Berkeley. The first triumphal presentation was of Puccini's *Turandot.* Phoebe Apperson Hearst would have been greatly pleased.

To make good use of these and other facilities, I assigned the income from a 2.25 million dollar endowment (the McEnerney Fund—named after Garrett W. McEnerney, regent from 1901–42, and former chair of the board) to the Committee on Drama, Lectures, and Music, which made fantastically good use of it. We became more competitive in our cultural life with other leading universities.

Years later I saw Gerald Holton again at a conference at the Institute of Advanced Studies in Princeton. I asked him whether he remembered our conversation. He said that he did. Then I said that we had become more like Athens. He said, "I know that, and we have become more like Sparta." And Harvard had moved forward in science. Then we talked about how, in competitive situations, competitors often tended to become more like each other.

The Campus as a Park

We put great stress on landscaping, which costs so little for so much. We started watering to keep the lawns green in summer. We turned spotlights on the Campanile every night. We got a landscape architect (Ari Inouye) on the staff of the business manager for the first time ever at Berkeley, and he was very talented. We also got the regents to appoint the first supervising landscape architect in campus history, Lawrence Halperin, and we had our first landscape plan written by December 1953 with the advice of a very active and even enthusiastic subcommittee of the BCDC on landscaping. We later arranged for Thomas Church, a world famous landscape architect, to be our consultant. The brush was cleared out along the branches of Strawberry Creek, and maintenance was improved generally. Trees with spring blooms or fall color were added around the campus—I take particular pleasure in the planting of *Magnolia soulangea* in the area above the Life Sciences Building and cherry trees (*Prunus* Akibono) below Sather Gate along Strawberry Creek. My wife, Kay, took particular interest in renewing the rose garden adjacent to the President's House (now University House). Among his many other contributions, Church emphasized the importance of trees to create a sense of privacy between and among buildings—

a 100-foot redwood tree was the equivalent of a 100-foot expanse of lawn. As an avid gardener, I have walked the campus noting the constant progress.

Failures and Unexpected Consequences

Along with all these advances, I regret several failures of campus planning—of unequal scale—each of which actually occurred after I left the chancellorship and had become president of the university.

The loss of the world's most beautiful white eucalyptus tree by the Life Sciences Building along Campus Drive. After I was no longer chancellor, some committee ordered that a parking lot be installed around its base, which was guaranteed to kill it, given its surface root system.

The tragedy of the architecture of Wurster Hall. Bill Wurster wanted the campus to be an "architectural museum"—as in fact it was with buildings representing the style of each age when they were built. A good idea. But the style in our age was brutalism, and Wurster Hall was at the very summit of its age. Bill said he wanted a building that "the regents will hate." He got his wish. The regents did hate it, and I was one of those regents.

What went wrong was, first, that the campus chancellor recommended that the College of Architecture be allowed to build its own building via a committee; and, second, that the regents approved this unusual, even unique, procedure on my advice. I advised it because the chancellor was strongly committed to it, and because the College of Architecture argued that it would be a vote of no confidence if it could not build its own building. Compounding all this was the faculty review process based on "senatorial courtesy" toward the work of colleagues. Additionally, Bill Wurster was a great architect and had done some very attractive buildings in the Bay Area, and he supported the design. Wurster also had been an effective dean of the College of Environmental Design, which he had built out of architecture, landscape architecture, city and regional planning, and decorative arts. And he was the best of friends—so well remembered by so many people on campus and in the community, and by Don McLaughlin and by me in particular. Furthermore, two of the three members selected for the design committee had recently developed beautiful buildings for the Berkeley campus (the Student Union by Vernon DeMars and the Pelican Building by Joe Esherick). Also, when the regents saw the drawings of the building, it was surrounded by trees, with an occasional glimpse of a building hiding behind them.[4]

Then, when it was built, nothing masked the brutal reality. Don McLaughlin and I were aghast. Part of the tragedy of Wurster Hall is that it is so totally contrary to the personality of Bill Wurster—humane, warm, responsive, enthusiastic. I sometimes dream that I am planting blue gum eucalypti all around this building and then watering them! And then, if my dream goes well, I go on to review the many places of real beauty on campus that have given so many of us so much joy.

In addition, there were at least three unexpected results of our plans. One arose from the great Sproul Plaza—with its massive expanse leading up to Sather Gate—at the entrance to campus, creating an ideal setting for the then unforeseen political theatrics. And, on the north, surrounding the plaza were buildings for the social sciences and humanities whence issued many of the students, teaching assistants, and faculty members who were leaders and participants in the demonstrations of 1964 and later—so convenient to the theater in the streets.

A second unexpected development was the internal arrangement for Barrows Hall (named after David Prescott Barrows, university president from 1919–23). Barrows Hall was intended as a large step ahead for the social sciences (and business administration), as a recognition of the forward thrust of the social sciences at Berkeley previously ignored as claimants for space. But the long halls pulled faculty members apart. Not that long halls were anything new at Berkeley, as witnessed by Wheeler Hall (1917), Life Sciences Building (1930), Dwinelle Hall (1952), and other buildings. Their environments were less congenial than three departments, in particular, had previously enjoyed: economics, political science, and business administration. They each had "bull pens" in South Hall, which as a student and faculty member I knew so well and the memories of which I so treasure. Faculty members held their student office hours there and saw one another on an almost daily basis. They disliked the move to Barrows, and there was (and continues to be) much grumbling—and I agree with it. The fact is, however, that the grumbling was and is misdirected. Faculty committees have control over the interiors of buildings. I once pointed this out to one complaining faculty member located in Barrows who looked startled and then said, "That's right. I had not thought of that. I was chair of that committee." But state controls were a problem too—"bull pen" space would have had to usurp some other use; and the Barrows site also lent itself to the design of a long building.

A third unplanned development was the massive size of the math building

(Evans Hall) that now dominates the central campus. It did not loom so large when originally planned, but the federal government kept giving money for additional floors and the campus kept accepting it all, for floor after floor after floor.

Goals for Accomplishment

On reflection, the work of the McLaughlin-Wurster-Kerr committee resulted in bigger innovations than we fully realized at the time: campus planning was made an ongoing internal process—no longer conducted by an outside and changing "supervising architect"; physical planning was centered around academic concerns and not only around architecture, and faculty members were fully associated in the process for the first time; and planning started with a series of agreed-upon goals of what we expected the campus to provide as a physical environment for those who centered their lives on it, including, as far as possible, a parklike atmosphere, a center of culture as well as of learning, a more inclusive community for the "whole" student. Overall, it was a far better approach to campus planning than anything that had gone before—including the Bénard plan—"internal organic" rather than "external periodic." And the Berkeley planning process became something of a model for other campuses within the university and across the nation.

Our specific goals included:

Building on only 25 percent of the land, keeping much as a park, and greatly improving the landscaping.

Keeping building heights relatively low—no skyscrapers (the mathematics building escaped this rule).

Putting most parking off campus; making the campus more oriented toward pedestrians—and more pleasing to sight and hearing.

Merging some new developments into the city (as with the residence halls), rather than taking over a whole contiguous district.

Providing more facilities for student life and for the cultural life of the entire campus.

Now there was an ongoing Berkeley campus plan, and not a series of plans identified by the names of successive campus supervising architects, each of whom wanted to leave his own personal imprint. It was a better plan and one that has lasted longer (now forty years), representing as it does, the considered judgment of the campus community. This was fortunate for, with the cap on enrollment, this plan has become the most influential single plan in Berkeley campus history—the most nearly permanent plan. And it resulted from the best process for permanent planning.

One of my treasured items hanging on a wall in my home is a framed copy of the Berkeley 1956 plan signed by Don McLaughlin and reading: "To Clark, With affection and admiration and happy memories of the planning committee. Don." In his oral history (Regional Oral History Office, University of California, Berkeley), he says: "It was a very happy and interesting experience—three close friends working on something that they were all deeply interested in." I fully concur.

A story:

At faculty meetings, when I was chancellor, one or more persons would get up and say, "What is the chancellor doing about parking?" Finally, in exasperation, I said I'd concluded that the chancellor's job had come to be defined as providing parking for the faculty, sex for the students, and athletics for the alumni (Berkeley had just had a panty raid and the university was also going through the great corruption crisis in the Pacific Coast Conference). I then added that this was a commentary not only on the way I spent my time but also on the average age and consequent interests of the three groups involved! This to the middle-aged faculty seated before me—and taken as an insult, although it was intended as a statement of fact.

This remark was picked up by *Time* and then by *Playboy*. I got back from a regents' meeting late one night to find on the top of the pile on my desk at home a copy of *Playboy* and a letter from the editor saying they had come across this statement and were featuring it in their current issue—the copy was opened to this marked page (page 2). Then there was a postscript to the letter. It read: "We are so impressed with this statement that we are going to name you in our next issue as 'Playboy of the Month.'" Then came a post-postscript: "We consider this such a signal honor that we are sending a copy of this letter to each member of your Board of Regents." On a more careful look, I noticed that the postscript and post-postscript had been written on a different typewriter and concluded that my administrative assistant, Gloria Copeland, was indulging her sense of humor. I did not then find it all that funny.

As I walk the campus today and enjoy it greatly, I think of the Witter report of 1944 that endorsed university-initiated residence halls at Berkeley for the first time in history, of the GIs' dissatisfaction in fall 1946, of the alumni-sponsored report of 1948 *(Students at Berkeley),* of the support of leaders in the classes, particularly of 1954, 1955, 1956, and 1957 in endorsing the recommendations in the alumni report, of the initiative supplied by the Pepper report, of the work of the BCDC under the leadership of C. W. Brown and Sanford Elberg, of the devoted and highly professional work of Evans, DeMonte, and Wagner as staff, of the vision of Thomas Church of the campus as a park, and of the many meetings of the committee that Don McLaughlin chaired. The campus is both more useful and more beautiful. I also think of the devoted and skilled attention given over the years by the members of the staff of grounds and buildings in keeping the campus so clean, so well maintained, so beautiful.

Forty Years Later

The 1956 physical development plan has been accomplished almost in its totality. Even all the temporary buildings in the central glade have now been removed.

The process that led to the plan has been continued.

The big additions beyond the 1956 plan have been the replacement of Cowell Hospital by the fantastic Haas School of Business, and the building of the new Tang student health center to take its place on Bancroft Way—both gifts!

The class of 1954 made a gift of a beautiful North Gate entrance—an area that had earlier been entirely nondescript. This gift stands with the class of 1914 fountain at the College Avenue entrance and the class of 1928 new Campanile bells as the greatest class gifts to the physical enhancement of the campus, and now the West Gate by the class of 1953.

Beautiful and highly useful renovations have been made to the Valley Life Sciences Building and to the Doe Library. The classes of 1945, 1946, and 1947 (including the special wartime classes) have made a gift of a Memorial Glade just north of Doe to enhance the library renovations.

Parking and athletics are no longer such hot issues on campus.

The one tragedy has been People's Park. This area some two blocks south of the main campus had been purchased for a residence hall. It was taken over by students and street people in a campus riot, after Ronald Reagan became governor in 1967. The National Guard was called in, fully armed. There were some 150 casualties and one death. The campus was sprayed by a potent tear gas from a helicopter. In practice, the area has been held ever since by street people and only partially reclaimed by the campus and the city. It became, for a time, a center for drug dealing and petty crime. This plot (2.8 acres) is, I believe, the only area relinquished to street people on any U.S. university or college campus—relinquished by Governor Reagan's Board of Regents.

I prefer to think instead of the accomplishments of the McLaughlin-Wurster-Kerr Committee:

- A physical planning process based on an academic plan and involving very considerable faculty and student input, rather than a regental-led process centered on changing external architectural advice.

- More facilities for student life: residence halls and intramural sports fields, the Haas Recreational Center, the student union complex, and the Clark Kerr Campus.

- More facilities for the cultural life of the campus: the art museum and motion picture theater, the Zellerbach Auditorium and Playhouse, and the renovated Greek Theatre.

- A campus that is more of a beautiful park and less of an ugly parking lot.

- A campus that doubled student enrollment and doubled the total building space without feeling overcrowded.

- A campus with more cooperative relations with its surrounding community.

- A plan that resurrected the vision of Phoebe Apperson Hearst. Hail to Phoebe Apperson Hearst! Her spirit still animates the Berkeley campus.

Responding to
Some Post–Loyalty
Oath Legacies

Nineteen fifty-two had not been the very best of years to inaugurate chancellorships at UCLA and Berkeley—particularly at Berkeley.

The regents had divided bitterly over the loyalty oath controversy.

The president of the university found himself in a weakened position vis-à-vis many of the regents and even some of his once loyal faculty, as a result of his initiation of the loyalty oath and then his retreats in reference to it.

The faculty had grown disheartened and discouraged, and politically sensitized.

As chancellor, my central approach was to see that there were no more conflagrations—not if I could help it. My efforts landed me in several skirmishes. I felt I had to be always on the alert and ready to intervene to the extent I could.

The series of responses to one of the major themes of the times (anticommunism) set forth below began before my years as chancellor and continued into my presidency. My successful attempts to heal old wounds also opened new ones that festered until my dismissal as president in 1967 and continue even to this day.

■

When Ray Allen and I became the first chancellors at UCLA and Berkeley in 1952, we were introduced into a supercharged atmosphere of a divided board of regents and a divided faculty, and more so at Berkeley than at UCLA because the oath controversy had been more concentrated at Berkeley. As the more liberal of the two chancellors, I was also the more vulnerable to criticism from the conservative factions in the state and in the Board of Regents. And, as a liberal, I was also subject to special criticism from Berkeley's influential radical left.

The regents were more touchy on some issues that came before them than they might otherwise have been and so, potentially, was the faculty.

The "Red Chancellor" of the "Red Campus"

I encountered many minefields and exploded several anti-personnel mines, the legacies of which profoundly affected my chancellorship and my university presidency after 1958. One of the first was a confrontation I began with the California Senate Committee on Un-American Activities (the Burns committee) the very day I was introduced as chancellor to the Berkeley community in Dwinelle Plaza. It happened on the day of the first university meeting of the new academic year—October 1, 1952. President Sproul had just announced my appointment as "contact man" with the state senate committee. I expressed my reservations about the arrangement and never did, in fact, so serve. But my antagonistic, and very distant relationship with the state committee lasted throughout my period in university administration. It also made my relationships with President Sproul and Vice President Corley more uneasy. I reserve until later *(Political Turmoil)* my account of this complex and most regrettable story when I set forth the intertwined internal and external political environment of those years of McCarthyism and its repercussions in California. I walked straight into this conflict with the most powerful reactionary force in the state (the Burns committee) with my eyes wide open.

In the wake of the oath controversy, a second obstacle was McCarthyism's chilling effects on free speech and association among faculty members. Several (perhaps ten) came in to see me as chancellor, one by one, asking for my permission to join one group or another, or sign one petition or another, or give one speech or another. In each case I would say that the decision was their own, not the chancellor's. I would add, however, that if I were in their place, I would do exactly what I wanted to do as a free American citizen.

After the first few such inquiries, I decided to set an example. An initiative to place the Levering Act oath adopted by the legislature in 1950 into the state constitution was before the voters of California in the fall of 1952. It passed with more than a two-thirds majority (2,700,000 to 1,200,000).[1] A group of Bay Area Quakers was opposing this initiative for inclusion in the permanent constitution of the state and asked me (also of the Quaker persuasion) to join them. I did so in public pronouncements. I knew the possible consequences and they came quickly, including several from regents. The most dramatic was at the next meeting of the board. The chair of the board (Edward Dickson) came to my office and seized me by the coat lapels. He said I was being viewed as the "Red Chancellor" of the "Red Campus," and he wanted me to retract what I had done. I refused. I said that I had acted as a citizen in an off-campus context; that I had not given up my rights as an American citizen when I became chancellor; that I never would; and that the regents should know this. Regent Dickson turned his back to me and walked away.

A third issue was the pressure being put on librarians around the state to acquire only politically acceptable books. A lecturer at Berkeley (Marjorie Fiske) published a study on the subject, suggesting that the pressure came from conservative groups. I considered this charge to be very likely true. At one of my first meetings with the board as chancellor, several regents wanted to do something to her in retaliation. What that action might be was never made clear. I defended her and prevailed.

A fourth controversy concerned the California Labor School, an allegedly Communist front activity (and I agreed that it was from my knowledge of it and its sponsors), which was going out of business and wanted to give its archives to the university. This raised some strong opposition within the board, again at one of the earliest meetings I attended. I defended acceptance on the grounds that historical records should be preserved, and again I succeeded.

A fifth issue arose, after the California State Supreme Court ruled the university loyalty oath invalid (October 17, 1952), over the question of back pay for the nonsigners. I immediately supported back pay in discussions with the regents (at their meetings on November 21, 1952, and January 20, 1953) on the grounds, in part, that the courts would subsequently require back pay in any event. I based this argument upon my experience in industrial relations. I also argued that for the board, on its own, to grant back pay would be a gesture welcomed by the faculty and would help bind up the wounds. Some agreed. Some disagreed. Others thought it was "wiser" for the courts to so rule than for the board to so act because the latter course of action would arouse needless controversy within the board and in some quarters externally; and so my effort failed. Later, however, back pay was agreed to by the board (March 1956) as a case brought by the dismissed faculty members lay before the Superior Court in Sacramento. I also tried personally to persuade nonsigners to return, promising that they would in no way be discriminated against.

A sixth obstacle touched on tenure for a faculty member in political science (Harold Winkler). His colleagues in the department voted to deny him tenure, although the chair of the department supported him. Shortly after that action, Winkler addressed a student group at the Hillel Foundation (the center for Jewish students at Berkeley) and was reported in the press to have urged students to consider joining the Communist Party. The reports on what he said were subject to dispute, and his actual comments were never fully clarified. The reports, however, drew headlines.

The issue of dismissing Winkler forthwith first came up at a meeting of the board to which I had not been invited. Some regents reacted violently to the reports. They may have remembered that Winkler had been one of the "not cleared" nonsigners, affecting their strong initial reactions. President Sproul postponed a vote to the next meeting of the board (January 29, 1954) and said I would be specially invited to attend. Here was another case in which a difficult issue came up; the universitywide reaction was, "That's why we have a chancellor," as with the "contact man" idea and several other issues. The president did not commit himself, either when inviting me or later, when I asked him what his position would be. I finally rode alone with him in the elevator at the Crocker Building in San Francisco where the regents occasionally met and were meeting that day. I told him I really had to know his position. He said that he would give me a chance to argue against dismissal but he thought I should know in advance that I would lose.

I was terribly worried. Friends had warned me that the Berkeley faculty was becoming aroused, that another minor oath controversy might be in the offing. I had taken the precaution of visiting Regent Neylan in his baronial castle on his estate in Woodside. I had gone over the case with him and how the university should act most carefully—no more oath controversies. At the board meeting, I argued that Winkler had spoken off campus as an individual, that he had a right to his opinions, and that his future at the university had already been determined on academic grounds and thus that any action by the regents would be both redundant and very distressing to many faculty members. When the vote was taken I did not lose and Regent Neylan ended up voting with me—in fact, he introduced the motion to accept my report. Only the chair of the board (Regent Dickson) voted "no." Winkler, of course, was furious. He was not a heroic martyr (like Mulcahy in Mary McCarthy's *Groves of Academe*), but an academic reject.

Another controversy started with the federal government's ruling that all Reserve Office Training Corps (ROTC) participants would be made ineligible if they belonged to any one of a long list (approximately 200) of suspect organizations ("the attorney general's list"). ROTC was still compulsory for freshmen and sophomore men in the university, and that meant that any such participants would become ineligible to continue as students. When the issue came before the regents, the president once again declared that this was a campus issue and that he had referred it to the chancellors. I said that the list was very suspect; that to dismiss some male students would be discriminatory because women and foreign students were exempted; and that, moreover, the federal government had no right to interfere with the constitutional authority of the university to govern itself. A majority of the regents agreed. Regent Neylan stated to the board that, while he had voted against my position, he admired my willingness to stand up and state my position while others had refused to do so. His oblique references were to Chancellor Allen, who had left the meeting early to return to UCLA (the board was meeting in Santa Barbara), and to President Sproul (Neylan was pounding one nail into the chancellor's coffin; another was for the cross onto which he had already been nailing Sproul). The minutes of the Board of Regents (September 24, 1954) record that "Chancellor Kerr was commended for his prompt and courageous action in dealing with the situation." Had we started dismissing students or even seriously considered the possibility, many other students would have risen in righteous wrath; also some faculty members—including me.

Yet another obstacle arose from an attempt to stop faculty contacts with the FBI: a faculty member (David Rynin of philosophy) in May 1958 asked the Berkeley Academic Senate to declare "not permissible" any reports by faculty to the FBI or other investigative agencies on "the beliefs, attitudes, activities and associations of a student regarding religion, politics and public affairs." This broad proposal took specific aim at comments to FBI agents. It was referred to the Committee on Academic Freedom chaired by Frank Newman of the law school and became a project he sponsored. The proposal was accepted at a lightly attended senate meeting on October 28, 1958. The regents were alarmed and particularly the most liberal of all regents, Jesse Steinhart. He thought it was a "gag rule" affecting faculty freedom and was a "police state approach." Many faculty agreed. I was also alarmed and objected to the proposal on the senate floor. I asked: were there any actual abuses? None were alleged. And did the Academic Senate have any authority to so control individual faculty contacts and conversations? The attorney for the regents ruled that it did not. Then I asked: how could the university go about enforcing such a rule? There was no answer. And last, I noted that, in my experience, faculty comments were almost always helpful to students in such circumstances—universally so in my own experience. I thought it better to leave such matters to the individual judgment of faculty members. Frank Newman came to see me the Sunday before a subsequent senate meeting to discuss the proposal. We talked in the patio at my house outside my study. He said that I would "shoot him down in flames" and that he wanted me to know that he would not put up much resistance. That is the way it finally turned out. The action of October 28, 1958, was rescinded on May 25, 1959.

But passions for a time did run high. Regent Steinhart at the next meeting of the regents complimented my actions. An unpleasant confrontation between the senate and the regents had been avoided.

In most of these cases, and others, I was doing my best to guide regental and faculty actions away from any new controversies that would arouse highly sensitized participants. No more oath controversies or even shadowy reflections of them! I would try to step in between.

"Sins" and Sensitivities

I was vulnerable in the atmosphere of those times. I had committed a number of "sins" from the point of view of right-wing regents, faculty members, alumni, and legislators. These "sins" were brought to my attention then and later, including in a series of interviews by federal security agents, particularly after the Radiation Laboratory at Berkeley came to be placed under my nominal supervision. (Actually Ernest Lawrence reported directly to the Board of Regents.) I needed (and obtained) a "Q" clearance, which was the highest level of all.

LEAGUE FOR INDUSTRIAL DEMOCRACY

As a graduate student at Stanford, I belonged briefly to the Walrus Club when it petitioned (early fall of 1932) to become affiliated with the League for Industrial Democracy associated with the Socialist Party of Norman Thomas. I had met and liked Norman Thomas at Swarthmore. Debates at Swarthmore were not only with teams from other colleges (including Oxford and Cambridge) but also with national leaders. In the latter category I drew, as captain of the debate team, Norman Thomas (spring 1932). My faculty coaches claimed that I had won the debate held in the Friends' Meeting House, but the important thing for me was the favorable impression I had personally of Norman Thomas. In the election in November 1932, however, I turned my political sympathies to the New Deal and voted for Franklin Delano Roosevelt; but I very briefly did have a "socialist" connection—very democratic socialist and very anti-Communist (the Communists called Norman Thomas a "social fascist" as they did me much later when I was at the University of Washington).

PAUL TAYLOR

As a graduate student at Berkeley, I worked with Paul Taylor (see chapter 1) who was considered a "radical" by conservative agricultural interests in the state. Actually Paul was a radical conservative—he wanted to go back to the kind of 160-acre family farm where he was raised, and so did I. On the 140-acre farm in eastern Pennsylvania where I was raised, we were at least half self-sufficient in providing our living. Paul came from Wisconsin and Iowa. All his life he stayed with his vision of the return of the family farm. I did too, as an ideal, but came to think that the future in California, realistically, lay with the "factories in the fields." Paul and I wrote a report on the bloody cotton pickers' strike of 1933 in the San Joaquin Valley, for which I did most of the fieldwork.[2] If there were a definitive event marking the transition in California from Thomas Jefferson's (and Taylor's and my) vision of the independent yeoman farmer as the backbone of democracy to the agricultural factory operator with transient laborers, it was that strike.

INSTITUTE OF INDUSTRIAL RELATIONS

In 1945 I became the first director of the Institute of Industrial Relations at Berkeley. This was an institute started on the initiative of Governor Earl Warren, who got the idea from a similar institute Governor Tom Dewey of New York had initiated at Cornell. The institute was the first agency of the University of California (except for one lecturer in University Extension long before) to establish teaching contact with organized labor. The leaders of several employers' associations in the Bay Area called on me, warning that if the institute kept on working with the trade unions, they would use their influence to cut off our funding in Sacramento. I replied that I hoped they would reconsider and decide against doing this; but, if they went ahead, I thought they would not succeed. If they did succeed, I was prepared to take the consequences. They did, in fact, reconsider.

A further challenge to me and to the institute came at a conference at the

Ahwahnee Lodge in Yosemite Park, where representatives of employer associations from southern California, including the powerful Merchants and Manufacturers Association—more anti-union than in the north—were present. Congressman Richard Nixon preceded me as a speaker. He associated trade unions with communism. In my reply, I associated them with the American right to freedom of assembly and said that, with a few exceptions, they were implacably anti-Communist; and this view has been verified by history.

LLOYD FISHER

As my associate director of the institute, I chose Lloyd Fisher. Lloyd had one of the best minds I have ever met. It flowed so freely, like mercury, and was a delight to observe as he went from idea to idea and discipline to discipline. Lloyd, however, did not have a Ph.D. and thus was handicapped in academic life. John Dunlop, a professor at Harvard and later dean of the faculty of arts and sciences, and I later arranged for him to attend Harvard and get his degree. He wrote a brilliant dissertation that the Harvard University Press published in 1953, *The Harvest Labor Market in California.* But Lloyd, before joining the Institute of Industrial Relations, had been research director for Harry Bridges and the ILWU. Because Bridges had been under investigation as an alleged Communist subject to deportation, many people jumped to conclusions about Lloyd. I had never seen any such implications—quite the contrary. One clear indication to the contrary came shortly after World War II during a meeting in New York in which we both participated. We attended, on Lloyd's initiative, a presentation of Arthur Koestler's *Darkness at Noon*—a devastating portrayal of Stalinist destruction of an "old Bolshevik," allegedly Bukharin. It was a play Communists hated. Lloyd occasionally jokingly referred to himself as a "theoretical, nonpracticing anarchist." He was both— doubting but not attacking all authority.

Lloyd advised me in drafting a June 1952 commencement speech at Swarthmore and also at Stanford that was later published in *Fortune* (July 1953), "Whatever Became of the Independent Spirit?" It was rather on the libertarian side and received an award from the Freedom Foundation of Valley Forge that greatly pleased Regent Dickson. Fisher also advised me on my introductory public speech, arranged by the regents before a large invited audience at the Mark Hopkins Hotel in San Francisco shortly after I became chancellor (December 10, 1952), on the theme of "heresy—yes, conspiracy—no" which was clearly against the then conspiratorial policies and actions of the Communist Party. It followed the line of a recent article by Sidney Hook.[3]

Lloyd was one of my very best friends at Berkeley and I admired him greatly. He was a free-thinking skeptic who doubted all ideologies.

For an exposition of my general views on economic issues at that time, see my chapter, "An Effective and Democratic Organization of the Economy," in *Goals for Americans*,[4] which was included in the report of the eleven members appointed by President Eisenhower of a commission so named, which included James Conant, president of Harvard; Crawford Greenewalt, president of DuPont; General Alfred M. Gruenther; Judge Learned Hand; and myself, among others. I supported a system of checks and balances in the economic system to parallel the political checks and balances in the American constitution. I note this as a statement of my centrist position at a time when I was subject to suspicions of radicalism.

PACIFIC COAST WATERFRONT

Additionally, I served (1946–47) as Impartial Chairman for the Pacific Coast Waterfront from Canada to Mexico. It was said by some that I had been "Harry Bridges' arbitrator." Actually, I arbitrated between the ILWU and the Waterfront Employers Association, under an appointment made by the United States secretary of labor. When you worked in between those enemies at the time of the "old look" of class warfare, you were a long way away from anybody.

To illustrate the atmosphere: One day the case placed before me was a reopening of the contract on wage issues. I asked if the parties had tried to negotiate the dispute between themselves. They looked at me as though I did not know the waterfront and said, "Negotiate?" I added that I might be somewhat old-fashioned, but that negotiations should precede arbitration, and I would not accept the case until they had negotiated. They reluctantly agreed. So I got up to leave. They said, "Sit down, this won't take long." So I sat down. Frank Foisie for the waterfront employers said: "Mr. Bridges, we do not know what you are going to demand, but, by God, the answer is no." Bridges replied: "To tell you the truth, Mr. Foisie, we have not yet finally decided on our demands but, by God, we will never take no for an answer." So the parties turned to me and told me that here was my case, that they had negotiated!

I was really arbitrating on behalf of the U.S. government on behalf of peace on the waterfront under conditions of class warfare, which I totally rejected in a democracy. I once ordered the rough, tough ILWU to live by a contract to which it had orally agreed but tried to get out of on the grounds it had never formally signed it. And it did live with it for a whole year on my order.

SUPPORT OF NONSIGNERS

Also, as the regents well knew, I had opposed the dismissal of "nonsigners" who had refused to sign the "regents' oath." I was a signer. I was sympathetic with those Quakers who would not take any oaths but I never saw all that much difference between an "oath" and an "affirmation" that they would make instead. I had signed oaths before when working for the U.S. government. In fact, I considered, and continue to consider, the U.S. Constitution to be the greatest nonreligious document in world history. I voted in 1950 in favor of the position taken by the Academic Senate against employment of faculty members who were proven members of the Communist Party under the conditions then surrounding party membership. I did not look on the "nonsigners" as suspect people. As I knew them, and as was confirmed in their appearances before the Committee on Privilege and Tenure on which I served, they were independent people who did not like to be pushed around and did not like to be singled out as suspicious characters.

I understood the type well. My father came from a family of pioneers in the Appalachian mountain valleys of central Pennsylvania where his ancestors had homesteaded (Raccoon Valley, Perry County) before the American Revolution. He was a totally independent spirit. He hated FDR for subjecting farmers to federal controls. He believed that nothing should ever be unanimous. He would vote "no," on principle. He would let any tramp sleep in our barn with a caution not to light a fire and also would give him a warm meal. But when the principal of the high school where my father taught, in addition to running our farm, asked for "100 percent support" for the Community Chest, my father would each year be the one person to refuse.

At Berkeley, any actual Communist would be among the first to sign the oath—and at least three did, as I describe later *(Political Turmoil)*. I quietly arranged for their immediate resignations when President Sproul told me he had received full proof of their memberships. It was the independent free spirit that refused. Thus I had been an opponent of the pro-oath regents who wanted to and did fire all the nonsigners. In addition, I was irate that the regents had gone back on the agreement to permit an affirmative appearance before the Committee on Privilege and Tenure as an alternative to signing the oath. In the world of industrial relations from which I came, the one cardinal sin was to repudiate an agreement. In that "jungle," this was almost never, never done. My very few responses of anger in my life have been when I thought agreements or informal understandings were being broken.

These were among my vulnerabilities at that time of American "red hysteria" and of conflict within the university. They help explain why, as chancellor, I wanted to live in my own house and to continue my teaching and writing. To retain my sense of integrity, I had to be prepared to be expendable. Kay, with a strong Quaker heritage from the maternal side of her family, agreed. I had to be willing to take a stand against the regents or against the faculty or between the faculty and the regents to try to hold them off from renewed conflict, and not just to stand aside and let conflicts intensify.

These vulnerabilities, of course, came back to haunt me when Senator McCarthy and the FBI were followed by the Un-American Activities Committee of the California State Senate and by Governor Reagan.

I earlier raised the question of why President Sproul proposed my appointment as chancellor (chapter 3). A related question is why the Board of Regents accepted it at that time in history. My guesses have been, first, that after the oath controversy, the regents were inclined, as a gesture of conciliation, to accept a faculty-originated nominee at Berkeley; and, second, they did not expect the position at Berkeley to amount to much. Two pro-oath regents (Ahlport and Neylan), however, did abstain in the vote appointing me.

Let me return for a moment to Regent Dickson. He was publisher of a newspaper in Los Angeles—the *Evening Express*. He was a member of the Board of Regents for forty-three years (1913 to 1956)—longer than anyone else in history. At the next board meeting one month after the encounter I noted above where he referred to me as the "Red Chancellor," he came up to me. He said he had been thinking about what I had said and had come to agree with me that I should never give up my rights as an American citizen to speak out. He added, however, that he wished I would be more discreet and that, if I were, I could have a great future within the University of California. We became good and respectful friends but were still not in full agreement.

In any event, I felt sympathy for Maggie in *Cat on a Hot Tin Roof*. Berkeley felt like a hot tin roof from time to time during those years, and I felt vulnerable.

An End to the Oath Controversy

When I became president of the university in July 1958, I continued to be concerned that the oath controversy be put to rest once and for all. I took several actions.

It had been burned into my soul that only the University of California faculty, among all the great universities in the United States, had no recognized right of lifetime tenure—that it was the *annual* contracts that were not renewed for nonsigners during the oath controversy. I began immediately to work informally among the regents, as the new president, to develop support for the first formal continuous lifetime tenure policy in the history of the university. By the September meeting of the regents (September 18, 1958), I was ready to move and introduced a proposal calling for "continuous tenure" with dismissal only for "good cause" after a hearing by the appropriate committee of the Academic Senate. The regents voted unanimously for this in December. Regent Jesse Steinhart, in particular, was enormously helpful. Regents Edward Carter and Don McLaughlin were also very helpful. During the discussion in September, Carter had said that this action would "close an ugly chapter in university history." It did, in part.

It never occurred to me at the time that I would be the first beneficiary of continuous tenure. After I was fired as president, and over the objections of Governor Reagan, the regents returned me to my professorship on the grounds that I had continuous tenure.

I also proposed to the regents an honorary degree for Edward Chace Tolman, distinguished professor of psychology and a nonsigner of the oath. Approval was not a foregone conclusion. The case against the regents for the dismissal of nonsigners was *Tolman* v. *Underhill* (Robert Underhill was secretary of the regents). It was incomprehensible to some regents that anyone who had sued the regents would be given the university's highest honor. To make this possible, it was necessary for me to get a change in the rules from unanimous consent for honorary degrees to a three-fourths majority vote in secret ballot. Regent Pauley took this especially hard because of his support for the oath but also because he thought that the senior regent (which he by then was), in particular, should have a right of a personal veto. The regents approved the honorary degree for Tolman, and I was proud to confer it on him on March 20, 1959, my first Charter Day at Berkeley as president. I later persuaded the regents to name Berkeley's new education and psychology building Tolman Hall (1962).

This action of mine had substantial consequences. It began a long battle for survival between Regent Pauley and me. Pauley was very determined about his standing as senior regent and his asserted possession of certain privileges. He hated my action in taking away from him one of these claimed privileges. Later I proposed a policy of rotating chairs of the board. Pauley thought that the senior regent had a lifetime claim to chair of the board, as had been the case with Regent Dickson. My proposal was accepted. Pauley detested this outcome. He made me his number one enemy. He began charging me as being "pro-communist." I always thought that his opposition was really based on his view that I was anti-Pauley. He did serve twice as chair of the board but never on a lifetime basis. To him, being chair of the board was the crowning glory of his life, and I took it away from him. He was a devoted and, in many ways, a good and supportive regent. He was also an alpha male par excellence, and I had challenged his dominance, and I was never to be forgiven. In the end, he destroyed me as president. In the meantime, however, the Board of Regents operated in a more civilized manner than it would have with Pauley as lifetime chair of the board.

During the oath controversy, the dean of the law school at UCLA (L. Dale Coffman) had supported the pro-oath regents and had referred to the law school at UCLA as "an island in a red sea." As a reward, and with the acquiescence of President Sproul, Coffman got the regents to take from the Academic Senate the right to approve of the UCLA law school's courses or to review its academic appointments and promotions or budget proposals (January 1952). The law school at Berkeley then received the same exemption. As chancellor at Berkeley, I told the dean of the law school (William Prosser) that I could get advice from any source I wanted and that I would always want it from the Academic Senate, and I always insisted on it in practice. The feeling that I had infringed upon the school's autonomy lasted for years. As president, I got the regents to put both law schools back under the Academic Senate with one exception. The exception was the review of courses by the Committee on Courses. I made this exception because the Committee on Courses seldom really reviewed any courses (it mostly just approved whatever was presented to it)—and because the law school, in any event, had its own entirely separate curriculum and student body. I wanted the law schools fully back in the senate not only because I valued senate advice, but also because I wanted law school faculty to be fully accepted in the affairs of the senate and in the governance of each campus. A law school faculty member later became chancellor at Berkeley. I also did not want other professional schools to attempt similar escapes. Some regents argued that senate power over professional schools mitigated against "excellence of our professional schools" (Regent Carter at the Board of Regents meeting, May 18, 1962). This was a common complaint of professional school deans and of Chancellor Murphy at UCLA. I argued that "the pressure of the Academic Senate is always in the direction of distinction, not the contrary." This view prevailed.

In these several ways, the oath was finally put to rest. Or was it? The two most active regents who later on worked for my dismissal as president of the university were the two remaining pro-oath regents, Edwin Pauley and John Canaday. There were some costs.

10

Reprise and Prelude: Three Struggles over the University's Orientation— 1870, 1900, and 1950

The University of California has gone through three periods that, in particular, defined its structure and its purposes. The first, following its founding in 1868, involved a conflict over whether it was to be a university with Yale as the model, or a trade school associated with agriculture, mining, and the mechanic arts. The second defining period came with the appointment of Benjamin Ide Wheeler as president in 1899. The third followed World War II.

■

The Yale-Gilman Model

I identify the solution to the first battle over the orientation of the University of California as the Yale-Gilman model. The University of California was originally founded by Yale alumni, and the first influential president, Daniel Coit Gilman (1872–1875), came from Yale, at that time the dominant American university. Gilman wanted to build the Yale of the west. In this new frontier state there was, however, another vision: a trade school for farmers and workers, supported by the Grange made up of farmers and the Workingmen's Party of organized labor. The federal Land-Grant Act of 1862 had offered grants of public lands to each state that would establish a college teaching "agriculture and the mechanic arts." However, the College of California, established in 1855 by Yale alumni, had offered its Berkeley site to the new university on the condition that an "academic college with courses of instruction equal to those of eastern colleges" be included.[1] The Yale-Gilman model eventually emerged victorious, particularly when Eugene Waldemar Hilgard became professor of agriculture and persuaded agricultural interests that a scientific emphasis at the university would be of greater benefit to them than a trade school teaching standard agricultural skills. By the end of the century, the University of California was considered one of the Big Six universities along with Yale; and agriculture did benefit.

The Wheeler-Sproul-Academic Senate Model

The first major reorientation of the university following the controversies of its first thirty years occurred when Benjamin Ide Wheeler became president in 1899. He and his successors created what I call the Wheeler-Sproul-Academic Senate model. New directions at first included:

A clear victory for the "academic" university over the "populist" university, or trade-school serving agriculture and the mechanic arts, concluding the thirty-year battle, 1868–1899.

Transfer of academic authority from the Board of Regents to the president. The regents, however, retained control of nonacademic affairs. Control of both types of activities continued to be highly concentrated. The university became a presidential-regental run institution rather than an exclusively regental dominated enterprise, and more oriented in an academic direction.

Further development of the university on the German model, with implications particularly for student life and for an emphasis on science and the classics.

This original Wheeler 1899 model continued to 1950 with three directional changes:

An upward thrust of the physical sciences to academic supremacy on the campus at Berkeley marked particularly by the appointment of G. N. Lewis as dean of chemistry in 1912 and of Ernest O. Lawrence to the physics faculty in 1928.

The devolution of important academic authority from the regents to the Academic Senate in 1919–20. President Sproul (1930–58) in particular accepted and worked with the Academic Senate; President Wheeler and his successor, President David Prescott Barrows (1919–23), had been opposed.

A temporary return to a "populist" (this time right-wing) orientation for the university with the imposition of the 1949 loyalty oath by the regents, and with President Sproul's 1952 "contact man" concession to the California State Senate Committee on Un-American Activities. The first "populist" orientation had been left-wing under pressures from labor unions and from the Grange of small farmers. In 1949 the faculty rebelled, asserting its joint ownership of the university. In 1952, I rebelled as the new chancellor at Berkeley.

By 1950, the university was vastly bigger, vastly more distinguished, and highly oriented toward the controlling figure of the university president: Wheeler and then Sproul, both exercising micromanagerial control.

The Twenty-First-Century Federal Model

Then came a whole series of reorientations. They began with the regents. In 1951 the board began a process of devolution of authority from the statewide university to the two big campuses, Berkeley and Los Angeles, where chancellorships were established. This devolution was hesitant and confused, but it was a beginning. Los Angeles was its point of origin, but it was Berkeley that came to take leadership. By 1951 there were six campuses (Berkeley, Davis, Los Angeles, Riverside, San Francisco, and Santa Barbara), not just one, and in prospect was the advancing tidal wave of enrollments.

A second new direction began with the faculty when it revolted against the imposition of a loyalty oath in 1949. The revolt against right-wing forces continued when I, as chancellor at Berkeley and then as president, began a long drawn-out confrontation with the state legislative Committee on Un-American Activities.

The university in both instances was asserting its autonomy and its academic freedom. The university was maturing as an academic institution.

There followed a whole series of new directions that originated within the administration—many of them when I was chancellor at Berkeley. These developments at Berkeley then set patterns for other campuses.

A transformation took place in student life from the German model to the English model. This meant building residence halls, student union facilities, intramural sports fields, and much else.

Cultural facilities were added on the campus—an art gallery, facilities for dramatic performances, a symphony hall, and more; and an emphasis on the social sciences and the creative arts helped add academic balance.

Control of physical planning was transferred from the Board of Regents to the campus and was based on academic planning, not just on architectural concepts advanced by changing external architects. Also the campus was turned from a parking lot into a park.

Berkeley began to compete academically with the best of the private universities instead of only with the best of the public universities (Michigan), and by 1964 came to be rated ahead of Harvard as the "best balanced distinguished university." Berkeley became more Ivy League, less Big Ten.

Then the reorientation process passed in 1958 from the Berkeley chancellor's office to the universitywide academic authorities:

Control of business and other nonacademic affairs shifted to academic authorities and away from the vice president–business (the Corley Empire) and from the Board of Regents.

Most authority was transferred from universitywide agencies to the campuses—from centralized to dispersed management, with widespread consultation. Administration was now less monolithic and more pluralistic while avoiding disintegration of the university.

There was a new approach to student life that included voluntary ROTC, nondiscrimination by fraternities and sororities, introduction of equality of opportunity programs, and study abroad provisions. Authority to select outside speakers was turned over to student groups, and controversial speakers— even Communists—were permitted on campuses.

Qualified faculty members received continuous tenure, replacing the one-year contracts that had permitted introduction of the loyalty oath.

These last two items resulted in the American Association of University Professors conferring the Alexander Meiklejohn Award for Contributions to Academic Freedom on the president and regents of the University of California in 1964.

All of these reorientations helped bring about the better balanced and more complete university being planned for the year 2000, but they also created opportunities for right-wing elements in the state to mount another "populist" invasion of the university, resulting in my dismissal as president in 1967. Much of the "red hysteria" in California after World War II came to center on me as university president.

The orientations of 1870, 1900, and 1919–20 were internally controlled. The university was in charge of its own future. By contrast, the new directions of 1950 and later were more in response to external events, to what society demanded. And what society wanted included:

The designation by the federal government during and after World War II of American universities as the servants of the "endless frontier" of science with vast funds for research, bringing many consequences including reconstitution of the San Francisco campus toward science and creation of military-oriented laboratories administered by the university at Berkeley, Livermore, and Los Alamos.

The movement to a national policy of universal access to higher education, of which the California Master Plan of 1960 was a major component, and the resultant enrollment tidal wave of the children of the GIs that gave rise to three new campuses of the university (San Diego, Irvine, Santa Cruz) and new orientations for three others (Davis, Riverside, and Santa Barbara). Fortunately, the national labor market was expanding to absorb the new graduates.

The enormous explosion of the Los Angeles metropolitan area economically, politically, and culturally that gave rise to a policy of "equal opportunities" for UCLA and subsequently for all campuses. The University of California chose the model of multiple "flagship" campuses instead of the standard one "flagship," and six UC campuses by 2000 were members of the Association of American Universities; no other state had more than two public campuses as members, and the balance had only one. The UC campuses were put in full competition with one another.

A preference for creating public "systems" of higher education instead of freestanding campuses reporting individually to state authorities. In 1919 there were only 2 major public systems—New York and California; in 1940, 16; in 1990, 120. This introduced a whole new layer of governance and conflicts over how to structure it, as in California. In 1950, the University of California was still mostly Berkeley. As it entered the twenty-first century, it was nine largely self-administered campuses. An effort in 1965 to break up the university into nine separately chartered universities was totally defeated.

A worldwide movement of liberation for colonial peoples, for ethnic groups, for women, and for students that disrupted and improved many segments of societies, including several campuses of the University of California.

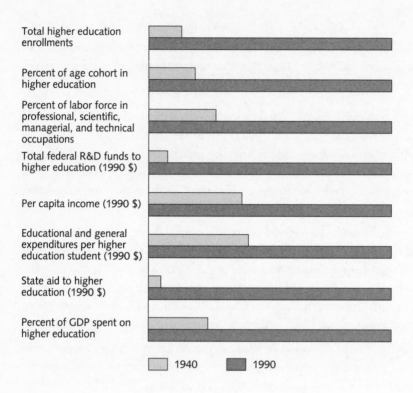

FIGURE 3. Transformations in U.S. Higher Education, 1940–90.

Altogether, these post-1950 reorientations have led to the twenty-first-century model for the University of California that exists today. It is less monolithic, more attentive to student life, better balanced in its academic programs, more combative in its resistance to right-wing political forces, more liberal in its internal political rules, higher ranking in its academic ratings, more concerned with service to all major geographic areas of the state and all elements of society, more oriented toward research and service and the labor market and less to a liberal undergraduate education, and more externally oriented than the models that preceded it. (For statistical data illustrating some of the recent changes, see Figure 3 and Table 14.)[2]

The most influential persons and institutions on the University of California have shifted dramatically. In the second half of the nineteenth century, they were the Yale founders, the Board of Regents, and the political forces of the

TABLE 14

Transformations in Higher Education, 1940–90

	United States		California		UC	
	1940	1990	1940	1990	1940	1990
Total higher education enrollments	1.5 million	13.8 million	120,000	1.8 million	30,000	165,000
Percentage of age cohort (18–24) in postsecondary education	9	52	15	53	Not applicable	
Percentage of labor force in professional, scientific, managerial, and technical occupations	7.5	30	Not available	32 (in 1995)	Not applicable	
Percentage of GDP spent on higher education	0.6	2.6	Not available	2.3[a]	Not applicable	
Total federal R&D funds to colleges and universities[b]	405.2 million[c]	9 billion	Not available	1.3 billion	8 million[d]	800 million
Per capita income[b]	5,500	14,400	7,700	20,700	Not applicable	
Educational and general expenditures per higher education student[b]	3,260	8,260	Not available	7,240	4,500[e]	13,800
State aid to higher education	1.6 billion	43.4 billion	75.6 million	5,500 million	50 million	2,150 million

[a]Percentage of gross state product.
[b]In 1990 dollars.
[c]All federal funds to colleges and universities; most was for R&D.
[d]All operating funds to UC from federal government.
[e]All current fund expenditures.

state, particularly the Grange and the Workingmen's Party; in the first half of the twentieth century, they became the presidents (Wheeler and Sproul) and the Academic Senate; and, in the last half of the century, the federal government, the campus chancellors, and activist students. What next?

These two volumes, *Academic Triumphs* and *Political Turmoil,* are centrally concerned with development of the twenty-first-century model and repercussions of its realization: a university less parochial in its orientation, more in accord with the structures and concentrations of the other great research universities of the world, more externally influenced—a world university rather than the earlier regional university attuned mostly to California.

PART III

The Presidency of the University: Overarching Issues, 1958–67

A New Agenda for
the Reorientation
of the University

As the nation approached the 1960s, the major research universities and much of the rest of higher education in the United States (though least of all the private liberal arts colleges) faced three unique developments. (1) Sputnik (a great surprise) entered the skies in the fall of 1957 and the Cold War took on a new intensity, with the research universities on the front line. (2) The tidal wave of students (no surprise) was on its inevitable course, and the community colleges would be most involved. (3) The United States was enjoying the greatest economic prosperity in all of its history (a modest surprise). And the state colleges were the most involved in helping build the necessary technostructure that the new age of industrialism required.[1]

Enormous as was the transformation for higher education in the United States at large, it was even greater for California. The impact on the state from the defense industry and defense-related university research was huge—twice the national average. In-migration to the state doubled the flow of students above the nationwide demographic tidal wave. California was producing new resources (and prosperity) at a faster rate than the nation as a whole.

I concentrate in this chapter and in most of parts III through VI on "the future to anticipate." The early 1960s became a golden age of planning and preparing for what turned out to be a glorious academic future for the university; but fate alone did not foreordain it. Fortunately, the governing authorities of the state of California were very supportive. Fortunately too, the regents, the university and campus administrations, and the faculties mostly confronted the future aggressively, but not uniformly so.

■

My introduction to the presidency of the University of California was a mirror image of my introduction to the chancellorship at Berkeley. I did not have to create an agenda: there was one in place, and it was one I could be enthusiastic about. And, instead of resistance, I was welcomed with encouragement. Under more normal conditions, however, I would have preferred to remain chancellor at Berkeley or to return to my professorship. A campus chancellor is more in contact with individual faculty members and students, and generally more a part of academic life than is the far-removed systemwide president. Also, a chancellor has a more supportive constituency than the president. Both positions are surrounded with potential adversaries but only the president has no rooting section—only potential assailants, except for the members of his or her own personal staff and, possibly, the regents.

My appointment at the meeting of the regents on the Davis campus in October 1957 did not come as a surprise to me. I was alerted several weeks in advance by the chair of the board, Edwin Pauley of Los Angeles, who had participated actively in the selection process, that I should start thinking about the possibility.

The appointment was a great and even devastating disappointment to my friend and fellow chancellor at Los Angeles, Raymond Allen. No one had bothered to warn him. He flew up to the Sacramento airport on his way to Davis fully expecting the appointment, as he told Dean McHenry, who sat beside him in the airplane. Allen had been president at the University of Washington and had several additional attributes going for him. By training a physician, he had been very successful with a new medical school at the University of Washington. UCLA was not only still developing its new medical school, but other new medical schools within the university were in the offing (at Davis, Irvine, and San Diego). His firing of alleged Communists at the University of Washington had made him invulnerable to right-wing attacks, and the California State Senate still had its active Un-American Activities Committee to placate. Allen had been brought to UCLA in 1952 with the implied promise that he would be the next president of the University of California. Sproul was then expected to announce his retirement in 1955, after twenty-five years of service in that position.

Five years later, when Sproul finally did announce his retirement in 1957, the southern regents in particular believed that Allen had shown himself too accepting of a centralized administration in Berkeley. He had prepared (or had prepared in his name) physical and academic plans for UCLA that the regents found unacceptable or only marginally acceptable, and he had shown no inclination to suppress or, later, correct scandals in intercollegiate athletics at

UCLA that so embarrassed the regents. The chair of the regents' Committee on Educational Policy, Edward Carter, who lived in Los Angeles and was a graduate of UCLA, was outspoken in his criticism of Allen. Also, several times, Allen had avoided taking forthright positions before the regents on controversial issues. The regents seemed to prefer opinions they opposed (like some of mine) to no opinions at all or to vacillating opinions designed to please them. Ray and his career sank after his 1957 rejection for the presidency of the university. He was a decent, friendly, and considerate person. It was a great personal tragedy.

In any event, I was chosen president with no votes in opposition. When the committee informed me of the board's action, a member of the selection committee assured me that the one vote that most concerned me had been affirmative. This was the vote of my predecessor. Given Sproul's great popularity with Berkeley alumni and with many leaders of the state, and the loyalty of the universitywide administrative staff, it would have been disastrous for me to have word be passed around that Bob Sproul had voted negatively or had abstained. The member of the selection committee, Jesse Steinhart of San Francisco, who had handled this delicate issue, was a close and longtime friend of Sproul. He assured me that all was well. In his effort to obtain this result, Steinhart had talked with Earl Warren, former governor of California and by then chief justice of the United States, who Steinhart said supported my appointment and sent me his best wishes in advance. The chair of the board also informed me that I had been the unanimous first choice of the faculty committee representing all campuses, including UCLA. In addition, he told me that the regents' selection committee, which toured the leading universities of the nation seeking names and interviewing prospects, was repeatedly advised to look for its nominee at home, a recommendation also offered by other prospects interviewed for the presidency.

But all was not so well. At the garden party at Provost Stanley Freeborn's house after the regents' meeting was concluded, James Corley, longtime vice president and the university's representative in Sacramento, and his chief assistant, James Miller, were courteous. Several members of Corley's staff, however, came up to me in concert and poured their drinks on the ground at my feet after they heard the news and then silently walked out. I considered them to have resigned, and each subsequently did so with my full acceptance and even encouragement. A long and bitter battle with the Corley empire had begun, or, more accurately, had accelerated. Sproul, on the contrary, was totally cooperative during the transition. He told me he would never interfere after I became president. And he never did. Fortunately, he kept his great backlog of items to work on and kept issuing decisions for the next two years—all of them predated to June 30, 1958. Otherwise I would have been deluged. Of those decisions I came to see, I would not have changed a single one, including a very intricate university regulation on irregular faculty titles and arrangements.

Much to Do about Everything

The October 1957 meeting at Davis was historic: the regents decided to proceed with *plans for three new campuses* and declared their intent to establish a fourth at some later date. These new campuses were thus placed high on the agenda for the new president.

On the agenda also (less dramatically) were questions about the *futures of the six existing campuses.* Still to be decided were what to do with Davis, largely oriented toward agriculture; with Riverside, badly split between the original Citrus Experiment Station and the newer liberal arts college; with Santa Barbara, halfway through a change from a teachers' college to a liberal arts campus; with San Francisco, which was a good regional medical center concentrating on training in a medical world fast opening to research; with UCLA, still smarting from being the university's "southern branch" and demanding equal treatment with Berkeley; and with Berkeley itself—the great rising star in the firmament of universities nationwide and even worldwide—but which would soon be sharing its privileges with eight siblings. This last question of the traumatic transition for Berkeley was high on the actual agenda but, sadly, I did not recognize it until much later.

The regents had still another agenda item in mind when they selected me. This was the *decentralization of the governance of the university,* which they had initiated when they created the chancellorships at Berkeley and Los Angeles in 1951, and for which I had demonstrated my support. It was taken for granted that I would proceed in that direction.

A fourth item on the agenda was the *chaos in higher education in the state,* with a smoldering battle over who should do what—a battle particularly between the University of California and what were then called the "state colleges." The regents knew about this issue, but it was not yet at the very top of their list of problems. The regental members of the liaison committee between the university and the state colleges, however, were particularly well aware of it and knew of its importance.

A fifth agenda item was placed there by the changing times and the changing mentalities of students and faculty members. It centered on the issue of *rules on student involvement in politics*. The McCarthy period had drawn to an end, and a backlash against it by students and faculty members was endemic. Activist students also protested compulsory ROTC, discrimination by fraternities and sororities, and other practices affecting students. The regents only consciously faced this agenda item of changing mentalities when I brought individual aspects of it to their attention. We dealt with most of the historic issues in this area, but one slipped by, largely because no one, including me, realized that it had come along until it was too late. This hidden issue was the shift from free speech to free advocacy as an extension of free speech.

These, then, were the major items on the agenda. Some remained so for the next eight and one-half years, and many other more minor items were added along the way. All of these original major items were urgent, so we needed to work on all at once and all together. There was too much to do too quickly. In retrospect, all of those ninety-hour weeks for me under intense pressure, and no vacations of more than two or three days at a time, were a great mistake. I became too tired. I still am perplexed to explain how I survived it all.

STAFF—DRAMATIS PERSONAE

Fortunately I had excellent assistance.

I brought Dean McHenry from UCLA, where he had been dean of social sciences, and appointed him head of academic planning. He had chaired the committee that produced the McHenry report on new campuses, which the regents, in effect, had adopted at their October 1957 meeting. He was the staff person in charge of both academic planning for the three new campuses and the detailed negotiations for what became the Master Plan for Higher Education in California—with the aid of one assistant (Charles Young) and one secretary! Dean was also my major source of ideas about the university of the future and particularly about the role of UCLA.

Dean, who had been the president of the Associated Students of UCLA, alerted me to the bitterness of alumni, faculty, and students at UCLA over its subservient position to Berkeley. He also persuaded me that the suppressed sit-

158 · *The Presidency of the University*

uation of UCLA was not politically compatible with the rise of southern California in the power structure of the state and that this inferior position for UCLA could not be continued indefinitely. I also knew that Dean had lobbied effectively in Sacramento to get Ph.D. degree programs and professional schools for UCLA, and how easy that had been. Thus he was instrumental in my subsequent support for "equal opportunity" for UCLA and then also later for all the other campuses of the university, which was so central to the academic ratings of the campuses of the university at the end of the century. I concluded, under Dean's tutelage, that "bitterness" could destroy the University of California and that a policy of equal opportunities was the best antidote.

McHenry was already giving advice to other systems of higher education, including those in Nevada and Missouri. The new directions for the university (1960–2000) were worked out in detail mostly in the McHenry-Kerr collaborations. We were the planning team.

I chose as vice president of the university (a long-unfilled position) Harry Wellman, who was already vice president–agricultural sciences. He was an agricultural economist whom I had known since my student days in economics, and he had served on the committee for my orals for the Ph.D. in 1939. He knew the university extremely well, had good judgment, and a most friendly and noncombative manner. Only later did I come to realize how, from his position as vice president of agriculture, he had already become a central figure in the emergence of the new University of California. He had been instrumental in starting the College of Letters and Science at Davis, in reorienting the Riverside Watkins college in the direction of research, in supporting the development of the School of Science and Engineering at San Diego, and in anticipating its transition to a general research university. Harry had also initiated plans for a new approach to the budget of the university. I already knew how sympathetic he had been toward my efforts to create an effective chancellorship at Berkeley.

I was appointed president of the university on a Friday, and that weekend I went to Harry's house to ask him to be vice president of the University of California. He agreed. I learned later that Harry had been the faculty committee's second choice for president of the university. It was the administrative team of Wellman-Kerr that carried the University of California into its most golden age.

In addition to McHenry and Wellman as essential appointments, I took along Gloria Copeland, my administrative assistant when I was chancellor.

Gloria had excellent judgment, was very conscientious and hardworking. I trusted her completely.

I had essential help also from John W. Oswald. Jack, too, came from agriculture and, on the suggestion of Harry Wellman, had been a faculty assistant to me when I was chancellor. The regents, with some amusement, would note my bias for people with agricultural backgrounds—"Here comes that list from agriculture again." They were right. I often did look there first. On the average, such persons, I thought, were more practical in their outlooks and more oriented toward university service than those from any other single field; they had their feet on the ground and their eyes on service. Jack was in charge of the general flow of work to and from the campuses, and to and from the regents. With Jack in charge, the work did flow. No more long delays waiting for "statewide" to act—after my experience as chancellor, I was obsessed with prompt action.

Virginia Smith, as an assistant vice president, was also of great help. I had first known her as an undergraduate student at the University of Washington. Later, after she secured a law degree, she served as my graduate assistant when I taught a summer course there. Virginia reviewed all specific items going to the Board of Regents with meticulous attention to detail; nothing went without her clearance, in which I had full trust. She participated in the later stages of administrative decentralization in 1965–66 and was very helpful in crucial aspects of the mid-1960s' student controversies. She later worked with me in the Carnegie Commission on Higher Education and subsequently served as president of Vassar and then of Mills College.

I relied more heavily on the advice of Dean, Harry, Gloria, Jack, and Virginia than on that of anyone else. They were indispensable. So also was Loren Furtado, the university's assistant controller. Harry and I selected Loren to be the new head of the budget office—a crucial position. The prior person working with Bob Sproul had concentrated on line-item budgets. We were turning to analytical budgets—an entirely different approach. Loren accepted this approach and had the good judgment and the intellectual ability to make it work. Instead of withholding information, as though it was his personal property, as had his predecessor, he shared it with the chancellors in working out acceptable solutions to budget problems. He also could be tough when he had to be. The new budget process was far superior to the old, and Loren made it work.

Eugene Lee also had an essential role. He had worked with me when I was chancellor and served with me during my presidency as vice president–executive assistant. Gene had a particular interest in reorganization of the university. He had worked on the Public Administration Survey of 1948. He took an especially central role in the reorganization of 1965 (chapter 14) and was a great source of general advice. Like McHenry, Gene had been president of the Associated Students at UCLA and was a varsity football player. Charles ("Chuck") Young, who worked so closely and effectively with McHenry, had been president of the Associated Students at Riverside.

Before I could get well started on the new agenda, there was a long series of inaugurations—two or three days on each campus with lunches, dinners, receptions, speeches. The Board of Regents seemed intent on declaring that there was a new president with a new agenda.

My inaugural address at UCLA (September 26, 1958) set forth the theme that "in this administration, the burden of proof will always rest with the centralizers." At Berkeley, speakers included the president of Harvard, Nathan Pusey, and the president of Stanford, Wallace Sterling—both good friends of mine. Both represented, along with Berkeley, what were shortly to become the "big three" of American higher education. The San Francisco Opera presented *Medea* in Berkeley's Hearst Greek Theatre. I gave no thought to Medea's singing, "What greater grief than the loss of one's native land" as a possible bloody augury of things to come at the end of my presidency. The series of inaugurals concluded at La Jolla with the "university fleet" sailing by, the last vessel a rowboat with a faculty member. The outpouring of effort and goodwill by many people on each of the campuses in welcoming Kay and me was overwhelming.

A Favorable Context

The context for the new agenda was generally good. At the national level, the signs all seemed auspicious for higher education. The coming tidal wave of students would triple enrollments over the next two decades; and, while it brought problems of planning and of accumulating financial resources, it also created opportunities for expanding in new directions and for improvements.

The country's economy was experiencing its greatest period of prosperity. The historic rate of productivity increases per hour of work had averaged 2 percent since the Civil War. It jumped to 3 percent after World War II and that made possible a doubling of per capita income every twenty-five years on a cumulative basis. This rate of productivity increases fell to 2 percent during the years of the OPEC crises in the 1970s and to the subsequent level of about 1 percent that marked the succeeding period of 1980 to 1995.

Sputnik in 1957 placed an immense new emphasis on basic research that so benefited the nation via the great research universities. The rise of the electronics industry, in particular, and of a heightened concern for the creation of more "human capital," in general, called attention to the need for training highly skilled professionals.

The national political mood was good. President Eisenhower had smoothed the antagonisms of the McCarthy years that had so upset higher education, and President Kennedy's "New Frontier" was about to raise great hopes for the future. Higher education in general, and the research universities in particular, faced a golden age.

And at the state level, the signs were almost equally favorable. California's population was rising by half-a-million a year (nearly two-thirds of it—300,000 out of 500,000—by in-migration), and the California system of higher education had to keep up with both its share of the national rise in the birthrate and new arrivals into the state. Growth added excitement and opened up new opportunities. The economy of the state was even stronger than the nation's with the rise of what would become Silicon Valley in the north, and of defense industries both south and north, which increased related employment to twice the national proportions.

In November 1958 a new governor was elected and became one of the greatest supporters the University of California ever had. At first, however, Pat Brown took a cautious approach to the university's budget; we got only 93 percent of our budget request for 1959–60. One of his assistants (Fred Dutton, later a regent of the university and a special assistant to President Kennedy) argued that the University of California was a "Republican institution" and "the wave of the past" and that the state colleges were the "wave of the future"—they were institutions of the people, which meant Democratic. How much these views influenced the governor, I do not know. The governor's other top assistants, William Coblentz (also later a regent and chair of the board and a leading attorney in San Francisco) and Warren Christopher (later president of the board of trustees at Stanford and secretary of state in the Clinton administration), were entirely friendly, as was Bernice, the governor's wife who had attended Berkeley. So also were Hale Champion as the director of the California Department of Finance, and the highly competent and deeply respected Alan Post as legislative analyst serving the legislature.

At the suggestion of Regent Pauley, we would postpone the presentation of the president's report at regents' meetings until such time as the governor arrived (the governor is also the ex officio president of the board; he rarely appeared at the meetings' scheduled starting time). This report set forth some of the research and other accomplishments of the university during the prior month—such as scientific breakthroughs, awards and honors received by faculty members, and highly acclaimed publications—and they were very impressive, especially to the governor. The governor, as he told me several times, was also influenced by how other governors across the nation envied the state of California for the high quality of the university it supported. Pat Brown became a greater and greater convinced friend of "my university," as he called it. Its rising stature in the academic world owes much to Brown's growing conviction of its importance to the state. The state legislators also had excellent leadership, including Senator George Miller, Jr., as chair of the all-important Senate Committee on Finance.

Additionally, and most importantly, the regents were more united than they had been for at least the twelve prior years (the first break some of them had with Sproul had come over decentralization at the end of World War II). The oath controversy (which began in 1949) was over, although not entirely forgotten. There were no longer two more or less equal blocs on the board—one largely southern and conservative, the other largely northern and moderate; one largely anti-Sproul, and one largely pro-Sproul. The regents had come together to agree nearly unanimously on an agenda for the future, particularly on new campuses and administrative reorganization, and on a new president. The board had a spirit of commitment that matched that of the Berkeley faculty after the loyalty oath controversy (chapter 3).

Based on my personal experience and a reading of university history, I consider the Board of Regents from 1958 to 1966 to have been the board with the greatest record of accomplishments in the entire history of the university. That board variously supported and improved upon proposals for three new campuses, a massive reorganization of the university, the rise in academic stature of several of the campuses, the liberalization of a series of student rules and practices, and continuing tenure for the faculty. It was a hard-working board with many members who carried statewide public stature and influence, and it represented a wide range of political viewpoints and sensitivities. It must rate with the best of all boards in the history of American research universities. This board was dominated by appointees of Governors

Earl Warren and Pat Brown. (See Appendix 1 section K for a list of regents, 1958–66.)

I recall with great pride, when there was a conflict with Governor Brown over whether the state or the university should keep the stipend for managing the federal laboratories at Berkeley, Livermore, and Los Alamos, how, on very short notice, twenty-three of twenty-four regents broke into their busy schedules to attend a dinner in the governor's mansion in Sacramento—the old Lincoln Steffens home—to discuss the issue. Only one, who was in Europe, did not attend.

From my own point of view, I had had six years on the sidelines as chancellor, watching the regents collectively and individually, noticing the problems solved and those still to be solved. I calculate that my familiarity with the personalities and the problems gave me at least a one year lead over any possible external alternative candidates for the presidency, and I could and did begin in November 1957, long before my official July 1, 1958, starting date as president, working on universitywide problems—thus I had a two-year advantage.

Introducing New Styles of Administration

One of my conclusions, as a close-in observer, was that the style of the presidency that had worked so well for so long needed reworking. Circumstances had changed, and the president's and regents' detailed case-by-case decisions made for each campus, based on the work of a large universitywide administrative staff, had become unwieldy. A related change was to establish clear policies and rules within which administration could be decentralized to campus levels and decision-making speeded up.

A further change was to move toward a more consultative style of governance. The regents were restive, and some hostile, that decisions were made on important matters without their full input. I started discussions of the next budget nine months before its adoption rather than present a budget to the board after it had already been submitted to the governor, and moved from a line-item to an analytical budget that the regents could better understand. Regent Carter, at a regents' meeting in Davis, had once taken the old line-item budget and thrown it across the table at President Sproul. It was very heavy and missed its mark.

I also began the practice of sending out the agenda for each regents' meeting with my recommendation on each item. Previously the regents had to wait for the meeting itself to know what the president would propose. With this advance knowledge, regents could react with more careful consideration to what was to be proposed. I also had a policy to alert key regents, particularly committee chairs and also potential opponents, in advance of major developments: take no one by surprise!

I also set up other new consultative procedures: an advisory council of chancellors that met monthly; a "cabinet" of universitywide officials that also met monthly; a council of student body presidents that met several times a year. I also encouraged the creation of a universitywide Academic Assembly of the Academic Senate with which to consult, instead of the split senate-north and senate-south. I persuaded the regents to invite the chair and vice chair of the Academic Council to attend and participate (but without vote) in all but confidential executive sessions. I also turned the Cal Club of student leaders from all campuses into more of a discussion group. I continued the annual all-university faculty conferences started by President Sproul.

All this was to replace a system of mostly one-by-one presentations to the president by petitioners, who then often had long waits for decisions. Where I still had specific decisions to make, I provided prompt replies and affirmative ones wherever possible. As an illustration, when Paul Dodd, longtime dean of letters and science at UCLA, retired to Rossmoor Village, he had a huge peg board on which he had pinned the most important documents of his life. In the center was a note from me that said, "Paul, Yes. Clark," with no date. It had frayed edges and looked as though it had been well used.

Item-by-item decision-making became much more localized and policy making more consultative, and they have remained so ever since. There was a structural revolution: decentralization; and a cultural revolution: consultation.

Instead of a system oriented to one-man authoritarian decision-making, I concentrated on seeking consensus, or at least consent—meaning that all points of view had to be considered and that the decision was acceptable even if not fully supported by all or most participants. This approach required time and lengthy discussions. It worked well where there was plenty of time and reasonable and friendly groups of people. It did not work well, or at all, in emergency situations or where some people were totally opposed for reasons of ideology or personal ambition. Several such situations did arise, and my approach failed. I did not have the inclination or the ability to shift to a more dominating style. I was more the conciliator.

Problems Appearing on the Horizon

Not all was for the best in the best of all possible worlds. I recognized the identifiable endemic problems within the University of California and within the state. What I did not know was how serious some of them could become, and several of them came together at the end. The end was inherent in the beginning.

There remained a small band of what might be called "post-McCarthy regents" centered around Regent Pauley and Regent Canaday, who had been strongly pro-oath. The members of this group, fluctuating in number from two to six, and variously composed of old and new regents, were concerned to patrol and control the suspected radicalism of some faculty members and students and administrators, including the president. Regent Pauley also thought that, as senior regent, he had special privileges, including the right to be the permanent chair of the board, as Regent Edward Dickson had been from 1948 to 1956, and that the chair of the board was the CEO. So two battles were built into the situation—over suspected faculty, student, and administration radicalism and over power.

There also existed what I thought of as an "empire" centering around James Corley, longtime vice president–business affairs and, crucially, in charge of university affairs in Sacramento. Campus business officers historically had reported to him, and Corley was in charge of architects and engineers and other important groups universitywide. Shortly after I entered the presidency, he came to my office saying he would like to continue the role he had under President Sproul, which he presented to me as follows: Sproul handled the regents and the faculty, and Corley was in charge of everything else, particularly Sacramento and nonacademic administration—two presidents, in effect, both reporting directly to the Board of Regents. Sproul and Corley had worked in tandem, and Corley offered to continue that cooperative arrangement. That was not the way I had seen Corley's role under Sproul (Corley's view greatly diminished Sproul's role as I had observed it—there had been *one* president, not two, and Robert Gordon Sproul was that president); nor was it the way I saw Corley's future role.

The empire was in evidence after each regents' meeting, when Corley held a reception for his adherents universitywide and from the several campuses. With its passionate belief in a centralized university and in the old policies and old ways, this cohesive unit became my internal opposition. Corley also had two spheres of great influence—in Sacramento and among the Berkeley alumni (he was class of 1926 and a track star). Many leading Berkeley alumni, as they later told me, came to see my presidency through his eyes and his comments. Let me add that Corley was always a gentleman and had great loyalty to his vision of the university. But he was without comprehension of or loyalty to my vision of the university of the future.

California's legislature, while mostly very friendly and supportive, had two points of danger. One was Senator Hugh Burns, president pro tem of the senate and chair of its Committee on Un-American Activities, with whom I had parted company over the "contact-man" arrangements at the start of my chancellorship. The other was the otherwise highly desirable one-person one-vote decision of the U.S. Supreme Court in October 1964, which shifted control from the university's longtime friends from the rural counties to new people in the suburbs with less historic knowledge of and allegiance to the university. The population of the state was 55 percent rural in 1850 and 5 percent in 1960, and agricultural interests around the state had been the strongest supporters of the university since its founding. By 1960, there were also 300,000 newcomers to the state each year without knowledge of the historic position and role of the University of California. The university never found a way to make contact with the suburbs as it had with the agricultural counties.

The McCarthy era of the late 1940s and early 1950s that had given rise to the loyalty oath controversy gave birth to a backlash among students and faculty members that reached a peak in the 1960s. That, in turn, gave rise to the even greater backlash of the Reagan years as governor starting in January 1967. This sequence of actions and reactions was built into the historical process. I had seen such movements and countermovements in my study of the vagaries of the history of industrial relations in the United States, and I was familiar with Hegelian theories of thesis and antithesis (but never a permanent synthesis). The impacts on the University of California of these swings of the political pendulum were inevitable.

Also, the university in 1958 had the most conservative policies governing on-campus political engagement by faculty and students of any major university in the United States (particularly via Rule 17) in a state that had elements of political instability (left and right) beyond those in any other state— an explosive combination.

On another front, the university had troubled relations with the University of Southern California. USC resented the rise of UCLA as a competitor, particularly in professional fields, including law, medicine, and business administration, and in intercollegiate athletics, where USC had been supreme. I tried early in my presidency to reduce this antagonism by two agreements with the private colleges and universities in the state: the University of California would limit competitive private fund-raising efforts to already university-related potential donors (particularly alumni and related business interests, such as agriculture), and we would limit efforts to recruit faculty members from private California institutions. Both agreements had full regental support but both eroded over time. Also, of a more public nature, were the battles over the conduct of intercollegiate sports—over rough play on the field and illegal recruiting off. (To its credit and advantage, USC has since become a model of fair play in both arenas.) It was California and Stanford versus USC and we prevailed, but not without costs. One cost came when every single member of Governor Reagan's famous "kitchen cabinet," his group of close advisors, was a member of the board of trustees of USC.

I knew all the above facts and issues full well. They affected my approach to the presidency. I also knew from reading history, from accounts by older faculty members, and from my own observations that no president of the university, and there had been eleven, had ever left the presidency under entirely friendly conditions—all had been in one kind of trouble or another, including Daniel Coit Gilman, Benjamin Ide Wheeler, and Robert Gordon Sproul. I also knew that, while college and university presidents are appointed ostensibly for life, they serve at the pleasure of several constituencies—and that pleasure comes and goes. The standard presidential term then was about ten years in the more famous universities, but it had been falling for half a century. Sproul with his twenty-eight years was a great exception. So I thought of myself as a faculty member temporarily otherwise engaged, as an "interim" president in a long line of interim presidents with still more to follow. As during my chancellorship, Kay and I and our children lived in our own home and maintained a faculty standard of living. I kept up (at a reduced level) my scholarly publications. I felt more independent that way and more secure and more prepared to adapt to the inevitable.

It turned out to be the wise course of action: to be prepared for the end as one entered the beginning. At all times, the urgent issue was: how much could I accomplish and how well in whatever time was available? This intense pressure of time was both externally and internally imposed.

There was, however, temporarily a wide-open "window of opportunity" for the university. How long would it remain open? It is never open forever: economic and political conditions change. And in the academic world, like any other, there is a "law of accumulating grievances" (grievances just accumulate since they are seldom forgotten). Sproul escaped the consequences of this law for a very long time, until 1946, when his trouble with some of the deans and regents began. But five of those years were the war years with academic life in abeyance— thus he really escaped for about eleven years (1930–41). Wheeler escaped for about fifteen years, from 1899 until World War I, when his pro-German sympathies and authoritarian inclinations began to catch up with him. The other presidents of the university served only about three to five years each. I escaped for about twelve of my total of fourteen and one-half years as chancellor and president.

My general expectation in 1958 for the open "window" was about ten years. I was wrong. The economic window was open about fourteen years until the OPEC oil crises of the early 1970s. The political window, however, was open only six and one-half years until the student revolts in the fall of 1964 and two years more until the California state election for governor in fall 1966. But those six and one-half years were among the best of all possible times for the University of California to advance.

The challenge was to make good use of such time as there was. There was always this feeling that time was short (and uncertain) and that the agenda was long and demanding. Napoleon once remarked to his generals: "You can ask for anything you like, except time."

A BROAD OUTLINE OF THE MOST PRESSING PROBLEMS

The agenda before us included the creation of a master plan for higher education in California, reorganization of the university to facilitate faster and better decisions by making the chancellors, in reality, the executive heads of their campuses, and preparation to accommodate what looked in advance to be a prospective 214,000 students by the year 2000 at three new campuses and the four reoriented campuses, while helping Berkeley and Los Angeles hold to their self-chosen sizes. As we carried out this agenda, we developed a more workable system of university governance; found out which academic innovations were more viable and which less; achieved spectacular consequences in the rising national academic rankings of the nine campuses; and, in total, created the most watched and most admired higher education system in the United States—accomplishments of heroic proportions.

Overall policy was set forth particularly in the Master Plan for Higher Education in California (1960), which approved three new campuses and access to the university for the top 12.5 percent of high school graduates in the state; and in UC's growth plan of 1960 and the academic plan of 1961, both of which followed up on the master plan.[2]

The master plan made enrollment projections to 1975, the UC growth plan to 2000. The latter gave us a projected enrollment figure of 214,000 in the year 2000 within a total state population of 45 million (Table 15 has a 1988 revision of the figure for 2000). We then distributed the figure over the existing and projected campuses. Top enrollment at Berkeley and UCLA had already been set at 27,500 and 32,500. Three new campuses were to be added and enrollment at the smaller campuses was projected to expand to 15,000 at Davis and Santa Barbara, and 10,000 at Riverside. As early as 1960, San Francisco was encouraged to have a "broadened mission to include upper-division and graduate work oriented toward the biological sciences."

We were also concerned with the rate of growth on each campus. We advised, particularly because of the problems in carefully recruiting faculty members, that no campus should be expected to grow at a rate that would result in more than 100 new faculty members per year except for already very large campuses. We thought it would take 15 years for a new campus to reach 7,500 students after the date of site acquisition. We then thought that each of the three new campuses would reach 27,500 students by 2000. The 1960 growth plan ended by saying that "Times change and plans must change too." Both have.

The 1960 growth plan was endorsed by the Academic Senate Committee on Educational Policy and by the Board of Regents. Next came the academic plan, in July 1961. This plan added the possibility of a need for two additional new campuses by or shortly after 2000, one in southern and one in northern California. And it suggested the desirability of acquiring land well ahead of time. The Board of Regents by that time had seen the problems of securing adequate sites in a state rapidly filling in its large, good sites for new campuses, and of the overload of effort in building more than one campus at a time. The 1961 academic plan also stressed the importance of "diversity" of programs and "personalities" among campuses and noted that "diversity" required more "thought, consultation, and self-discipline" than conformity to the standard model, which it clearly does.

The last plan I helped develop was the Academic Plan of the University of California 1966–76 (November 1966). This plan reviewed the many changes

TABLE 15

Enrollment Projections to 2000

Campus	1959	1960	1988	1995
	Actual Enrollment	*Projection for 2000*	*Projection for 2000*	*Actual Enrollment*
Berkeley	19,805	27,500	29,450	29,630
Davis	2,404	15,000	26,850	23,092
Irvine	0	27,500	26,050	17,261
Riverside	1,258	10,000	18,050[a]	8,906
San Diego	44	27,500	26,050	18,315
San Francisco	1,660	7,500	4,000	3,640
Santa Barbara	2,865	15,000	20,000	18,224
Santa Cruz	0	27,500	15,000	9,923
UCLA[b]	16,443	27,500	34,500	34,713
Total	**44,479**	**214,000[c]**	**199,950[d]**	**163,704**

Sources: for 1959 and 1960, University of California Office of the President, "Recommended Plan for Growth of the University of California" (June 1960); for 1988, University of California Office of the President; and for 1995, "UC Statistical Summary of Students and Staff" (fall 1995).

[a]*As modified by the regents in 1991.*
[b]*Including medical school.*
[c]*The state Department of Finance projection to 1975 (for a total state population of 45 million) as extended to 2000 by Van Beuren Stanberry, a state government consulting demographer; we adjusted it to get the size of the college-going age cohort, then multiplied by .125 (the proportion made eligible for admittance to UC), and then by .50 because historically about half the eligible students were admitted by and actually attended UC. The total included an anticipated 29,000 students at "additional campuses."*
[d]*The revised projection within a total population of 36.5 million reflects slower growth than the rate predicted in 1975.*

that had taken place since 1961, including the impact of preparing for year-round operations. The one new element in the 1966 plan was to state more specifically that the San Francisco "Medical Center might be expected to build upon its existing strength in human biology and to take advantage of the resources of its urban situation to develop a university center with a commitment to the concept of man as a biological entity within the city as a meaningful unit" of the human environment.[3]

The plan concluded by saying:

The place of the university in society is itself changing in fundamental ways. Once among the most isolated of social institutions, it is being drawn inevitably into a more intense and intimate relation with the society it serves. This is more than a matter of the degree to which new knowledge through research is necessary for economic progress [and or] . . . the astonishing numbers of persons who must be educated to higher levels for the occupations and leisure activities of an increasingly automated industrial economy. . . . [The university also] must educate young people to deal with change in their lives not as fearsome uncertainty but as opportunity which they can adapt to their needs. It must continue to nourish that critical independence of mind and spirit that is the essence and the ferment of the good university and the thriving democratic community alike.[4]

The great American dream after World War II meant many things to many people. Perhaps it was, above all, a dream of universal and increasing affluence. But it was also a dream of equality of opportunity. The dream of the University of California was to contribute to affluence through research and the training of highly skilled people; and to equality of opportunity particularly by supporting the community colleges and by holding open half of its upper-division student places for community college transfers. For a time the dream's supporting conditions were favorable. And the following chapters here are mostly about dreams being realized. Yet dreams and plans "gang aft a-gley," and some did, as I shall note.

And dreams for some can be nightmares for others. UCLA felt San Diego to be a threat, as Berkeley did UCLA. The four campuses in transition viewed the three new campuses as upstarts and interlopers, diverting attention and resources from them. The large campuses looked down on the small. Berkeley and UCLA viewed the six expanding campuses as a rescue mission taking enrollment pressures off them but also as thieves taking away resources they thought might otherwise be theirs. The general attitude of unwelcome acceptance was evident in a letter that Lawrence Clark Powell, former librarian at UCLA, wrote in April 1968 to Donald Coney, librarian at Berkeley. It said in part, "Don't let those pygmy campuses emerge too far." This general rallying cry of the old met the rallying cry of the new: "We want equality—and now." The golden age was also an age of recriminations. "Every unhappy family is unhappy in its own way" (Leo Tolstoy, *Anna Karenina*), and the University of California had its "own way," which I shall attempt to describe.

A Master Plan for Higher Education in California

We had to do everything all at once: set up new campuses and renovate some of the older ones, reorganize as well as administer the university—and each was a full-time task in itself. Our basic task in preparing for the future, however, was to determine the role of the University of California within the totality of higher education in the state. As of 1958, this was much in dispute.

Working to develop an outstanding statewide system of higher education and to keep the university's place as the great center for graduate instruction and research within that system, while considering both the public welfare and the private interests of the several segments, we created the Master Plan for Higher Education in California. Ex post, the plan looks like a grand design to achieve great purposes: equality of opportunity through universal access to higher education; provisions for supplying the highest-level skills and the most advanced knowledge to serve both wealth and welfare; concern for the full labor market needs of a technologically advancing society; and preservation of the self-governing ability within institutions of higher education.

It is a grand design: one of the most studied plans for higher education and, perhaps, the most influential. California was the first state in the nation to guarantee universal access. With the rest of the states following in one way or another, the United States became the first nation so committed. California also developed the largest number of high-level research campuses—the envy of the academic world. And higher education preserved its autonomy by planning its own future.

Ex ante, however, the plan looked to those of us who participated in its development more like a desperate attempt to prepare for a tidal wave of students, to escape state legislative domination, to contain escalating warfare among its separate segments. This it also was. And the preparation, the escape, and the containment in each case was barely in time and barely succeeded. The master plan was a product of stark necessity, of political calculations, and of pragmatic transactions.

The tidal wave was coming. Nothing could stop it. It was huge. It carried enrollments in the University of California from 50,000 in 1960 to 100,000 in 1968. State colleges' enrollment went from 95,000 to 210,000; the enrollment in community colleges increased from 340,000 to 665,000; the total in public higher education grew from 485,000 to 975,000. It had taken the university nearly one hundred years to go from zero to 50,000 enrolled students, and only ten to go from 50,000 to 100,000. Half of the university of 1968 had been planned and built since 1958, and the situation was roughly similar for the rest of public higher education in the state. By 1968, half of the life of the University of California, measured in total student years on campus, had been experienced since 1960.

The tidal wave in California was composed of three parts: the great increase in the birthrate nationwide after World War II; the historic change across the country from a mass-access system of higher education (access for 10 to 50 percent of an age cohort) to one marked increasingly by universal access (access for 50 and possibly approaching 100 percent of high school graduates); and the in-migration to California of over 300,000 people per year. It really was three waves, one on top of another. Nothing like it, proportionately, had ever happened before or is likely ever to occur again.

The university of 1958 was not prepared, nor was higher education in California more generally. The community colleges (then known as junior colleges) were administratively part of secondary education—not of higher education. The state colleges were under the state Board of Education, which also supervised the elementary and secondary school systems, and this board looked upon the colleges primarily as sources of teachers. The state colleges had advanced enormously since the founding of San Jose State in 1857 (before the University of California in 1868). Originally, they operated as normal schools (to 1921), on an "apprenticeship basis" of training teachers largely for the primary schools. Then they added "general culture" and more emphasis on subject matter, particularly in the rapidly expanding preparation of high school teachers—thus joining letters and science to teacher training. Then the state colleges added other "white-collar" occupations, including bookkeeping, social work, and nursing. Just prior to the development of the master plan, they were expanding into "polytechnic" professions—engineering, business administration, computer science, for example—particularly into engineering (1953).

Leaders of some state colleges wanted their institutions to have university status. Those of their faculty members who had Ph.D.'s from leading research universities might well view the state colleges as graveyards of disappointed expectations—they would rather be located in the research universities whence they had come. Several state college presidents (also with Ph.D. degrees) were recruiting new faculty members with the promise that they could assure them university status in the (not very distant) future. A few state colleges in other states (particularly agricultural colleges, and preeminently Michigan State) were moving toward university status. UCLA, then known as Los Angeles Normal School, had been taken over by the University of California in 1919 and was on its way to becoming a world-famous research university. There was much "academic drift" upward at that time in history. Arnold Joyal, president of Fresno State in 1960, says in his California State University (CSU) oral history that "we were looking to the day when the institution would be recognized as a university. . . . We knew . . . that was bound to happen."[1] They were hiring Ph.D.'s with this in mind.

The University of California did not know whether it would continue to be the sole source, within public higher education, of the Ph.D. degree and other high professional training and of basic research. It was as fearful of the future as some of the state colleges were hopeful.

Robert Wert, vice president of Stanford, member of the master plan survey team, and first chair of the subsequent coordinating committee, says in his CSU oral history that the situation was approaching "a state of anarchy."[2]

In the absence of understandings within higher education, the state legislature was getting ready to take control of higher education with many bills under consideration (some twenty-five to fifty in early 1959 including individual bills to create nineteen new state colleges). It had just created a new state college in the little Central Valley town of Turlock, home to the legislator who was chair of the Senate Committee on Education. Since the town was known as the "turkey capital" of the world (and turkeys' aspirations toward higher education were not at issue), there seemed little to justify the legislative action.

Facing the Crisis

What to do? The tidal wave was on its way. So was the state legislature.

I went first to the regents—specifically the Committee on Educational Policy under Edward Carter as chair. Ed was a UCLA graduate (1932) with an

M.B.A. from Harvard and was a fast-rising department store executive and highly influential person in the Los Angeles community. I came to rely on him for advice and support more than on any other single regent. He had great strengths in the areas of educational policy, finance, and administrative organization. I told Ed of my concerns and he agreed they should be considered by the board. The first discussion was at his home, where the Committee on Educational Policy was meeting in August 1958. This was my second meeting with the board as the new president of the university, and it came to be a historic meeting. I reviewed with the committee the current stalemate and explained how no segment of higher education could make plans with any assurance. Jim Corley, as our representative in Sacramento, spoke of how the legislature was starting to move in on unsettled issues, and of how the aspirations of the state colleges and their political power were both rising fast.

There was in existence a liaison committee between the regents and the state Board of Education (started in 1945), on which several members of the regents' committee had served or were serving, and they had experienced the deteriorating situation at firsthand. From sitting in as an observer at several meetings of that committee, I considered the situation to be a disaster. The state colleges came in with their demands for expanded programs. The university usually voted "no." Then the state colleges, if at all possible, found a way around the "no" by one subterfuge or another. The atmosphere was getting more and more adversarial. We needed a new approach. The regents agreed.

I went next to Roy Simpson, state superintendent of public instruction and an ex officio member of the Board of Regents. Roy was an essential building block of the master plan. Without him, it would never have been achieved. He had knowledge, wisdom, and courage; he was strategically placed but took no initiatives. We agreed on each major step to take.

Why was he so agreeable? He knew the university well and admired it. He looked on the state colleges primarily as a source of teacher training and did not share their aspirations to metamorphose into university campuses, leaving behind in the dust what he considered was their most essential function. Roy was devoted to primary and secondary education, and to the state colleges mostly as substantial supports for teaching at these levels. He looked at education in its totality and had no commitment to defending his own bureaucratic turf. This turned out to be of fundamental importance when he supported a separate board of trustees for the state colleges. Roy was an educational statesman—as thoughtful as he was quiet.

The state colleges had two distinct personalities. One integrated the interests and convictions of the superintendent of public instruction with the state Board of Education. The other personality splintered into the twelve college presidents, one for each campus. Some held one view, some held another. Each president was an independent force—the sole source of authority on campus, without checks and balances. Joyal of Fresno called campus governance an "enlightened dictatorship."[3] The presidents had an informal council of their own but one without any coordinating authority.

Paul Leonard, the longtime president of San Francisco State (1945 to 1957), once told me that he had the best college presidency in the United States— no organized faculty, no organized student body, no organized alumni association, and—since the state Board of Education paid little attention to the colleges—no board of trustees. Paul went east once a year to hire new faculty. He worked through the deans of graduate studies in leading universities. He sent them lists of open positions in advance to guide the appointments they arranged for him with likely candidates. He hired on the spot and informed the departments involved of what he had done when he got back. They had no choice but acceptance.

I decided early on to sound out the presidents of the potentially most involved state colleges. San Jose, San Francisco, Fresno, and San Diego colleges were in areas the regents had designated for possible new campuses. These presidents had met in advance and had chosen John Wahlquist as their spokesman. We met in my office in Berkeley. John was president of San Jose State, the oldest, largest, and best established of the state colleges. He took a very hard line. The state colleges wanted research university status. They had earned it. They expected to get it. And all that federal R&D money, after *Sputnik,* was out there for the asking, and they wanted their share of it. They had the greater political influence around the state. The new governor, so they claimed, would support them.

I raised the possibility of whether any of them might possibly wish to take the "Santa Barbara route," which had been transfer by legislative action (in 1944) from state college to university status. Wahlquist said that absolutely never again would that be allowed to happen. Santa Barbara had been condemned to languish by the university (true). The university's Academic Senate would only slowly and reluctantly give the colleges their proportionate share of Ph.D. programs (certainly also true), whereas the state colleges could get their "fair share" overnight by making their system a university system through political action. Aside from that, they wanted nothing to do with any academic senate coming onto their campuses. I knew this already. When I was chancellor at Berkeley, I had once been invited to spend an evening with their council of presidents when they met in San Francisco. They wanted my advice on how to forestall initiatives for an academic senate of their own or, as an alternative, a faculty union. I said they were talking to the wrong person, because I strongly favored the Academic Senate in the University of California and recommended one to them. So we went home early.

I knew that the presidents were divided—Arnold Joyal of Fresno, Glenn Dumke of San Francisco, and Malcolm Love of San Diego did not take as strong a position as John Wahlquist of San Jose—and I knew that one powerful president, Julian McPhee of San Luis Obispo ("Cal Poly"), liked his emerging polytechnic status. Dumke would later sign the master plan as a member of the survey team, and Love would give good support for the new UC campus in San Diego. Joyal was publicly friendly to the possibility of a UC campus in the San Joaquin Valley (but not too close to Fresno!). The presidents were divided, I concluded, and would stay that way.

I calculated that the state Board of Education, under the leadership of Roy Simpson and its chair, William Blair, was not divided and was not likely to divide; and that the members of the board, not the presidents, would cast the deciding votes in any event. It was important to be nice to the presidents but even more important to be very nice to the members of the board.

But what about the new governor, Pat Brown? I was not convinced of his full commitment to university status for the state colleges, although he may have indicated, as alleged by the state college presidents, some support in a speech at Chico State during the campaign of 1958. I did know that one of the governor's staff assistants, Fred Dutton, favored the state colleges; but not his other chief assistants—William Coblentz and Warren Christopher. The regents, and particularly Edwin Pauley, a powerful and wealthy political supporter of the governor, were very helpful in carrying a persuasive case for one and only one research university system. Governor Brown took little active part in the early development of the master plan but, to the extent he did, favored the evolving solution. He later became an ardent supporter of the master plan and considered it one of the greatest accomplishments of his terms as governor. "I was responsible for the Master Plan of Higher Education."[4]

Within the Board of Regents, there was one minor problem. One regent, John Canaday of Los Angeles, with some polite but not vigorous support by a few other regents, favored combining the university campuses and the state colleges into one total system under the Board of Regents. This arrangement would assure the board's control of what happened. I was totally opposed. The system would be too large and too diverse for effective governance, and its internal dynamics would lead, I thought, to a homogenization in a downward direction. The idea was abandoned.

Among the chancellors, there was also a problem. Early on, the university chancellors and college presidents comprised a joint advisory committee; the UC campus heads were from Berkeley, UCLA, and Davis. Without advance discussion or warning, the advisory group from the university side agreed that state colleges should have the right to award the Ph.D. degree. They had apparently decided they would rather compete with a long list of less prestigious state college Ph.D. programs than the potentially more prestigious programs on new and transformed campuses within the university. Giving the three campus heads no more advance discussion or warning than they had given me, I replaced them on the committee with three other chancellors. That ended not only the tentative and unapproved offer but also the active life of the joint advisory group.

The strategy of the university was clear. Our three new campuses (with Fresno proposed for later on), along with the expansion of programs at Davis, Santa Barbara, and Riverside, were adequate to fill an anticipated void in facilities for training Ph.D.'s and conducting research and in the political map of fast-growing population areas without a UC campus. We did not want to share resources with sixteen additional "university" campuses (the twelve established state colleges and four more then being developed) who would then claim lower teaching loads for their faculties and higher research subsidies at great cost. And we did not want to watch the state colleges abandon their highly important skill training functions for teachers in the hot pursuit of the holy grail of elite research status. The state did not need a higher education system where every component was intent on being another Harvard or Berkeley or Stanford. An upward drift was desirable in quality but in the direction of several models. What we needed were three improved models—the open-access model, the polytechnic model, and the research university model. If the state colleges "went university," some new colleges would have to be founded to serve the polytechnic role.

Developing the Master Plan

So I went back to Roy Simpson. We quickly agreed on the following points:

- To replace the liaison committee between regents and board of education with a new coordinating mechanism.

- To bring into the discussions the junior colleges and the private colleges and universities. Each of these segments had an interest in the solutions. We also thought that four segments—three state systems plus the private colleges and universities—could more easily concentrate on the welfare of the state than an already confrontational two had managed to do.

- To ask the state legislature to give us a year to work out a solution and to hold in abeyance all legislative actions for that year. Simpson and I went before the legislature together and obtained agreement in spring 1959 (the assembly in May and the senate in early June). Jim Corley drafted the joint resolution to accomplish this. Corley was very helpful throughout. He had seen the growing political aggressiveness of the state colleges in Sacramento. He totally agreed on preserving the historic status of the University of California.

- To go ahead with three new campuses for the university and four additional new campuses for the state colleges. (There was a brief misunderstanding later at a public meeting when Simpson suggested seven new college campuses, without prior private consultation, but he quickly reversed himself.)

- To prepare a plan with clear differentiation of functions among the three public segments. This plan would include universal access to the community colleges, expanded polytechnic programs in the state colleges, and a greater concentration on Ph.D. training and research in the university system.

- To ask Arthur Coons, president of Occidental College, to chair a survey team to work out the specific terms. There were, in the end, sixty-three master plan recommendations—all unanimously agreed upon. At the time, an invitation to private institutions to participate in the discussions on a basis of equality was considered rather daring. It was threatening to some to put the president of a private college in a commanding position to influence the future of public higher education in the state. There was no danger. Coons was a wise, public-spirited person with great knowledge about all of higher education in California. Simpson and I never had a doubt about his potential effectiveness and chose him as the one best person to represent the *overall* welfare of higher education in the state and to do so with diplomacy and determination. We were so fortunate that he was available. (Incidentally, two members of his board of trustees at Occidental were powerful members of the Board of Regents, Ed Carter and Dorothy ["Buff"] Chandler of the family that owned the *Los Angeles Times*.)

The master plan survey team began its work on June 16, 1959, and completed its report in December 1959. Coons was an excellent chair. Dean McHenry was a superb representative of the university with good judgment and outstanding persuasive skills. He and I had jointly developed in our discussions the idea of a master plan. It was his idea as much as or more than mine. McHenry and I were in constant contact as the plan developed. Tom Holy was the second representative of the university. He was coauthor of the *Additional Centers* report for the liaison committee, which had recommended establishing additional campuses of the university and the state colleges. Holy had great familiarity with all the segments of higher education and was a rich mine of information. Dumke was a fair-minded leading participant for the state colleges. Everything went along rather smoothly, until the very end, with full efforts to bring in active participation by state officials and leaders of the legislature. We worked most closely with Dorothy Donohoe of Bakersfield, who was chair of the Assembly Committee on Education, and her chief assistant, Keith Sexton (the resultant legislation was named the Donohoe Act), and with the powerful George Miller of Martinez, who was chair of the Senate Committee on Finance, and the equally powerful Jesse Unruh of Los Angeles, a fast rising leader of California's State Assembly.

Last-Minute Resistance and a "Summit"

But then, at the end, it looked as though it might all have been in vain. Some state college presidents were in revolt. Reportedly, they took Dumke for a long automobile ride (to Sacramento and back) and persuaded him to withdraw from the developing agreement. The possible breakdown within the survey team surfaced at a joint meeting of the Board of Regents and the state Board of Education in the regents' room at Berkeley on December 18, 1959.

I called a "summit" meeting late that afternoon in my office. I made one last concession: the university would be willing to offer joint Ph.D. programs on a case-by-case basis with the state colleges. I got this idea from Herman

Wells, longtime president of Indiana University, who had worked out a similar arrangement with Ball State College. This "sweetener" was intended to help Dumke placate his faculty members most intent on university status. It, and a second point on teaching-related research (research within the time and campus resources provided for a teaching program), gave him proofs of a triumph in his negotiations on behalf of state college faculties.

The superintendent of public instruction and the chair of the state Board of Education, who were present at the summit, were quite persuasive in their discussions with Dumke. Both Simpson and Blair argued for the central importance of completing the plan. Senior members of the survey team were there too, McHenry, Coons, and Dumke. And as always Don McLaughlin, chair of the Board of Regents, was diplomatic and charming, with an impressive understanding of academic life through his background as a faculty member at Harvard and Berkeley. In the end, Dumke agreed to vote in the affirmative. There was a "plan"!

But there was still one uncertainty: a new chair of the state Board of Education would be replacing Blair in the new year. Louis Heilbron, a 1928 Berkeley alumnus, had been appointed to the board in March 1959 by Pat Brown and then—in January 1960, when everything still hung in the balance—was elected as its new chair. In these roles he advised the governor, presided over the board to which Simpson reported, and then became chair of the state colleges' board of trustees that later appointed Dumke chancellor of the state college system. I say "still hung in the balance" because, while Pat Brown presided at the December 18 meeting, he had not clearly committed himself. Heilbron was also there as a new member of the state Board of Education and had said that the university's ownership of doctoral degrees should be protected from "unreasonable search and seizure." However, some of the college presidents and many leading faculty members were irate at the summit's results. We knew that they were exerting unreasonable pressure on the members of the Board of Education and particularly on its new chair. Would they and would he hold firm?

Lyman Glenny says in his CSU oral history that "all those faculty associations were after the Ph.D. Every one of them."[5] This in spite of having achieved a joint doctorate. And in his own CSU oral history Dumke says that "there were many members of the faculty who simply didn't approve of our not becoming research-oriented universities. . . . They wanted to become baby Berkeleys. They were, I think, unrealistic." "And a lot of faculty members wanted to go full bore for the doctorate."[6] Faculty votes were taken on at least nine state college campuses. Votes varied on the separate parts of the master plan. On an overall basis, three large campuses voted against the master plan (Sacramento overwhelmingly so, Los Angeles, and Long Beach) and six in favor (including San Francisco, which Dumke carried—also overwhelmingly). The proposal for their own independent board was particularly popular. By a 95 percent favorable vote, however, the state college faculty expressed the conviction "that basic and applied research are a proper professional function of any scholarly faculty"—a nearly unanimous rejection of the differentiation of research functions as between the state colleges and the University of California.

At a crucial meeting held at Berkeley in March 1960, Heilbron (in my mind I can still see where he sat in the regents' room) made a statement giving unequivocal support to the draft of the master plan. Among other things, he said that UC should keep the "crown jewels": basic research and training for the Ph.D., the M.D., the law degree, and other advanced degrees. I heaved a big sigh of relief. The last piece of a complicated puzzle was now in place. Heilbron then joined others of us (including Simpson, Carter, and me) later in March in appearing in Sacramento before the assembly and the senate to support the plan. Heilbron was steadfast throughout, although some of the state college presidents and many faculty members continued in revolt.

Our master plan was then adopted, with only one dissenting vote among the 120 members of the two houses of the legislature, and was signed into law by the governor on April 27, 1960.

What the Master Plan Did

The plan was a "treaty," but it was not a treaty universally supported. Some state college presidents and many faculty members (and their successors) never accepted it. For example, Fred Ness in 1966 (then president at Fresno State) said that "our fellow citizens are ultimately going to require the state colleges to offer some form of the doctorate."[7] Neil Smelser, who wrote the best outside analysis of the master plan, noted that many of the state college leaders felt "locked" into a status they did not accept.[8] Dumke, as chancellor of the new system, however, accepted the plan, and carried it out during his term (1962 to 1982) in good faith, although he supported and secured a change in name from "state college" to "state university" but without any change in functions.[9] Holding to the master plan and particularly to the differentiation of functions cannot have been easy for him. Dumke and Simpson and Blair and Heilbron and Governor Brown were in the most difficult political situations. Thus, to them belongs the chief credit for making the master plan a reality. For the rest of us it was comparatively easy from a political point of view, although hard in terms of time taken and worry endured.

Our plan included these provisions in addition to those indicated above:

- It set admission policies: the community colleges were to make places for all of California's high school graduates and all others equally qualified; the state colleges for the top 33.3 percent of high school graduates instead of the prior 50 or 60 percent; the university for the top 12.5 percent instead of the prior 15 percent. At my suggestion, there would be "special procedure" admissions to the university of 2 percent. I did think—as critics said—about places for "tackles on the football team." But I was interested too in students who could make special contributions to campus life, as in music, theater, and leadership (for example, high school class presidents); and students who had shown ability to overcome disadvantages and deserved "equal opportunity" consideration (this 2 percent figure was later raised to 6 percent).

- Each segment would provide transfer opportunities for students to move within the overall system.

- Community colleges were to be established within commuting distance of virtually all residents of the state. This coverage would require twenty-two new colleges (eventually nearly fifty on top of the sixty-four then in existence).

- The state colleges would be given the same constitutional and thus fiscal autonomy as the university (regretfully never fully realized); access to M.A. degrees across-the-board on their own choice; and their own board of trustees. Also, two additional state colleges would be needed on top of the four already being planned.

- The California State Scholarship Program funding for tuition would be greatly expanded—of particular interest to the private institutions.

- A coordinating council of all four segments would be established to continue the process of consultation and coordination (never fully effective). This council was to be advisory to the segments and to state agencies. We did not want a public "super board" with final authority. We wanted higher education to continue to control its own destiny.

- The new differentiation of functions should be made a part of the state constitution (never accomplished).

Some dissidents said that the university had "out-negotiated" the state colleges. The master plan was even called "a thieves' bargain."[10] Lyman Glenny, who was then (1960) at Sacramento State but later at UC Berkeley, says that the University of California "won the whole thing"; that Simpson could "have gotten a lot more." To the question, "The University won this fight?" he replied, "Absolutely . . . absolutely."[11] I entirely disagreed—though in political advantages we were ahead. We had the better historic relations with the junior colleges and with the private colleges and universities. And the state did not need over twenty more (very costly) research universities. California had 9 percent of the nation's population but by the mid-1960s had 15 percent of its research universities: of the then about eighty "research universities" nationwide (Carnegie classification), the state had UC's nine campuses, and with Stanford, USC, and Cal Tech, twelve in total.[12]

There was an enormous gap between state college aspirations and reasonable expectations. The state colleges actually got quite a lot. In particular, they obtained their own Board of Trustees, and that made them an independent segment of higher education, instead of an attachment to primary and secondary education. (But for the college presidents, independence had a downside. They now had a chancellor and an active board above them, and they thus lost some of their prior free-wheeling autonomy.) Additionally, the colleges had the whole polytechnic area opened up to them with across-the-board access to M.A. degrees and teaching-related research. By the 1990s, two-thirds of their degrees were in polytechnic areas. They were no longer primarily teachers' colleges.

I thought at the time that the colleges did not fully appreciate the great opportunities offered to them. They were so concentrated on the academic prestige of the Ph.D. degree and of basic research that they ignored the new possibilities of serving a highly technological society and thus gaining public support. My field of specialization was labor economics and I was fully aware of the movement of the American labor force in the direction of development of higher technology and related skills. And, with a farm background, I had high appreciation of technical skills. But "academic prestige" was the chosen goal, not service to an advancing technological society. In the period since 1960, polytechnic institutions have prospered the most among all institutions around the academic world in advanced nations. The recent leadership of CSU (Barry Munitz was its chancellor until 1998) fully recognized this. The California state universities have the whole world of the "techno-structure" to create and to serve. The downside, however, has been that the "polytechnic" assignment is an in-between and less well defined assignment than "equal opportunity" (the community colleges) and Ph.D. and advanced professional degrees and basic research (University of California).

The Plan in Operation

Heilbron and Dumke got the new state college system off to an excellent start. Once the system was under way, Heilbron set the central theme: "We must cultivate our own garden" and not just continue to covet someone else's. And "our own garden" was a huge estate. It encompassed all the polytechnic skills at the operational level of an advancing industrial economy. Enrollments went from 60,000 in 1960 to 350,000 in 1990. The grounds of this estate came to be well cultivated.

But work in one area, the joint Ph.D. degree, went slowly. Some college presidents and faculty members, as well as Ann Reynolds, Dumke's immediate successor as chancellor, felt that it would proceed only at the expense of their ultimate access to full "university status."

RESOURCES

The report of the survey team, among many other things, weighed how to finance the plan. It concluded that resources would be available because it made two assumptions. One was that productivity per hour of work would continue to rise at approximately the average rate of recent years—then 2.5 to 3 percent, and the master plan survey team assumed 2.5 for the future. This scenario was not to be. Regent Carter and I, in our private discussions, took the historic rate of 2 percent to be more realistic, but it too was off. The other assumption was that there would be much better use of resources, as, for example, in weeklong and year-round utilization of plant, and heavier reliance on the community colleges for lower-division education. This fared as the first scenario had. Opportunities for conserving resources still exist in many forms and are extensive in their totality. The efficiency of society went down from annual increases in labor productivity of 3 to 2 and then to 1 percent per year. Increases, if any, in efficient use of higher education's resources are not measurable.

PROCESS

The plan we were drawing up was not a "plan" in the usual sense. Rather, it was a process that made specific planning possible within the several segments of higher education. It set parameters for individual segment-by-segment and campus-by-campus plans and involved all four segments, the governor's office, and the legislature. Internally, we consulted with campus heads and faculty leaders. We kept the press informed. We considered all major problems. We looked at the long run. We did it ourselves rather than through consultants. It was our plan, not the Strayer report (1948) or the McConnell report (1955).

What if there had been no agreement and no plan? The battle between the university and the state colleges would have intensified. The legislature would have taken over the planning function. Higher education would have lost much of its essential autonomy. Campus-by-campus planning would have rested on a very uncertain basis. The vision of a higher education system committed to both equality of opportunity and higher academic merit would not have become such a successful reality. Higher education in California would have continued on its 1950s path toward a greater mess—anarchy compounded.

The Vision

The plan was a treaty and it was a process. It was also a vision. It was a vision that within a single overall system of higher education there would be greatly expanded opportunity for all youth, greatly extended provisions for the training of "polytechnic" skills in an evolving economy with a more highly skilled labor force, and the highest level of advanced professional training and basic research. The vision was to serve an egalitarian democracy, a technocratic economy, and a meritocratic society. It was Thomas Jefferson's vision of equality of opportunity for all and of service to all combined with contributions to the development of what Jefferson had called an "aristocracy of talent." It was Benjamin Franklin's vision of the value of *all* "useful knowledge" and all useful skills. It was also a vision of "a nation of educated people."[13] It was a characteristically all-American vision.

The plan was also a continuation (with revisions) of prior history. It built effectively on the past.[14] As the survey team wrote, "California can and will, as in both the past and present, provide adequate support for an efficient program of public higher education designed to meet fully the rapidly changing needs of society."[15]

To the extent there can be said to have been a predecessor report, it was *Higher Education for Democracy* by the president's Commission on Higher Education for Democracy (the Zook commission) in 1948.[16] This report stated that "education is the foundation of democratic liberties" and that education is the biggest and most hopeful of the nation's enterprises. It called for one-third of all young people completing four years of college or more, and one-half completing two years, which is about the way it has turned out half a century later. At that time, some of the most eminent leaders of American universities were suggesting, instead, that "mental ability" limited a maximum range of individuals going to college to something like 25 percent.[17]

For a time at least, the California dream became a reality.[18] As a 1990 report from the Organisation for Economic Co-operation and Development (OECD) comments, the master plan was "a distinctive attempt to reconcile populism with elitism," an effort to combine "equality with excellence"; and "logic was superimposed on history" by integrating "both populist and elitist forces into one system."[19] We did, at that moment, "seize upon history and shape it rather than being overrun by it. At the time, it felt like the *Perils of Pauline*. In retrospect, it looks more like the triumph of collective good judgment."[20]

The OECD report states that the master plan is "the most advanced effort through state action to organise mass higher education for a tripling enrolment by 1975 while maintaining a quality of research and education at the top which was unsurpassed anywhere among OECD countries and probably in the world."[21]

The master plan became a central building block of the California dream of a technologically advanced society with equality of opportunity for all.[22]

The Master Plan Forty Years Later

At the formal level of announced policies, the Master Plan for Higher Education in California remains virtually intact today. It has had good results. It reduced the warfare between UC and what became CSU. Each segment knew its assignments and could plan within them. Nearly all the other forty-nine states have come to imitate this plan to one degree or another—the sincerest form of flattery, with a universal access segment, a designated research segment (a "flagship" campus), and a polytechnic segment. Within California, it increased opportunity for students; saved money by placing more of the burden on the less expensive (per capita) community colleges and by avoiding the creation of twenty or more unneeded research universities at high cost; and fully served the labor market, particularly through the CSU with its polytechnic programs.

Yet there has been gradual but significant erosion of the original plan:

Tuition, defined as charges for academic programs, has cropped up and increased in all segments.

The state scholarship program, of particular interest to the private institutions, has atrophied.

The community colleges have generally reduced their emphasis on transfer programs to UC and CSU.

The joint doctorate program, while falling short of our original expectations, has had substantial results. Programs were authorized involving five UC campuses: San Diego (7), Davis (3), Berkeley (3), Los Angeles (1), and Santa Barbara (1); and seven CSU campuses: San Diego (11), Chico (1), Fresno (1), Long Beach (1), Los Angeles (1), San Francisco (1), and San Jose (1). Altogether, from 1990–97, 193 joint degrees were awarded. In 1997, 307 students were currently participating—170 of them in programs with UC-San Diego participation.[23]

The coordinating council has been less effective than once expected, and control and responsibility have shifted away from representatives of the segments to the public members.

Efforts to achieve better use of resources, including by year-round operations and other proposed actions, have remained in almost total neglect.

The plan's big test now lies in the next twelve to fifteen years. The test is whether enough student places, at reasonable tuition levels, can be created to continue universal access and full service to the labor market. The next ten years' Tidal Wave II of students will be about as large in absolute numbers as was the earlier one but far less in proportion, since it will come on top of a

TABLE 16

Percentages of California State General Fund Expenditures to Four-Year Higher
Education, Prisons, and Medi-Cal

Year	UC and CSU	Prisons	Medi-Cal
1960	11.3	2.4	0
1990	9.4	5.3	10.0
1995	7.8	7.1	14.0

Source: State of California, "Governor's Budget" (year varies).

greatly enlarged base. It will call for an expansion of total student places by at
least 25 percent. How can this be financed? New resources per capita are being created at a slower long-run rate than in the 1960s—by 1 percent per year
from 1970 to 1995 instead of the earlier 3 percent, although the rate has risen
to 3 percent since 1995. There is also more competition for the use of these resources, particularly from prisons and from support of medical expenses for
an aging population. Prisons alone now take nearly as much of the state general fund as does four-year higher education (CSU and UC; see Table 16).

There have been plenty of warnings of difficulties to come, but too little
advance planning.[24] Solutions must draw on several sources. Students will need
to take advantage of enhanced opportunities in high school for advanced placement or remedial courses; they will need to make faster progress toward a degree in college; and they will need to pay higher tuitions (based on financial
circumstances). Institutions of higher education will need to make much better use of resources. The state will have to face the need for increased appropriations for higher education from the general fund. The contribution from
each of these sources may need to approximate one-quarter from students,
one-quarter from institutions, and one-half from the state.

A great deal is at stake for the state's youth, its high technology industries,
its political tranquillity, and, since California has been the model state in developments in higher education, for higher education across the United
States. A continuing rate of productivity increases of at least 2 percent would
be of enormous value, as would be a continuation of a full employment economy. As of the end of the 1990s, productivity increases are rising closer to 2
percent or even 3 percent and full employment is being approximated. Also,

state authorities, starting with the university's 1994–95 budget year, began to consider long-term policies for financing the university.

Higher education met head on and conquered the crisis of the 1960s. Now it faces a new crisis. Will it rise to the occasion once again? (For a discussion of "Paradise" being "lost" and the need to pursue "Paradise Regained," see my 1999 presentation to a joint legislative committee reviewing the master plan; also see Schrag.)[25]

13

Moving from Unitary
to Pluralistic Decision-
Making (1957–59)

As President Sproul's term of office drew to a close in the late 1950s, all admin-
istrative control resided in the Board of Regents, the president, and the vice pres-
ident–business affairs. An earlier university president once complained that the
university had three presidents: "the president eo nomine, *the secretary of the*
regents, and the professor of agriculture";[1] in 1958, the triumvirate was the presi-
dent, the vice president–business affairs, and the professor in charge of atomic
energy projects.

Because the burden of item-by-item decision-making had grown enormously
with more and more faculty, new campuses to build and old ones to reorient, and,
by now, a huge research enterprise to administer, adjustments were necessary. The
result was the most extensive revision of administration in the history of the univer-
sity. The revised basic structure has held now for nearly forty years but with some
changes in both structure and operational conduct, as I note later (chapter 15).
This was act 4 in the history of the governance of the university (see chapter 4).

∎

George Strauss, professor of business administration and former director of the
Institute of Industrial Relations at Berkeley, was going through the back files of
the institute a few years ago and found the following correspondence. I had written President Sproul asking for a $6 reimbursement. I had landed at the Oak-
land airport after midnight at the end of a trip to Los Angeles on university
business. All public transportation had closed down, and I had a class to meet
early the next morning, so I took a taxi home. Some weeks later I received a letter from Sproul saying the request was reasonable, and he was approving it.

As the university grew, and particularly as it faced the oncoming tidal wave
of students, such attention to detail came closer and closer to impossibility

even for a person with the enormous energy and devotion to detail of Robert Gordon Sproul. Delays got longer and more burdensome. The system still kept a personal sense of touch and concern between the president and the entire faculty, but it was becoming less and less viable.

Favoring decentralization was, most importantly, the logic of the situation. The regents, overall, recognized this logic, including Sproul's best friends and most loyal supporters within the board. Campus heads and campus deans also, quite uniformly, were in support, as were many faculty members, although they were less directly involved. In totality, the support for a new system of governance was overpowering. Once there was a new president, the outcome was never in doubt.

At the center of the controversy was the issue of what is the "natural" unit of attachment in academic life. For students and alumni, it is the individual campus, as it is for attached professional groups such as medical doctors and agribusiness leaders and journalists. For most faculty members, it is first of all the department and their colleagues in the nationwide discipline outside the department, and then, but only then, the campus. For nonacademic staff members at the campus level, it is the campus, and many of them tend to be the most loyal of all. The universitywide system has no alumni, no students, no faculty, no sports teams, no one to cheer for it. To the extent that any individuals at all feel personally attached to it, they are the trustees and the systemwide officials and employees. Yet the system can be a unit of usefulness in protecting institutional autonomy from direct state control, in obtaining funds, and in assisting in their effective distribution and use.

Campus heads, by the nature of their positions, are basically entrepreneurs for their campuses. They may also have some, even great, attachment to the system out of prudence when they consider the alternatives, out of altruism toward its welfare, out of personal loyalty to its head, or out of expectations of preferment. Or again they may not. Chancellors, by the nature of their positions, are at least ambivalent about the system and the presidency or, at worst, opponents. The young and the new campuses and their chancellors are more likely to feel appreciation for the system than the old and the large. Also, longtime faculty members, in particular, may come to have a personal concern for the system's general welfare. And, in general, faculty members are more likely to have a professional concern for what is good and useful for the system than campus heads with their more competitive orientations—competitive with one another and with the system's presiding officer. The professional judgments of faculty members, I have concluded, are a better base for impartial views about what is good for the system than are the more particularistic concerns of campus heads. The University of California, historically, has been very fortunate in having so many faculty leaders devoted to the advancement of the university as well as to their own campus units within it. This has been one of our hidden but great sources of strength. It showed up most dramatically in contributions from faculty leaders of the older campuses to the startup of the three new campuses in the early 1960s, and in the solidarity of the universitywide senate leadership during the student troubles at Berkeley in the middle and late 1960s.

It was my conviction, both as chancellor and as president, that the campus was the basic loyalty unit; that "universitywide" was an essential superstructure in service to the campuses; that we needed "one university" but one university with a pluralistic system of governance; that the campuses should control item-by-item decision-making under general policy guidance unless there was a good reason to the contrary; that the chancellors should be the "executive heads" of their campuses as the Board of Regents had decided in 1951.

There then resulted the most basic administrative reorganization of the University of California in all of its history and, potentially, in all of its future. Decentralization of governance was necessary. It was inevitable.

And it was also, sometimes and in some ways, painful. Hansena Frederickson of UCLA, who saw so much of the history of UCLA as administrative assistant to provosts, campus administrative committees, and chancellors (1936 to 1968), gives her views (UCLA oral history):

> [Kerr] just wiped Sproul's staff completely out . . . as far as clerks and stenographers and secretaries and all that goes, they were just without a job. As far as Kerr was concerned, he couldn't care less, and so the Personnel Office had to find jobs for as many as they could, and fortunately, we eventually acquired Sproul's head file clerk here. . . . Fumi Iwata, and she's very bitter about the way Kerr just kicked her out of the job of file clerk. Of all the jobs, it seems to me he could have kept her on. So she finally left Berkeley and came down to Los Angeles. . . . But the fact is that Kerr was just not going to have any of Sproul's people continue with him at all.[2]

I know that is the way it looked to some observers who had participated in the old order, but it was not the way it really was. The fact is that I took only four people with me from the chancellor's office: my administrative assistant, my secretary, and two faculty members who served as part-time faculty assistants. All the rest of the remaining systemwide employees were from Sproul's staff. We were cutting the universitywide staff from 1,025 to 275, even as the university doubled its enrollment. We turned 750 positions over to the campuses. Every person was provided a position and all kept their rates of pay. Almost no one chose to leave the university—not more than 10 out of 750. There was no way to decentralize decision making without decentralizing the people who made the decisions, including the file clerks who worked with them. We did care and we did suffer for it—working with 750 people, a few of whom were "bitter" and sometimes with good reason because of the impacts on their lives. There was no alternative.

Why were a few so bitter? They had jobs. None had reductions in pay. It was, in large part, a matter of status. They had worked for the all-powerful president. They had been at the center of action. Now some found themselves out in the provinces. Often they had to work with a new set of colleagues, and sometimes too, as in Fumi Iwata's case, they had to move their homes.

Additionally, when we decentralized, we set forth rules to guide actions. Previously, operations were mostly based on past practice and personal judgments on behalf of, with review by, and in the name of the president. Employees were now more a part of a "bureaucracy," acting in the name of the rules. Even the 275 who remained in universitywide status were affected through what happened to their friends, and the size of the staffs over which they presided, so their sense of personal influence was reduced. It was painful and there were residues of this pain throughout the early years of my presidency. Also, I was a new person with new ways of administration and not a familiar figure with twenty-eight years of standing and established patterns of conducting business.

The biggest impact was on Jim Corley and his supporters. As vice president–business affairs, Corley reported directly to the Board of Regents. He also always remained close to leaders among the older Berkeley alumni, and his views affected their views of what was going on. This was one of his bases of power. The second base was the legislature in Sacramento, where he began representing the university in 1940. He never permitted me to have much contact. His third base was the universitywide staff. Many of its members reported to him. Harry Wellman notes in his oral history that "James H. Corley, vice president of business affairs, was really the chief campus officer of each of the campuses with respect to all business matters."[3]

Corley totally opposed decentralization on principle—he thought it threatened the concept of one university. He also wanted to preserve his own personal position of power.

Historical Background

The first major decentralization had come in 1891. The Board of Regents assigned to the acting president (Martin Kellogg) the authority to care for the university grounds and to appoint janitors, provided he reported on his actions at the next meeting of the board; both authorizations were transferred from the secretary of the board. The board was an administrative board. It met twelve times a year and its finance committee, with full power to act on behalf of the board, met an additional eleven times. With twenty-three meetings a year and control over great detail, the finance committee became a supercommittee within the board and the chair of that committee as important as, or more important than, the chair of the board. This arrangement continued up until my presidency. On my recommendation in 1958, the regents cut out the mid-monthly meetings of the finance committee and reduced the detail going to the board.

The second big breakthrough against board domination after that by President Kellogg took place when Benjamin Ide Wheeler became president in 1899. He insisted, as a condition of acceptance, that faculty members report to the board through him rather than by direct contact. Some of this direct contact continued, although on a diminishing scale, up until and through my presidency—for example, as director of the Radiation Laboratory at Berkeley Ernest Lawrence always reported directly to the Board of Regents.

The next big breakthrough came at the end of World War I when the board required that the president consult with the Academic Senate on faculty appointments and promotions and delegated some of its own power to the Academic Senate.

The first broad movement at the campus level for further decentralization began at UCLA in the early 1940s (see chapter 4). Because UCLA was 400 miles away from Berkeley, it took exception to the continuing aura of being the "Southern Branch." And southern California in general resented the political and cultural supremacy of San Francisco and northern California. Blue Shield, an organization of UCLA alumni leaders (and not the health insurance organization), issued a statement on May 4, 1943, which said in part that its members "implore the Regents . . . to appoint . . . [a] full-time executive head of the University of California at Los Angeles, and that he have full authority in matters exclusively affecting the University of California at Los Angeles . . . and that the Board of Regents itself undertake to find the man and make the appointment—to act independently of President Sproul."[4] The committee of the Academic Senate's southern section on administrative reorganization endorsed this initiative and added that the executive head of the campus should have "general powers" over the campus, including appointments of faculty, preparation of budget requests, appointment of department chairs, and supervision of the business office (during my chancellorship and presidency, each of these four "powers" was assigned to campus heads). As Regent Dickson observed with implied opposition, "this, of course, would leave the campus only one short step away from an entirely separate institution, subject only to the Board of Regents."[5]

The movement continued to gather strength. The provostship of Clarence Dykstra at UCLA (1945 to 1950) was especially significant. Dykstra had been a university president (Wisconsin) and was incensed at what he considered demeaning treatment of the provost by UC's universitywide administration. Dykstra was popular with alumni, faculty, and students at UCLA. His death on the job was a galvanizing event at UCLA and among the southern regents. Sproul delayed naming a replacement for Dykstra and worked through a committee of three UCLA campus deans for two years. (He ignored and effectively suppressed a Public Administrative Service of Chicago report, calling in 1948 for extensive decentralization.)[6]

The loyalty oath controversy of the late 1940s and early 1950s was not only weakening Sproul's position among the pro-oath regents who had come to be the majority but also cutting into what had been his solid faculty support. In any event, he agreed in 1951 to a proposal to appoint chancellors at UCLA and at Berkeley. Ray Allen and I, the original nominees for the chancellorships, misinterpreted what was happening. We thought that Sproul, in his vote in favor of establishing the chancellorships and his actions in nominating us, demonstrated a basic change in his position. We were wrong, as I noted earlier. The war over decentralization was to be continued by other means. The board proposed but the president disposed.

Action

By the time I was appointed president (October 1957), the situation was this: the chancellors and provosts had authority (nominal) over the campus business manager and authority (real) over the selection of department chairs. The chancellors had their place in the stream of recommendations on faculty appointments and promotions on the way to the president and the regents, and also on budgets. By default at the universitywide level, they could lead in making academic and physical plans for the campuses. They had achieved access to important sources of information, including copies of the campus budget and open-session minutes of the board, and had the right to attend meetings of the regents. The chancellors and provosts did not, however, administer the campuses as "executive heads," as the regents had said they should.

Once I was appointed president, I immediately initiated action. At the December 1957 meeting of the board there was established, on my recommendation, a committee on administrative reorganization with the four most influential regents as members: Ed Pauley as chair, Ed Carter, Don McLaughlin, and Jesse Steinhart. Three of them were past, present, or future chairs of the board. President Sproul was also a member of the committee. He came to all meetings but took no active part. He must have suffered internally as he sat there silent and, I am sure, sad, witnessing the destruction of his system of governance. I too was a member. Regent Carter was the participant most experienced with large-scale organizations and was extremely helpful. The committee met frequently. All the recommendations it made were unanimous. All its proposals to the board were accepted unanimously. (On January 23, 1959, the basic vote to change the by-laws and standing orders was 23 to 0.)

The first action of the committee was to employ the management consultant firm of Cresap, McCormick and Paget, which, like any competent and well-paid advisory group, did exactly as it was told to do in terms of general policy. Additionally, it translated our general instructions into detailed plans in a very helpful way. The chancellors accepted the process without putting on any pressure. I had been a chancellor in favor of decentralization, and they now seemed to rely on my experience and judgment.

The essential process took about one year (1958), and here is what it accomplished.

THE PRESIDENCY

Decentralization strengthened the president's position in several ways. The vice president–business affairs now reported only to the president instead of also directly to the board. The position of vice president–finance replaced that of controller, and its occupant too reported only to the president. The closing of the Committee on Southern Schools, Colleges, and Institutions blocked a formal channel for UCLA campus administrative officers and faculty members since 1920 to go directly to board members around the president. It did not end informal contacts, however. This action, incidentally, was an unspoken vote of confidence by the southern regents that I would treat UCLA fairly. And in abandoning the finance committee's eleven meetings a year between board meetings, the regents were relying on the president to handle more of the details of management with less constant supervision. The position of vice president of the university, vacant for many years, was filled in July 1958 so that the president had assistance across the board and not just in specialized areas, and so that decisions could be made promptly whenever the president was traveling outside the state.

THE CHANCELLORSHIP

Decentralization enormously strengthened the chancellorship: it assigned most members of the former administrative staff of the president (750 out of 1,025) to the campus level, with all the enormous volume of decisions in which they had been engaged. The largest numerical transfers of personnel were in accounting, purchasing, admissions, architects and engineers, and the nonacademic personnel office. The most important transfers, from my point of view, were of business affairs personnel including grounds and buildings and architects and engineers, public relations staff, public ceremonies, the police force, and intercollegiate athletics. Each campus soon acquired a chancellor, not only Berkeley and Los Angeles. Each chancellor's office had its own public affairs officer. The campus business officers reported to the chancellor de facto as well as de jure, as did the deans of students. Each chancellor had the use of a "university house" in which to live and entertain (and thus there was no longer a President's House at Berkeley). The chancellors had full access to all information. The local alumni associations worked directly with the chancellors. Also, in those areas where reference to the president was still necessary, decisions came promptly. Chancellors no longer had to beg for action. And chancellors were expected, even required, to prepare academic, physical, and fiscal plans—not just seize such opportunities on their own if they so wished, as I had at Berkeley.

FACULTY GOVERNANCE

Decentralization made the Academic Senate more effective. Its alignment since 1933 into a northern and a southern section had been the source of two problems. One was the size of Berkeley and UCLA: they dominated their respective sections at the senate meetings (held on their campuses) and essentially disenfranchised faculty members on other campuses. The second problem came when the two sections did not agree or did not take action at the same time on the same issues, or both. As a faculty member during the loyalty oath controversy, I had observed this disjunction and thought it undercut the faculty's effectiveness in academic governance. In 1963, a universitywide senate governance mechanism replaced the northern and southern sections. Each campus also obtained its own graduate division with its own dean, instead of two divisions, north and south, with the two deans reporting to the president, and similarly with senate oversight by graduate councils at the campus level.[7]

The new alignment was to have a division of the Academic Senate on each campus with its own officers—no longer dependent on the president's availability to chair its meetings. The new alignment also called for a universitywide elected Academic Assembly, a smaller Academic Council of senate leaders, and a series of universitywide senate committees as on educational policy, academic personnel, and faculty welfare. The faculty as a whole could now speak more clearly and more promptly. Also, for the first time in University of California history, I got the agreement of the regents to invite senate leaders (specifically the chair and vice chair of the Academic Council) to attend their meetings, with the right to participate in regents' discussions but not to vote. The Academic Senate had been asking for this since 1919, as it had also for selection of its own presiding officers. These early actions of my presidency thus completed the 1919 agenda of the Berkeley faculty "revolution." Taken together, its 1920 and 1960 achievements were significant, but as a "revolution" it was, in reality, a mildly stated series of requests with welcoming responses by the regents.

BOARD OF REGENTS

Decentralization also made the Board of Regents more effective. By delegating most of its detailed decision-making to the president (and the president to the campuses) for the first time in its history, it could turn its time and attention more to policy making and performance review than to administration. Only the president, the secretary, the treasurer, and the general counsel reported to it directly.

A basic aspect of reorganization was a total change in the nature of the budget. It had been a line-item budget of enormous length and totally incomprehensible. We turned the budget into a short analytical budget that could easily be comprehended. It became a policy budget, not an accounting budget, and was part of the process of the board becoming a policy board.

Another change affected the board's chair. Past practice was for a chair to serve consecutive terms, as, for example, William Crocker (1926–37), James K. Moffitt (1942–48), and, in particular, Edward Dickson (1948–56) had. This practice had at least two consequences. One was that the chair tended to become very dominant within the board. The other was that the chair was in a position to act as though he were CEO, as Pauley thought he should be able to do when he served as chair. I arranged that the old practice be stopped. This resulted in Pauley serving for one term as chair (1956–58) and then being replaced by McLaughlin (1958–60). Pauley did serve a second term as chair, 1960–62, but not again. He was furious. My serious problems in relating to him, which led to his leadership of those regents seeking my dismissal in 1967, really began with this development. I once asked McLaughlin why Pauley was giving me so much trouble, and he answered: "POWER." And he was right. Pauley would have liked to be permanent chair. He later asserted a second reason for his authority and that was that he was the "senior" regent with a veto power, as in the case of the honorary degree for Edward Chace Tolman (see chapter 9). Again I denied his claim. It was better for the Board of Regents to have a circulation of chairs and no special privileges for a "senior" regent, but it was a disaster in my relations with Pauley. I had raised the issue of his power, and it came to stand between us.

When the special committee on reorganization went out of existence on June 10, 1960, its policies had fundamentally reshaped the university. In fact by that time the committee had turned into an unauthorized "executive committee" that I consulted on all important matters. The detailed implementation of the decentralization policies, however, continued over the next several years, but the basic decisions occurred in 1957 and 1958.

Some observers passed off the process of decentralization as just a reshuffling of staff positions, but the people who held these positions took many actions and participated in making many decisions. This most basic reorganization in the history of the university—with some important supplements in later years—attracted none of the fuss and fury that accompanied its next stage.

Consultation

Another important development beyond decentralization was a more pluralistic decision-making process. No system of decision-making groups had existed within the administration. One general purpose advisory group had met only occasionally: a large President's Administrative Advisory Conference with about thirty members drawn from the Academic Senate, campus heads, and universitywide officers. The president presided and listened to formal presentations and informal reactions. He listened. He did not engage in debate. Later on, he might or might not take action—we never knew at the end of a meeting with President Sproul what, if anything, might happen. Beyond that, any joint meetings in the absence of the president were considered acts of insurrection. Once I initiated a meeting of campus heads at the Faculty Club at Berkeley (1955) to talk about coordinating campus plans to honor the twenty-fifth anniversary of Bob Sproul's presidency. George Pettitt, assistant to the president, somehow heard about it, and he burst into our luncheon and demanded to know who had authorized us to meet. He made it clear that we should never do so again, regardless of the subject, without the permission and the participation of the president or his representative, and we never did meet again.

There was even some suspicion of faculty clubs. Some regents believed that the loyalty oath controversy was a product of the Berkeley Faculty Club. When I became president, I discussed the subject of faculty clubs informally with the regents and got them to agree that such clubs could be an affirmative presence on each campus. The view had been that it was better to keep campus heads and faculty members from associating with one another, however informally.[8]

I set up the following consultative groups and met with them regularly:

An advisory council of chancellors met once each month before regents' meetings (the first meeting was August 1958).

A cabinet of universitywide officers (including vice presidents and the three officers of the regents: the secretary, the treasurer, the general counsel) met similarly.

A council of ASUC presidents met about four times a year.

In addition, I encouraged periodic meetings of deans of students, deans of letters and science, deans of graduate divisions, librarians, and others to discuss areas of mutual concern among the campuses.

The Academic Senate was now better organized to participate in consultation, and I established the position of vice president–academic affairs in large part to consult regularly with the Academic Assembly, the Academic Council, and the universitywide senate committees. I continued the Cal Club of campus student leaders (which met twice a year) as well as the annual all-university faculty conference, both of which had been initiated by President Sproul.

The purpose of all this consultation was to share information, elicit suggestions, agree upon decisions, and get acquainted. There were face-to-face negotiations and a certain amount of conciliation to achieve consensus or at least consent. We followed the same process with the Board of Regents: bringing problems to the board's attention as soon as we identified them; supplying members with information and asking for their reactions as we began to make policy. Only at the very end of this consultative process would a formal recommendation go to the board. Solutions evolved. I also made a practice of giving the regents the bad news and not just the good news.

As an illustration of how this practice of advance consultation before final action gave the board a sense of ownership of decisions, consider the following case. The Board of Regents began discussions of the university budget on a monthly basis starting in March, and it came up for final action in October. In October 1960 there was a relatively new regent, Norton Simon. Norton was a very successful investor in many endeavors. He had a practice, I later found out, of taking over leadership of boards he joined by first attacking management.[9] He attacked my proposed budget in an area of personal interest to him, UCLA Extension, and he had been well briefed in advance. He probably expected that as president I would not know the details of the budget on one campus in such a peripheral area as the extension program. But I did. Simon sat across from me at the table (a sign of possible trouble) and fired at me details of the budget that he disputed. I replied without calling on staff assistance. This went on for quite some time, and the Board of Regents became restive. Finally, Regent Pauley said that he moved the budget in its entirety to seconds all around the table, and so the total budget passed with no further discussion.

That evening, at the usual regents' reception at Davis, I went up to Norton and said that I considered our debate to have been over a single issue and that

I looked forward to working with him for the welfare of the university. He grunted and walked away. However, at the next meeting of the regents, he came up to me and said he had thought about the events of the prior meeting and wanted to say that he was my friend, and he remained so ever after. Had I retreated under his attack or been ill informed, he would have pursued me repeatedly as he had management in many other enterprises. What Simon had not fully realized was that the budget had been under discussion since March and that the regents were already defensive of it as their own creation.

Consequences

In the change from a largely unitary to a largely pluralistic approach to administration, more decentralization of decision-making had occurred as a result of the basic decisions of 1957–59 than in the prior ninety years. The regents supported it unanimously, and the chancellors did too (Franklin Murphy, a strong advocate of further decentralization, had not yet been recruited to UCLA). The chancellorship at the campus level was now the central locus of administration, and chancellors were fuller participants in the making of policy. Each chancellor now had far greater authority than Ray Allen and I ever asked for beginning in 1952 or dreamed was possible. The administrative staff reporting to the chancellor at UCLA had gone from 38 in December 1958 to 277 in October 1963. It was a far cry from the days when the president had to approve a charge of taxi fare from the Oakland airport to Berkeley.

END OF THE CORLEY EMPIRE

In January 1959, on my initiative, Jim Corley became vice president–governmental relations, no longer business affairs. The new vice president–business, Elmo Morgan, had major responsibility for the physical development of the three new campuses and the enormous building programs throughout the university, and he was excellent. He fully accepted the chancellor's control of business affairs on each campus. Even earlier, I had transferred the university press from Corley to Wellman, vice president of the university. Before that time, both the press and the printing department had reported to Corley, resulting in years of controversy between Corley and the university press. As a result of the new assignments, the printing department was responsible to Morgan and the press to Wellman, and there was far less friction.[10]

In addition, Corley no longer reported officially directly to the regents, although, in practice, he made all his reports on Sacramento relations directly to the board and never to me. At the urging of the governor and lieutenant governor, I appointed Frank Kidner of the economics department at Berkeley as our representative in Sacramento under Corley. Brown and Lieutenant Governor Anderson urged the change, saying Corley's relations continued to be closer with conservative Republicans than with the more liberal Democratic leaders of both houses of the legislature, and that this was not helpful to the university. Corley had been instrumental both in introducing the 1949 loyalty oath for faculty members and in arranging the 1952 "contact man" assignment for chancellors with the state Senate Un-American Activities Committee—both of which the most reactionary members of the legislature favored (and I opposed).

The regents and I also wanted Corley to spend more time in Washington, D.C., because of our huge involvement with federal research grants and, particularly at that time, to try to get for the University of California a new atomic research system that had been planned at Berkeley (later, on political grounds, it was given to a midwest consortium). This project was of particular interest to Regent Pauley and the board's other proponents of atomic energy projects. I discussed this change of assignments with Corley and with the regents, and thought I had all-around agreement. However, Corley subsequently responded by resigning to the regents (July 1964) effective July 27, 1965. He may have seen his power base in Sacramento diminishing and he may have sensed likely failure on the big project assignment in Washington, subjecting him to criticism from Pauley and other regents. In any event, he resigned directly to the Board of Regents with no advance warning to me. Ironically, Corley spent his last year as "special assistant to the president" with no assignments from me but with full salary. Corley had been connected with the university for fifty-two years as student, staff member, comptroller, and vice president.

THE DETAIL OF DECENTRALIZATION

The great burden of actual detailed decentralization fell on the universitywide staff. Its members had the monumental and essential task of turning informal past practices into new policies known to all on the many matters decentralized to the campuses. This process involved translating past practice—set forth in item-by-item presidential and regental decisions—into open policies to guide campus actions. This, in turn, required endless consultations with campus authorities and much drafting and redrafting of policies. The heavy burden of this process was carried by Loren Furtado, Eugene Lee, Jack Oswald, and Virginia Smith at the universitywide level with great patience and good judgment. Gene Lee was the central person involved in reorganization efforts, both in my office as chancellor and in the universitywide administration under my presidency, particularly with the 1965 reorganization. Beyond that he participated in the original 1948 report and has been consulted by later presidents in all the years since 1966. He is the one great authority on the governance of the University of California.

The end result was not only decentralization of governance but also governance by law, not by personal decree. The big gain was the more effective functioning of the university. I know of no one who now favors a return to the old system prior to 1958. It is unthinkable.

A Second Look
at Decentralization (1965)
and a Failed Proposal

By early 1960 we had gotten rid of all the problems of campus and university-wide structures and decision making that once bothered me as chancellor. The chancellors were, in fact, the executive heads of their campuses. The central administration (or "Berkeley," as the other campuses referred to it) made few decisions on its own. Its almost sole function was to prepare materials for action by the Board of Regents, including recommendations. The president had, and exercised, great influence but kept almost no final item-by-item authority over the campuses. Thus, I thought, the governance issue was settled for all time: the president had voluntarily surrendered all of his power except to administer his own staff and advise the Board of Regents; the regents had given their unanimous support.

How wrong I was. What I came to realize only slowly was that to some chancellors use of the tools of authority meant use of all of its symbols as well; that nearly all chancellors would welcome both in their entirety; and that in micro-battles over power—which are everywhere and all the time—there is never a final solution.

Following on the reorganization of 1957–59, two areas came into dispute during the 1960s. They were of greatest concern to Chancellors Franklin Murphy at UCLA and John S. Galbraith at San Diego and became entangled in more controversy than the administrative reorganization itself, within a broader disagreement over whether there should be one federated university or nine independent universities in a confederation. The first specific issue was what items should flow to the Board of Regents for decision. The second involved use of the symbols of authority.

Actions by the Regents

By 1965 a substantial number of items still went to the regents each month for their action. They fell mainly into the three categories of applications for federal grants and contracts, the transfer of budgeted funds from one purpose to another, and faculty appointments and promotions at the tenure level. On their way to the board, proposals on academic personnel went to the president's office for review, grants and contracts to the secretary of the regents, and budget transfers to the vice president–finance. Their processing proceeded on the assumption of the regents' approving (as they always did) the president's recommendations. Consequently, there was only moderate delay, usually fourteen days or fewer, before formal confirmation by the board. Occasionally, campus proposals were challenged by requests for more information, and even more infrequently they were not supported.

All these actions were routine at the regents' level. And they were routine at the presidential level except for promotions and appointments to tenure, which I reviewed as had President Sproul before me. Actually, the preliminary detailed review was by Vice President Harry Wellman. I never even glanced at the grants and contracts or the budget transfers.

The processing of administrative recommendations through the board did have some positive effects. The board kept up with significant aspects of the university's operations. Particularly, I took the occasion of academic personnel promotions and appointments to call the board's attention to the accomplishments of the faculty members involved, and they were impressive. This helped build a regental pride in the faculty and emphasized the importance of a high-quality faculty in the life of the university. Given the history of lack of continuous tenure at the time of the loyalty oath controversy, I also felt tenure was more secure if the regents—not just the campus administration—conferred it case by case. Additionally, this review gave Wellman and me a chance to monitor campus actions. I had questions about judgments on tenure at two campuses: Riverside then proceeded too much on a lock-step seniority basis in promotions, and occasionally at first Santa Barbara seemed not to recognize what was expected of a person appointed to the faculty of the University of California. A further consideration was that the regents' approval meant that tenure was within the university and not solely at the campus. I had been involved in the discontinuance of three academic units, Home Economics at Berkeley, Industrial Arts at Santa Barbara, and Agriculture at UCLA.

In each case it was helpful to be able to find positions for persons within the university and not just at the campus affected—always by mutual agreement. Were such closure actions ever to be taken again, an effective use of faculty resources would be easier to arrange within the totality of the university and might even be impossible at the campus level alone. In any event, it was long established that these items went to the regents, and there were only minor costs and some advantages. Neither the regents nor I had or would have made a change on our own initiative.

A change was made, however, and for three related reasons. One was that I was concerned with how well the process of reorganization was working and had begun a survey of the chancellors to get their opinions of how it was going at the campus level and their views of the cooperation they were receiving at the universitywide level. We got many comments. I brought Eugene Lee back as vice president–executive assistant to lead this process as of February 1965.

The second reason was that Franklin Murphy strongly opposed any flow of decisions beyond his level of authority. He challenged all authority except his own. Murphy several times proposed that all items from UCLA go directly from his office to the Board of Regents, through the president's office but without universitywide review, as they had at the University of Kansas whence he came. I pointed out that this would turn the president's office into a "post office box." Presidential influence would, like presidential authority, be a cipher. Chancellor Murphy finally dropped the idea. His centripetal approach to power was like Robert Gordon Sproul's, except that the center for all concentration of authority was the chancellorship instead of the presidency.

The third reason was that we had to contend with the Byrne report.[1] The Byrne report came about as follows. During the course of the Free Speech Movement (FSM) in the fall of 1964, the regents set up a committee chaired by Regent William Forbes (December 1964) to probe into the controversy. The committee picked a Los Angeles attorney, Jerome Byrne, to assess the situation and make a report. For reasons unknown to me, in May 1965 Byrne submitted the report first to the press and only then to the regents. His report added urgency to our survey that was already under way.

The Byrne report complained that "the Regents have not in fact chosen to delegate most of their enormous powers." Instead of "being the government," the regents should be "providing for government." The report proposed that the positions of president and of chair of the Board of Regents be "merged

209 · A Second Look at Decentralization

into one." In effect, there would be a chair and no president. The merged position would have the power "now vested in the chairman," which was solely the power to preside.

This was the Kansas system—six institutions individually reporting directly to the board. Byrne's report went on to propose a division of the University of California into a series of "separately chartered" universities "as autonomous members of a university commonwealth" under chancellors "with complete responsibility for leadership and management of the university under his jurisdiction." (Again as in Kansas.) In the political arena the report was generally sympathetic to the FSM's point of view: student governments should be free to "take and announce positions on issues of importance to the membership, within or without the university." This idea contradicted the existing and continuing policies of the university that student governments with compulsory memberships and dues could not take positions on political issues external to the university. The university would not force students to belong to, and financially support, political action associations.

In gathering material for his report, Jerome Byrne never talked with me. Hansena Frederickson said, "And you've asked me if Dr. Murphy talked freely with Jerry Byrne. Well, he did."[2] Murphy also talked freely elsewhere about a confederation of universities replacing the University of California. Harry Wellman, in his oral history, said, "My impression is that Byrne got many of his ideas from Chancellor Murphy." He added, "I heard Chancellor Murphy talk about a commonwealth of campuses and about the president becoming chairman of the board."[3] Arthur Coons (president of Occidental College and chair of the master plan study committee) wrote about how he "heard one University campus Chancellor declare himself in the presence of many persons . . . that there should be nine universities rather than one."[4] Coons strongly disagreed. "There cannot be many presidents, only one; nor many Boards of Regents, only one."[5]

The Forbes committee, in effect, disowned the Byrne report and made it clear that it was not a report endorsed in whole or in part by the committee. Regent Philip Boyd, a member of the committee, gave an account of the history of the Forbes committee and the Byrne report at the regents' meeting in May 1965:

During this five months the Committee has never reached an agreement with Jerome Byrne as to his employment status. He refused to submit to direction or control and insisted that he was an independent contractor. Our disagreement on this subject continued throughout the past several months. . . .

The Committee is yet to receive its first statement of background information, its first page of research data, its first knowledge of how and where our Special Counsel and staff researched for opinions which supported his recommendations. We have no findings or evaluations, only recommendations. . . .

On May 11, our Committee met briefly at the Statler-Hilton Hotel with Jerry Byrne in attendance and taking active part in debate on our motions. This brief luncheon meeting was followed by a widely advertised press conference which was not approved by the Committee. . . .

These conditions do not justify the continuation of this Special Committee which would terminate on June 30, allowing too brief a period for thorough consideration of the charge which was our responsibility. . . . [6]

The minutes then note that the Board of Regents voted on a motion to end the work of the committee. "It was carried, and the Special Forbes Committee was discharged."

To my knowledge, no faculty group, or even any faculty member, came out openly in support of the Byrne report, except for two committee reports at Berkeley: the Jack Kent committee of October 1965 (chapter 24), and, much later in 1968, the Caleb Foote report.[7] Neither committee report found support at higher levels of the Academic Senate. Both quickly lapsed into oblivion.

The board received the Byrne report but never discussed it on its merits. No single regent spoke in support. Murphy too made no public comment. He preferred to work the phones, the halls, and the social gatherings in advance rather than engage in direct confrontations, particularly over lost causes. The only discussion by the board was of the claim for payment to Byrne, particularly for expensive wines—eventually approved. One regent, Don McLaughlin, voted against any payment at all.

During that May 1965 meeting I told the board I was planning to "formulate more specific plans" for delegation of board authority to the chancellors. The chair, Ed Carter, said to me as we sat side by side at the head of the table at the meeting in Riverside, "You make a proposal and the Board will approve it unanimously." Anticipating his comment, I had already prepared for the board a "preliminary" report on what might be done. It started out by saying "there will continue to be one University of California as provided in the Con-

211 · A Second Look at Decentralization

stitution of the State of California" and that "the Board of Regents will retain its historic position as the final governing authority of the University." My May 20, 1965, report, in effect, rejected two items of the Byrne report. It then suggested further delegation to the chancellors (through the president) of the board's authority in the areas of academic personnel, nonacademic personnel, construction, grants and contracts, and budget transfers.

Subsequently (December 1965) I did make a specific proposal to decentralize a series of actions to the campuses, and it passed unanimously and without discussion (as Regent Carter had said it would). This proposal was in response to our already ongoing review of reorganization, to the Byrne report, and to the urgings of the UCLA chancellor and several highly respected faculty members there concerning the chancellor's authority to make faculty tenure decisions. The one public reservation I had—and with which the regents agreed— was about one aspect of academic personnel actions, appointments and promotions to overscale salary status: in the absence of approval by the regents, one (San Diego) or more campuses might wish to out-compete other campuses. I had unstated reservations about removing the regents entirely from the process of approving appointments and promotions to tenure—the most important series of actions a university ever takes. To this day I regret that I did not ask for more detailed consideration of this basic change in university policy, but I did not: an annual presidential post-review of the quality of actions at the campus level and, perhaps, monthly reports would have kept the regents informed about the chancellors' actions and the quality of the faculty being developed. Actually, in practice, the campuses made better decisions than I had feared. But the change isolated the regents from this essential aspect of university life. Regent McLaughlin voted against the total cutoff.

No universitywide personnel were replaced or reassigned as the result of these actions to decentralize regental authority, although the processing requirements in the office of the secretary of the regents and of certain vice presidents were reduced. Through Vice President Wellman and later Vice President Angus Taylor, the president's office continued a low-key post-audit of faculty appointments and promotions as a check on quality and on the level of approved salaries. Generally, the campuses, which meant mostly the budget (academic personnel) committees of the Academic Senates, performed well. An occasional word of caution was given to a few chancellors and committees.

The Forbes committee disbanded. The Byrne report faded away. What I thought of as "Murphy's rebellion" had been put down. Murphy's attempt to

TABLE 17

Percentage Distribution of Full-Time Positions in General Administration, Student Services, and Institutional Services

	Universitywide	Campus-Level	Percentage-Point Gain (at campus level)
As of December 1957	46	54[a]	—
After 1958–59 reorganization	11	89	35
1965	9	91	2[b]

Source: University of California, Office of the President, "Growth and Distinction: The University of California 1958–1966," n.p.

[a]*Most changes were purely nominal.*
[b]*Changes were part of ongoing reorganization and not a result of 1965 decisions.*

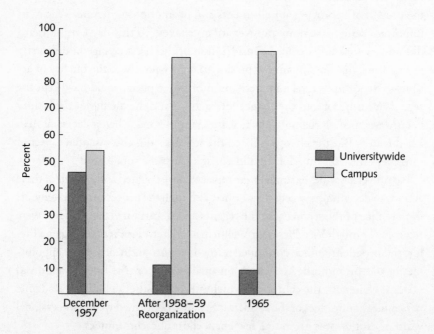

FIGURE 4. Percentage Distribution of Full-Time Positions in General Administration, Student Services, and Institutional Services.

TABLE 18
Percentage of Actions Subject to Chancellor's Final Approval

	Faculty Personnel Actions	Approval of Research Grants and Contracts	Budget Transfers
As of December 1957	2	0	0
After 1958–59 reorganization	75[a] (73)	80[b] (80)[c]	80 (80)
After 1965 reorganization	99 (24)	98 (18)	98 (18)

Source: University of California, Office of the President, "Growth and Distinction: The University of California 1958–1966," n.p.; University of California Office of the President, "Development and Decentralization: The Administration of the University of California, 1958–1966" (Berkeley, 1966), 5, 7; and "Progress Report: Administrative Reorganization of the University," University Bulletin 10, no. 37 (May 7, 1962): 197.

[a]*As of 1964.*
[b]*As of 1961.*
[c]*Figures in parentheses show percentage point gains.*

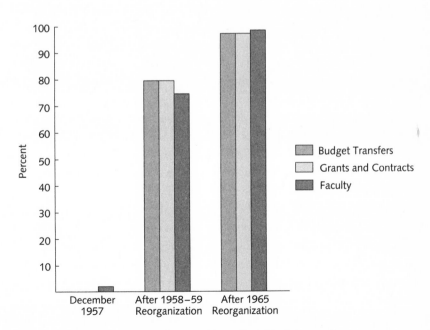

FIGURE 5. Percent of Actions Subject to Chancellor's Final Approval.

turn the federation of the University of California into a confederation of nine independent campuses had failed.

In the above discussion, I have paid considerable attention to the Byrne report because efforts to move toward confederation tend to recur within a federation approach to university governance. (See Tables 17 and 18 and Figures 4 and 5 for a summary of the relocation of authority.)

Regal Functions

Leadership in major university public events is what I call the "royalty" or "regal functions." Franklin Murphy referred to them as the "symbolic functions." Sproul performed them all and did so superbly. He had the booming voice and a great sense of presence. He also had energy and endurance: fall receptions for new students and faculty on each campus, Charter Day convocations and alumni banquets, commencements and the granting of all degrees, meetings of the southern and northern sections of the Academic Senate, meetings of citizens' associations as at Santa Barbara and Riverside and Picnic Day at Davis, university meetings at Berkeley and occasionally on other campuses, and the presentation of all-university athletic awards at the annual football game between Berkeley and UCLA. A career all by itself!

It served a purpose. The president became a familiar figure—a personality to large portions of the university community. He was a reminder that there was one university of several campuses with common interests. These occasions created opportunities rhetorically to present the university in historical perspective and to burnish the cherished ideals. More informally, the president had an opportunity to meet and converse with many people and to observe the quality of campus life, to hear concerns of participants, and to observe the performance of the campus head. These contacts also enhanced the flow of paperwork and of decision making, increasing the sense of dealing with a personality rather than just a faceless bureaucracy.

But as my presidency evolved there were nine campuses—not six—and each was much larger and more complex than formerly. Each now had a chancellor in charge, not a provost or committee or no one at all except the president (as at Berkeley for five years—1947–52); and the regents had provided that the chancellors at Berkeley and UCLA should preside at campus public events. I continued two or three public appearances on each campus each year, and on each occasion shared participation with the chancellor. This arrangement seemed to be acceptable (even welcomed) on all campuses—except at UCLA after Murphy became chancellor.

The first problem came at Murphy's first commencement as chancellor. Franklin and I headed the academic procession. We each had been handed our cue books. I had taken the opportunity to glance at mine during the robing ceremony. Franklin began reading his as the procession moved along. All of a sudden he jumped in front of me. The whole procession came to a halt. He said, "You are not going to confer degrees on my campus to my students." I said, "I noticed that, but the cue book was prepared in your office." He said, "You can give the honorary degrees," and I replied, "That's fine." The procession moved forward.

An account of another academic procession episode comes from Wellman's oral history:

> When President Eisenhower spoke on the UCLA Campus (Charter Day, 1963), the academic procession was headed by a triumvir: President Kerr on the left, Chancellor Murphy on the right and President Eisenhower in the middle. This was the first, and as far as I know, the last time that a chancellor of a UC campus assumed that his rank was equal to that of the president of the university.[8]

What happened was this: as the academic procession started its march, Murphy jumped forward from row two into row one. President Eisenhower was chatting with me and Murphy moved slightly in front of Eisenhower and tried to get his attention, but Eisenhower just kept on talking to me and paid no attention. It was embarrassing because the other person in row two, who was to be the recipient of an honorary degree, was left to march all by himself. I made no comment to Murphy then or later. I understood the sense of compulsion that impelled him forward. On our farm when I was a boy, we had a horse with the same kind of personality. Brownie had been a racehorse at county fairs early in his life and then became a riding horse for a wealthy person who lived in the nearby county seat. The horse was boarded with us and even abandoned to us when the owner went bankrupt during the Great Depression. He then became one of our farm horses. But Brownie still needed to keep his head out in front of the other member of the team as a racehorse should in order to win. But this meant that he pulled more than his share of the load—commendable but suicidal—working against a much heavier draft horse. So I lengthened the chains in his harness: he could appear to be the leader while the swingletree behind the two horses stayed even (and they were pulling equally).

On several occasions, Franklin proposed to me that I be allowed on the UCLA campus only after I made a formal request to him and secured his consent. I said that it would be rather strange if only one person in all of California was not allowed on a University of California campus except with the personal permission of the chancellor—and that person was the president of the university—but if he made a written request, I would take the issue up with the regents. That was the end of that proposal.

Franklin's general position was quite understandable, and it did not take me by surprise (though some of its details did). As noted above, he had been president of a university reporting directly to the trustees, and the campus was "separately chartered." The Academic Senate of the University of California also bothered Franklin; Kansas did not have a strong academic senate. He found it hard to adapt. During the course of his first year, the chair of the senate at UCLA (Earl Griggs) told me that Franklin faced a possible vote of no confidence if he did not accept the senate. I cautioned Franklin about the situation and, realist that he was, he adapted his behavior—but did not change his basic views. On several occasions, at meetings of the council of chancellors, he attacked the senate. He said that he had talked to enough regents to know that if I were to propose to the board a curtailment of senate powers the board would agree. Finally I said to Franklin that, if he would tell his senate what he had just told us, I would give him a chance to argue his case before the Board of Regents, but he should know, in advance, that I would speak in opposition, that I considered the senate one of the greatest strengths of the university. That too was the end of that.

Franklin had been not only a university president but a dean of medicine (also at Kansas). Deans of medicine, above all other deans, have traditionally had the greatest independent authority reflecting the status of their profession and the complexities of medical schools. And he was, by nature, admittedly combative. Frederickson says, "Everytime something was frustrated that [Murphy] was aiming for, he would call up one of the Regents, and he would *shout* over the phone at them."[9] He, however, made something of an exception of me. Frederickson notes, "But he doesn't yell at Dr. Kerr. He uses friendly persuasion for him. He does pick up the phone and call him and get to him." She goes on to say, "And Dr. Murphy can get to Dr. Kerr, and get a point over to him now, and he will endeavor to do a lot of the things that in the beginning he couldn't get done. . . . The relationship between the Los Angeles campus and Berkeley statewide is the best it's ever been in the history of the University, as far as I'm concerned."[10] I concur in full! And Frederickson was in the best position to know.

I admired Franklin greatly. He was just perfect for UCLA at that time and for the Los Angeles community. And we never disagreed over any academic policy. Yet I should have given more prior thought to Murphy's experiences at Kansas, and particularly to his direct reporting to the Kansas board.

In the end Murphy declared peace, saying he had "largely won."[11] What he referred to was further and extended progress in directions already undertaken. (For a general review of reorganization 1958–66, see Appendix 2 section C and, for my basic views on administrative reorganization, section D.)

In retrospect, I wish the 1965 decentralization had come more easily and earlier. What we did too late was inevitable and desirable, and Franklin was right: more detailed decisions could be transferred from the regents to the chancellors, and more regal functions could be transferred by the president to the chancellors.

The controversies of 1965 were partly a commentary on the slow and complicated progress of decentralization within the decision-making processes of the University of California. But they were also a commentary on Murphy's approach to decision making. His inclinations toward instant results, plus the southern-branch syndrome of UCLA alumni leaders and many faculty, was a powerful combination. Murphy favored full control and, to his great credit, always took full responsibility at his level of authority. Before his arrival at the University of California, his clashes with other authorities, particularly Governor Docking in Kansas, had been spectacular and bitter, and Murphy left Kansas as a result.[12] After he left the University of California, his controversies at the *Los Angeles Times* with Dorothy Chandler, whose family owned the newspaper, were also publicly known. Buff said, "He couldn't wait to get me out of there." The magazine story from which this quote is taken goes on to say, "And he did." Chandler noted, "He was very jealous of me." She added, "He should have been in politics," and she did not think well of politicians.[13] Murphy's controversies with me ended in a more friendly way than those with Docking and Chandler: the process of decentralization in 1965 came to completion, he said, "with Clark Kerr's full support."[14]

In July 1966 the *Los Angeles Times* reported: "In the past Dr. Murphy frequently has compared the University of California to a dinosaur, with a central nervous system unable to cope with its anatomical growth. However, in a recent interview he said, 'What we are seeing now is a splendid and successful attempt to match the nervous system to the body.'" The *Times* gave Murphy's view of the controversy over decentralization: "Everybody comes at this from a different vantage point. Clark Kerr had a terrible problem carving out the chancellor's job at Berkeley. He had lots of responsibility but very little authority. When he became president he was determined that this would change, and, from his point of view, a lot of things were decentralized. But I came in later and didn't know this history. I saw a lot of things that were still centralized that should not be, so I complained. A chancellor who comes into the system now sees still other areas where he thinks he should have more say."[15]

A comparatively happy ending. Murphy declared victory. The headline above this *Los Angeles Times* story was, "UCLA Autonomy Fight Believed Won." But the University of California system did not adopt the Kansas model.

Murphy concluded by saying, "This university system has done something no other university system has ever attempted. It has created new universities (Irvine, Santa Cruz and San Diego), expanded three others (Davis, Riverside and Santa Barbara) and has kept Berkeley and UCLA growing. That is a remarkable achievement."[16]

■

The intervening thirty-five years have made only moderate formal changes in the reorganized University of California system. It is generally considered to be one of the most successful systems in the nation, and other states have used it as a model. Nationwide, campuses within systems now include 80 percent of students in public higher education. The University of California pioneered in developing a system that was operationally effective: one university with pluralistic decision-making. A good test of the one-university system is whether there is a united approach to the legislature and governor in Sacramento. There was during my presidency and there still is. And this crucial policy is accepted by all chancellors and by all divisions of the Academic Senate.

Reconsiderations

In 1965, when the University of California finished the massive reorganization of its governance, it had become a federation of campuses, under a single board and president, instead of a consolidated nation state. As chancellor and president, my major contributions to the governance of the University of California were to help move it from a unitary administrative unit to a decentralized federated one and to resist its disintegration into a confederation.

The reorganization took place in three successive developments: 1951–58— creation of chancellorships at UCLA and Berkeley, and relatively small and reluctant delegations of authority to them (chapters 3 and 4); 1957–59—decentralization of most staff and decision-making from the president to the chancellors (chapter 13); 1965–66—substantial further decentralization of regental decision-making to chancellors, through the president, over grants and contracts, budget transactions, and academic tenure (chapter 14).

Now, half a century after the regents' action of 1951 creating chancellorships at UCLA and Berkeley, the university has not yet found universally satisfactory solutions to governance issues. Multicampus systems, such as the University of California, which now dominate public institutions of higher education in the United States, all seem to be in constant stages of adjustment. They are inherently very difficult to govern. There are 120 such systems with over half of all students in public and private higher education combined—they serve 8 million students in all.

And yet overall, the reorganization of the University of California since 1951 has worked out very well. There have been big gains and only small costs. In 1997, six of eight general campuses of the University of California were members of the Association of American Universities: no other state has more than two public universities in this association and only three states have that many. Also in 1997, new chancellors of the University of California included the current president of the American Association for the Advancement of Science (Santa Cruz), the recent provost of Harvard University (UCLA), and the recent president of the University of Texas at Austin (Berkeley)—all identified and re-

cruited by President Richard Atkinson. Without the reorganization, none of these developments would be likely.

Within the three major alternative approaches to organizing a system of institutions of higher education—a centralized system with a single source of decision making, like Napoleonic France or UC, 1868–1951; a decentralized system with several centers of administrative decision-making under a single constitution, like the United States with a federal government and 50 states, or UC, 1951 to now; or a confederated system with the constitutionally independent units delegating such authority as they may wish to a central body, like the United Nations, or the thirteen American colonies associated within the Articles of Confederation, 1777 to 1787, or as proposed for UC in 1965—continuing struggles between the center and the parts are inevitable. Sheldon Rothblatt has observed that "any federal system by the facts of its very existence undergo[es] periodic struggles for domination between the center and the parts."[1] So it has been within the University of California.

In my judgment, the pressures for constant extension of chancellorial dominance have reached the point of challenging the effectiveness of the center in assuring state authorities and the people of the state that their financial support is being used to the maximum benefit of the people of the state. And therefore we need to take a new look at the proper role of the center as well as at the autonomy of the parts.

For nearly half a century, the appropriate question has been, how much more power do the chancellors want and how much more should be given to them? The new additional question seems to me to be, how much authority should the president and the regents retain to assure that the regents can justify the constitutional autonomy granted to them in California's constitution of 1878? The regents represent the public welfare in the governance of the university.

Contrary to all other chapters in this memoir, this one chapter makes recommendations for specific changes in current policy. I was a primary agent in beginning the decentralization process and now confess to a major neglect in my view of this process. I did not sufficiently consider its ultimate limits. At what point does the center become too powerless? The current system works well when the president exercises his influence aggressively. It works less well when a president, as some have, mostly just presides. Thus I think the system now needs more formal checks and balances, such as the Board of Regents' advance approval of new developments and of disengagements, and subsequent review by required specified audits of both programs and finances.

In studying reorganization in industry, for example inside General Motors, I had observed a standard pattern—to decentralize too much and, when that did not work, to recentralize too much, and when this also did not work, to change again—a yo-yo process in perpetuity. And as we developed our policies on governance, I always asked myself, could we achieve a golden mean that would last? I naively thought we had done so by the end of 1965. But not so. I have concluded that there is no permanent golden mean, no single point of steady equilibrium, only constant tensions and adjustments that seem to be inherent in large organizations, as, for example, in the United States currently between the federal government and the states. Power struggles, macro and micro, are indeed ubiquitous and eternal.

■

Observations

AN APPRAISAL OF CHANGES, 1951–66

I believe these changes within the university were essentially sound. We were able to make decisions faster and closer to the origins of problems. The campuses became more dynamic entities. I have, however, one major qualification.

That qualification is the designation, beginning in 1958, of each campus (except San Francisco) as a "general campus." Some chancellors interpreted this phrase to mean an absence of limits on their campus endeavors. We intended the term "general" to mean the opposite of "specialized"—as Davis was in agriculture, San Francisco in health sciences, and La Jolla in oceanography—and certainly not "unlimited in scope."

AN APPRAISAL OF CHANGES SINCE 1966

As an external observer since 1966, I have sensed various further developments.

At the formal level there have been four developments. First, a decentralization of admissions policies to the chancellors of the individual campuses that took place beginning about 1967.[2] Second, a countermovement of recentralization of some large-scale purchasing that took place as the result of a report by a task force appointed by Governor Reagan.[3] Third, a decentralization of the auditing function to the chancellors that was authorized particularly during the presidency of David Saxon (1975 to 1983). And fourth, an allocation of "lump-sum" budgets to the chancellors subject to their specific determinations of uses that began in 1977 and greatly expanded in 1996. This latter expansion followed a series of cutbacks in universitywide budgets during the early 1990s when the chancellors had responsibility to allocate cutbacks and figure out how to absorb the losses. It gave them the more pleasant responsibility to allocate increases as well. There is now more attention to feedback of information, and fortunately so. It helps keep the president and regents aware of what is happening to budgets after decentralization, allowing them to represent the university more effectively to state authorities, including being certain that any agreements with the state are being carried out.

At the informal level there have been two developments. First, a change in the role of the chancellors as a collective has occurred. I did set up (1958) an *advisory* council of chancellors, and it was purely advisory. The president always presided. We never took formal votes. After my presidency, this became the Council *of* Chancellors as an increasingly independent body. The council began acting occasionally as though it were an emerging constitutional body. A common complaint of some chancellors came to be that "the president did not consult us properly," which meant "the president did not have our permission." The comparative status of the Council of Chancellors has depended greatly on the position of strength established and asserted by the individual presidents. The Council of Academic Vice-Chancellors has also become a very influential organization. These two councils, however, do serve to make all participants more conscious of the needs of the total university and involve them more in seeking agreeable solutions to problems.

The second informal development was a substantial withdrawal of the president as a presence on each campus. Some of this withdrawal was voluntary and some was encouraged by individual chancellors. Partly at the insistence of several chancellors, the universitywide Cal Club of student leaders and the all-university faculty conference were discontinued. Charter Day observances were discontinued except at Berkeley. The president came to figure in campus life more *in absentia* than in *propria persona*, attending receptions for new students and new faculty members, participating in charter days and commencements, attending divisional meetings of the Academic Senate. The president became more a position than a widely known person.

The combination, from 1957 to 1966, of decentralized administrative power to the chancellors and of open internal competition among "general" cam-

TABLE 19
Source of University of California Current Fund Revenues, Fiscal Year 1996*

Category	Campus-generated (%)	State-financed (%)
Student tuition and fees	11	
Auxiliary enterprises	6	
Teaching hospitals	23	
Educational activities	8	
Gifts, grants, and contracts	23	
Other	5	
State of California		24

Source: University of California Office of the President, "University of California Annual Financial Report, 1995/96" (November 1996), 18.

*Excluding federal laboratories.

puses has been a source of great strength to the University of California system, but it has also created governance problems. Since 1966, the chancellors' control over auditing and over lump-sum budgets has exacerbated the problems. As illustrations, one chancellor started to plan for a new medical school without any prior authorization, four campuses were found in 1995 to have set up their own admissions policies and procedures contrary to regental policy, and a number of financial scandals have come to public attention in recent years.

Together, the formal and informal changes since 1965 have created a new balance of power. Central influence has gone down, campus self-determination up. Chancellors have the campus administrative staffs, the alumni, the faculty, and the students as their constituencies. They have the lump-sum budgets, control of auditing, and the sports teams. And chancellors have the attention of the local press. In addition, their campuses generate more of the financing through tuitions, private fund raising, federal R&D projects, and auxiliary enterprises, all of which are not subject to as much central university influence as are state funds. State funds as a percentage of the total university budget went down from 47 percent in 1965 to 24 percent in 1996 (Table 19). The "campus-generated" percentage rose from 53 percent to 76 percent in the same period.

In the late 1950s, when Roger Revelle was riding high as the initiator of the new School of Science and Engineering at La Jolla, he said to me as chancellor at Berkeley that either he or I would be the next president of the university and, in either case, would be the last person who was in reality "*the* president" of "*the* university." His time frame was off, but on the direction of movement he was correct.

A struggle for power is still endemic today, as it was from 1951 to 1965. Above all, the campus is the natural unit of loyalty, not the statewide presidency or the Board of Regents. Though at one point several regents came to feel they had turned into a "rubber stamp," the Board of Regents still has the legal authority. The chancellors have the actual on-the-spot authority (and many of its symbols too). The president is in an ambiguous situation, with little of either.

This is not to suggest that the president is without influence if he wishes to exercise it, and several presidents have. The president has great influence over the budget that goes to the governor and legislature, over the selection and review of chancellors, and over the agenda of the Board of Regents. The president could, also, selectively withdraw delegations to chancellors if the president so decided. The president's essential role of influence, however, is as advisor to the Board of Regents. The other most essential role is as representative of universitywide faculty interests to the regents. The faculty is at the center of the enterprise and the university performs well only as the faculty performs well. Beyond that, the president is in charge of the general consensus that holds the institution together. The president is potentially powerful in influence but not in authority. To perform this role effectively, the president must be in contact with everyone but also be independent of everyone.

During my period as president, I always had in mind the concerns of Regent Edward Dickson and President Robert Gordon Sproul that the process of decentralization could result in the destruction of the University of California as one university. Dickson, then chair of the board, had said in 1950 that "The office [provost] is a *menace* to the unity of the University . . . and might conceivably lead to a movement for separation" (emphasis added).[4] Dickson changed his view, but Sproul never did. He continued to fear a move from a regental-presidential administration to a regental-presidential-chancellorial administration that, under pressure from the chancellors, could evolve into a regental-chancellorial administration, cutting out the president and threatening the concept, which Sproul so strongly supported, of "one university."

The reforms I largely led from 1952 to 1966 were directed too much, I now think, at empowering the chancellors and too little at building a Madisonian system of checks and balances. I should have paid more attention, in particular, to an episode I witnessed. It centered on the 1965 Byrne report's proposal for nine separately chartered universities and a president who took on the limited role of chairperson of the board, and Harry Wellman describes it in his oral history:

> The Byrne report came out in early May 1965. When I read it, I felt that it was so far fetched that nobody would pay any attention to it. But I was wrong. At the first meeting of the council of chancellors following the release of the Byrne report, I proposed that the chancellors go on record opposing it. Chancellors Murphy and Galbraith objected to that proposal. None of the other chancellors supported it; consequently I dropped it.[5]

Sometimes, quite naturally, chancellors have come to want *all* the tools of authority and *all* its symbols. I paid too little attention to how their aspirations might outrun reasonable attainments. Since 1966, in my judgment, there has been far too little interest in the question of how to build an effective system of checks and balances on the power of the chancellors.

Governance in Comparative Perspective

Academic governance, and not just within the University of California, is often an "omnium gatherum." The mock-Latin expression refers to "an unlikely collection of items of a heterogeneous nature." And this collection is in perpetual motion—an unstable compound with an occasional threat of decomposition. I undertake this digression in order to note that the University of California is not unique in having problems of governance; it is, rather, illustrative of the general situation.

The governance of a university may have aspects of a democracy (within the student body or the faculty), of a corporation (the trustees), of a guild (the faculty), of a monarchy (the president), of a bureaucracy (the nonacademic staff), of a political party (activist students), of an oligarchy (the full professors), and of a market (students as consumers).

Differing combinations of governance have flourished. The first university, Bologna, originally was a dictatorship of the students over the faculty; Oxford and Cambridge before the 1850s were guilds of the faculty (masters); Columbia in the 1920s was the monarchy of Nicholas Murray Butler; a modern community college is a marketplace making courses available in response to consumer demand. Prior to President Wheeler, the University of California was mostly a corporation run by the Board of Regents, then a monarchy under President Wheeler, then a monarchy working with the advice of a guild under President Sproul after the empowerment of the Academic Senate in 1920, and later an attempted revolutionary fortress in the 1960s under the FSM, and was also much else at each of these times.

Different participants have different ideal models of governance that have some constancy: the trustees' is the corporation; the faculty's is the academic guild; the nonactivist students', a market where the consumer is always right; and activist students', the revolutionary party. What makes it all work most of the time is mutual restraint; no group seeks total domination for its model. Even with restraint, however, there is constant tension; and there can be anarchy, "organized" or not[6]—but that has seldom happened. University governance is a protean formulation—fascinating to observe, frustrating to take part in. The president needs to be a juggler of all the movable parts or a makeup artist, or both.

Situations vary by types of institutions. The most stable institutions are religiously oriented private colleges and universities, where there is an accepted hierarchy—a theocracy. The next most stable institutions are the private nonreligious residential colleges held together by the mutual devotion of faculty, students, and alumni with most trustees drawn from alumni. Public institutions generally have less stable governance. There is no sanctified theocracy, and there are fewer bonds of loyalty among faculty, students, alumni, and trustees. Trustees in public institutions may owe whatever loyalty they have to their source of appointment, or to some element of the public, or to the perceived public at large, or to the institution. Without a common religion or a common loyalty, the public institution is almost inevitably a less integrated institution and is more a collection of groupings divided within as well as among themselves—diversity not unity. The existence of a federated "system" brings in additional points of tension: campus versus campus; and campuses versus central authority. The public system is the most likely, internally, to experience a breakdown of mutual respect and mutual restraint. Thus, when the University of California went from the unitary model of Wheeler and Sproul to a federated system, it became a more effective institution but also more open to internal conflict.

The University of California is among the more difficult systems to govern effectively because it is among those most subject to internal and external tensions. It is one of the larger systems and the most academically prestigious of them all, with individual campuses of national and international standing and proud of their positions. It has, along with the University of Michigan, the most autonomous Board of Regents, the most empowered Academic Senate of all universities as a result of the faculty's insistence in 1919–20, and a highly competent and somewhat arrogant student body. It has, in addition, a variety of campuses, each with its own characteristics and complexities.

Yet the University of California has become academically supreme above all other systems. If the measure of the quality of governance is not internal tensions but academic results, then the University of California has had superb governance despite its inherent handicaps, as I think it mostly has. No other multiple campus university has seen all of its campuses rated among the top twenty-five public research universities (see chapter 28; for some additional general comments on university governance, see Appendix 2 section E). Viewed externally in terms of results during the last half-century, the governance of the University of California is close to perfection. Viewed internally, however, in terms of processes, there are a few developments to be concerned about.

AUDITING

The chancellors have not handled audit well. There have been more abuses in financial affairs in recent years than probably in the entire prior history of the university. I think that there are several reasons for this. To begin with, the university is a much larger and more complex organization than in earlier times, and moral conduct on campus—like that in society at large—has not grown more noble. Also, some chancellors are too close to their subordinates to want to express suspicions of them by starting an audit, and if they should find any failures it reflects badly on their own performance as supervisors. In addition, a large central auditing staff can have more specialized experts, for example in hospital finance or research funds management, than can a smaller staff at the campus level. It is particularly important now, with lump-sum campus budgets, to set up a more adequate system to assure full accountability.

LONG-RANGE PLANNING

Planning to accommodate Tidal Wave II of students from 2000 to 2010 has been inadequate, except temporarily during the presidency of David Gardner

(1983–92) and currently of Richard Atkinson. The planning process in practice became one of decentralized growth without differentiation. Other opportunities have been lost, particularly to work with the high schools to provide more advanced placement courses and to make much better use of what is often the "lost" last year of high school, and to work with community colleges to provide more transfer programs.[7]

PARTICIPATION IN ACADEMIC GOVERNANCE

The actions on admission policy by the Board of Regents in 1995, whether intentional or otherwise and I think mostly otherwise, have called into question the role of the Academic Senate. Its role badly needs clarification, as does the reduced role of the president and the Board of Regents in a federated system, with less knowledge of what is going on.[8] I note, however, contrary to my views, that recent presidents of the university conclude that the president has enough potential influence to be fully effective if he or she chooses to utilize it.

Comments

A new look at the total governance structure of the University of California is, I believe, now in order. The place to start is not with the chancellorship, which is well established, but with the responsibilities of the total university to the people of the state (the Board of Regents and the office of the president working together, with the advice of the chancellors and the Academic Senate). The governance structure must be able to assure that taxpayers' financial support is effectively and efficiently spent and that there are no abuses; that long-range plans are well made and well coordinated to provide for excellent stewardship to the state through research, teaching, and service; that the administration is well staffed and competently led; that faculty members are carefully chosen and well paid and that their academic freedom is protected, and that they are fully consulted in all academic affairs. The conditions and quality of the faculty are the highest priority, since the faculty does the teaching, carries out the research, and conducts the service activities.

The best way to preserve the university's cherished autonomy, in the long run, is to preserve the ability of the total university to perform its many responsibilities effectively. Autonomy is constantly earned as well as originally granted. (For other specific comments on university governance, see Appendix 2 section F.)

ONE UNIVERSITY

The campuses of the University of California are better off, I believe, as part of one university than if they were nine "separately chartered" universities:

- "Separately chartered" universities would probably not receive the degree of autonomy that the University of California enjoys, within the state constitution.

- What would happen to the compact that the University of California joined, through the master plan, to serve the people of the state and assign differential responsibilities to the several segments of higher education?

- What would become of universitywide programs such as the unified library system, the education abroad program, and the natural land and water reserve system?

- How would separate campuses fare in facing a more unified California State University system? Or would that system too split up?

- Might the people of California not end up with both more duplication and more gaps in service?

- Nine separate universities might engage in antagonistic acts against one another or form blocs in internecine warfare—rather as Chancellor Murphy once suggested that Davis and UCLA do, to put down Berkeley, rather than support a common budget. Chancellor Mrak rejected this proposal.

The individual campuses and the total university, in my judgment, are better off with the decentralized administration in existence since 1958 than with the prior unified administration: the present system provides faster and better decision-making and more vitality at the campus level. It is also more effective than nine "separately chartered" universities would be. But the questions still remain of how far to decentralize and of who does what.

It is now half a century since the Board of Regents established chancellorships at UCLA and Berkeley in 1951. With the further granting of lump-sum budgets to the chancellors in 1996, the empowerment of the chief campus officers has probably about reached its limits within the parameters of one university. It may now be time to consider these elements of governance:

- Delineation of the president's responsibilities.

- Improvement of the university's long-range academic planning by the central administration. Also the recapture, within the campus lump-sum budgets, of presidential review and board approval of all new projects, and, in addition, a report to the president and board of all major reductions.

- Recapture of fiscal auditing by the Board of Regents and the president and its extension to program auditing as well, perhaps under the auspices of the regents' Committee on Finance and the Committee on Educational Policy respectively. President Atkinson has recently started a system of dual reporting by campus auditors to the president as well as to the chancellors.

- An annual report by the president to the Board of Regents on the process of academic personnel actions, including how satisfactory is the salary scale, the record on acceptances and refusals of new appointments, changes in faculty honors such as memberships in the National Academy of Sciences, and other indications of gains and losses.

- Preservation of the president's role as chief executive of the university, as chief advisor to the Board of Regents and to the chancellors, as chief representative to the regents of faculty concerns, as chief representative of the university to the people of the state, as chief planner of new academic endeavors, as chief reviewer of campus performances, and as chief leader of one university.[9]

    The elements above constitute what might be identified as an *ex ante* and *ex post*—or bookends—model of governance, with the president and Board of Regents in control, *ex ante*, of new plans and, *ex post*, of evaluations, and the chancellors in charge of operations within these parameters.

- The clarification of the central role of the Academic Senate in academic decision-making.

    In making this suggestion, I fully realize that faculty participation in academic governance is generally declining—at least in higher education systems that derive from the British experience—and the authority of government and of the university administration is rising.[10] This trend needs watching.

AN OVERALL REVIEW OF GOVERNANCE

I conclude that, if there is an appropriate time in the foreseeable future (and the appropriate time must be carefully chosen), there should be a careful overall consideration of the totality of the governance of the university:

> It is now eighty years since the agreement of the board and the Academic Senate on shared governance. It is also fifty years since the process of decentralization of governance to the nine campuses began. How well is shared governance now working? How well has decentralization developed?

> The state now supplies only one quarter of the funding of the university. Should it still have nearly 100 percent of basic control through gubernatorial domination of the Board of Regents? And the related question is, how are we to avoid one-party dominance of the Board of Regents?

> The University of California now faces increasingly intensive national and international competition for preeminence among research universities. How well situated is it in its governance to continue its position in the front ranks?

PART IV

Nine Campuses

Creation of
Three Campuses

Three new campuses all at once! This tremendous opportunity came along at the same time as reorganization of the university, which included transferring three-quarters of the universitywide staff to the campuses; and both came on top of the day-to-day operation of an already very large and very complex enterprise.

Development of the new campuses belonged to the regents and to the president and the president's staff for the first six to seven years (1958 to 1964–65). It involved decisions on sites, physical plans, and general academic directions, as well as the original leadership. Once the campuses were established, responsibility shifted quickly to the chancellors and their staff and then, increasingly, to the tenured faculty.

The chancellors' period of strong influence also averaged about six or seven years. It overlapped both the regents' and president's period and the tenured faculty's, but it covered roughly 1961 to 1968. In this period the chancellors chose and guided the original deans and other academic and administrative officers, recruited the initial faculty, planned and supervised the construction of all but the very first buildings, developed the academic plan, and established relations with the local community.

The third period was forever after. It began with the first undergraduate classes in 1964 or 1965 and involved conformance to university and national norms under faculty guidance. During this forever after, the campuses expected the universitywide administration to keep the money flowing and ask few questions, issue no orders, and offer little guidance. And the funding sources, the agencies of the State of California, expected the universitywide administration to ensure that the state's needs were well met without gaps or undue duplications of effort, that there was no fraud, that there was good leadership, and that the students behaved and that faculty members did not cause trouble. The contrast between what the recipients (the chancellors and the faculty) came to demand insistently and what the donors (the state agencies) insisted upon in perpetuity was enormous: complete campus autonomy versus substantial universitywide responsibility to the state.

This and the following chapter take up the first six or seven years of the new campuses when the universitywide administration had major direct responsibility, increasingly shared with the chancellors. The other chapters in this series of five evaluate the innovations at the three new campuses. I treat San Diego first, because it began first as the Institute of Technology and Engineering in 1958 and opened as a general campus in 1964 with its first undergraduate students. Irvine and Santa Cruz opened as general campuses in 1965. Both because Santa Cruz attracted national attention as an experimental campus and because its existence as such tells the most about American higher education in general and the context of the University of California in particular, I put it last. Also, I know the most about it.

■

Basic Decisions at the Universitywide Level

A series of reports and actions in 1957–60 had determined the *number* of new campuses. The first report was by the liaison committee between the state Board of Education and the regents of the University of California in March 1957;[1] the second, which drew strongly on the first, was "Size and Number of Campuses," a report from the McHenry committee (identified by the name of the chairman, Dean McHenry, formerly dean of social sciences at UCLA) at the eleventh all-university faculty conference in April 1957; the third was a recommendation from President Sproul to the regents' meeting at Davis in October 1957 and endorsed by them; and the fourth, and most authoritative, was the master plan that became law in April 1960.

Behind the decision to build three new campuses (and a possible fourth later in the San Joaquin Valley) lay two basic figures. The first was the size of the student body the university would need to accommodate, given the demographic projections and the university's commitment under the master plan to make places available to the top 12.5 percent of high school graduates (with one-half of those admissible expected to enroll). The calculated size was 214,000 by 2000 (actually it turned out to be 178,000 by 1999). The second basic figure was the maximum of 25,000 students at Berkeley, which the regents accepted on my recommendation at their meeting at Lake Arrowhead in August 1956, and which UCLA shortly adopted (plus a medical school). The 1960 master plan raised this figure to 27,500 as the maximum for both new and existing campuses. For planning purposes, eight general campuses at 27,500 each would provide sufficient capacity (220,000) at least to the year 2000. We were then thinking forty years ahead.

In my own private calculations, the State of California's share of research universities within the national total was at least eleven—eight general campuses inside the University of California plus three private universities outside it (Stanford, Cal Tech, and USC). The United States was in the process of creating about 100 research universities (as later defined in the Carnegie Commission's *Classification of Institutions of Higher Education* and counted as 92 institutions in 1970 and 104 in 1987).[2] California was already the second most populous state in 1960 with 9 percent of the national population and growing—which translated proportionately into eight to ten research universities. New York, with 9.5 percent of the population, had eleven. Additionally, the nature of industry in California called for at least a proportionate share of research universities. Thus a total of eight general campuses seemed reasonable for the University of California.

The reports and actions noted above also set the *general locations* of campuses: the central coast south of San Francisco, the eastern reaches of the Los Angeles metropolitan area, and the environs of San Diego. These were the areas of greatest population growth. All three were coastal areas and thus, the regents generally agreed in their informal conversations, more attractive to students and faculty members. The experience at Riverside, in an interior valley 60 miles east of Los Angeles with its drifting layer of smog, was clearly in their minds as they saw the conditions there in early fall (hot and dry) and in late spring (hot and dry—again). This experience was a factor also in delaying action on a San Joaquin Valley site.

The *amount of land* thought to be needed also reflected past experience. The Berkeley central campus was crowded on 300 acres, and the regents were buying additional land at very high prices; UCLA was impacted on 400 acres. The UCLA and San Francisco campuses also demonstrated the tremendous appetites of medical schools for space for hospitals, for laboratories, for parking. In addition, after the breakthrough at Berkeley when I was chancellor, the regents were now committed to residential campuses that required space for student housing, for parking, for intramural athletics, for student centers. The regents were also committed to more cultural facilities, again following the breakthrough at Berkeley. The Wheelock report (named after its chair, Admiral Charles D. Wheelock of the La Jolla campus, and submitted in January 1958) recommended a minimum of 1,000 usable acres for a campus, and the regents accepted that figure.[3] In fact, the land we obtained was 1,200 acres at La Jolla, 1,510 at Irvine, and 2,000 at Santa Cruz.

The Wheelock report also recommended "freedom from excessive heat," an easily "accessible" location for automobile traffic, a site of "natural beauty" in a "sympathetic" community, compatible local zoning and land use plans, adequate space for parking, athletic facilities and student housing, a cultural center serving the surrounding community, an assured adequate supply of water, and a location "beyond the area of influence of other existing campuses." In their discussions, the regents took particular account of their experiences with existing campuses: the lack of expansion space at UCLA and Berkeley, the gold coast around UCLA that pushed faculty out to more affordable housing at substantial distances from the campus, the horrible parking problems created by medical schools at UCLA and UCSF, and the hot climate and smog at Riverside. They knew what they did *not* want, and the Wheelock report identified what they came to wish.

The sites actually chosen met Wheelock's wish list and avoided the regents' concerns with these exceptions: the lack of easy accessibility to the Santa Cruz site from the metropolitan area of San Jose, and the lack of a politically "sympathetic" community in La Jolla next door to the San Diego site and in California's most conservative Orange County more generally. In commenting on the Wheelock report, Sproul added another wish for an adjacent "college town" (like Berkeley), which Santa Cruz had and the original plans for Irvine and San Diego included. The three sites chosen did have adequate land, a good climate and, especially at Santa Cruz and La Jolla, great "natural beauty."

Each new location was to become a *general campus*. This was also the conclusion reached for the three smaller existing campuses in Davis, Riverside, and Santa Barbara. Unfortunately, I did not carefully define "general campus" when I chose the term. Ideally, it meant that there would be both undergraduate and graduate students, and that there would be attention to each of the major intellectual areas of the physical sciences, the biological sciences, the social sciences, the humanities, and the arts. And it meant that there would be one or more professional schools. Over time, however, the campuses came to interpret the term to mean that each campus could have every specialty within each of the major areas—just as it wished!

This confusion led to a substantial amount of duplication in specialty fields. When UCLA got, by private gift, a chair in Armenian studies, Berkeley demanded one the next month—from state funds to be obtained by the central administration. Then UCLA became angry when we considered state funds for Berkeley: the donor at UCLA wanted to withdraw his gift if state funds were available for the purpose. The only other chair in Armenian studies anywhere in the United States at the time was at Harvard, and it was not filled. "General" had come to mean "unrestrained." I must take responsibility for a grave mistake in allowing the duplication. It would have been better to set up a mechanism to distribute specialties among campuses. If we had required the regents' approval before any planning for each new department and research institute as well as for each new professional school, we would have saved resources and created more high-quality centers of distinction. We made some early efforts to distribute language specialties and area studies specialties, in particular, and related library holdings too, but they were largely failures (see chapter 25).

In part, our decision to go the route of the "general campus" referred to the differentiation of functions of the California master plan. University of California campuses were to be those that had a concentration in graduate studies and research. A teacher's college at Santa Barbara or an undergraduates only college at Riverside did not fit this assignment. With the anticipated tidal wave of students, the university would need the capacity of eight general campuses to accommodate the undergraduates, the graduate students, and the research facilities authorized by the master plan. Additionally, if the university did not fully supply the "research university" functions, then those elements in the state colleges that aspired to "research university" status would face an inviting opening. It was better for the university to be prepared to overfulfill its responsibilities than to underfulfill them.

So the term was "general campus." It should have been "general—but with selective specialties subject to advance approval by the Board of Regents"; general but not necessarily totally comprehensive.

Each entirely new campus was to have *its own academic senate* on the Berkeley model. As a preliminary to this, I appointed faculty committees, with members drawn from existing campuses, for Santa Cruz, Irvine, and San Diego to advise on educational policy, on academic appointments, and on other areas of senate responsibility. These committees were very important in the early development of each new campus, and their members were extraordinarily devoted to their responsibilities.[4]

Each new campus was to have *its own personality,* its own character; so too the transformed existing campuses. The positive reasons were to give wider choices to students as they selected their campuses, to reflect the community in which each campus was located, and to serve the interests of nearby related professions, industries, and citizen support groups. The negative reason was to avoid setting up a whole series of intercampus feuds to mirror the UCLA versus Berkeley format. Without explicitly discussing it, the regents were all highly conscious of this intense rivalry. In my informal discussions with them, we took for granted that if each campus were to concentrate more on what it wanted to be and less on what each other campus had, the whole system would live in greater harmony or, at least, with less hostility. Each campus should be encouraged to have its own sense of identity, its own sources of pride, its own aspirations. This diversity of personalities was more likely to result from advance consultation than from unguided campus-level growth.

We did not set up a special bureaucracy to plan and to run the new campuses since the centralized roles in starting the new campuses were specific and temporary. Consequently, a few people assumed very heavy burdens. I did so. Both McHenry, as dean of academic planning, and his assistant, Charles Young, did too. Harry Wellman, as vice president of the university, absorbed very heavy responsibilities for the daily affairs of running the existing university. Vice Presidents Earl Bolton on site selection and Elmo Morgan on physical planning and construction played essential roles. Once the new campuses were under way, there was no universitywide staff left behind trying to hang on to authority—only people with somewhat lesser burdens to carry. All those ninety-hour weeks became less necessary. Once the new campuses assumed control of their own lives, everyone felt a sense of relief instead of postpartum depression.

Site Selection and Development

Site selection once made can never (or almost never) be changed. It is irrevocable—unlike almost everything else, even including the name of the institution. The site involves land, climate, access, topography, views, compatibility with the surrounding community, earthquake safety, and much else. The Board of Regents on its own had chosen the site for a campus only once before: under the leadership of Edward Dickson, the longest serving regent in university history (1913–56), who identified the site for UCLA. The Berkeley site was chosen by the preceding College of California; San Francisco by the preceding Toland Medical College and later by a gift of land from Adolph Sutro, mayor of San Francisco; Davis by concerned agricultural interests; Santa Barbara by legislative action designating Santa Barbara College as a UC campus; Riverside by the prior existence of the Citrus Experiment Station; La Jolla by private gift.

Contrary to earlier practice, the entire Board of Regents decided where to put the three new campuses, after an extensive search of alternative sites. Unlike the sites for Santa Barbara and to some extent Riverside, their locations had nothing to do with politics. Actually the decisions were counterpolitical. The governor and the lieutenant governor were Democrats, as were the majorities in both houses of the legislature. Yet the university chose to locate in three of the most overwhelmingly Republican counties of the state—Orange, San Diego, and Santa Cruz. Governor Brown and Lieutenant Governor Anderson, both board members, remarked to me that it would have been nice if at least one site had been in Democratic territory. The governor noted wryly, however, that perhaps the presence of a university campus would tilt a locality, over time, in a more Democratic direction. And there were unanticipated political repercussions. In bitter battles, the city of Santa Cruz did swing to the left wing of the Democratic Party as a result of the student vote. And the Irvine and San Diego campuses, during the student troubles of the late 1960s, found themselves in especially unfriendly confines. So whereas political considerations did not affect site selection, the sites selected affected the surrounding political ambience of each new campus.

SAN DIEGO

Site selection for the San Diego campus was difficult—even, in one respect, tragic.[5] There was only one good site—the bluff above the Scripps Institution of Oceanography in La Jolla, which had been established there in 1909 and became part of the University of California in 1912. Altogether 1,200 acres were available: land owned by the city of San Diego and an adjacent Marine Corps base, which was closing. It was a beautiful location above the Pacific Ocean. The Scripps Institution was a marvelous component from which to build a campus. But the site met the hostile and implacable opposition of the senior regent, Ed Pauley of Los Angeles. He proposed, instead, an attempt to obtain part of Balboa Park with the famous San Diego Zoo. This was an impossibility. I know of one sure reason why Pauley opposed the La Jolla site. Planes from the nearby Miramar Naval Air Base flew over the site. He owned Coconut Island off the coast of Oahu in the Hawaiian Islands, and the noise of planes landing or taking off from a nearby military base irritated him every time he visited there. He took a planeload of regents to Coconut Island just so they could hear how bad it was. But the Navy changed the flight pattern at Miramar, and the noise was never a problem once the campus was built.

Were there other reasons? I do not really know. Was he influenced by his friends on the UCLA faculty, particularly in the earth sciences, who felt competitive toward the prospective San Diego campus? Was he influenced by his friend who owned the Black estate between the campus site and the ocean and opposed the development of the campus because it would interfere with his own plans for development? Did it become a question of who would win once the battle was engaged? Pauley, as Herbert York, first chancellor at UCSD, wrote, "behaved as if he owned the university" and was "fully accustomed to getting his way in arguments with people he considered to be his subordinates."[6] Early leaders at San Diego referred to Pauley as a "pit bull." Was it a matter of his personal dislike for Roger Revelle, the director of the Scripps Institution and possible first chancellor at San Diego? Pauley did want his way with "subordinates." Revelle was, for his part, rather contemptuous of business-type trustees. In a presentation at Princeton, he once referred to the "ingenious American idea that a university should be owned and managed by a board of semi-literate trustees";[7] and he did often speak in this manner—which was common among many academics in the United States at that time.

The battle became very acid and very personal, and neither Pauley nor Revelle showed any empathy toward the other's feelings. I stood with Roger all the way on the issue of location and never made or implied any concessions to Pauley at all, but I was always careful to treat Pauley and his views with respect. Pauley did not forgive me for the position I took (he rarely forgot differences), but he did not respond to me on this issue with the anger he showed toward Roger, or as he did toward me later on other issues. In the end, the Board of Regents voted on May 15, 1959, "that the La Jolla site be approved for the development of a University campus." Regent Boyd, as chair of the Committee on New Campuses, and I, separately, went to Regent Pauley, once the vote had been taken, and asked that he not use his influence in Washington, D.C., to stop transfer of the Marine Corps land to the university. He said he would not, and he kept his promise.

Once the site was selected, the physical plan for the central campus was quite straightforward—to follow the spine of the ridge above the La Jolla bluffs.

IRVINE

Only one site was seriously considered: the Irvine Ranch.[8] This was a ranch of 100,000 acres located close to the Pacific Ocean and was the single possible site most distant from both UCLA and Riverside. It had the potential for planned development under one owner, including the possibility of a university village, and of planned space for high technology industries, including regional medical facilities and information processing enterprises. The ranch, however, was under split control. One force was Joan Irvine, the living spirit of her great-grandfather, James Harvey Irvine (1827–86), who had assembled the ranch. The other combined force was the Irvine Foundation under the leadership of Loyall McLaren and the Irvine Ranch under the direction of Charles S. Thomas, former secretary of the navy. Unfortunately, the two groups did not speak to each other. Fortunately, for different reasons both wanted a university campus. But the operation took some careful maneuvering around the personalities. Joan Irvine was devoted to the idea of an *Irvine* campus and became a very good friend of its development. McLaren and Thomas were more interested in what the campus would do for the effective use of the total property on its way from orange groves and grazing land to a great metropolitan high technology center.

There were two sticking points with some of the regents, particularly the governor, the lieutenant governor, and Norton Simon. One was unjust enrichment. The ranch was willing to give us 1,000 acres for the campus. The university wanted another 510 acres—an "inclusion area" for related developments such as faculty housing (avoiding another gold coast as around UCLA) and religious centers for students. For this, the ranch wanted a commercial price ($25,000 to $35,000 per acre). The concerned regents thought a commercial price would result in unjust enrichment, because the campus brought so many advantages in developing the surrounding area. The treasurer of the regents, Robert Underhill, who was also land agent, was negotiating a commercial appraisal price. In the minds of many regents, the price was unacceptable. The second sticking point was a perceived "exclusionary policy" by the ranch that prohibited sales to persons in disapproved racial and religious categories. Ranch officials now deny having had such a policy. Such policies or practices were no longer enforceable in the courts but were enforceable by mutual consent. The governor and lieutenant governor said they could never support either point in Sacramento or in their own minds. Norton Simon and other regents agreed.

So the regents took the negotiations away from Bob Underhill and turned them over to me (a great blow to Underhill, who prided himself on his negotiating skills and never forgave me for taking his place). In early 1963 Regents Donald McLaughlin (chair of the Board of Regents), Philip Boyd, and Gerald Hagar, as well as Daniel Aldrich (the chancellor-designate), and I met with McLaren, Thomas, and others from the ranch. It was heavy going. At one point, Aldrich asked me to step out into the hall with him. He said, "You are losing me my campus." He was white in the face. I said, "Danny, I am winning you your campus." And I did. All parties finally agreed on an end to the exclusionary policy or practice on all the ranch's acreage and a price of $6,500 per acre for the inclusion area. This result was accepted by the Board of Regents in January 1964 in a unanimous vote. The Irvine campus site was dedicated in June 1964 with President Lyndon Johnson as major speaker, as arranged by Regent Pauley.

Then there was a question of how best to use the site. William Pereira, the campus planning architect, and Aldrich came to see me in Berkeley to talk about how we might start. I remembered a book I had read as a graduate student in economics on how to plan a model city (Johann Heinrich von Thunen, *Der isolierte Staat*, 1863). Von Thunen had a series of concentric circles starting out with central city buildings and going out to industrial, housing, and agricultural areas. I drew a rough sketch based on a central circle with a library and classroom buildings for the social sciences, physical sciences, biological sciences, and humanities and arts. The biological sciences started a spoke going out to a medical school, the physical sciences to an engineering school, and so forth. Then there were to be outside rings of residence halls, sports fields, and parking areas. Aldrich and Pereira liked it, and it became the basic plan (see Figure 6). Inside the first circle was to be a park—which came to be named Aldrich Park.

SANTA CRUZ

Each campus site selection was, to a degree, controversial. Santa Cruz was the least so.[9] My own early preference was the beautiful Crystal Springs area run-

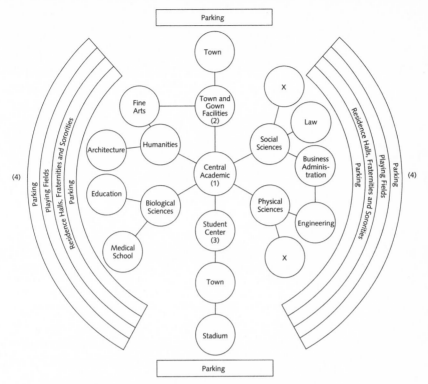

(1) Plaza, library, central classrooms, faculty club, administraton
(2) Theater, gallery, auditorium, concert hall, conference center
(3) Student union, cafeteria, gym, recreation center, Greek theater, international house
(4) Laboratories and field stations outside the central campus

FIGURE 6. Sketch of the Original Physical Layout for the Irvine Campus.

ning in the low hills between the San Francisco Bay and the Santa Cruz Mountains, and almost halfway between Stanford and San Francisco. But runoff from a campus would have polluted the lakes. Also, it was on an earthquake fault (the Berkeley campus is on another). And the site was too close to Stanford. We gave serious consideration to three other sites. One was in the community of Evergreen, east of San Jose and favored by Governor Brown, but it faced the hot western sun. The second was the beautiful Almaden Valley, west of San Jose. It started out as my own and the regents' considered choice, but

246 · *Nine Campuses*

there were some seventy or eighty parcels involved, owned by many different individuals and groups—including one large piece owned by the Catholic Church. We could not have put the site together in time. Also, smog levels were building up and land prices were rising fast. The third possibility was the Cowell ranch in the hills northwest of Santa Cruz. It was a site of great beauty with hills, meadows, and forests of Douglas fir and redwood over-looking Monterey Bay. The regents chose this third site with great relief. They had visited Evergreen and Almaden in buses on a very hot, smoggy July day in 1960. The cool breezes from the ocean when they reached Santa Cruz across the mountains made the convincing argument. (They did not, however, take an official vote to accept the Cowell ranch site until March 1961.)

The Santa Cruz site had a great impact on the campus. Dean McHenry, already the potential chancellor and in charge of university academic planning including for the new campuses, originally preferred a site near San Jose, as I would have if Almaden had been more easily available. Almaden was closer to a large population base with both enrollment and political implications, and to a fast-growing high-tech industrial area that would have encouraged the early creation of colleges of engineering and business administration. In time, it would have attracted a more vocationally oriented student body, as well as faculty members aware of consulting opportunities for themselves and attractive employment for spouses. And so almost by default I came to favor Santa Cruz but also because I had the conviction that its site would make it highly attractive in recruiting a faculty and drawing students from all over the state. The terrain was more conducive to an experimental and unique uni-versity campus, which McHenry and I both favored and, in fact, developed. Another argument was that year-round campus operations, then a major in-terest of the regents, would be much more compatible with the Santa Cruz than the San Jose climate.

Once selected, the site required a plan. The first plan called for development on the great meadow facing the town of Santa Cruz. An alternative plan, sug-gested by Thomas Church, the famous landscape architect, called for group-ing each college's buildings at the edges and into the forests on the top of the hill, and Church's plan came to be preferred and was a wise choice, particularly because we wanted a series of semi-independent colleges and they fitted better into the environment of the forests. But what should the colleges look like?

The design for the first college was a set of buildings scattered among the trees. One regent said it looked like a "series of motels on the shores of Lake

Tahoe," and it did not fit the site. I agreed and made a countersuggestion that led to an entirely new design. That prior summer Kay and I had been traveling in the south of France and had stayed in the old port city of Aigues-Mortes, from which the sixth crusade had set forth. The port is now silted in and the walled city is surrounded by forests. I suggested this as a model—each one a concentrated college isolated from other colleges by groups of trees. When you were in the college, you were in the college; and when you were in the trees, you were in the trees. This approach also appealed to McHenry, a passionate defender of each giant redwood and stately Douglas fir. However, shifting to the new design did cause delay in getting ready for the first students. Thus the design of the campus began to evolve: concentrated colleges, isolated from one another, each with its own architectural design—some much better than others.

■

So between July 1958 and 1961, we had three approved sites—all on outstanding pieces of property. San Diego and Irvine turned out to be ideal locations— no second thoughts. Santa Cruz was ideal for the kind of campus it turned out to be, but not for the more standard research university it might have been except for its remoteness on the other side of the Santa Cruz mountains, perhaps too idyllic, too sensuously competitive with dry-as-dust scholarship, more suited to Dionysus than Minerva.

Early Leadership

Many names have gone into the list of great and dominant founders of new campuses across the United States: Gilman at Johns Hopkins, Jordan at Stanford, Harper at Chicago, and White at Cornell. The list now also includes McHenry at Santa Cruz, Aldrich at Irvine, and Revelle at San Diego. These leaders are commemorated by the McHenry Library at Santa Cruz, the Aldrich Park at Irvine, and Revelle College at San Diego.

ROGER REVELLE

One indispensable ingredient in developing the San Diego campus was Roger Revelle. Roger had been associated with Scripps Institution of Oceanography since 1931 and became its director. He also served as dean of the short-lived graduate program in science and technology at La Jolla. He was more a states-man of science with a very broad view of developments in all the sciences than a line-item scientific investigator. He had great energy and enthusiasm. Roger had wanted a graduate institute (or school) in science and technology but adapted quickly to the idea of a general campus with a science emphasis. His great strengths were in identifying talent and then recruiting it, and in leav-ing it up to me to persuade the regents and to find the money. He was superb at both.

Then why was he never chancellor? This is a sad and complex story. As noted earlier, he had a bitter battle with Regent Pauley over the selection of the site and alienated not only Pauley but some of Pauley's close friends on the board. And in breaching the exclusive "gentlemen's agreement" in La Jolla real estate, Revelle angered many local conservatives (but had my full support). I pro-posed changing the name of the campus from La Jolla, as it had been identified for Scripps, to San Diego partly because of the association of La Jolla's name with attitudes antagonistic to minority racial and religious groups, and too because the city of San Diego was the donor of land for the campus. The re-gents accepted this change.

Members of the citizens' committee of the local chamber of commerce that had sponsored the campus and been very instrumental in securing the land from the city and the Marine Corps considered Roger too "radical" in general— as several of them complained to me, Revelle was hiring "Jews and Commu-nists"—and too arrogant for their tastes. The regents were well acquainted with Jim Archer, the former alumni regent from La Jolla who hated Revelle for his opposition some years earlier to the loyalty oath and to exclusionary clauses— one of the complaints Archer also had against me. Archer was a terror when his sense of national patriotism was aroused. I viewed Archer and Pauley as Revelle's most active opponents.

The San Diego citizens' committee, very unfortunately, came to think it owned the campus, and some of its members had friends among the regents. One member of the committee, who had once had polio and was a fervent supporter of Jonas Salk, was particularly belligerent. At one point I found my-self in the middle of a confrontation between Revelle and Salk at the home of James Archer over whether the Salk Institute might take some very desirable San Diego land Revelle wanted for the campus. There was much shouting back and forth, and I put Revelle and Salk in separate rooms. In this matter, I did not support Revelle. I thought the Salk Institute would strengthen the campus, which it came to do; the land did belong to the city of San Diego, not to the campus, and the city favored the Salk Institute. Once the site issue was settled, Revelle gave a full welcome to the Salk Institute to work in cooperation with the campus.

Members of the citizens' committee also were appalled at how unbusinesslike Revelle was in his conduct of campus affairs and relations with the community. In retrospect, I think we paid too much attention to the citizens' committee. It played an important role in getting the land but its views had a conservative bias, and I should have canvassed more widely for community opinion. Roger had community supporters as well, but the regents and I heard almost entirely from his opponents.

In addition, Roger had not made friends among the other chancellors—all of whom had their contacts on the board—because he made it clear that San Diego inhabited a different and superior world. The observations of Roger by the regents, as he presented budgets and other administrative affairs to the board, coincided with those of the members of the citizens' committee and they were also supported by some longtime members of the Scripps staff who went out of their way in making comments to regents and to me, that Roger was "disorganized." This charge counted heavily against him because the regents were faced with investing half a billion dollars in buildings and equipment, including library materials, in the first twenty-five years of the existence of UCSD. They were very concerned with effective administration. Roger's strengths obviously lay elsewhere and they appealed more to academic types like me than to businessmen. I thought that the talents he had were precious and unique, and that those he lacked were available at both lower and higher levels of the administrative hierarchy. I thought too that to label Roger a radical was preposterous. I saw him as a standard-brand academic liberal. And, among other evidence, he had the highest security clearance for the secret military research at Scripps.

What was best for the campus? Roger had already recruited the basic core of scientists to the faculty, and it was excellent. Increasingly, the recruiting would fall more to deans and department chairs. There were more and more buildings to build, a large staff to assemble and administer, and many operating decisions to be made. Perhaps I could have pushed through Roger's name as chancellor, as Roger thought I could have and should have done. I never counted all the votes among the regents, but it would have been an angry and drawn-out affair that would have affected the board's consideration of many future aspects of campus development. After talking widely with leaders of the regents, I told Revelle that he would not be chancellor. He was heartbroken. He spoke of how he had walked the site of the prospective campus on moonlit nights visualizing what one day might rise there in all its splendor. I shared a few very sad moments with him. Later I saw to it that he was properly honored with the naming of Revelle College. I also made him University Dean of Research—though he chose not to throw his scientific expertise at representing the nation's leading university research system into the position. He went to Harvard instead.

Fortunately, Herbert York was available, and the regents knew him well and greatly respected him. York became the first chancellor on July 1, 1961, and served with great effectiveness through to the opening of the general campus in the fall of 1964. Herb had been on the Berkeley faculty and was the founding director at the Lawrence Livermore National Laboratory, and then an assistant secretary of defense in charge of research. He had high status in the scientific world and was a superb administrator with good judgment and a steady hand; and he was a realist. York rounded out the faculty beyond the original scientific stars recruited by Revelle and began the recruitment of faculty in the social sciences and humanities, built the buildings, established an efficient administration, and started the medical school. The campus opened on time.

The San Diego campus kept on its upward course toward its special destiny. The regents' approval continued at a preferential level, unimpeded by a continuing controversy. York, however, withdrew from the chancellorship, on the grounds of a setback to his health (from which he did fully recover) and his frustrations with endless academic feuding, to accept appointment by President Johnson as vice chair of the president's Science Advisory Council.

While in Washington, York negotiated the crucial test ban treaty with the USSR. He returned later to San Diego and became head of a very important Institute on Global Conflict and Cooperation, and served as acting chancellor in 1970–71. Roger Revelle was the creator of the San Diego campus; Herb York was its builder as a fully operational campus. The university needed both of them. Among subsequent chancellors, Richard Atkinson served for the longest time (1980–95) and with a very high sense of purpose until he was appointed president of the university in 1995.

The San Diego campus saw Revelle at his best in envisioning the future campus and recruiting the distinguished corps of early faculty members, and at his best is how he will go down in history. What he accomplished, and not the titles he held, comprises the record. A subsequent chancellor, after York, once commented to me, "Why would anyone care about the title of chancellor when he was already God?" Roger accomplished miracles. So did Herb. So did Dick.

In his farewell television interview, Revelle concluded by saying: "Clark Kerr was a great big powerful force here too as well as me. He had a vision of doing the right thing, and he supported what we wanted to do wholeheartedly. It was a beautiful collaboration between him and me."[10] And Roger was in the best position to make this judgment.

DANIEL ALDRICH

Aldrich fitted Irvine to perfection. I never considered any other possibilities for recommendation to the regents. Dan was reluctant at first. One aspect of his personal life disqualified him, he told me. But he seemed so perfect that I talked to him a second time—without wanting to intrude into any secrets— was he really disqualified? He said, "Yes." The reason was that he not only did not drink alcohol but did not allow it to be served in his home. I said, "Dan, there is more to being a chancellor than drinking alcohol, and people will respect you for your principles." And so he became the first chancellor at Irvine. Years later, when visiting at his home, I noticed that he was serving alcoholic beverages, and I said to him, "Dan, you may not know it, but you've just taken the first big step toward skid row," and we laughed.

He was ideal for Irvine. He came out of the land-grant tradition (he was then serving as the universitywide dean of agriculture), and he liked the idea of a land-grant university for the twenty-first century, which I was supporting. He knew the university so well, having served at Davis, Berkeley, and Riverside, as well as universitywide. Dan would get along well with the Irvine leaders with their mutual interests in agriculture; he was committed to academic freedom and would be an excellent defender of it in a community unaccustomed to the idea; he was practical in his approach to problems and would learn as he went along. He could, and he did. When I walked the campus with Dan after the first students had arrived, I saw a student with long hair, no shoes, and wearing a long white robe. I asked "Who is that?" and Dan said, "Oh, that's Jesus Christ." Very matter of fact. We needed Dan Aldrich in Orange County. Jack Peltason, one of the early vice-chancellors, once said that his most important task in the area of Orange County was to keep Aldrich talking and the faculty thinking (but never talking). Peltason served as president of the university from 1992 to 1995.

DEAN MCHENRY

Few faculty members have contributed more to the history of the university than Dean McHenry. As a student at UCLA, he was president of the ASUC there. He received his Ph.D. at Berkeley and was a longtime member of the UCLA faculty and dean of social sciences. He participated in two reports that are among the handful of crucial documents in the history of the university: the McHenry report on new campuses and the report of the master plan survey team. He was, in my judgment, one of the four university undergraduates who made the greatest contributions to its future glories, the others being Robert Gordon Sproul (Berkeley 1913), Glenn Seaborg (UCLA 1934), and Charles Young (Riverside 1955).

Dean brought to the chancellorship at Santa Cruz a deep knowledge of the operations of the university and total loyalty to it, and a gift for personal contacts. He and I shared a vision of the campus, in the context of its chosen environmental site, which became the "dream" to which so many of the alumni of the early years of the campus are still so fervently attached.

SPOUSES

I have referred here to the chancellors and not to their spouses, and I do so later on in talking about the leaders of other campuses. On the new campuses the spouses had an especially significant role in planning the original University Houses, in making initial contacts with the community, in organizing activities for faculty spouses. They also had traditional central roles in managing social affairs for the campus and in creating a supportive and sympathetic environment at home for the chancellors and their families. The University of California had a remarkable group of chancellors' spouses, many of them superb personalities. As the president's wife, Kay brought them all together at each regents' meeting to share experiences.

The selection of campus leaders is always a gamble. Their assignments are many-sided and necessarily put them in the midst of contentious constituencies. The three new campuses were most fortunate in their founding leaders.

I used to tell the regents that what they saw first about a new or prospective chancellor was the least important thing and what they would see last was the most important. First, they saw how an individual met other people at a reception and dressed, what he or she looked like. Next, they saw the chancellor make a speech or present a report. Still later, they saw her or him choose associates, prepare a budget, and make long-term plans. Last of all, they (or their successors) would see how well each individual had given academic leadership to the campus as shown by the quality of the faculty and the success of new programs. This last view might not come until twenty or even thirty years later, long after the chancellor had left the job. I also said that allowance needed to be made for how difficult the particular assignment was and what special unforeseen impediments might arise, and the inherent difficulties in starting a new campus are extensive.

17

Original Directions
and Problems at
the New Campuses

The distinctive vision of each new campus had an impact on the course of events there, as did the process of adjusting its development to fit the commonality of its faculty's predilections.

■

San Diego

The central theme for San Diego was scientific research. This was set by the history of the Scripps Institution and the short-lived Institute of Technology and Engineering, by Roger Revelle's interests and available federal R&D funds, and by the changing industrial composition of the San Diego community.

San Diego was an instant success. It came to be one of the four American research universities that started out in the front ranks. The three others were Johns Hopkins in the 1870s, and Stanford and Chicago in the 1890s. These others came out of the era of the great rise of the American research university. Each had great private resources devoted to its building. Each had outstanding early leaders. All of the twenty leading research universities in the United States today began Ph.D. programs before 1900—except for two: UCLA and UC-San Diego; and only one of these, UC-San Diego, was originally founded as an institution after 1900.

How did UC-San Diego break into this magic circle? It had the reputation of the University of California; the resources of a then prosperous state of California; access to the federal funds that followed Sputnik; an original building block in the world-famous Scripps Institution of Oceanography; and the charismatic leadership of Revelle, who had a gift for identifying and recruiting academic talent.

It also had something else. It received clear preference in the assignment of new resources (for faculty appointments and book acquisition funds) from the regents and from the president of the university—preference over the two other new campuses, over the metamorphosing campuses of Davis, Santa Barbara, and Riverside, and even over Berkeley and UCLA. No vote had established this preference. It was the result of an unspoken acceptance.

Why was there this silent consent? San Diego was the third great population center of the state. Even with its great resources, California's budget allowed the university to go absolutely all out on only one campus at a time. The regents and the president were willing to make discriminatory choices, not just act with equal across-the-board distributions of resources. As a result, San Diego was able to recruit heavily at the full-professor (and above-scale salary) level while the other campuses usually had to hold to the assistant-professor level. During San Diego's crucial founding years, 50 percent of its new faculty appointments were at the full-professor level or above, as against 15 percent for the university as a whole, and that 15 percent included the 50 percent at San Diego.[1]

One of the first recruits at San Diego was Harold Urey, a Nobel Prize winner in chemistry from the University of Chicago. Additional faculty of great distinction from Chicago included James Arnold in chemistry, who was chair of the Academic Advisory Committee at San Diego in the early years, and quite a few others at San Diego and on other UC campuses. When the vice president at Chicago, Gerhard Casper (who was later president at Stanford), introduced me at a program during the University of Chicago's centenary celebrations, it was as "the former president of the University of Chicago in California." His point was apt; we did give many Chicago faculty new opportunities, but mostly on their own initiative.

This preference—"favoritism," the other campuses called it—was particularly unpopular at Irvine and Santa Cruz and even at Berkeley and especially Los Angeles. (As of 1960–61, 57 percent of the faculty members at San Diego were full professors with 67 percent of them at overscale; as against 43 percent and 29 percent at Berkeley, and 40 percent and 32 percent at UCLA.[2]) The arrogance of some faculty members and academic leaders at San Diego added salt to the wounds, with references to UCLA as "the pits."

San Diego was both instant headache and instant success. Not only was there resentment of San Diego's special assistance on the other campuses; some faculty at San Diego felt, and even insisted, that they were being denied their full birthright. At one early faculty meeting, sustained applause accompanied the shouted charge that I was trying to hold San Diego "down to the low levels of Harvard and Berkeley." This was unacceptable! We struggled in Sacramento to explain San Diego's requests for support levels unknown elsewhere within the University of California (or anywhere else). The new campus had not yet earned this special preference. It came from the regents and the president. Obviously we were not the worst enemies the new campus had, as some early leaders (but never Revelle or York) asserted.

The headache was worth it. San Diego would never have been so dramatically successful if the regents and president had treated all campuses alike. It was better to have given preference to the best prospect. And later, by its own actions, San Diego warranted this preference. Its triumph was not, as the local myth later asserted, the result of its own efforts alone against resistance by the regents and president's office. Still, this interpretation of history—"we did it all on our own against opposition"—has added to the special personality of San Diego.

The history of Scripps had a large impact on the early attitudes at San Diego. Scripps had looked upon itself for half a century as less a part of the rest of the university than any other campuses or sub-campuses. It had been started with a private gift in 1909. It had gotten most of its financial support not from the state but from private and federal sources. It had lived within its own world of oceanography. It was a small, self-governing community, enjoying the larger university's benign neglect.

To find itself subject to university governance and to university plans came as a shock for Scripps. Suddenly foreign entities had turned its own plan for a small graduate-level school of restricted scope into plans for a vast research university with thousands of undergraduates (even lower-division students). Now it had "Berkeley" and "Sacramento" to deal with too, as it experienced the shift to a large research university first set out in 1957 by a special planning committee appointed by President Sproul and chaired by Harry Wellman, then vice president of agricultural sciences.[3]

The new campus started in 1957 as an Institute of Technology and Engineering (later School of Science and Engineering). San Diego's first faculty member was hired on a grant from General Dynamics, as of July 1, 1957. This institute (school) was intended to be a graduate-level Cal Tech. But the anticipated universitywide enrollment and the city's presence warranted a full-line research university. The plan for San Diego quickly shifted from an institute to a school to a university. There was some resistance. At one faculty meeting, a faculty member, again to sustained applause, shouted at me that there should be, not only no undergraduates, but also no graduate students: "Only post-docs—send all those run-of-the-mill Ph.D. candidates to San Diego State." That sentiment quickly vanished, and Ph.D. candidates and even undergraduates came to be well accepted.

Because the campus started from the top down—graduate students first, with my full support—it was able to begin with a few faculty and students in a limited number of departments and then spread out gradually into more departments and more students and faculty. It did not need to wait for ten or twenty departments to come into existence in order to start instruction, as had to be done at the undergraduate level. Also, science at the graduate level takes only current and recent journals and not a substantial library of books accumulated over the years.

Revelle's early plans for San Diego, with my encouragement, had two other special features. One was a series (ten to fifteen) of residential colleges with about 2,000 to 2,500 students each, in order to break the campus into smaller human communities. The second was that faculty members should affiliate with research institutes as interdisciplinary intellectual communities, each with its own personality—one concentrating at a more theoretical level, Alfred North Whitehead; another at a more practical level, Benjamin Franklin; and a third more concerned with historical evolution, Charles Darwin.[4] The residential colleges did come about, though they had far less than the two-thirds of undergraduate instruction first anticipated. The structured transdisciplinary research communities, however, did not develop as planned.

San Diego always asked for the best. On three occasions, the university-wide administration, particularly myself as president and Wellman as vice president of the university, thought it was asking for too much and too fast, and there were open public disputes.

One occasion involved the *medical school,* first planned in June 1960 and estimated to require an original investment of $26.5 million. All of a sudden, under John S. Galbraith as chancellor (1965–68) this sum escalated to $120 million—all from state funds. At that time, the investment cost at UCLA, from state and federal and private funds, was $80 million—the most "gold-plated" medical school start-up in history. In the end about $63 million of state and federal funds was negotiated for San Diego, the maximum acceptable to the regents and in Sacramento. Along the way, a bitter dispute erupted in the public press.

A related matter under dispute was an early effort to concentrate more on a molecular biology research program than on a medical school. David Bonner, the spiritual leader of the San Diego program, looked upon the more traditional programs at UCLA and San Francisco as "second-rate." He favored a strong research background for medical doctors on the grounds that an interest in research would lead them to keep more up-to-date as they conducted their practices than if they remained bound to the knowledge they had encountered as students—a good point. The compromise that resulted was very successful.

The second instance of public conflict concerned the *universitywide library plan*. It called for two central libraries at Berkeley and Los Angeles serving the whole system, with San Diego—in part because of its distance from UCLA—to receive an extra allowance beyond any of the other campuses except Berkeley and UCLA. There was a disagreement over how much this extra allowance should be. Once again, before we could work out a solution in private the dispute surfaced in the press. The allowance was increased. We gave UCSD a book budget of $475,000 for 1965–66, as against $110,000 at UCSC and $135,000 at UCI, the other new campuses. The next year the figure was $719,000 at UCSD, $239,000 at UCSC, and $482,000 at UCI. Wellman and I had agreed that UCSD should have the "third great library" in the UC system. Local partisans interpreted the phrase to mean instant parity with Berkeley and UCLA. The UCSD library, however, served only itself, while the UCLA library also served Santa Barbara, Riverside, Irvine, and San Diego with daily bus service. Berkeley similarly served San Francisco, Davis, and Santa Cruz. Also, UCLA and Berkeley had far more faculty and students than San Diego.

The third occasion was the scheduled presentation of the *library building's physical plan* to the Board of Regents. At the last moment, Elmo Morgan, vice president in charge of construction at the new campuses, identified some structural problems and requested a one-month delay. Unfortunately, Morgan talked to me just as Wellman and I were leaving for a hearing in Sacramento, so I asked Morgan to talk to John Galbraith. As it turned out, Galbraith felt that bad news like this should come directly to him as chancellor from the president and not from some lesser individual. Many years later (1985), he wrote to Wellman that "I believed, and still believe, there should have been direct communication from the President, rather than transmission through a Vice President." I agree, and that was my practice, but circumstances had not permitted this nicety. What I should have done was give Galbraith the alternatives: either hold the presentation for a month while we worked out our disagreements, or leave it on the agenda but reserve Morgan's right to present directly to the regents his hesitancies over the structural strength of the underpinning of this huge building. The regents would have accepted Morgan's advice, embarrassing San Diego and Galbraith.

This episode caused a brief resignation by Chancellor Galbraith, who chose to submit it to the chair of the board and not to the president. By the next regents' meeting, the solutions suggested by Morgan were accepted by the campus and the project went ahead. In the meantime, the brief resignations of the chancellor and the vice-chancellor for business affairs, Robert Biron, came into public dispute. Neither the board nor I had taken their resignations seriously. Wellman notes in his oral history, "contrary to their expectations, a majority of the regents would have voted to accept them."[5] The resignations reflected the general sensitivities at San Diego over the process of universitywide review; no similar controversies arose on any other campus, to push momentary disagreements so quickly to such public and personalized attacks.

I had known John Galbraith for some years as a leading faculty member at UCLA, chair of the southern division of the Academic Senate, and chair of the department of history—one of the leading departments in the entire university. John had been born in Glasgow and was a scholar of British history. When we were beginning to plan for the new campuses, I asked him to head a committee to travel to Great Britain and see what Britain was doing with its new campuses. He wrote a very good report. Later, I asked him to chair the committee that helped guide the founding of Irvine before a local senate was established there and subsequently nominated him to be the first vice-chancellor at San Diego. What I had not observed was an aspect of Galbraith's character that Hansena Frederickson noted when he was on the UCLA faculty: "Galbraith wants it right now, and he gets mad and won't wait."[6] A friend of his at UCLA later told me that Galbraith had a "collision course" personality; that in faculty committees where he was losing, he would pick up his papers and walk out. If I had been alerted to this trait earlier, I would have been more sensitive in my dealings with John. Perhaps we would have been able to work out the trio of problems above with fewer public fireworks.

John gave good leadership at San Diego. He took the faculty along the course York had set, toward the social sciences and humanities and away from concern only with the sciences. He also built a great library somewhat faster than would otherwise have happened. I respected him highly but regret his quick resort to dramatic explosions. When he resigned as chancellor in September 1967 (effective summer 1968), I wrote to him saying that I was sorry to see him leave and "sorry also that we could not have been of more help to each other. San Diego developed favorably under your leadership. You can be proud of your contributions." Many years later (September 11, 1995) John wrote me a letter on other matters that concluded, "You acted in a manner befitting an outstanding leader."

The combination of John's impatience, plus his longtime unsatisfactory experience with the status of the "southern branch" of UCLA vis-à-vis Berkeley, and the very high expectations of the early UCSD faculty constituted an explosive mixture. At the time I had thought that Galbraith regretted his public attacks on me, which included his repeated resort to contacts with the most reactionary elements on the Board of Regents and in the local community to get support for his views, against mine. However, he told Nancy Scott Anderson, who wrote a history of the San Diego campus, that he "did admit he was well aware of germinating attempts to unseat Kerr. And knowing how his actions had fed that effort, he could not say he would not do it again."[7]

Irvine

Irvine was much less complicated. Because it was to be a land-grant university for the twenty-first century, one aspect of its central theme (which I suggested) was an emphasis on off-campus extension and cultural programs—paralleling earlier land-grant programs' emphasis on agricultural extension and 4H Clubs—in an extension program that started at Irvine even before there was a campus. And a cultural center was planned.

The other aspect was new emphases within knowledge and new ways of organizing knowledge, as with the land-grant emphases on science and on departmental disciplinary organization. Irvine was to put heavy emphasis on environmental studies, and on new ways of organizing knowledge on a vertical rather than on a horizontal approach in biology. In literature it would focus on comparative literature rather than language-by-language segmentation, and in administration on the "administrative sciences" rather than on area-by-area specializations (business, public policy, schools, hospitals, etc.). Also, there was to be intensive experimentation with the new electronic technology.

Irvine came to pride itself on being a "homegrown" success rather than a quick-fix "hothouse" product, as it came to refer to San Diego. "Homegrown" both in its recruitment of younger scholars who made their records at Irvine and in its own choice of variations on the model of the "multiversity," to which I shall return in chapter 18.

Santa Cruz

The Santa Cruz campus was the most significant educational experiment in the history of the University of California. David Riesman and Gerald Grant called it "a genuine innovation in academic structure."[8] Thus, of the roughly 1,300 new campuses started in the United States between 1945 and 1975, its background and early stages are of more than usual interest.

The idea of Santa Cruz goes back to the ancient Greeks, to the Academy of Plato and the Lyceum of Aristotle: a place for high-level contemplation and discussion of the human experience in its manifold complexities, among small groups of teachers and students. A more modern version was set forth by John Henry Newman in his *Idea of the University*. A university training, said Newman, "aims at raising the intellectual tone of society, at cultivating the public mind, at purifying the national taste, at supplying true principles to popular enthusiasm and fixed aims to popular aspiration, at giving enlargement and sobriety to the ideas of the age, at facilitating the exercise of political power, and refining the intercourse of private life." It prepares a person "to fill any post with credit, and to master any subject with facility."[9]

THE ORIGIN OF THE "DREAM"

There were, more importantly, some more proximate sources of the Santa Cruz idea.

I had met Dean McHenry, the founding chancellor at Santa Cruz, accidentally. We stood together, by chance, in the registration line at Stanford in the fall of 1932 and started talking. We began comparing UCLA, from which he had come, and my Swarthmore, arguing the advantages of each. We often resumed our discussion over the next several years when we roomed together as graduate students at Stanford and Berkeley. He argued the advantages of the great library and the active cultural programs at UCLA, and I the broad learning experience and sense of community at Swarthmore. We always came to the consensus that both were worthwhile and could be combined.

By 1958, McHenry had been a faculty member at Williams College and then at UCLA, later becoming dean of social sciences there and chair of the McHenry committee on new campuses. He was a natural to become universitywide dean of academic planning in charge of developing the new campuses when I became president. We wanted each campus and particularly each new campus to have its own personality. One personality attractive to both of us was a big UCLA with a series of small Swarthmores or Williamses inside it.

We were not the only people with such thoughts. Stephen Pepper at Berkeley (see chapter 7) had thought this way and wanted the new residence halls at Berkeley to become mini-colleges, similar to the "houses" at Harvard. So had Gordon Watkins at Riverside (see chapter 22). So, earlier, had the leaders of the outstanding Claremont Colleges system in southern California, with its series of diverse colleges and a single high-quality graduate program.

At Berkeley, as chancellor, I had listened to students in my open office hours complain about large classes in highly specialized subjects. You could learn about everything in detail but about little in its totality of relationships. I had tried, as Chancellor Glenn Seaborg did after me, to encourage the new residence halls to become small undergraduate colleges, but without any success. Santa Cruz was an opportunity to start fresh, to create neoclassical colleges within a "multiversity." As a professor, I had always put great emphasis on teaching my undergraduate courses in a broad fashion while carrying on research, service, and graduate instruction. I did not feel it impossible, and I thought most faculty would not. Could we not do better with the undergraduates while serving well the graduate students and our research? I thought we could.

THE GODKIN LECTURES

I note that just as I was describing the rise of the "multiversity" in my Godkin lectures at Harvard (1963), and, to a degree, celebrating it, I was plotting, along with McHenry, a counterrevolution at Santa Cruz. In my Harvard lectures I described the "multiversity" as a "series of communities and activities held together by a common name, a common governing board, and related purposes," contrasting it with the older concept of a university as a single community. In those same lectures I also set forth my concerns with the multiversity, in part, as follows:

> Harold Orlans, who conducted the excellent Brookings study of federal aid to universities, concludes that federal research aid "has accelerated the long-standing depreciation of undergraduate education at large universities." This is

my own observation, with one exception—that a very few private institutions with long traditions of very high quality undergraduate instruction have been able to maintain their standards; and this is to their great credit.

The reasons for the general deterioration of undergraduate teaching are several. Teaching loads and student contact hours have been reduced. Faculty members are more frequently on leave or temporarily away from the campus; some are never more than temporarily on campus. More of the instruction falls to teachers who are not members of the regular faculty. The best graduate students prefer fellowships and research assistantships to teaching assistant-ships. Postdoctoral fellows who might fill the gap usually do not teach. Average class size has been increasing.

There seems to be a "point of no return" after which research, consulting, and graduate instruction become so absorbing that faculty efforts can no longer be concentrated on undergraduate instruction as they once were. This process has been going on for a long time; federal research funds have inten-sified it. As a consequence, undergraduate education in the large university is more likely to be acceptable than outstanding; educational policy from the undergraduate point of view is largely neglected. How to escape the cruel paradox that a superior faculty results in an inferior concern for undergraduate teaching is one of our more pressing problems. . . .

The undergraduate students are restless. Recent changes in the American university have done them little good—lower teaching loads for the faculty, larger classes, the use of substitute teachers for the regular faculty, the choice of faculty members based on research accomplishments rather than instruc-tional capacity, the fragmentation of knowledge into endless subdivisions. There is an incipient revolt of undergraduate students against the faculty; the revolt that used to be against the faculty *in loco parentis* is now against the faculty *in absentia.* The students find themselves under a blanket of im-personal rules for admissions, for scholarships, for examinations, for degrees. It is interesting to watch how a faculty intent on few rules for itself can fash-ion such a plethora of them for the students. The students also want to be treated as distinct individuals.

If the faculty looks on itself as a guild, the undergraduate students are coming to look upon themselves more as a "class"; some may even feel like [part of] a "lumpen proletariat." Lack of faculty concern for teaching, end-less rules and requirements, and impersonality are the inciting causes. A few of the "nonconformists" have another kind of revolt in mind. They seek, in-stead, to turn the university, on the Latin American or Japanese models, into a fortress from which they can sally forth with impunity to make their attacks on society.

If federal grants for research brought a major revolution, then the resultant student sense of neglect may bring a minor counterrevolt, although the target of the revolt is a most elusive one.

The big state universities are most vulnerable to charges of neglect of students. The private universities, tied more to tradition, to student tuition, to alumni support, to smaller size, have generally far better preserved their devotion to undergraduate life.[10]

OTHER INSPIRATIONS

Demands for new approaches came also from some faculty members, partly out of nostalgia for a vanishing world as the multiversity took over, partly from guilt at abandoning their undergraduate students, partly from awareness that scientists and professionals were dominating their institutions—and causing alarm to their colleagues in the humanities and arts and concern to those in the social sciences.

The multiversity was making great contributions to research and to science, but it had its pathologies as well. Could we keep the contributions and reduce the pathologies? That was what Dean and I hoped Santa Cruz might do: restore attention to the undergraduates and to liberal learning while simultaneously advancing research and service. But "counterrevolution," as I called it above, puts it too strongly. What we had in mind, rather, was a course correction, not a total reversal.

We paid particular attention to the Claremont system of associated undergraduate colleges with a central graduate program and to a series of new universities in Great Britain. Most of them had the same two concerns McHenry and I had: to create smaller, face-to-face communities of faculties and students; and to make greater intellectual contact across disciplinary specializations to encourage broader general learning experiences for both students and faculty. The exception to this pattern among the new universities in Great Britain was Warwick University, which took the American university as a model and later turned out to be the most successful of them all as a research enterprise. In the United States, Michigan and Michigan State were starting internal undergraduate colleges; Columbia and Stanford had their "Great Books" and western civilization courses; Yale was developing Harvard-style houses; Harvard had its "Red Book" report of Paul Buck recommending reforms in undergraduate education and later its "core courses" under Henry Rosovsky's guidance as dean of letters and science.

Both McHenry and I visited most of the new universities in Great Britain and we were greatly impressed. Also, I organized two tours of them, one by the committee of faculty members (under Galbraith of UCLA as chair), and another of several regents and top executives of the university. The new British universities were then the most exciting developments in higher education around the world—with the traditions and prominence of Oxford and Cambridge to encourage them—and, in the United States, we still cherished our British heritage in higher education. In California we had, as the closest equivalent, the Claremont system.

THE PLAN AND ITS EARLY DIFFICULTIES

The emphasis at Santa Cruz was to be on obtaining the advantages both of large scale (a big central library, centralized science laboratories, a wide range of cultural programs) and small scale (smaller size human and more integrated intellectual communities). To realize both we would build a series of colleges (500 to 1,000 students), each teaching some version of the liberal arts, each college with its own provost, and each faculty member with a college connection. Fifty percent of the students, not the standard University of California 25 percent, would be residential. Here was the skeleton of the plan.

The Santa Cruz plan started out in an especially difficult situation. The campus was located in the shadow not only of Berkeley but also of Stanford, and was bound to remain in their shadows for a very long time to come and perhaps forever. So it needed a distinctive personality to attract and retain students and faculty members, and it had to flourish as first rate within its own type. McHenry and I offered it such a possibility. As it turned out, too many faculty members wanted to revert to the type of multiversity institution they had known in their graduate schools; a few others just wanted to frolic with the students in the redwoods. The "Santa Cruz dream" eroded, and no other new dream came along to take its place. During the late 1960s, however, Santa Cruz was the most popular campus in the University of California, attracting students even from those who otherwise might have applied to Berkeley.

Santa Cruz's popularity had certain drawbacks. Experimental campuses draw experimental people—some of them uninterested in or intolerant of any experiment other than their own, others highly critical of the surrounding society, including the university—and Santa Cruz was the most experimental of the eight general campuses. The lack of students and faculty members in engineering and business administration, who tend to be more conservative in both the internal educational and the external political areas, intensified its distinctive cast (plans for both of these schools were later canceled at universitywide levels). Also McHenry and I, both farm boys, were not sensitive to how students and faculty members might react to its trees and meadows—a place for relaxation.

Because this academic experiment was taking place in the 1960s with its widespread student activism, it shared the unrest of campuses across the nation. Santa Cruz, almost alone among the experimental campuses, survived with strands of its dream intact. And the early alumni are among the most enthusiastic and loyal I have ever seen, matching those of the Hutchins college at Chicago and of Swarthmore under Aydelotte.

Santa Cruz was not a replay of the Watkins college at Riverside. Unlike it, Santa Cruz was planned to carry its full share of the anticipated undergraduate enrollment and to have graduate studies and research. Early on, I considered the possible transfer of forestry from Berkeley to Santa Cruz and did transfer the Lick Observatory on Mount Hamilton from Berkeley to Santa Cruz affiliation, where it came to find a congenial home, though the Berkeley astronomy department had thought of Lick as its own adjunct enterprise and Lick thought it belonged to itself and to the universe and to no one else. Santa Cruz also developed a strong research program in marine biology and early proposed a concentration on Pacific area studies (subsequently allotted to San Diego).

Santa Cruz was intended to "seem smaller to the individual student even as the campus and the university became larger." These were our central goals: to provide a broad general learning experience for undergraduate students in an intellectual world of fiercer and fiercer specializations and small living communities in the midst of a massive university. These were our dreams for new frontiers for higher education.

Mass Transformations and Administered Alterations

The 1960s were favorable to change: within the "New Frontier" and "Great Society" of Presidents John F. Kennedy and Lyndon Johnson, the period's unsurpassed growth in economic productivity per employed person helped make America the new world leader in economic, intellectual, cultural, political, and military affairs. For many it was a time of absolute faith in assured progress toward a better world. The United States and California—where whatever happened elsewhere happened first and hardest—were "on a high."

An enrollment explosion and massive increases in resources resulted in new campuses and expanded old campuses and augmented the conviction that there was no limit to what could be imagined as possible. There resulted, as Grant and Riesman say, "as volatile a period of educational reform as America has ever experienced" *(emphasis added).[1] The University of California participated in this explosion of aspirations.*

■

Popular Demand

This ferment in educational reform had two major sources. One was "popular demand" as expressed in public policy and in the desires of masses of people. The other was "administered" or "telic" change in the sense of having a specific goal *(telos)* and being originated by one or a few persons in positions of authority or influence on campus. Popular demand had the greater force behind it and had, by all odds the greater impact. I include the following as its major themes:[2]

THE RESEARCH UNIVERSITY'S RISE. Federal research support dollars in the hundreds of millions were available to our universities. I spoke about the new world of the "federal grant" university in my Godkin lectures at Harvard in 1963.[3] I noted the rise of the multiversity, with its expanse of often unrelated activities; the resulting new attention to graduate studies and research; and the neglect of undergraduates and the humanities. Along with the great successes in research and service, I discussed the pathologies of the multiversity: restless undergraduates, dissensions within the faculties, the rise of more and more restricted specialties, and the loss of a sense of an integrated intellectual community. Radical commentators thought I was celebrating too enthusiastically the rise of the military-industrial-university complex. I was even accused of setting up the multiversity. What in fact set up the multiversity was the federal government's investment of research dollars and faculty members' efforts to receive those dollars. The multiversity was a reform by popular demand par excellence, the greatest such reform since the land-grant movement of the 1860s.

EMPHASIS ON EQUALITY OF OPPORTUNITY. Open-access community colleges spread across the nation. California introduced its Master Plan for Higher Education. Support funds became available, as never before, for students from lower income families. Efforts were made to attract students from disadvantaged minority group backgrounds.

MORE VOCATIONAL STUDIES. Jobs in primary and secondary teaching were opening up as never before, along with new jobs that required tertiary education as in engineering, business administration, and computer science. The state colleges absorbed the greatest volume of this new demand. Liberal education faded.

THE COUNTERCULTURE. In loco parentis rules came under attack and disappeared nearly everywhere. Required courses similarly made way for individual student choices. "Participatory democracy" was a new theme. Political dissent flowered. It was a great period of human, and academic, liberation. These were the greatest of the mass transformations arising from popular demand.

Administered Academic Innovations

The other great source of change was internal individuals and groups—solutions advanced by established elites or new elites that seized power. These were planned, purposeful programs. In part they were reactions against the popular transformations, against a perceived overemphasis on research, against a neglect of undergraduates, against the concentration on the specialized expert as compared with the broadly educated person, against the neglect of the humanities and the arts. The solutions took the form of "cluster colleges" for undergraduates, of neoclassical educational programs, of concentrations on the arts.

These elitist, administered solutions really had little chance. The popular demand directions of movement overwhelmed attention and captured resources. The popular demands, also, were so contrary in their emphases to the administered solutions: for example, research instead of teaching, jobs instead of general knowledge, electives instead of planned requirements, the future instead of the past.

I choose the phrase "academic innovations," instead of "academic reforms," as the more neutral designation. The word "reform" asserts an improvement. But what is improvement to some is poison to others. As Francis Cornford once wrote, in academic life "nothing should ever be done for the first time."[4] Many faculty members are dubious about all innovations. There is a word of advice on the wall of the Director's Room of the Berkeley Faculty Club: "When it is not necessary to change, it is necessary not to change." This comment sets forth an eternal theme of academic life. The 1960s, however, were an aberration. Change, instead of continuity, was the great theme. Innovations were rampant.

I divide innovations into the following categories, drawing on Grant and Riesman, in their path-breaking book, *The Perpetual Dream:*[5]

"Popular" innovations that are initiated on the basis of mass pressures both internal and external.

"Telic" innovations that have a stated purpose and are initiated within existing or newly introduced internal governmental processes—what I call "administered innovations" and in turn divide into

"segmental telic" innovations that apply only to one part of a campus—to a single department or college or activity, as at the Irvine campus in particular; and

"holistic telic" innovations that apply to a campus in its entirety or to a major segment of a campus, as at San Diego and Santa Cruz.

Grant and Riesman then set forth four holistic telic models:[6]

"Neo-classical," with an emphasis on a broad liberal education—a reversion to earlier practices.

"Aesthetic-expressive," with an emphasis on creativity—Bohemia inside the university.

"Communal-expressive," with an emphasis on the whole person within a tribal family.

"Activist-radical," with an emphasis on societal change planned and organized within the university.

Within the University of California, these last two types of these telic programs were established by groups that seized influence rather than by already established authority, as with Kresge College at Santa Cruz and Lumumba-Zapata College at San Diego.

Among the new University of California campuses, Irvine accepted the standard university model of the time, making adjustments, some quite substantial, to individual segments of the model, but these were generally in the flow of broader movements, as in biology. Irvine led all American universities in such segmental adjustments.

San Diego was critical of the existing multiversity model in general and made adjustments to it in response to its already evident pathologies. It paid more attention to undergraduates, to teaching, to contacts among the disciplines while accepting and advancing attention to science, to research, to graduate studies. In my judgment, San Diego made the most successful modifications to the totality of the standard model, staying mostly with the neoclassical telic model.

Santa Cruz started out more nearly to confront the standard model than to modify it, particularly in its rejection of departmental hegemony. As the most experimental of the three new campuses and of the country's research universities, it set up "boards of studies" on the British model that often included more than a single discipline. It also initially gave one-half of the control of faculty appointments and promotions to the colleges, not the departments. It emphasized the humanities and social sciences, and undergraduate teaching. Later on Santa Cruz backed off from some of its more confrontational stands and ended up with an experimental lower-division program that takes a small step toward correcting the greatest single pathology of the research university: its inattention to lower-division students. It achieved modifications rather than confrontation.

All campuses of the University of California were involved in both popular and telic initiatives, although to quite differing degrees.

Irvine's Adjusted Model

Segmental telic innovations Irvine undertook included:

Breaking up the standard college of letters and sciences into *divisions* of physical sciences, biological sciences, social sciences, humanities and arts. The combined college was good at budgetary allocations, at review of academic appointments and promotions, and at selection of department chairs, but it was weak in attention to innovations within the separate areas and at encouraging interdisciplinary efforts. I had suggested such a breakup when I was chancellor at Berkeley, and it occurred later. At Riverside and at Santa Cruz and San Diego, as well as at Irvine, separate colleges or divisions replaced a unitary letters and sciences college. One result of the divisional structure was to involve the deans more in departmental academic affairs. Some departments had had more autonomy within the old format and disliked the change.

Organizing *biology* by levels of life instead of by kinds of species. This also happened on all UC campuses—most slowly at Berkeley. It resulted from the evolution of the field toward biochemistry and the advent of new instruments of study including the electron microscope that aided microbiology.

Setting up a new field of *administration* to encompass business and public health and educational administration and not business alone. This happened also at Davis and Riverside.

Making *comparative literature,* not literature on a language-by-language basis, a single department. This had earlier been done as an add-on at Berkeley but it was easier to do at Irvine in the absence of established departments organized around individual languages. Comparative literature at Irvine came to be rated as one of the best in the nation in the 1993 National Research Council rankings.

Dividing *psychology* into social psychology in the social sciences and psychobiology in the biological sciences.

Orienting the *arts* more toward performance and less toward history and criticism alone. This had previously been done at Riverside.

Emphasizing *creative writing,* a field not usually taught in traditional English departments.

Blending an early emphasis on the *environment* with a new field of *social ecology.*

Putting strong emphasis on *computer engineering.*

Experimenting heavily with the *new electronic technology* in teaching.

All the above initiatives at Irvine I was glad to try to encourage to the extent (often minor) that I could. All were successful as far as I can determine, with two exceptions.

> The first exception was administration. In each case (Irvine, Riverside, and Davis) the attempt to consider administration in its many settings, and not just business alone, failed as a result of perceived external rejection. Employers in the business world did not seem to like the combination of "business enterprise" with "governmental bureaucracy" and with other nonprofit orientations, which they looked at unfavorably. This reaction, they thought, had an impact on students' choice of schools. Thus the designation of each school became "management" or "business" instead of "administration." "Public administration" was seen as an enemy.

> The second exception was the new electronic technology. The hardware for computerized instruction was then available but not enough good software. We started with the hardware alone but soon discovered that we needed to make provision for students to discuss each lesson, preferably with a discussion leader, and this was not part of our planning.

All these innovations at Irvine were within the confines of the standard model of the multiversity, in a new campus without set structural patterns; and all were compatible with what was beginning to happen in the nationwide university world. They were mostly good things to do and most were also sure things. As the most innovative research university of any in the United States on a systematic basis at the time, Irvine had an early and attractive personality of its own. The process of segmental telic change, however, did not long continue.[7]

San Diego's Modified Model

Both San Diego and Santa Cruz carried out holistic telic campuswide innovations that went outside the standard multiversity model. Many criticisms of the emerging multiversity model focused on the university's primary concern with research and graduate studies; its view of the campus as one massive organism but with faculty and students who lived largely or even entirely separate lives; and the department's supremacy in the intellectual life of the campus along with an emphasis on more and more minute specializations. Robert Hutchins at Chicago was the most famous critic in the United States, assailing departments and the dominance of research activity. Columbia developed its "Great Books" program[8] as Stanford did its "Western Civilization" sequence. Harvard introduced broadly oriented "core courses"; Michigan and Michigan State started experimental undergraduate colleges; earlier, Swarthmore had introduced undergraduate "honors seminars." The Claremont system in southern California developed a more total alternative approach of affiliated independent colleges with a common graduate school.

In partial imitation of Oxford and Cambridge, several of the new postwar universities in the United Kingdom organized into "cluster colleges" with several common characteristics, mostly neoclassical: they were relatively small, emphasized undergraduate teaching, and offered courses of broad intellectual understanding (under boards of studies) instead of more and more specialization and vocational emphases. San Diego and Santa Cruz fell into this same approach of criticism of and resulting experimental responses to the emerging standard multiversity pattern, but to quite different degrees and under different circumstances.

The original San Diego plan included some fundamental departures. The first was growth from the *top down,* starting with self-contained departments at the graduate level that could be instituted one at a time. This followed on the earlier plans for a graduate-level school of science and engineering. It worked well.

The second departure was development of *internal colleges for undergraduates* originally with 2,000 to 2,500 students each. They became successful residential and social communities for students and centers for organized activities by students, but they did not become as successful as centers for faculty-student interactive intellectual life as had first been hoped. Faculty members, by and large, did not enter into college activities.

Each college, however, did develop its own general education requirements—breadth requirements and skill requirements—and, along with the departments, set graduation requirements. The general education requirements mostly consisted of the customary introductory courses taught by faculty from within the established departments. I have always looked upon breadth requirements as an easy but unsatisfactory approach to a liberal education, using introductory courses to a discipline as though they constituted a broad survey of the field.

In addition, Revelle College developed a strong liberal arts theme, a five-course sequence concentrating on the humanities (history and literature) to go along with its emphasis on science—an effort to bridge the two-culture gap then recently set forth by C. P. Snow.[9] Thurgood Marshall College established a three-course theme centered on multicultural understanding (with credit for off-campus service activities). The theme of Eleanor Roosevelt College became "global perspectives" with a six-course sequence. These were colleges 1, 3, and 5. The in-between colleges, 2 and 4, have had less strong themes, perhaps in each case in reaction to the predecessor college's strong emphasis on a central theme. John Muir College (number 2) has come to draw students in a balanced way from the arts and humanities as well as the sciences, and Earl Warren (number 4) in an unbalanced way from engineering. Muir has put great emphasis on a two-course sequence in writing. It alone has no math requirement. Warren has a one-course theme curriculum of "ethics and society." The required theme courses, across the colleges, constitute about a tenth or less of undergraduates' class hours. Originally it was expected that undergraduate students would take about two-thirds of their courses within their colleges.

The third departure, originally planned by Roger Revelle, was *organization of research around themes,* as with oceanography at Scripps, rather than around departments. This was, I thought, a very attractive idea. However, to my regret, actual practice came mostly to follow the standard mono-disciplinary form.

The colleges at San Diego now stand (1997) as follows.[10] There are five colleges with a sixth in prospect. The number of students per college has risen from the original plan for 2,000–2,500 to 3,000 or more. The colleges, in general, have performed well in creating residential accommodations for one quarter of all students, mostly freshmen and sophomores. They provide a great wealth of standard student activities, far beyond, on a per capita basis, those available in a monolithic campus of equivalent total size. They also are centers for academic and personal advising beyond what is available on the standard campus, and for social and cultural functions. The colleges handle occasions such as an orientation period for new students, a parents' day, and commencements. As smaller and more complete communities for residential students, and to a much lesser extent for commuters, they have met the expectations for them.

As academic units, however, their performance is much more mixed. All faculty members are assigned to a college but only about 25 percent (as a modal estimate of the provosts) actually participate in any significant way. Each college is in charge of general education as defined above as well as liberal education defined as being organized around themes of broad intellectual understanding: "great books" or "great ideas" or "great epochs" of all civilizations or "broad learning experiences" about human activities from a multidisciplinary point of view.

Most course instruction at San Diego is by or under the direction of faculty members who are appointed by and promoted within their separate departments. College provosts—as academic deans of general and liberal education, and deans of students for their colleges—can and often do make comments on the "service" of faculty members who participate in college affairs, and these comments have varying influences in specific cases in the course of promotions. The provosts serve as proponents of teaching and of undergraduate interests in general, and San Diego does appear to pay more attention to both than does the standard multiversity. Provosts, however, universally wish they had more resources to encourage faculty to provide assistance to their general and liberal education endeavors. The only instrument of persuasion the provosts now have is that departments get credit for the students they teach in the college courses and this adds to their total departmental full-time equivalent (FTE) faculty positions. Nonfaculty personnel assigned to the colleges by the central administration handle academic advising and student affairs.

A look at one college illustrates the movement of San Diego over time. Marshall College, once called Lumumba-Zapata College, had an early period when some students sought to make it into a college devoted to the "theory and practice of revolution." The college broke into feuding factions and also drew the attention of the central administration seeking a reorientation of the program. This attempt at a revolutionary theme was never successful and temporarily affected the public's view of the total campus. On the positive side, Marshall College did increase campus attention to the needs of minority students. Provost Joseph Watson is widely credited with having "saved" that college.

The overall movement of the San Diego campus has been back toward the standard multiversity model with dominance of faculty activity by the departments. The original dreams have lost some of their drawing power, particularly among the newer and younger faculty members. Yet San Diego does stand as one public university that pays more than the usual attention to undergraduates, to teaching, and to interdisciplinary teaching and research activities. Nevertheless, the individual colleges seem to be moving toward more disciplinary concentrations: in Revelle to the biological sciences, in Marshall and Roosevelt to the social sciences, and in Warren to engineering.

The colleges, in their totality, still stand for balance: against total domination by the disciplines, and for general and liberal education. They also give undergraduates more flexibility of choice: among academic requirements, and among intellectual and cultural environments.

In contrast to Santa Cruz, San Diego stepped in faster to contain Lumumba-Zapata College than Santa Cruz did with the original Kresge College. Also, the scientists at San Diego seemed much more devoted to maintaining hard-core academic discipline than the more permissive (and less confident) humanists and social scientists at Santa Cruz. Interestingly enough, liberal education seemed to fare better in San Diego's hands.

Innovations and
Reactions at Santa Cruz

Santa Cruz challenged the multiversity model head on. It attempted a basic holistic telic reform that was battered but survived in small part. The experience taught us a lot about American higher education and about the University of California.

We began with a "dream" that Page Smith, the original provost of Cowell College at Santa Cruz, set forth in his "Statement of Aims" (undated) for the college in a quote from my Harvard Godkin lectures:

> *One [task] is the improvement of undergraduate instruction in the university. It will require the solution of many sub-problems: how to give adequate recognition to the teaching skill as well as to the research performance of the faculty; how to create a curriculum that serves the needs of the student as well as the research interests of the teacher; how to prepare the generalist as well as the specialist in an age of specialization looking for better generalizations; how to treat the individual student as a unique human being in the mass student body; how to make the university seem smaller even as it grows larger; how to establish a range of contact between faculty and students broader than the one-way route across the lectern or through the television screen; how to raise educational policy again to the forefront of faculty concerns. . . . Another major task is to create a more unified intellectual world. We need to make contact between the two, the three, the many cultures; to open channels of intelligent conversation across the disciplines and divisions; to close the gap between C. P. Snow's "Luddites" and scientists; to answer fragmentation with general theories and sensitivities.[1]*

These were very large aims!

∎

In November 1964 the original academic plan for Santa Cruz with its colleges received the approval of the statewide Academic Senate Committee on Educational Policy. But the committee had reservations: "A college transmits knowledge; a university creates it." Shortly later the committee advised "more formal organization of faculty by departments." The relevance of these observations is even more obvious in retrospect, as is the fact that our aims went beyond faculty acceptance at that time. And yet I would argue that a university both transmits and creates knowledge—and should do both well. There is a place for the college as well as the department.[2]

An Outline of the Original Santa Cruz

The initial challenge to the standard university model of departments based upon academic disciplines was the decision to have broadly oriented "boards of studies" instead of departments at Santa Cruz. The boards of studies and the more interdisciplinary "committees of studies," intended at coalescing several academic fields, offered freedom for faculty members to explore broader horizons, some of them potentially highly productive. Broader horizons were also attractive to independent-minded students who were not yet willing to settle on narrow specializations. However, the boards suited the humanities and social sciences better than they did the sciences—but the former were in retreat as the latter advanced. Also, many fields, including the arts, require special facilities for their activities (as in traditional departments rather than interdisciplinary boards). The scientists and artists led the attack in breaking away from boards to develop departmental connections. In fact the boards were never fully developed. Most of the early ones were actually limited to a single discipline while others gradually evolved in this direction, and divisions were set up to house them (and the departments that took their place). The original divisions were in the sciences, the social sciences, and the humanities. The divisions—rather than the colleges—became the most important administrative subunits under the chancellor. But how did this reversal of the original intent come about?

As the campus grew, most new faculty members wanted standard departments. They had been trained in and received their Ph.D.'s from established departments across the nation and the world. To ask a young faculty member to step into a board of study was to encourage him or her to become familiar with a larger body of information and analysis, even though the requirements of a single discipline, or even subdiscipline, were already often overwhelming. What to read? Where to publish? Where to look for another job? These are always central questions for young faculty members. Departments supply specific answers. Boards of studies do not. Also, students on their way to graduate study elsewhere could find themselves less of a known commodity when they emerged from a board of study.

Santa Cruz's second challenge to the standard university model was the college system. It was, however, less of a departure than the original boards of studies. Oxford and Cambridge had their internal colleges, and Harvard and Yale their houses, and the Claremont system its independent colleges. Yet the colleges have tended to wither away as a curricular influence, at Santa Cruz and at Oxford and Cambridge too. Why? The original college core courses were required courses, and students in the 1960s were fighting against requirements. And core courses often require some cooperation among faculty members, even team teaching—something akin to getting two painters to work on a single portrait. In addition, the colleges required two affiliations from faculty members instead of one, and two contrasting focuses of evaluation. One loyalty, to the college, was to teach and counsel students; and the other, to the department, was to do research—with consequent disagreements over performance evaluations, and lost time and lost dispositions in disputations. Also, teaching was hard to evaluate, and research comparatively easy. And because a college's format promises more faculty attention to students than does the university's, students at Santa Cruz overwhelmed faculty members with consultations in the early days, and many faculty members increasingly preferred to view themselves as "university" faculty. They found that while they mostly did like students, they also did not wish to perish through lack of publications. They retreated from college contacts. College teaching came to be viewed as an "overload."

More recently, another big change affecting the colleges has been to turn each college's business and administrative affairs over to an administrative officer who reports to a campuswide officer and not to the provost. Some provosts felt they were "hotel keepers" and disliked the role. But this move reduced their realm of influence as well as their administrative load. In addition, each college now has a corps of student advisers, tutors, writing supervisors, and discussion leaders that makes up its student-oriented *non*faculty faculty (outside the "ladder faculty" of full, associate, and assistant professors). So the role of the college as a center for regular faculty affiliation and for administrative activity has diminished but has not totally disappeared. In particular, the provost has little to do as provost—bereft as she or he may be of both academic contact at the faculty level and administrative responsibilities.

The process of change was confused and the negotiations labyrinthine. But in the end—which was an early end—the colleges limited their academic involvement to one core course taught by nonladder faculty. For lower-division students, colleges also provide advising at the nonmajor level and arrange for a changing menu of topical courses. The departments and divisions are in charge of the majors, of academic personnel actions, and of the budgets. What is left now for the colleges? A lower-division core course in writing and in group discussions (in sections of fifteen to twenty students under mostly nonladder faculty leadership), and smaller and more human living and activity centers for students within the colleges. Each of these, in my judgment, is an improvement on the customary multiversity model, where undergraduates, and especially lower-division students, can feel neglected, compared to graduate students and faculty research interests.

History Was Destructive

The search for a location for the campus began after suitable and readily available sites in the Santa Clara Valley (Silicon Valley) had already been taken. This led us to a rural site across the mountains to the south, with certain consequences already noted (chapter 16).

The big impacts of the subsequent history of the 1960s and 1970s have been the rise of the student counterculture, followed by a shift of students to a labor market vocational orientation, and a shift of faculty tastes increasingly to the multiversity model. Santa Cruz was greatly affected by the first, not prepared for the second, and susceptible to the third.

A NEOCLASSICAL MODEL AND ITS DEMISE

The Santa Cruz campus opened in the fall of 1965. The student-led political revolt of the 1960s was already under way (as at Berkeley in the fall of 1964) and so also the contemporary but quite different cultural revolution. Santa Cruz was planned, however, as a neoclassical campus with solid and cohesive academic liberal learning programs as in the first three colleges: Cowell (1965)—six courses in a core sequence, "World Civilization"; Stevenson (1966)—three courses in the sequence "Self and Society"—great ideas in the social sciences; and Crown (1967)—three courses in a sequence on "Science, Culture, and Man."[3] These were the three first-flight colleges planned while I was still president of the university.

We intended each college to be somewhat similar to Swarthmore, Williams, Pomona, Oberlin, or Reed, and its broad core curriculum to resemble the undergraduate liberal learning courses at Columbia and Stanford and earlier at Chicago. But the period of founding successful neoclassical colleges was long past and the neoclassical model ran up against the student counterculture and political revolts, against requirements of any sort, and particularly up against the canons of *Western* civilization. "Great books" were no longer thought to be "relevant" to the modern problems of class, gender, and race and, in any event, students said they had been written by despised "dead white males." Many Santa Cruz students were affected by the counterculture, as were some of the younger faculty, while other faculty felt an obligation to go along with their students whether they agreed with them or not.

COUNTERCULTURAL PROGRAMS

The next flight of colleges included Merrill (1968)—third-world studies and somewhat "activist-radical"; Porter (1968)—the visual and performing arts— "aesthetic-expressive"; and particularly Kresge (1970)—"communal-expressive," as Grant and Riesman describe it. The subsequent last flight of colleges was somewhat more traditional, somewhat less countercultural but still "relevant": Oakes (1971), under the leadership of the African-American sociologist J. Herman Blake, originally concentrated on hard-core skills and subjects for minority students and on credit for community service ("Oakes serves"); and College Eight (1972), which focused on the environment.

I give most attention in what follows to Kresge because it was, for awhile, the most extreme in its orientation and the most prominent in the general public's awareness, though it was the first and only Santa Cruz college clearly to fail totally in its original format. Founded in 1970, Kresge lasted with remnants of its original plan only to 1979. The first provost was Robert Edgar, a scientist from Cal Tech and, as it turned out, a devotee of Carl Rogers. Rogers was a psychotherapist who practiced "client-centered" psychotherapy. This translated into student-centered education: the students would lead the way and the faculty would follow as "facilitators." Rogers had "a profound distrust of all external authority" and believed that each individual was bound to obey "only the laws he regards as sound and just, and to disobey those he sees as unsound and unjust."[4] A recipe for total anarchy. A recipe for Kresge.

Edgar had written to Dean McHenry in advance that he wanted to create a "participatory, consensual democracy."[5] In practice this meant that the most activist faculty and students would take over, that the nonactivists would end up on the sidelines or leave the college, and that decay would result; and this is what happened.

Additionally, Kresge's education was intended to be concerned with training all the senses—not just the cognitive—seeing, hearing, feeling, tasting, smelling, touching. "The Heart and the Body were not to be cut off from the Head"—and that involved "the body erotic."[6] Cynics insisted that the Kresge College environs were the only place in the world where, if you kicked a poison oak bush, it would kick you right back. Students were encouraged to experience, however vicariously, all the sensations of life from birth to death. Death meant digging your own grave and climbing into it, having friends throw clods of dirt on your body and give farewell speeches.[7] Thus the "touchy-feely" perception of the college and of the campus. This approach was in full bloom only four years, until a new chancellor (Mark Christensen, 1974–76) was brought in. But the damage was done. Most of the faculty and students quickly fled from this approach, which resulted in leaving only a "corner of the college" with four faculty members and forty-eight students going along with their "sensitivity training."[8] In 1979 Chancellor Sinsheimer finally disbanded this remnant.

The "Kresge experiment" occupied only a small corner of the Santa Cruz campus. However, the central administration became very nondirective. The second-flight policy was to hire provosts and tell them: "do your own thing; we may or may not like it, but whatever it is we will support you in doing it." Thus much of the campus did come to have a Kresge flavor and a tendency toward Grant and Riesman's "activist-radical" model. But it was badly located for this development—out of range of TV crews and distant from metropolitan newspapers. The Berkeley campus came to best represent that type of activity.

Santa Cruz became more the counterculture campus—a campus with students and faculty members who "mellowed out" among the redwoods.[9] The emphasis on the humanities and on the social sciences was one source of this tendency. Another was the semirural setting that repelled those from big cities interested in getting jobs and susceptible to what one called "asphalt deprivation." Instead Santa Cruz attracted "Anglo" students and faculty from affluent suburban backgrounds who were avoiding the stress of highly competitive atmospheres.[10] The second provost at Cowell, an art historian who hated industrial society, turned that college from "world civilization" to the practice of preindustrial arts and crafts. Crown College, which started with a carefully organized series of courses on the history and methods and impacts of the sciences and set forth the cutting edges of each major scientific field, ended up with a one-term course that concentrated on multiculturalism, "California: Images and Realities of the Golden State." In its totality, the Santa Cruz campus came to have multiculturalism as its central theme. Defenders of the campus say this was because the students both needed and wanted increasing multicultural understanding. Most students came from segregated situations and for the first time were living and working in a nonsegregated community.

Much more importantly, however, but less noticed at the time, most faculty were actually moving in a hard-working multiversity direction, emphasizing their research interests. Berkeley was the common model for many students and many faculty—radical activism for the first group and the multiversity for the second. Support for the Berkeley model came not only from within the Santa Cruz faculty. Especially in the early days, faculty members from other campuses, and particularly Berkeley, were invited to sit on promotion and appointment committees at Santa Cruz. They quite uniformly advanced adherence to "Berkeley standards" of performance as the only way for the campus to develop and sustain the respect of faculty colleagues on sister campuses. Also, early emphasis on a campuswide Academic Senate was a centralizing force as against the intended emphasis on decisions within cluster colleges.

BACKLASHES

Many parents and prospective students became suspicious of Santa Cruz. The student generation of the 1960s was followed by the "me" generation of the 1970s that wanted jobs and money at a time of recessions and a reduction in employment opportunities. The vocationally oriented students who might otherwise have entered Santa Cruz found that there were no engineering or business administration programs and few other directly job-related specialties to turn to. Also, a series of grisly murders in the Santa Cruz mountains put a blight on the campus. Applications fell off and entering SAT scores dropped from an average of 1250 in the early 1970s (the same level as Pomona) to 1050 in the early 1980s (the UC average, although Santa Cruz had been above even the Berkeley level in earlier years).

The Sinsheimer period (chancellor, 1977–87) built on the internal and external backlashes. Robert Sinsheimer was a scientist from Cal Tech. His real interests were in science and research. He seemed to be intent on the transformation of Santa Cruz into a Berkeley or large-scale Cal Tech as fast as possible. He put all academic personnel actions in the departments (as of 1979, a "reaggregation" turned over faculty appointments and promotions entirely to the departments and the higher levels of the administration, relocated faculty offices to achieve departmental concentrations, and gave the departments full control of the curriculum). Additionally, reaggregation gave most budgetary authority over the departments to the divisions, originally set up in 1964 under vice-chancellors (later deans) simply to coordinate interdisciplinary work among faculty from different departments.

Sinsheimer also reoriented Kresge College and pushed hard for more effective recruitment of students. Santa Cruz was moving fast toward the dominant model of the multiversity. The counterculture was in almost total retreat. So also was the dream of neoclassical undergraduate colleges in the context of the modern research university.

STABILIZATION IN A MULTIVERSITY DIRECTION

Santa Cruz in the 1990s remains a campus of colleges as centers of social life and of student-oriented activities (there are eight colleges—with two more in prospect), with some residual academic efforts. SAT scores have stopped falling, and the campus has advanced substantially in academic rankings as a center of research. An engineering school, as well, was launched in 1997. The campus reached a plateau of comparative stability under the chancellorship of Karl Pister (1991–96). In 1991, a *Report on the Intellectual and Cultural Life of the Colleges,* coauthored by Carol Freeman (a subsequent provost of Cowell) and Carolyn Clark, was accepted, but not overwhelmingly, by the Santa Cruz Academic Senate. It endorsed the continuation of the college system. It also called for more courses within the colleges and suggested that each faculty member at Santa Cruz should be expected to teach at least one *additional* course for one term within a college at least once every three years (the average teaching load, or primary class workload per regular-rank FTE, at Santa Cruz—a campus intended to put an extra effort into teaching—had fallen to 4.19 as compared with 5.46 at Berkeley. This negative variation by one-quarter gave Santa Cruz the lowest teaching workload among the eight general campuses).[11] The senate, however, revised the Freeman report's recommendation to call for an additional course within a college *or a department* (most of these courses, in practice, were for only one or two units). But the change would increase the academic role of the colleges to the extent individual faculty members elected to teach these courses within the colleges and not the departments. Acceptance of the Freeman report was later rescinded in its entirety with enthusiasm by the Academic Senate.

The likelihood is that the colleges will not regain their originally intended central role in undergraduate liberal education, although I still hope that one or more of the colleges (in addition to Stevenson, which has a neoclassical three-term program on "Self and Society") might wish to do at least as much in the way of broad learning sequences as Revelle, Marshall, and Roosevelt Colleges at San Diego. Such sequences of courses might, however, be also at the upper-division level. They might constitute an optional "minor" to go along with the disciplinary major. A common faculty view seems to be, however, that broad learning sequences of courses are not necessary, that the total curriculum at Santa Cruz is full of broad learning courses, and that students who want to do so can fashion their own sequences.

I have gone over the core course outlines for several of the colleges and find most of the readings to be generally rather contemporary avant-garde items and scattered in their academic content. The assigned readings do appear, however, to be rather challenging as a basis for writing assignments and for class discussions about contemporary American civilization. Students' evaluations seem strongly to support the value of these courses as an introduction to the skills required for a university education—the ability to write clearly and to engage actively in intellectual discourse. As such, the core courses serve as good entrance vestibules to the enterprise of higher education. Some faculty members, however, consider them to have been "dumbed down" to the high school level. The colleges also provide opportunities for student- and faculty-originated low-unit (one or two units) courses, some crossdisciplinary, and mostly of a topical nature. General breadth requirements are set on a campuswide basis and are quite standard. The full transition of power from colleges and boards of studies to departments has taken much of the last three decades.

The four stages in the life of Santa Cruz—the neoclassical, the countercultural, the backlashes, and the stabilization—complicate its history, and shifts from one stage to the next have left behind residues of resentment among those who have disliked one or more of the shifts. The broad movement at Santa Cruz has been from neoclassical themes to a central campus concern for multiculturalism.[12]

Personal Impressions

Kay and I went to Santa Cruz in September 1965 to participate in the first full meeting of students and faculty in the field house, which served at first as a dining hall. Afterward we went from trailer to trailer where the students were housed pending completion of residence halls. It was a beautiful evening with warm breezes blowing in from the ocean. There was a full moon. The students welcomed us with such enthusiasm and expressions of appreciation for what we were doing for them. Some wrote poems for us. It was for Kay and me one of the greatest evenings of our lives.

Four years later, in June 1969, I accepted an invitation from these same students to give the address at their commencement: I was then the university's former president, they were the first four-year graduating class. Recalling that earlier enchanted evening, I went with high expectations. I found the situation totally changed. As students received their diplomas and then walked by Chancellor McHenry and me on the stage, some of them expressed their contempt for us and the campus by throwing their diplomas at us. Then a group of students took over and turned the occasion into guerrilla theater. Their leaders said that McHenry and I had planned and created Santa Cruz as a capitalist-imperialist-fascist plot to divert the students from their revolution against the evils of American society and, in particular, against the horrors of the Vietnam War. They gave an "honorary degree" in absentia to a Black Panther (Huey Newton) who was in jail charged with murder. They then turned to the audience asking it to rise in appreciation of the contributions of this Black Panther. The students mostly all rose. The leaders then motioned to the parents sitting in a large circle behind the students, but no one rose. Then they turned to the faculty in front and almost all members rose one by one until nearly all were standing except for a small group surrounding Kenneth Thimann, the provost of Crown College.

When I was called upon to speak, I put aside my written comments and spoke to the occasion. I said that it had been a long and "hot" afternoon and I was not going to add to either the length or the heat of the occasion. That, however, I would like to make two brief comments. One, with reference to Alice in *Through the Looking Glass*—when she asked a man gazing into the far distance what he saw, he replied, "Nothing," and Alice then said what wonderful eyesight he must have to be able to see nothing and at such a great distance!—was what wonderful eyesight McHenry and I must have had in the 1930s as graduate students at Stanford, when the "Santa Cruz dream" first occurred to us, to see the Vietnam War and student revulsion when we were so far away. The second comment was that I was in sympathy with their views about the Vietnam War (it was a bad war for Americans to be in, and I was by that time national chair of an antiwar but pro-American group called Committee for a Political Settlement in Vietnam) but thought that their means of protest against the war were very counterproductive and hoped that they would give some thought to whether or not the means they used were in accord with the high ideals they professed to hold. I then sat down. Several years passed before I visited the campus again. What most impressed me was how such a high proportion of the faculty had stood on their feet to applaud the students who were attacking the campus the faculty had by then created. It was one of the worst afternoons of my life.

I should not have been so surprised by the Santa Cruz commencement. Just the day before, I had attended the commencement at Oberlin. The main speaker was the radical minority mayor of a midwestern city. He castigated Oberlin as an example of a racist education—Oberlin of all places, given its history. The students stood up in wild applause; parents and friends sat in stunned opposition. Then I heard some rustling noises on the stage behind me and turned around to see what was going on. I watched the faculty rise, row by row, to join the students in their rejection of Oberlin—yet they were the purveyors of this education! A year or two before, I had been to a commencement at Brandeis. There the student speaker attacked the president as the "Brandeis Hitler"—the harshest possible criticism in that setting. Again the students had risen to applaud, the rest of the audience had remained seated, but so had the faculty. Why was I so surprised at Santa Cruz? I remembered our plans for neoclassical colleges and the students' poems that September evening. And I had not yet fully absorbed how the counterculture and political rebellion had swept so much of American higher education, including this "Swarthmore in the redwoods."

I then reflected on Santa Cruz. I thought of our hopes for the undergraduate colleges with their more human scale and their broader combinations of subject matters across the traditional disciplines, but then also of the tensions between the colleges and the departments; of the hopes for more attention to teaching, but also of faculty desires for more research time in a research-oriented university; of the needs of the undergraduates but also of the attractiveness to faculty members of teaching graduate students; of the idealistic hopes but also of the realistic costs. The hopes had sometimes been disappointed and the costs, though mostly known to exist in advance, had sometimes been greater than earlier estimated. But Santa Cruz, I concluded, was a better campus for its individuality, and the University of California a more diverse institution for the presence of Santa Cruz within the system.

Reconsiderations on Attempts at Academic Change

Heraclitus said that "nothing endures but change." About the historical university it might be said, instead, that everything else changes, but the university mostly endures. About seventy-five institutions in the Western world established by 1520 still exist in recognizable forms, with similar functions and with unbroken histories, including the Catholic church; the Parliaments of the Isle of Man, of Iceland, and of Great Britain; the governance structures of several Swiss cantons; the Bank of Siena; and some sixty-one universities. . . . [These universities] are mostly still in the same locations with some of the same buildings, with professors and students doing much the same things, and with governance carried on in much the same ways. There have been many intervening variations on the ancient themes, it is true, but the eternal themes of teaching, scholarship, and service, in one combination or another, continue. Looked at from within, universities have changed enormously in the emphases on their several functions and in their guiding spirits, but looked at from without and comparatively, they are among the least changed of all institutions.

How can this be so? Universities still turn out many of the same products—members of the more learned professions of theology, teaching, medicine, and the law, and scholarship. Universities have not yet been subject to any major technological changes, as have industry and agriculture and transportation. Faculty members continue to operate largely as individual craftspersons. Universities, traditionally, like the churches, have usually had a degree of autonomy from political and economic control that is quite remarkable, partly because they have been protected by the upper classes, however constituted, at nearly all times in almost every type of society. They have, on occasion, through what has gone on within them, helped change the world but have themselves been much less changed than most of the rest of the world.[1]

Though I first made these remarks in 1986, they still apply today. Since the founding of Harvard in 1636, there have been four major mutations on the standard American models of the liberal arts college, the liberal university, and the teachers' college: the land-grant model university, incorporating the German research university; the two-year community college, concentrating on vocational preparation; the polytechnic institution, adapting the teachers' college; and the multiversity.

The University of California attempted in the 1960s to offset some of the pathologies of the multiversity by setting up liberal arts colleges within it, at San Diego and Santa Cruz. This chapter evaluates the fate of the cluster colleges at these new campuses and concentrates on Santa Cruz, as the greatest challenge to the multiversity model.

■

One big early decision—to block efforts to set up a school of engineering at Santa Cruz for which Chancellor Dean McHenry had already recruited an excellent dean—was a mistake. UC President Charles Hitch (1968–76) took this action on the strong advice of the California Postsecondary Education Commission. But the decision, in turn, discouraged efforts to start a school of business or other professional schools, which tend to attract less radical and "expressive" students and faculty and to enjoy higher public confidence and standing. Also, "participatory democracy" by students and faculty, as at Santa Cruz, was much less conducive to management of telic neoclassical innovations than an environment of administration-faculty shared governance as at San Diego and Irvine. It is a strange circumstance that neoclassical educational programs draw heavily on the humanities and social sciences but are more likely to prosper under the guidance of the sciences and professional schools, as at MIT.

Another early mistake was to recruit faculty for Santa Cruz mostly at the assistant-professor level. At this level, faculty members must concentrate on achieving tenure. They are, in addition, often not yet broadly oriented enough intellectually to engage fully in the liberal learning activities of the neoclassical college. We should have provided for more tenure-level faculty in the pioneer days, and for more faculty with experience in liberal arts colleges.

Third, the practice at Santa Cruz, particularly after the first three colleges, was to appoint a charismatic provost and then to let him or her and the associated faculty and students work out an academic theme for the college as they went along. This policy was, I thought, like taking an unidentified sprout from a forest floor and planting it in your garden and taking your chances. I wish I had insisted harder than I did on having a "charter" for each college to help it set up the core curriculum and to choose a provost and faculty members who would know what they were expected to do.[2] Charters would, at least, have forced discussion of the knowledge most worth knowing and provoked debate on educational policy for the undergraduate years, which no longer takes place on most university campuses in the United States. They would also have created documents subject to review within committees of the Academic Senate and by higher levels of the administration.

I did not think that any large group of academic people could any longer agree on what constituted the one and only "liberal education"—that body of knowledge most worth knowing, or what was once called "universal knowledge." I did think that we could, however, provide some "broad learning experiences" that would help students think in terms of more than one discipline in approaching broad issues.[3] Students' academic majors orient them toward vertical thinking, but throughout their lives as citizens and also at higher levels in their careers they need to think horizontally. Concentrations—"great books" as with Hutchins or "great issues" as suggested by Ortega y Gasset,[4] or "great epochs" in the history of Western or world civilization, global perspectives, or more specific theme courses such as the environment, Asian civilizations, or the origins and the impacts of the city on human development—encourage the broader perspective.

Each college charter at Santa Cruz could have concentrated on the study of some body of cohesive and durable knowledge, to give students a neoclassical liberal education or a broad interdepartmental learning sequence. Some of the colleges at San Diego, starting with Revelle College, did so. The general San Diego approach was based, however, more on the solid sciences and less on the increasingly disoriented humanities.[5] Scientists have stronger convictions that what they are doing is the right thing to do and that they are doing it the right way. They deliberately try to concentrate on "truth," not on opinion and taste. But the second-flight policy at Santa Cruz (after Crown) was the exact opposite of "charters": it subcontracted the Santa Cruz dream to the individual provosts' idiosyncratic interpretations. Also, the original plans of the founders had been subject to regental and senate review; the subcontracted plans were subject to no review at all.

Alternative Approaches

No single approach fits all students equally well. We might have planned charter themes with less demanding required course hours for scientists than for humanists. Nor does collegiate life fit all faculty. We could have invited faculty members to join a college, with some system of rewards, rather than universally assign all new faculty to a college. And we might have given each college or division a set of faculty positions to bargain with—perhaps 10 to 20 percent of all FTEs—to encourage the departments to recruit faculty members able and willing to teach courses for "nonmajors": for example, an engineer to talk about the physical structure of the city, or a social scientist or a humanist to discuss the history of Venice or the culture of Vienna or the arts of Beijing. Then, even with most faculty appointments and promotions in the hands of departments, colleges or divisions could offer a series of three to six courses in a liberal or broad learning sequence. Provosts and deans, in addition to making suggestions for first appointments, could be encouraged to comment on teaching and college service to promotion committees and to chancellors.

I would, on reflection, also have put less emphasis on "narrative evaluations" by faculty members instead of letter grades—perhaps making the evaluations available only on request as a supplement to a letter grade. Some students came to think that such evaluations made it more difficult to get into graduate schools, and, as time went on, they often became rather routinized.

We should have put more emphasis on facilities for nonresident students in the colleges—lounges, study rooms, reading libraries, lockers, facilities to wash up and change clothes.

To make more allowance for the extra costs of our approach, we might have set up a separate budgetary division for the colleges. Extra state subsidies were probably not possible, but supplements to tuition and residence hall charges on the basis of ability to pay, or more aggressive fund raising even in the absence of high-income alumni, would have helped offset the costs of a college atmosphere. Porter College greatly benefited from its substantial endowment.

McHenry and I were in agreement on the overall plan for Santa Cruz. However, we did disagree on two important points. Aside from my preference for charters with neoclassical themes and McHenry's for the colleges' growth into whatever they wanted to be, I wanted a diversity of the student mix among the colleges while McHenry favored a more or less equal representation of stu-

293 · Reconsiderations on Attempts at Change

dents and faculty in all departments (labeled a two-by-two "Noah's ark" approach). My emphasis would, it is true, have led to more artists one place and more scientists another. McHenry was concerned that the colleges would become what he called "ghettos."[6]

With more time to work together, the two of us would have found common and possibly better solutions. One of my great regrets is the loss of this option. Also, McHenry was left all alone under a countercultural tsunami that overtook the campus, and he felt Puritanical outrage at some things that went on. (From the fall of 1964 I was heavily involved in other affairs and then, in January 1967, dismissed as president.) It would certainly have been helpful, also, if the next two presidents (Charles Hitch and David Saxon) had been more favorable toward the Santa Cruz experiment.

McHenry, looking back on the developments at Santa Cruz, concluded that the "division of academic functions between colleges and disciplinary groups was left vague" and attributed the haziness to his "humility": "I simply did not know enough." He also said he did not want to be too directive in his leadership—"I wanted to wait to see how faculty members felt and to judge the competence of those who would bear responsibility." He noted that "before we were out of the 1960s, the trend was clear: the colleges were truncating core courses . . . the faculty grew tired of teaching them, and the students' complaints about compulsion were telling."[7] All true.

One advantage of the developing college system is to offer feedback from the early colleges on how to improve the performance of newer ones. The campus can thus change as it grows—not just become more set in its ways. If Santa Cruz should decide or be required to grow to its originally planned size of 27,500, perhaps additional colleges will be added. They can be better colleges than those that came from our attempts. Santa Cruz can be a campus of the future as well as of the past. It can, in part, be born again, particularly now, with its new engineering school and its reaching out to the San Jose metropolitan area, where it already has 50,000 extension enrollments.

Evaluations

SANTA CRUZ COMPARED WITH WHAT?

The innovations at Santa Cruz have been and will be evaluated in many ways. Trying to ignore nostalgia for what might (or might not) have been, I shall comment on four possible approaches.

The first is a *comparison,* the approach Grant and Riesman took in *The Perpetual Dream.* They looked at several innovative campuses including St. John's in Annapolis and Santa Fe, New College of the University of South Florida, the College for Human Services in lower Manhattan, and Santa Cruz; and they were familiar with a number of other such experimental efforts, as they mention in their book. They called Santa Cruz a "genuine innovation in academic structure."[8] With reference to what I called the counterculture and backlash at Santa Cruz, they stated, "despite its recent reverses, Santa Cruz . . . continues to be, one of the most genuine successes of the last decade" (253). They concluded:

> In its curricular pluralism, its establishment of colleges with dramatically different architectures and personalities, the enthusiasm of its students about the quality of teaching and of faculty interaction, Santa Cruz seems to have actualized its ideals to an extraordinary degree. . . .
>
> We can think of few campuses where there is more genuine attention to educational issues, of no university that has achieved a more vibrant pluralism in the forms of intellectual, social, and aesthetic experience for undergraduates. (287, 290)

From a comparative vantage point, Santa Cruz could be viewed, in 1976, when Grant and Riesman concluded their fieldwork, as "one of the most genuine successes of the last decade," but then most other of the innovative campuses either did not survive at all or were clear failures.

A second evaluative approach is from the point of view of the *original intent.* As noted above, Grant and Riesman set forth four intentions of the founders, and I add my comments:

A climate for "innovation in academic structure"—achieved at first, yes, but much less so in more recent times.

A "curriculur pluralism" in college environments—yes, but not all academically oriented.

An emphasis on "the quality of teaching"—at first yes, and to a degree continuing.

An enriched "faculty interaction" with students on a campus that would continue to seem small as it grew larger—yes, but to a declining degree.

I have tried to take to heart the warning of Martin Trow, if "the judgment of failure is made not by any reasonable comparison with other institutions of higher education, but rather against the utopian criteria that the founders had in mind when they created the institution. Against those criteria, only failure is possible."[9] Reality will always fall short of dreams. Yet Santa Cruz is still a partial success from a student's point of view: the teaching of undergraduates and facilities for their on-campus lives are comparatively superior, as are opportunities for undergraduates to engage in research activities. And from the faculty viewpoint, the departments have won out and research production has risen in both quality and quantity.

My greatest surprise has been the vulnerability of the campus to changing circumstances. We had thought we were tying into a tried and true enterprise—the neoclassical college for undergraduates. Yet our version of it was particularly hard hit by political and cultural radicalism in the late 1960s and early 1970s. This unexpected but natural vulnerability reflected the context: a new and experimental campus, a young and offbeat faculty with an aversion to administrative authority, a heavy emphasis on humanities and social sciences, a physical campus that was congenial to the "heart and body" and the Dionysian aspects of human nature—a beautiful location with a mild climate for those few who chose to become lotus-eaters in the elysian fields. And all benefited from the high salaries and low teaching loads the hard-working and prestigious faculty at Berkeley had earned for the entire University of California. Many lotus-eaters, fortunately, took official early retirement in the early 1990s.

A third approach to evaluation is to ask the question: how well did Santa Cruz adapt to *its context of time and place?*

Our original assumptions about a Santa Cruz student body with high levels of scholastic aptitude—at first it was at or above Berkeley levels—and about the faculty's willingness to teach at least one nonmajor course around some broad theme but within the borders of their own discipline did not fit the context. In the course of its development, Santa Cruz drew students with lower scholastic aptitude scores (falling from 1250 to 1050, as noted earlier). Students needed improved skills in writing and oral argumentation and an introduction to the discussion modes of higher learning far more than a rigorous encounter with high thought about the great issues of humankind. In addition, many students were alienated from the surrounding society and needed some recognition of their alienation. As time went on, the faculty was increasingly drawn to the attractions of the standard University of California model with its attention to research, and to the security of departmental affiliations.

Santa Cruz had to adapt to these realities, and it did so. It combined the standard model for upper-division and graduate work and research with an enriched lower-division program taught, however, mostly by nonladder faculty and aimed at higher academic skills and improved motivation. There is more than the usual attention to teaching and advising students and to developing intellectual contacts across the disciplines, and these attributes of the lower-division program carry over to upper-division and graduate levels too. There is also more flexibility than usual at all levels in creating new courses, responding to new needs, and in encouraging student and faculty initiatives.

Chief Justice John Marshall, in *McCullough* v. *Maryland* (1819), wrote that the constitution must be "adapted to the various crises of human affairs." Santa Cruz has had its share of crises, and it has, in my judgment, adapted well. It pays special attention to what has been the greatest disaster area of the multiversity: the poverty of the lower-division environment.

A fourth approach is to look at how well the faculty at Santa Cruz has performed in meeting *the faculty's own self-chosen goal of high-level research*. It now has been found to rank, overall, in the top fifteen public universities in the United States, on a per capita basis, and first in the social sciences (see chapter 28).

The skeptics who once confidently asserted that within a year or two Santa Cruz would look like and be like any other large university campus anywhere, and the critics who once thought that the campus should be closed to save money for other campuses, have been proved in error. The teaching arts have been given a higher order of priority. Some of the individual colleges have proved that they can develop and retain their own personalities, their own sense of community. Contact across the "iron curtains" that so often separate the great streams of thought, across what has been called the "Snow line" after C. P. Snow's famous essay on "The Two Cultures," endures. In its attention to undergraduates and contact of faculty members across disciplines, the campus is much closer to the original dream than the more formal arrangements by departments suggest. Some of the spirit remains although the structure has changed.

And the future, not just at Santa Cruz but more generally, still lies, I think, with a heightened attention to teaching, with efforts to break massive organizations into more humane components, with giving individuals more choices among diverse options, with broader contemplations of the human condition and more integrated analyses of the human prospect. And in particular—among the alternative arrangements discussed above—I include consideration of a separate budgetary division for the colleges; and of "bargaining chip" FTEs for colleges, allowing them to create upper-division liberal or broad learning sequences to supplement major requirements and perhaps replace breadth requirements. For Santa Cruz still points toward the future. Drawing on the title of Grant and Riesman's book, it continues to pursue the "perpetual dream."

As an indication that experience at Santa Cruz in some ways has been joined in pointing a possible future for the entire University of California, note the Smelser report of June 1986, "Lower Division Education in the University of California," which called for a "core general education requirement" and recommended possible core emphases on "internationalization" and the "diversification" of cultures. And the Pister report of June 1991 on faculty rewards, which called for more attention to, and rewards for, good teaching of undergraduates.[10] And I note that Princeton, even with its small size, has created internal colleges for its lower-division students.

Recently I was visiting the undergraduate residential unit called the Clark Kerr Campus at Berkeley with its 850 students. The director took me to see a new "academic resources" unit with a computer room and an academic assistant in charge of advising students and arranging for tutorials by highly successful students for less successful students. The director said this was an effort to make the campus into more of a "living-learning" experience for the students. I asked the academic assistant where he came from. He said "Santa Cruz," and added that he had served in a similar role at Porter and Kresge Colleges.

LESSONS WE LEARNED AT THE THREE NEW CAMPUSES

- Change comes hard in higher education. Faculty members are highly attached to past practice. Consequently, change must be carefully thought through in advance. Goodwill alone is not enough. Robert Sinsheimer, Santa Cruz chancellor from 1977 to 1987, in his generally unfavorable evaluation of Santa Cruz, says that it was "incompletely conceived" and that we planners knew more what we were "against" than what we were "for."[11] I agree.

- You cannot ignore time or place. A time of popular innovations is not a good time for telic change and may well overwhelm it, as the counterculture and the multiversity overwhelmed the neoclassical college. New York City helped create the personality of City College of New York; redwood groves, Santa Cruz.

- There is eternal conflict (within the university) between teaching the "cultivated person" and training the "expert" (to use Max Weber's terms), and between creating and transmitting knowledge. How much of each and how?

- Faculty members and students vary greatly, and it is better to give them choices instead of one standardized required program.

- Faculty members, with few exceptions, are not willing or able to teach outside their disciplines. The best that can be expected is that they will teach one course for nonmajors but within their own discipline.[12] There are few "all-around" faculty members.

- The attractive power of the standard model of the multiversity, as at Berkeley, shapes faculty expectations and choices.

- The absence of agreement on a single definition of a "liberal education" clears the way for a series of courses each setting forth liberal or broad learning experiences. Having more than one definition of liberal education available helped calm the "culture wars" at both San Diego and Santa Cruz.

- It is easier to innovate on the standard model of the university, segment by segment as at Irvine, than to modify the model as at San Diego or to challenge it, if only in part, as at Santa Cruz. Eric Ashby, former vice-chancellor of Cambridge and a biologist, once observed that small mutations are more likely to survive than are large mutations in academic life as in biological life.[13] Make the smallest changes possible to get the results.

- Departments are the supreme organizational units of the research university; do not tread on them.

- Count the costs realistically. Sinsheimer says of Santa Cruz that "no one was willing to pay for it."[14] I agree.

- Beware of too heavy a superstructure of authority or one that is too divided or too inadequate or missing entirely.

- To enrich all the groups that compose it, a university must reconcile the multiversity for the faculty and the graduate students, with the neoclassical liberal arts college for the undergraduates.

One thing we did not learn was the best size for a college—very large and influential as at San Diego or smaller and more intimate and providing more alternative environments as at Santa Cruz. We did learn, however, that colleges for undergraduates within the multiversity are an improvement over the mass monolithic campus.

A Dream Too Far?

The "Santa Cruz dream" was a wonderful dream: that it should be possible to combine in the same public institution the best research and graduate training and the best circumstances for the intellectual and personal development of undergraduates, as at Oxford and Cambridge in the early twentieth century or at the Chicago of Hutchins or at the Harvard of Buck and Rosovsky, or at the Claremont Colleges. For the first few years at Santa Cruz, the original highly talented students and equally talented and motivated faculty realized this dream. But then it faded. The time was not congenial: an age of Dionysus and of Che Guevara, and of millions of federal research dollars.

The place was not sufficiently compatible with the dream: a public university devoted to research and graduate study and dominated by its subject matter departments. A student body increasingly intent at first mostly on the counterculture and then on good jobs, and drawn from middle-income families not able or willing to finance added facilities, such as reading libraries; and a student body whose composition was shifting from high-ability toward middle-ability intellects. A university with a high ratio of students to faculty members and a low ratio of resources to students, as compared with the best private universities.

McHenry and I were too impressed with Williams College where he had taught and with Swarthmore where I had studied, and too conscious of student complaints at UCLA where McHenry had studied and been leader of the student body and taught, and at Berkeley where I had studied and taught and listened to student grievances during my hundreds of open office hours as chancellor. And we were too confident that we could do better.

Given a better time (normality) and a better place (a wealthy private university with excellent students wanting a broad orientation to life and to thought), then the cluster college idea with neoclassical academic programs might have worked out better.

I still hope, however, that it may be possible to develop "broad learning experience minors" to stand alongside narrow learning majors spread over the full four years of undergraduate life or at least the years 2, 3, and 4. That may not be a dream too far.[15]

In the end, I have concluded that the best that can be expected realistically of Santa Cruz is the goal set by M. R. C. Greenwood in her inaugural address as chancellor on May 23, 1997: "Solidify our position as one of the best universities in the nation in which to gain a baccalaureate degree." Only I would say more cautiously, solidify our position as one of the best *public* universities in which to gain a baccalaureate degree.

There is an "afterglow" to the original dreams at Santa Cruz that makes this goal more possible. Many faculty members and students of today at Santa Cruz call attention to the comparatively greater concern for the welfare of individual students and the willingness of faculty members to step across disciplinary boundaries that still give Santa Cruz a special ambience.

However, in the end, I must confess my responsibility for the failure of the original Santa Cruz dream, for pursuing a dream too far, while noting that Santa Cruz is one experimental campus that has survived and that has many accomplishments to its credit and a bright future.

Postscript

Reactions on returning from the thirtieth reunion of the Pioneer Class at Santa Cruz on April 17, 1999: one-third of all the alumni of that class were there. Their spirits were so high and their memories so warm about what the campus has meant to their lives. I have been to many class reunions many places. None has ever matched the thirtieth of Santa Cruz's pioneer class. All was for the best, in retrospect, with their particular worlds. The Santa Cruz dream lives on in their lives, as Swarthmore 1932 does in mine—"Swarthmore in the Redwoods" did exist for at least those few years.

Addendum: Clark Kerr's Remarks to UCSC Pioneer Class Reunion (April 17, 1999)

Greetings to the Pioneers on your Thirtieth Anniversary. I wish that Dean McHenry could join with me tonight in extending these greetings. He poured so much of his remarkable life into creating this campus.

You had one of the great student experiences in the history of American higher education in participating in the creation of one of the greatest academic experiments in public higher education:

- Small cluster colleges within a larger and more impersonal university, and the better chance to create lifetime friendships.
- Core courses in liberal education to help you to understand important aspects of the civilization in which you were to live instead of only a miscellany of largely unrelated specialized courses.
- A chance to live in a beauty spot of all geography on our planet.
- The leadership of that impressive pioneer faculty and those memorable founding provosts.

I know from talking with many of you that those early years, by themselves, made the whole experiment worthwhile.

And my wife, Kay, and I look back on that night when we first met you in September 1965 in the field house and visiting with you in your trailers afterward as one of the most enchanted evenings of our lives. The moon was shining and a soft breeze was wafting in from Monterey Bay. The redwoods were standing so tall. And the "Santa Cruz Dream" was drawing us forward. The years pass on but that memory never fades.

21

Transformations at
Davis and Santa Barbara

As of July 1958 the University of California had, as it then counted them, eight campuses: its six actual campuses plus two nominal campuses, the Scripps Institution of Oceanography in La Jolla and Lick Observatory on Mount Hamilton. Scripps became the founding source of the new San Diego campus, conferring its prestige, its high standards of scholarship, and its leadership on the new endeavor. And Lick found a favored and congenial home as part of the new Santa Cruz campus.

Four of the six actual campuses were undergoing transformations: Davis, Santa Barbara, Riverside, and San Francisco (in the order I present them). Each was in a special situation.

■

The opportunities for transformations at Davis, Santa Barbara, Riverside, and San Francisco came from several sources. Expanding enrollments, an explosion of federal research funding, and the postwar prosperity affected all the campuses and led, across the nation, to a great expansion of research universities from twenty to about one hundred.

There were additional factors at work in California. Under the master plan (1960), with its differentiation of functions, two campuses (Santa Barbara and Riverside) were destined, if they were to remain within the university system, to become research universities instead of solely undergraduate colleges. Agriculture was less dominant in the state's economy and politics and no longer warranted a campus all its own (Davis), plus half of another campus (Riverside). Medical schools all over the country were growing away from the local medical profession and becoming more constituent parts of the scientific community and thus of their universities, a development that greatly affected San Francisco.

The Board of Regents was ready, and even eager, to move ahead into new territory, and it had just selected me to press forward across the range of university endeavors. Beyond that, California's recently elected governor, Pat Brown, became increasingly supportive of the university, and the theme of the next president of the United States, John F. Kennedy, would be the "new frontier." The total situation was favorable to fresh opportunities and assignments but also, as it turned out, to the advent of novel and disconcerting concerns.

What was less favorable was an underlying sense of urgency. We at the university realized that all the favorable circumstances would not last forever. What we did not know in 1958 was that the opportunities would fade in fewer than ten years—with the election of Ronald Reagan as governor in 1966. We did feel, nevertheless, the great pressure of passing time to get done what needed to be done. We were driven hard and drove ourselves hard. Full speed ahead!

Davis—A Contented Campus

Davis made its transition to expanded responsibilities with ease. It had progressed from a farm school in 1905 to a branch of the College of Agriculture at Berkeley in 1909 (with sixteen farm school students). A full four-year course in agriculture was introduced in the early 1920s. A school of veterinary medicine was established in 1946. A college of letters and science was added in 1951, when the campus enrolled 1,500 students. The campus head (Knowles Ryerson, 1937–52) was an assistant dean of agriculture reporting to the dean and vice president for agriculture at Berkeley (Claude Hutchison). Stanley Freeborn then served, mostly with the title of provost, from 1952 to 1959. In 1958 Davis had 2,500 students.[1]

Then came the great explosion. On my recommendation, on October 23, 1959, the regents voted that Davis was to become a "general campus," originally scheduled on its way to 18,500 students and later to 26,800. Its letters and science college was to become a college in its own right and not just in service to agriculture, with a full chance to develop its own specialties. Then came the College of Engineering in 1961, the School of Law in 1963, a medical school in 1965, and the School of Administration (later Management) in 1981. Neither the city of Davis nor the campus welcomed this rate of growth but—after making efforts to hold down the rate and ultimate scope of the increases—the Davis campus generally accepted the inevitable with its usual attitude of pragmatism and cooperation in meeting the needs of the University of California and the state of California.

A special feature of the College of Engineering was a graduate program in applied science jointly at Davis and at the Lawrence laboratory at Livermore. It was the Livermore laboratory director Edward Teller's idea and was often called "Teller Tech." The plan was to use senior scientists at Livermore to help instruct M.A. and Ph.D. candidates, thus helping young scientists at Livermore and at Davis advance their competencies. Originally, Berkeley and Livermore were to take part in the program, but there was resistance within the Berkeley faculty to Livermore's military purposes and to the political views and personality of its leadership. In fact many faculty members at Berkeley and at Davis had reservations. Davis offered to step in, mostly as a result of the efforts of Chancellor Emil Mrak and Dean Roy Bainer of the College of Engineering. Thus began the first academic, as compared with scientific and administrative, connection between Livermore and the university. The theme was joint development of skills in science *and* engineering, something like the Department of Applied Science at Harvard. A number of regents took a special interest in this development. And I always thought it was a good idea to use the talents at Livermore for teaching and to make Livermore more an intellectual part of the university community.[2]

I had two fears, at first, about Davis. One was that the agricultural industry might suspect that it was losing the campus that had belonged to it. We took great pains to promise that agriculture would continue to be a central concern of the campus and that a general campus with strong liberal arts and basic science departments would increase, not decrease, the excellence in agriculture, particularly in the biological sciences. Organized agricultural opposition never developed although there was some grumbling at first; and Harry Wellman, as the former vice president–agricultural sciences and, beginning in 1958, vice president of the university, was most helpful in giving agricultural interests a sense of assurance. So also were the efforts of prominent alumni of the Davis campus who were leaders in the agricultural industry.

My second fear concerned the possible loss of the "Hi, Aggie!" tradition as the campus got bigger. The Davis campus had always had more community spirit than any other, and more faculty children from all campuses, including one of our sons, enrolled at Davis than any other campus. This spirit, fortunately, endured. Tradition is one reason. Another is the character of the adjoining community: Davis is more nearly a "college town" than any other community where a University of California campus is located. Programs like Picnic Day in the spring of each year that attract many friends to the campus are still another. Picnic Day was (and is) totally run by students and emphasizes agricultural activities such as my favorite, sheep dog trials.

Chancellor Mrak (1959–69) was a very large part of the answer to my fears. We chose him most carefully. We needed someone from agriculture but with much broader interests than agriculture alone. We also needed someone who would help represent the whole university to the legislature in nearby Sacramento. Emil was a Berkeley graduate (B.S., M.S., Ph.D.) and totally loyal to the university and not just to Davis. Wellman knew Mrak well and suggested I review his work and qualifications carefully after I rejected the number one person on the original list advanced by the local faculty search committee. So to Emil's astonishment I spent a whole day with him at Davis, ostensibly showing an enormous interest in the Department of Food Science and Technology, of which he was chair, and in yeast, which was his specialty. At the end of that day I agreed with Harry that Mrak was just right. Emil told me later that his reaction was, "Is this the way the new president plans to waste his time?"

But I had trouble with some regents. Emil did not have the urban sophistication to which some regents were more accustomed in chancellors. I had to take him back three times to see the regents before I got the board's reluctant acceptance. Several regents said he did not *look* like a chancellor. In exasperation, I told them that if they would describe what they thought a chancellor should look like, I would try to find such a person. They withdrew the comment. Later the regents became as devoted to Emil as I was. He was "agriculture" to the agricultural interests. He was the Aggie spirit to students and staff. He was an excellent goodwill ambassador to Sacramento, as in the wine-tasting seminars he held for legislators. The legislature had earlier voted that Davis could not sell any of its agricultural products competitively. But, we pointed out, it was "un-American" just to waste them. So we invited legislators to help us solve the problem by attending the wine-tasting seminars Mrak held at Davis with the assistance of Professor Maynard Amerine, a world-famous authority on wine, and some legislators were inordinately happy to do so.

Emil was also a very good personal friend. On my way back from Sacramento I would often stop by to see Emil, who always lifted my spirits. He traditionally fed me a combination of candied kumquats prepared by the Department of Home Economics and Muscato Amabile from the Louis Martini vineyards. I always left feeling that Davis at least was all right with the world.

Emil started Davis on its broader trajectory better than any one else could possibly have done. We needed someone with vision, with energy, with a dedication to public service to found the new Davis. We needed someone who would continue the campus spirit—this was for me almost the number one priority—and Emil personified it. As an illustration, Emil's office in an old single-story building had a big plate glass window; he sat behind it and waved to students as they passed by on the sidewalk outside. Also, with the great scramble for money among now nine growing campuses, we needed a person who could represent the whole university to legislators in Sacramento. That person was Emil Mrak. I once told him, drawing on Orwell, that to the president of the university all campuses are created equal, but that one was more equal in my view than all the others—and it was Davis. I was thinking of its sense of loyalty to the whole university and spirit of service to the state. But I was thinking most particularly of Emil himself—his loyalty and his sense of service surpassed that of all others. Emil became a leader among the chancellors and a great ambassador to legislators who respected his opinions and advice.

Davis was an all-around joy. It had its own special place in the university as the primary center for agricultural research—one of the best in the nation and even in the world, I discovered as I traveled abroad. Managers of sheep ranches in Australia and vineyards in France spoke of Davis as the center of research in their specialties. It had professional and academic respect. It also had its own strong, unified personality. Unlike UCLA, it had no "hang-ups" about Berkeley and was proud of its older sibling. There were always joint appointments of faculty members at Davis and Berkeley.

The Davis campus and the town formed a congenial face-to-face community. Campus colleagues were neighbors. New members of the academic staff became friends. Also, Davis was very resourceful in working out problems. In agriculture, theory aided practice and practice energized theory. Thus new professional schools found no resistance at Davis (though they did at Riverside, Santa Cruz, and Santa Barbara). It was, above all other campuses, an integrated human and intellectual community. The new medical school, however, was harder to absorb, particularly because medical professors and administrators from other institutions were not accustomed to supervision by an academic senate. But Davis had so much to be contented about.

I last saw Emil at Davis on March 9, 1987, shortly before he died. We talked about how it had all turned out at Davis—very well indeed, we both thought; even the Aggie spirit was still alive among the students and most of the faculty. Emil was pleased and proud of the results. He had had little exposure to cultural activities earlier in his life and came greatly to enjoy a whole world that their development at Davis opened up to him. Over the years Davis had become a cultural center for the Sacramento area in art, in music, in dramatic performances. We both thought that Superior Court Judge Peter Shields would have shared our sense of accomplishment. (Shields was, in 1899, secretary to the State Agricultural Society and a strong proponent of an agricultural school in California. He is considered the founding father of Davis.)

Emil did say, however, that he had learned more than he ever wanted to know about hospitals, particularly county hospitals, after we added the medical school. He had several concerns. One was that the university, across-the-board, was less involved with service to and contact with the people of the state than had once been the case and than he thought was wise. Another was that some faculty members were by then not full members of the Davis academic community—living at great distances from the campus in Berkeley or even San Francisco, performing only specifically assigned duties, and neglecting their obligations to the Academic Senate at the heart of the university. Emil saw too that Davis was becoming part of the great urban complex centered in Sacramento and feared the intrusion of drugs and crime—it was not the Davis of old. Noting the decline of agriculture in the life of the state and the university, he was concerned that Davis should maintain its momentum of diversified growth, in quality as well as quantity. Good concerns to remember.

Emil and I then talked about how lucky the university had been at the time of the great expansion to have had Pat Brown as governor and Alan Post as legislative analyst; of what a wonderful group of chancellors we had had in those golden years; of how helpful Harry Wellman and Jack Oswald—both with strong Davis connections—had been in the president's office; of the devoted regents we had worked with; of the outstanding friends of the university in the state legislature and, in particular, George Miller, chair of the Senate Committee on Finance; of the wise leaders of the Academic Senate; of the great builders among the deans. I noted how Emil had always chosen persons who had his same helpful attitude and the same "let's get it done" spirit in solving problems—and we talked about his excellent vice-chancellors: Everett Carter, Vernon Cheadle, Chester McCorkle; and his equally excellent staff assistants, including Edwin Spafford and John Hardie.

During our conversation, I sat there thinking of Erik Erikson's "eight ages of man," each age with its challenges, from a baby's need to establish a sense of trust to the adult's need to develop a sense of integrity and dignity at life's end despite the regrets and concerns that engulf so many of us. Meeting this last challenge is the final "fruit" of life that comes, according to Erikson, only when an individual surmounts all the earlier challenges.[3] I interpret this last task as that of coming to peace with one's life. I sat there thinking that Emil had met it as well as all the other challenges along the way. He was clearly at peace with his life.

Whoever served as chancellor at Davis during the golden years of the campus was bound to be a key person, even *the* key person, in its history. But to become the great legendary figure in the life of the campus—only Emil could manage it and he did. At those wonderful universitywide Cal Club affairs of student leaders, the Davis students always depicted Emil in their skits as the kindly white-bearded "little old wine maker from Davis." With his belief in the goodwill of others that encouraged them to be almost as good as he thought they were, with his personal freedom from arrogance despite all he had accomplished, Emil Mrak was the ideal chancellor for Davis at the most important time in its history.

Davis became more "equal" than all others.

Santa Barbara—A Cinderella Campus

Santa Barbara was an unwanted child in a mandated adoption. The state legislature had compelled the University of California to accept Santa Barbara State College as a campus it had not asked for. Following this legislative action in 1944, a universitywide faculty committee chaired by Gordon Watkins, longtime dean of the College of Letters and Science at UCLA, had recommended that Santa Barbara be accepted into the University of California but only as a "regional college" with its own separate and lower faculty salary scale and with the condition that its faculty not be permitted to join the Academic Senate. The committee said "it should be definitely understood that such regional colleges [and the following words were doubly underlined] are not miniature or embryo universities." Shortly later, President Sproul declared that Santa Barbara should be a "model state college" located within the university.

The 1944 adoption of Santa Barbara was advanced by prominent members of the local community, and the bill in Sacramento was introduced by local Assemblyman Alfred W. ("Bobby") Robertson, longtime member of the legislature, after whom Robertson Gymnasium is named. The prominent members of the local community were particularly Pearl Chase, an early and very effective environmentalist, and Thomas Storke, the publisher of the *Santa Bar-*

bara News Press from 1901 to 1964. Storke was a Republican senator from California (appointed by Governor Frank Merriam), a close friend of Governor Earl Warren, and later a regent of the university. And Santa Barbara was a strongly Republican county.

The Santa Barbara campus was then allowed to exist within the university as Santa Barbara College with the actual standing of a teachers' college. Founded in 1909 as the Santa Barbara State Normal School of Manual Arts and Home Economics, it had its roots as a crafts training school for women starting in 1891. It was being shunted from home to home—from the Riviera compound on the hill, to the Mesa campus in the flats, to the abandoned Marine Corps facilities at Goleta on the coast (the last move began in 1954).[4]

What to do with Santa Barbara? The crucial act in its transformation came on September 19, 1958, when the Board of Regents voted to accept my recommendation, as the new president of the university: "The Santa Barbara campus will become a general campus of the university . . . with graduate programs leading to the highest degrees"; and that included the Ph.D. Santa Barbara gave its first Ph.D. in 1963. By 1966 there were twenty doctoral programs. It took thirty-two years from that first Ph.D. until membership in the Association of American Universities (AAU) in 1995. UCLA had taken thirty-six years, from its first Ph.D. in 1938 to AAU membership in 1974.

An early task after Santa Barbara became a general campus was a reorganization of its activities. The best known part of the inherited college was the Department of Industrial Arts. Some of the regents (Regent Pauley in particular) looked upon this program ("shop work") as an insult to the university. In any event we eliminated it, over protests from similar departments in colleges and universities around the nation and from high schools around the state, which considered it an excellent source of industrial arts teachers. We placed all the industrial arts faculty in other positions within the university under Wellman's careful guidance. A second task was the creation of a college of letters and science (1961) as the new center of the campus. The School of Education was started in 1962 to absorb what was left of teacher training, and the School of Engineering was added the same year.

One urgent issue, or at least policy action, was to expand as fast as possible so that the new "university" faculty would overwhelm the old "college" faculty. Student enrollments increased from 2,500 in fall 1958 to 11,000 in fall 1966.

Another issue was to determine Santa Barbara's new personality. At that time the university was interested in developing a study abroad program, as many other institutions were doing. The city of Santa Barbara had a multicultural history with its Spanish origins. The community had a substantial number of residents, many of them retired, with histories of service and travel abroad. As well as being publisher of the *Santa Barbara News Press* and a United States senator, Tom Storke was part of a family (the Ortegas) with a long history in Santa Barbara and had broad cultural and international interests. So I proposed that our education abroad program be located at Santa Barbara. I hoped that the campus might develop a special international emphasis within its then anticipated schools of engineering, business administration, and law directed, in part, toward training people for international service as the United States became more of an international economic, political, military, and academic power. This expectation has been realized only to a very small degree.

Santa Barbara needed new leadership as well as a broader program. Clarence Phelps, president of the state college (1919–44) who had guided it into the university, was provost from 1944 to 1946. Then came Harold Williams, who had been director of summer sessions at UCLA. He continued to live in Los Angeles while serving as provost from 1946 to 1955. His home's distance from the Santa Barbara community was a particular irritant to the faculty. The academic year 1955–56 marked the temporary leadership of a new provost in residence who, however, quickly disappeared under less than glorious circumstances. Then for three years the acting provost was Elmer Noble (1956–59). By 1959 the campus had had no steady leadership, in residence and in good repute and with a permanent title, for fifteen years. So much for how much the university cared about Santa Barbara.

After the vote had been taken in October 1957 at Davis appointing me president of the university, Regent Tom Storke came up to me. He pushed an index finger into the middle of my chest, which meant he was really serious about what he was going to say (and he often had a great deal to say): "Don't forget Santa Barbara." He said it twice: "Don't forget Santa Barbara." I replied, "Tom, I can't forget Santa Barbara and I won't. The university needs Santa Barbara now." And thus, for the first time, we declared that Santa Barbara had become a prospective asset and not a liability. My first official response, at my third monthly meeting with the regents as president, was to propose that Santa Barbara become a "general campus," as noted above. Santa Barbara's new and permanent goal was to be a research university.

Santa Barbara in 1958 had 2,500 students. It had recently moved to the Goleta campus and had a reputation with students as a "party school," with a mile-long stretch of ocean beach and surfing. It had a few M.A. programs but none at the Ph.D. level. The library had 101,000 volumes. The campus faculty's research output was minimal, and the faculty had finally been admitted into the Academic Senate only in 1956. Admission requirements were not yet at the University of California levels. They reached them in 1959.

I looked long and hard for a chancellor who would lead Santa Barbara into the future. I then had two particular concerns. One was to get someone with experience of a study abroad program, and the other was to get someone able to bring the campus into contact with the local community. The latter attribute was particularly important to Regent Storke. I recommended Sam Gould, then president of Antioch College. He had started a successful education abroad program at Antioch and was an outstanding speaker and skilled at public relations. He took office as chancellor in 1959 and served until 1962. He did start an excellent study abroad program and brought the campus into the life of the community as never before. However, the faculty never fully accepted him—he was not a "scholar" ready to lead them immediately into the scholarly world of the University of California. They wanted instead, several of them told me, a Nobel Prize winner as chancellor, just as Berkeley had in Glenn Seaborg. Also, though his expectation was not clear to me at the outset, Gould thought he would move rapidly upward within the hierarchy of the university to another more prestigious campus and was disappointed when this did not happen at Berkeley or UCLA. He later became chancellor of the fast-expanding State University of New York.

Gould invited community leaders to join the Santa Barbara Affiliates and initiated an active alumni effort. He also began the planning for Campbell Hall, which was to serve, among other things, as a cultural center for the entire community of Santa Barbara; he set up the College of Engineering with a contingent of faculty drawn from Yale. To attract a higher academic level of students to meet the admission requirements after 1959, Gould visited high schools all over the state successfully calling attention to the new Santa Barbara.

Then it fell to Santa Barbara's next chancellor to lead the campus into its research university age. Vernon Cheadle (1962–77) became chancellor at Santa Barbara this way. Part of his duties as vice-chancellor at Davis was to be the Cal Club advisor. And each year during the universitywide convention, students put on skits mostly aimed at the faculty present (someone wearing a skin-tight bathing cap always played me; in fact, I took a few extra caps along with me each time in case the students had come unprepared). At one convention, the Santa Barbara chapter presented a takeoff on Cheadle, their Davis host. I sat there thinking: Cal Club→Cheadle→Santa Barbara→chancellor! and—on the informal nomination of those campus student leaders—it came to be Chancellor Cheadle's Santa Barbara.

When Cheadle was at Davis, Emil Mrak spoke highly of him. He was a Harvard Ph.D. and a scholar of international distinction who had served as president of the Botanical Society of America (1961). Cheadle was a very competent administrator. With the spectacular assistance of William Allaway, he expanded the education abroad program on a worldwide basis with great skill and devotion. He steadily added faculty members with higher levels of scholarship and not only accepted but welcomed the Academic Senate. He liked working with students and the campus staff, got along well with the community, and became a great favorite of Regent Storke as well as Pauley, who also took a special interest in the Santa Barbara campus. With good judgment and a very steady hand, Vern created the University of California at Santa Barbara.

To the list of individuals who gave the faculty such good leadership I should like to add Russell Buchanan and Elmer Noble. Buchanan had a Ph.D. from Stanford. He served variously as dean of letters and science and vice-chancellor of academic affairs. Noble had a Ph.D. from Berkeley. He served as dean of liberal arts, as it was then called, and later as acting provost. Both wanted desperately to see Santa Barbara justify, academically, its membership in the University of California, to be an honored member of that great intellectual community. They both worked quietly, devotedly, and with great energy, as perhaps did a dozen others of those who had suffered from their deep humiliation at being unwanted by the University of California, of being relegated to the status of a "regional college," of being at first denied membership in the Academic Senate, and of being held to a lower salary scale. They fought for every additional book in the library, every additional teaching assistant, every new faculty member. They inched their way up the university's totem pole. Buchanan and Noble were the first among many other largely unsung faculty heroes from the old teachers' college to have a vision of a possible glorious future, as the humiliation of Santa Barbara became the miracle of Santa Barbara—with membership in the AAU. At first, that vision had seemed almost pathetic. Later, it appeared very daring. Now, it has obviously become triumphant, an apt outcome for the campus set on its beautiful lagoon at the foot of the spectacular Santa Ynez mountains.

Transformations
at Riverside and
San Francisco

Two additional campuses, Riverside and San Francisco, had a more difficult progress to distinction than Davis and Santa Barbara.

■

Riverside—A Split Personality

Riverside holds several puzzles. The Citrus Experiment Station (1907) was never one of them. The station was well located for the purpose of studying semi-desert and irrigated crops. It became the best citrus research facility in the world, as I heard in glowing terms when I visited the world's largest citrus plantation in the northern Transvaal of South Africa. The experiment station later evolved into the College of Agriculture (1960) as UCLA withdrew from agricultural research and service, and we concentrated agricultural studies at Riverside in the south and at Davis in the north. Riverside, however, was never fully equivalent to Davis because it did not have agricultural economics or agricultural engineering or veterinary medicine. Alfred Boyce, who had been director of the Citrus Experiment Station, became the college's first and very dominant dean of agriculture and led it into new areas of exploration, in air pollution and dry lands crop production.

The early success of "Watkins college" was likewise easy to trace. As a liberal arts college, intended for 1,500 students, it was authorized in 1949 and opened in 1954. It carried the name of University of California but got its popular designation because of Gordon Watkins, a longtime and very popular dean at UCLA, who was its first provost. The college provided university-level salaries to teachers of undergraduate students. It had low university-level hours of teaching without high expectations for scholarly output. It was thus very attractive to highly skilled and devoted teachers of undergraduate students.

These faculty members, in turn, along with comparatively low tuition, attracted very high-quality students. Charles Young was one of these early outstanding students. Chuck was the first president of the student body, which is how I met him. Later, after he completed his Ph.D. in political science at UCLA, I brought him to the universitywide office in Berkeley at the suggestion of Dean McHenry. When Franklin Murphy became chancellor at UCLA, he wanted someone to assist him who knew the universitywide staff. McHenry and I suggested Young. He later became a longtime and powerful chancellor at UCLA.

At one time Riverside led all campuses, including Berkeley, in the measured academic quality of its entering students;[1] and it was ranked by some observers in a 1956 national study as one of the ten best liberal arts colleges, and the only one of public origin.[2] It also became a comparatively strong source of undergraduate students who later achieved Ph.D.'s, at about the same level (measured on a per capita basis) as Columbia University.[3]

Three puzzles did confront me at Riverside. The first one intrigued me most: why did the University of California set up a single liberal arts college (prospectively of no more than 1,500 students) as it got ready for the next wave of students numbering in many tens of thousands? And why put it in the area of California most saturated with good liberal arts colleges (including the Claremont Colleges group), which would resent the competition, particularly with Riverside's high salaries and low teaching loads? In fact Riverside took its first dean of the physical sciences, Conway Pierce, from Pomona (part of the Claremont group) under its protest. The private colleges were alarmed. A partial answer to this question is the political and community interest in the location of a campus in the Riverside area. Assemblymen Philip Boyd (1945–49, later a regent) and John Babbage, along with Senator Nelson Dilworth, pushed hard to pass the necessary legislation. There was a very strong citizens' committee in support of this action and much local interest in its potential favorable impacts on the real estate market and the community at large. Also, the Strayer report (1948) had proposed a liberal arts college in Riverside with 1,500 students and a possible maximum of 3,000.[4]

But why, I wondered then, was the original physical plan of the Watkins campus based on broad expanses of lawn, like New England's colleges, in a climate where Mediterranean patios, shade trees, and fountains (as in Granada and Seville) were a more sensible solution, particularly for the hot early fall and late spring seasons? And why, as a third puzzle, was there such animosity between the Citrus Experiment Station and the new college? The experiment station was like Scripps to La Jolla—or might have been—bringing it worldwide scientific prestige. And the new college brought a larger academic community, with its cultural attractions, to the experiment station as Santa Cruz did for Lick Observatory. But instead, as I saw it, the station feared the intruder's negative impact on its budget and on its control of the campus and its land. And the new college faculty looked down on these "applied types" and sometimes even referred to them as "clodhoppers." As a former Pennsylvania farm boy, I shuddered with alarm when I first heard that awful appellation.

An early battle was over the location of the biological sciences. Dean Boyce of agriculture wanted them included with the Citrus Experiment Station, soon to become a college of agriculture (1960), and this was the eventual solution. But Provost Watkins preferred placing them in the new college (which was the original arrangement). It was a shotgun marriage.

Then came a seismic shock. The regents voted on my recommendation on April 17, 1959, to turn the new college into a "general campus" with vast potential numbers of undergraduate students and with graduate students and professional schools. The college faculty was already split. Faculty members in the divisions of the physical and biological sciences generally favored university status as they were more research oriented. But members in the humanities and social sciences leaned more to teaching and almost universally wanted to keep the college format. The new status would put pressure on the humanists and social scientists to undertake more research and then compete for promotion. The bulk of the students supported them.

The Watkins "dream" of undergraduate liberal arts education was being destroyed, and the original promises to liberal arts faculty members were not being kept. True. Some faculty members were alienated—forever, and they had good reason for their unhappiness. The crucial issue was this: would they rather have been transferred to the state college system in accord with the differentiation of functions under the master plan—with lower salaries, higher teaching loads, and lesser prestige? Certainly not. But Riverside, for them, was no longer the best of all possible academic worlds.

Actually, the basic decision to abandon the dream had come earlier than 1959—in 1956 when Watkins was retiring. President Sproul and the regents took the action, on the recommendation of Harry Wellman as vice president–agricultural sciences, with the concurrence of Watkins as provost. When a faculty advisory committee was asked, as usual, to suggest a list of recom-

mended persons for consideration as provost to succeed Watkins, it had submitted only one name (Robert Nisbet, dean of letters and science). In effect
the committee was trying to name the provost rather than to advise the president on possible names. The students too mostly supported Nisbet. I knew
and greatly admired Nisbet from his earlier days as a faculty member and friend
at Berkeley.

President Robert Gordon Sproul, however, quite understandably responded
by looking beyond that one and only name. He asked Wellman to search further. After much consultation within both letters and science and the experiment station, Wellman came up with a new name—that of a scientist already
on the faculty, Herman Spieth. That Herman favored the university model
was well known. Faculty supporters of the college model felt betrayed.

It was a great surprise to me to learn much later that Watkins had supported
Spieth to Sproul over Nisbet. Did he then realize that he was, in reality, supporting the end of Watkins college, and did Sproul fully realize what he was
doing? In the atmosphere of hostility and even vindictiveness that met Herman Spieth, a friendly and civil person, he decided it was not a good atmosphere for an inaugural ceremony and never scheduled one.

Thus the chair of the division of life sciences and a supporter of university
status was appointed to be the new provost. Spieth favored close cooperation
with the experiment station, as did Pierce, chair of the division of physical sciences. The lines of conflict intersected, with Spieth, provost (1956–58) and then
chancellor (1958–64), at the center. Three passionately incompatible groups
faced him: the experiment station, the divisions of life and physical sciences,
and the divisions of social sciences and humanities. Spieth came to me during the 1963–64 academic year to say, with tears in his eyes, that he had had
enough of constant combat. We worked out his transfer to Davis, where he
returned to his very productive research career and a more pleasant life, and
he loved it there. He was more enamored of his fruit flies, he said to me, than
of faculty members. But what happened to Spieth at Riverside was sad. I had
not realized, as I wish I had, the great burdens placed on Herman by his appointment as chancellor during the changeover. And I did not give enough
thought to how to reduce them—if that were possible. Herman, however,
shared in the vision of creating a university campus, and he never complained
about the magnitude of this assignment.

In developing the university model, Spieth's efforts were worth it. In particular, he made great contributions to the physical attractiveness of the campus.

Its original building looked to me like a high school displaced from an older New England environment, but later buildings won prizes and the landscaping became gorgeous. Regent Dorothy Chandler was very helpful in supporting the move to a Spanish or Moorish style campus with patios and shade trees.

Ivan Hinderaker was the next chancellor (1964–79) and the creator of the full-blown *university* at Riverside. He had been vice-chancellor at Irvine when it was being founded. Before that he was a leading faculty member and department chair in political science at UCLA, a department that had long been one of the most distinguished within the university and was, I considered, the second best all-around department in the university after chemistry at Berkeley (I drew two chancellors from that UCLA department—Ivan Hinderaker at Riverside and Dean McHenry at Santa Cruz). Ivan continued the task of trying to unite the two factions within the college, and the college faculty with the experiment station. Also he led the development of a series of professional schools.

At a very early age, Hinderaker had been a member of the Minnesota state legislature and was no stranger to political disputes. He was patient and persistent, at once in and above the battles of the day, and saw Riverside become a much more united campus of greatly expanded size and more widely distributed scholarly activity.

Hinderaker faced other problems than a split campus personality. After initial successes, Riverside had difficulties in recruiting students, and many of those who enrolled there transferred to other campuses. The city of Riverside, with its Victorian ambience, proved to be something of a cultural desert from a 1960s student's point of view. And, particularly in the late 1960s and early 1970s, the Riverside area had to live with the news media's transfer of the "smog capital of the world" image from Los Angeles to its own hazy skies. The damage to the city and to the campus (in student enrollment decline and, thus, in budget) was severe. At the same time, the campus had to compete with three new University of California campuses, each in a more appealing geographic location. (When David Saxon, a later president of the university, let it be known that he was considering closing down the Riverside campus, local faculty members came to refer to it as the "Hard-Luck Campus.")

Hinderaker held the campus together and helped improve its academic standing in research. He oversaw the integration of agriculture (both the experiment station and the College of Agriculture) into the academic mainstream of the campus in 1968 with the creation of the College of Biological and Agricultural Sciences. This involved removing the Division of Life Sciences from the College of Letters and Science. Then in 1974 the physical sciences were incorporated into a combined College of Natural and Agricultural Sciences. And a College of Humanities and Social Science that included arts, humanities, and social sciences was also established. The new arrangement reflected the on-the-ground reality at Riverside.

Of all the chancellors within the university with whom I worked, only Roger Heyns at Berkeley (1965–71) had a more tormenting assignment than Spieth and Hinderaker had at Riverside. The campus will always carry the marks of their superb leadership during the crucial years of its transition from Watkins's college to research university. By the 1980s, the consolidation was over, and Hinderaker had worked what in advance appeared to be a miracle. But some original faculty members, until and after they retired, felt betrayed. I visited Gordon Watkins in retirement in Santa Barbara, and this once cheerful and effervescent personality was mute and despondent. Under other circumstances, he could have created one of the most distinguished of liberal arts colleges. But a split was inherent in his own plan for "a student-centered college" and a faculty with "a keen interest in research." The faculties in arts and humanities and the social sciences had, from the beginning, gone mostly one way and those in the sciences another, with agriculture joining the sciences. Yet the split was not part of everybody's plan. Claude Hutchison, the dean of agriculture, to whom Riverside then reported, had told the *Riverside Press-Enterprise* (May 26, 1948), "The University of California at Riverside is to be a university, not a liberal arts college." And that is what it became.

At one point during the traumatic changeover I was so concerned with how things were going that I gave Riverside a special grant of $100,000 to plan its future. It slowly came up with a plan (1966) that included a college for general education, with the faculty committee's recommendation for a comprehensive interdisciplinary lower division. But not enough of the faculty seemed to be interested to make it a feasible possibility. Had this program come along sooner and with more local support, the Watkins college could have continued as a college of lower-division liberal learning within the larger university campus, like the Hutchins college at Chicago. I would have welcomed and given it strong support. Riverside had always done well with disciplinary learning at the upper-division level, department by department, but had never worked out an effective plan for liberal education at the lower-division level.

Riverside had a very difficult series of transitions: from the early triumph of the Watkins college, to a divided and unhappy general campus, to gradual recovery, and finally to high national standing as a research university. Hard as Santa Barbara's progress was, it was easier than the Riverside roller coaster of early success, stall, and climb toward the academic heights. The Riverside of today rose from the once-upon-a-time possibility of hurtling to disaster.

San Francisco—A Revolt and a Coup

The San Francisco campus in 1958 was due for a change. But it came faster and harder than I had expected, and it emerged from within the faculty rather than at the president's and regents' external initiative.

San Francisco began as the private Toland Medical College (1864) and became a part of the University of California in 1873. The first two years of instruction were transferred to Berkeley after the great San Francisco earthquake and fire in 1906 and remained there, in large part, until 1958. Before 1954 the deans at San Francisco (of medicine, pharmacy, dentistry, and nursing) reported directly to the president in Berkeley. At that point, an advisory committee for on-campus coordination was established with the dean of the medical school as chair but with each dean still reporting directly to the president. When I became president in 1958, I gave the title of provost to the chair of the advisory committee, John B. deC. M. Saunders, and then turned the title into chancellor in 1964. Not until 1958 did a head of the San Francisco campus have any real authority, except when Sproul himself served as dean of the medical school, 1941 to 1942.

As of 1958, the medical school was one of the better regional medical schools in the nation, then rated by other deans as in the range of twenty-fifth to thirty-fifth. Los Angeles was rated about number fifteen or twenty. The disparity in ratings between San Francisco and the Berkeley campus across the bay with which it had long been affiliated worried me.

Medical schools in the United States had been changing for a century. In the late nineteenth century Johns Hopkins and Harvard led the way in becoming higher-level and more academic institutions. The Flexner report to the Carnegie Foundation (1910) accelerated the movement, urging higher standards for medical schools, and then after World War I the Rockefeller Foundation helped introduce more scientific research. San Francisco took a delayed and subdued part in these developments. In 1958 its ambience was still as much a part of the local medical profession as of the University of

California. When the provost and I were talking about increasing the size of the entering class at the San Francisco Medical School, Saunders's remark that he would have to "clear" that decision with the local medical association disturbed me. The University of California was not accustomed to having to clear its decisions with anyone except the governor and state legislature. The mentality at San Francisco was still, strongly, that of a proprietary school tied to the local profession—like a guild, and not that of a participant in a vast endeavor tied to scientific discovery.

The long-term trend of the best American medical schools, on the contrary, was to broaden the scope of patient care to emphasize more research. Heavy federal funding after World War II had greatly accelerated the shift and, beginning in 1958, I watched the trend from my place on the board of the Rockefeller Foundation, which supported the new research emphasis. Reading an ancient Greek comment on medicine's four aspects—what we would now call self-care, public health, medical treatment, and research—I became convinced that the future lay with an increasing emphasis on self-care, on public health, and on research; the quality of medical treatment was already at a high level.

The UCLA Medical School had started with a heavy emphasis on research in 1947, as did San Diego in 1964. The Stanford Medical School in 1959 had moved, at great expense, from San Francisco to Palo Alto to be more a part of Stanford University and of the world of research. UC's San Francisco campus was a laggard. It was still so heavily concentrated on treatment alone that some national observers advising me even called it a "trade school." At some point, it would have faced a transformation even without a limited faculty revolt in 1964.

THE FACULTY'S UNREST

The change at San Francisco began, particularly, with William Reinhardt when he became dean of medicine in 1963 and carried on into 1966. I had set a policy as chancellor at Berkeley, which as president I extended to all campuses, that department chairs and deans were to serve for three to five years or, subject to a special review, beyond five years. They would not serve for life, as some still did, particularly in medical schools on the German model. The policy allowed Reinhardt to review all department chairs and to make several important changes. He also quietly began bringing in more research-oriented faculty members. I gave him full support and when, many years later, he received the

UCSF Medal, he wrote me a note saying, "In my mind, I am sharing it with you." (I was later awarded one of my own.) I heard rumors that the new elements Reinhardt had brought in were unhappy with the chancellor at San Francisco, but in November 1964 I was surprised when some of them asked for an appointment to discuss the future course of the campus. They made this request in what I shall refer to as the "manifesto" dated November 20, 1964.[5]

I asked Wellman to meet with these faculty members. I had learned not to intervene too much or suggest too much presidential interest until I knew more about a protesting group's concerns. On November 27, 1964, twelve persons came to meet with Harry.[6] Harry told me that they were an impressive group, that they were quite serious in their intentions, and that their complaints merited consideration. It took a high level of conviction and courage to be a signer of the manifesto and to attend that meeting. Based on Wellman's report and subsequent experiences, I was particularly impressed by the stature, the balanced approach, and the reasoned arguments of J. E. Dunphy and L. H. Smith.

The chancellor, Saunders, was a longtime faculty member at Berkeley and San Francisco. I knew him well even when I was a young faculty member at Berkeley after World War II. John was from South Africa and had fascinating tales about that country. He was one of the best raconteurs I have ever known. I admired him as a personality and we became friends. John had graduated from Rhodes University in Grahamstown and took his medical degree at Edinburgh. He became a member of the Department of Anatomy (then at Berkeley) in 1931 and was chair from 1937 to 1956. He was then dean of the medical school from 1956 to 1963, and also provost from 1958 to 1964, and subsequently the first chancellor from 1964 to 1966.

When I was Berkeley's chancellor, I had thought of John in San Francisco as "royalty"—presiding with great authority and sense of personal presence. Observers on campus saw him as a micromanager who made, for example, the most minor decisions about assignments of space—all very much in the Robert Gordon Sproul mode. Space was a vexing issue at San Francisco at the time because of the move of faculty members from Berkeley, the great increase in research programs based on federal grants, and the opening of the two science towers on the campus. Space was not only space, it was also recognition of prestige and of the favor of the chancellor.

Franklin Murphy at UCLA, himself a former dean of a medical school, was very critical of the San Francisco school and made his views known aggressively to individual regents along with his pride in the medical school at UCLA.

He had a special friend in the San Francisco Medical School (Julius Comroe) who was one of its greatest scientific stars and an avowed open opponent of Saunders. Several of the regents, particularly from the south, became very insistent that a change be made.

I consulted carefully externally and internally, particularly with Dr. Morton Meyer who was later chair of the clinical faculty at San Francisco and my personal physician, and with Charles E. Smith, dean of public health at Berkeley. I had great confidence in both men's judgment. I concluded, regretfully, that a change would help assure the medical school's future and, in the short run, avoid the possible departure of faculty members who were essential to the school's welfare. The dissidents, however, were a clear minority within the total faculty—possibly no more than 10 percent.

In addition to many internal consultations through Vice President Harry Wellman and Vice President John Oswald, I made careful explorations externally on my own. Robert Brode, a faculty assistant to the president, canvassed the deans of medical schools across the nation. They confirmed the comparatively low standing of the San Francisco Medical School—twenty-fifth to thirty-fifth out of the then eighty schools in the nation. I discussed the issue with (among others) George Packer Berry, dean of the Harvard Medical School; Robert H. Ebert, a later dean at Harvard (and, like me, a member of the Rockefeller Foundation board); Lowell T. Coggeshall, vice president of medical affairs at Chicago; William N. Hubbard, Jr., dean at Michigan; Gordon Meiklejohn, chair of the Department of Medicine at Colorado; and Robert J. Glaser, dean at Colorado and Stanford. All thought that a change in direction of the school was urgent.

As part of the medical school's accreditation, an August 1964 evaluation by the American Medical Association reported, "The program is not of the distinction that characterizes other fields in the University of California." Its authors found no feeling of vitality and expressed "disappointment." I gave a copy of this external evaluation to Saunders, who brushed it off.

Coggeshall of Chicago chaired a special advisory committee I set up. Its oral report to me stated that Saunders was an "impediment" and should be shifted as soon as possible to be director of libraries for the entire University of California because of his interest in historical records. The committee also recommended the choice of an "outsider" to replace him in such a way that "nobody won or lost." It said, as an afterthought, that the school had "great prospects" for the future if the appropriate changes were made.

The internal complaints, I concluded, had substance. These included long delays in making decisions. And then, it seemed, the basis of Saunders's decisions was more a faculty member's support for or opposition to the chancellor than the merits of the requests—particularly in the assignment of space and actions on promotions. Saunders talked endlessly and listened only spasmodically, critics said, and so I observed. In his conversations with me, he stated that his opponents were all "radicals" (and referred to American blacks as "Kaffirs"). When I talked with each of the other deans at UCSF, I was impressed that none really supported John though they did not join in open opposition. There was also much unhappiness among department chairs, all of whom I consulted in private.

When Howard Naffziger retired as a regent in 1961, after ten years of service on the board, Saunders had lost his one crucial supporter. Naffziger was a distinguished brain surgeon who had been a member of the San Francisco faculty from 1912 to 1952. President Sproul had deferred to Naffziger on all important matters at San Francisco. Naffziger's power was enhanced because he was a swing vote in a divided board and Sproul needed his support.

A resultant coup from above changed the medical school's leadership. John was bitter and particularly at me, as he made clear in many conversations, literally around the world, that his listeners told me about. According to the reports, I had started a personal vendetta against Saunders even as he was giving me his full support during the Free Speech Movement at Berkeley in 1964–65.

The controversy became front-page news in San Francisco. On Saunders's side were most of the clinical faculty (about 1,200 in total), who favored continued emphasis on the training of doctors and who owed their appointments, in part, to Saunders. The appointments were without pay, but they led to enhanced prestige in the profession and greater appeal to an affluent clientele. Saunders had also cultivated support in political circles, particularly with a leading member of the state senate who was a physician. To my knowledge, only one regent spoke out openly in his favor, and she was already growing critical of my administration during the FSM affair at Berkeley. The regents more generally, however, had misgivings about Saunders because of Murphy's criticisms and Saunders's handling of the Franklin Hospital dispute (1956–62). The dispute had centered on the chancellor's seeking an affiliation between the hospital and the medical school without adequately consulting the Academic Senate. This incurred the senate's opposition. In the end, the regents re-

324 · *Nine Campuses*

jected the Saunders plan and had to make a $250,000 payment to the Franklin Hospital, which they did not like.

The faculty in the basic sciences, including some who had moved from Berkeley, opposed Saunders. Recently appointed scientists in a series of new research institutes opposed him as well. These groups were emboldened by the federal R&D funds pouring into medical research, giving them nation-wide opportunities. Medical schools generally were moving in the direction of science and research. The avant-garde members of the San Francisco faculty were ready to lead the charge.

A REALIGNMENT

With all the above considerations in mind, I decided in favor of the research model, and the regents supported that. The chair of the board, Edward Carter, and I met with Saunders to discuss his future. Saunders would receive a sabbatical from which he would not return as chancellor. J. E. Dunphy, a signer of the faculty manifesto, assumed the post of interim chancellor and Professor Stuart Cullen, who also signed the manifesto, became dean of the medical school. As the new vice-chancellor of academic affairs, Leslie Bennett, long assigned at Berkeley, eased the realignment at UCSF with his great skill, devotion, and quiet demeanor. I arranged for Saunders to have the newly created Regents' Chair of Medical History, which he long held with distinction. He was an authority, among other things, on Egyptian medicine.

The major hero of the historic change was Dean William Reinhardt. He brought in most of the dissidents who became intellectual stars of the School of Medicine. He never took an open part in the rebellion (though he did sign the manifesto), but Saunders's friends and supporters held him responsible for it. They insisted that Reinhardt must go as dean if Saunders left, and I arranged for this as part of the solution—nobody should "win." In my mind Reinhardt was the heroic leading casualty (stepping down as dean of the medical school), and I greatly regretted and continue to regret the university's loss.

San Francisco prospered as never before. UCSF rose faster and farther than at any other time in its history or than any other health science center in the United States at that time. The Cardiovascular Research Institute continued to flourish under the direction of Julius Comroe. Recruitments in biochemistry and biophysics and microbiology created the groundwork for the discovery of recombinant DNA and the rise of the biotechnology industry in the San Francisco Bay Area, leading the nation. Enterprising research work in virology, neuroscience, imaging technologies, pediatric surgery, and kidney transplantation positioned UCSF as a premier American academic medical center and a top contender for federal research dollars.

We were very fortunate that Willard Fleming, the dean of dentistry, was available to be the next chancellor. He had received his D.D.S. degree at San Francisco in 1923 (he had been a student leader on campus) and was a faculty member from 1933 and dean of dentistry beginning in 1939. He became vice-chancellor of the campus in 1965 and served as chancellor from 1966 to 1969. Bill was universally liked and respected. He had a rare sense of humor that stood him, and the campus, in good stead during the era of student disturbances. He took nothing either more or less seriously than it deserved. Bill began the process of healing the wounds and moving the campus in new directions. Francis Sooy, as the next chancellor, continued the process with superb leadership. San Francisco became an assured member of the university intellectual community.

A Vision of the Future

I had a vision that San Francisco might become a specialized "general campus" of the university, centered on the health sciences and biology but reaching out to related fields such as medical economics, medical engineering, city and regional planning as related to the environments within which people live, medical history, and health science administration. It would be an all-encompassing health care and biological science university. The campus might spread up San Francisco's Parnassus Heights like a modern Mont-Saint-Michel. The regents joined me in 1966 in looking also at other possibilities for expansion. We considered the Presidio and Fort Mason on the San Francisco waterfront, both potentially available.

As early as 1960, the Board of Regents had accepted my growth plan for the university that included an expansion of San Francisco into upper-division instruction in the biological sciences. The 1966 academic plan repeated this goal. But enthusiasm at San Francisco was very muted, except for that of Philip R. Lee, chancellor (1969–72) and later assistant secretary for health and human services in Washington, D.C. He created a program in health policy studies in 1972, which later became the Institute for Health Policy Studies, but organized programs for fields such as medical economics, medical engineering, and human ecology never materialized. I thought San Francisco could become the health care capital of the western United States, as Boston had long been for the eastern half. Beyond that, I had hopes that the university's expanded health care endeavor might help take the place of agriculture as a point of contact with the people of the state, advising and keeping doctors and other health care professionals around the state up-to-date through training and retraining programs, preparing general health care letters to go to all citizens throughout the state, putting all local doctors on-line electronically with specialists as they encountered difficult problems in their practices. One result was the Area Health Education Center (AHEC) at Fresno and, later, a federal program for AHECs nationwide.[7]

I note, in conclusion, how difficult health science centers are to administer. They require large sums of money, heavy contact with both state and federal agencies, and, unlike any other part of the university, are an important part of the health care industry to which they closely relate. They not only train professionals and carry on research and service but actually administer an important part of the health care industry: their hospitals. I developed a strong conviction that the university's most demanding post was dean of a medical school or chancellor of a health science center (aside from the presidency itself).

23

A Place in the Sun
for UCLA

UCLA and Berkeley were both affected by the development of the nine-campus university. Both lost influence and dominance of activities within the university (see Table 20). They no longer had a monopoly on graduate work, in the south or in the north, or veto power in the Academic Senate. Countering their loss of influence within the University of California, both gained in local autonomy and in national academic standing, Berkeley spectacularly and UCLA more modestly.

The major change for UCLA was that in 1958 it achieved a policy of "equal opportunities" with Berkeley. As the policy quietly and gradually spread to the other six "general" campuses, the University of California became the only system of higher education in the United States that gave up its one "flagship" campus approach. The new policy put all campuses in competition, each with its own chancellor, with similar decentralized decision-making authority, each (except San Francisco) with "general campus" status, each operating under the same general formulas for receiving state funds, including salary schedules. And each was encouraged to have its own personality. As chapter 28 indicates, it was an experiment that worked. Other campuses received general-campus status in the following order: Santa Barbara in 1958; Davis and Riverside in 1959; San Diego in 1964; Santa Cruz and Irvine in 1965. In June 1960 San Francisco received— but never accepted—a charter to become a biology-centered campus.

The shift in status happened campus by campus. The central importance of this series of actions is fully apparent only in retrospect. It led, among many other distinctions, to six campuses of the University of California being members of the Association of American Universities by 1996. A 1997 report showed the University of California with seven of its eight general campuses among the top fifteen public research universities in the nation and all eight in the top twenty-six. Only two other states—New York and Illinois—have as many as two public campuses among the top twenty-six.[1]

It all started with UCLA becoming a second flagship campus. Roger Geiger

TABLE 20

Changing Dominance in Activities of Berkeley and UCLA within the Nine-Campus University, 1960–90

	1960	*1990*
Total UC students	49,940	166,541
Berkeley	21,939	30,632
UCLA	19,006	36,427
Other UC campuses	8,995	99,482
UC total state funds	$98,630,000	$2,227,000,000
Berkeley	29,239,000	343,071,000
UCLA	25,741,000	438,901,000
Other UC campuses	31,095,000	1,162,503,000
UC total federal R&D	$58,430,000*	$830,164,000
Berkeley	25,594,000	123,983,000
UCLA	21,679,000	176,735,000
Other UC campuses	11,157,000	525,664,000

Total for 1963.

states in his history of *American research universities, "The year 1958 was the beginning of a revolution for UCLA and for the University of California."*[2]

■

UCLA in 1958 was poised to ride its manifest destiny into further recognition both within the ranks of the top American research universities and in the Los Angeles metropolitan community. It had already come a long way. The campus had begun as a normal school in 1881. It became a part of the university in 1919 as the Southern Branch. It moved to its spectacular site in Westwood located in the fast expanding westward reaches of the Los Angeles area in 1929. It awarded its first Ph.D. degree in 1938. By 1958, it had professional schools of agriculture, education, business administration, engineering, medicine, nursing, law, and social welfare.

UCLA had strong support. The dominant founder was Edward Dickson, who served on the Board of Regents for forty-three years (1913–56) and as chair for eight (1948–56). He was a graduate of Berkeley and one-time owner and publisher of the *Los Angeles Evening Express*. He was the board's leading pro-

329 · A Place in the Sun for UCLA

ponent of a university campus in Los Angeles, and he identified and helped secure the Westwood location. He served as chair of the Committee on Southern California Schools, Colleges, and Institutions (1920 to 1948, when he became chair of the board), which devoted attention particularly to the development of UCLA.

Once the Westwood campus was well established, a powerful alumni association developed. It promoted a graduate school (1935) and professional schools for UCLA, particularly business administration (1937), engineering (1943), medicine (1947), and law (1947). The alumni association, along with the local Chamber of Commerce, lobbied on its own initiative in Sacramento for several of these developments. I was well aware of this activity from the very start. My graduate school roommate at Stanford and Berkeley was Dean McHenry, former president of the Associated Students of UCLA. He was an active lobbyist for UCLA in Sacramento during the academic year 1933–34.[3]

The UCLA Alumni Association also constantly urged autonomy for the campus to escape dominance by Berkeley. It was the only alumni association within the university with which I consulted as though it were a quasi-board of regents, as, for example, in the selection of a new chancellor. The committee of past presidents of the alumni association was a major force in the governance of UCLA and had well earned this status.

In addition, and very importantly, by 1958 half of the appointed members of the Board of Regents came from southern California. Regent Dickson had been the first in 1913, and the chair tended to rotate between north and south. Thus UCLA had, from these several sources, political support far beyond the academic resources and respect that had been accorded to it within the university. There was a clear imbalance between actual political power and potential academic standing versus received financial support.

I was fully familiar with the triumphs of UCLA in Sacramento in the 1930s and 1940s against the implacable opposition of Jim Corley. I did not find out until much later, through reading Verne Stadtman's history of the university, that local supporters of a UC campus in Los Angeles had lobbied for a political solution to their aspirations even earlier.[4] A petition to the legislature in 1915 requested the establishment of a state university in southern California. Shortly later, a "movement to locate a branch of the University in Los Angeles threatened to ask the legislature for authority to create a municipal college with an independent board of directors if the Regents turned down their proposal." Legislative creation of UCLA came in April 1919, the regents' en-

330 · *Nine Campuses*

dorsement in June 1919. Political action, in fact, was part of the creation of UCLA. The Board of Regents only signed the marriage contract after the baby was born. What should have been done with enthusiasm and goodwill was done with reluctance and out of necessity.

UCLA never had fully effective campus leadership until 1960—but not because it had not tried. For two periods (1942–45 and 1950–52) it was administered by committee. Clarence Dykstra, former president of the University of Wisconsin, was provost for five very unhappy years—1945–50. He held the title of provost but had no more authority or influence than the committees that preceded and succeeded him. Under the leadership of Stafford Warren, the medical school (founded in 1947) was quickly rising to be rated among the top twenty in the United States. And the UCLA campus was moving forward academically, especially in letters and sciences. It had two exceptionally able deans, Gordon Watkins (1936–45, and later founding provost at Riverside) and Paul Dodd (1946–60), who led the faculty in pushing the campus forward. Paul and I were among the few labor economists on the West Coast, and he nominated me for positions on the wartime Labor Board. I came to know him well when he was director of the Institute of Industrial Relations–south. He later became president of San Francisco State College, now University.

In 1952 the regents gave the campus more control of its own affairs. Under pressure from UCLA advocates, they established the position of chancellor and only incidentally set up a similar position for Berkeley. As first chancellor (and possible subsequent president of the university) they picked Raymond Allen, who had been president of the University of Washington (1946–52). Ray was willing to accept only modest authority for the chancellor at UCLA (perhaps, in the general expectation of Robert Gordon Sproul's retirement in three years, not wishing to antagonize him and his supporters among the northern regents). In any event, he never energetically tried to take charge at UCLA.

By the time I became president, the regents, both north and south, and the leaders of the Academic Senate, again both north and south, had come to accept that UCLA needed a new opportunity to move ahead. I agreed. I had first come to know UCLA in 1932–33 through McHenry when there were four buildings on 400 mostly open acres, which McHenry proudly showed me. He also made me conscious of the deep bitterness at UCLA. Even then I had begun to marvel, nevertheless, at how much was being accomplished so quickly.

Sitting on the sidelines at regents' meetings for six years as chancellor at

Berkeley, I had seen UCLA move steadily ahead and concluded that it had earned more nearly equal treatment with Berkeley, and that southern California was enough of a factor in California and in the regents' politics to make this status inevitable. I also concluded that early agreement on its status would forestall new eruptions of antagonisms between south and north within and outside the university.

Before my appointment as president the regents in general, and the southern regents in particular, never discussed with me collectively or individually what my attitude toward UCLA would be, nor did they pressure me afterward in any way or even talk to me about the status of UCLA. They seemed to be willing to rely on my judgment of what was good for UCLA within the university and for the university as a whole—a great leap of faith in my willingness to look impartially at the welfare of all the campuses. And UCLA faculty members had joined in my nomination as president over that of their own chancellor. So, as a Berkeley faculty member (and graduate) and former chancellor, I acquired a large degree of responsibility over the fate of UCLA at a crucial time in its history.

Decisive Actions

I decided to do several things. The regents agreed, first informally and then by formal action, on each of the items below—this included all regents, both north and south. There was no disagreement. The time had come.

The *first action* (July 1958) was to go ahead with a proposal already made by President Sproul to give UCLA "equal opportunities" with Berkeley, rather than hold it to a lower level of support. The regents had discussed the future of the two campuses at an Arrowhead Conference Center meeting on August 15, 1957. As the regents compared the two campuses' academic plans, they were not impressed by UCLA's. And following President Sproul's request, discussions of the future of UCLA then took place formally in the Academic Senate's universitywide Committee on Educational Policy and, informally under Regent Carter's leadership as chair, in the regents' committee of the same name. Both of these committees and President Sproul generally agreed that UCLA should have equal treatment with Berkeley.

At my first regents meeting as president (July 1958), I proposed, in accordance with the expressed views of the two committees noted above, that UCLA and Berkeley should have "equal opportunities for developing programs which, although not identical but rather complementary, are of equivalent quality," and that budget allocations should reflect this policy.

This was the basic action that gave UCLA its full place in the sun for the first time in its history. It had the strong support of the senate committee, including the members from Berkeley. The policy was "equal opportunities." Later, leaders at UCLA claimed that the policy was "equal distinction," which is quite something else and depends too on the quality of the faculty's own future efforts.

The history of this earth-shaking development within the University of California is of great importance. While it fell to me, as the new president, to make the formal proposal for "equal opportunities," the two chief players had been Regent Carter and President Sproul. They deserve most of the credit, or the blame, as the case may be. At the August 1957 Arrowhead regents meeting, Carter had strongly criticized the UCLA academic plan and said it would condemn UCLA to second-class academic status. In response to this attack, President Sproul on September 9, 1957 (very fast action for him), asked the universitywide senate Committee on Educational Policy to consider and make recommendations on both the Berkeley and UCLA plans. The senate report called the Berkeley plan "a rigorously and constructively critical document." With respect to UCLA, the committee noted "that the rapidity of growth has made it difficult to develop on this campus the kind of intellectual climate and degree of faculty morale for the highest distinction." The committee called for "the recruitment of outstanding scholars in greater numbers, the development of a notable research library" and a "faculty center" (faculty club) and "student housing" at UCLA. Most important was the following recommendation: "Plans for the future and budget allocations for the Berkeley and Los Angeles campuses shall be based on the principle that the two campuses should be comparable in size and have *equal opportunities* [emphasis added] for developing programs which, although not identical but rather complementary, are of equivalent quality."

The senate committee also expressed the view that it was essential "to preserve inviolate the dominant principle of one university." Its report was unanimous. The committee's members were:

Ex officio members
Frank Kidner (Berkeley, economics)
Vernon Cheadle (Davis, botany)

Henry D. Moon (San Francisco, pathology)
Franklin P. Rolfe, vice chair, Academic Senate, southern section (Los Angeles, English)

Appointed members
B. Lamar Johnson, Chair (Los Angeles, education)
Robert Brode (Berkeley, physics)
Bertrand H. Bronson (Berkeley, English)
John C. Clendenin (Berkeley, civil engineering)
Hugh G. Dick (Los Angeles, English)
Russell Fitzgibbon (Los Angeles, political science)
John W. Green (Los Angeles, mathematics)
Thomas L. Jacobs (Los Angeles, chemistry)
James A. Jenkins (Berkeley, genetics)
Victor Jones (Berkeley, political science)
Thomas R. McConnell (Berkeley, education)
Marian E. Swendseid (Los Angeles, nutrition)
Ronald N. Walpole (Berkeley, French)
Harold F. Weaver (Berkeley, astronomy)
Marion A. Zeitlin (Los Angeles, Spanish and Portuguese)
Louis J. Zeldis (Los Angeles, pathology)

I assumed that the Berkeley faculty accepted UCLA's new status. The nine Berkeley faculty members cast their affirmative votes after eight months of deliberation. The first proposal of "equal opportunities" for UCLA came from a committee of which they were members, and their prestige on the Berkeley campus must mean that the new status for UCLA was acceptable to the Berkeley faculty. President Sproul made a similar assumption when he took the votes of the Berkeley faculty members of the senate committee he consulted on the loyalty oath to be a commitment on behalf of the Berkeley faculty (see *Political Turmoil*, forthcoming). We were both wrong. Faculty members speak one by one and reserve the right to change their minds one by one. The paradox of faculties is that they can simultaneously hold a collective commitment to the welfare of the university and function as fiercely independent individuals.

The Senate report was dated May 19, 1958. President Sproul wrote to me on June 10, 1958, asking for my reaction as chancellor at Berkeley, and I promptly gave my support of the report in writing. President Sproul then submitted the senate report to the regents' Committee on Educational Policy on

June 19, 1958, noting "the endorsement of Chancellors Kerr and Allen." The minutes of the committee meeting state, "Because of the importance of the policy statement, the members felt that it should be given further study and then submitted to the full Board for endorsement. Upon motion of Regent Steinhart, seconded by Regent McLaughlin, action on the statement was deferred pending further study by the Committee."[5] At the meeting of the Board of Regents on July 18, 1958, I resubmitted President Sproul's recommendation of June 19, and it passed the board in a unanimous vote. The motion for adoption was made by Regent Carter (south) and seconded by Regent Steinhart (north). This crucial action, thus, had the unanimous support of the Board of Regents, the senate Committee on Educational Policy, and two presidents (Sproul and Kerr). It, however, caused prolonged controversy at Berkeley.

The *second action,* in April 1961, was to equalize UCLA library acquisition funds with those at Berkeley. This new policy for libraries had been under discussion since early in my presidency (see chapter 25). We also went ahead with a "faculty center" at UCLA and residence halls, as the senate committee had recommended.

The *third action* was to encourage UCLA to mark out its own path rather than to follow Berkeley but always a few steps behind it. For example, in July 1960 UCLA was pushed to establish a College of Fine Arts, and all-out universitywide support went to its foreign language instruction, which came to be more broadly based than in any other American university. Language programs were a special interest of Dodd's. I also fully supported the development of schools of dentistry (1958), librarianship (1960), public health (1961), and architecture (1965). No longer did the office of the president stand in opposition as it earlier had in objecting to the establishment of engineering, business administration, law, and medicine, thus encouraging UCLA supporters to go directly to Sacramento. I had seen how effectively UCLA could obtain in Sacramento what it had lost within the university decision-making processes, and I strongly wanted to stop the process of going outside the regents and the president to get results. This never happened while I was president, in part because I avoided encouraging such initiatives and, too, because I insisted that such action was "off limits."

The *fourth action* was to get new campus leadership. I had observed Raymond Allen as a fellow chancellor for six years and decided that he could not give UCLA the aggressive guidance it needed at that stage in its history. In consultation, I found that all but one of the southern regents agreed with my evaluation, as did most of the leaders of the UCLA Academic Senate. So Regent Carter and I persuaded Ray to terminate his occupancy of the chancellorship. It was hard going. Instead of being the new president of the university, as he had once expected, he was the outgoing chancellor at UCLA. Regent Carter gave me good support in achieving this result, but it was a traumatic process for Ray and for me.

THE SUGGESTION OF GENERAL MARK CLARK AS CHANCELLOR

I knew I had to proceed carefully in choosing Allen's successor. I had heard rumors of the difficulties before Chancellor Allen's appointment. They were later confirmed when I read a memo dated May 1951 that President Sproul wrote in longhand. It started out by saying,

> About nine months ago a group of Regents resident in southern California began to meet outside of regular committee meetings, and without the knowledge of the President "to discuss procedures to be followed in the selection and appointment of a Provost at UCLA," and to consider candidates for that office. In the course of the meetings of this group, the name of General Mark Clark was suggested and evoked much interest.

General Clark, among other assignments, had been a commander of U.S. ground forces in Europe during World War II. Regent Pauley invited him to visit UCLA and to tour the campus and to examine the provost's house. Salary and renovation of the house were discussed. Regent Pauley negotiated General Clark's potential separation from the armed forces. President Sproul noted that "General Clark said that he would accept the University appointment if it were offered to him." Individual regents made these "arrangements," Sproul stated, without the president or the university's knowledge.[6]

A story about the initiative was broken in a southern California newspaper. The faculty members from the southern section of the Academic Senate who were advising the president on the choice of a chancellor at UCLA then reported that appointing General Clark was "quite unacceptable to a great majority of the faculty." Individual faculty members also wrote to General Clark opposing his appointment. He withdrew his name. President Sproul ended his longhand memo by calling this episode part of a "guerrilla war" by a faction of the regents. It was that.

It was also the worst case, to my knowledge, of sabotage by board members against a president and the presidency of the university. The action reflected some regents' long-standing concern for greater autonomy for UCLA and for greater discipline over what they perceived as radical tendencies of UCLA faculty and students. These regents, however, placed the governance of the university in grave disorder.

One implication of this intrusion into the president's authority greatly alarmed Sproul: a possible move to separate UCLA from the university. Feeling that the heavy burdens of his position had become almost "unbearable," he contemplated the most decisive and ultimate action available to him in his relation to the university. It was a precarious moment in the university's history—near anarchy at the highest levels of university governance—a rebellious action by powerful regents totally outside constitutional boundaries. Unconscionable![7]

One inference I was careful to draw in considering a successor for Chancellor Allen was the importance of consulting with southern regents on the appointment.

NOT "CONTROVERSIAL" IN ANY RESPECT

A report on the character of a potential UCLA chancellor had laid out the qualities several regents judged essential. Regent John Canaday, in association with Regents Ahlport and Hansen, presented it to the regents' Committee on Southern California Schools, Colleges, and Institutions on October 11, 1950: "He should be one whose patriotism and devotion to the fundamental principles of Americanism is unquestioned. This qualification is considered of paramount importance in view of recent events and the prolonged and widespread criticism (whether justified or not) of the University as a 'hot bed of communism.' He must definitely not be a controversial figure in any respect." I paid attention to this admonition, as had President Sproul in picking Chancellor Allen.

I also made a mental note that Regent Canaday and perhaps other regents would apply this test (of being noncontroversial) to me as president, and he and they did. I did not accept or meet this test. Canaday was a member of the class of 1927 at UCLA and later manager of the UCLA Alumni Association. As such, he became obsessed with the Southern Branch designation of what became UCLA and with its early reputation as "the little red schoolhouse" in Westwood. Regent Canaday participated in Sacramento in getting improved opportunities for UCLA within the legislative process, and he had been chair of the regents' committee that first recommended a chancellorship at UCLA. He later became a vice chair of the Lockheed Corporation, the biggest industrial giant in southern California.

I started the search for a new chancellor at UCLA by talking informally and individually with southern regents. To my surprise, they told me they had consulted informally on choosing a new chancellor and did not want to consider any of the excellent internal candidates, that to do so would result in factional fighting on campus. They wanted a careful external search. In particular, their wishes ruled out Dean Paul Dodd, who would have been my first choice. Dodd had had some bitter disagreements with southern regents including over the issues of the loyalty oath, of the continuance of the dean of the Law School (Dale Coffman), and of retention of an alleged lesbian in the Department of Physical Education. So, on my nomination, the regents appointed Vern Knudsen, dean of the graduate division, to serve as chancellor for one year only (1959–60) to give us more time for a nationwide search. Knudsen served with grace and distinction and full cooperation with me in this crucial transition year for UCLA. We worked closely to establish the College of Fine Arts.

RALPH BUNCHE

Early on during our national search I raised the possibility of appointing Ralph Bunche, a fellow member of the Rockefeller Foundation board. He was a UCLA graduate and athletic hero, a Nobel Peace Prize winner as undersecretary of the United Nations, and an African-American. Ralph had indicated to me, in response to my inquiry, that he might possibly be interested. Dominant regents and alumni leaders, however, believed that his appointment was too advanced an action for that time and place—to my great regret. UCLA was, after all, the campus of Jackie Robinson, who broke the racial barriers in professional sports, and later of Arthur Ashe.

FRANKLIN MURPHY

My search came to concentrate on the chancellor and former medical dean at the University of Kansas (I also gave careful consideration to Meredith Wilson, president of the University of Oregon and later president of the University of Minnesota, but alumni leaders vetoed him as having been anti-

UCLA in the ongoing disputes over practices within the Pacific Coast Athletic Conference).

I had come to know Murphy when we were both members of the Association of American Universities and of the Conference on Higher Education in the American Republics. Franklin was bright, energetic, full of ideas. He was, in the opinion of mutual friends whom I consulted, also considered to be "brash" and "pushy." And his mortal enemy in Kansas was the Democratic governor of the state. But in all, however, he seemed to me to be perfect for UCLA. The regents came to agree; and he was perfect. The still developing medical school needed careful consideration, and he could give it. He had a great interest in the arts (later becoming chair of the board of the National Gallery of Art in Washington, D.C.), which was an asset in relation to the fast developing Los Angeles cultural community. He had a proven interest in library affairs, as he had shown at Kansas, and one attraction for him at UCLA was that I had already decided that the library there should be equal in acquisition funds to that at Berkeley. The new College of Fine Arts, just opened, was also attractive to him. Other attractions were UCLA's "equal-opportunities" policy, set by the regents in July 1958, and the massive decentralization of administration in 1958–59.

Franklin had the charismatic and self-confident personality to make his way in both the business and cultural communities of the greater Los Angeles area, and he did so spectacularly. UCLA had been on the fringes of southern California's loci of power and influence, and Franklin put it at the center. Franklin and I went over, in advance, the details of the historic decentralization of the university that had already taken place, and this seemed to satisfy him. Everything seemed to be in good shape. And Franklin was available. His nationally known conflicts with Governor Docking had led him to explore the market elsewhere. In addition, Lawrence, Kansas, offered a small stage for a person with his great talents and ambitions. Los Angeles, with Hollywood, Beverly Hills, and Bel Air, appealed to him. It did not take much persuasion to obtain his acceptance.

Once he joined us, Franklin agreed with me that UCLA should develop its own personality. I said to him, "Any time you ask me for something solely because Berkeley has it, I will say no. Any time you ask me because Columbia or Michigan has it, I will take a careful look. Any time you say this proposal specially fits UCLA, I will say yes."

We never disagreed on any substantive issues affecting the future of UCLA, including operating and construction budgets and academic plans (chapter 14 explored our differences over administrative processes). Franklin also agreed with me that the University of California should approach Sacramento with a single budget and program of new endeavors, and a unified all-campus team approach—no more backdoor approaches as in earlier years, and he kept to this arrangement completely.

So Franklin became the first de facto, as against de jure, chancellor in UCLA's history. He presided over its continuing academic advancement and great rise to stardom in the Los Angeles metropolitan community. The Cal Club members from UCLA had long sung a refrain that UCLA wanted its "place in the sun." Now it had that place—in budget treatment, in library acquisition funds, in its own personality, and in its leadership. And it prospered in the sun.

UCLA became the dominant educational institution in southern California—more dominant than those in the nation's other greatest metropolitan centers, Columbia University in New York City in the cultural and professional life of the community, or the University of Chicago in the Chicago area. Of almost equal importance was the impact on faculty members at UCLA. UCLA was no longer a second-rate "southern branch" but a first-rate campus in its own right.

UCLA continued to grow nationally and internationally in its visibility in the university world. Franklin Murphy emerged as a leading figure in the business and cultural life of Los Angeles, and he became the giant in the history of UCLA, followed by Chancellor Charles Young. He was not, however, as was said of him, the person who "forced the decentralization of the University of California and made the Westwood campus an equal partner to Berkeley."[8] John Galbraith, a faculty leader at UCLA during its rise (1948–64) and later chancellor at San Diego and a Murphy supporter, has written in his oral history:

> And after all Kerr was the president. He felt, and I think justifiably so, that he had shown his belief that UCLA should have parity with Berkeley—he had shown that before Murphy arrived. . . . In substantive terms, in budgetary terms, he made provision for UCLA, substantially, on an equality with Berkeley. That was something he dedicated himself to; and he didn't have to be pushed to do that. And I think he felt wounded that the assumption was that he was the Berkeley president; he wasn't. He'd been the Berkeley chancellor, but he was quite courageous in stating this view, that UCLA had the right to aspire to the same status as Berkeley, and he would do what he could to promote it. That antagonized him with people on the Berkeley campus; so I think it was admirable.[9]

TABLE 21

Academic Rankings, 1934 and 1957

1934[a]		1957[b]	
1	Harvard	1	Harvard
2	Berkeley	2	Berkeley
	Chicago		
	Columbia		
		3	Columbia
		4	Yale
5	Wisconsin	5	Michigan
6	Cornell	6	Chicago
7	Yale	7	Princeton
8	Michigan	8	Wisconsin
	Princeton		
		9	Cornell
10	Johns Hopkins	10	Illinois
11	MIT	11	Pennsylvania
12	Minnesota	12	Minnesota
13	Cal Tech	13	Stanford
14	Illinois	14	UCLA[c]
	Ohio State		
	Stanford		

Sources: for 1934, Raymond S. Hughes, "Report of the Committee on Graduate Instruction" [American Council on Education], Educational Record 15, no. 2 (April 1934): 192–234; for 1957, David S. Webster, "America's Highest Ranked Graduate Schools, 1925–1982," Change 15, no. 4 (May–June 1983): 23. Based on Hayward Keniston, Graduate Study and Research in the Arts and Sciences at the University of Pennsylvania (Philadelphia: University of Pennsylvania Press, 1959); the study was done in 1957.

[a] *The 1934 list was based on number of departments rated "distinguished." UCLA was not included in the 1934 survey as it had no Ph.D. programs at that time.*
[b] *In 1957, "the list did not include technical schools, like the Massachusetts Institute of Technology and the California Institute of Technology, nor state colleges, like Iowa State, Michigan State or Penn State, since the purpose was to compare institutions which offered the doctorate in a wide variety of fields" (Keniston, Graduate Study and Research, 115).*
[c] *Institutions ranked in both the 1934 and 1957 studies that UCLA surpassed in the top rankings by 1957 were Northwestern, Johns Hopkins, and Ohio State.*

Murphy wrote me on March 17, 1964, as follows:

The University has indeed given good support to the Los Angeles campus and its development. I have said so privately and publicly, in your presence and when you have not been present. I have made this comment to members of the faculty individually and collectively. For example, I have told many

TABLE 21 *(continued)*

1934[a]	*1957*[b]
	15 Indiana University
	16 Johns Hopkins
17 Pennsylvania	17 Northwestern
Iowa State	
	18 Ohio State
19 University of Iowa	19 New York University
20 (10 universities tied:)	20 University of Washington
Brown	
Bryn Mawr	
Clark University	
Northwestern	
Purdue	
Rutgers	
University of North Carolina	
University of Rochester	
University of Texas	
Washington University	

members of the faculty the kind of courage it took for you to support the special library growth at Los Angeles in view of pressures laid upon you at Berkeley and elsewhere. I shall continue to do so for I am, in fact, grateful, and I am aware that many of the things that happened here would not have happened had they not received your unstinting support.

SPROUL AND THE UCLA DEANS

Looking backward, I am impressed with how far UCLA had already developed under the leadership of its several deans and of President Robert Gordon Sproul. I think their roles have been greatly neglected. In the Keniston survey of 1957, UCLA was ranked number fourteen in academic reputation. It had not been included in the last prior such survey in 1934 because it had no Ph.D. programs then (see Table 21). The year 1957 was just under twenty years after the granting of the first Ph.D. at UCLA in 1938. The individuals chiefly involved were:

L. M. R. Boelter, dean of engineering, 1944–65
Paul Dodd, dean of letters and science, 1946–60
Dean McHenry, dean of social sciences, 1947–50

Neil Jacoby, dean of business administration, 1948–68
Vern Knudsen, dean of graduate studies, 1934–58
Edwin A. Lee, dean of education, 1940–57
Lawrence Clark Powell, librarian, 1944–61
Franklin P. Rolfe, dean of humanities, 1947–61
Stafford Warren, dean of medicine, 1947–62
Gordon Watkins, dean of letters and science, 1936–45
William Young, dean of physical sciences, 1947–57

I also add Gustave O. Arlt, dean of the graduate division–southern section, 1952 and again 1958–62. While situated at UCLA, Arlt was responsible for graduate work on all the southern campuses, reporting directly to President Sproul as had Vern Knudsen before him.

Among them all, I particularly note Dodd, Knudsen, Warren, Watkins, and Young. The progress at UCLA by 1957 was spectacular and—in view of the constraints on campuswide leadership—belongs mostly to the contributions of the several deans. UCLA's standing in 1957 also raises doubts about whether Sproul had held the campus back during his twenty-eight years as president as much as many of UCLA's supporters alleged. So I add the names of Robert Gordon Sproul and the twelve deans to the list of those to honor; also Regents Dickson and Carter.

SUBSEQUENT ACADEMIC RANKINGS

But there still was much to do. Murphy was followed as chancellor by Charles Young, who served from 1968 to 1997. This made him one of the longest serving heads of a leading American research university in the twentieth century.[10] Chuck also served as chair of the AAU (1983). Murphy and Young raised UCLA to become the most influential institution of higher education in southern California and, after Stanford and Berkeley, in all of California and even in the entire western United States. And the two were among the most visible and influential leaders in the vast Los Angeles metropolitan area. There may, however, have been another side to their concentration on the external community. Vern Knudsen in his oral history says:

> Murphy, you know, succeeded me, and I was very enthusiastic about his appointment as chancellor, and I haven't had occasion to regret it. I think the total record of Murphy is outstanding. Naturally, I'm inclined to be a little

sensitive about the claim which was repeatedly made and has been echoed a great deal, that [though] it was a good university when Murphy came here, he was going to make it a great university; and I think in many respects he has contributed to greatness. He has contributed to greatness especially in the public image that has been created of the university, and this is important; his public relations, I think, on the whole have been very good. His understanding of the problems of the students I think was good and had much to do with the relative absence of confrontations that plagued the university, especially since 1964 when the troubles erupted at the Berkeley campus. And there's no doubt that Murphy's administration had much to do about that.

The matter of recruiting of faculty is something that I've spoken about already, and I would say if there's any shortcoming with the Murphy administration it was the failure to press sufficiently for the recruitment of top scholars. . . .

I think the accent then, in large part because of the need for distinguished scholars to build up our Graduate Division, was on building up the faculty, and I believe that if you look at the number of distinguished professors that we have in the university here, you will find that we haven't been as ardent in pressing that very important requirement as took place in the earlier years.[11]

In confirmation of Knudsen's evaluation, it should be noted that UCLA's rise in the academic rankings from 1934, when it had no Ph.D. programs, to 1957 was faster than in the next thirty years from number fourteen to number ten (based on number of departments rated "distinguished" in 1993; see Tables 28 and 29 at the end of chapter 28).

It should also be noted that, while the rate of rise in academic rankings slowed considerably, the competition intensified as the campus rose. Murphy emphasized the professional schools that he thought had been neglected and had to put great amounts of time and energy into building relations in the business and cultural communities. One result of the comparative emphases on professional schools was that, as of 1997, UCLA was closer to Berkeley in its ratings of professional schools than it was in letters and science and engineering, which are the areas of comparison in the most used academic rankings (see Table 22).[12]

Triumphs

UCLA and the Los Angeles metropolitan community got what they were entitled to: one of the great university campuses of the nation and of the world,

TABLE 22

Comparative Rankings of Professional Schools, Berkeley and UCLA, 1997[a]

	Berkeley	*UCLA*
Law	9	17
Business administration	10	17
Medicine	4 (San Francisco)	11
Fine arts	29	19
Education	3	5
Film	—	3
Architecture	6	13
Social work	3	14
Average	9.14	12.38
Letters and science and engineering (1993)[b]	1	12

[a] U.S. News and World Report, *March 10 and March 17, 1997.*
[b] *The 1993 National Research Council ratings (based on Marvin L. Goldberger, Brendan A. Maher, and Pamela Ebert Flattau, eds.,* Research-Doctorate Programs in the United States: Continuity and Change *[Washington, D.C.: National Academy Press, 1995]) did not include professional schools, except for engineering. Webster and Skinner combined the NRC programmatic rankings to derive their institutional rankings for arts and humanities, biological sciences, engineering, physical sciences and mathematics, and social and behavioral sciences (David S. Webster and Tad Skinner, "Rating Ph.D. Programs: What the NRC Report Says . . . and Doesn't Say," Change, 28, no. 3 [May–June 1996]).*

and one well integrated into the surrounding community due particularly to the efforts of Chancellors Murphy and Young. In my judgment, no one in American university history, except for Van Hise at Wisconsin in the early 1900s, has managed community integration better than did Murphy at both Kansas and UCLA and Young at UCLA.[13] As another consequence of its changed status, UCLA became more reconciled to its membership in the University of California community of campuses, less resentful of being "held back" and "controlled" by Berkeley and more willing to view it as a colleague rather than as an enemy. At the state level, UCLA and its advocates became more supportive of the welfare of the total university in the legislative halls of Sacramento and less inclined to push its own welfare or try to select its own leaders through independent action outside approved university administrative channels. And UCLA came to look upon itself as one of the two brightest stars in a constellation made up of nine academically highly reputable campuses.

In viewing UCLA history, I see five major stages:

1919–29	Vermont Avenue Campus	Southern Branch—status resented
1929–58	Westwood	Fights for equality of opportunity within UC
1958–61	Westwood	Secures equal opportunities with Berkeley, including in library acquisitions
1961–99	Westwood	Becomes leading intellectual and cultural institution in southern California
1999–	Westwood	New opportunity to rise in academic rankings nationwide

I feel confident in my description of this fifth stage in UCLA history for these reasons among others:

1. UCLA, in the 1993 National Research Council study, was tied with Michigan as the third highest ranking public research campus in the United States (in faculty quality across all programs).

2. UCLA, in this same study, was ranked sixth in across-the-board "strength" among all universities public and private—strength defined as number of departments either classified as "strong" or "distinguished." This places it in a very favorable position to move toward more departments ranked as "distinguished."

3. UCLA has made excellent use of the UC policy of "equal opportunities" of July 1958 and the library plan of April 1961 to raise the ranking of its library to number two in 1997 among all university libraries in the United States. Since library rankings affect future academic rankings so directly, this implies an opportunity to rise further in academic rankings: a distinguished library is a major source of a "distinguished" academic ranking. A library ranked number two implies a future academic ranking at least among the top six in the long-run future, as does the high ranking of overall "strength"—point 2 above (in library resources, Berkeley dropped from number two in 1995 to number five in 1997, reflecting the impacts of a series of inadequate state budgets in the early 1990s. Chancellor Young deserves great credit for protecting the UCLA library under similar financial handicaps and improving its ranking so dramatically).[14]

4. The new chancellor at UCLA, Albert Carnesale, has had successful experience at Harvard in competing at the highest levels of American university life for academic talent, and he follows in the steps of two outstanding chancellors, Murphy and Young. In his inaugural address on May 15, 1998, Chancellor Carnesale said, "it is our potential to rise to greater heights." I agree.

5. Los Angeles is the second most populous metropolitan area in the United States and also the second highest ranking cultural community after New York City.

But it will not be easy going. The competition ahead of UCLA is very strong and mostly composed of private institutions that are now in excellent financial situations. Nevertheless, in my judgment, UCLA will make it clearly into the top ten within the foreseeable future.

In any event, UCLA already has its place in the sun.

Clouds Obscure
Berkeley's Sun

During the creation of three new campuses, and the transformations at the other four general campuses, I had not entirely forgotten Berkeley. However, it seemed absolutely secure. Feedback across the nation showed me that the reputation of Berkeley was rising, as was later evident in the 1964 rating of Berkeley as "the best balanced distinguished university" in the country. And, as it insisted and as I had insisted as its chancellor, beginning in 1958 Berkeley had far more control over its own affairs than ever before in history. With what I saw as its basic advantages—location in the San Francisco Bay Area, close competition and cooperation with Stanford, and a long history of academic distinction—Berkeley contrasted favorably with any other campus. Also the office of the president and the Board of Regents gave full consideration in budgetary allocations to the maintenance of Berkeley's distinction. What they did not do, however, was any longer hold back the other campuses to forestall rivalry with Berkeley. Berkeley had to compete more actively in raising its own resources and in using effectively what state resources it got. The Berkeley faculty, however, wondered what was happening to Berkeley's cherished preferred treatment.

■

Why was I not more sensitive earlier to the developing negatives at Berkeley in reaction to developments on other campuses? I had idolized Berkeley since my days as a graduate student. It had so much: its location, the resources of the state of California, the quality of its faculty, and its established place in history. I was also very busy with the three new campuses and changes at the five other older campuses—several of which had grievous problems beyond anything I thought existed at Berkeley, and with negotiating the Master Plan for Higher Education in California, and I thought Berkeley was in unexcelled condition.

In what Lincoln Constance, the longtime dean of letters and science who knew Berkeley so intimately, called the "only child" syndrome, Berkeley had long regarded itself as the only campus that really counted. Robert Gordon Sproul had effectively cultivated this syndrome, and UCLA reinforced it by constantly complaining about its own inferior treatment. Now eight others really counted too, as a result of the new circumstances. But I never thought that the newly enriched Berkeley might not have the same confidence I did in its future, like that of other campuses with several generations of inherited advantages, such as Harvard and Yale. Berkeley had become the Harvard of the west and would remain so, I thought (and it did).

I did know, however, of Henry Adams's listing as one of history's truths that a "friend in power is a friend lost."[1] I had a corollary of my own that a "friend in power loses friends." I knew that grievances accumulate against those in power, and particularly those in power who once held the place of the best of friends, as I had as Berkeley's chancellor. And friendships did start fading away. Yet it all happened so slowly, with no single climactic event until 1964–65. I largely ignored faint early signs of problems. UCLA had always watched Berkeley. Now Berkeley was watching UCLA. When UCLA obtained a chair in Armenian Studies by private gift, Berkeley wanted one right away, and the same with a Space Sciences Center.

Other broad developments in the background should have alerted me to the changing mood at Berkeley. Berkeley enrollment was reaching 27,500 students and the prospective end of fast growth in new faculty and new buildings, while other campuses were still growing. Roger Heyns, chancellor at Berkeley from 1965 to 1971, once talked with me about the meaning of this end to growth. I said to him, "You must now grow qualitatively instead of quantitatively," and he left my office shaking his head—"grow qualitatively not quantitatively, what does that mean?" It was a "change of life" period for Berkeley.

Housing costs were rising in Berkeley, driving faculty to purchase homes in outlying areas. Berkeley was less a "campus town," less a community of friends. There was more intense competition among the now eight general campuses, each watching all the others with jaundiced eyes; and Berkeley saw the other seven receive more new resources, which these campuses were earning by enrolling thousands of new students. There were those at Berkeley who would have welcomed these same resources but not at the cost of the accompanying enrollment. (On the shift in comparative enrollments at UC campuses from 1960–97 see Appendix 3 section A.)

The Berkeley faculty had been politicized by the loyalty oath controversy (1949–52) beyond any other American university, resulting in some disenchantment with the regents and the top university administration, and some faculty members were on the alert for new grievances. Before Chancellor Edward Strong (1961–65) took office, I had been assured, both formally and informally, that he was clearly the faculty's first choice. But he was not the leader that the departing chancellor, Glenn Seaborg, had been. In presentations before the regents, Strong was not competitive with the new chancellor at UCLA (Franklin Murphy) nor with several of the other chancellors including Emil Mrak at Davis, and the regents began to doubt his ability to handle the job. He was drawing into seclusion under the pressures of the burdens of office. In addition, Strong developed what was for me a difficult and often frustrating tendency to blame everything that went wrong on higher authority. I had many experiences with Berkeley people asking me why I had done this or that and saying that Strong told them it was on my orders. This was believable because, under Sproul's longtime model of governance, all orders came from the president. Most of the items called to my attention, however, I had never even heard about. It felt like a thousand small stings.

Irritations and Rivalries

Science was king at Berkeley, and the humanities and social sciences were resentful. Several departments were in internal turmoil for one reason or another—in the biological sciences, economics, psychology, and political science, as illustrations (see chapter 6). The plans I had helped make as chancellor to move parking places from the Berkeley central campus to the edge of the campus, and then charge for them, still rankled. And, as I explained in chapter 23, it fell to me in July 1958, at my first Board of Regents meeting as president, to present the UCLA "equal opportunities" proposal that Sproul had already submitted in June. I had no fear that Berkeley was threatened. In fact, the possibility never occurred to me. Berkeley was so far ahead of UCLA and, in fact, has stayed far ahead over the intervening years. But many Berkeley faculty members thought it was a grave error to equate UCLA's "opportunities" with Berkeley, particularly in library acquisitions (Berkeley's library rated second only to Harvard in national ranking until very recently, and the campus lost this ranking by its own actions).

There were now nine independent graduate divisions in competition across the campuses, not just two. Berkeley no longer dominated graduate studies on all northern campuses nor UCLA on all southern campuses. Actually the objections I heard at the time to nine graduate divisions came more from UCLA than Berkeley, because of fear there over competition from San Diego. The argument was that only control by Berkeley and UCLA could maintain graduate "standards." Gus Arlt, the graduate dean in the south, was the one who objected most strenuously. Berkeley and UCLA were happy to have the new and expanding campuses take on the heavy load of more undergraduates as "feeder schools," but they were very defensive about their roles in graduate education.

Berkeley did not want to change from a semester to a quarter system to make better use of the physical facilities throughout the academic year, despite the fact that all other campuses had accepted it; so had Berkeley on a plurality, but not a majority, basis.

The Berkeley campus did not like to lose its veto over Academic Senate actions. Under the old senate structure, the northern and southern senate divisions had this power and were dominated by Berkeley and UCLA. Under the new system, no single campus had a veto. UCLA, equally affected, did not complain to me about this.

Berkeley no longer (as of 1958) took care of the first two years of medical training in cooperation with San Francisco, while UCLA had a fast growing medical school. Berkeley also lost Lick Observatory to Santa Cruz. The Bodega Bay Marine Laboratory had been placed under Davis, as was "Teller Tech" at the Livermore laboratory. Santa Barbara developed the study abroad programs.

UCLA was becoming more dominant in intercollegiate athletics—of serious concern to many Berkeley alumni.

A big difference was in the vantage point. I was looking at Berkeley from the point of view of its place in national academic life, which was advancing fast. Many Berkeley faculty members, however, seemed to see mostly its place within the University of California, which was declining. And some held that the other campuses were unfairly advantaged by the salary levels earned by Berkeley, not by their own efforts. Thus Berkeley was contributing greatly to their advances while losing its own comparative dominance. For Berkeley, was it the best of times or was it the worst of times? It was both.

Two developments were going on at the same time, and they were confused. The first was decentralization of administrative authority to the campus chancellors, a change that greatly advantaged Berkeley as well as all the other campuses. The second was the creation of a federal system of campuses with equal opportunities for all. The federal system involved separate academic senates on each campus, rather than an Academic Senate–North and an Academic Senate–South. This meant that Berkeley and UCLA lost control over the other campuses north and south, and each could now be outvoted in the new nine-campus senate that was also put in place in 1963. Thus it was not decentralization that was "holding Berkeley down" (as Carl Schorske says in his oral history[2]), but the development of a federal system of nine largely self-governing campuses. Berkeley lost its dominance over Davis, San Francisco, and Santa Cruz in the Northern Section of the Academic Senate, as well as its veto over policies that might originate in the south. From Berkeley's point of view, it was held down; but from the point of view of Davis, San Francisco, Santa Cruz, Santa Barbara, Riverside, Irvine, and San Diego, they were liberated. And with their new freedom, Davis, Santa Barbara, Irvine, and San Diego all rose to membership in the American Association of Universities. The chancellors, for the first time, became the real executive heads of their campuses. There came to be nine academic senates, not two.

A Controversy over Autonomy

The new organization of the Academic Senate had been accepted, in principle, in January 1963 in a mail ballot sent to all senate members. It called for separate divisions on each campus and a universitywide Academic Assembly and a universitywide Academic Council. The vote in the north was 796 "yes" in favor of senate reorganization to 170 "no," and in the south 530 to 70— overwhelming. However, not all the senate reorganization language had yet been worked out. At the last minute, some of the most respected leaders of the Berkeley faculty began to worry: did the end of the senate's northern and southern sections' veto mean the Berkeley faculty would also lose power even over actions affecting only Berkeley? The new rules said that the university-wide senate had "jurisdiction" over "legislation substantially affecting more than one division of the statewide university." How was "substantially" to be defined? Could it be interpreted to reduce "desirable campus autonomy"?

A meeting of the northern section of the Academic Senate was scheduled for Monday, May 20, 1963. On May 14 Frank Newman of the law school and four others decided to press for a "resolution of postponement" of the senate reorganization from July 1, 1963, to February 1, 1964, in order to give time to work out more specific understandings. Under the rules, it was too late to place the proposed action to postpone on the agenda of the May 20 meeting, as the chair of the northern section pointed out. But with the consent of those members of the northern section in attendance—a small minority of the total—the group brought up the issue under new business. Berkeley's chancellor, Ed Strong, spoke in opposition, but the resolution of postponement passed 34 to 8. To make it effective, the full universitywide senate had to agree. At the already scheduled meeting of the universitywide Academic Assembly on May 28, the representatives of all campuses, except Berkeley, voted unanimously against postponement, and the Davis and San Francisco representatives, in particular, noted their disagreements with Berkeley.

The Berkeley faculty had lost veto control in the senate for the first time in university history. I became involved in this affair at the last minute. I heard of the May 14 development on Friday, May 17, with action set for Monday, May 20. I was still potentially involved as president of the Academic Senate and as the informal initiator of the senate's reorganization to follow along with the administrative reorganization of the university in general. I got in touch with leaders of Frank Newman's group of five urging withdrawal of the postponement resolution. I did so on the grounds that the time was long past for such action, and, in any event, there would be opportunities to agree on specific language after the new senate structure had gone into effect, and that the language in dispute did not mean "the end of the Berkeley senate as an effective body," as one proponent of postponement had argued. I thought that was a gross exaggeration.

The group of five met for luncheon on Monday, May 20, and decided to withdraw its resolution. However, word did not get out to all supporters and the proposal was presented from the floor with the results already noted. I took the matter seriously not only because of the procedural question about hasty, last-minute actions, but also because it looked to me as though Berkeley might be trying to get back its historic veto and that the whole enterprise of Academic Senate reform might be put in jeopardy. The reorganization effort was so far along, had taken so much effort in the protracted negotiations, and was so essential, I thought, to good operation of the senate. I was also discouraged to see the resistance to change at Berkeley and the resentment of the other campuses toward Berkeley. Could the university be held together? Sensitivities were running so high—Berkeley over possible loss of control, the other campuses over independence from past domination by Berkeley.

THE KENT REPORT

The accumulated Academic Senate grievances at Berkeley were assembled in the fall of 1965 in a report submitted on October 11 by a committee chaired by Jack Kent of the Department of City and Regional Planning.[3] Among other things, this report suggested that the Berkeley division should accept as gracefully as possible its defeat on the calendar question (year-round operations on campus) but that it continue its efforts to obtain greater "campus autonomy" within the university. It specifically endorsed the "'commonwealth' conception of the Byrne report" (released in May 1965; see chapter 14)—the only faculty group to do so within the entire university, except for another Berkeley report much later that also went nowhere.[4] The Kent report interpreted the Byrne report to mean that the Board of Regents' sole function would be to "raise revenues and determine bloc-grant budgets" for each campus. The committee favored a system under which the chancellor and the divisional senate would be "partners" in running the campus. It raised the possibility that there would be no "need for a university-wide Academic Senate in any form." It suggested, instead, consideration of a system operated by "nine chancellors and nine academic senates." Now Berkeley, instead of UCLA, was contemplating disassociation. The committee also took particular exception to the action of Governor Brown and the legislature in the 1965–66 budget for the university in reducing funding for teaching assistants, thus putting more teaching burdens on the regular faculty. This legislative action had been taken in response to student complaints of excessive use of teaching assistants and to the perception that teaching assistants had been very supportive of the student revolts of the prior year.

The Kent report was discussed informally by the Board of Regents at its meeting at Davis on October 22, 1965. The minutes record that "the chancellor [Roger Heyns, 1965–71] did not agree with the basic posture of the committee report"; nor did any of the regents who spoke about it. The chair of the board, Edward Carter, said the "tone" of the report was "one of anger and disrespect." Carter added that "the chancellor feels that the more responsible people at Berkeley will be able to forestall the adoption of the report, and he was inclined to rely on the good judgment of the Chancellor." And that is what happened. The report was never acted upon by the Berkeley senate, but it did represent, I thought, a substantial body of opinion at Berkeley.

While the Berkeley campus came generally to accept the senate reorganization, an apprehensive and sometimes even a resentful mood lingered within elements of the Berkeley faculty. Yet Berkeley also gained from the new situation. Politically it was better protected than if it had stood by itself, exposed and more vulnerable, during the student revolts of the 1960s when some legislative leaders in Sacramento would have liked to punish it specifically but could not do so constitutionally. There is also the far distant prospect that the equal-opportunity policy might someday come to protect Berkeley as southern California becomes more dominant within state governance. Berkeley could also hold more nearly to its chosen size of 27,500 students, which I as chancellor at Berkeley had fought to get as the limit, than if the tidal wave of students had been channeled solely to it and to UCLA. And it could better respond to its developing desire for student "diversity" than if it were inexorably forced below a 12.5 percent level of access for California's high school graduates. Suppose that figure were 6.5 percent instead? How academically elite can a campus become and still attract strong public support?

Berkeley lost. Berkeley gained. At least in the years of more plentiful resources, the gains were, in my judgment, clearly the greater; and the new arrangements had mutual advantages for Berkeley and for the other campuses under the circumstances. The circumstances of the early 1990s, however, did demonstrate the vulnerabilities of Berkeley.

Berkeley, however, earlier than that felt that it was suffering. Neil Smelser, a leading Berkeley social scientist wrote in 1974 (and I agree):

> The Berkeley campus, in short, struck a posture of opposition—varying in strength from issue to issue—to measures that would decentralize features in which Berkeley had always had a leading position, would standardize procedures for all campuses, and would centralize administrative and faculty authority in the university-wide system . . . [, acting] toward the remainder of the system in much the same way the university acted toward the state colleges—as a conservative elite resisting standardization and further overlapping of functions. . . . Furthermore, the series of defeats in the early 1960s— over libraries, governance, graduate studies, and the calendar—may have increased the Berkeley faculty's displeasure with the university administration in these years and may have predisposed them to regard the 1964 student rebel-

lion against the administration with more favor than they might have felt a half-dozen years earlier.[5]

Smelser makes a rather "soft" presentation of what were often "hard" feelings.

I, much too slowly, came to understand this sense of suffering. Berkeley continued to be number one, not only in the University of California but also in the nation. It was not, however, any longer the only campus that counted in the University of California. Inexorable forces leading to a vast expansion of higher education in California were at work. No one in the universitywide administration sought to reduce the stature of Berkeley within the university, quite the contrary. But perspectives varied greatly. From my perspective as president, the university had become a university of nine campuses with Berkeley supreme among them. I thought it would continue that way, and of course it did. The best situation for Berkeley has been a stronger University of California, and the best possible situation for the other campuses has been a stronger Berkeley.

At the time, however, Berkeley faculty members saw only "centralization" in the hands of a distant administration they no longer solely controlled. They did not see—and did not care about—the massive decentralization to the campuses in the flow of microdecisions. They were quite correct, although I did not understand the implications at the time, that more policy macrodecisions were being made by the president, the regents, and the universitywide senate, and the historic privileges of the Berkeley campus were being extended to the other campuses. Berkeley was part of a macrosystem as well as more in control of microdecisions, but the faculty was concerned only with the former.

The long-held fears at Berkeley, dating back to July 1958 and earlier, however, were justified, at least in part, by two events in the 1990s. The first event came in the early 1990s. The university started an early retirement program to persuade older and better paid faculty members to move into retirement to be replaced by younger faculty, and some were not replaced at all. In the course of this process, a few faculty positions were moved from Berkeley to other campuses. In certain basic votes on the third round of the retirement program (1993), Berkeley was outvoted eight to one in the Council of Chancellors and fifteen to one in the Academic Council. I never thought I would live to see this—even Davis voted against Berkeley. Berkeley was the great source of academic prestige, of the level of faculty salaries and teaching loads, of the influence of the Academic Senate—of benefit to every other campus.

Berkeley had given and was still giving so much to others, yet the other campuses seemed to show so little concern for Berkeley's welfare. I thought their action was disrespectful, even disgraceful.

The second event, in 1995, came as the Board of Regents revised admissions policies for the university, forbidding "affirmative action" for members of underrepresented racial or gender groups in the admissions process. Berkeley, the campus most devoted to "diversity," was more affected than any other campus because it had the most pressure on admissions (some campuses were still taking all eligible students). The regents had not sought the Academic Senate's advice, and Berkeley protested. The other campuses did not support the Berkeley protest in an effective way. Yet the future of the Academic Senate was potentially at stake.[6] As a Berkeley faculty member, I was irate at both of these actions.

Overall what might we have done in the mid-1960s to assuage feelings at Berkeley? There was no way to take back the "equal opportunities" among campuses policy already extended to UCLA and then to the other campuses. Nor could there have been different timing of introduction of the policy to slow down its application to the other campuses so that Berkeley might continue to feel more advantaged. It would have been possible, however, to give more personal assurances to leaders of the Berkeley faculty that every reasonable effort would be made to preserve the standing of Berkeley in the national ratings—which is in fact what was being done and continues to be done. Would this have been enough? I rather doubt it.

I concluded the chapter on UCLA by indicating my belief that UCLA could rise modestly further in the academic rankings. I now conclude this chapter on Berkeley with a series of assurances that Berkeley will hold its position at the top of the academic pyramid:

Rankings change slowly. Eighteen of the top twenty universities in 1993 were on the similar list in 1964.

Berkeley entered the top six in the ratings by 1906 and has remained there, rising to the top, ever since.

The state of California has recently recovered in its economic performance and is well situated for the future.

I note, however, that several of the professional schools at Berkeley need to rise more nearly to the rankings of letters and sciences and engineering (see Table 22, chapter 23). This is one of the great challenges ahead. I also note

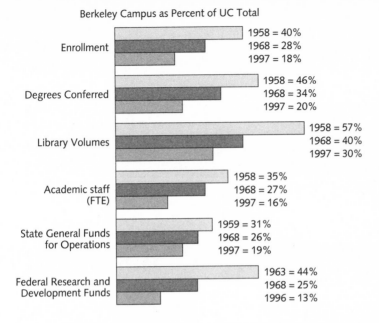

Berkeley Campus as Percent of UC Total

Enrollment	1958 = 40% 1968 = 28% 1997 = 18%
Degrees Conferred	1958 = 46% 1968 = 34% 1997 = 20%
Library Volumes	1958 = 57% 1968 = 40% 1997 = 30%
Academic staff (FTE)	1958 = 35% 1968 = 27% 1997 = 16%
State General Funds for Operations	1959 = 31% 1968 = 26% 1997 = 19%
Federal Research and Development Funds	1963 = 44% 1968 = 25% 1996 = 13%

FIGURE 7. Berkeley as a Diminishing Proportion of the University of California: 1958, 1968, and 1997.

that the Berkeley library has fallen from a rank of two to five, while UCLA rose to two (1997) but subsequently (1998) fell to six, below Berkeley.

Figure 7 indicates some of the changes that were taking place as Berkeley became a diminishing proportion of the total university during the 1960s. Berkeley's "share," in all dimensions, dropped more between 1958 and 1968 than in the average of the three subsequent decades. It was a tough decade for Berkeley.

In any event, I felt very disturbed in the late 1960s and early 1970s by the distress of Berkeley faculty members and particularly at my perceived contributions to that distress. It took me a long time to overcome my misery and to return to participation in Berkeley campus affairs.

But overall: Berkeley, in 1868, had aimed at becoming the Yale of the West. In 2000, Harvard has become ranked as the Berkeley of the East. No American university can do better than that.

PART V

Universitywide Innovations

Academic Affairs

On July 1, 1958, only Berkeley and UCLA had across-the-board or "general campus" programs. The other four University of California campuses—Davis, Riverside, Santa Barbara, and San Francisco—had specialized programs. Berkeley had already been ranked second to Harvard in academic distinction (1957); UCLA was ranked fourteenth. All other campuses were unranked. With its 45,800 students on six campuses, the university was, and always had been, administered on a highly centralized basis.

In broad perspective, during my presidency we established the 1960 master plan for higher education, clarifying the assignments of the major sectors of higher education in the state (chapter 12); decentralized the administration (chapters 13, 14, and 15); created three new campuses (chapters 16 to 20) and expanded the assignments of four others (chapters 21 and 22) to accommodate what came to be 128,500 students in 1975 and 163,500 in 1995; gave UCLA equal consideration with Berkeley in resources while maintaining the high distinction of Berkeley (chapters 23 and 24); and procured resources to finance all the above (Table 23). Tremendous effort went into securing resources. The high prosperity of the United States and a favorable atmosphere of support in Sacramento made all this possible. The possibilities turned into realities because higher education was serving such high national and state purposes.

The chapters that follow take up the developments that supplemented our accomplishments. In the area of academic affairs, these included:

A library plan encompassing all campuses.

A health sciences program involving medical schools on five campuses of the university.

Actions to expand other areas of university concerns, specifically enlarging the cultural programs of the university and starting a natural resources preservation and study program.

Some of these academic initiatives were controversial, the library plan inordinately so.

TABLE 23
Support for the University of California

	1958–59	1966–67	1984–85	1995–96
Federal support for science[a]	100,177	594,947	650,452[b]	928,171
Operating support from state general fund[a]	422,740	950,874	1,769,969	1,623,335
Construction funds from state[a]	300,460	486,414	373,167	421,224
State general fund support per student[c]	9,000	10,900	12,100	9,900
per FTE[d] academic staff member[c]	60,074	73,466	82,251	57,712
Percentage of state general fund to UC	7.37	8.05	5.67	4.22

[a]*In thousands of 1990 dollars.*
[b]*For research and development only.*
[c]*In 1990 dollars.*
[d]*Full-time equivalent.*

■

The Library Plan—
Academic Success, Political Disaster

I subscribed to the view of Thomas Carlyle (1841) that "the true university of these days is [first of all] a collection of books." Immediately after I became president I set out to improve the university's library resources. But I had two qualifications of Carlyle's opinion: books matter more for the humanities and the social sciences than for the sciences, where current journals are more important; and quantity and quality are of equal value—what use is an old volume nobody has read for decades and nobody is likely to read ever again? Yet *total number* of books is the usual quality test—a worship of numbers.

Improving the libraries of the university was one very important action that could be taken to encourage the humanities and social sciences at a time when the federal government was doing so much to encourage the sciences.

I started out with great enthusiasm for the project but soon learned that no welcomed solutions were easily attainable. Everybody wanted every library resource on every campus—and yesterday. No compromises! I had looked on librarians as quiet, meek individuals. I learned, instead, that they are rapacious and belligerent and devious, beyond even deans of medical schools. In exasperation, I once told the assembled librarians of the university that I had a dream about the ultimate end of the world if librarians were to have their way. Book titles were then doubling around the world every fifteen years, and librarians never throw any books away. In my dream, the planet eventually was covered by one huge library. The last four people for whom there was room still available were an author, a typesetter, a printer, and a librarian. The last person left was the librarian who placed the last book on the last opening on the last shelf and then committed suicide—in triumph, the ultimate *Liebestod.*

I went first to the librarians of the several campuses. Each wanted, as a minimum, a Library of Congress on their individual campus. No concessions; not even that it would take a long time. Their agreed way to a solution was clear—there was no agreeable solution. So I went to the council of chancellors but with the same result.

So, one weekend in early 1960, I sat down at my desk and worked out a new plan on my own. I then moved it through the council of chancellors, the librarians, and the Academic Senate Committee on Educational Policy. I got from each, I thought, consent to go ahead, but not agreement on particulars. In any event, I finally took a plan to the regents in April 1961—by then consideration of the matter had been in progress for over two years. It had the following features:

The library holdings of the university would grow from about 5 million volumes in 1961 to 10 million in 1971. They would constitute the largest holdings by one university in the world, and would stand second among all American libraries to the Library of Congress. Huge sums of money would be required—estimated at $75 million in then current dollars by 1971.

There would be two central libraries—at Berkeley and UCLA. Both Berkeley and UCLA would also create off-campus storage libraries, north and south, for seldom used books. Each campus would have a list of the holdings at Berkeley and UCLA and at each of the other campuses—a union catalogue. It should be noted, as set forth in chapter 23, that in July 1958 the Board of Regents, with the support of the Academic Senate and on my recommendation as the new president, had adopted a policy to give UCLA equal library acquisition resources to Berkeley on its way to comparable academic opportunities. Libraries were a central consideration, even *the* central consideration, in the newly developing equal-opportunities policy. UCLA did turn equal opportunities into equal, and later greater, distinction in its libraries, under the leadership of Chancellors Murphy and Young and Librarians Lawrence Clark Powell and Robert Vosper. The policy of two central libraries, one for five general campuses in the south and the other for three general campuses in the north, would have led to a policy of equal acquisition funds for UCLA with Berkeley even if the equal-opportunities policy for UCLA with Berkeley had not already been put in place.

Daily buses would travel back and forth between the two central libraries and other campus libraries in their geographical areas carrying books and book requests, and there would be accommodations on the buses for faculty members and students taking part in seminars and consultations on another campus.

The allocation for library expenditures from the universitywide account for educational and general expenditures was raised by 21 percent from 4.3 percent in 1959–60 to 5.2 percent in 1966–67. Actual educational and general expenditures in total rose by 175 percent and library expenditures by 231 percent. This was a substantial increase in the fiscal support for libraries.

San Diego would have the "third major library" but not one equal to Berkeley and UCLA—full equivalency was never promised though sometimes claimed. San Diego was chosen for special treatment because it was in the third major population area of the state and the farthest removed from either of the two central libraries. But it would not serve as a "central library" for other campuses (as Berkeley did for three and UCLA for four, including San Diego) or have as many students and faculty members as Berkeley and UCLA.

The other campus libraries would grow as fast as we could get resources. We planned a minimum of 3 million volumes each at UCLA and Berkeley by 1971; and 4 million among the other seven libraries, to be distributed in general proportion to the numbers of students and faculty members, with intentions of at least 500,000 each for Davis, Santa Barbara, and Riverside.

In accordance with provisions of the master plan of 1960, faculty members at other state and private campuses throughout California would have free access to the holdings of the University of California.

The librarians of the nine campuses were asked to work out a distribution of specialized strengths among the libraries to reduce duplication and to add to total usefulness. No progress occurred in this area.

At the same time we were developing the general library plan, we put into effect—at San Diego's initiative—a separate program to obtain an initial undergraduate library of 75,000 volumes each for the three new campuses then being built. By purchasing copies for all three libraries simultaneously, we substantially reduced acquisition costs. The list of contents for these three libraries was based on the holdings of the Lamont Library at Harvard and the undergraduate library at Michigan. This list later became a model for many liberal arts colleges across the United States.

In total, an expansive and integrated plan, but . . .

- Berkeley rebelled at it, even though the Berkeley chancellor had given his consent as a member of the council of chancellors. The Berkeley history department made a belated protest (March 7, 1962) and all the other departments in the social sciences and humanities joined in. The central statement was: "If the University of California is to create a research library that can compete with those of the East, . . . it can do so successfully only *if its efforts are concentrated on one campus. For historical and practical reasons, this must be the Berkeley campus*" (emphasis added). The chair of the economics department and my good friend, Robert Aaron Gordon, wrote to me urging that "the quality of the Berkeley Campus not be sacrificed in the course of building up the other campuses." The Berkeley librarian said that my plan would have "disastrous results." At the next all-university faculty conference held at Santa Barbara (April 16–18, 1962), the Berkeley letter was widely circulated among the participants, and an angry debate resulted.

- UCLA also had an anticipatory rebellion of its history department in reaction to an early draft of the plan. On March 11, 1960, it referred to a "shocking betrayal" because equivalency to total holdings with Berkeley was not to be instantaneous. Lynn White, a highly distinguished historian at UCLA, former president of Mills College, and a longtime friend of mine, wrote to me (September 16, 1960) to endorse the charge of "shocking betrayal" and to add that this betrayal added to the "long accumulated anger on this campus." UCLA's Department of Art wrote a similar letter. Theirs, however, was not the general UCLA reaction. Chancellor Franklin Murphy wrote to me (December 13, 1960) that the general "reaction" at UCLA was "ecstatic." He noted that this action greatly advanced the policy of the regents of July 1958 to assure UCLA what he called "comparable distinction" to Berkeley.

- San Diego interpreted the "third major" library as meaning instant equality with Berkeley and UCLA, and the chancellor (Galbraith) at one point refused to go ahead with his inauguration in protest that inadequate resources were being made available to San Diego.

- The other campuses were all irate to be forever subordinate to Berkeley, UCLA, and San Diego.

How did it all work out? The university library system did have 10 million volumes in 1971 as promised, and 28 million in 1997. UCLA met the promised figure of 3 million volumes in 1971 compared to 1,500,000 volumes in 1960. Robert Vosper, who had been librarian at UCLA at the time we completed our library plan, wrote to me on June 30, 1985. He enclosed a report on the recent ranking (1983–84) by the Association of Research Libraries (see Table 24). UCLA was ranked number two; Harvard number one; Berkeley number three; Yale and Stanford tied for number four. His note said: "The enclosure reveals what you precipitated for 'our' great library. Pretty fancy!"

Berkeley did not suffer under the 1960 plan. In 1994–95 Berkeley was again ranked second to first-place Harvard, according to the Association of Research Libraries, and UCLA was third. And thus, it turned out, there could be more than one great library within the University of California. In the 1997 rankings, however, Berkeley did suffer when it fell behind UCLA, Yale, and Toronto, as well as Harvard, into fifth place. But by this time the individual campuses were allocating library resources, and thus Berkeley must accept responsibility for its surprising drop. Universitywide policies had helped Berkeley advance to second place behind Harvard. Campus policy allowed it to fall. As funds from total state financial support dropped by one-third, Berkeley campus policy slashed library staff and made substantial cuts in new acquisitions. The percentage of educational and general expenses allocated to libraries fell to a low of 4.2 percent in 1999.[1] The progress of half a century turned into a quick retreat. UCLA, at the same time and under similar circumstances, protected its library budget.

The interlibrary program for the circulation of books worked well.

The library plan, as fully realized, made a significant contribution to the academic advancement of the whole University of California. When the library plan was started in 1960, Berkeley stood number six nationwide in to-

TABLE 24
Association of Research Libraries Library Rankings*

	1983–84	*1994–95*	*1996–97*
Harvard	1	1	1
UCLA	2	3	2
Yale	4	4	3
Toronto	8	6	4
UC-Berkeley	3	2	5
Illinois	7	5	6
Stanford	4	9	7
Michigan	10	8	8
Texas	6	10	9
Columbia	9	7	10
Cornell	11	11	11
Washington	13	12	12
Indiana	19	14	13
Minnesota	14	15	14
Pennsylvania State	20	18	15
Wisconsin	12	13	16
North Carolina	17	19	17
Princeton	16	17	18
Chicago	22	16	19
Pennsylvania	24	22	20
Ohio State	15	26	21

Source: for 1983–84, Association of Research Libraries, ARL Statistics 1983–84 (Washington, D.C., 1985), 27. For 1994–95 (based on ARL index), "Holdings of Research Libraries in U.S. and Canada, 1994–95," Chronicle of Higher Education 42, no. 34 (May 3, 1996): A18. For 1996–97 (based on ARL index), "Holdings of Research Libraries in U.S. and Canada, 1996–97," Chronicle of Higher Education 44, no. 36 (May 15, 1998): A22.

*The ARL notes that these index scores are only a summary description of library resources based on five quantitative measures (ten in 1983–84); the scores do not assess the quality of the libraries' collections, services, or operations.

tal volumes and UCLA number thirteen. In 1980, when the first American Library Association rankings (based on numbers of volumes and some additional factors) came out, Berkeley was rated number three and Los Angeles number four—very substantial gains in such a short time. These figures later rose to two and three. The library plan of 1960 and the higher priority given to libraries among university endeavors had a quick and substantial payoff. A

TABLE 25

Research Library Rankings (1997) and Academic Rankings (1993) for Top American
Research Universities

Institution	Academic Rank (1993)	Library Rank (1997)	Library Rank Higher (+) or Lower (-) than Academic Rank
Berkeley	1	5	-4
Stanford	2	7	-5
Harvard	3	1	+2
Princeton	4	18	-14
MIT	5	70	-65
Yale	6	3	+3
Columbia	7	10	-3
Cornell	7	11	-4
Chicago	9	19	-10
Cal Tech	10	*	n.a.
Michigan	10	8	+2
Pennsylvania	12	20	-8
UCLA	12	2	+10
UC-San Diego	12	43	-31
Washington-Seattle	12	12	0
Wisconsin-Madison	16	16	0
Duke	17	24	-7
Illinois-Urbana	17	6	+11
Johns Hopkins	19	39	-20
Texas-Austin	20	9	+11

*Sources: for academic rank (based on number of programs rated "distinguished"), Marvin L. Goldberger,
Brendan A. Maher, and Pamela Ebert Flattau, eds.,* Research-Doctorate Programs in the United
States: Continuity and Change *(Washington, D.C.: National Academy Press, 1995). For library rank,
"ARL Membership Index, 1996–97, Based on Five ARL Variables,"* Chronicle of Higher Education
44, no. 36 (May 15, 1998): A22.

*Not an ARL member; not ranked.

great accomplishment! (Appendix 3 section B shows the changing status of libraries on each UC campus and on some other principal campuses.)

UCLA is particularly well situated to improve its academic ratings in the
future because of the high ranking of its library, in addition to its access to
other libraries in the University of California system. Its academic rating (1993)
is twelve and its library rating (1997) is two, a difference of ten places. The
other major universities with large positive gaps are Illinois with figures of sev-

enteen and six (eleven places) and Texas with twenty and nine (also eleven). These two, in particular and in addition to UCLA, may potentially be pulled up by the rankings of their libraries (see Table 25).

The general rule is that a highly ranked library is associated with a highly ranked academic institution for two reasons: a great library draws a great faculty, and a great faculty insists on a great library. Table 25 shows that fifteen of the top twenty ranked research universities also have libraries ranked in the top twenty. The big exceptions to the general rule are highly scientific institutions (MIT, Johns Hopkins, Cal Tech, and UC-San Diego).[2]

Medical School Developments

The medical school program was more a matter of evolution than of coordinated planning. As of 1958, the University of California had two medical schools, in San Francisco (1873) and at UCLA (1947). The unification of the medical school in San Francisco with the basic sciences program in Berkeley was dissolved in 1958 and the size of the medical school class stood at 100; at UCLA the figure had risen from 28 in the first class to 56 in 1958. There were then four other medical schools in California: Stanford, University of Southern California, Loma Linda (Seventh Day Adventist), and the College of Osteopathic Physicians and Surgeons (commonly referred to as the California College of Medicine).

The state then seemed clearly to need more capacity to train medical practitioners. California was relatively underserved in places for medical school students. It had 8.4 percent of the nation's population, but enrolled only 5.5 percent of the first-year medical school students. The population of the state was growing rapidly, as was the demand for more health care per capita. The population was aging, the average income level was rising, and the capacity of doctors to advance health was growing. I heard it said several times, at meetings of the board of trustees of the Rockefeller Foundation, that in 1900 the chances of being aided rather than hurt by a visit to a doctor were about 1 to 1 but by the year 2000 the chances would be at least 100 to 1.

But medical schools cost money. Medical schools also are very complex institutions and a source of many problems. At one Rockefeller meeting I heard the old story of a university president being greeted by St. Peter at the Pearly Gates and told he was being sent to hell and his assignment there was to serve as a university president. The newcomer agreed because, he said, as a university president on earth he'd gotten used to hell. But St. Peter replied, "No, you are not really prepared. *This* university has a medical school!" UC ended up with five of them.

The legislature asked us for a plan for medical schools and expressed its preference for new medical schools at Long Beach and Sacramento. We prepared no overall formal plan for the health sciences but agreed that the university should place greater emphasis on this area.

First of all, we expanded the medical school class at San Francisco to 128 by 1966 and at UCLA to 127 by 1971. Next we planned new medical schools at San Diego, which was the third largest population center in the state, and at Davis serving Sacramento and the vast Central Valley area. The San Diego school was to be developed on a research model in consonance with the scientific concentration of the general campus. We already knew that there was a shortage of training facilities for general practitioners as compared with specialists, and so oriented Davis to concentrate on general practitioners. We looked on the Davis Medical School as a welcome connection with legislators in Sacramento, who would make use of it as they had earlier of the medical school located less conveniently in San Francisco. Our legislative representatives in Sacramento, James Corley and his successors, arranged referrals of legislators and members of their families to both medical schools.

Our fifth medical school, which ended up as part of the Irvine campus, was a totally different story. The California College of Medicine was about to fail financially. It was located next to the Los Angeles County Hospital. The only physician in the state senate was Stephen Teale, a graduate of the college. He was widely influential and had been named chair of the Senate Committee on Finance. Teale called to my attention how difficult it would be for him to support with enthusiasm the expansion of the UCLA and San Francisco medical schools and the new schools in Davis and San Diego if the University of California were willing to let an existing school go out of existence. Also, the legislature had indicated a preference for a new medical school in the Long Beach area. It was not difficult to conclude that the welfare of the total medical program of the university depended on the survival of the California College of Medicine. So we proposed that the college be taken over by the new Irvine campus, which was not far from Long Beach. Had we been acting solely on our own, we would have preferred to limit the university to four medical schools or to create an entirely new one with a faculty of our own choice. Chancellor Aldrich agreed, somewhat reluctantly, to take over the California College of Medicine and Senator Teale gave good support to our total medical school program.

We also planned a health education center in California's Central Valley and picked Fresno as its site. In October 1957 the Board of Regents had designated Fresno as the location of a fourth new campus center but we had gone ahead first with the other three locations. Fresno community leaders were very disappointed. To show the university's interest in the area, I decided to do two things. One was to start the Area Health Education Center (AHEC). It became one model for a national system as proposed by the Carnegie Commission on Higher Education, which I later chaired.[3]

My other decision was to expand the already existing Kearney Agricultural Experiment Station in Fresno County managed by the Davis campus. I dealt particularly with Milo Rowell, a member of the family that included Chester Rowell, a regent for thirty-four years and once editor and publisher of the *Fresno Republican* and later longtime editor of the *San Francisco Chronicle*. Chester Rowell had been a member of the committee of regents that granted the Academic Senate its major role in the governance of the University of California in 1920. Fresno and the Rowell family had a strong claim on the interest of the university.

It took several years for the AHEC project to get under way, but it became the first of nearly twenty in the state of California, each affiliated with one or more of the state's eight medical schools.[4] These projects helped train, retrain, and advise health care personnel in their surrounding regions. I had great hopes for this endeavor as contributing to better health care for the people of the state and bringing them into more direct contact with the university.

The growth of the UC medical system is shown as follows:

	1958–60	1969–70
Number of medical schools	2	5
Student places per entering class	171	428
Annual instructional expenditures (medical school only; current $000)		
UCSF	3,652	13,097
UCLA	3,768	10,836
UCSD	0	4,954
UCD	0	3,605
UCI	0	3,209
Total	7,420	35,701

The total state cost of construction of physical facilities for medical schools (all at UCLA and UCSF) from 1958 to 1968 was about $60 million. No other American university acted as quickly to meet what was then considered to be a national crisis in the preparation of medical doctors. The building of the medical school system, along with affiliated schools of dentistry, pharmacology, and nursing, was a project of epic proportions.

Cultural Programs—The Arts and Humanities

A dominant national priority in 1958 was support for the sciences and, to a much lesser extent, the more statistical aspects of the social sciences. Student choices at the time were moving heavily toward the professional schools. Thus the arts and humanities experienced almost universal neglect. The best thing the university could do for the humanities was to have outstanding library resources, and that project was already under way. But what about the arts? The arts, particularly the performing arts, had been neglected in the University of California, for reasons I have already noted in chapter 8. I thought we could and should do better, first, because a strong cultural program is an added attraction in recruiting faculty members and their spouses, and, second, because I had an additional concern for public service. Public service for the University of California throughout most of its first century had meant service to agriculture. But agriculture was now in comparative decline, and its composition had changed away from the family farm and toward agribusiness. What might replace this service? I thought two of the best possibilities were health care and cultural programs. As models for cultural programs, I looked upon what we had done at Berkeley to advance the performing arts for our on-campus audiences, and what was being done at UCLA through university extension for external audiences. The extension program there was under the superb guidance of Abbott Kaplan, and I thought it was the best in the nation. Abbott later became the president of the Purchase campus of the State University of New York specializing in the performing arts.

What could we do at the universitywide level to encourage the arts? We did two things. One was to increase the activity of the Intercampus Committee on Arts and Cultural Exchange. I provided a budget of $100,000 for 1962–63. This committee engaged in block-booking for the several campuses of individual artists, associated groups of artists, and art exhibitions. One year

(1959–60) we brought to the university such famous artists as Jean Renoir, Jascha Heifetz, and Pablo Casals. The 1962–63 grant underwrote a student arts festival, an all-university traveling faculty art exhibition, concerts, and a faculty lecture series on each campus under the active leadership of Travis Bogard of Berkeley's dramatic arts department, who was chair of the committee. Second, we created in 1968 an Institute of the Humanities with an initial grant of $250,000 from the National Endowment for the Humanities.

Our overall objective was to make the entire university a center for activities in the creative and performing arts. These efforts intensified when David Gardner was president (1983–92). What we did mostly, however, was to encourage all the campuses to place a higher priority on cultural programs for their campuses and their surrounding communities. Davis did particularly well.

A Natural Reserve System

The state of California is blessed with an unusually wide range of ecological microsystems from seashores to mountain tops, from marsh lands to high deserts. By midcentury many of these areas of diversity were under pressure from expanding population and industry, and this impact came to be an increasing concern among biologists within the University of California. On June 4, 1963, I received a letter from the zoologist Kenneth Norris of UCLA and later UCSC, proposing that the University of California start a program to preserve, in perpetuity, selected examples of ecosystems both for their own sake and as a resource for biological investigations. Such investigations would, of course, be more of the Linnaean classification type (that is, taxonomic) than of the more modern scientific biochemistry analysis type, but the new biology has been supplemental to, rather than a total replacement for, the more traditional "naturalist" biology.

I reacted to Norris's initiative with enthusiasm and appointed a university-wide faculty committee, chaired by him. In December 1964, on my recommendation, the Board of Regents established the Natural Land and Water Reserves System. In that year the university acquired the first of what became by 1985 a system of twenty-six reserves. The first major property was a gift from Regent Philip Boyd—a 16,000-acre reserve extending from the floor of the Coachella Valley to the peak of the Santa Rosa Mountains in southern California, with a small remaining flock of bighorn mountain sheep.

Most parcels of University of California reserve lands have been private gifts. The hope is eventually to have one or more examples of each of the many microsystems of the state. No other university in the United States has anything comparable to this reserve system. Faculty leadership has been outstanding, including particularly, in addition to Norris, Mildred Mathias of UCLA. So too was the administrative leadership of Roger Samuelsen, who had been president of the ASUC at Berkeley in his undergraduate days.[5]

Student Life

Student life was subject to reexamination in several areas during my time as president. All of the changes were innovations within the context of the University of California; some of them also were controversial. The new initiatives in student life included the following:

Improving physical facilities for student life on all campuses

Establishing education abroad programs

Introducing equality of opportunity programs

Making ROTC voluntary

Reducing discrimination in the sororities and fraternities

Taking university control of intercollegiate athletics

(I discuss changing rules on political activism on campus in Political Turmoil*).*

■

Improving Physical Facilities

The biggest innovation was the immense increase in facilities for student life that followed the breakthrough at Berkeley when I was chancellor (see chapter 7). The policies were first established at Berkeley and then, with new money available from federal and state sources, applied to all the campuses. Facilities for students were an integral part of physical plans for the three new campuses— San Diego (1964), Irvine (1965), and Santa Cruz (1965). Between 1958 and 1970, across the nine campuses, the number of student places in university-financed residence halls and apartments increased from 2,900 to 18,750, and to 42,000 in 1995. Universitywide assignable square feet in student union facilities increased from 302,450 in 1958 to 538,000 in 1980 and to 645,000 in 1995; the number of intramural sports fields grew from 8 to over 20 in 1980 and then to 35 in 1995 (some large enough to accommodate 8 or more teams playing simultaneously); and the number of tennis courts increased from 35 to 97 and to 130 in 1995. Residence halls, student union buildings, and sports fields flourished on every general campus.

Establishing Education Abroad

A second important initiative was the study-abroad program. Such programs were being developed all over the United States at that time. Our biggest stimulation came from the Stanford Overseas Study Program, which was started in June 1958.

My wife and I had experienced our own study-abroad program in the 1930s at the graduate level under fellowships from the American Friends Service Committee and the economics department at Berkeley. We were students at the Rappard Institute affiliated with the University of Geneva and twice at the London School of Economics. Both Kay and I thought we had learned and experienced a great deal, including a better understanding and appreciation of the American way of life.

I wanted a UC-organized education abroad program for undergraduates and persuaded the Board of Regents to authorize one (May 19, 1961). As noted in chapter 21, I chose Santa Barbara to administer the program rather than locate it universitywide or on one of the two major campuses where I thought it might get lost. The chancellor on a smaller campus could devote more time to its establishment. Sam Gould at Santa Barbara, with his experience at Antioch, got the program well started. He secured William Allaway to administer the program, and Allaway had the energy, the resiliency, the personal skills, and the convictions to make it a great success. Allaway engaged in endless negotiations, with spectacular results. We decided, contrary to Stanford, to work with foreign universities rather than establish our own mini-UC programs in old châteaux or hotels. Our students went to classes with local students and studied under local faculty members and, whenever possible, in the local language—French, German, Italian, Japanese, Spanish. They lived in university residence halls or in family homes.

Kay and I participated in inaugural ceremonies at several of the cooperating universities, including Bordeaux, Göttingen, Padua, Hong Kong, and Tokyo. We always took several regents with us, which built up the board's confidence in the program.

In many places, there were local people who remembered kind treatment

377 · Student Life

TABLE 26
University of California Education Abroad Programs, 1998–99

Region	Number of Institutions with Programs
Africa (sub-Sahara)	4
The Americas	10
Asia	24
Australia/New Zealand	18
Europe	53
Middle East	3

by Americans and were seeking to show their appreciation to the United States. Our first program was at Bordeaux in fall 1962. The rector at Bordeaux was Professor Jean Babin. He had been seven years old at the end of World War I and had observed the American troops who were stationed near the village in northeastern France where he lived. He got to know one American, who was very kind to him and became his friend. However, this soldier was killed in an advance against the Germans. Babin still visited his grave when he went back to his home village. Babin took a special interest in our students, as the American soldier had once taken an interest in him.

Our most heart-rending experience was at Padua. We had just finished an informal discussion with our students when the national television began playing sorrowful music. This was a customary signal that something terrible had happened. We were still talking with a few remaining students when the announcement came of the assassination of President John F. Kennedy. With tears streaming down their faces, the students all straggled back to the hotel lounge where we had met and we mourned together for a long time.

As of 1998, there were over a hundred Education Abroad programs with more than 1,500 students in thirty-three countries worldwide.[1] Each program was under the supervision of a University of California faculty member. (See Table 26 for a regional breakdown of the programs.) The great concern of the regents has always been for the safety and welfare of university students in strange cultures and sometimes insecure situations. Fortunately, there have been no calamities. By 1998, 27,000 UC students had participated in our Education Abroad programs.

Advancing Equality of Opportunity

The university had always had open doors to students from all segments of California's population, as well as low fees and tuition. But the opportunity to enter those doors was not equally available to all. At one meeting of the Rockefeller Foundation in early December 1963 we considered proposals from two famous eastern universities (Dartmouth and Princeton) for outreach programs to help disadvantaged young persons become eligible for entrance. I was much impressed. I returned to California convinced that we should follow their example. I had seen how unequal opportunities were, particularly when I helped prepare and serve breakfasts in the ghettos of north Philadelphia in my student days at Swarthmore and when I worked in the San Joaquin Valley with Paul Taylor, studying agricultural labor (chapter 1).

I took a proposal to the regents (December 13, 1963) to create an equal opportunity program for our campuses and suggested the use of funds received from managing the Atomic Energy Laboratories. I argued that we could make an important contribution to long-term national defense by finding and advancing talent from all sources in our society. We would support special programs on campuses of the university to increase the interest of disadvantaged youth in attending the university and encourage their preparation to do so. The funding would be matched by faculty, students, and other university community members, with the money used to contact high school students in time for them to recognize that the university was indeed an option, and to prepare them to meet admission requirements before high school graduation. The first proposal was submitted by the mathematics and statistics departments at Berkeley to help students in Oakland inner city schools meet our mathematical requirements for admission.

The regents agreed. In December 1963, the regents' finance committee voted unanimously to allocate $100,000 (an appreciable sum thirty years ago) to be used in 1964–65 to provide scholarships to talented California high school students who might not otherwise have an opportunity for a university education.

Our first approach was outreach: to contact students, through our Office of Relations with Schools, which then maintained contact with schools throughout the state, at the eighth-grade level to encourage them to prepare to enter the University of California and to advise them of what they needed to do to be fully prepared, and then to help them get prepared.

I had been most impressed with the argument of Ralph Bunche, also a member of the Rockefeller board, that the worst thing you could do was to start people up a ladder when they had little chance to reach the top, only to have them meet deep disappointment along the way. It was better to get them ready to start up the ladder with adequate preparation and with continuing encouragement and assistance as they climbed up step by step. The real test was not how many got on the first step but how many reached the top.

Our UC outreach program was hard hands-on work and the immediate results were minimal. It shortly became obvious (this was after my time as president) that an easier and quicker approach was to adjust entrance practices. Outreach efforts were gradually replaced by more emphasis on proportionality among racial and other groups in admissions decisions. The university, as a result, quickly developed a much more diverse student body. But there were problems of continued high drop-out rates among students from some underrepresented minority groups, and of increasing charges of reverse discrimination against "Anglo" and Asian students. In the 1990s, the university reconsidered its approach. It had, however, been the first public research university in the nation to take formal action to advance equality of opportunity. And this was before the Great Society program of President Lyndon Johnson. I found only support in the Board of Regents—no opposition.

The timing of the program's introduction was unfortunate. We began our program in 1964 but soon the attention of the administration and the regents turned to student unrest. What a sad note that a student movement aimed, in part, at equality of opportunity should have interfered with the attention given to an actual program aimed at greater opportunity. Also unfortunate were our early expectations of overcoming problems quickly and rather easily, of needing just a few new policies and a little money and special effort, and a few years. We had the goodwill but understood too little of what was needed.

The nature of the original program we had in mind is shown by the following excerpt from a report I made to the regents on March 16, 1964:

> To be optimally successful, the program must start with the youngster not later than the eighth grade, before he has embarked upon a non-college course and before he is over-awed by impending cultural and financial barriers . . . and it must follow him through high school. . . .
>
> That part of the program which takes place on campus must include non-minority youngsters. . . . The program must not perpetuate, on campus, the child's vision of the ghetto. . . .

Junior high school and high school counselors must be consulted in designing the program and selecting the participants.

The program must be broader in scope than introducing the student to the curricular, student activities and physical facilities of higher education. It must be supplemented by an introduction to cultural and social activities normally beyond the interest and the horizon of these students' parents, e.g., attendance at good motion pictures, the opera, plays, the symphony and trips to museums, etc. must be included.[2]

The university spent $137 million on its outreach programs in 1998–99.

Making ROTC Voluntary

The University of California had required compulsory military training since its founding in 1868, according to the terms of the Morrill Land-Grant Act of 1862. This requirement had been a source of student complaint since at least 1933 when I was a graduate student and began following student affairs at Berkeley. I heard about it most when, as chancellor, I held my weekly open office hours. I heard more complaints about compulsory ROTC than any other issue, of how dull and useless was basic parade ground drill—"Hut 2, 3, 4, hut 2, 3, 4"—three hours a week for two years.

By the time I became president of the university, I had long felt that compulsory ROTC needed careful review. As I started my second year as president (September 17, 1959), I told the educational policy committee of the Board of Regents that I thought compulsory ROTC was "academically unsatisfactory" and needed careful study and possibly consultation with the Department of Defense. The board agreed. There followed three years of almost constant discussion with the Board of Regents, reports by faculty committees, presentations by student leaders, consultations with the Department of Defense, and then action by the board. Slow, steady consultation and persuasion, step by step. Along the way I met much opposition to even raising the issue, from alumni and other supporters of the university. One particularly important letter in opposition was from a former regent and high naval officer, Admiral Chester Nimitz. At one point, I had in my office the current national commander of the American Legion and four former national commanders—all highly opposed to eliminating compulsory ROTC. The University of California was taking leadership in discussions with the Department of Defense over the future of ROTC. Whatever UC did, as the outstanding leader among public universities, would have impacts across the nation. At that time only one public university, Minnesota, had abandoned compulsory ROTC. Such an action by UC would be far more important. Thus the public controversy.

I started the discussion with the regents over whether the two compulsory years of basic training were of the academic quality of University of California courses. The answer was clearly "No." Then we went on to consider how ROTC fit into the University of California program. At that time, 60 percent of our upper-division students were transfers and thus not eligible for advanced training because they had not had access to basic training. In any event, basic training better fitted a summer camp than it did the Berkeley campus. So we made an alternative proposal: would it not be better to have a basic-training "summer camp" available for continuing students and transfers who wanted to enter advanced training at the upper-division level? We made a comparison of upper-division training programs at Ohio State under a compulsory basic-training program with that of Minnesota with a voluntary program—almost identical proportions of students participated in advanced training.

We then began discussions in Washington, D.C., with the Department of Defense. Robert McNamara, secretary of defense, was a Berkeley graduate and a friend of mine. We asked the question, "Is compulsory basic ROTC at the undergraduate training level necessary to the development of the officer corps of the U.S. armed forces?" The navy and air force rather quickly agreed that it was not. The army took much longer to reply. In the end, however, the Department of Defense agreed that "properly organized and supported elective programs" would be adequate. Along the way, we had always said we were prepared to work with the military in making the advanced programs of higher academic quality.

If an elective program was acceptable to the Department of Defense, and if a compulsory basic program was not academically acceptable to the university, and if the university was prepared to help improve advanced training, then the answer seemed clear. The Board of Regents, on motion of Regent Carter, voted on June 22, 1962, to make basic training voluntary. The vote was 20 to 0 with one abstention. Along the way, one of the most helpful people was Robert Brode of the Department of Physics at Berkeley and a faculty assistant to the president, who wrote many reports and memos and who consulted closely with the Academic Senate Committee on Educational Policy within the university and, outside the university, with Department of

Defense officials in Washington—always persuasive and reasonable and never confrontational.

Particularly helpful regents included Edward Carter, chair of the regents' Committee on Educational Policy, Donald McLaughlin, chair of the board when the discussions began, and Edwin Pauley, who must not have liked the parade ground training when he was an undergraduate at Berkeley. Pauley thought UC's best contribution to the national defense was through our work at our national laboratories and not through "Hut 2, 3, 4" outside Harmon Gym. Pat Brown was helpful too. The students, knowing these efforts were under way, did not act in ways that would have been objectionable to the Board of Regents, legislators, or the public at large. But it did take three years of hard work.

Total enrollment in advanced training at Berkeley in spring 1965 was 250 as compared with 305 in spring 1962. Enrollment in Air Science went up; in Naval Science it remained about even; and Military Science declined.

The essential ingredient was that moderates were in control of the key positions in the Board of Regents, in the top leadership of the student bodies, in the governorship, in the Department of Defense, and the U.S. presidency. We had time and an atmosphere for reasoned consideration of alternative solutions, and we were able to handle a politically explosive issue in a nonexplosive way all around. Contrast this with the subsequent FSM-Reagan period when instant no-compromise solutions became the style on both sides.

I shudder to think what the situation might have been at the time of the FSM and the Vietnam War had ROTC still been compulsory. The actual situation by that time of voluntary participation was better for both the University of California (and many other public universities that followed along) and for the military recruiting services than if there had been no change. Everyone won in the long run.

Reducing Discrimination

The first fraternity (Zeta Psi) in the University of California was founded at Berkeley in 1871. By 1960 there were over a hundred fraternity and sorority chapters on the five then-existing general campuses. Particularly at Berkeley and UCLA, the fraternities and sororities dominated the social, athletic, and political life of the campuses. Some of these chapters were still subject to the rules established by their national organizations against admitting members of certain identified minorities, although the practices were in the process of changing. In fact, however, most nationals, including my own fraternity (Kappa Sigma), which had been founded in Virginia just after the Civil War, had such exclusionary rules.

Although as an undergraduate I was head of my fraternity, I had developed doubts by the time I was a senior about fraternities at a small school like Swarthmore (500 students). I came, however, to appreciate their value on a big campus like Berkeley in creating smaller communities to which individual students could relate. I mention this because it affected how I reacted when the general counsel of the Board of Regents reported to the board that Governor Brown, as one of his last acts as attorney general, had "issued an opinion that the university can in no way discriminate or officially recognize groups which practice discrimination."

The general counsel recommended that "there should be developed a wall of separation between the university and the fraternity and sorority system." This was in June 1959. I told the regents that I did not want to go that far. I suggested, instead, that the regents adopt a policy "requiring nondiscrimination by student organizations and in approved housing"; and that we would give sororities and fraternities four years (to 1964) to get changes in the policies of their national organizations if such were required. I pointed out that the university already had a policy of not recognizing any new fraternities and sororities that had discriminatory clauses in their charters.

Jim Corley was very angry and bitterly opposed to doing anything. He had been a fraternity member as a Berkeley undergraduate. I was amazed at the antagonistic reactions we got from many fraternity and sorority alumni, particularly from UCLA, many as bitter as those of Corley. I was personally challenged and condemned by many such alumni. Current active student members were much more understanding. All the local UC chapters did obtain changes in the policies of their nationals or exemptions from them by 1964. The problem generally faded away but not all the personal antagonisms. Some alumni thought this was my first step in a program to order fraternities and sororities to accept against their will people whom they considered undesirable; that they were going to lose their autonomy. I was astonished at the vindictiveness and at the suspicions of an evil plot in the making.

The Board of Regents, however, unanimously approved my proposal on July 17, 1959.

Taking Control of Intercollegiate Athletics

Another issue that disturbed some alumni was removing the historic control of intercollegiate athletics from the Associated Students of the University of California at Berkeley and Los Angeles. The proposal was a consequence of the scandals in the Pacific Coast Athletic Conference already noted in chapter 7. UCLA was particularly involved.

Alumni groups at both campuses, in fact, had come to exercise substantial influence over athletic policy. The undergraduate officers of the two student associations, serving mostly one-year terms, were in no way up to the task of controlling athletic directors and coaches and their alumni supporters, and alumni committees had taken over. To restore integrity, we had to turn control over to the campus chancellors—taking it away, in fact, from the alumni. Here was another source of resentment that some alumni never forgot. The Board of Regents on June 17, 1960, however, voted 21–0 to approve my proposal. There have been no great public athletic scandals since that time at the University of California.[3]

Structural Adjustments

Our initiatives and innovations included:
  An improved retirement plan
  A more competitive faculty salary scale
  An abandoned plan for year-round operations
  Efforts to reduce duplication of programs in area studies and language training
  Flexible retirement ages
  Rotation of department chairs and deans
  A weighted system of counting students by levels of their programs.

■

Efforts to Recruit and Retain Faculty— Generally Successful

During the university's whole period of great growth, we were engaged in intense competition in the academic labor market. The University of California added approximately 4,500 faculty positions in the 1960s and 1970s and lost very small but uncounted numbers of faculty members to other institutions. Two important aspects of this intense competition were the comparative attractions of our retirement plan and of our faculty salary scales.

RETIREMENT

By 1957 there was much debate about what to do with the existing retirement plan. It was facing the prospect of insolvency and there was increasing dissatisfaction within the faculty. One group, led by the top officers of the university, Robert Gordon Sproul, James Corley, and Robert Underhill, favored joining the State Employees Retirement System (SERS). This group had the general support of the northern regents led by Jesse Steinhart, Gerald Hagar, and Donald McLaughlin, and of the faculty—a senate mail ballot in March 1957 showed faculty support of 1,200 to join SERS versus 240 to keep an independent university system. The basic argument of the pro-SERS group was security. The state had the power to tax; the university did not. The state retirement system also had the powerful political support of the California State Employees Association, a union with 600,000 members.

The opposition favored maintaining an independent university retirement system—the University of California Retirement System. Regents Pauley and Carter, who led this group, had the backing of most of the southern regents. Their basic argument related to the autonomy of the university from state control. The university, they said, could invest more effectively whatever funds were available than could the state, and it could fashion its benefits more in line with faculty desires. As I listened to the two groups, I realized that some regents felt strongly that joining the state system would create an inviting opening for faculty members to be part of the state employees' union—a union that was the political guardian of SERS.

As discussions ranged over the issues I was grateful to the efforts of Constantine Panunzio of UCLA, who was a special friend of mine—his interests in sociology and mine in economics overlapped, and he had been a source of advice and encouragement to me in the 1930s when I was doing fieldwork in southern California for my doctoral dissertation. He quietly patrolled the halls at every meeting of the Board of Regents arguing for better treatment for retired faculty members and particularly for their spouses. He would discreetly talk with individual regents, reminding them about former professors they had long known and greatly respected.

At a meeting of the regents in March 1957, when I was still chancellor at Berkeley and not yet serving as the next president of the university, I was asked for my views. I generally supported continuation of UC's retirement system but with major revisions. I thought this approach would strengthen the university's autonomy and independence, and that the regents could handle investments better than could the state of California. But I particularly argued that the state should be willing to give UC the same subsidy whether we were inside or outside SERS, and that we could develop a plan "more satisfactory" to the faculty. I noted three concerns. The first was that the state plan did not accommodate our system of sabbaticals, since anyone on leave did not accumulate service credit in the SERS and sabbaticals were defined as being on leave. The second was that the state mandated retirement at age seventy, while the university had arrangements to keep some faculty members beyond that age; I favored more use of such arrangements. Third, the state had no cap on the maximum amount to be paid under the plan. The formula was that retirement pay was calculated on number of years worked times 2.5 percent of salary. Thus, individuals with over forty years' service would get over 100 percent of the average of their three highest salary years. The university had a cap of 80 percent. The state plan, however, did not do very well by spouses. I said I thought that the faculty would prefer a plan with an 80 percent cap that used the funds saved to be more considerate of spouses. The minutes of the meeting then say: "The Chancellor thought that with a certain amount of independence, The Regents could develop a system which would not cost more than the State System but would be more satisfactory to members of the faculty and fit more clearly their particular needs. With respect to the chancellor's proposal, Associate Counsel [John] Landon stated that it represented an entirely new concept and would require special legislation."[1]

This proposal eventually emerged as the accepted solution after a great deal of consultation, including with the Welfare Committee of the Academic Senate, mostly conducted by Harry Wellman. On April 20, 1961, by which time I was president, I reported to the regents' committee on faculty and staff relations that the cabinet of universitywide officers almost universally suggested joining SERS (I was the lone dissenter), but that the faculty and the chancellors now generally supported an independent system as revised to meet faculty concerns, and that I recommended an independent system. Regents Steinhart, Hagar, and McLaughlin supported pending legislation to allow a transfer into the state plan and, among other long-term faculty members, Wellman too continued to favor SERS.[2]

On the above date the Board of Regents supported my recommendation and voted for an independent system. In addition to all of the faculty, all newly hired UC nonacademic personnel were included in the UCRS in 1961. However, continuing nonacademic employees could elect to remain members of the state retirement system, under which they had been covered since 1937.

This new system has worked very well. It is among the best retirement systems in American higher education and has been helpful in both recruiting and retaining faculty members. Among other things it has been better adapted than SERS to a variety of the faculty's needs, as noted above. Also, the regents have invested the funds very profitably, allowing the university to provide opportunities for early retirement in the 1990s as a way to exchange faculty with high salaries for those with lower ones, at substantial savings. The negative side of this switch has been the loss of many outstanding scholars as well as a large portion of the established leadership of the Academic Senate—a disaster.

FACULTY SALARIES

Comparability of salaries was under intense scrutiny, particularly during the 1960s. The demographic surge of students pushed the national demand for faculty members ahead of supply, especially of "stars" who did well in the competition for federal R&D funds.

The University of California had a salary scale and tests of performance (research, teaching, university service, professional service) that aimed at "internal justice." Harvard too had this policy. But there were at least two other competitive approaches. One was to respond mostly to "external market offers," as did the University of Chicago. If you wanted to keep a person, you matched the offer plus a bonus. If you did not, you took no action and let the person involved make the decision to stay or to leave. The second competitive approach was to compete on the basis of the "total package" instead of salaries alone, as Princeton did so successfully. There, a whole set of possible responses figured in the offers: to make available an attractive house that the family wanted—and Princeton owned many—or to provide a special sum for book purchases or an annual trip to Rome or a personal secretary, and so forth. This required knowledge of what each faculty member most wanted and left great freedom to adjust responses on a strictly personal basis. Dean Douglas Brown at Princeton was a genius at fashioning such packages.

The UC approach of internal justice promised young faculty members fair treatment in prospect, reduced envy among older faculty members, and minimized the need for faculty members to shop around. But it was difficult for UC to handle special cases where the Chicago and Princeton approaches had advantages. Hence we made increasing use of our system of overscale salaries. In any event, our salaries had to be fully competitive with salaries offered by other major research universities.

We negotiated with Sacramento an original list of comparison institutions that included Columbia, Yale, Chicago, Michigan, and Harvard. This list was subsequently renegotiated and now includes Harvard, MIT, Stanford, SUNY-Buffalo, Illinois–Urbana-Champaign, Michigan, Virginia, and Yale. By 1966, the Berkeley campus stood above the average of its five comparison institu-

TABLE 27

University of California Faculty Salaries: Percentage below Comparison Institutions, 1965–66 through 1997–98

Year		Year		Year	
1965–66	*	1976–77	-4.6	1987–88	-2.0
1966–67	-2.5	1977–78	-5.0	1988–89	-3.0
1967–68	-6.5	1978–79	-8.0	1989–90	-4.7
1968–69	-5.5	1979–80	-12.6	1990–91	-4.8
1969–70	-5.2	1980–81	-5.0	1991–92	-3.5
1970–71	-7.2	1981–82	-5.8	1992–93	-6.7
1971–72	-11.2	1982–83	-9.8	1993–94	-6.5
1972–73	-13.1	1983–84	-18.5	1994–95	-12.6
1973–74	-6.4	1984–85	-10.6	1995–96	-10.4
1974–75	-4.5	1985–86	-6.5	1996–97	-10.3
1975–76	-11.0	1986–87	-1.4	1997–98	-6.7

Sources: California Postsecondary Education Commission, Fiscal Profiles, 1995 (Sacramento, Calif.), Display 59; for 1996–97 and 1997–98 data, University of California Office of the President.

*For Berkeley alone, since there are no universitywide figures available, the scale was slightly above "parity" (see chapter 6, Table 8).

tions (see chapter 6). By the end of the governorships of Ronald Reagan and Edmund G. ["Jerry"]) Brown (1983), the UC scale stood at 18.5 percent below the comparison average; at the end of the governorship of George Deukmejian and the presidency of David Gardner (1992), it stood at only 3.5 percent behind and had been as little as 1.4 percent behind (1986); by 1994–95, the low point of the recession of the early 1990s, it stood at 12.6 percent below the comparison institutions' average.[3] As of 1998 there was an understanding with Sacramento to achieve parity once again (see Table 27 and Figure 8).

Efforts to Make Better Use of Resources— Mostly Disappointments

About forty years ago, when we prepared the master plan and the universitywide growth plan that followed it, the immensity of the potential needs for resources was appalling. As a consequence, while having promised a tenth campus (in the Fresno area), we wanted to avoid it as long as possible. We were overwhelmed in the early 1960s with starting three new campuses and trans-

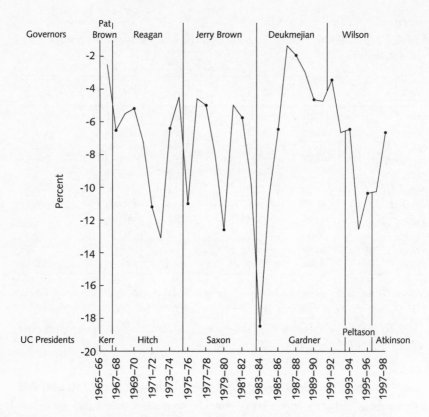

FIGURE 8. University of California Faculty Salaries: Percent below Comparison Institutions, 1965–66 through 1997–98.

forming four others, and also with giving UCLA more nearly equal opportunity to Berkeley, while keeping Berkeley out in front. We were very concerned about the problems of securing the necessary operating and construction funds from the legislature and of bond issue construction funds from the state's voters. We knew full well that we would be called upon to show that we were making good use of existing resources.

There were two major areas of vulnerability: we used our physical resources fully for only about thirty-two weeks a year—two semesters of about sixteen total weeks each—and we had many (growing) areas of duplication, particularly at the levels of graduate instruction and research centers (see chapter 16's discussion of the "general campus" problem). We were already hearing about these vulnerabilities in Sacramento, in the press, and in the Board of

Regents, and were bound to hear more. As an economist, I was very concerned about the need to make good use of resources and sympathetic to some of the criticisms.

Our efforts, however, were a fiasco, at least in the medium run. I say "fiasco" because so little was accomplished and so much controversy was introduced into the university. In retrospect, it would have been better from a political point of view to do nothing about effective use of resources, as the university had done for nearly a hundred years and would do for at least the next third of a century, and as most universities always do. I was caught, as an economist, believing in effective use of resources, while this concept was anathema to most faculty members—an absolute abomination. Faculty members tend to neglect or reject concerns for campuswide efficiency, although they are very careful to conserve resources under their own direct control. I should have known this better than I did.

I locate the fiasco in the medium run, because with Tidal Wave II of enrollments facing the university in the first decade of the twenty-first century, it may again have to face resource problems and, with seven general campuses already on a four-quarter system, it may be better situated to make year-round use of facilities than if all eight campuses were still on a two-semester basis. The criticism about duplication of efforts has, in addition, intensified. The highest and best forms of efficiency are not, however, the highest and most spontaneous concerns of the faculty world anywhere, including in the University of California. However, faculty concern for equality of opportunity for disadvantaged minority students might lead to a change in attitude. Year-round operations would add 10 percent to student places without any additional physical facilities. Might the regents and the state be willing to dedicate this 10 percent to disadvantaged minorities if faculty members would accept year-round operations? Or might the necessity for an additional campus be avoided?

YEAR-ROUND OPERATIONS

The University of California had had a summer session since the 1890s. It had been self-supporting and charged tuition. In 1960, at Berkeley, summer-session enrollment was at a level of about one-third of the regular semesters. Berkeley had had a three-semester, year-round operation during World War II but went back to the traditional two semesters after the war ended. The existing two-semester calendar was strongly criticized by students because two weeks of classes, then examinations, followed the Christmas break (from the middle of December to after New Year's Day). The students claimed they couldn't enjoy their Christmas vacations. The faculty, however, was content.

The master plan of 1960 looked ahead particularly to 1975. In anticipation of a vast increase in student enrollments, it called for "fuller use of the state's higher education physical facilities" and recommended that the higher education institutions "offer academic programs in the summer months of unit value equivalent to one-quarter of a year, or one-half or three-quarters of a semester." While the master plan was strongly endorsed within faculty circles in the University of California, this provision was hardly even noticed, if noticed at all. The University of California administration and regents, however, took their commitments seriously. The California State University system, on the contrary, allowed each campus autonomy in working out solutions, which was also the ultimate UC solution.

Within the University of California, the regents became the great supporters of year-round operations. I was always hesitant. My original recommendation to the regents was for an augmented summer session (in effect, for terms of 16, 16, and 12 weeks), a solution involving the least change. The regents originally accepted this recommendation in February 1961. I consistently told the regents that, without coercion, we could not expect more than 40 percent use of summer sessions (or summer quarter). They wanted 100 percent use. I based this 40 percent figure on the experience within the University of California but particularly on that of the two universities with the most successful summer programs within my knowledge: Stanford and Chicago. A 40 percent usage by regular degree-seeking students would add over 10 percent to year-round capacity and, in the longer run, eliminate the cost of creating a tenth campus or at least postpone it substantially. It would create places, and thus opportunities, for an additional 20,000 students within the existing nine campuses. A more nearly year-round operation would have additional advantages:

> It would help us finance the gigantic residence hall system then being planned. Hotels work more efficiently on an operational basis of forty-eight weeks than thirty-two.

> It would give students a chance to accelerate their progress toward a degree by assuring a more well rounded sufficiency of essential courses in the sum-

mer, especially for engineers and others who wished to avoid one more year of debt accumulation.

It would make participation in the newly inaugurated Education Abroad program more feasible for students without drawing out their enrollment period beyond four years.

More younger faculty members could earn extra income, and older faculty members would have more flexibility to arrange their work, for example, to teach in the summer and then take two semesters' leave in a row, followed by an additional summer.

It would make possible reduced costs to students since there would be no tuition in summer session.

California was an attractive place for faculty from other universities and colleges to teach. This arrangement would bring in extra talent for students to take advantage of (a summer-session course from Alvin Hansen, from Minnesota and later Harvard, was of great benefit to me as a Stanford graduate student), and it would give UC a chance to look over and perhaps to recruit the most attractive visitors.

At that time, year-round operation was particularly on the minds of college and university trustees because of the Ruml report of 1959, which appealed to trustees looking for better use of resources. Beardsley Ruml stated, "The Trustees, therefore, must take back from the faculty *as a body* its present authority over the design and administration of the curriculum."[4] This became a trustees' battle cry. Dean Lincoln Constance of Berkeley called it a "businessman's approach" that disliked "very expensive plant just sitting vacant in the summer." He added his suspicion that "Kerr was told to put this into force and not to let the faculty try to squirm out of it."[5] It is true that Regent Carter "stated that it should be impressed upon the faculty that the Regents are determined to institute year-round operations" by fall 1964.[6] And not just Regent Carter. The regents were unanimous. One regent, William Forbes, at one point stated that he would never vote for another new building until we put year-round operations in place.

I was "told," but I also agreed with the necessity, in relations with Sacramento, of instituting year-round operations. I was hesitant, however, about how much we could expect to accomplish (certainly not 100 percent summer usage), and about what was the best calendar approach. I was aware of the importance of full consultation with the faculty and I hoped for their essential consent across the board. Constance said he thinks I should have told the faculty, "This is the regents' decision, and we don't have any other choice." I did not do this because I did not want, after the loyalty oath controversy, to see another confrontation between the regents and the faculty. So I took most of the blame and tried to work out an agreement over what we might do.

The discussion started with my 16 + 16 + 12 proposal with the possibility that the 12 might have within it an option of two sessions of 6 weeks each during the summer. But many problems came to our attention. Two in particular were how to develop equivalent academic programs for students for the 12-week period in summer as against a 16-week semester, and how to develop an acceptable faculty pay schedule on a 16 + 16 + 12 basis. So we turned to considering the four quarters, 12 + 12 + 12 + 12, alternative. This approach was straightforward from the above two points of view.

In spring 1963 there were straw votes on several of the campuses to see how faculty and students felt about various options. In April students at Berkeley voted 1,674 to 1,065 for a quarter system over a trimester plan while UCLA and Riverside students preferred the latter. Faculty on five campuses preferred (May 1963) three terms to four terms a year. Berkeley faculty narrowly favored (47 percent of those expressing a preference among three alternative options offered) a four-quarter calendar. However, in a second ballot 55 percent favored the "status quo" as against any kind of "year-round" operations. On December 13, 1963, the Board of Regents, on a motion by Regent McLaughlin, unanimously reaffirmed their commitment to year-round operations and chose the quarter system calendar to go into effect in fall 1966 at Berkeley and later elsewhere. This action was accepted on all campuses except Berkeley, where the faculty had voted for it on a plurality (47 percent) but not quite a majority basis.[7]

In summary, students universitywide generally seemed to favor four quarters, the universitywide Academic Senate Committee on Educational Policy favored three terms, the universitywide Academic Senate Budget Committee favored four quarters, the chancellors (unanimously) favored four quarters, and the regents (unanimously) favored four quarters.

In March 1965, as the 1966 date of initiation loomed, the Berkeley faculty voted 167 to 78 to ask for a one-year delay for the inauguration of year-round operations on that campus. The regents promptly dismissed this request. The battle lines were drawn.

If I had to do it over again, I would have more vigorously opposed this dismissal action by the regents and would have voted in dissent. I would argue to let Berkeley go its own way, or at least take its own time, letting it face the possibility that the regents and Sacramento might take a more critical view of its new construction requests than they might otherwise be inclined to do, and that campuses making better use of their physical resources would have their cooperation taken into account. Berkeley would have had to face this reality.

Also, I would try to persuade the regents to give the Berkeley faculty the option of a 16 + 16 +16 alternative to 12 +12 + 12 + 12, as strongly recommended by the campus Senate Committee on Educational Policy, ably chaired by the highly regarded Davis McEntire.

I never thought, as many at Berkeley argued, that academic quality or academic freedom was at stake. Among many others, Chicago and Stanford and Cal Tech were all on a quarter system, and Harvard and Berkeley and many others on a semester system. I had been a student under both the semester system (Swarthmore and Berkeley) and the quarter system (Stanford and the London School of Economics). I had taught under the quarter system (Stanford and the University of Washington) and the semester system (Berkeley). I saw no significant differences in academic quality. Some longtime faculty members at Berkeley asserted heatedly that there were important differences. Generally, faculty members in the humanities and social sciences favored two or possibly three 16-week terms, and those in the sciences three or four 12-week terms.

What was really involved? Berkeley wanted its independence, its right to go its own way, its right not to be homogenized. All faculty members had to change their reading and laboratory assignments and their lecture notes for every course they taught. They found the move from 16- to 12-week terms onerous. Whatever the reasons, as Constance later said, "Most faculty abhorred it"—at least at Berkeley.

Some Berkeley arguments I found less persuasive:

There was too little consultation. In fact, consultation was universal and long drawn out. Wellman comments on the point: "that charge seemed to me to be entirely unfounded."[8]

The faculty had no chance to vote on keeping the semester system but only on picking a quarter or a trimester system. In fact, the first ballot at Berkeley on April 17, 1963 was on the "status quo" versus "year-round" operation (420 votes vs. 349), the second ballot was on three alternatives as set forth by the senate itself: a three-term calendar with equal-length terms (114 votes); a three-term calendar including a twelve-week summer term (296); a four-term calendar (362).

All nine campuses were scheduled to go on the quarter system, and the three new campuses opened in 1964 and 1965 on that calendar. By fall 1966–67, which was a traumatic year at Berkeley in more ways than one, all nine campuses had three quarters per year. Only two campuses, however, ever moved to year-round operations that included a summer quarter—Berkeley for three years (1966–69) and UCLA for two (1967–68 and 1968–69).

Governor Reagan refused to endorse the budget increases necessary to make the change effective. To set up a tuition-free summer quarter and give its academic program the breadth to equal the other three quarters' would—as I had always informed the regents—involve short-run financial costs. In fact I warned the regents that "the initial cost will be substantial."[9] Later on, after Governor Jerry Brown refused to finance a fourth-quarter program, President David Saxon gave Berkeley its choice of calendars, and it chose to go back to the "old" Berkeley calendar of the period before World War II that started in August (after the wheat harvest was completed) and ended before Christmas. It worked very satisfactorily.

I end this discussion with two cautions: efficiency in use of campuswide resources does not rank high among the most cherished values of faculty members and even of most academic administrators; and it is not wise to upset all faculty members at one and the same time on the same subject, and changing the calendar does this. Robert Hutchins of Chicago once remarked that trying to change a curriculum, which a calendar change requires, was like trying to move a graveyard.

Major changes are not popular. Mostly, the status quo will win out in faculty votes. It did so in Berkeley's first ballot (420 vs. 349). What was amazing was that 45 percent of faculty members at Berkeley who expressed a preference should have voted for the move to year-round operations. And more than half the faculty did not seem to care enough to vote.

I had a great hope that the introduction of a new calendar would create an opportunity to improve undergraduate education, which was already being increasingly neglected and turned over to teaching assistants. UC then had, on the average, four teaching assistants for every faculty member. Teaching assistants provided about one-half of the total contact hours with lower-division students. Many years later the deterioration of undergraduate education became a matter for national attention. The evidence of student complaints, however, was already accumulating, as I had learned from my student office hours at Berkeley. Possibilities for improvements in the course of a calendar change included new or improved courses and methods of teaching, seminars for freshmen students, and curricula for a broader understanding of history, of society, of the natural world.

One consequence of the effort to introduce year-round operations was that it gave faculty members an opportunity to reduce their teaching loads—once on the way in (as in the moving from a semester to a quarter system) and again on the way out (as when Berkeley returned to the semester system in 1983–84). Another consequence was to produce resentment that faculty members could take out by reducing their teaching assignments.

Much might be done. In fact, some things were done in the short experiments at Berkeley and UCLA. The UC academic plan of November 1966 (see chapter 11) noted the academic revisions and changes that had taken place in the course of developing year-round operations. Berkeley, for example, reported that "some 36% of . . . courses have been revised, 13% have been eliminated, while 26% of the courses are new. . . . The end result must be recognized as the most thoroughgoing reappraisal of courses and curricula ever attempted on this campus." UCLA reported that the change had "offered an unusual and rare opportunity . . . to effect a major and needed revision in the basic structure and total detail of our instructional program."[10]

I persuaded the Board of Regents to set aside $500,000 for such program changes, including released time for faculty members to work on such improvements. The money was there, the opportunity was there, but the spirit was lacking. The results were minimal, although much curricular reexamination did take place at both Berkeley and UCLA.

DUPLICATION OF PROGRAMS

One potential advantage of a "system of campuses" is that different campuses may have different emphases with complementary centers of excellence, while the system as a whole can have a greater variety of first-rate programs.

We tried to get a systemwide approach in three curricular areas, and in only one of these were we successful. The successful area was agriculture, administered on a universitywide basis by a vice president–agricultural sciences. Faculty members and administrators in agriculture (being, as it happens, unusually sensible and practical-minded persons) agreed to eliminate agriculture at UCLA and concentrate our southern California efforts at Riverside and, in the north, to move programs gradually from Berkeley to Davis. Riverside and Davis had large amounts of land. Los Angeles and Berkeley did not. The two counties where they are located, both once strong centers of agricultural production, were almost totally urbanized—housing tracts, shopping malls, streets, and parking lots. And Harry Wellman, with his detailed knowledge of agriculture and of the personalities involved, the trust in which he was held by agricultural interests, and his conciliatory approach, greatly added to the ease of the transitions. Our agricultural efforts were concentrated.

The other two attempts were failures—much controversy and no results. They were in "area studies" and in language specialties, both intellectual dominions of then substantial contemporary growth in American research universities. The first major area studies program had been initiated in the University of London in 1916: the famous School of Oriental Studies. Now it was the turn of American universities, beginning with the University of Chicago and its prestigious Oriental Institute in 1919. There was a whole spate of new programs after World War II. By 1960, within the University of California, Berkeley had great strength in Asian Studies, and UCLA in African. Along came the Ford Foundation with an offer of a $4 million grant (July 22, 1960) to help the university expand its area studies programs. Suddenly, both Berkeley and UCLA wanted all areas of the whole world as their assigned provinces, and Santa Cruz was interested in claiming the South Pacific, where Dean McHenry had a special interest, as did San Diego later. Middle Eastern studies, Slavic studies, and Latin American studies were claimed by everybody. Universitywide battles ensued, while the staff of the Ford Foundation, with the best of intentions, now seemed to encourage one element and then another. The harvest was a crop of mutual resentments. The formal solution was that Berkeley got Asian and Slavic studies, and UCLA Middle Eastern and African, but actually each campus went ahead to expand across the board. With our $4 million grant, I got a $4 million headache.

The University of California had strong offerings in the foreign language area, particularly at UCLA. I had a survey made of our language offerings by Professor Russell Fitzgibbon of UCLA (later Santa Barbara) and a part-time academic assistant to the president.[11] He found a total of 127 languages and major dialects taught within the university, 85 at Berkeley with particular strengths in Asian languages, and 95 at UCLA with major strength in African languages. Fifty-seven languages were taught at both Berkeley and Los Angeles. He also made a study of eighteen other leading research universities in the United States. They averaged 40 languages with the maximum number on any other campus at 67 versus UC's 85 (Berkeley) and 95 (UCLA). Thirty-six languages were taught only within the University of California. In addition, I arranged (1961), in negotiations with the Defense Language Institute in Monterey, California, access for up to thirty UC faculty and students at any one time on a space available basis to participate in their intensive language training. The institute offered five languages not available within the University of California. UC also developed by far the largest number of language training programs with the Peace Corps of any American university. The competition within the University of California between Berkeley and UCLA undoubtedly led to stronger offerings on each campus as compared with those at other leading American research universities, but with much duplication and some gaps.

We tried to get an agreement for further expansion of our offerings (we were, for example, particularly lacking in the teaching of Quechua) with selected strengths at individual campuses, but with negative results. So also with library specializations by geographic areas and by language groups.

Given campus cooperation, we might have come out of this period with an even broader totality of area studies programs and language training—although already clearly the most comprehensive within the United States. Instead we ended up with more duplication than desirable and less in the way of distinguished programs than might have been possible. Each campus stood its ground. The university suffered.

OTHER ITEMS

I note in passing three other initiatives. The first was to provide for *flexible retirement* possibilities. In cases of exceptional merit, faculty members could continue teaching after age seventy—one at Berkeley (Joel Hildebrand in chemistry) kept teaching until he was almost one hundred and another (Stefan Riesenfeld in law) until he was past ninety. We provided for a review of performance good for three years at first and then, as age advanced, for one year at a time.

The second was to arrange, on a universitywide basis as I had done when I was chancellor at Berkeley, for *rotation of department chairs and of deans* as against a prior practice, as in Germany, of lifetime appointments. Chair appointments were set at three to five years, and deans at five to seven. Chairs in departments with heavy external commitments, as in agriculture and medicine, were to be treated the same way the deans' were.[12] In each case, by special action, terms could be extended. More faculty were willing to serve for the shorter terms, and it was easier to move out unsatisfactory incumbents.

The third initiative was to devise a *new method of counting teaching loads* with a credit of 1 for lower-division students, 2 for upper-division students, 3 for M.A. candidates, and 4 for Ph.D. candidates. Wellman developed this formula to reflect the amount of time actually allocated by faculty members to student teaching at each level. As of 1997 it is no longer in effect, and teaching of all students, regardless of status, is being accorded the same weight. This change is said to be intended to encourage more attention to undergraduates—I doubt it.

PART VI

Outcomes at the End of the Century

Pure Gold and Some Dross

During the late 1950s and early 1960s, we were looking forty years ahead. We were beginning to build the University of California that would enter the twenty-first century. Specifically, we planned to create enough places for all eligible students up to the year 2000. We gave each campus competitive opportunities to advance as rapidly as it could, with its own chancellor, with decentralized decision-making, with the same salary scales, with approximately the same student to faculty ratios, and with access to the same enormous library resources.

Now we have reached the year 2000. How well has the University of California done in the academic rankings? (This is the test that counts the most in national and international academic competition.) Spectacularly, in academic rankings—summa cum laude—for research and graduate training; not so splendidly for undergraduates.

Let me note quickly that there is more to the evaluation of a university than research ratings alone, including its commitment to intellectual integrity, the morale of the faculty, the distinction of its alumni, the quality of its undergraduate teaching programs and of its student life, and the level of public respect.

Caveat: The University of California in the middle of the twentieth century underwent a great transformation. Before World War II, it was basically a teaching university as so well described in Robert Nisbet's Teachers and Scholars.[1] *The most famous faculty members on campus were best known as teachers: Henry Morse Stephens, Charles Mills Gayley, Ira B. Cross, Joel Hildebrand, among many others. After World War II, the stars were the Nobel Prize winners. The University of California had become a research university, as was true of all of the best of the public universities. The best of the private universities instead became teaching plus research universities. With their great resources and particularly their low ratios of students to faculty (8 or 10 to 1), they could add an enormous research effort without so neglecting undergraduate students. The University of California, with ratios of 15 or 20 to 1, was not so fortunate. Something had to give, and it was attention to undergraduate students.*

What happened, in brief, was this: The research effort of faculty members increased many times over as did consultation with industry and government. Also there was a shift to more graduate students—from 25 to 35 percent of the student body at Berkeley—and they absorbed more and more of faculty teaching effort. The university's push toward research excellence meant that it was now competing with the best of the private universities for faculty members and thus had to match their lower teaching loads.

Teaching loads of senior faculty were reduced by one-half—the "flight from teaching," first in the sciences and then, on the basis of "internal justice," in all segments of the campus. And the subsequent shift to year-round operations created a welcomed opportunity to reduce teaching hours. More and more teaching contact with undergraduates, and particularly lower-division students, was by teaching assistants until they handled one-half of all faculty contact hours with lower-division students.

These developments encouraged dissatisfaction by the neglected undergraduates in a period of increasing political turmoil. The replacement of older and more conservative faculty members by more liberal and progressive teaching assistants and junior faculty also affected the orientation of undergraduates. In addition, some humanists and some social scientists in the faculty were embittered by their comparative neglect—thus the flight into political dissent. This process began before, went on during, and continued after the events of fall 1964.

The academic triumphs celebrated in this chapter thus contributed to the political turmoil, which is the subject of the next volume. The triumphs were a source of the turmoil. The benefits had their costs. The glories of the academic triumphs were directly connected to the disasters of the political turmoil. Research replaced teaching; new and junior faculty and teaching assistants replaced senior faculty as student advisers. Celebration was in order but also consternation.

■

Academic Rankings

Berkeley first entered the national rankings in 1906, when it was rated one of the best half-dozen research universities (Table 28; this and subsequent tables are at the end of this chapter). It tied with Chicago and Columbia for number two in the rankings in 1934 and moved past Columbia and Chicago, as sole owner of the number two ranking, in 1957. Harvard was number one in both 1934 and 1957. Then in 1964 Berkeley was elevated, and by a substantial margin, to the status of the "best balanced distinguished university."

(In each case, the year given is the one in which the study was made and—since reputations lag behind reality—reflects the situation at least two years earlier.)

UCLA gave its first Ph.D. in 1938 and was first ranked in 1957 when it came in as number fourteen—an enormous jump in the course of twenty years. It rose to a tie for number ten in 1993 with Cal Tech and Michigan. San Diego, given university status in 1965, entered the rankings in 1982 tied at number twenty-one and in 1993 was ranked at number thirteen tied with Penn and Washington. No other American university campuses have advanced faster in the course of the entire twentieth century than Los Angeles and San Diego.

Some caveats:

Most rankings reflect the perceived views of respondents of the quality of graduate programs and scholarly research. They bear an unknown relation to the quality of the undergraduate curriculum and of undergraduate teaching (but sometimes possibly negative).

They relate mostly to performance in letters and science and engineering. As a consequence, they disadvantage Harvard, which has great strength in almost all its professional programs except engineering, and advantage Berkeley, with a strong engineering school.

The perceptions of those who do the rankings depend on the depth of the knowledge and the reasonableness of the respondents' judgments. And they are not up-to-date. This factor most certainly was of advantage to the University of California in the rankings published in 1995. A huge program of early retirements from 1990 to 1993 had a particular impact on the Berkeley campus, where there were a total of 455 early retirements out of a faculty of 1,650 when the program began.

Also, ideological commitments of some respondents certainly enter into judgments, as for example, for and against political correctness and multiculturalism, particularly in the humanities.

"MOST DISTINGUISHED"

The most recent and most careful ratings took place in 1993, under the auspices of the National Research Council.[2] Among universities with the largest number of programs rated "distinguished," Berkeley rates first with 33 (Table 29). Stanford follows (30), then Harvard (25), Princeton (24), MIT (21), and

Yale (19), together constituting the current Big Six. Only Berkeley and Harvard continued from the Big Six of 1906. The others in 1906 were Columbia, Chicago, Cornell, and Johns Hopkins.

In percentage of programs rated distinguished (Table 30), MIT (91 percent) is first and Berkeley (89 percent) second, followed by Harvard, Princeton, Cal Tech, and Stanford. UC San Francisco comes in seventh, UC San Diego thirteenth, and UCLA ties for fourteenth with Penn.

"BEST BALANCED"

Next, which are the "best balanced" research universities measured by the percentage of all departments ranked as "distinguished" and "strong"? I show (Table 31) the total list of the top twenty and then the ranking of those UC campuses not in the top twenty. Berkeley, Princeton, and UC-San Diego have all their departments ranked "distinguished" or "strong." Other highly rated universities in terms of balance are Cornell, Harvard, Chicago, Stanford, and the University of Michigan; UCLA just trails Michigan at number nine. Stanford and Michigan ranked at the top of the total number of programs labeled "distinguished" or "strong." Campuses well situated to move upward because of their many already "strong" programs are Texas (Austin), with twenty-seven; North Carolina (Chapel Hill), with twenty-six; Michigan twenty-four; Illinois and Northwestern, twenty-three; Wisconsin (Madison), twenty-two; UCLA, Washington, and Irvine, all with twenty. Campuses with fewer than twenty-five ranked departments are not included (MIT has only twenty-three).

Only Berkeley ranks as both most distinguished and best balanced.

Rankings of professional schools, other than engineering, are much less reliable than the rankings of the National Research Council.[3] However, they seem to show that this additional set of rankings would raise the overall rankings of several of the private universities, including Harvard. Also, they might place UCLA in a slightly closer balance with Berkeley rather than at an appreciably lower level. I noted earlier (chapter 23, Table 22) that UCLA had taken more of a professional school route than Berkeley.

Another way to view the general level of distinction among universities is by the percentage of programs ranked in the top ten (Table 32). Here Berkeley is far out in front, followed by Harvard and MIT. UCSF comes in as number seven, San Diego as number eleven, and UCLA as number fourteen. These four UC campuses, with the University of Wisconsin at Madison, are the only public campuses in the top fifteen; Michigan and Washington come in as sixteen and seventeen.

Table 33 looks at changes since 1964 on the basis of number of programs in the top six, which was the test used in 1964. Berkeley is clearly first in all four surveys, followed by Stanford and Harvard—the "big three." UCLA comes in tied at fourteenth in 1993 and below only Berkeley, Michigan, and UC-San Diego among public institutions. This table shows movement over a period of thirty years. The biggest gainers here have been Stanford, Cornell, MIT, Duke, and UC-San Diego, followed by UCLA, UC-San Francisco, Princeton, Chicago, and Penn. The big losers have been Wisconsin and (to a lesser degree) Illinois—both public institutions. And in general public institutions have lost position, aside from Virginia, Michigan, Washington, and campuses within the University of California, which have risen. There are good reasons for this realignment. Some of the public campuses became enormously larger and, apparently, less effective while private institutions benefited from smaller size and from the redistribution of income toward the wealthier segments of the population. Lower marginal income taxes and a shift in the labor market favoring the most skilled made it possible for those persons most advantaged to make larger gifts and to pay higher tuitions.

Table 34 shows, as of 1993, faculty quality as averaged over all fields. MIT comes in first and Berkeley second. UC-San Diego comes in as number ten with UCLA tied with Michigan at number twelve. UC-San Francisco would be tied at nine with Cornell if it were a general campus. Four of the five highest rated public institutions (including UCSF) are campuses within the University of California. Irvine (27), Davis (35), and Santa Barbara (41) are all within the top fifty.

PER CAPITA STRENGTH

Still another way to look at rankings is to assess per capita strength. Big departments, and thus departments on large enrollment campuses, have an advantage in most rankings because of their total strength. Each faculty member is likely to add strength if only in topical coverage or in the handling of departmental chores that relieves others to concentrate on research. Average per capita contribution to scholarship is an important method of evaluation in its own right, giving credit to small departments where everyone is first-rate. The basic study of per capita productivity was undertaken by Graham and Diamond, covering the period 1980 to 1990.[4] It has the additional value of being based on facts, not judgments. The facts used are the per capita receipt of federal R&D funds, and the per capita publication rate in leading scholarly journals.

The University of California rates very well on all of its campuses, among public universities (see Table 35). The study shows Berkeley and Santa Barbara as the top two overall, with seven University of California campuses making up almost half of the top fifteen. The four post–World War II campuses in this group of fifteen are Stony Brook in the State University of New York system and San Diego, Santa Cruz, and Irvine in the University of California. Davis is the only one of the eight general UC campuses not in the top fifteen and its rank as twenty-six leads the other still basically land-grant campuses on the list: Purdue, Penn State, Ohio State, and North Carolina State.

Berkeley (1), Santa Barbara (2), UCLA (3), Riverside (5), and Santa Cruz (6) show up very well in the arts and humanities; Santa Cruz (1) and Riverside (6) in the social sciences; and San Diego (1), Berkeley (2), Irvine (3), and Santa Barbara (6) in the sciences.

Among the rising public research universities, UC-Santa Barbara ranked first, UC-Riverside and UC-Santa Cruz are fourth and fifth, UC-Irvine is seventh, and UC-Davis is fifteenth.[5] Graham and Diamond's study makes these additional comments about UC campuses:

UCLA   "Prior to World War II the faculty and administration in Berkeley regarded the aspirations of the Los Angeles campus with open contempt . . . in the 1950s and 1960s [UCLA] became the nation's first true 'second flagship' campus." (149)

UCSD   "UC San Diego has become, arguably, the national exemplar of accelerated hothouse incubation." (213)

UCSB   "Perhaps the system's [UC] unprecedented achievements in building research universities are best symbolized by Santa Barbara." (213)

Overall, Graham and Diamond say, "Judged by the comparative results, California designed the nation's most effective system for building research universities."[6]

OTHER COMPARISONS

Table 36 compares the nine campuses of the University of California with the
Big Ten (plus Penn State) in number of programs rated in the top ten in the
National Research Council study. UC has 78 and the Big Ten (with Penn State)
has 59. A clear superiority.

Table 37 shows the public campuses, state by state, with membership in
the Association of American Universities—an honor the AAU gives out only
after careful study. Six campuses are from the University of California. Only
four other states have as many as two: Indiana, Iowa, Michigan, and Pennsylvania. Three UC campuses have become members since 1995: Santa Barbara, Davis, and Irvine. I was once chair of the admissions committee of the
AAU and know firsthand of the intense scrutiny given each new member
(in its early history, however, the AAU admitted some members more to
achieve regional balance rather than on the basis of academic distinction
alone).

Table 38, again based on the 1993 survey of the National Research Council, shows the movement up and down of programs within UC from 1982 to
1993. Irvine and San Diego have been doing particularly well, and UCLA not
so well. The total university has been doing very well.

Table 39 shows the departments by campus within the University of California that were accorded "distinguished" status in the 1993 study. They are
the departments that have added most to the academic prestige of the University of California.

Table 40 shows how Davis ranks among all U.S. universities that still concentrate heavily on agricultural and technical (engineering) programs—the
original land-grant emphases. Davis ranks second to Purdue and tied with Penn
State in the 1993 National Research Council study.

Table 41 ranks medical schools by test scores of entering medical students
and by receipt of National Institutes of Health (NIH) grants for research and
development. UC-San Francisco does very well in both of these measures: it
ranks fourth, after Harvard, Yale, and Johns Hopkins. The 1960s transformation of UC-San Francisco has clearly been worth it. UC-San Diego and UCLA
also come out well.

Table 42 lists the number of faculty members in 1997 who were members
of the National Academy of Sciences or received Nobel Prizes, among the private and public research universities of greatest academic distinction. These

numbers are a measure of highest contributions in the area of science, including economic science. Berkeley and San Diego have done particularly well.

Overall, in reviewing the above data, I conclude that the Boston and San Francisco areas hold the two great concentrations of academic talent in the United States—at Harvard and MIT and at Berkeley and Stanford—and that the state most favored is California.

Table 43 shows, state by state, per capita cost of higher education from state tax funds. California ranks thirty-three. Several of the lower ranked states rely comparatively heavily on enrollments in private institutions (for example, New York, Connecticut, and Massachusetts).

Table 44 sets forth data for the University of California, campus by campus, on enrollments and receipts of federal research and development funds.

Rankings by Test Scores and by Persistence Rates

The final rankings I present (Table 45) relate to the ability of campuses to attract and keep students throughout their undergraduate education. Here the UC record is more adequate than glorious. No UC campus ranks with the best private universities and colleges; and only Berkeley ranks with the best of the public universities. The variations among UC campuses are dramatic. Berkeley is clearly in front followed by Los Angeles, San Diego, and Davis. Santa Cruz, Santa Barbara, and Irvine follow, and Riverside trails.

The variations serve as a strange commentary on the two campuses that first started out to give undergraduates in general and lower-division students in particular more attention—Riverside (Watkins college) and Santa Cruz—but end up with the lowest SAT scores of entering students and the lowest graduation rates after six years. Perhaps what attracts students to a campus and keeps them there is what they perceive as the faculty's academic quality and the quality of the specialized training within their anticipated majors rather than the opportunity to receive a good liberal arts education and a well-rounded campus life. Or is it more the campus's advantages: a bigger library, a more diversified cultural life, and the prestige of a more recognized degree—the attractiveness of the Brand Name above all? Both Riverside and Santa Cruz did very well in attracting well-qualified undergraduates in their early years of operation when they had the most liberal arts in their programs. And yet for students who want a good liberal education, public campuses cannot compete with the best of the private liberal art colleges. Of course the physical climate of Riverside and the isolation of Santa Cruz may be other factors, but my conclusion is still sad. The University of California tried and failed to match the environments that attract undergraduates of the highest quality to the best private colleges and universities. And the best of the private universities demonstrate that it is possible to be very good both at the research level and the undergraduate level. Having caught up with the best at the research level, UC now faces the challenge of attracting and keeping the most qualified undergraduates. In Virginia and Michigan, for example, states that do not have strong private universities, the public universities do much better than most of the UC campuses have done.

Thus Table 45 shows that the University of California has a long way to go to match the best private universities and even the best public universities. UC is the best balanced and most distinguished university system in research and graduate training but not in the attractiveness of its undergraduate programs—a major challenge for the next century.

A SUMMARY

The research status of the state of California's public system of higher education in its totality is outstanding. UC is clearly the best among public research universities, more than equal to the total of the Big Ten plus Penn State. CSU, in my judgment, is the best system of state colleges and is universally considered to be among the very best. The community colleges have the most complete coverage of any state. Put together, the state of California gets the most quality and quantity for almost the least cost.

The University of California has, by a wide margin, the greatest total academic strength of any public university system in the United States. Four UC campuses (Berkeley, San Diego, UCLA, and UC-San Francisco) rank with or above all other public universities in the nation (UCLA ranks with Michigan). Berkeley spent many years trying to match Michigan. Now UCLA has also accomplished that goal.

Berkeley has held its position as the leading American research university and perhaps the world leader in academic distinction for over one-third of a century. Berkeley, with Harvard, has been ranked in the top six American research universities for almost one full century.

UCLA and San Diego constitute the greatest academic successes of the twentieth century. UCLA matches Michigan as the best of the public universities after Berkeley. UCSD is now in the top dozen universities, private and public.

Over thirty years UCSF has rebuilt its mid-level medical center into one of the four best in the nation at attracting the best qualified students and the most NIH support.

Irvine is rising fast.

Santa Barbara has advanced from a teachers college to a distinguished research university in forty years.

Davis is at the top of the continuing land-grant campuses. It now needs to rise higher among the ranks of distinguished research universities.

Riverside and Santa Cruz have done well under difficult circumstances and deserve disproportionate consideration for the future. On a per capita basis, in Graham and Diamond's survey, Santa Cruz rated number one for social sciences, number six in arts and humanities, and Riverside number five in arts and humanities and number six in social sciences, among public universities—indications of brighter futures.[7] *Science Watch* (November 1990), in its article "Small Can Be Beautiful, Too," reported that Santa Cruz "ranked first in the physical sciences and twelfth in the biological sciences" in citations per paper. Harvard was second and Princeton was third in the physical sciences; Santa Barbara fifth and Berkeley twelfth.[8] Santa Barbara has a remarkable record for a new university-level campus.

In total, over the past half-century the University of California has had the most spectacular rise in academic distinction, certainly in American and perhaps even in world history. (See David S. Webster and Tad Skinner's rating of UC's doctoral programs in the addendum to this chapter.)

Hugh Graham, coauthor of the survey I cite above, said in a 1997 presentation to the Board of Regents, "Building the University of California has been an achievement without parallel in the history of the world."[9]

I conclude also that the two great assemblages of distinguished universities are the Ivy League and the University of California. These two assemblages helped give the United States world educational leadership.

Conclusion

The twentieth century was one of triumph for the American research university. In 1900 the German university was a model for the world. Then, after World War II, Oxford and Cambridge returned to their status as the most admired universities. Now, in 2000, the best of the American research universities have few peers and no foreign institutions to envy. Harvard has led universities in the United States for most of the century and still does so when its outstanding professional schools are taken into account. However, within the smaller world of letters and science and engineering, Berkeley for the past third of a century has been ranked ahead of Harvard, and the University of California system, in its totality, far outpaces any other American public university system. What our new century may hold, no one can tell. But, for the time being, Berkeley and the University of California constitute one of the greatest centers of academic life worldwide.

In my mind I hear the late Victorian rhetoric of Benjamin Ide Wheeler or Robert Gordon Sproul, exhorting the people of California, "We have given you a university to match our mountains. Treasure it"; or Daniel Coit Gilman again admonishing governors in their relation to the university "to be quick to help and slow to interfere."

How has the University of California reached these heights?

- The state has generally given it good financial support.

- The agricultural and high technology industries of California have prospered economically, to the university's benefit.

- The Board of Regents has had constitutional autonomy, particularly a "lump-sum" budget subject to internal distribution.

- The Academic Senate has acted wisely in evaluating appointments and promotions over the years. This achievement stands above all other factors. In most universities, departments and deans make and evaluate appointments without campuswide faculty input. The academic record set forth above is the great payoff for the policy of shared governance authorized by the Board of Regents in 1920.

- The Berkeley campus has shared the prestige and the high salaries and low teaching loads it earned with all the other campuses.

- Berkeley has gained greatly from the existence of Stanford across the bay as colleague, competitor, and cooperator.

• The new university policies of the late 1950s and early 1960s gave all campuses more effective local leadership through chancellors and decentralized governance. Rather than set aside one or two flagship campuses, as most other systems do, the new policies created the conditions for each campus to compete on more or less equal terms for academic distinction: establishing "equal opportunities" for UCLA and then for the other campuses, starting three campuses, and transforming four existing campuses.

Our policies of the 1950s and early 1960s opened up possibilities. To assure their realization, the support of Governor Pat Brown (1959–66) gave the University of California high priority for distribution of state funds, a most favorable faculty/student ratio, and comparatively high faculty salaries—all at historically very advantageous levels. Then Presidents Charles Hitch (1968–75) and David Saxon (1975–83) guided the university through some difficult years. Governors Ronald Reagan (1967–75) and Jerry Brown (1975–83) were more critics of the university than friends and supporters, but Hitch and Saxon succeeded in minimizing the damage done by a reduced level of financial resources—they and Jack Peltason (1992–96) had to ride out declining trends, while Sproul, Kerr, Gardner, and Atkinson rode the rising trends.

Under President David Gardner (1983–92), a wonderful combination of circumstances literally saved the university from academic decline. The economy of the state improved substantially, creating enhanced state resources. The new governor, George Deukmejian (1983–91), had campaigned for office on a program of support for education. Gardner saw the possibilities of the situation, took the risk of proposing, and then securing, the passage of an almost one-third increase in state funds for the university in a single year. His triumph equalized faculty salaries (they had fallen 18.5 percent below those of comparable institutions; see Table 27) and made possible many other gains. That convergence of circumstances and Gardner's efforts led to the academic rankings of 1993. Gardner, as I observed the process, also restored the effectiveness of the university's presidency, which had deteriorated over the prior twenty years (and a most advantageous budget President Atkinson secured for 1998–99 also helped offset prior shortfalls).

The early 1990s were difficult years for the university as state general fund support fell by about $340 million over three years, which amounted to 16 percent of the 1989–90 state general fund appropriation. At the same time, the university had to cope with inflation and workload growth, translating into a $900 million budgetary shortfall.

A major turning point came when Governor Pete Wilson agreed to a four-year compact with higher education to provide fiscal stability. While the compact proposed to provide the university with average annual increases of 4 percent, the 1998–99 state budget provided a 15.6 percent increase in state general funds for the university. This 15.6 percent increase was a consequence of a great increase in the general fund as a result of improved economic conditions and a rise in the percentage of the general fund going to the university, from 4.21 to 4.32 percent.

The university was saved twice from financial disaster, once by President Gardner and Governor Deukmejian and once by President Atkinson and Governor Wilson.

See Figure 9 for the impact of governors on the resources available to the university and on the opportunities and the problems confronting presidents of the university and Figure 10 for the impact of governors on the ratio of students to faculty.

THE BEST TEMPERED BY THE WORST

There were favorable circumstances for the programs of the University of California during the second half of the twentieth century, but there were hardships as well. The unique story of the University of California is not only how it benefited from the former but also how it escaped from the latter. A separate volume, entitled *Political Turmoil,* explores how it endured the hardships:

- The McCarthy period's devastating impact: the loyalty oath controversy within the University of California.

- The fiercest attack by any state un-American activities committee: the Burns committee reports on the University of California.

- The first and one of the most disruptive incidences of student unrest among American universities: the so-called Free Speech Movement at Berkeley.

- The assaults on the university by Governor Ronald Reagan (and later by Governor Jerry Brown) that were among the most severe by any governors on any universities in U.S. history.

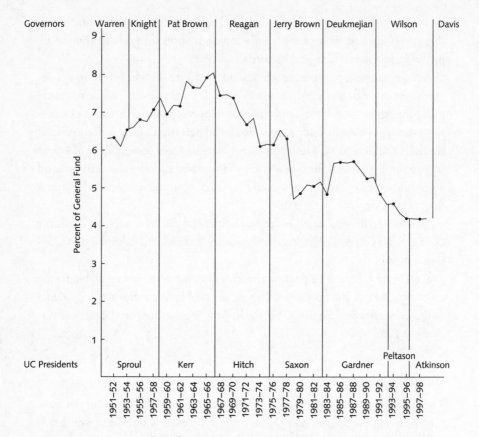

FIGURE 9. University of California General Fund Expenditures as Percent of State General Fund.

Political Turmoil tells how the University of California in general, and Berkeley in particular, experienced and survived what, taken all together, were the worst political storms—external and internal—to assail an American university in the more than three centuries since the founding of Harvard. Gilman in 1874, as an early president, thought that the political "foundations" of the university were too "unstable" to support a great university.[10] They have continued to be unstable but a great university evolved.

The state of California has had several gold rushes. The first came in 1849. The next was the rise of citrus culture in southern California and viticulture in northern California toward the end of the nineteenth century. Then came Hollywood and the motion picture industry at the start of the twentieth cen-

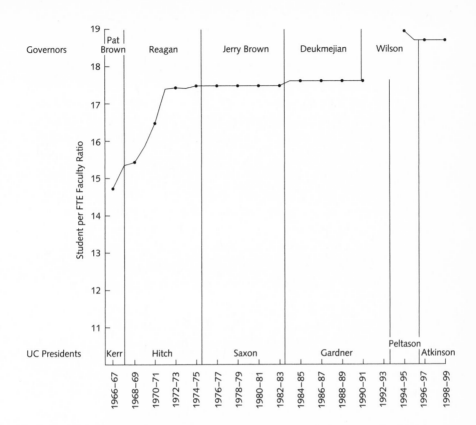

Note: The years 1991–92 through 1993–94 were ones of severe state funding cuts; there was no agreement with the state regarding budgeted enrollment and faculty.

FIGURE 10. Students per Budgeted Full-Time-Equivalent Faculty Member at Berkeley Campus. *Source: University of California, Office of the President, budget, February 18, 1998.*

tury, followed by the military-related industrial development during and after World War II, then by Silicon Valley. The most recent gold rush in California has been the rise of the biotechnology industry, which is so important for the future of the state, an industry led by Stanford, Cal Tech, and the campuses of the University of California.

With Stanford, Cal Tech, Berkeley, UCLA, San Diego, and San Francisco among the top twenty universities in the United States and, perhaps, the top thirty in the world, California has replaced Massachusetts as the national and world center in the production of new knowledge.

The first California gold rushes drew on the physical resources of the state—the precious metal itself, the agricultural largesse of citrus and wine, and the excellent year-round climate of southern California that spawned the spectacle of motion pictures. The most recent gold rushes have, however, been based on the state's human resources—scientists and factory workers, technicians and file clerks in the military-industrial-scientific complex during and after World War II, then in the electronics industry of the 1960s and later, and in biotechnology today.

It is unlikely that any future gold rushes will depend only on the state's physical resources. Now and for the future, California must rely on its human resources. Its electronic phase drew primarily on engineering at Stanford University and, to a slight degree, at Berkeley; its biotechnological phase now depends on Stanford, Cal Tech, Davis, Berkeley, UC-San Francisco, and UC-San Diego. Thus the central importance of the state's education system to the improvement of the future human resources of the state. As goes education, so goes the future of the state of California.

PARADISE LOST: IS THE VIEW OF GOLD COMING TO AN END?

Has paradise already been lost or is it in the process of being lost? Paradise, for these purposes, is defined as the 1960 Master Plan for Higher Education in California and what it implied. The master plan contained a vision for higher education, but it was also a vision for the entire state—to spread opportunity to all its young citizens and to integrate them into society. And it involved raising the skill level of human resources—the greatest renewable resource in the state. The master plan called for extending educational opportunity and for raising academic research quality. It was forward looking. It was uplifting. It was for everybody.

Peter Schrag, the longtime editorial-page editor of the leading newspaper in the great valley of California, the *Sacramento Bee,* has written (1998) that this was the great vision and that it has already been lost.[11] Schrag must be taken seriously. He has seen more California politics at close hand and for longer than almost any other observer. I respect his judgment. But I do not, as yet, concede his conclusion. I do think, however, that he sounds a warning that we will ignore at our peril. Major decisions must be made in the next ten to twenty years. If paradise is really lost, will it ever be regained? The University of California played a major role in establishing the vision of 1960. It may

TABLE 28

Rating of UC General Campuses in Major Surveys, 1906–93

Campus	1906	1934	1957	1964	1969	1982	1993
Berkeley	6	2[a]	2	1	1	1	1
UCLA			14	14	10	8[b]	10[c]
Davis							37[d]
Irvine							37[d]
Riverside							e
San Diego						21[f]	13
Santa Barbara							24[g]
Santa Cruz							37[d]

Sources: for 1906, James McKeen Cattell, "A Statistical Study of American Men of Science," Science, *2d s., 24 (1906): 739; for 1934 (based on number of departments rated "distinguished"), Raymond S. Hughes, "Report of the Committee on Graduate Education" [American Council on Education],* Educational Record, *15, no. 1 (April 1934): 192–234. For 1957–82, rankings based on David S. Webster, "America's Highest Ranked Graduate Schools, 1925–1982,"* Change, *15, no. 4 (May–June 1983): tb. 11 on 23; for 1993 (based on number of programs rated "distinguished"), Marvin L. Goldberger, Brendan A. Maher, and Pamela Ebert Flattau, eds.,* Research-Doctorate Programs in the United States: Continuity and Change *(Washington, D.C.: National Academy Press, 1995).*

[a] *Tied with Chicago and Columbia.*
[b] *Tied with Wisconsin and Michigan.*
[c] *Tied with Cal Tech and Michigan.*
[d] *Seventeen institutions tied for number 37, each with one program rated "distinguished."*
[e] *Not ranked; no programs rated "distinguished."*
[f] *Tied with Penn and Washington.*
[g] *Tied with five other universities.*

still be able to play a role in renewing this vision as higher education becomes ever more central to the economy and society of the state. Or will we have lost a second chance to guide history? I take comfort, however, in Plato's observation: "When the wheel [of education] has once been set in motion, the speed is always increasing . . ." (*Republic*, book 4). Will the speed keep on increasing in California in the twenty-first century?

TABLE 29

Most Distinguished Research Universities, 1993, by Number of Programs
Rated "Distinguished"

	Campus	Number Rated "Distinguished"
1	Berkeley	33
2	Stanford	30
3	Harvard	25
4	Princeton	24
5	MIT	21
6	Yale	19
7	Columbia	
	Cornell	
	Chicago	18
10	Cal Tech	
	Michigan	
	UCLA	15
13	UC-San Diego	
	Pennsylvania	
	Washington	14
16	Wisconsin-Madison	13
17	Duke	
	Illinois-Urbana	10
Other UC campuses		
	Santa Barbara	3
	Santa Cruz	1
	Irvine	1
	Davis	1
	Riverside	0

Source: Marvin L. Goldberger, Brendan A. Maher, and Pamela Ebert Flattau, eds., Re-search-Doctorate Programs in the United States: Continuity and Change *(Washington, D.C.: National Academy Press, 1995).*

TABLE 30

Most Distingushed Research Universities, 1993, by Percentage of Programs Rated "Distinguished"

	Campus	Percentage of Total Programs Rated "Distinguished"	Total Number Rated	Number Rated "Distinguished"
1	MIT	91.3	23	21
2	UC-Berkeley	89.2	37	33
3	Harvard	83.3	30	25
4	Princeton	82.7	29	24
5	Cal Tech	78.9	19	15
6	Stanford	69.8	43	30
7	UC-San Francisco	66.7	9	6
8	Yale	63.3	30	19
9	Chicago	56.7	30	17
10	Columbia	50.0	36	18
	Rockefeller	50.0	4	2
12	Cornell	48.6	37	18
13	UC-San Diego	48.3	29	14
14	UCLA	38.9	36	14
	Pennsylvania	38.9	36	14
16	Washington	36.8	38	14
17	Michigan	36.6	41	15
18	Wisconsin-Madison	33.3	39	13
19	Duke	30.3	33	10
20	Illinois-Urbana	27.0	37	10
Other UC campuses				
	Santa Barbara	9.4	32	3
	Santa Cruz	5.9	17	1
	Irvine	4.2	24	1
	Davis	3.8	26	1
	Riverside	0.0	19	0

Source: Marvin L. Goldberger, Brendan A. Maher, and Pamela Ebert Flattau, eds., Research-Doctorate Programs in the United States: Continuity and Change (Washington, D.C.: National Academy Press, 1995).

TABLE 31

Best Balanced Research Universities, 1993, by Percentage of Programs Rated "Distinguished" and "Strong"*

	Campus	Programs Subject to Ranking (1)	Programs Rated "Distinguished" (2)	Programs Rated "Strong" (3)	Total of Columns 2 + 3 (4)	Column 4 as Percentage of Column 1
1	Berkeley	37	33	4	37	100.0
	Princeton	29	24	5	29	100.0
	UC-San Diego	29	14	15	29	100.0
4	Cornell	37	18	18	36	97.3
5	Chicago	30	17	12	29	96.7
	Harvard	30	25	4	29	96.7
7	Stanford	43	30	11	41	95.3
8	Michigan	41	15	24	39	95.1
9	UCLA	36	14	20	34	94.4
10	Texas-Austin	37	7	27	34	91.9
11	Columbia	36	18	15	33	91.7
	Pennsylvania	36	14	19	33	91.7
13	Northwestern	30	4	23	27	90.0
	Yale	30	19	8	27	90.0
15	Wisconsin-Madison	39	13	22	35	89.7
16	Washington	38	14	20	34	89.5
17	Illinois-Urbana	37	10	23	33	89.2
18	Duke	33	10	18	28	84.8
19	North Carolina–Chapel Hill	34	2	26	28	82.4
20	Johns Hopkins	34	8	19	27	79.4
Other UC campuses						
	Davis	26	1	16	17	65.4
	Irvine	24	1	20	21	87.5
	Riverside	19	0	5	5	26.3
	San Francisco	9	6	1	7	77.8
	Santa Barbara	32	3	17	20	62.5
	Santa Cruz	17	1	6	7	41.2

Source: Marvin L. Goldberger, Brendan A. Maher, and Pamela Ebert Flattau, eds., Research-Doctorate Programs in the United States: Continuity and Change (Washington, D.C.: National Academy Press, 1995).

*Institutions ranked 1–20 include only institutions with at least 25 programs subject to ranking. This criterion eliminated MIT (which had only 23 programs rated), as well as UC-Irvine.

TABLE 32

Faculty Quality, by Percentage of Programs in Top Ten, 1993

Campus	Total Programs	Number in Top Ten	Percentage in Top Ten	Percentage Rank in Top Ten
UC-Berkeley	37	36	97	1
Harvard	30	26	87	2
MIT	23	20	87	2
Princeton	29	22	76	4
Stanford	43	32	74	5
Cal Tech	19	13	68	6
UC-San Francisco	9	6	67	7
Yale	30	19	63	8
Chicago	30	18	60	9
Cornell	37	29	51	10
UC-San Diego	29	14	48	11
Pennsylvania	36	15	42	12
Columbia	34	14	41	13
UCLA	36	13	36	14
Wisconsin-Madison	39	14	36	14
Michigan	41	14	34	16
Washington	39	11	28	17
Illinois-Urbana	37	10	27	18
Johns Hopkins	34	9	26	19
Duke	33	8	24	20
Northwestern	30	6	20	21
Purdue	25	5	20	21
Texas-Austin	37	7	19	23
Virginia	32	5	16	24
Minnesota	39	5	13	25
UC-Santa Barbara	32	4	13	25
Georgia Institute of Technology	16	2	13	25
Other UC campuses				
Davis	26	1	3.8	
Irvine	24	2	8.3	
Riverside	19	0	0	
Santa Cruz	17	2	11.8	

Source: Marvin L. Goldberger, Brendan A. Maher, and Pamela Ebert Flattau, eds., Research-Doctorate Programs in the United States: Continuity and Change *(Washington, D.C.: National Academy Press, 1995).*

TABLE 33

Leading Graduate Institutions in 1964, 1969, 1982, and 1993, by Number of Programs in Top Six in Each Field

Campus	1964 (T=29)	1969 (T=36)	1982 (T=32)	1993 (T=41)
UC-Berkeley	28	34	26	27
Stanford	10	19	14	22
Harvard	23	27	17	21
MIT	10	14	14	18
Princeton	13	14	12	18
Yale	13	15	16	15
Chicago	8	14	14	11
Cal Tech	9	12	8	10
Cornell	2	4	6	10
Michigan	9	14	8	9
Columbia	7	6	6	8
Duke	0	1	1	8
UC-San Diego	n.a.	0	1	7
Pennsylvania	3	5	6	6
UCLA	1	1	8	6
Illinois-Urbana	7	9	4	5
UC-San Francisco	0	0	1	5
Wisconsin-Madison	9	12	8	3
Washington-Seattle	2	2	3	3
Virginia	0	0	2	3
Other UC campuses				
Davis	1	1	3	1
Santa Barbara	0	0	0	1
Santa Cruz	n.a.	0	0	1

Sources: for 1964, Allan M. Cartter, An Assessment of Quality in Graduate Education *(Washington, D.C.: American Council on Education, 1966); for 1969, Kenneth D. Roose and Charles J. Andersen,* A Rating of Graduate Programs *(Washington, D.C.: American Council on Education, 1970); for 1982, Conference Board of Associated Research Councils,* An Assessment of Research-Doctorate Programs in the United States *(Washington, D.C.: National Academy Press, 1982).*

TABLE 34

Rankings of Faculty Scholarly Quality in All Fields, 1993

Rank	Campus*	Number of Programs	Average Rating
1	MIT	23	4.60
2	Berkeley	37	4.49
3	Harvard	30	4.40
4	Cal Tech	19	4.29
	Princeton	29	4.29
6	Stanford	43	4.21
7	Chicago	30	4.13
8	Yale	30	4.08
9	Cornell	37	3.95
10	UC-San Diego	29	3.93
11	Columbia	34	3.92
12	UCLA	36	3.85
	Michigan	41	3.85
14	Pennsylvania	36	3.79
15	Wisconsin-Madison	39	3.70
16	Texas-Austin	37	3.63
17	Washington	39	3.60
18	Northwestern	30	3.58
19	Carnegie-Mellon	15	3.56
	Duke	33	3.56
	Illinois-Urbana	37	3.56
	Johns Hopkins	34	3.56
Other UC campuses			
	San Francisco	9	3.94
	Irvine	24	3.35
	Davis	26	3.18
	Santa Barbara	32	3.08
	Riverside		2.72
	Santa Cruz		2.71

Source: David S. Webster and Tad Skinner, "Rating Ph.D. Programs: What the NRC Report Says . . . and Doesn't Say," Change, 28, no. 3 (May–June 1996): tb. 1 on 26; for San Francisco, Marvin L. Goldberger, Brendan A. Maher, and Pamela Ebert Flattau, eds., Research-Doctorate Programs in the United States: Continuity and Change *(Washington, D.C.: National Academy Press, 1995).*

Institutions rated in the top twenty have 15 or more programs.

TABLE 35

Research 1* Public Universities Ranked by Combined Index Rankings for Top-Science, Top–Social Science, and Arts and Humanities

			Rank on Qualitative Indexes		
Rank	Campus	Combined Rank	Top-Science	Top–Social Science	Arts & Humanities
1	UC-Berkeley	11	2	8	1
2	UC-Santa Barbara	15	6	7	2
	SUNY-Stony Brook	15	5	2	8
4	UCLA	23	7	13	3
5	Wisconsin-Madison	25	9	5	11
	Michigan	25	15	3	7
7	Illinois-Urbana	28	8	11	9
8	UC-San Diego	30	1	19	10
	Indiana	30	22	4	4
10	Colorado	34	4	15	15
11	UC-Santa Cruz	39	32	1	6
12	UC-Riverside	40	29	6	5
13	North Carolina–Chapel Hill	44	20	10	14
14	Washington-Seattle	46	10	14	22
15	UC-Irvine	47	3	26	18
16	Texas-Austin	48	16	16	16
17	SUNY-Albany	52	24	9	19
18	Maryland-College Park	54	14	20	20
19	Iowa	55	21	22	12
20	Virginia	56	18	25	13
21	Arizona	61	11	29	21
	Minnesota	61	19	17	25
23	Pittsburgh	62	26	12	24
24	Utah	65	13	24	28
25	Illinois-Chicago	66	31	18	17
26	UC-Davis	70	17	30	23
27	Purdue	71	12	28	31
28	Penn State	75	25	21	29
29	SUNY-Buffalo	77	23	27	27
30	Ohio State	80	27	23	30
31	North Carolina State	85	28	31	26
32	Alabama-Birmingham	94	30	32	32

Source: Hugh Davis Graham and Nancy Diamond, The Rise of American Research Universities *(Baltimore: Johns Hopkins University Press, 1997), tb. 6.7 on 167.*

Graham anad Diamond's classification of institutions is based on receipt of federal research and development funds and on their "publications index." See their book, 144–52, for details on the Research 1 Public Universities category, which contains the 32 universities listed above.

TABLE 36

Number of Programs in Top Ten—UC vs. Big Ten (with Penn State)

UC		Big Ten	
Berkeley	36	Illinois	10
Davis	1	Indiana	0
Irvine	2	Iowa	0
San Francisco	6	Michigan	14
San Diego	14	Michigan State	0
Santa Barbara	4	Minnesota	5
Santa Cruz	2	Northwestern	6
UCLA	13	Ohio State	2
Riverside	0	Penn State	3
		Purdue	5
		Wisconsin	14
Total	**78**	**Total**	**59**

Source: Marvin L. Goldberger, Brendan A. Maher, and Pamela Ebert Flattau, eds., Research-Doctorate Programs in the United States: Continuity and Change (Washington, D.C.: National Academy Press, 1995).

TABLE 37

Public Members of Association of American Universities, Campuses by State, 1997

State	Campus	Date Joined AAU
Arizona	University of Arizona	1985
California	UC-Berkeley	1900*
	UCLA	1974
	UC-San Diego	1982
	UC-Santa Barbara	1995
	UC-Davis	1996
	UC-Irvine	1996
Colorado	University of Colorado-Boulder	1966
Florida	University of Florida	1985
Illinois	University of Illinois–Urbana-Champaign	1908
Indiana	Indiana University	1909
	Purdue University	1958
Iowa	University of Iowa	1909
	Iowa State University	1958
Kansas	University of Kansas	1909
Maryland	University of Maryland–College Park	1969
Michigan	University of Michigan	1900*
	Michigan State University	1964
Minnesota	University of Minnesota–Twin Cities	1908
Missouri	University of Missouri-Columbia	1908
Nebraska	University of Nebraska-Lincoln	1909
New Jersey	Rutgers, the State University	1989
New York	State University of New York-Buffalo	1989
North Carolina	University of North Carolina–Chapel Hill	1922
Ohio	Ohio State University	1916
Oregon	University of Oregon	1969
Pennsylvania	Pennsylvania State University	1958
	University of Pittsburgh	1974
Texas	University of Texas-Austin	1929
Virginia	University of Virginia	1904
Washington	University of Washington	1950
Wisconsin	University of Wisconsin-Madison	1900*

* In founding group.

TABLE 38

Rank of Programs at UC Campuses, 1993 vs. 1982*

Campus	Programs Up	Programs Down
Berkeley	10	8
Davis	10	7
Irvine	10	2
Los Angeles	11	15
Riverside	7	6
San Diego	10	5
San Francisco	0	1
Santa Barbara	8	9
Santa Cruz	2	1
Totals	68	54

Sources: for 1982, Conference Board of Associated Research Councils, An Assessment of Research-Doctorate Programs in the United States (Washington, D.C.: National Academy Press, 1982); for 1993, Marvin L. Goldberger, Brendan A. Maher, and Pamela Ebert Flattau, eds., Research-Doctorate Programs in the United States: Continuity and Change (Washington, D.C.: National Academy Press, 1995).

All programs are ranked in both surveys.

TABLE 39
UC Departments Ranked as "Distinguished" (by campus), 1993

Campus	Department	Campus	Department
Berkeley (33)	Arts and humanities	Los Angeles (*continued*)	Physical sciences and mathematics
	Art history		Chemistry
	Classics		Geosciences
	English language and literature		Mathematics
	French language and literature		Physics
	German language and literature		Social and behavioral sciences
	Music		Economics
	Philosophy		History
	Biological sciences		Political science
	Biochemistry and molecular biology		Psychology
	Cell and developmental biology		Sociology
	Ecology, evolution, and behavior	San Diego (14)	Biological sciences
	Molecular and general genetics		Biochemistry and molecular biology
	Neurosciences		Cell and developmental biology
	Engineering		Molecular and general genetics
	Biomedical engineering		Neurosciences
	Chemical engineering		Pharmacology
	Civil engineering		Physiology
	Electrical engineering		Engineering
	Industrial engineering		Biomedical engineering
	Materials science		Mechanical engineering
	Mechanical engineering		

Physical sciences and mathematics
Astrophysics and astronomy
Chemistry
Computer sciences
Geosciences
Mathematics
Physics
Statistics and biostatistics (2 programs)
Social and behavioral sciences
Anthropology
Economics
History
Political science
Psychology
Sociology

Davis (1)
Biological sciences
Ecology, evolution, and behavior
Arts and humanities
Comparative literature

Irvine (1)
Arts and humanities
English language and literature
Philosophy

Los Angeles (14)
Biological sciences
Biochemistry and molecular biology
Physiology

Physical sciences and mathematics
Geosciences
Mathematics
Oceanography
Physics
Social and behavioral sciences
Political science
Psychology

San Francisco (6)
Biological sciences
Biochemistry and molecular biology
Cell and developmental biology
Molecular and general genetics
Neurosciences
Physiology
Engineering
Biomedical engineering

Santa Barbara (3)
Engineering
Materials science
Physical sciences and mathematics
Physics
Social and behavioral sciences
Geography

Santa Cruz (1)
Physical sciences and mathematics
Astrophysics and astronomy

Source: Marvin L. Goldberger, Brendan A. Maher, and Pamela Ebert Flattau, eds., Research-Doctorate Programs in the United States: Continuity and Change *(Washington, D.C.: National Academy Press, 1995).*

TABLE 40

Davis and Other Universities with Strong Agricultural and Technical Programs, in Rank of Faculty Quality, 1993

Campus	Rank among All Universities, Average Faculty Quality*
Purdue	29
Davis	35
Penn State	35
North Carolina State	46
Texas A&M	47
Georgia Tech	52
Michigan State	55
Iowa State	57

Source: Marvin L. Goldberger, Brendan A. Maher, and Pamela Ebert Flattau, eds., Research-Doctorate Programs in the United States: Continuity and Change *(Washington, D.C.: National Academy Press, 1995).*

*Among the better known institutions, all others had lower rankings including Oregon State, Washington State, and Nebraska.

TABLE 41

Leading Medical Schools in National Institutes of Health Grants and Test Scores of Entering Medical Students, 1994

Rank by MCAT Scores	Campus	Average MCAT Score	Total NIH Research Funds	Rank by NIH Research Funds
	Washington University (Missouri)	11.4	$132,056,813	10
2	Harvard	11.0	412,800,000	1
	Yale	11.0	208,286,834	2
	Johns Hopkins	11.0	188,037,185	4
	UC-San Francisco	11.0	158,860,845	6
	UC-San Diego	11.0	139,700,000	9
	Vanderbilt	11.0	70,991,271	15
8	Duke	10.8	123,798,546	11
	Stanford	10.8	114,002,000	13
10	Pennsylvania	10.7	160,522,000	5
	Columbia	10.7	154,431,888	7
	Michigan-Ann Arbor	10.7	88,215,586	14
13	UCLA	10.5	150,721,792	8
	Cornell	10.5	123,235,000	12
15	Washington	10.0	195,425,225	3

Source: "Research-Oriented Medical Schools," U.S. News & World Report 118, no. 11 (March 20, 1995): 98.

TABLE 42

National Academy of Sciences Members and Winners of Nobel Prizes among
UC Campuses and Other Leading Universities, 1997

Campus	Number of NAS Members[a]	Number of Nobel Prize Winners
Harvard	110	21
Berkeley	108	8
Stanford	107	12[b]
MIT	98	11
Yale	64	2
Cal Tech	60	4
Chicago	50	6
Princeton	45	7
Cornell	45	4
UC-San Diego	42	4
Wisconsin	39	0
UCLA	30	1
Illinois	29	0
Michigan	20	0
UC-San Francisco	18	2
UC-Santa Barbara	16	0
UC-Davis	15	0
UC-Irvine	13	2
UC-Santa Cruz	9	0
UC-Riverside	4	0

Source: 1997 National Academy of Sciences membership roster; for Nobel Prize winners, public affairs offices of respective institutions.

[a]*Includes emeritii.*
[b]*Does not include three Nobelists affiliated with Hoover Institution.*

TABLE 43

Appropriations Per Capita of State Funds for Operating Expenses of Higher Education, 1995–96

State	Appropriations (in $1,000)	Per Capita ($)	Rank
Hawaii	339,282	287.77	1
New Mexico	466,462	282.02	2
Alaska	169,254	278.39	3
Wyoming	129,401	271.85	4
North Carolina	1,758,713	248.76	5
Mississippi	659,292	247.02	6
Iowa	673,423	238.04	7
Nebraska	385,709	237.65	8
North Dakota	151,210	237.01	9
Minnesota	1,066,898	233.61	10
Alabama	948,630	224.85	11
Utah	424,899	222.69	12
Idaho	237,309	209.45	13
Kansas	525,115	205.60	14
Delaware	143,052	202.62	15
Wisconsin	971,644	191.19	16
Washington	1,002,851	187.69	17
Arkansas	451,851	184.20	18
South Carolina	660,048	180.14	19
West Virginia	327,173	179.57	20
Texas	3,278,313	178.38	21
Kentucky	677,125	176.93	22
Michigan	1,672,447	176.12	23
Tennessee	901,253	174.16	24
Georgia	1,224,076	173.50	25
New Jersey	1,369,244	173.23	26
Arizona	697,602	171.19	27
Indiana	975,726	169.63	28
Oklahoma	548,153	168.25	29
Illinois	1,970,664	167.69	30
Maryland	815,618	162.93	31
South Dakota	116,890	162.12	32
California	5,072,800	161.39	33
Colorado	579,950	158.63	34
New York	2,833,060	155.93	35
Nevada	224,143	153.84	36
Connecticut	501,942	153.26	37
Oregon	471,892	152.91	38

TABLE 43 *(continued)*

State	Appropriations (in $1,000)	Per Capita ($)	Rank
Ohio	1,679,546	151.28	39
Massachusetts	912,525	151.06	40
Virginia	980,781	149.69	41
Maine	179,883	145.07	42
Montana	122,620	143.25	43
Louisiana	593,858	137.63	44
Missouri	722,038	136.80	45
Pennsylvania	1,642,340	136.27	46
Florida	1,830,847	131.22	47
Rhode Island	128,092	128.48	48
Vermont	55,711	96.05	49
New Hampshire	83,185	73.16	50
Total	**44,354,550**	**170.74**	

Source: Edward R. Hines and J. Russell Higham III, State Higher Education Appropriations 1995/96 *(Denver: State Higher Education Executive Officers, March 1996).*

TABLE 44

Comparative Statistics on Size of Enrollment and Receipt of Federal R&D Funding at the University of California Campuses

| | Enrollment | | | | Federal R&D Funding ($000), 1995 |
| | 1965 | | 1995 | | |
Campus	Total	Graduate	Total	Graduate	
Berkeley	26,834	10,224	29,630	8,433	142,338
Davis	7,907	1,731	23,092	4,281	98,932
Irvine	1,589	140	17,261	2,788	67,079
Los Angeles	25,676	9,064	34,713	9,302	216,423
Riverside	3,544	834	8,909	1,324	20,978
San Diego	1,438	569	18,287	2,849	239,078
San Francisco	2,227	1,590	3,729	2,538	201,770
Santa Barbara	9,570	929	18,224	2,279	59,737
Santa Cruz	652	0	9,923	1,015	21,026

Sources: for enrollment, University of California Office of the President, "Statistical Summary of Students and Staff" (various years); for federal R&D, U.S. National Science Foundation, Federal Science and Engineering Support to Universities, Colleges, and Nonprofit Institutions: Fiscal Year 1995 (NSF 97-330), Washington, D.C., 1997, tb. B-15.

TABLE 45

SAT/ACT Scores and Graduation Rates, University of California and Selected Other Institutions

Campus	SAT/ACT Scores, Entering Students (25th–75th percentile)	Percentage Graduating in Six Years (1996)
University of California		
Berkeley	1180–1430	80
Los Angeles	1130–1360	77
San Diego	1120–1340	77
Davis	1048–1270	76
Santa Cruz	1020–1260	65
Santa Barbara	1020–1220	70
Irvine	970–1240	72
Riverside	930–1180	67
Cal Tech	1430–1580	82
Harvard	1390–1580	97
Princeton	1350–1550	94
MIT	1370–1540	89
Yale	1360–1550	93
Stanford	1310–1520	94
Williams	1310–1520	95
Amherst	1310–1500	98
Chicago	1280–1470	81
Swarthmore	1260–1490	91
Cornell	1240–1430	89
Virginia	1210–1400	91
Michigan-Ann Arbor	1140–1340*	84
North Carolina–Chapel Hill	1120–1320	82
Illinois–Urbana-Champaign	1110–1300*	78
Wisconsin-Madison	1110–1300*	72
Texas-Austin	1100–1320	66
Colorado-Boulder	1070–1270	66
Iowa	1030–1220*	63
Minnesota	1030–1220*	52
Washington	1020–1260	69
Utah	990–1220*	38
Arizona	980–1220	51
California State University		
Cal Poly, San Luis Obispo	910–1225	54
Humboldt State	950–1170	56

Source: "America's Best Colleges," U.S. News & World Report 123, no. 8 (September 1, 1997) 100–102, 106.

*SAT equivalents as in "Concordance" (American College Testing Research Division, Iowa City, Iowa, January 1998); they are based on ACT scores.

Addendum: Excerpts from David S. Webster and Tad Skinner's Report on the University's Outstanding Rankings

The University of California (UC) system rated extraordinarily well in many areas, as did two of its campuses, UC-Berkeley and UC-San Diego.

UC-Berkeley

UC-Berkeley rated exceptionally high any way you look at the *Report's* figures. It achieved the second highest overall mean rating (4.49) of all 274 institutions rated, below only MIT. It had more programs rated in the top 10 in their disciplines (36) than did any other institution, ahead of Stanford (32), Harvard (26), Princeton (22), and MIT (20). It also had the highest proportion of its programs rated in the top 10 in their disciplines (36 of 37, or 97 percent), ahead of Harvard (26 of 30, 87 percent), MIT (20 of 23, 87 percent), Princeton (22 of 29, 76 percent), and Stanford (32 of 43, 74 percent)—the only other institutions that had more than 70 percent of their programs rated in the top 10. Of Berkeley's 37 programs included in the *Report,* five were first, or tied for first, in their disciplines. Berkeley was rated first in chemistry and German and was tied for the rank of 1.5 in mathematics as well as in statistics (although it rated lower in biostatistics) and for the rank of 2.0 in English. Twenty of its programs were rated anywhere from second to fifth (including any ties) in their disciplines, and 11 more were rated from sixth to 10th. The only Berkeley program that rated lower than 10th was cell and developmental biology (13th).

UC-San Diego

UC-San Diego rated extraordinarily well, particularly for an institution that became a UC campus as recently as 1964. It was rated 10th in mean score (3.93) for faculty scholarly quality—higher than older and larger UCLA, higher than any public university campus in the United States except Berkeley, and higher than such highly regarded private universities as Columbia, the University of Pennsylvania, and Northwestern. Two of its programs—in neurosciences and oceanography—rated first in the United States. Three more programs at UC-San Diego rated from second to fifth, and nine more from sixth to 10th, for a total of 14 of its 29 doctoral programs (48 percent) that were rated in their discipline's top 10.

The UC System

Impressive as are the ratings of UC-Berkeley and UC-San Diego, the showing of the UC system as a whole is even more remarkable. Of its 229 programs included in the study, 119—or 52 percent—rank in the top 20 in their disciplines. The nine UC campuses represent only 3 percent of the 274 institutions included, and the eight UC campuses (all but UC-San Francisco) that have 15 or more programs rated represent only 8 percent of the 104 institutions in this category. Remarkably, however, these nine house 15 percent of the nation's top 20 programs, 19 percent of its top 10 programs, and fully 20 percent of its top five programs. Six of the nine UC campuses placed one or more programs in the top five in their disciplines, and eight of the nine—all but UC-Riverside—placed one or more programs in the top 10.

The eight UC campuses with 15 or more programs rated, taken as a group, achieve a higher mean score than do the 11 schools in the Big Ten. They score an average of 3.55 in faculty scholarly quality, compared to the Big Ten's 3.37, and 3.38 in program effectiveness, compared to the Big Ten's 3.32. This performance is astonishing, considering that the Big Ten universities, taken as a group, are much older than the UC campuses and have much larger faculties (reputational rankings of doctoral programs generally correlate quite highly with the size of program faculty). It is all the more astonishing when one considers that eight of the Big Ten universities—all except Indiana, Michigan State, and Northwestern—are, according to the *Report,* the highest-rated public research universities in their states.

In the past 40 years or so, many states that long had only one state university campus have established one or more other campuses, and some states are developing their new campus(es) to eventually achieve parity with the flagship campus. As of now, however, none of these non-flagship campuses has achieved anything approaching parity with any of the UC's five highest-rated non-flagship campuses. . . .

Of the 12 non-flagship campuses that have 15 or more programs rated, fully seven are UC campuses. The highest rated non-flagship campus that is *not* part of the UC system, the University of Illinois at Chicago, falls behind five non-flagship UC campuses. In addition the other four non-flagship campuses—the SUNY campuses at Buffalo, Albany, and Binghamton, and the University of Wisconsin-Milwaukee—score below all seven UC non-flagship campuses that had 15 or more programs rated. California, with a 1994 population of about 31 million, thus had a state university system in which five of its non-flagship campuses with 15 or more programs included rated above *any* similar campuses in such populous states as Texas (18 million), New York (18 million), Florida (14 million), Pennsylvania (12 million), and Illinois (12 million).

UC's rating is all the more noteworthy considering that in 1978 California passed Proposition 13, which lowered property taxes and is regarded as having severely hurt public higher education. It is even more impressive considering that the Committee polled faculty members for its reputational ratings in May

1993, just after UC had lost many of its most senior faculty members due to attractive financial incentives it had offered in 1990 and 1991 to induce faculty members to retire early. (Since many other major universities—especially public universities—offered attractive buy-outs to their most senior faculty just *after* the Committee polled faculty members for its reputational rating, the *Report* may have been well out-of-date by the time it was published last September.) ["RATING PH.D. PROGRAMS: WHAT THE NRC REPORT SAYS . . . AND DOESN'T SAY," *CHANGE* 28, NO. 3 (MAY–JUNE 1996): 36, 37, 39, 40.]

Honor Roll
of University Leaders

A. Ranking of Deans and Chairs of Colleges, Schools, and Departments in Top Six in Field, 1952–62 (from 1964 Survey)

DEAN, COLLEGE OF CHEMISTRY
Kenneth S. Pitzer (1951–60)
Robert Connick (1960–65)

DEAN, DEPARTMENT (LATER COLLEGE) OF ENGINEERING
Morrough P. O'Brien (1943–59)
John R. Whinnery (1959–63)

Chairs, Engineering

Civil Engineering	Harold B. Gotaas (1952–53)
	Thomas R. Simpson (1953–54)
	Harmer E. Davis (1954–59)
	Howard D. Eberhart (1959–62)
Electrical Engineering	Thomas C. McFarland (1949–53)
	Paul L. Morton (1953–56)
	John R. Whinnery (1956–59)
	Robert M. Saunders (1960–62)
Mechanical Engineering	Richard G. Folsom (1949–53)
	Everett D. Howe (1953–58)
	Clyne F. Garland (1958–60)
	Samuel A. Schaaf (1960–64)

DEAN, LETTERS AND SCIENCE
A. R. Davis (1947–55)
Lincoln Constance (1955–62)

Chairs, Humanities

Classics	Louis Alexander McKay (1949–53)
	Arthur E. Gordon (1953–59)
	Murray B. Emeneau (1959–62)

English   Willard E. Farnham (1952–55)
James D. Hart (1955–57)
Henry N. Smith (1957–60)
Mark Schorer (1960–65)

French   Clarence D. Brenner (1952–57)
Ronald N. Walpole (1957–63)

German   Edward V. Brewer (1945–54)
Robert T. Clark, Jr. (1954–57)
C. Grant Loomis (1957–62)

Philosophy   George P. Adams (1952–53)
Stephen C. Pepper (1953–58)
Edward W. Strong (1958–59)
William R. Dennes (1959–60)
Karl Aschenbrenner (1960–63)

Spanish   Lesley B. Simpson (1952–53)
Robert K. Spaulding (1953–56)
Arturo Torres-Rioseco (1956–61)
Edwin S. Morby (1961–64)

Chairs, Social Sciences

Anthropology   Theodore D. McCown (1951–55)
David G. Mandelbaum (1955–56)
Robert F. Hizer (1956–58)
George M. Foster, Jr. (1958–61)
Sherwood L. Washburn (1961–64)

Economics   Paul S. Taylor (1952–56)
Andreas G. Papandreou (1956–59)
Robert A. Gordon (1959–63)

Geography   Carl O. Sauer (1923–54)
John B. Leighley (1954–60)
James J. Parsons (1960–66)

History   John J. Van Nostrand (1952–53)
James F. King (1953–56)
George H. Guttridge (1956–58)
Delmer M. Brown (1958–62)

Political Science   Peter H. Odegard (1952–56)
Charles Aikin (1956–61)
Robert A. Scalapino (1962)

Sociology   Herbert G. Blumer (1952–58)
Reinhard Bendix (1958–61)
Kingsley Davis (1961–63)

Chairs, Biological Sciences

Anatomy	John B. deC. M. Saunders (1937–56)
	William O. Reinhart (1956–58)
Bacteriology/Microbiology	Sanford S. Elberg (1952–57)
	Edward A. Adelberg (1957–61)
	Roger Y. Stanier (1961–62)
Biochemistry	Wendell M. Stanley (1948–53)
	Hermann O. L. Fischer (1953–56)
	Esmond E. Snell (1956–62)
Botany	Lee Bonar (1947–54)
	Lincoln Constance (1954–55)
	Adriance S. Foster (1955–61)
	Leonard Machlis (1961–67)
Entomology	E. Gorton Linsley (1951–59)
	Ray F. Smith (1959–64)
Physiology	James M. D. Olmsted (1952–53)
	Leslie L. Bennett (1953–58)
[department combined with Anatomy, 1958]	
	Sherburne F. Cook, cochair for Physiology (1959–64)
	C. Willet Asling, cochair for Anatomy (1959–64)
Psychology	Clarence W. Brown (1949–55, 1961–64)
	Edwin E. Ghiselli (1955–57)
	Leo J. Postman (1957–61)
Zoology	Richard M. Eakin (1952–57)
	Morgan Harris (1957–62)

Chairs, Physical Sciences

Astronomy	Otto Struve (1950–59)
	Louis G. Henyey (1960–63)
Chemistry [chair same as dean of College, 1952–56—see above]	
	Isadore Perlman (1957–59)
	Robert E. Connick (1959–60)
	Richard E. Powell (1960–66)
Chemical Engineering [part of department of Chemistry through 1957]	
	Theodore Vermeulen (division chair, 1952–53)
	Charles R. Wilke (division chair, 1953–57)
Geology	Perry Byerly (1949–54)
	Francis J. Turner (1954–59)
	Charles M. Gilbert (1959–62)

Mathematics	Charles B. Morrey, Jr. (1949–54)
	Derrick H. Lehmer (1954–57)
	John L. Kelley (1958–60)
	Bernard Friedman (1960–62)
Physics	Raymond T. Birge (1932–55)
	August C. Helmholz (1955–62)

B. Members of the Berkeley Academic Senate's Academic Personnel Committee, 1952–62

Member	Departmental Affiliation
1952–53	
L. Constance, chair	Botany
N. S. Buchanan	Economics
H. E. Davis	Civil Engineering
G. H. Guttridge	History
T. D. McCown	Anthropology
1953–54	
T. D. McCown, chair	Anthropology
N. S. Buchanan	Economics
J. Cason, Jr.	Chemistry
H. E. Davis	Civil Engineering
F. L. Kidner	Economics
R. H. Walpole	French
1954–55	
F. L. Kidner, chair	Economics
H. B. Gotaas	Civil Engineering
C. Stern	Zoology
R. N. Walpole	French
H. Williams	Geology
1955–56	
F. L. Kidner, chair	Economics
A. H. Miller	Zoology
T. Vermeulen	Chemical Engineering
R. N. Walpole	French
H. Williams	Geology

1956–57

A. H. Miller, chair	Zoology
R. G. Bressler, Jr.	Agricultural Economics
S. C. Pepper	Philosophy and Art
T. Vermeulen	Chemical Engineering
H. Williams	Geology

1957–58

T. Vermeulen, chair	Chemical Engineering
R. M. Eakin	Zoology
S. S. Hoos	Agricultural Economics
S. C. Pepper	Philosophy and Art
J. Verhoogen	Geology

1958–59

R. G. Bressler, chair	Agricultural Economics
R. M. Eakin	Zoology
M. B. Emeneau	Classics
E. S. Morby	Spanish
E. R. Parker	Metallurgy
J. Verhoogen	Geology

1959–60

E. R. Parker, chair	Metallurgy
W. D. Gwinn	Chemistry
M. Moonitz	Business Administration
E. S. Morby	Spanish
R. L. Usinger	Entomology

1960–61

H. Williams, chair	Geology
W. D. Gwinn	Chemistry
S. J. Maisel	Business Administration
E. S. Morby	Spanish
R. L. Usinger	Entomology

1961–62

S. S. Hoos, chair	Agricultural Economics and Business Administration
S. J. Maisel	Business Administration
P. L. Morton	Electrical Engineering
E. G. Segrè	Physics
E. Tuveson	English
R. L. Usinger	Entomology

C. Members of the Berkeley Academic Senate's Committee on Committees, 1952–62

Robert B. Brode, 1954–58, Physics
Bertrand H. Bronson, 1952–53, English
James R. Caldwell, 1954–56, English
Milton Chernin, 1952–56, 1961–62, Social Welfare
Robert E. Connick, 1956–58, Chemistry
Lincoln Constance, 1953–54, 1955–56, Botany
John W. Cowee, 1958–61, Business Administration
Harmer E. Davis, 1955–57, 1960–62, Civil Engineering
Malcolm E. Davisson, 1954–56, Economics, Business Administration
William R. Dennes, 1956–58, Philosophy
Stephen P. Diliberto, 1958–62, Mathematics
John E. Dorn, 1959–61, Mineral Technology
Willard C. Fleming, 1955–57, Dentistry
Harold B. Gotaas, 1953–54, Civil Engineering
August C. Helmholz, 1954–55, 1959–60, Physics
Sidney S. Hoos, 1959–61, Agricultural Economics
Arthur E. Hutson, 1953–54, 1958–60, English
Francis A. Jenkins, 1952–53, Physics
James A. Jenkins, 1958–59, Genetics
Frank L. Kidner, 1953–55, 1957–59, Economics, Business Administration
Arthur F. Kip, 1961–62, Physics
Gordon Mackinney, 1959–60, Food Science and Technology
Donald W. MacKinnon, 1958–59, Psychology
Theodore D. McCown, 1961–62, Anthropology
Sanford A. Mosk, 1956–58, Economics
Emil M. Mrak, 1952–53, Food Technology
Kenneth S. Pitzer, 1952–55, Chemistry
Richard E. Powell, 1958–59, 1960–62, Chemistry
Armin Rappaport, 1961–62, History
Wendell M. Stanley, 1952–54, Biochemistry
Edward W. Strong, 1952–53, Philosophy
Theodore Vermeulen, 1961–62, Chemical Engineering
Ronald N. Walpole, 1953–60, French
William W. Wurster, 1952–53, Architecture

D. Members of the Berkeley Academic Senate's Committee on Educational Policy, 1954–58

Reinhard Bendix, Sociology and Social Institutions, 1955–56
Raymond G. Bressler, Agricultural Economics, 1954–55

Robert B. Brode, Physics, 1957–58
Bertrand H. Bronson, English, 1955–58
Robert E. Connick, Chemistry, 1954–55
Lincoln Constance, Botany, 1954–55
Howard D. Eberhart, Civil Engineering, 1954–55
Ralph Emerson, Botany, 1954–55
William E. Farnham, English, 1954–55
Harold B. Gotaas, Civil Engineering, 1955–57
George H. Guttridge, History, 1954–56
James A. Jenkins, Genetics, 1956–58
B. Lamar Johnson, Education, 1954–55, 1956–57
Victor Jones, Political Science, 1956–58
Thomas R. McConnell, Education, 1957–58
Emilio G. Segrè, Physics, 1955–56
Edward W. Strong, Philosophy, 1955–57
Robert C. Tryon, Psychology, 1955–57
Ronald N. Walpole, French, 1957–58
Harold F. Weaver, Astronomy, 1957–58

E. Members of the Academic Advisory Committee, 1954–58

Charles Aikin, Political Science, chair, Courses of Instruction, 1955–56
Robert Brode, Physics, vice chair, northern section of Academic Senate, 1955–58
Clarence W. Brown, Psychology, chair, Administrative Committee on Buildings and Campus Development, 1954–55, 1956–58
Robert E. Connick, Chemistry, chair, Academic Senate Committee on Educational Policy, 1954–55
Lincoln Constance, Botany, dean of letters and science, 1955–58
John W. Cowee, Business Administration, chair, University Welfare Committee, 1956–57
A. R. Davis, Botany, dean of letters and science, 1954–55, and vice-chancellor, 1955–56
Malcolm Davisson, Economics, chair, Graduation Matters, 1955–56
William R. Dennes, Philosophy, dean of the graduate division 1952–53, 1954–55; vice chair, Council of the Graduate Division, northern section, 1954; chair, Committee on Committees, Berkeley division and chair, Graduation Matters, 1956–58
Sanford S. Elberg, Bacteriology, chair, Building and Campus Development Committee, 1955–56
Willard E. Farnham, English, chair, Courses of Instruction, 1956–57
E. T. Grether, Business Administration, chair, northern section of Academic Senate, 1954–55
James D. Hart, English, vice-chancellor, Academic Affairs, 1957–58
Emily H. Huntington, Economics, chair, University Welfare Committee, 1957–58

Joe W. Kelly, Civil Engineering, chair, Academic Senate Committee on Courses, 1954–55

Clark Kerr, Business Administration and Economics, chancellor, Berkeley Campus, 1952–58

Frank L. Kidner, Economics, chair, Committee on Budget and Interdepartmental Relations, 1955–56

Theodore McCown, Anthropology, chair, Committee on Budget and Interdepartmental Relations, 1954–55

Alden H. Miller, Zoology, chair, Committee on Budget and Interdepartmental Relations, northern section, 1956–57

Sanford A. Mosk, Economics, chair, Committee on University Welfare, 1954–55

Edward S. Rogers, Public Health, chair, Committee on University Welfare, 1955–56

Morris A. Stewart, Parasitology, dean of the graduate division and chair, Graduate Council, northern section, 1954–58

Edward W. Strong, Philosophy, chair, Committee on Educational Policy, 1955–56

Theodore Vermeulen, Chemical Engineering, chair, Committee on Budget and Interdepartmental Relations, Berkeley division, 1957–58

F. Individual Faculty Honors, 1962–63

BERKELEY FACULTY AWARDED NOBEL PRIZES (MEMBERS OF THE FACULTY AS OF 1962–63)

Name, Department	*Year of award*
Melvin Calvin, Chemistry	1961
Owen Chamberlain, Physics	1959
William Francis Giauque, Chemistry	1949
Donald Glaser, Physics	1960
Edwin M. McMillan, Chemistry	1951
John H. Northrop, Chemistry	1946
Glenn T. Seaborg, Chemistry	1951
Emilio G. Segrè, Physics	1959
Wendell M. Stanley, Chemistry	1946

BERKELEY FACULTY WHO WERE MEMBERS OF THE NATIONAL ACADEMY OF SCIENCES IN 1962–63

Name, Department	*Year of election*
Luis Walter Alvarez, Physics	1947
Daniel I. Arnon, Botany	1961
Arnold Kent Balls, Biochemistry	1954
Horace A. Barker, Biochemistry	1953
Frank A. Beach, Psychology	1949

Raymond T. Birge, Physics	1932
Leo Brewer, Chemistry	1959
Robert B. Brode, Physics	1949
Perry Byerly, Geology and Geophysics	1946
Melvin Calvin, Chemistry	1954
Owen Chamberlain, Physics	1960
Ralph W. Chaney, Paleontology	1947
Shiing-shen Chern, Mathematics	1961
Geoffrey F. Chew, Physics	1962
Michael Doudoroff, Bacteriology	1962
Herbert M. Evans, Anatomy	1927
William Francis Giauque, Chemistry	1936
Donald A. Glaser, Physics	1962
William Z. Hassid, Biochemistry	1958
Joel H. Hildebrand, Chemistry	1929
Charles Kittel, Physics	1957
I. Michael Lerner, Genetics	1959
Daniel Mazia, Zoology	1960
Edwin M. McMillan, Physics	1947
Alden H. Miller, Zoology	1957
Rudolph L. Minkowski, Astronomy	1959
Charles B. Morrey, Jr., Mathematics	1962
John H. Northrop, Bacteriology	1934
Glenn T. Seaborg, Chemistry	1948
Emilio G. Segrè, Physics	1952
Esmond E. Snell, Biochemistry	1955
Wendell M. Stanley, Virology	1941
Curt Stern, Zoology	1948
Edward Teller, Physics	1948
Francis J. Turner, Geology and Geophysics	1956
John Verhoogen, Geology and Geophysics	1956
Howel Williams, Geology and Geophysics	1950
Robley C. Williams, Virology	1955

Source: National Academy of Sciences of the United States, Membership–July 1, 1962 (653 members at the time).

G. Members of California Alumni Association Board and Alumni Project Committee, 1947–49

1947–48

President	Stanley M. Barnes ('22)
First Vice President	William J. Hale ('14)

Second Vice President	Mrs. Beatrice Ward Challiss ('23)
Treasurer	James H. Corley ('26)
Executive Manager	Robert Sibley ('03)
Councilors	Sidney Anderson ('21)
	Harold Breakenridge ('30)
	Mrs. Alice Kohlberg Geballe ('11)
	Carroll G. Grunsky ('20)
	Mrs. Ella Barrows Hagar ('19)
	Miss Ruth Hardison ('20)
	I. W. Hellman ('20)
	E. C. Lipman ('14)
	Stanley McCaffrey ('38)
	O. Cort Majors ('21)
	Mrs. Helen Reef Maynard ('15)
	Sumner Mering ('20)
	James Mills ('17)
	Robert Mulvany ('24)
	William H. Park ('28)
	Albert M. Paul ('09)
	E. J. Power ('15)
	Edward G. Sewell ('19)
	Fred Stripp ('32)
	B. A. Swartz ('11)
	John P. Symes ('21)
	Maynard J. Toll ('27)
	Harold Tower, D.D.S. ('34)
	M. E. Van Sant ('23)
Ex Officio	James W. Archer ('30)
	Floyd A. Blower ('36)
	Victor E. Breeden ('12)
	William C. Deamer, M.D. ('23)
	Girard G. Johnson ('23)
	Don Lang ('48)
	Gus Olson, Jr. ('38)
	Mary O. Scroggs ('22)
	George E. Steninger, M.D. ('25)
	Jean C. Witter ('16)

1948–49

President	William M. Hale ('14)
First Vice President	Maynard J. Toll ('27)
Second Vice President	Mrs. Beatrice Ward Challiss ('23)

Treasurer	James H. Corley ('26)
Executive Manager	Robert Sibley ('03)
Councilors	Sidney Anderson ('21)
	Harold Breakenridge ('30)
	Everett Brown, Jr. ('31)
	Mrs. Camille Johnston Ehrenfels ('05)
	Alfred G. Fry ('36)
	Mrs. Ella Barrows Hagar ('19)
	I. W. Hellman ('20)
	Stanley McCaffrey ('38)
	O. Cort Majors ('21)
	Mrs. Helen Reef Maynard ('15)
	Sumner Mering ('20)
	James Mills ('17)
	John Monninger ('38)
	Robert Mulvany ('24)
	William H. Park ('28)
	E. J. Power ('15)
	Edward G. Sewell ('19)
	Fred Stripp ('32)
	B. A. Swartz ('11)
	John P. Symes ('21)
	Harold Tower, D.D.S. ('34)
	M. E. Van Sant ('23)
	Lloyd Whitman ('40)
Ex Officio	Jack Andrew ('49)
	James W. Archer ('30)
	Stanley N. Barnes ('22)
	Floyd A. Blower ('36)
	Arch B. Davison ('14)
	William C. Deamer, M.D. ('23)
	Girard G. Johnson ('23)
	Gus Olson, Jr. ('38)
	Mary O. Scroggs ('22)
	George E. Steninger, M.D. ('25)
Alumni Project Committee	Fred Stripp, chairman ('32)
	Emery E. Stone ('32)
	John P. Symes ('21)

Source: Students at Berkeley: A Study of their Extracurricular Activities with Suggestions for Improvements On and Off the Campus to Broaden their Preparation for Citizenship *(L. Deming Tilton, project director) (Berkeley: California Alumni Association, 1948), ii.*

H. ASUC Presidents and Vice Presidents, 1952–53 to 1957–58

	Presidents	*Vice Presidents*
1952–53	Dick Holler	Marjorie Coombs
1953–54	Ralph Vetterlein	Gene Donnely
1954–55	Dick Marston	1st VP Claude Rohwer
		2d VP Carol Mixter
1955–56	Bob Hamilton	1st VP Mike Savage
		2d VP Barbara Levin
1956–57	Jim Kidder	1st VP Paul Erickson
		2d VP Pat Marsh
1957–58	Roger Samuelson	1st VP Scott Sherman
		2d VP Colette Morgan

Sources: Blue and Gold, *various years.*

I. Members of Buildings and Campus Development Committee, fall 1953 to spring 1956

Name	*Affiliation*
Clarence W. Brown Chairman	Chair, Psychology
Sanford S. Elberg Acting chairman, fall 1955	Bacteriology
A. W. Baxter Secretary	
Charles Aikin	Political Science
Edward W. Barankin	Statistics
Donald S. Berry	Transportation Engineering
Robert A. Cockrell	Forestry
Donald Coney	Librarian
Frederick W. Cozens	Physical Education
William B. Fretter	Physics
Fred O. Harris	Dramatic Art
Franklin M. Henry	Physical Education
Walter W. Horn	Art
Joseph W. Hutchison	Superintendent, Grounds and Buildings
Richard W. Jennings	Law
Paul F. Keim	Civil Engineering
T. J. Kent, Jr.	City and Regional Planning
Myron E. Krueger	Forestry
Edwin G. Linsley	Accounting Officer, Controller's Office

Marion A. Milczewski	Assistant Librarian
William W. Monahan	Business Manager
Richard H. Nedderson	Assistant Business Manager, Residence Hall Supervisor
Lucretia Nelson	Design
Stephen C. Pepper	Philosophy and Art
Richard E. Powell	Chemistry and Chemical Engineering
David A. Revzan	Business Administration
Francis E. Violich	City and Regional Planning and Landscape Architecture
Harold F. Weaver	Astronomy
Harvey E. White	Physics
Helen M. Worden	Assistant librarian
William W. Wurster	Dean, School of Architecture

Student Members
Elizabeth Waldie
Tom Morrish
Hans Palmer
Bernice Pence
Roslyn H. Puterman
Bill Somerville

Technical Advisers

Lawrence H. Boyd	Assistant Architectural Draftsman, Architects and Engineers
Louis A. DeMonte	Principal Architect, Architects and Engineers
Robert J. Evans	Chief Architect, Architects and Engineers
Ralfe D. Miller	Associate Supervisor, Physical Education
Charles E. Routsong	Planning Analyst, Architects and Engineers
Albert R. Wagner	Assistant Planner, Architects and Engineers

J. University Liaison Committee with City of Berkeley

Walter W. Horn, Art
T. J. Kent, Jr., City and Regional Planning
Stephen C. Pepper, Philosophy
Francis Violich, City Planning
H. Leland Vaughan, Landscape Architecture
William W. Wurster, College of Architecture
    (chair, 1953–55)
Richard Jennings, Law (chair, 1956–58)

K. Members of the University of California Board of Regents, 1958–66

Robert E. Alshuler (Sherman Oaks), 1962–63

Glenn M. Anderson (Hawthorne), 1959–67, lieutenant governor of California

James W. Archer (La Jolla), 1961–62

Philip L. Boyd (Palm Desert), 1957–70: chair, new campus sites, 1958–61; board vice chair, 1967–68

Edmund G. Brown (San Francisco/Sacramento), 1959–67, governor of California

Ralph M. Brown (Modesto), 1959–61, Speaker of the Assembly

John E. Canaday (Rancho Palos Verdes), 1950–51; 1958–74

Edward W. Carter (Los Angeles), 1952–82: chair, educational policy, 1958–62; chair, finance, 1962–64; board chair, 1964–66; board vice chair, 1972–73, 1976–77, 1980–81

Dorothy B. Chandler (Los Angeles), 1954–68: chair, grounds and buildings, 1962–64 and 1965–66; board vice chair, 1966–67

William K. Coblentz (San Francisco), 1964–80: board vice chair, 1973–74; board chair 1976–78

William Thomas Davis (Beverly Hills), 1964–65

Frederick G. Dutton (San Mateo), 1962–78

William E. Forbes (San Marino), 1960–61; 1962–77: chair, grounds and buildings, 1964–65

Gerald H. Hagar (Oakland), 1951–64: board chair, 1962–64

Cornelius J. Haggerty (Los Angeles), 1950–66

Harry R. Haldeman (Los Angeles), 1966–67, 1968–69

Victor R. Hansen (Los Angeles), 1946–62

Catherine C. Hearst (Hillsborough), 1956–76

Edward H. Heller (Atherton), 1942–58; 1960–61: chair, finance, 1961

Elinor H. Heller (Atherton), 1961–76: board vice chair, 1968–69, 1971–72; board chair, 1975–76

DeWitt A. Higgs (Chula Vista), 1966–82: board chair, 1968–70; board vice chair, 1970–71, 1974–75, 1978–79

Laurence J. Kennedy, Jr. (Redding), 1964–68

Clark Kerr (El Cerrito), 1958–67, president of the university

Goodwin J. Knight (Los Angeles), 1947–59, lieutenant governor and governor of California

Luther H. Lincoln (Oakland), 1955–59, speaker of the assembly

Arthur J. McFadden (Santa Ana), 1943–59: chair, agriculture, 1958–59

Donald H. McLaughlin (San Francisco), 1951–66: chair, finance, 1958–59; board chair, 1958–60; chair, grounds and buildings, 1960–62; chair, educational policy, 1962–66; board vice chair, 1964–65

John R. Mage (Pasadena), 1965–66

William Gladstone Merchant (San Francisco), 1949–61

Theodore R. Meyer (San Francisco), 1962–69: chair, finance, 1964–66; board chair, 1966–68

Samuel B. Mosher (Los Angeles), 1956–68

Einar Mohn (Menlo Park), 1966–68

Howard C. Naffziger (San Francisco), 1952–61

G. Norris Nash, Jr. (Berkeley), 1963–64

Gus Olson (Clarksburg), 1951–60

Edwin W. Pauley (Beverly Hills), 1940–72: chair, finance, 1958–60; board chair, 1956–58, 1960–62

Harold J. Powers (Eagleville), 1953–59, lieutenant governor of California

Max Rafferty (Carmichael), 1963–70, superintendent of public instruction

William M. Roth (Sausalito), 1961–77: board vice chair, 1965–66

Norton Simon (Los Angeles), 1960–76

Roy E. Simpson (South Pasadena/Sacramento), 1945–62, superintendent of public instruction

Mortimer B. Smith (Berkeley), 1959–60

Jesse H. Steinhart (San Francisco), 1950–62: chair, grounds and buildings, 1958–60; chair, finance, 1960–61

Thomas More Storke (Santa Barbara), 1955–60

Jerd Francis Sullivan, Jr. (San Francisco), 1958–64

Jesse W. Tapp (Los Angeles), 1964–67

Jesse M. Unruh (Inglewood), 1962–68, speaker of the assembly

John Vernon Vaughn (Pasadena), 1958–59

John S. Watson (Petaluma), 1959–63

Arthur E. Wilkens (San Francisco), 1961–62

University of California Administration and Governance

A. A Recipe for Mutual Discord: The 1951 Administrative Reorganization Plan, and My Comments on It

EXCERPTS FROM THE MINUTES OF THE BOARD OF REGENTS (BERKELEY, MARCH 30, 1951)

A meeting of The Regents of the University of California was held this day at 2:00 P.M. in the Administration Building on the Berkeley campus.

Present: Regents Ahlport, Canaday, Dickson, Fenston, Griffiths, Heller, Jordan, McFadden, McLaughlin, Merchant, Nimitz, Pauley, Sproul, and Steinhart (14).

In attendance: Mr. Maynard Toll, Secretary and Treasurer Underhill, Vice President–Business Affairs Corley, Attorney Calkins, Assistant Secretary Woolman, Controller Lundberg, Engineer Weaver, Architect Evans, Mr. Maynard Morris of the Office of Public Information, newspaper representatives and guests.

AMENDMENT TO STANDING ORDERS PERTAINING TO OFFICERS OF THE UNIVERSITY AND THEIR DUTIES:

12. Pursuant to notice served at the last meeting of the Board, President Sproul moved that Chapters VIII and IX of the Standing Orders and By-Laws of The Regents of the University of California, reading as follows:

2. *Duties of the Vice Presidents*
(a) The Vice President of the University shall be its executive vice president, and shall perform such duties of the President as the President shall designate, except as herein otherwise provided. In the absence of the President from the State, or in the event of the President's disability, or while the President is on vacation, he shall have and exercise all the duties and powers of the President, but he shall not during the term of office of the President act as a Regent.

(b) The Vice President–Agricultural Sciences, the Vice President–Medical and Health Sciences, the Vice President–University Extension, and such other vice presidents as The Regents may authorize, shall advise and assist the President in connection with the divisions of the University indicated by their titles.

3. Duties of Chancellors, Provosts and Directors

(a) The Chancellor, Provost or Director of each campus shall be the executive head of all activities on that campus, except as herein otherwise provided, and except the offices of Admissions, Personnel, Relations with Schools, and Vice President–Business Affairs; the Division of Vocational Education; University Extension, University Press, and such others as may be designated by The Regents as statewide activities; and with reference to these on his campus he shall be consulted. In all matters relating to the business operations on his campus, excluding construction other than repairs, maintenance and minor alterations, he shall have administrative authority within the budgeted items for the campus, consistent with policies for the University as a whole as determined by the Vice President–Business Affairs, and subject to the approval of and direction by The Regents. He shall be responsible for the organization and operation of the campus under his jurisdiction, including summer sessions and intersessions, its internal administration and its discipline; and his decisions made in accordance with the provisions of the budget and with policies established by The Regents or the President of the University shall be final. He shall nominate through the President all faculty members and other personnel of the campus under his jurisdiction in accordance with the provisions of Chapter IX, sections 1(c) and 3(d).

(b) The Chancellor, Provost or Director shall preside at all formal functions on his campus. At the Commencement exercises and the ceremonies in celebration of the Charter Day anniversary he shall present the President, who, as the University's chief executive, shall function in accordance with the University's rules for protocol and procedure.

(c) The Chancellor, Provost or Director on each campus shall appoint an Advisory Administrative Council (of which he shall be Chairman), to assist him as he may request in the administration of his responsibilities. The Advisory Administrative Council shall consist of the Chancellor, Provost or Director, the deans of the colleges and schools under his jurisdiction, the Business Manager, and the officer in charge of Public Information on the campus, and shall meet once a week, or oftener at the call of its Chairman.

(d) The Chancellor, Provost or Director on each campus shall appoint all instructors deemed necessary by him, for the conduct of instruction in any summer or intersession of the University, and may fix their remuneration in accordance with the provisions of the budget established by The Regents.

4. Duties of the other Officers of the University

(a) All officers of the University, other than those whose duties are defined in the Standing Orders or by resolution of The Regents, shall perform such duties and shall have such powers as the President shall prescribe.

5. Nothing in the Standing Orders or the By-Laws or any act or failure to act by

The Regents shall be construed or operate as an abridgment or limitation of any rights, powers or privileges of The Regents.

President Sproul explained that the amendment sets forth a plan of administrative reorganization of the University, which was prepared by the Special Committee on Administrative Reorganization in conference with the Committee on Southern California Schools, Colleges and Institutions. It was designed (1) to streamline the administrative machinery of the University, (2) to define clearly the duties of the University officers and (3) to give to the different campuses the maximum degree of autonomy consistent with unity.

Regent Fenston asked the President if he was thoroughly in accord with the proposed amendment, and the President replied that he was.

The motion was seconded by Regent Jordan and unanimously adopted, Regents Ahlport, Canaday, Dickson, Fenston, Griffiths, Heller, Jordan, McFadden, McLaughlin, Merchant, Nimitz, Pauley, Sproul, and Steinhart (14) voting "aye", voting "no" none.

Commentary—in particular, note:

1. Item 2 above. The provision for a "Vice President of the University." It remained unfilled for the duration of President Sproul's term of office.

2. Item 3(a) above. The general exemption, in particular, of the areas under the Vice President–Business Affairs from the authority of the Chancellor as "executive head" of the campus, while giving the Chancellor general "administrative authority" over all "business operations." Did this mean "no" or "yes"?

3. Item 3(c) above. The creation of an "Advisory Administrative Council" including all deans (which came to be known as the "Council of Deans"). This acknowledged the efforts of the deans at UCLA and later Berkeley to create the chancellorships, and emphasized that the deans were to report directly to the chancellor and not to the president. It also gave the deans an opportunity not previously available to receive information, to be consulted, and to give advice.

4. Item 5 above. The Regents retained all of their "rights, powers or privileges."

5. The consultation with the Committee on Southern California Schools, Colleges and Institutions—the regents' committee watching out for UCLA.

6. The question by Regent Fenston at the end of the minutes and the reply. Sproul was "thoroughly in accord."

EXCERPTS FROM PRESIDENT SPROUL'S OFFICIAL EXPLANATION OF THE PLAN

The Vice President–Business Affairs is responsible to the Regents and to the President.

The duties of the President are essentially the same as they have been for many years. As executive head of the University of California he is directly responsible for its organization and operation, its internal administration, its discipline, and the care of its grounds and property.

One new provision, which formalizes what has hitherto been the practice of the

President is this: the President shall invite the Chancellors of the Berkeley and Los Angeles campuses, or other administrative officers, to attend Regents' meetings or committee meetings dealing with matters affecting their respective campuses or interests.

Duties of the Chancellors, Provosts or Directors—chief administrative officers of the various campuses—include the nomination through the President of all faculty and administrative personnel, and the executive direction of all activities on their campuses except those of a state-wide nature such as University Extension, Relations with Schools, University Press, etc. Their decisions on local matters made in accordance with provisions of the budget and policies established by the Regents or the President will be final.

The administrative reorganization plan which the Regents adopted on my motion formalizes the larger degree of local autonomy which the President of the University has been gradually transferring to campus administrative officers—especially on the Los Angeles campus—as the various campuses have grown in size and in their responsibilities."

Source: Faculty Bulletin *20, no. 10 (April 1951): 79, 82–83.*

Commentary—in particular, note:
1. The reference reminding that the vice president–business affairs is an officer of the regents, and reports directly to them as well as to the president.
2. The emphasis on the duties of the president as being "essentially the same" as before the reorganization.
3. The comment that the action of the regents merely formalizes "the larger degree of local autonomy" already transferred by the president to campus officers.

MY OVERALL COMMENTARY

The two documents taken together posed some problems from the start:
1. The chancellor of the campus "shall be the executive head of all activities on that campus" and "shall be responsible for the organization and operation of the campus under his jurisdiction." But—
2. The regents retain all their extensive controls.

The duties of the president are "essentially the same."

The responsibilities of the vice president–business affairs, reporting, in part, directly to the regents, are an exception to delegations to the chancellor as "executive head." Most nonacademic activities and personnel at that time came under this vice president. In addition, all nonacademic personnel, whether under the vice president–business affairs or not, were outside the authority of the "executive head."
3. While "business affairs" was an exception to delegation to the chancellor, yet the campus business officer is a member of the Council of Deans, the chancellor is to be "consulted" on business affairs, and the chancellor has "administrative authority" over "all matters relating to business affairs" (with some specified exceptions).

4. Question—was it an administrative reorganization plan or an administrative reaffirmation plan? There was now a fourth major actor (along with the regents, the president, the vice president–business affairs), namely the campus "executive head." However, the prior three major actors all retained their status quo ante positions.

5. A recipe for the internecine warfare that developed! Were there to be changes or were there not? It could be read either way. It was read both ways. The Board of Regents on March 30, 1951, after long consideration, acted unanimously but to do what?

B. Excerpts of Remarks by Joel H. Hildebrand to the Academic Senate, Northern Section, April 5, 1943: "University and Faculty Welfare"

There is growing apprehension among us that the welfare of our great university is in jeopardy and we cannot look complaisantly upon trends which, if unchecked, threaten a decline from the high position attained during recent years. . . .

Equally serious, and even more dangerous, is the sense of a gulf between faculty and administration. This is not personal. The complaints have to do not with the President but with the administration. . . .

The fact is that the President divides his attention between seven campuses and numerous public affairs. He has but limited time, therefore, to devote to any one of the scores of departments directly responsible to him. His contacts with members of the faculty are rare. Even a department chairman may have to wait days for an interview and weeks for a decision. The administration seems to be trailing its business rather than steering it. There is little leisure for long-range planning. There is little delegation of authority, even when the President is absent. The government is then carried on by mail. There is no administrative officer whose business it is to sit down and discuss with a department chairman the work, welfare and future of his department. . . .

I believe the Senate must take the initiative. This University has been made great chiefly by the labors of able and devoted members of its faculty. . . .

We must revive the courage and vision of earlier years and assume more of the responsibility necessary to the survival of this as a great University during the troubled days of war and reconstruction.

Our basic need is a change in the form and function of the university administration to provide for delegation of authority to persons who can gain and hold the confidence both of the President and of the members of the faculty with whom they deal. Those men should form a presidential, academic cabinet. They should confer frequently so as to reach agreement regarding general policies, but the individual officers should then be left free to make final and prompt decisions on all ordinary matters. Men worthy of such responsibility and confidence are surely available. This will require willingness on the part of the faculty to deal normally with a cabinet officer, instead of with the President, for the sake of prompt decision and efficient action. It will, likewise require a willingness on the part of the President to delegate authority to the proper officers. . . .

I move that the remarks just made be spread upon the minutes, and that the Committee on Committees be directed to appoint a special committee to consider the present organization of the University, particularly as it affects the units under the jurisdiction of the Northern Section of the Academic Senate; to confer at its discretion with the President, and to report its findings as soon as practicable to the Northern Section of the Academic Senate.

Source: UC Archives *[CU–9, v. 31]. Minutes of the Academic Senate, northern section, April 5, 1943, series II, 5:202–5.*

C. Administrative Decentralization of the University of California: A Chronology of Major Steps, 1958–1966*

1958–59
Regents amend Standing Orders to place Vice President–Business Affairs and Controller under jurisdiction of the President.

Chancellorships established for the Davis, Riverside and Santa Barbara campuses, instead of the title Provost, indicating status as general campuses of the University.

Council of Chief Campus Officers (now Council of Chancellors) and Cabinet (University-wide) established to meet monthly under chairmanship of the President.

Provost established at San Francisco.

Campus Accounting Offices transferred from University-wide line jurisdiction to the Chancellors.

Chancellors' authority to transfer funds within budget totals greatly expanded, permitting campus approval of over 80 per cent of all transfers.

Campus Personnel Offices transferred from University-wide line jurisdiction to the Chancellors.

Chancellors delegated authority for Environmental Health and Safety activities.

1960
Campus offices of Architects and Engineers transferred from University-wide line jurisdiction to the Chancellors.

Campus Planning Committees established on each campus.

Campus Purchasing Offices transferred from University-wide line jurisdiction to Chancellors.

Chancellors authorized to solicit and accept gifts up to $100,000.

Admissions administration delegated to the Chancellors.

---

* *While this listing deals almost entirely with delegations to the Chancellors, many parallel delegations have been made to the University Dean of Agriculture and the Dean of University Extension.*

Campus offices of Educational Placement transferred from University-wide line jurisdiction to the Chancellors.

Campus Police Departments transferred from University-wide line jurisdiction to the Chancellors.

Institute of Transportation and Traffic Engineering and Institute of Industrial Relations transferred from University-wide line jurisdiction to the Chancellors at Berkeley and Los Angeles.

Environmental Health and Safety personnel transferred from University-wide line jurisdiction to the Chancellors.

1961

Northern and Southern sections of the Graduate Divisions abolished and separate Graduate Division established on each campus to be administered by a Graduate Dean responsible to the Chancellor.

Campus publications programs transferred from University-wide line jurisdiction to the Chancellors.

Chancellors authorized to solicit and accept research contracts and grants not exceeding $100,000, bringing approximately 80 per cent of the total number of such contracts and grants under campus control. (This followed action of The Regents increasing President's authority from $15,000 to $500,000.)

Chancellorships established at San Diego and Santa Cruz campuses.

School of Public Health transferred from University-wide line jurisdiction to the Chancellors at Berkeley and Los Angeles.

1962

Chancellorship established at Irvine campus.

1963

Academic Senate Northern and Southern sections abolished; campus divisions and a University-wide Academic Assembly established.

1964

Chancellorship established at San Francisco campus.

University Extension Directors established on each campus (within University-wide Extension system).

Chancellors authorized to approve all merit salary increases up to and including Step 3 of the Professorship, representing approximately 75 per cent of tenure salary decisions.

1965

Chancellors authorized to execute purchase orders up to $100,000.

Chancellors authorized to solicit and accept research contracts and grants up to $500,000.

Chancellors authorized to adopt campus regulations governing students and student organizations in accordance with University-wide policies.

Chancellors authorized to transfer funds within the Minor Capital Improvement Program and to approve rental agreements and leases not exceeding $10,000 per year.

Chancellors authorized to approve siting of individual buildings in accordance with approved physical development plan.

Chancellors' authority to approve transfer of funds within budget totals further expanded, permitting campus approval of approximately 95 per cent of all transfers.

Chancellors authorized to appoint Regents' Lecturers.

1966

Chancellors authorized to make appointments and promotions to tenure ranks and to approve all in-scale merit increases.

Chancellors authorized to make initial appointment of professor and associate professor at off-scale rates.

Chancellors authorized to solicit, approve and execute research contracts and grants up to $1,000,000.

Chancellors authorized to award and execute construction and equipment contracts and change orders without dollar limitation but within appropriated funds.

Chancellors authorized to appoint executive architects and to approve building plans for all projects not specifically designated by The Regents as requiring Board approval.

Chancellors authorized to solicit and accept gifts up to $1,000,000 and to make allocations of such gifts in accordance with the gift terms and approved University programs and policies. (To be effective.)

Source: Development and Decentralization: The Administration of the University of California, 1958–1966, *Report of the President (Berkeley: University of California, 1966), appendix A, 7–8.*

D. Excerpt from Clark Kerr's 1958 Inaugural Address at UCLA: "Unity and Diversity in the Statewide University of California" (September 26, 1958)

I have suggested what seem to me to be basic needs of any university—money, freedom, an external climate of sympathy, an internal atmosphere of enthusiasm. Now I should like to add one that arises from the unique structure of the University of California. We have our several campuses—and we shall soon have several more—all of them members of the same university, but all of them unmistakably different in style and atmosphere. This is an invaluable asset. An institution can be greater than the mere sum of its parts only if those parts have diverse personalities, each making its own characteristic contribution—and that is precisely what our different campuses do. But this also means that we have to find the proper balance between unity and diversity—unity without uniformity, diversity without chaos.

The whole university must be united in purpose and basic principles, united on such fundamental matters as the standards governing the appointment of faculty and admission of students, united in academic planning to prevent unnecessary duplication and at the same time to assure that somewhere in the university system there will be programs to meet even the most varied educational needs of our students.

But within this framework each individual campus should enjoy as much autonomy as possible. Initiatives that can be taken locally, decisions that apply individually, belong on the local campus. Our campuses today are zestful and vigorous, largely because they have been able to develop their strikingly individual characters. The variety of our campuses broadens the choices which lie before students entering the university. It greatly extends the range of curricular offerings and research activities.

The spontaneity, responsibility and sense of achievement which are important to our successful expansion would be thwarted by too much centralization and conformity. In practice, it is always difficult to define and achieve the appropriate balance, but, in this administration, the burden of proof will always rest with the centralizers. Nothing could be more appalling than the vision of ten or more University of California campuses cut from the same pattern.

E. Additional Comments on University Governance

1.   No one likes to be supervised in their production efforts. This is particularly true in the academic world where each individual likes to feel in control of his or her total situation. The seemingly eternal academic model for governance is the historic Oxford and Cambridge where faculty members and the executives they selected were in full charge until the middle of the nineteenth century, when a series of royal commissions intervened. Governmental authority in Great Britain has been in the ascendancy over the past century and a half—excessively so currently, I believe. The guild system of producer supremacy in the Middle Ages, out of which Oxford and Cambridge grew, failed because it was too oriented toward producer interests and too little toward those of consumers and the public at large. Oxford, Adam Smith once observed, was run too much for the sake of "the ease of the masters." But the idea of guild control by the faculty in higher education has reemerged as a cherished solution in various forms from time to time ever since, including through unionization. Total guild control is not compatible, however, with the pluralistic system of checks and balances found throughout the modern world, particularly in the United States. It follows that guild-like arrangements will continue to be attractive to produc-

ers but are not viable in modern societies, where other interests demand consideration. I assume that students as consumers are free to make choices, and that regents, president, and state authorities serve, in part, to represent the public welfare. Together they constitute the essential checks and balances. Nevertheless, an effective academic guild is an essential component within any university of distinction.

2. Government authorities generally are not willing to grant public funds without the right to approve the purposes for which they are to be spent or to audit their uses. Authorities may, however, be willing to delegate supervisory authority to intermediate agencies, such as boards of trustees of colleges and universities.

3. Supervisory control by a board of trustees is preferable to control by a government agency as a method of oversight, since trustees generally will be more independent in their judgments, better informed, more skilled, and more devoted to the specific institution than most government agencies.

4. One alternative to either state or board supervisory authority is "privatization" via competitive markets for students and private gifts and federal student and R&D support. It should be noted in this connection, however, that to operate the Berkeley campus as a private enterprise would mean giving the physical plant to the faculty free of charge and foregoing yearly state support of over $300 million— both highly unlikely. A supervisory board of trustees, too, may be found to be an advantage even in a privatized institution.

5. Another alternative is "state related" status as Lincoln University, Penn State, Temple, and the University of Pittsburgh have with Pennsylvania. Lump-sum support is negotiated each year subject to local distribution. This support may be problematical, however, in periods of tight budgets and high political concern over the conduct of higher education, and it may require periodic frenzied political activity. This is a "contract model" and both parties can make demands. "State related" support is, nevertheless, a more realistic possibility than "privatization."

6. Government authorities prefer to deal with one representative of a system of colleges and universities rather than with each separate campus, particularly when the campuses are numerous. Thus, systems of higher education institutions are now the rule in most of the fifty states of this nation, as well as around the world.

7. Systems can plan the effective use of resources, without gaps or duplications, better than competitive individual campuses; can reduce or control intercampus conflicts; and can protect new and weak campuses from the old and the strong. Systems can encourage and protect diversity among campuses, while competition otherwise may result in homogenization as each campus imitates every other campus.

F. Further Suggestions for the University's Review of Governance

SELECTION OF REGENTS

The Board of Regents should take an active interest in the selection of new regents. Specifically I suggest that the board, when an opening occurs or is about to occur, advise the governor that it would welcome consultation by the governor with the board chair and/or the president. These board members will know better than any governor what geographical locations, skills, and aspects of personality are most needed on the board at that time. I note this has sometimes, but not always, been the informal practice.

I totally oppose direct popular election of board members. Experience shows that public election of trustees is likely to become selection by members of highly organized and motivated groups, not by the informed will of the people at large. If the selection process is to be changed, I favor having more sources of appointment, for example appointments by the superintendent of public instruction or the chief justice of the state supreme court, and/or more appointments by alumni associations or by faculty senates.

CONSULTATION WITH ACADEMIC SENATE

The board might set up a direct discussion process with the universitywide Academic Senate, with the president as chair. For example, the Regents Committee on Educational Policy might meet at intervals with the Academic Senate's Committee on Educational Policy, and with the senate Committee on Academic Personnel.

The board might ask the president, as part of the annual audit process, to prepare a candid appraisal of academic personnel actions, campus by campus, to be submitted to the Committee on Educational Policy, possibly meeting jointly with the senate Committee on Academic Personnel. The board is now almost completely isolated from participation in or knowledge about the most important series of decisions made within the university—the hiring and promotion of its faculty.

CREDIT FOR UNIVERSITY SERVICE

In addition, I suggest that the Academic Senate and the chancellors might give more attention to "university service" when appointing and promoting faculty members, including considering a faculty member's unwillingness to accept appointment on faculty committees or, once appointed, to serve actively. The senate suffers from some self-inflicted wounds. Increasing numbers of faculty members are unwilling to take the time to serve on senate committees, to attend meetings, or to participate actively if they do attend. They are increasingly tied to their research and consulting work, to contacts outside the university. Some are simply bored by committee work or wish to avoid the pressure cooker of conflicts over policies and appointments and promotions in the new ambience of "political correctness," and to avoid losing friends. There are still, however, many devoted senate members. And departmental governance still remains largely effective.

MEMORIALS TO THE REGENTS

There are more ideological splits among faculty than ever before. Consequently, I suggest that all Academic Senate memorials to the Board of Regents be based on mail ballot votes. Each division of the senate should also have the right to submit memorials to the regents on its own, subject to comment by the university-wide Academic Council.

SELECTION OF CHANCELLORS

It is of the utmost importance to select as chancellors persons who are willing to participate in a system of shared governance.

Indicators of Growth in the University of California

A. Comparative Enrollments at UC Campuses, 1960–97

Year	Berkeley	Los Angeles	Davis	Riverside	San Francisco	Santa Barbara	Irvine	San Diego	Santa Cruz	UC Campus Total
1960	21,860	17,331	2,883	1,635	1,842	3,511		107		49,169
1961	23,713	17,968	3,500	1,979	1,913	4,130		156		53,359
1962	25,092	20,189	4,116	2,173	1,976	4,865		205		58,616
1963	26,756	21,890	4,956	2,641	2,040	5,938		283		64,504
1964	27,431	23,724	6,444	3,109	2,120	7,879		560		71,267
1965	26,834	25,676	7,907	3,544	2,227	9,570	1,589	1,438	652	79,437
1966	26,963	26,898	9,218	3,882	2,240	11,245	2,385	2,335	1,294	86,460
1967	28,863	29,070	10,161	4,183	2,338	12,201	3,423	3,070	1,983	95,292
1968	28,132	28,997	11,454	4,565	2,441	12,619	4,123	3,811	2,638	98,780
1969	28,088	30,657	12,594	5,361	2,526	13,733	5,049	4,864	3,163	106,035
1970	28,525	28,920	13,362	5,991	2,601	13,644	6,367	5,851	3,772	109,033
1971	27,712	27,903	14,005	6,168	2,675	12,916	6,879	6,475	4,396	109,129
1972	28,483	29,637	15,279	5,481	2,842	12,300	7,384	7,068	4,796	113,270
1973	29,909	31,086	15,622	5,376	2,921	12,526	8,384	7,950	5,080	118,854
1974	29,730	31,958	16,243	5,018	3,089	13,277	8,754	8,811	5,576	122,456

1975	30,004	33,236	17,217	5,050	3,295	14,584	9,399	9,598	6,103	128,486
1976	29,084	32,132	17,201	4,989	3,473	14,691	9,531	10,168	6,134	127,403
1977	28,097	31,623	17,249	4,872	3,567	14,588	9,330	10,375	6,097	125,798
1978	29,063	31,709	17,511	4,600	3,710	14,473	9,925	10,794	5,879	127,664
1979	30,445	32,953	17,952	4,615	3,812	14,785	10,030	11,159	6,085	131,836
1980	30,875	34,026	18,886	4,707	3,779	15,450	10,222	11,410	6,466	135,821
1981	30,405	34,609	19,274	4,764	3,739	15,706	11,058	12,312	6,859	138,726
1982	29,296	34,568	19,321	4,787	3,819	16,158	11,270	13,102	6,817	139,138
1983	30,009	34,751	18,969	4,706	3,644	16,752	11,908	13,658	6,892	141,289
1984	30,007	34,503	19,541	4,855	3,632	16,935	12,684	14,295	7,137	144,589
1985	31,482	34,378	19,837	5,227	3,612	17,414	13,554	14,837	7,616	147,957
1986	31,463	34,423	19,809	5,726	3,608	18,003	14,532	15,912	8,589	152,065
1987	32,055	35,435	20,847	6,554	3,681	17,879	15,139	16,589	9,152	157,331
1988	31,609	35,730	21,838	7,487	3,760	18,571	15,902	17,226	9,396	161,519
1989	31,123	36,378	22,568	8,220	3,711	19,082	16,152	17,587	9,784	164,605
1990	30,632	36,427	23,898	8,715	3,812	18,391	16,817	17,797	10,052	166,541
1991	30,145	36,366	23,302	8,890	3,756	18,519	16,950	17,956	10,136	166,020
1992	30,357	35,407	22,889	8,805	3,746	18,655	17,187	18,238	10,255	165,539
1993	30,341	34,447	22,486	8,677	3,731	18,581	16,815	17,851	10,173	163,102
1994	29,435	35,110	22,442	8,591	3,729	17,834	17,073	17,774	10,117	162,105
1995	29,630	34,713	23,092	8,906	3,640	18,224	17,261	18,315	9,923	163,704
1996	29,797	35,594	23,931	9,063	3,589	18,531	17,888	18,110	10,215	166,718
1997	30,290	35,558	24,250	9,898	3,522	18,940	17,808	18,657	10,638	169,862

Source: Statistical Summary of Students and Staff of the University of California (*fall, various years*).

B. Annual Net Increases in Bound Library Volumes Held

University of California Libraries

Year	Berkeley	Davis	Irvine	UCLA	Riverside	San Diego	Santa Barbara	Santa Cruz
Total volumes in 1957								
	2,226,359	145,597	0	1,231,238	93,243	30,620[a]	94,271	22,394[b]
Volumes added								
1958	78,762	13,990	0	69,837	15,085	511[a]	7,006	664[b]
1959	91,996	14,581	0	78,093	12,128	1,105[a]	10,071	618[b]
1960	105,070	14,424	0	85,306	12,166	3,350	13,123	477[b]
1961	94,339	20,102	0	104,635	18,508	10,270	17,684	281[b]
1962	105,160	30,683	2,167	150,250	26,576	21,673	26,221	550[b]
1963	116,846	40,524	16,150	147,292	27,678	43,699	64,241	21,757
1964	146,555	43,575	30,089	140,168	55,258	68,804	41,064	30,047
1965	81,891	61,181	37,080	190,356	47,724	79,672	45,485	29,751
1966	132,645	85,824	33,539	136,267	46,118	77,107	67,320	20,007
11967	49,493	72,625	92,473	136,368	49,369	83,940	69,666	33,264
1968	157,261	93,774	55,557	166,339	57,138	94,052	74,476	52,502
Total volumes in 1997								
	8,628,028	2,949,213	1,973,972	7,010,234	1,850,932	2,531,418	2,396,611	1,195,529
ARL rank in 1997								
	5	36	72	2	100	43	60	n.a.

Sources: for University of California libraries, Office of the President, "University of California Library Statistics" (annual). For other research libraries, 1957–68, Robert E. Molyneux, The Gerould Statistics: 1907/08–1961/62 (Washington, D.C.: Association of Research Libraries, 1986). For 1997 volumes and rank except at UCSC (based on ARL data), "Holdings of Research Libraries in U.S. and Canada, 1996–97," Chronicle of Higher Education, May 15, 1998, A22; for 1997 data at UCSC, Office of the President, "University of California Library Statistics" (forthcoming).

[a]*Total for La Jolla prior to establishment of UCSD.*

[b]*Total for Mt. Hamilton prior to establishment of UCSC; for 1963 and later, Mt. Hamilton is included within UCSC.*

Other Research Libraries

Year	Total UC	Columbia	Harvard	Illinois	Michigan	Stanford	Wisconsin
	3,843,722	2,218,641	6,225,447	3,049,741	2,532,849	1,414,611	1,227,335
1958	185,855	69,062	162,186	88,067	92,561	48,772	49,456
1959	208,592	73,802	142,677	93,461	68,523	78,085	55,263
1960	233,916	79,954	204,651	93,908	98,291	80,463	58,173
1961	265,819	89,707	151,524	95,246	107,952	92,945	64,674
1962	363,280	85,875	82,658	142,436	119,976	71,323	78,664
1963	478,187	97,430	195,577	108,823	125,756	108,119	72,536
1964	555,560	103,143	241,221	118,451	135,894	101,381	149,397
1965	573,140	123,311	257,631	150,466	134,811	181,745	135,792
1966	598,827	121,894	208,534	197,190	142,859	177,684	108,647
1967	687,198	137,395	222,569	241,441	178,406	204,053	136,225
1968	751,099	132,281	234,247	181,544	185,421	195,450	129,783
	28,195,937	6,905,609	13,617,133	9,024,298	6,973,162	6,865,158	5,824,639
		10	1	6	8	7	16

List of Documentary Supplements

Selected Tributes

1.1 Gloria Copeland, January 16, 1994.

1.2 E. T. Grether, March 24, 1994.

1.3 Milton Chernin, November 1, 1987.

1.4 Harry Wellman, August 30, 1997.

1.5 Glenn T. Seaborg, March 27, 1999.

1.6 Charles E. Young, Spring 1994.

1.7 Edmund G. "Pat" Brown, April 19, 1995.

1.8 Angus E. Taylor, May 27, 1999.

Academic Organization of University of California, Santa Cruz

2.1 Excerpt from Dean E. McHenry, "Academic Organizational Matrix at the University of California, Santa Cruz," in Dean E. McHenry and Associates, eds. *Academic Departments* (San Francisco: Jossey-Bass, 1977), 101–10.

Selected Comments

3.1 Clark Kerr, "The University: Civil Rights and Civil Responsibilities," Charter Day speech, University of California, Davis, May 5, 1964.

3.2 Clark Kerr, remarks at Ninety-Third Charter Day Ceremonies, University of California, Berkeley, March 20, 1961.

3.3 Katherine A. Towle, statement to Presidents or Chairmen and Advisers of All Student Organizations, September 14, 1964, regarding provisions of the policy on "Use of University Facilities."

3.4 Katherine A. Towle, addendum to p. 242 of Oral History, *Administration and Leadership,* clarifying the sequence of events of September 16, 1964.

3.5 Katherine A. Towle, statement, October 9, 1964, concerning the application of university policies and Berkeley campus regulations at the Bancroft-Telegraph entrance.

3.6 Clark Kerr, "Perspective on the Prophets of Doom," Commencement Address, University of California, Berkeley, June 12, 1965.

3.7 Transcript of Clark Kerr's remarks to the press, January 20, 1967.

Regulations Concerning Use
of University of California Facilities

4.1 Robert Gordon Sproul, "Academic Freedom," University Regulation No. 5, February 15, 1935.

4.2 Robert Gordon Sproul, "Use of University Facilities," University Regulation No. 17 (revised June 1, 1949).

Documentation on "Contact Man"

5.1 Excerpts from Hugh Burns's Oral History, "Legislative and Political Concerns of the Senate Pro Tem, 1957–70."

5.2 "A Recipe for Mutual Distrust: A Documented History of the 'Contact Man' Episode," with comments by Clark Kerr.

Documentation on Events of 1964–65

6.1 Petition to Dean of Students, September 18, 1964, by SLATE, Campus CORE, University Society of Individualists, DuBois Club of Berkeley, and others.

6.2 Report of the Ad Hoc Committee on Student Conduct (I. Michael Heyman, Chair) to the Berkeley Division of the Academic Senate, November 12, 1964.

6.3 Introduction by Mario Savio in Hal Draper, *Berkeley: The New Student Revolt* (1965).

Notes

Preface

1. The Institute of Governmental Studies Press and the Center for Studies in Higher Education, University of California, Berkeley, have published a series of "Chapters in the History of the University of California" that includes Henry F. May, *Three Faces of Berkeley: Competing Ideologies in the Wheeler Era, 1899–1919* (1993); Gunther Barth, *California's Practical Period: A Cultural Context of the Emerging University, 1850s–1870s* (1994); Geraldine Joncich Clifford, *"Equally in View": The University of California, Its Women, and the Schools* (1995); Eugene C. Lee, *The Origins of the Chancellorship: The Buried Report of 1948* (1995); Roy Lowe, *"A Western Acropolis of Learning," the University of California in 1897* (1996); Kent Watson, "William Hammond Hall and the Original Campus Plan," and Peter Van Houten, "The University and the Constitutional Convention of 1878," both in *The University in the 1870s* (1996); Gene A. Brucker, Henry F. May, and David F. Hollinger, *History at Berkeley: A Dialog in Three Parts* (1998).

Chapter 1

1. An earlier version of the first part of this chapter appeared in the 125th anniversary edition of Irving Stone, ed., *There Was Light: Autobiography of a University: A collection of essays by alumni of the University of California, Berkeley, 1868–1996*, rev. Jean Stone (Berkeley: University Relations, University of California, 1996), 24–34.

2. I wrote a chapter, "Paul and Dorothea," in *Dorothea Lange: A Visual Life*, ed. Elizabeth Partridge (Washington, D.C.: Smithsonian Institution Press, 1994), 36–43.

3. Enrollment figures throughout are based on "opening fall enrollments" as tabulated by the office of the registrar. These figures may differ from total numbers of students in any year.

4. James Bryant Conant, *My Several Lives: Memoirs of a Social Inventor* (New York: Harper and Row, 1970), 86.

5. A popular book by a psychologist whose scholarly reputation I do not know (Thomas A. Harris, *I'm OK—You're OK: A Practical Guide to Transactional Analysis* [New York: Harper and Row, 1969]) identified me as an "impressive adult" (253) seeking solutions in the course of the student troubles at Berkeley, as against the "frightened, anxious child" (160) or the "self-righteous parent" (17).

Chapter 2

1. *Robert Gordon Sproul Oral History Project,* an oral history conducted 1984–85, Regional Oral History Office, Bancroft Library, University of California, 2 vols. (Berkeley, 1986).

Chapter 3

1. "John Kenneth Galbraith," in *There Was Light: Autobiography of a University: A collection of essays by alumni of the University of California, Berkeley, 1868–1996,* ed. Irving Stone, rev. Jean Stone (Berkeley: University Relations, University of California, 1996), 17.

2. See *National Geographic,* June 1981, 831. See also Galen A. Rowell, *Bay Area Wild* (San Francisco: Sierra Club Books, 1977), ch. on "Living Visionaries."

3. Eugene C. Lee, *The Origins of the Chancellorship: The Buried Report of 1948,* Chapters in the History of the University of California 3 (Berkeley: Center for Studies in Higher Education and Institute of Governmental Studies, University of California, 1995).

4. For this and future references to documentary supplements, see *Documentary Supplements to The Gold and the Blue* by Clark Kerr (Berkeley: Institute of Governmental Studies, University of California, forthcoming).

5. John Walsh and Garth Mangum, *Labor Struggle in the Post Office: From Selective Lobbying to Collective Bargaining* (Armonk, N.Y.: M. E. Sharpe, 1992), 193.

Chapter 4

1. Eugene C. Lee, *The Origins of the Chancellorship: The Buried Report of 1948,* Chapters in the History of the University of California 3 (Berkeley: Center for Studies in Higher Education and Institute of Governmental Studies, University of California, 1995).

2. Robert Gordon Sproul, president, comments on the subcommittee report of October 13, 1950, "Appointment of a Provost at U.C.L.A.," to the Committee on Southern California Schools, Colleges, and Institutions (University of California Archives, presidential correspondence and papers, CU-301, Box 11, 7–8; hereafter UC Archives, CU- . . .).

3. Hansena Frederickson, "UCLA Administration, 1936–1966" (Department of Special Collections, Oral History Program, University Research Library, University of California, Los Angeles 1969), 102 (hereafter Oral History, UCLA).

Chapter 5

1. Hayward Keniston, *Graduate Study and Research in the Arts and Sciences at the University of Pennsylvania* (Philadelphia: University of Pennsylvania Press, 1959).

2. Allan M. Cartter, *An Assessment of Quality in Graduate Education* (Washington, D.C.: American Council on Education, 1966), 107.

3. Abraham Flexner, *Daniel Coit Gilman: Creator of the American Type of University* (New York: Harcourt, Brace, 1946), 48–49.

4. See Appendix 1's list of deans of schools and colleges rated in the top six in their fields, and the chairs of departments similarly rated; the names of members of the Academic Senate Committee on Budget and Interdepartmental Relations (academic personnel committee); members of the elected Committee on Committees, which played such a central role in appointing members of the academic personnel committee and all other senate and faculty committees; and the names of Berkeley faculty members holding Nobel Prizes and those with memberships in the National Academy of Sciences, 1962–63.

5. Stephen R. Graubard, "Notes toward a New History," in *The Research University in a Time of Discontent,* ed. Jonathan R. Cole, Elinor G. Barber, and Stephen R. Graubard (Baltimore: Johns Hopkins University Press, 1994), 384.

Chapter 6

1. H. H. Semans et al., *A Study of the Need for Additional Centers of Public Higher Education in California* (Sacramento: California State Department of Education, 1957).

2. "Size and Number of Campuses," report of study committee 1 (Dean E. McHenry, chair) *Quality of Education in Relation to Numbers: Proceedings of the University of California Twelfth All-University Faculty Conference,* Highlands Inn, Carmel, California, April 4–6, 1957 [University of California, 1957]), 9–18.

3. T. R. McConnell, T. C. Holy, and H. H. Semans, *A Restudy of the Needs of California Higher Education* (Sacramento: California State Department of Education, 1955).

4. Sanford S. Elberg, "Graduate Education and Microbiology at the University of California, Berkeley, 1930–1987" (Regional Oral History Office, Bancroft Library, University of California, Berkeley, 1990), 108.

5. See Maresi Nerad, *The Academic Kitchen: A Social History of Gender Stratification at the University of California, Berkeley* (Albany: State University of New York Press, 1999).

6. "Report of the Commission on Education" (Neil J. Smelser, chair), transmitted to Vice-Chancellor Roderic Park, May 13, 1981.

Chapter 7

1. *Students at Berkeley: A Study of Their Extracurricular Activities with Suggestions for Improvements On and Off the Campus to Broaden their Preparation for Citizenship* (L. Deming Tilton, project director) (Berkeley: California Alumni Association, 1948).

2. Clark Kerr, "The Total Student," inaugural address, University of California, Santa Barbara, October 3, 1958.

3. For a discussion of these developments, see Glenn T. Seaborg and Ray Colvig, *Roses from the Ashes* (Berkeley: Institute of Governmental Studies, University of California, 2000). Also see IGS Documentary Supplement for my memorial tribute to Seaborg.

Chapter 8

1. "Planning the Physical Development of the Berkeley Campus" (prepared by the Office of Architects and Engineers, University of California, December 1951).

2. See Sally Woodbridge, "The Physical Evolution of the Berkeley Campus, 1868–1956" (Berkeley: Institute of Governmental Studies, University of California, Berkeley, forthcoming).

3. Stephen C. Pepper, "Art and Philosophy at the University of California, 1919–1962" (Regional Oral History Office, Bancroft Library, University of California, Berkeley, 1963), 327, 328.

4. The presentation of the Wurster drawings was not the first or, probably, the last such episode in the history of the Berkeley campus. See, for example, the following account:

> As Maybeck tells the story: One day in 1896 there appeared in President Martin Kellogg's office, a charming woman. This woman identified herself as the widow of Senator George Hearst. It was her feeling that since Mr. Hearst had accumulated a great fortune through the mining industry of the West, it would be fitting that an adequate sum be given to the University for a mining building which would be a memorial to her husband and would further growth and research in mining. There she was with the money in her hand, and like a good executive, President Kellogg assured her the University would be delighted to accept her offer and that if she would return in a day or two he would be able to show her what they could do with the money. A hurried call to the engineering department found no talent to produce in twenty-four hours a drawing of an imaginary building. But someone did recall that there was that architect fellow, Maybeck, around and if an architect was good for anything maybe this was it. "Ben" Maybeck was put to work on the sketch and as he says, "a miserable sketch it was." And the next afternoon when Maybeck saw the sketch sitting in the office of the President, "looking very sad and very miserable," he was sure it would never convince the good lady to give money for such a building. However, Maybeck had an inspiration. He hurried to his own home, removed a pair of plush hangings from a window in spite of his wife's protestations, and grabbed a number of potted geraniums from the garden. Maybeck said later—"when Mrs. Hearst saw the drawing of the building with the plush hangings at its sides and a row of potted geraniums in front—how could she resist? After all, she was a woman!" True or not, Mrs. Hearst did approve of the sketch. *(Kenneth Cardwell and William C. Hays, "Fifty Years from Now," California Monthly 44 [April 1954]: 20–21).*

Chapter 9

1. The Levering Act oath required every civil defense worker and public employee in California to swear to or affirm the following:

I, _____, do solemnly swear (or affirm) that I will support and defend the Constitution of the United States and the Constitution of the State of California against all enemies, foreign and domestic; that I will bear true faith and allegiance to the Constitution of the United States and the Constitution of the State of California; that I take this obligation freely, without any mental reservation or purpose of evasion; and that I will well and faithfully discharge the duties upon which I am about to enter.

And I do swear (or affirm) that I do not advocate, nor am I a member of any party or organization, political or otherwise, that now advocates the overthrow of the Government of the United States or the State of California by force or violence or other unlawful means; and within the five years immediately preceding the taking of this oath (or affirmation) I have not been a member of any party or organization, political or otherwise, that advocated the overthrow of the Government of the United States or the State of California by force or violence or other unlawful means except as follows: _____

_____

_____

(if no affiliations, write in the words, "no exception")
and that during such time as I am a member or employee of the

_____

(name of public agency) I will not advocate or become a member of any party or organization, political or otherwise, that advocates the overthrow of the Government of the United States or the State of California by force or violence or other unlawful means. *(David P. Gardner,* The California Oath Controversy *[Berkeley: University of California Press, 1967], 219).*

2. Paul S. Taylor and Clark Kerr, "Documentary History of the Cotton Pickers in California, 1933," in *Violations of Free Speech and Rights of Labor,* hearing before a subcommittee of the Committee on Education and Labor, United States Senate, 76th Congress, 3d sess., S.Res. 266 (74th Congress), part 54 (Washington: U.S. Government Printing Office, 1940), 19945–20036.

3. Sidney Hook, "To Counter the Big Lie—A Basic Strategy," *New York Times Magazine,* March 11, 1951, 9, 59–64.

4. Clark Kerr, "An Effective and Democratic Organization of the Economy," in *Goals for Americans: Programs for Action in the Sixties,* report of the U.S. President's Commission on National Goals (Englewood Cliffs, N.J.: Prentice-Hall, 1960), 149–62.

Chapter 10

1. Verne A. Stadtman, *The University of California 1868–1968* (New York: McGraw-Hill, 1970), 31.

2. For a discussion of these developments from a national point of view, see also Clark

Kerr, *The Great Transformation in Higher Education: 1960–1980* (Albany: State University of New York Press, 1991).

Chapter 11

1. I have written of the changes in higher education that resulted from these developments, in Clark Kerr, *The Great Transformation in Higher Education: 1960–1980* (Albany: State University of New York Press, 1991).

2. The 1960 growth plan is "A Recommended Plan for Growth of the University of California" (Berkeley, June 1960); and the academic plan, "A Proposed Academic Plan for the University of California" (Berkeley, July 1961).

3. "The Academic Plan of the University of California 1966–1967," (Berkeley, November 1966), 63.

4. Ibid., 85.

Chapter 12

1. Arnold Joyal, "A Presidential View of the Master Plan," interview conducted by Lawrence B. de Graff in 1987 (Oral History Program, California State University, Fullerton, June 1988), 13 (hereafter Oral History, CSU-Fullerton).

2. Robert Wert, "Creating the Master Plan: An Independent College Perspective," interview conducted by Judson A. Grenier in 1988 (Oral History, CSU-Fullerton, 1989), 3.

3. Joyal, "Presidential View," 8.

4. Edmund G. "Pat" Brown, "The Master Plan and State Educational Policy," interviews conducted by Judson A. Grenier in 1981 and 1988 (Oral History, CSU-Fullerton, November 1988), 1.

5. Lyman Glenny, "State Government and the State Colleges Before the Master Plan," interview conducted by Judson A. Grenier in 1988 (Oral History, CSU-Fullerton, 1989), 26.

6. Glenn S. Dumke, "Creating the California State Colleges," interviews conducted by Judson A. Grenier in 1981 and 1987 (Oral History, CSU-Fullerton, July 1987), 14 and 23.

7. Office of the Chancellor, California State Colleges, "Papers Presented at the Conference on Educational Philosophy," (Los Angeles, January 18, 1966), 25.

8. Neil J. Smelser, "Growth, Structural Change, and Conflict in California Public Higher Education, 1950–1970," in *Public Higher Education in California,* ed. Neil J. Smelser and Gabriel Almond (Berkeley: University of California Press, 1974), 71.

9. Ibid., 73.

10. Ernest G. Palola, Timothy Lehmann, and William R. Blischke, *Higher Education by Design: The Sociology of Planning* (Berkeley: Center for Research and Development in Higher Education, University of California, Berkeley, 1970), 98.

11. Glenny, "State Government," 23 and 30.

12. For a listing of the 83 research universities in 1963–65, see Clark Kerr, *The Uses of the University,* 4th ed. (Cambridge, Mass.: Harvard University Press, 1995), tb. 1 on 119–22. That listing is based on criteria for classification of research universities set forth in Carnegie Council on Policy Studies in Higher Education, *A Classification of Institutions of Higher Education,* rev. ed. (Berkeley, 1976), which considered level of federal financial support and number of Ph.D.'s awarded.

13. Howard R. Bowen, *The State of the Nation and the Agenda for Higher Education* (San Francisco: Jossey-Bass, 1982), 101–2.

14. See John A. Douglass, *The California Idea and American Higher Education: 1850 to the 1960 Master Plan* (Stanford: Stanford University Press, 2000).

15. Master plan survey team (Arthur G. Coons, chairman), *A Master Plan for Higher Education in California 1960–1975* (prepared for the liaison committee of the state Board of Education and The Regents of the University of California, Berkeley and Sacramento, February 1960), 227.

16. *Higher Education for Democracy: A Report of the President's Commission on Higher Education* [George F. Zook, chairman], vol. 1, *Establishing the Goals* (New York: Harper and Bros., 1947).

17. For example, one of the supporting appendices to Vannevar Bush's famous 1945 report to the president on postwar policy quoted a 1944 study that said, "It is generally assumed that pupils with intelligence quotients above 110 are good college material" (W. Lloyd Warner, Robert J. Havighurst, and Martin B. Loeb, *Who Shall Be Educated: The Challenge of Unequal Opportunities* [New York: Harper and Bros., 1944]. Quoted in Office of Scientific Research and Development [Vannevar Bush, director], *Science, the Endless Frontier* [Washington, D.C.: U.S. Government Printing Office, 1945], Appendix A, 164). If all those with an IQ over 110 attended college, there would be a cohort participation of about 25 percent.

18. See Sheldon Rothblatt, ed., *The OECD, the Master Plan and the California Dream: A Berkeley Conversation* (Berkeley: Center for Studies in Higher Education, University of California, 1992).

19. Organisation for Economic Co-operation and Development, *Higher Education in California* (Paris: OECD, 1990), 36.

20. Clark Kerr, "The California Master Plan of 1960 for Higher Education," in *The OECD, the Master Plan and the California Dream,* ed. Sheldon Rothblatt (Berkeley: Center for Studies in Higher Education, University of California, 1992), 60.

21. OECD, *Higher Education in California,* 32.

22. Peter Schrag, *Paradise Lost: California's Experience and America's Future* (New York: New Press, 1998).

23. California Postsecondary Education Commission, *From Compromise to Promise: A Status Report on the Joint Doctorate in California* (Sacramento, 1998), displays 1 and 3.

24. See for example, Clark Kerr, "Preserving the Master Plan: What Is to Be Done in a New Epoch of More Limited Growth of Resources," in *Who Will Take Responsibility for the Future of California Higher Education? A Statement by Clark Kerr to the Cal-*

ifornia Postsecondary Education Commission, October 25, 1993, commission report 93-21 (Sacramento: California Postsecondary Education Commission, 1993), Appendix A (statement to the CSU trustees and the regents); John Immerwahr and Jill Boese, *Preserving the Legacy: A Conversation with California Leaders,* prepared by Public Agenda for the California Higher Education Policy Center, report 95-3 (San Jose, 1995); David W. Breneman, Leobardo F. Estrada, and Gerald C. Hayward, *Tidal Wave II: An Evaluation of Enrollment Projections for California Higher Education,* technical report 95-6 (San Jose: California Higher Education Policy Center, 1995); California Higher Education Policy Center, *Shared Responsibility: Strategies for Quality and Opportunity in California Higher Education,* report 96-3 (San Jose, 1996); and Michael A. Shires, *The Future of Public Undergraduate Education in California* (Santa Monica: Institute on Education and Training, RAND, 1996); California Citizens Commission on Higher Education (John Brooks Slaughter and Harold M. Williams, cochairs), *A State of Learning: California Higher Education in the Twenty-First Century* (Los Angeles, 1998); and Schrag, *Paradise Lost.*

25. Clark Kerr, Testimony before the Joint Committee to Develop a Master Plan for Education, Kindergarten through University (Senator Deirdre W. Alpert, chair), Sacramento, California, August 24, 1999; Schrag, *Paradise Lost.*

Chapter 13

1. Edward S. Holden, president of the University of California from 1885 to 1888, quoted in Verne A. Stadtman, *The University of California 1868–1968* (New York: McGraw-Hill, 1970), 104.

2. Hansena Frederickson, "UCLA Administration, 1963–1966" (Oral History, UCLA, 1969), 140.

3. Harry R. Wellman, "Teaching, Research, and Administration, University of California 1925–1968" (Regional Oral History Project, Bancroft Library, University of California, Berkeley, 1976), 75–76 (hereafter Oral History, UCB).

4. "Resolution Adopted by Blue Shield May 4, 1943" (UC Archives, administrative reorganization III, CU-5, Box 1163).

5. Robert N. Underhill, Memorandum on "Administrative Reorganization" [n.d.] (ibid.).

6. Eugene C. Lee, *The Origins of the Chancellorship: The Buried Report of 1948,* Chapters in the History of the University of California 3 (Berkeley: Center for Studies in Higher Education and Institute of Governmental Studies, University of California, 1995), 32–46.

7. For a more complete description of the senate's history and role, see Angus E. Taylor, *The Academic Senate at the University of California: Its Role in the Shared Governance and Operation of the University* (Berkeley: Institute of Governmental Studies, 1998). See also Russell H. Fitzgibbon, "The Academic Senate of the University of California" (Office of the President, University of California, 1968).

8. Regents allocated campus sites to faculty clubs in the early years. However, assistance in construction funding was not provided by them until the late 1950s. The following table shows regental financial support for club facilities:

Campus	First regental funding for club construction/expansion
Berkeley: The Faculty Club	1958
Berkeley: Women's Faculty Club	None received*
San Francisco	Space allocated
Davis	1964
Los Angeles	1958
Riverside	1960
Santa Barbara	1965
Irvine	1966 (furnishings only)
San Diego	1965
Santa Cruz	[No faculty club]

9. Freeman Lincoln, "Norton Simon, Like Him or Not," *Fortune* 48, no. 6 (December 1953), 142–44ff.

10. See discussion in August Frugé, *A Skeptic Among Scholars: August Frugé on University Publishing* (Berkeley: University of California Press, 1993), 43–46.

Chapter 14

1. Jerome C. Byrne, "Report on the University of California and Recommendations to the [Forbes] Special Committee of the Regents of the University of California" (mimeo, Los Angeles, May 7, 1965).

2. Hansena Frederickson, "UCLA Administration, 1936–1966" (Oral History, UCLA, 1969), 203.

3. Harry R. Wellman, "Teaching, Research, and Administration, University of California 1925–1968" (Oral History, UCB, 1976), 135.

4. Arthur Coons, *Crisis in California Higher Education* (Los Angeles: Ward Ritchie, 1968), 74.

5. Ibid., 75.

6. Minutes of meeting of the Regents of the University of California, Riverside campus, May 21, 1965.

7. University of California, Berkeley, Study Commission on University Governance, *The Culture of the University: Governance and Education* (San Francisco: Jossey-Bass, 1968).

8. Wellman, "Teaching, Research, and Administration," 173.

9. Frederickson, "UCLA Administration, 1936–1966," 203.

10. Ibid., 204.

---

* Although the regents granted a campus site to the club.

11. William Trombley, "UCLA Autonomy Fight Believed Won: Chancellor Murphy Cites Shift of Authority to Campus Level," *Los Angeles Times,* July 25, 1966, 1.

12. "Asked in January, 1958, about the policy differences between himself and Murphy, Docking replied, 'I want the schools run on an efficient basis. It's mainly a battle between the salesman and the auditor.' With that view of himself Docking said that the regents must 'simplify the curriculum, reduce its size, and raise its quality' by surveying all courses to see how many could be eliminated or consolidated 'so that the maximum utilization of the faculty can be obtained'" (Clifford S. Griffin, *The University of Kansas: A History* [Lawrence: University Press of Kansas, 1974], 533).

13. Lally Weymouth, "The Word from Mamma Buff," *Esquire* 88, no. 5 (November 1977), 206, 205.

14. Trombley, "UCLA Autonomy," 1.

15. Ibid., 3.

16. Ibid., 1, 3.

Chapter 15

1. Sheldon Rothblatt, *The Modern University and Its Discontents* (Cambridge: Cambridge University Press, 1997), 288.

2. John A. Douglass, "Setting the Conditions of Undergraduate Admissions: The Role of University of California Faculty in Policy and Process" (report to the Task Force on Governance, University of California Academic Senate, 1997).

3. *Governor's Survey on Efficiency and Cost Control* (report on University of California, Sacramento, February 1968).

4. As quoted in Eugene C. Lee, *The Origins of the Chancellorship: The Buried Report of 1948,* Chapters in the History of the University of California 3 (Berkeley: Center for Studies in Higher Education and Institute of Governmental Studies, University of California, 1995), 49.

5. Harry R. Wellman, "Teaching, Research, and Administration, University of California 1925–1968" (Oral History, UCB, 1976), 134.

6. Michael D. Cohen and James D. March, *Leadership and Ambiguity: The American College President* (New York: McGraw-Hill, 1974).

7. For discussions of these lost opportunities, see Clark Kerr, *Who Will Take Responsibility for the Future of California Higher Education?* commission report 93-21 (Sacramento: California Postsecondary Education Commission, 1993); and Patrick M. Callan, *The California Higher Education Policy Vacuum* (San Jose: California Higher Education Policy Center, 1993).

8. See "The Report of the Governance Advisory Group on the Regents, Berkeley Division, Academic Senate," May 14, 1996.

9. Several of the possibilities set forth here are already (1998) under consideration by the Board of Regents, the president, and the Academic Council of the Academic Senate.

10. See the discussion in A. H. Halsey, *Decline of Donnish Dominion* (New York: Oxford University Press, 1992); and Peter Scott, *The Meanings of Mass Higher Education* (Buckingham: Society for Research into Higher Education, 1995), ch. 2.

Chapter 16

1. Liaison Committee of the State Board of Education and The Regents of the University of California, "A Study of the Need for Additional Centers of Public Higher Education in California" (1957).

2. Carnegie Commission on Higher Education, *A Classification of Institutions of Higher Education* (Berkeley, 1973); Carnegie Foundation for the Advancement of Teaching, *A Classification of Institutions of Higher Education* (Princeton, 1987).

3. "University of California New Campus Location Criteria," report by Administrative Committee (Charles D. Wheelock, chair), January 1958 (UC Archives, CU-5, Series 5, Box 9).

4. Members of faculty committees for new campuses:

UC-San Diego	*James Arnold, chair, San Diego*
	Gustaf Arrhenius, San Diego
	Gifford Ewing, San Diego
	Martin Kamen, San Diego
	Robert Nisbet, Riverside
	Stephen Pepper, Berkeley
	Lynn White, Los Angeles
UC-Irvine	*John S. Galbraith, chair (summer 1964), Los Angeles, later San Diego*
	H. T. Swedenberg, chair, Los Angeles
	Carl H. Eckart, San Diego
	James S. Gillies, Los Angeles
	Robert F. Gleckner, Riverside
	William F. Kennedy, Santa Barbara
UC-Santa Cruz	*Gordon Mackinney, chair, Berkeley*
	Malcolm Davisson, Berkeley
	Leslie Bennett, San Francisco
	Siegfried Puknat, Davis
	Daniel J. Crowley, Davis

5. For a spicy and perceptive account of the early developments at San Diego, see Nancy Scott Anderson, *An Improbable Venture, A History of the University of California at San Diego* (La Jolla: UCSD Press, 1993). See also William J. McGill, *The Year of the Monkey: Revolt on Campus, 1968–69* (New York: McGraw-Hill, 1982).

6. Herbert F. York, *Making Weapons, Talking Peace: A Physicist's Odyssey from Hiroshima to Geneva* (New York: Basic Books, 1987), 208.

7. Roger Revelle, "The Multiple Functions of a Graduate School" (address delivered during the seventh conference, Association of Princeton Graduate Alumni, Princeton University, December 27–28, 1958).

8. For a participant's careful history of the early years at Irvine, see Samuel Clyde McCulloch, *Instant University: The History of the University of California, Irvine, 1957–1993* (Irvine: University of California, Irvine, Alumni Association and Samuel C. McCulloch, 1996).

9. Sources to consult for further information on the Santa Cruz campus: Gerald Grant and David Riesman, *The Perpetual Dream: Reform and Experiment in the American College* (Chicago: University of Chicago Press, 1978); Christopher Hudson, *Spring Street Summer: The Search for a Lost Paradise* (New York: A. A. Knopf, 1993); Dean E. McHenry, "Academic Organizational Matrix at the University of California, Santa Cruz," in *Academic Departments* (San Francisco: Jossey-Bass, 1977), 86–116; Robert Sinsheimer, *The Strands of a Life: The Science of DNA and the Art of Education* (Berkeley: University of California Press, 1994); Angus E. Taylor, *Freely Speaking: A Scholar's Memoir of the University of California* (Berkeley: Institute of Governmental Studies Press, 2000).

10. Roger Revelle, "Statesman of Science," television interview, KPBS, San Diego, 1992.

Chapter 17

1. Nancy Scott Anderson, *An Improbable Venture, A History of the University of California at San Diego* (La Jolla: UCSD Press, 1993), 93.

2. See "A Proposed Academic Plan for the University of California" (Berkeley, July 1961).

3. "The special planning committee recommended and the Regents approved (1) the establishment of a general campus in the San Diego–La Jolla area and (2) the expansion of faculty and facilities of the La Jolla campus to provide a graduate program in science and technology together with the necessary undergraduate instruction to support that program" (Harry R. Wellman, "Teaching, Research, and Administration, University of California 1925–1968" [Oral History, UCB, 1976], 101).

4. Roger Revelle, "The Multiple Functions of a Graduate School" (address delivered during the seventh conference, Association of Princeton Graduate Alumni, Princeton University, December 27–28, 1958).

5. Wellman, "Teaching, Research, and Administration," 181.

6. Hansena Frederickson, "UCLA Administration, 1936–1966" (Oral History, UCLA, 1969), 115.

7. Anderson, *An Improbable Venture,* 103.

8. Gerald Grant and David Riesman, *The Perpetual Dream: Reform and Experiment in the American College* (Chicago: University of Chicago Press, 1978), 3.

9. John Henry Cardinal Newman, *The Idea of a University* (New York: Longmans Green, 1947), discourse 7, section 10, "Knowledge Viewed in Relation to Professional Skill."

10. Clark Kerr, *The Uses of the University,* 4th ed. (Cambridge, Mass.: Harvard University Press, 1995), 1, 48–49, 77–78.

Chapter 18

1. Gerald Grant and David Riesman, *The Perpetual Dream: Reform and Experiment in the American College* (Chicago: University of Chicago Press, 1978), 1.

2. For my prior effort to set forth and explain these themes, see Clark Kerr, *The Great Transformation in Higher Education: 1960–1980* (Albany: State University of New York Press, 1991).

3. See Clark Kerr, *The Uses of the University,* 4th ed. (Cambridge, Mass.: Harvard University Press, 1995), ch. 2 ("The Realities of the Federal Grant University").

4. Francis M. Cornford, *Microcosmographia Academica: A Guide for the Young Academic Politician* (1908; reprint, Arlington, Va.: Beatty, 1969), 23.

5. I take these categories from Grant and Riesman, *Perpetual Dream.*

6. Ibid., 384.

7. For further discussion of these developments at Irvine, see Samuel Clyde McCulloch, *Instant University: The History of the University of California, Irvine, 1957–1993* (Irvine: University of California, Irvine, Alumni Association and Samuel C. McCulloch, 1996).

8. For a fascinating tour of and reaction to this program, see David Denby, *Great Books* (New York: Simon and Schuster, 1996).

9. C. P. Snow, *The Two Cultures and the Scientific Revolution* (New York: Cambridge University Press, 1959).

10. I draw here heavily on a series of interviews on campus in fall 1996 by Marian Gade, my research associate; as also for Santa Cruz in winter and spring 1997.

Chapter 19

1. Clark Kerr, *The Uses of the University,* 4th ed. (Cambridge, Mass.: Harvard University Press, 1995), 89–90.

2. Readers interested in Santa Cruz can do no better than read Gerald Grant and David Riesman, *The Perpetual Dream: Reform and Experiment in the American College* (Chicago: University of Chicago Press, 1978), chs. 4 and 8.

3. Dean E. McHenry, "Academic Organizational Matrix at the University of California, Santa Cruz," in *Academic Departments* (San Francisco: Jossey-Bass, 1977), 107–8.

4. Richard L. Evans, *Carl Rogers—The Man and His Ideas* (New York: E. P. Dutton, 1975), 166.

5. Grant and Riesman, *Perpetual Dream,* 80.

6. See Michel Kahn, "The Kresge Experiment," *Humanistic Psychology* (spring 1981).

7. See Grant and Riesman, *Perpetual Dream,* 95–96.

8. Kahn, "The Kresge Experiment."

9. Grant and Riesman, *Perpetual Dream,* 274. Additionally, for a fond look at Santa Cruz's counterculture stage, see Christopher Hudson, *Spring Street Summer: The Search for a Lost Paradise* (New York: A. A. Knopf, 1993). In 1976 he had seen the campus "as a model for higher education in its best and purest form" (85), where the "outside world is out of sight and out of mind" (127). Santa Cruz "was utopian in that it offered an ideal alternative to the commercial corruption of other university campuses." However, "paradises are too beautiful and restful to encourage prolonged intellectual labour" (128). And "things had changed" and he had changed when he went back thirteen years later: "UCSC had fallen prey to the commercialization it had struggled so valiantly to avoid" (234–35). "The job market was shrinking" and the "business community had no preference for quizzical, sceptical, highly educated graduates. They wanted, and still want, specialized talents and narrow-focused minds" (236). He "was coming to realize" that it was "as pointless to devise ideal blueprints for the future as it was to imagine golden ages in the past" (237). He concluded that "paradise" was "illusory" (257). He ends up watching a locomotive "monster" rushing by on a new-laid track in what he and his girlfriend had, on his first visit, called their "Garden of Eden" (259). To the degree that this verdict is true, it represents a triumph of markets for both students (jobs) and faculty members (research grants) over the dream that a single university can both prepare "the educated citizen" and train the "expert."

10. "Santa Cruz freshmen are twice as likely as others to cite 'avoiding pressure' as a 'very important' factor affecting their choice of career" (Grant and Riesman, *Perpetual Dream,* 273).

11. S. Geiser, Planning and Analysis Unit, Office of the President, University of California (April 20, 1997).

12. For an on-the-spot discussion of the colleges' decline, see the as yet unpublished essay by Professor Carlos G. Noreña, "The Rise and Demise of the UCSC Colleges."

Chapter 20

1. Clark Kerr, "Accumulated Heritage Faces Modern Imperatives," in *Higher Education Cannot Escape History: Issues for the Twenty-First Century* (Albany: State University of New York Press, 1994), 45. (This chapter is based on a lecture I gave in Rome on January 27, 1987, under the auspices of Agenzia di Richerche e Legislazione. An earlier version of this chapter appeared as "A Critical Age in the University World: Accumulated heritage versus modern imperatives," *European Journal of Education* 22, no. 2 [1987]: 183–93.)

2. See, for example, the comments of Gordon Mackinney (chair, Faculty Committee on Development of Santa Cruz) in a memorandum to President Kerr, October 31, 1963.

3. See the discussion in Carnegie Council on Policy Studies in Higher Education, *Missions of the College Curriculum: A Contemporary Review with Suggestions* (San Francisco: Jossey-Bass, 1977).

4. José Ortega y Gasset, *Mission of the University* (1944; New Brunswick, N.J.: Transaction Publishers, 1992).

5. See several of the discussions in *Daedalus* (winter 1997) concerning the state of humanities after the 1960s.

6. For McHenry's reflections on Santa Cruz, see Dean E. McHenry, "University of California, Santa Cruz," in *Important Lessons from Innovative Colleges and Universities,* ed. V. Ray Cardozier, *New Directions for Higher Education* 82 (San Francisco: Jossey-Bass, 1993), 37–53; also Dean E. McHenry, "Academic Organizational Matrix at the University of California, Santa Cruz," in *Academic Departments* (San Francisco: Jossey-Bass, 1977) (the latter is set forth in the Documentary Supplement 2).

7. McHenry, "Academic Organizational Matrix at Santa Cruz," 107–8.

8. Gerald Grant and David Riesman, *The Perpetual Dream: Reform and Experiment in the American College* (Chicago: University of Chicago Press, 1978), 3.

9. Martin Trow, "From Institution Building to Steady State: A Note on the Early Years of Innovative Colleges," in *Proceedings of the Anglo-American Conference* (Cambridge, Mass.: Massachusetts Institute of Technology, 1978), 101–18.

10. "Lower Division Education in the University of California: A Report from the Task Force on Lower Division Education" (Neil J. Smelser, chair), University of California, June 1986; and "Report of the Universitywide Task Force on Faculty Rewards" (Karl S. Pister, chair), Office of the President, University of California, Oakland, June 26, 1991.

11. Robert Sinsheimer, *The Strands of a Life: The Science of DNA and the Art of Education* (Berkeley: University of California Press, 1994), 272.

12. See the similar conclusion in Joseph Tussman, *Experiment at Berkeley* (New York: Oxford University Press, 1969). "My efforts to recruit a staff from among the regular Berkeley faculty failed completely" (14). See also Joseph Tussman, *The Beleaguered College* (Berkeley: Institute of Governmental Studies, University of California, 1997). Tussman concluded, thirty years later at a seminar at Berkeley, that any liberal education program for undergraduates that is worthwhile is not possible; and that any program that is possible is not worthwhile. I do not agree, but then I have more relaxed standards of what is worth doing. Nevertheless, I consider that the Tussman reports on his experiment are the best I have ever read on academic innovations. For a favorable review of the Tussman program from the point of view of the students who went through it, see Katherine Bernhardi Trow, *Habits of Mind* (Berkeley: Institute of Governmental Studies, University of California, 1998). I still think it is possible to build a worthwhile broad learning program as follows:

1. Use only tenured faculty. Ask them to teach only within their own discipline.

2. Ask each faculty member to teach his or her own segments of a liberal or broad learning sequence on a nonmajor basis for the general student. Teaching is a "one-man show" (Tussman, *Beleaguered College,* 28).

3. Give the liberal-learning college a series of FTE appointments—bargaining

chips—with which to persuade departments to appoint faculty members willing to teach, in part, on a nonmajor basis.

4. Give faculty members who teach within a liberal-learning program extra rewards and recognition.

5. Put the liberal-learning program under the control of scientific and professional school faculties.

6. Give students a choice among alternative liberal-learning programs.

7. Allow lower-division students time to meet their other requirements, including prerequisites for the major.

8. Operate the liberal-learning program over the full four years.

9. Secure the appointments and promotions of faculty members through the disciplinary departments.

10. Create "teaching centers" as counterparts to "research institutes."

13. Eric Ashby, *Masters and Scholars: Reflections on the Rights and Responsibilities of Students* (London: Oxford University Press, 1970), 6.

14. Sinsheimer, *Strands of a Life,* 163.

15. See Carnegie Council, *Missions of the College Curriculum.*

Chapter 21

1. For a history of Davis as an agricultural campus, see Ann Foley Scheuring, with Chester O. McCorkle and James Lyons, *Science and Service: A History of the Land-Grant University and Agriculture in California,* UC Division of Agriculture and Natural Resources special publication 3360 (Oakland: ANR Publications, University of California, 1995).

2. Marilyn B. Ghausi, *Collaboration in Higher Education: The Lawrence Livermore National Laboratory and the University of California, Davis* (written under the auspices of the U.S. Department of Energy by Lawrence Livermore National Laboratory under Contract W-7405-Eng-48) (Washington, D.C.: U.S. Government Printing Office, 1990).

3. Erik Erikson, *The Life Cycle Completed: A Review* (New York: W. W. Norton, 1982).

4. For a history of the Santa Barbara campus from its beginning, see Robert Kelley, *Transformations: UC Santa Barbara, 1909–1979* (Santa Barbara: ASUC-SB, 1981).

Chapter 22

1. Of Riverside's entering students 8.5 percent had 4.0 grade point averages in the solid courses on which admission was based, as compared with 7.5 percent at Berkeley (Ivan Hinderaker, "Talk to the Faculty at the College of Letters and Science," University of California, Riverside, December 1, 1966).

2. *Chicago Tribune,* April 28, 1957, Part I, 8.

3. Carol H. Fuller, "Ph.D. Recipients: Where Did They Go to College?" *Change* 28, no. 6 (November–December 1986): 42–51. Data are adjusted for institutional size and are for Ph.D.'s earned during the years 1951–80.

4. For the Strayer report, see "A Report on a Survey of the Needs of California in Higher Education" (March 1, 1948), submitted to the Liaison Committee of the Regents of the University of California and the State Department of Education.

5. The faculty "manifesto" read as follows:

> Dear President Kerr:
>
> In the immediate future decisions will have to be made that will determine much of the future course of this Campus. We, the undersigned, urgently request an appointment to see you at your earliest convenience for a high-level decision of utmost importance to this campus.
>
> Sincerely yours,

The signers were Julius H. Comroe, Jr., Professor of Physiology, and Director, Cardiovascular Research Institute; S. C. Cullen, Associate Dean, School of Medicine, Professor and Chairman, Department of Anesthesia; J. E. Dunphy, Professor and Chairman, Department of Surgery; I. S. Edelman, Professor of Medicine and Physiology, and Chairman, Committee on Educational Policy, Academic Senate; R. M. Featherstone, Professor and Chairman, Department of Pharmacology; A. Margulis, Professor and Chairman, Department of Radiology; A. Simon, Professor and Chairman, Department of Psychiatry; L. H. Smith, Professor and Chairman, Department of Medicine; M. Sokolow, Professor of Medicine, and Chairman, Budget and Interdepartmental Relations Committee, Academic Senate; and W. O. Reinhardt, Dean, School of Medicine.

6. The group consisted of the signatories to the November 20, 1964, letter plus E. Page, Professor and Chairman, Department of Obstetrics and Gynecology; and E. Jawetz, Professor and Chairman, Department of Microbiology.

7. Malcolm S. M. Watts and Clark Jones, *The Story of the California AHEC System: California Area Health Education Centers: 1972–1989* (Fresno: California AHEC System, 1990); Charles Odegaard, *Eleven Area Health Education Centers: The View from the Grass Roots* (Berkeley: Carnegie Council on Policy Studies in Higher Education, 1980); and Carnegie Commission on Higher Education, *Higher Education and the Nation's Health: Policies for Medical and Dental Education* (New York: McGraw-Hill, 1970).

Chapter 23

1. Hugh Davis Graham and Nancy Diamond, *The Rise of the American Research Universities: Elites and Challengers in the Postwar Era* (Baltimore: Johns Hopkins University Press, 1997), 167.

2. Roger Geiger, *Research and Relevant Knowledge: American Research Universities since World War II* (New York: Oxford University Press, 1993), 143.

3. Dean E. McHenry, "Childhood, Education, and Teaching Career, 1910–1958" (Oral History Project, University of California, Santa Cruz, 1972), 1:138–40.

4. Verne A. Stadtman, "Expansion in the Southland," in *The University of California 1868–1968* (New York: McGraw-Hill, 1970).

5. Minutes of Committee on Educational Policy of the Board of Regents of the University of California, Lake Arrowhead, California, June 19, 1958, 280.

6. Handwritten memorandum of Robert Gordon Sproul, dated May 1951 (UC Archives, CU-301, Box 11, admin.).

7. As I shall note in *Political Turmoil*, Regent Pauley later sought to recruit outside normal channels, John McCone, head of the CIA, as my successor as president.

8. *Los Angeles Times*, June 17, 1994.

9. John S. Galbraith, "Academic Life and Governance of the University of California" (Department of Special Collections, Oral History Program, University Research Library, University of California, Los Angeles, 1982), 83.

10. The 20-year-plus club of presidents among the top ten research universities includes

Berkeley:	Benjamin Ide Wheeler, 1899–1919
	Robert Gordon Sproul, 1930–58
Chicago:	Robert Maynard Hutchins, 1929–51
Harvard:	Charles William Eliot, 1869–1909
	Abbott Lawrence Lowell, 1909–33
	James Bryant Conant, 1933–53
	Derek Bok, 1971–91
Michigan:	James B. Angell, 1871–1909
	Alexander Grant Ruthven, 1929–51
Princeton:	John Grier Hibben, 1912–32
	Harold Willis Dodds, 1933–57
Stanford:	David Starr Jordan, 1891–1913
	Ray Lyman Wilbur, 1915–42
UCLA:	Charles E. Young, 1968–97
Yale:	Arthur Twining Hadley, 1899–1921

A list of giants.

11. Vern O. Knudsen, "Teacher, Researcher, and Administrator" (Department of Special Collections, Oral History Program, University Research Library, University of California, Los Angeles, 1974), 3:1290–92.

12. For a somewhat similar appraisal of UCLA progress to that given above, see Geiger, *Research and Relevant Knowledge,* ch. 5.

13. See IGS Documentary Supplement 1.6 for my tribute to Young.

14. The 1998 ARL library rankings put Berkeley at number five and UCLA at number six.

Chapter 24

1. Henry Adams, *The Education of Henry Adams* (1918; New York: Modern Library, 1931), ch. 28.

2. Carl E. Schorske, "Intellectual Life, Civil Libertarian Issues, and the Student Movement at the University of California, Berkeley, 1960–1969," Regional Oral History Office, Bancroft Library, University of California, Berkeley (2000), 45.

3. "Report of the Committee on Senate Policy: State of the Campus Message," in *Notice of Meeting,* Berkeley Division, Academic Senate, October 11, 1965. Committee members were T. J. Kent, Jr. (city and regional planning), chair, I. M. Heyman (law), D. W. Louisell (law), M. E. Malia (history), J. R. Searle (philosophy), R. Y. Stanier (bacteriology), and S. S. Wolin (political science).

4. This was the Caleb Foote report, done in 1967 (University of California, Berkeley, Study Commission on University Governance, *The Culture of the University: Governance and Education* [San Francisco: Jossey-Bass, 1968]).

5. Neil J. Smelser, "Growth, Structural Change, and Conflict in California Public Higher Education, 1950–1970," in *Public Higher Education in California,* ed. Neil J. Smelser and Gabriel Almond (Berkeley: University of California Press, 1974), 76–77.

6. See the report of the Governance Advisory Group on the Regents, Berkeley Division, Academic Senate, May 14, 1996.

Chapter 25

1. In calculating the 1990s' library expenditures as a percentage of educational and general expenditures, teaching hospitals, auxiliary enterprises, and student financial aid have been excluded from total E&G.

2. As we go to press, the 1998 ARL rankings have been released, indicating some change in the UC campuses' positions. UCLA and UC-San Diego succumbed to the system's budgetary trend, moving to numbers 6 and 46, respectively. Berkeley stayed at number 5 from 1997 to 1998. No other institution in the top 20 changed its rank by more than two places except Stanford, now number 3, moving closer to its academic standing ("Holdings of University Research Libraries in U.S. and Canada, 1998–99," *Chronicle of Higher Education* 46, no. 37 [May 19, 2000]: A23; based on index developed by the ARL).

3. Charles E. Odegaard, *Area Health Education Centers: The Pioneering Years, 1972–1978* (Berkeley: Carnegie Council on Policy Studies in Higher Education, 1979); and Carnegie Commission on Higher Education, *Higher Education and the Nation's Health: Policies for Medical and Dental Education* (New York: McGraw-Hill, 1970).

4. For a history of this project, see Malcolm S. M. Watts, M.D., and Clark Jones, *The Story of the California AHEC System: California Area Health Education Centers: 1972–1989* (Fresno: California AHEC System, 1990).

5. For a list of properties, as of 1985, see the following report on this initiative: Uni-

versity of California, Office of the President, "Natural Reserve System: The First Twenty Years" (n.d., but internal evidence suggests 1985).

Chapter 26

1. List of the program's host institutions in Africa—*Ghana:* University of Ghana, Legon; University of Science & Technology, Kumasi. *South Africa:* University of Cape Town (pending final approval); University of Natal, Pietermaritzburg. • In the Americas—*Barbados:* University of the West Indies, Cave Hill. *Brazil:* Pontifical Catholic University of Rio de Janeiro. *Canada:* University of British Columbia, Vancouver. *Chile:* Pontifical Catholic University of Chile; University of Chile, Santiago. *Costa Rica:* Monteverde Institute; University of Costa Rica, San José. *Mexico:* Monterrey Institute of Technology; National Autonomous University of Mexico, Mexico City and Taxco; San Nicolás de Hidalgo University of Michoacán, Morelia. • In Asia—*China:* Beijing Normal University; Peking University, Beijing; Tsinghua University, Beijing. *Hong Kong:* Chinese University of Hong Kong; Hong Kong University of Science and Technology. *India:* University of Delhi. *Indonesia:* Gadjah Mada University, Yogyakarta; Indonesia Institute of the Arts, Yogyakarta. *Japan:* National Universities—Hitotsubashi University, Tokyo; Kyoto University; Osaka University; Tohoku University, Sendai; Tokyo Institute of Technology; University of Tokyo, Hongo and Komaba campuses; University of Tsukuba; Private Universities—Doshisha University, Kyoto; International Christian University, Tokyo; Meiji Gakuin University, Yokohama; Sophia University, Tokyo. *Korea:* Yonsei University, Seoul. *Singapore:* National University of Singapore. *Taiwan:* National Taiwan University, Taipei. *Thailand:* Chiang Mai University; Chulalongkorn University, Bangkok. • In Australia/New Zealand—*Australia:* Australian National University, Canberra; Flinders University of South Australia, Adelaide; La Trobe University, Melbourne; Monash University, Melbourne; University of Adelaide; University of Melbourne; University of New South Wales, Sydney; University of Queensland, Brisbane; University of Sydney; University of Western Australia, Perth; University of Wollongong. *New Zealand:* Lincoln University, Canterbury; Massey University, Palmerston North; University of Auckland; University of Canterbury, Christchurch; University of Otago, Dunedin; University of Waikata, Hamilton; Victoria University of Wellington. • In Europe—*Austria:* University of Vienna. *Denmark:* University of Copenhagen. *France:* École normale supérieure, Paris (rue d'Ulm); École normale supérieure at Fontenay/St-Cloud, Paris region; Institut d'Études politiques (Sciences Po), Paris; Paris Center for Critical Studies; University of Bordeaux; University of Grenoble; University of Lyon; University of Toulouse. *Germany:* Free University, Berlin; Georg-August University of Göttingen; Humboldt University, Berlin; Technical University, Berlin; University of Bayreuth; University of Potsdam, Berlin metropolitan area. *Hungary:* Central European University, Budapest; Eötvös Loránd University, Budapest. *Ireland:* National University of Ireland, Cork and Galway; University of Dublin (Trinity College). *Italy:* Bocconi University, Milan; Scuola normale superiore, Pisa; University Institute of Archi-

tecture, Venice; University of Bologna; University of Italian Studies for Foreigners, Siena; University of Padua; University of Venice. *Netherlands:* Maastricht University (pending final approval). *Russia:* European University, Moscow. *Spain:* Autonomous University of Barcelona; Autonomous University of Madrid; Complutense University of Madrid; University of Alcalá; University of Barcelona; University of Granada. *Sweden:* Lund University. *United Kingdom:* England—University of Birmingham; University of Bristol; University of East Anglia, Norwich; University of Essex, Colchester; University of Exeter; University of Kent; University of Lancaster; University of Leeds; University of London (Queen Mary and Westfield College; King's College); University of Nottingham; University of Sheffield; University of Sussex, Brighton; University of Warwick, Coventry; University of York. Scotland—University of Edinburgh; University of Glasgow; University of St. Andrews; University of Stirling. • In the Middle East—*Egypt:* American University in Cairo. *Israel:* Ben-Gurion University of the Negev; Hebrew University of Jerusalem.

2. Office of the President, "University of California Programs and Activities to Further Equality of Opportunity" (March 19, 1964), 3.

3. See the extended and totally factual discussion in Glenn T. Seaborg and Ray Colvig, *Roses from the Ashes* (Berkeley: Institute of Governmental Studies, University of California, 2000).

Chapter 27

1. Minutes of a dinner meeting of the Special Committee to Resurvey the Pension and Retiring Annuitants, Alumni House, Berkeley campus, March 13, 1958.

2. Harry R. Wellman, "Teaching, Research, and Administration, University of California 1925–1968" (Oral History, UCB, 1976), 228.

3. California Post-Secondary Education Commission, *Fiscal Profiles,* 1995 (Sacramento), Display 59.

4. Beardsley Ruml, *Memo to a College Trustee: A Report on Financial and Structural Problems of the Liberal College* (New York: Fund for the Advancement of Education and McGraw-Hill, 1959), 13.

5. Lincoln Constance, "Versatile Berkeley Botanist: Plant Taxonomy and University Governance" (Regional Oral History Office, Bancroft Library, University of California, Berkeley, 1987), 240.

6. Minutes of the Board of Regents, November 16, 1962.

7. The Berkeley ballot of April 17, 1963, may be summarized as follows (leaving out abstentions):

First ballot
Status quo	55 percent
Year-round operations	45 percent

Second ballot

Three equal-length terms	15 percent
16 + 16 + 12 calendar	38 percent
Four equal-length terms	47 percent

8. Wellman, "Teaching, Research, and Administration," 149.

9. Minutes of the Board of Regents, November 16, 1962.

10. "The Academic Plan of the University of California 1966–1976," 5.

11. [Office of the President], "Foreign Languages at the University of California" [1964].

12. See memorandum from Office of the President, "Appointment and Review of Department Chairmen" (March 29, 1960).

Chapter 28

1. Robert Nisbet, *Teachers and Scholars: A Memoir of Berkeley in Depression and War* (New Brunswick: Transaction Publishers, 1992).

2. Marvin L. Goldberger, Brendan A. Maher, and Pamela Ebert Flattau, eds., *Research-Doctorate Programs in the United States: Continuity and Change* (Washington, D.C.: National Academy Press, 1995). "Distinguished" programs received a score on faculty quality of 4.01 or higher; "strong" programs scored 3.01–4.00. Overall, 11 percent of all rated programs received "distinguished" ratings and 32 percent were "strong" (tb. 3-1, NRC).

3. Some of these studies are Rebecca Zames Margulies and Peter M. Blau, "America's Leading Professional Schools," *Change* 5, no. 9 (November 1973): 21–27; Peter M. Blau and Rebecca Zames Margulies, "The Reputations of American Professional Schools," *Change* 6, no. 10 (winter 1974–75): 42–47; "The Cartter Report on the Leading Schools of Education, Law, and Business, *Change* 9, no. 2 (February 1977): 44–48; "America's Best Graduate Schools," *U.S. News and World Report,* March 22, 1993, 51–73; "America's Best Graduate Schools," *U.S. News and World Report,* March 18, 1996, 79–103.

4. Hugh Davis Graham and Nancy Diamond, *The Rise of the American Research Universities: Elites and Challengers in the Postwar Era* (Baltimore: Johns Hopkins University Press, 1997).

5. Ibid., 193.

6. Ibid., 213.

7. Ibid., tb. 6.7 on 167.

8. "Small Can Be Beautiful, Too: UC Santa Cruz, Univ. Oregon Rank Among Scientific Elite," *Science Watch* 10, no. 10 (November 1990): 1–8.

9. Office of the President, University of California, "UC excels in research excellence, productivity at all campuses," *UC Focus* 12, no. 1 (August–September 1997): 1.

10. Quoted in Fabian Franklin, *The Life of Daniel Coit Gilman* (New York: Dodd, Mead, 1910), 162, 163.

11. For a highly informed and rather pessimistic discussion of the future of California, see Peter Schrag, *Paradise Lost: California's Experience and America's Future* (New York: New Press, 1998).

Acknowledgments

I am indebted to the following persons who gave so generously of their time in meeting with me to share their personal and institutional perspectives and in reviewing and commenting on the draft manuscript in its entirety or parts of it. This work was vastly improved with the aid of their helpful insights and corrections of facts. All of them have had careers within the University of California or have been associated with the university in some way and are insightful observers of and participants in its life. It should be noted that many of them have different views than mine both about details and about overall developments. All of them have helped me in my own understandings, but none should be held responsible for any of my opinions or statements of facts.

Many current UC staff members also took time out of their busy schedules to answer research questions and to provide and update information and statistics. They are too numerous to name, but their assistance is greatly appreciated.

Interviewees

(Those persons who were interviewed by my research associate, Marian Gade, are denoted by an asterisk [*])

Daniel G. Aldrich, Jr., chancellor, UCI, 1962–84

David Anthony,* provost, Oakes College, UCSC

James Arnold, professor emeritus of chemistry and biochemistry, UCSD

Jacquelynn Baas, director, Berkeley Art Museum and Pacific Film Archive, UCB, 1989–99

Frederick E. Balderston, vice president–budget and planning, 1966–70; academic assistant to the president, 1970–75, UC; professor emeritus, Haas School of Business, UCB

Al Baxter, former staff member, chancellor's office, UCB

Leslie L. Bennett, M.D., chair, department of physiology, UCB/UCSF, 1953–66; vice-chancellor, academic affairs, UCSF, 1966–71

Travis M. Bogard, chair, department of dramatic art, 1958–64; chair, Committee for Arts and Lectures, UCB, 1973–80

Earl C. Bolton, vice president–university relations, 1961–64; vice president–administration, 1964–66; vice president–governmental relations, 1966–68, UC

F. Thomas Bond,* provost, Revelle College, UCSD

Edmund G. "Pat" Brown, governor, State of California, 1959–67

Walter Burroughs, editor of leading newspaper in Orange County at time of UCI's founding

Edward W. Carter, UC regent, 1952–88 [chair, Educational Policy Committee, 1958–62; chair, Finance Committee, 1962–64; chair of board, 1964–66]

Hale Champion, press and executive secretary to Governor Edmund G. Brown, 1958–60; director, department of finance, State of California, 1961–66

Vernon I. Cheadle, chancellor, UCSB, 1962–77

William K. Coblentz, UC regent, 1964–80 [chair of board, 1976–78]

Robert W. Cole, director, CAL Performances, UCB

Lincoln Constance, dean, College of Letters and Science, 1955–62; vice-chancellor, 1962–65; professor emeritus of botany, UCB

Gloria Copeland, administrative assistant to the chancellor, UCB, 1953–58; executive assistant to the president, UC, 1958–67

Michael Cowan,* chair, American Studies, UCSC

Ann L. Craig,* provost, Eleanor Roosevelt College, UCSD

Deborah Day,* archivist, Scripps Institution of Oceanography, UCSD

Louis DeMonte, campus architect, UCB, 1964–73

John Dizikes,* professor, American Studies, UCSC

Paul Dodd, dean, College of Letters and Science, UCLA, 1946–60

David Dodson,* chief administrative officer, Oakes College, UCSC

Sanford S. Elberg, dean of the graduate division, 1961–78; professor emeritus of public health, UCB

Robert J. Evans, university architect, 1939–72

Kathy Foley,* provost, Porter College, UCSC

Carol Freeman,* provost, Cowell College, UCSC

Loren M. Furtado, budget officer, 1964–65; assistant vice president and director of budget, UC, 1965–79

John S. Galbraith, chancellor, UCSD, 1965–68

W. F. Goldfrank,* provost, College Eight, UCSC

M. R. C. Greenwood, chancellor, UCSC

E. T. Grether, dean, College of Commerce (later School of Business Administration; Graduate School of Business Administration), UCB, 1941–61; vice chair, Assembly of the Academic Senate and Academic Council, 1964–65; chair, 1965–66

Roger W. Heyns, chancellor, UCB, 1965–71

Ivan H. Hinderaker, chancellor, UCR, 1964–79

Charles J. Hitch, vice president–university administration, 1966–68; 13th president, UC, 1968–75

John Isbister,* provost, Merrill College, UCSC

David K. Jordan,* provost, Warren College, UCSD

J. R. K. Kantor, university archivist, the Bancroft Library, UCB, 1964–84

Dana M. Kawaoka,* student, Oakes College, UCSC, 1994–98

Walter Kohn, chair, department of physics, UCSD, 1961–63; chair, San Diego division, Academic Senate, 1965–66; professor emeritus of physics, UCSB

Leo F. LaPorte,* associate vice-chancellor for undergraduate education and provost, Crown College, UCSC

Patrick J. Ledden,* provost, Muir College, UCSD

Cecil W. Lytle,* provost, Thurgood Marshall College, UCSD

Errol W. Mauchlan, administrative assistant to chancellor, 1958–61; assistant to chancellor, 1961–63; assistant chancellor, 1963–72; assistant chancellor–budget and planning, UCB, 1972–91; acting associate chancellor–planning and budget, UCSC, 1991–93

Dean E. McHenry, academic assistant to the president, 1958–60; university dean of academic planning, UC, 1960–63; chancellor, UCSC, 1961–74

Samuel C. McCulloch, professor emeritus of history, UCI

Morton A. Meyer, M.D., assistant then associate clinical professor of medicine, UCSF, 1951–65; chief of medicine, Cowell Hospital, UCB, 1959–92; clinical professor of medicine, UCSF, 1965–96; chair of clinical faculty, School of Medicine, UCSF, 1986–95

Martin Meyerson, acting chancellor, UCB, 1965

Elmo Morgan, vice president–physical planning and construction, UC, 1965–67

Ernie Mort,* dean of student affairs, Revelle College, UCSD

Emil Mrak, chancellor, UCD, 1959–69

Walter Munk, professor, Institute of Geophysics and Planetary Physics, Scripps Institution of Oceanography, UCSD

John W. Oswald, vice president–executive assistant, 1961–62; vice president–administration, UC, 1962–63; later president, University of Kentucky and Penn State; chair of Association of American Universities

William H. Parker,* associate executive vice-chancellor, UCI

Jack W. Peltason, chancellor, UCI, 1984–92; 16th president, UC, 1992–95

Karl S. Pister, chancellor, UCSC, 1991–96

A. Alan Post, legislative analyst, California legislature, 1950–77

William O. Reinhardt, M.D., chair, department of anatomy, UCB/UCSF, 1956–63; dean, School of Medicine, UCSF, 1963–66

Roger Revelle, director, Scripps Institution of Oceanography, 1951–64; dean, School of Science and Engineering, UCSD, 1959–61; university dean of research, UC, 1962–64

William M. Roberts, university archivist, the Bancroft Library, UCB, 1985–

Nancy Rockafellar, director, UCSF Campus Oral History Program, department of the history of health sciences, UCSF, 1994–

William M. Roth, UC regent, 1961–77

M. Lea Rudee,* former provost, Warren College; professor/coordinator, material science, electrical and computer engineering, UCSD

Paul D. Saltman,* former provost, Revelle College; professor of biology, UCSD

Glenn T. Seaborg, UCB faculty representative to Pacific Coast Conference, 1952–58; chancellor, UCB, 1958–61; University Professor of Chemistry, UC

Norton Simon, UC regent, 1960–76

Paul Skenazy,* provost, Kresge College, UCSC

Neil J. Smelser, assistant chancellor for educational development, UCB, 1966–68; University Professor of Sociology, UC; director, Center for Advanced Study in the Behavioral Sciences

Lloyd H. Smith, M.D., chair, School of Medicine, 1964–85; associate dean, School of Medicine, UCSF, 1985–

C. Page Smith, provost, Cowell College, UCSC, 1964–70

Sandra Smith,* assistant vice president for planning and analysis, UC

Virginia B. Smith, assistant vice president, UC, 1964–67

F. Edwin Spafford, former assistant to chancellor, UCD

Herman T. Spieth, provost, 1956–58, chancellor, UCR, 1958–64

Verne A. Stadtman, editor, *The Centennial Record of the University of California;* author, *The University of California 1868–1968*

Robert Stevens, chancellor, UCSC, 1987–91

John L. Stewart,* founding provost, Muir College, UCSD

Paul K. Stumpf, professor emeritus of biochemistry, UCD

R. Michael Tanner, executive vice-chancellor, UCSC

Angus E. Taylor, chair, department of mathematics, UCLA, 1958–64; chair, Assembly of the Academic Senate, UC, 1964–65; chair, Academic Council, UC, 1964–65; vice president–academic affairs, 1965–74; vice president–academic affairs and personnel, 1974–75; university provost, UC, 1975; acting chancellor then chancellor, UCSC, 1976–77

Louise Taylor, principal clerk, accounting office, then office of planning and analysis; later director, office of planning and analysis, UCB, 1964–98

Martin A. Trow, professor, department of sociology, 1953–93; director, Center for Studies in Higher Education, 1976–88; professor emeritus, Graduate School of Public Policy, UCB

Robert D. Tschirgi, university dean of academic planning, UC, 1964–66

Joseph Tussman, professor emeritus of philosophy, UCB

Larry N. Vanderhoef, acting chancellor then chancellor, UCD, 1994–

Peter S. Van Houten, director, Graduate School Services, UCB, 1973–99

Joseph W. Watson,* former provost, Thurgood Marshall College; vice chancellor–student affairs, UCSD

Harry R. Wellman, vice president–agricultural sciences, 1952–58; vice president of the university, 1958–67; acting president, UC, 1967

Garff Wilson, director, Office of Public Ceremonies, 1943–76; professor emeritus of rhetoric and dramatic art, UCB

Sally Woodbridge, architectural historian and writer

Herbert F. York, chancellor, 1961–64; acting chancellor, 1970–71; director emeritus, Institute for Global Conflict and Cooperation, UCSD

Reviewers

The following persons read, reviewed, and commented on one or more chapters. Those who had an opportunity to read and to review the manuscript in its entirety are set in boldface. Nearly all made specific suggestions about the manuscript. A very few made general comments only, although they did have the opportunity to comment in detail if they so wished.

Maynard A. Amerine, professor emeritus of enology, UCD

Richard C. Atkinson, chancellor, UCSD, 1980–95; 17th president, UC

Frederick E. Balderston, vice president–budget and planning, 1966–70; academic assistant to the president, 1970–75, UC; professor emeritus, Haas School of Business, UCB

Irving Bernstein, professor emeritus of political science, UCLA

Joseph F. Bunnett, professor emeritus of chemistry, UCSC

Patrick M. Callan, executive director, California Higher Education Policy Center; president, National Center for Public Policy and Higher Education

Albert Carnesale, chancellor, UCLA, 1997–

Everett Carter, vice-chancellor, UCD, 1959–63; university dean–research, UC, 1964–66

Carol Christ, executive vice-chancellor and provost, UCB, 1994–2000

Burton R. Clark, Allan M. Cartter Professor of Higher Education Emeritus, UCLA

Raymond Colvig, public information officer, UCB, 1964–91

Lincoln Constance, dean, College of Letters and Science, 1955–62; vice-chancellor, 1962–65; professor emeritus of botany, UCB

Gloria Copeland, administrative assistant to the chancellor, UCB, 1953–58; executive assistant to the president, UC, 1958–67

John Cummins, assistant chancellor–chief of staff, chancellor's office, UCB

Deborah Day, archivist, Scripps Institution of Oceanography, UCSD

Louis DeMonte, campus architect, UCB, 1964–73

John Dizikes, professor, American studies, UCSC

John A. Douglass, executive director, UCSB Academic Senate, 1991–97; policy analyst, universitywide Academic Senate, 1997–98; research fellow, Center for Studies in Higher Education, UCB, 1997–

Sanford S. Elberg, dean of the graduate division, 1961–78; professor emeritus of public health, UCB

Robert J. Evans, university architect, 1939–72

Kathy Foley, provost, Porter College, UCSC

William Forbes, UC regent, 1962–77

Carol Freeman, provost, Cowell College, UCSC

Loren M. Furtado, budget officer, 1964–65; assistant vice president and director of budget, UC, 1965–79

John Kenneth Galbraith, Ph.D., UCB, 1934; Paul M. Warburg Professor of Economics Emeritus, Harvard University

David P. Gardner, 15th president, UC, 1983–92

W. F. Goldfrank, provost, College Eight, UCSC

M. R. C. Greenwood, chancellor, UCSC

Louis H. Heilbron, chair, California State Board of Education, 1960–61; first chair, California State College System Board of Trustees, 1960–63

Ivan H. Hinderaker, chancellor, UCR, 1964–79

David K. Jordan, provost, Warren College, UCSD

J. R. K. Kantor, university archivist, the Bancroft Library, UCB, 1964–84

Dana M. Kawaoka, student, Oakes College, UCSC, 1994–98

Catherine Kerr, environmentalist; presidential spouse

Leo F. LaPorte, associate vice-chancellor for undergraduate education and provost, Crown College, UCSC

Patrick J. Ledden, provost, Muir College, UCSD

Eugene C. Lee, vice president–executive assistant, UC, 1965–67; professor emeritus of political science, UCB

Gerald Lowell, university librarian, UCSD, 1993–98; university librarian, UCB, 1998–2000

Errol W. Mauchlan, administrative assistant to chancellor, 1958–61; assistant to chancellor, 1961–63; assistant chancellor, 1963–72; assistant chancellor–budget and planning, UCB, 1972–91; acting associate chancellor–planning and budget, UCSC, 1991–93

Chester O. McCorkle, Jr., acting vice-chancellor, 1963–64; vice-chancellor–academic affairs, UCD, 1964–66; vice president, UC, 1974–78; professor emeritus of agriculture and resource economics, UCD

Samuel C. McCulloch, professor emeritus of history, UCI

Dean E. McHenry, academic assistant to the president, 1958–60; university dean of academic planning, UC, 1960–63; chancellor, UCSC, 1961–74

Duncan Mellichamp, chair, Academic Council, UC, 1996–97

Morton A. Meyer, M.D., assistant and associate clinical professor of medicine, UCSF, 1951–65; chief of medicine, Cowell Hospital, UCB, 1959–92; clinical professor of medicine, UCSF, 1965–96; chair of clinical faculty, School of Medicine, UCSF, 1986–95

Martin Meyerson, acting chancellor, UCB, 1965

Meredith Michaels, director of the budget, internal coordination, UC

Theodore R. Mitchell, dean, School of Education and Information Studies, UCLA; vice-chancellor, academic planning and budget, and vice-chancellor, external affairs, UCLA, 1992–98

Barry Munitz, chancellor, the California State University, 1991–97

Jack Peltason, chancellor UCI, 1984–92; 16th president, UC, 1992–95

Karl Pister, chancellor, UCSC, 1991–96

A. Alan Post, legislative analyst, California legislature, 1950–77

John R. Raleigh, vice-chancellor–academic affairs, 1969–72; professor emeritus of English, UCB

Richard Randolph, professor emeritus of anthropology, UCSC

David Riesman, Henry Ford II Professor of Social Sciences Emeritus, Harvard University

William Roberts, university archivist, the Bancroft Library, UCB, 1985–

Nancy Rockafellar, director, UCSF Campus Oral History Program, department of the history of health sciences, UCSF, 1994–

Sheldon Rothblatt, dean, division of freshman and sophomore studies, College of Letters and Science, 1982–83; director, Center for Studies in Higher Education, 1989–96; professor emeritus of history, UCB

Paul D. Saltman, former provost, Revelle College; professor of biology, UCSD

David Saxon, 16th president, UC, 1975–83

Glenn T. Seaborg, UCB faculty representative to Pacific Coast Conference, 1952–58; chancellor, UCB, 1958–61; University Professor of Chemistry, UC

Eli Silver, chair, Santa Cruz division, Academic Senate, UCSC, 1966–97; professor of earth sciences, UCSC

Daniel L. Simmons, associate provost, educational relations, UC, 1996–97

Neil J. Smelser, assistant chancellor for educational development, UCB, 1966–68; University Professor of Sociology, UC; director, Center for Advanced Study in the Behavioral Sciences

Lloyd H. Smith, M.D., chair, School of Medicine, 1964–85; associate dean, School of Medicine, UCSF, 1985–

Verne A. Stadtman, editor, *The Centennial Record of the University of California;* author, *The University of California 1868–1968*

Paul K. Stumpf, professor emeritus of biochemistry, UCD

Virginia B. Smith, assistant vice president, UC, 1964–67

R. Michael Tanner, executive vice-chancellor, UCSC

Angus E. Taylor, chair, department of mathematics, UCLA, 1958–64; chair, Assembly of the Academic Senate, UC, 1964–65; chair, Academic Council, UC, 1964–65; vice president–academic affairs, 1965–74; vice president–academic affairs and personnel, 1974–75; university provost, UC, 1975; acting chancellor then chancellor, UCSC, 1976–77

Louise E. Taylor, director of planning and analysis, UCB

Chang-Lin Tien, chancellor, UCB, 1990–97

William Trombley, former education writer, *Los Angeles Times;* senior editor, California Higher Education Policy Center and National Center for Public Policy and Higher Education

Martin Trow, professor, department of sociology, 1953–93; director, Center for Studies in Higher Education, 1976–88; professor emeritus, Graduate School of Public Policy, UCB

Joseph Tussman, professor emeritus of philosophy, UCB
Peter S. Van Houten, director, Graduate School Services, UCB, 1973–99
Harry R. Wellman, vice president–agricultural sciences, 1952–58; vice president
   of the university, 1958–67; acting president, UC, 1967
John W. Whinnery, dean, College of Engineering, UCB, 1959–63
Sally Woodbridge, architectural historian and writer
Herbert York, chancellor, 1961–64; acting chancellor, 1970–71; director emeritus,
   Institute for Global Conflict and Cooperation, UCSD
Charles E. Young, chancellor, UCLA, 1968–97

Credits

The following publishers have generously given permission to use extended quotations from copyrighted works. FROM *There Was Light: Autobiography of a University: A Collection of Essays by Alumni of the University of California, Berkeley, 1868-1996,* edited by Irving Stone, updated by Jean Stone. Copyrighted 1970, 1996 by The Regents of the University of California. FROM "Fifty Years from Now," by Kenneth Cardwell and William C. Hays. *California Monthly,* April 1954, 20–21. FROM *The Perpetual Dream: Reform and Experiment in the American College,* by Gerald Grant and David Riesman. Copyright 1978 by the University of Chicago Press. FROM *Higher Education Cannot Escape History: Issues for the Twenty-First Century,* by Clark Kerr. Copyright 1994 by the State University of New York Press; all rights reserved. FROM "A Critical Age in the University World: Accumulated heritage versus modern imperatives," by Clark Kerr. *European Journal of Education* 22, no. 2 (1987): 183–93. Used with the permission of Carfax Publishing Limited, P.O. Box 25, Abingdon, Oxfordshire OX14 3UE, United Kingdom. FROM *The Uses of the University,* by Clark Kerr. Copyright 1963 by the President and Fellows of Harvard College. Reprinted by permission of Harvard University Press. FROM *Research-Doctorate Programs in the United States: Continuity and Change* by Marvin L. Goldberger, Brendan A. Maher, and Pamela Ebert Flattau, eds. Copyright 1995 by the National Academy Press, Washington, D.C. FROM *The Rise of American Research Universities,* by Hugh Davis Graham and Nancy Diamond. Copyright 1997 by The Johns Hopkins University Press. FROM David S. Webster and Tad Skinner, "Rating PhD Programs: What the NRC Report Says . . . And Doesn't Say," *Change* 28, no. 3 [May–June 1996]: 36, 37, 39, 40). Copyright 1996 by Heldref Publications, 1319 18th St., N.W., Washington, D.C. 20036–1802; reprinted with permission of the Helen Dwight Reid Educational Foundation.

The Regents of the University of California and the following depositories have also given permission to use extended quotations. FROM the oral histories of Lincoln Constance, Sanford S. Elberg, Stephen C. Pepper, and Harry R. Wellman, in the Regional Oral History Project, Bancroft Library, University of California, Berkeley, 1963–90. FROM the oral histories of Hansena Frederickson, John S. Galbraith, and Vern O. Knudsen, in the Department of Special Collections, Oral History Program, University Research Library, University of California, Los Angeles 1969–82.

Index

activism, student *(continued)*
280, 281–83, 286–87, 293, 294, 295;
Sherriffs vs., 107; vs. teaching assistants instead of faculty, 263, 404.
See also politics
activist-radical model, 270, 281, 282
Adams, Henry, 348
Additional Centers report (1957), 79–80,
180
administration, 14, 23, 225–28; of academic innovations, 268–76; constant
adjustments in, 219, 220, 225; full-
time positions (1957–65), 212*table*,
213*table;* health science centers, 326;
innovations in, 279–80; Lee as authority on, 205; micromanagement/
line-item, 17, 19, 145, 159, 163, 191–92,
200, 321; models of, 60, 90, 93–105,
143–44, 145, 225–31; Sproul methods,
17–20, 23, 25, 40, 46–47, 51, 52, 93,
145, 191–92, 196, 201, 226; universitywide, 155, 164, 192–94, 199–205, 211,
222, 235–40, 258. *See also* Academic
Senate; administration courses; budget; chancellorships; committees,
faculty; deans; decentralization; governance; planning; presidency; pro-
vostships; regents; reorganizations
administration courses, 271, 272, 303.
See also business administration
admission policies: governance of,
221, 223; Master Plan, 183; regents
forbidding affirmative action (1995),
228, 356; Santa Barbara, 311. *See also*
equal opportunities for students;
open access
aesthetic-expressive model, 269, 281
affirmative action, regents vs. (1995),
228, 356
AFL-CIO, 7
African Americans: Bunche, 337; on chancellor's staff, 25; Philadelphia, 13
African-American studies, 350
African studies, 398
agenda, administrative, 29, 153–71
agriculture: Aldrich at Irvine and, 251;

Berkeley campus, 85, 88, 303, 398;
Davis campus, 18, 85, 303–7, 313, 371,
398; Davis community, 304–7; faculty rankings, 432*table;* Kerr appointments from, 159; labor, 4–5, 14, 135,
378; public service related to, 372;
Riverside campus, 313, 315, 317–18,
398; Taylor views, 135; UC benefits
to, 143–44, 413; UCLA discontinuance of, 207–8, 313, 398; universitywide approach, 397–98
Ahlport, Brodie, 44, 139, 336
Aigues-Mortes, 247
Albany Village, 94
Aldrich, Daniel, 244, 247, 251–52,
370–71
Aldrich Park, Irvine, 247
Alexander Meiklejohn Award for Contributions to Academic Freedom, 146
Allaway, William, 312, 376
Allen, Raymond, 47–51, 154–55, 196, 330,
334–36; and loyalty oath/communism,
48, 129, 133, 154; and presidency, 48,
50–51, 154–55, 335
Almaden Valley site, 245–46
alumni: and fraternities and sororities,
383; Santa Barbara, 311; Santa Cruz,
300; UCLA, 19, 48, 195, 329, 337–38,
384. *See also* Berkeley alumni
American Association of University
Professors, 27, 31, 62, 146
American Council on Education, 57
American Friends Service Committee
(AFSC), 4, 13, 376. *See also* Quakers
American Library Association, 367
American Medical Association, 322
Amerine, Maynard, 305
Anderson, Nancy Scott, 260
Annis, Barbara, 30
Antioch College, 12, 311
arbitration, industrial relations, 14, 34,
47, 137–38
Archer, James, 248–49
Architects and Engineers Office, Berke-
ley, 114, 115
architecture: Berkeley campus, 111, 112,

budget *(continued)*
366; line-item, 159, 163, 191–92, 200; lower-division courses and, 83; lump-sum, 68–69, 222, 223, 230, 413; medical school, 369–70, 372, 409; planning, 82; presidential instead of regental, 39; and rankings, 68–69, 347; retirement, 386–88; Riverside campus, 318; San Diego campus, 255, 256, 257, 258; Santa Cruz campus, 298; scandals, 223; Scripps Institution of Oceanography, 256; Simon-Kerr debate over, 202–3; Sproul and, 17, 54, 159, 191–92; for student facilities, 93, 94, 99, 102, 105; student fees, 102; for teaching assistants, 353; UCLA, 17, 329, 332, 339; and university property ownership, 119; year-round operations, 396, 397. *See also* federal funds; finance committees; salaries; state funds

budget committees, Academic Senate, 28, 63, 65, 211, 394

Buildings and Campus Development Committee (BCDC), 28, 72–73, 102, 106–7, 114, 117, 122

Bunche, Ralph, 337, 379

Burdick, Eugene, 31

Burns, Hugh, 166

Burns committee (Senate Committee on Un-American Activities), 139, 154, 415; "contact man" on campus, 19, 130, 132, 145, 166, 204

business administration: academic planning and, 86–87; physical space, 114, 120, 124, 127; telic innovations, 271, 272

business affairs: regent responsibility for, 203. *See also* finance committees

business manager, campus, 49–50

Butler, Nicholas Murray, 225

Byrne, Jerome, 208, 209, 210

Byrne report (1965), 208–11, 214, 225, 353

Cal Band, 107

Cal Club, 93, 104; decentralization and,

164, 202; UCLA, 109, 339; university-wide, 222, 308, 311–12

California: constitution, 130, 220; defense industry, 153, 161; economics, 56, 78, 153, 189–90, 356, 414; gold rushes, 416–18; in-migration, 153; and loyalty oath, 8, 19; population, 72, 161, 237, 369; research universities, 172, 184, 237, 239; State Supreme Court, 9, 131; university support, 56, 78, 79, 153, 161–62. *See also* Board of Education; California legislature; governors; Master Plan for Higher Education in California; state college system, California

California Alumni Association, 98. *See also* Berkeley alumni

California College of Medicine, 369, 370–71

California Hall, 112

California Labor School, 131

California legislature: Corley and, 50, 166, 194, 204, 329, 370; and higher education planning, 174, 175, 179, 180, 182, 186; and loyalty oath, 8, 19, 130, 139; and medical schools, 370; Mrak/Davis campus and, 305, 306; physical development planning and, 119, 120; Post as analyst for, 161, 307; and Riverside campus, 314; and Santa Barbara campus, 308; Senate Committee on Finance, 162, 180, 307, 370; and student revolts (1960s), 354; and UCLA, 329–30, 334, 339, 344; united UC approach to, 218. *See also* Burns committee; state funds

California Postsecondary Education Commission, 290

California State Polytechnic College (Cal Poly), San Luis Obispo, 177

California State Scholarship Program, 183, 188

California State University (CSU), 174, 181–82, 185, 187–88, 411. *See also* state college system, California

Cal Performances, 53

Davis campus, 18, 20, 145, 147, 156, 302, 303–8; AAU membership, 351, 409; Academic Senate, 306, 307, 352, 355; agricultural studies, 18, 85, 303–7, 313, 371, 398; Bodega Bay Marine Laboratory under, 350; chancellorships, 305–8, 349; College of Letters and Science, 18, 158, 303; community spirit, 304–5, 306; cultural programs, 306–7, 373; and enrollment growth, 72, 169, 303; as general campus, 238, 303, 327; joint doctorate program, 188; library, 364; medical school, 154, 306, 307, 370; rankings, 407, 408, 409, 410, 412, 432table; Shields founding, 307; site selection, 241; specialized programs, 361; Spieth transfer to, 316; student residences, 94
Dazai, Osamu, 26
deans: academic, 27, 56, 63, 320, 400; of medicine, 216; of students, 32, 52, 106, 107; terms of, 320, 400; UCLA, 340–42; of women, 107. See also Council of Deans
decentralization, 39–40, 43–55, 191–231, 414; Berkeley privileges and, 351, 355; changes (since 1966), 221–25; Corley and, 194, 203–4; first major (1891), 39, 195; in industry, 221; during Kerr presidency (1957–59), 40, 160, 163–64, 191–219; Murphy vs., 203, 206, 208, 209, 211–18, 225, 338; reconsiderations of, 219–31; regents and, 19, 39–40, 156, 192–214, 220, 224, 227, 230; second look at (1965), 206–18; Sproul and, 19, 20, 40, 44, 196, 197, 224. See also autonomy; centralization; reorganizations
defense industry, 153, 161. See also Department of Defense, U.S.; military research; ROTC
Defense Language Institute, Monterey, 399
DeMars, Vernon, 123
DeMonte, Louis A., 115
Department of Defense, U.S., 380–82

departments, 67–70, 192, 298; academic planning and, 83–89; chairs, 50–51, 64, 65, 320, 400; deans, 27, 63, 320, 400; with "distinguished" rankings, 345, 405–6, 409, 430–31table; ladder faculty, 69, 88table; Santa Cruz campus and, 278–79; size, 75–76
Deukmejian, George, 414, 415
Deutsch, Monroe, 23, 30, 34, 42, 43, 45, 49, 53
Dewey, Tom, 135
Diamond, Nancy, 408, 412
Dickson, Edward A., 43, 139, 328–29; anticommunism, 48, 130–31, 132; and decentralization, 196, 224; and Kerr commencement speech, 136; and regent chairmanship, 141, 165, 200, 328; and UCLA, 43, 48, 240, 328–29, 342
Dilworth, Nelson, 314
discrimination, 382–83; in fraternities and sororities, 109, 146, 382–83; loyalty oath and, 131, 133, 138–39. See also equal opportunities for students; exclusionary policy
diversity: ecological, 373; of programs and personalities, 169; student, 354, 356, 379. See also equal opportunities for students; multiculturalism
Docking, governor of Kansas, 338, 486n12
doctorate. See Ph.D. training
Dodd, Paul, 17, 164, 330, 334, 337, 341, 342
Doe Library, Berkeley, 112, 127
dogs, campus, 7, 41, 42
Donohoe, Dorothy, 180
Donohoe Act, 180. See also Master Plan for Higher Education in California (1960)
Duke University, rankings, 407
Dumke, Glenn, 177, 180–81, 182–83, 185
Dunlop, John, 136
Dunphy, J. E., 321, 324
duplication of programs, among campuses, 239–40, 390–91, 397–99

programs at UC campuses, 429*table;* reputational (1906), 59*table;* reputational (1964), 58*table;* Riverside, 314, 408, 410, 411; ten best liberal arts colleges, 314; by test scores, 410–12, 433*table,* 438*table;* top twenty, 340–41*table,* 356, 406, 417; Webster and Skinner report on, 439–41. *See also* Berkeley academic rankings; Big Six research universities; Harvard University rankings; research universities; UCLA academic rankings

Rappard Institute (Geneva), 376

Reagan, Ronald, 166, 303, 382, 414, 415; and faculty salaries, 389; vs. Kerr, 36, 139, 140; and People's Park, 127–28; and recentralization, 221; Sherriffs as adviser to, 32; USC connections, 167; and year-round operations, 396

"reaggregation," Santa Cruz campus, 284

red hysteria, 129–42, 146. *See also* communism; loyalty oath

regal functions, presidential, 214–18, 222

regents, 39–40, 146, 148–50, 231; and academic planning, 74–75, 78, 82, 86, 142; vs. affirmative action (1995), 228, 356; Allen rejected by, 154–55, 334–35; and athletics, 109, 384; autonomy, 227, 413; Berkeley's distinction maintained by, 347; and California Board of Education, 79, 175, 179, 180, 236; chairs, 141, 165, 200, 244, 328; chancellorships created by (1951), 39–40, 139, 145, 219; Clark initiative by, 335–36; commitment and accomplishments (1958–66), 162–63; Committee on Educational Policy, 78, 155, 174–75, 230, 331, 333–34, 380, 382; consultative style and, 163–64, 201, 202; and Davis chancellorship, 305; and decentralization, 19, 39–40, 156, 192–214, 220, 224, 227, 230; and equal opportunities for campuses, 147, 158, 327, 330–34, 338, 339, 344, 345, 349–57, 363–66; and equal opportunity for

students, 109, 146, 185, 186, 268, 378, 379; and faculty appointments and tenure, 63, 140, 207, 211; and faculty clubs, 201, 485n8; and faculty retirement plan, 385–87; and faculty revolt (1919–20), 8–9, 61; finance committee, 24, 195, 198, 230, 378; and fraternities and sororities, 383; Hearst (Phoebe) as, 112–13, 115–17; and Kent report, 353–54; and Kerr appointments from agriculture, 159; Kerr appointment to presidency, 154–56, 160; and Kerr chancellorship, 9, 24, 25, 27, 28, 36, 39–40, 45–50, 54, 139; Kerr dismissal from presidency, 140, 141, 142, 200; and libraries, 363–64; and loyalty oath, 8–9, 35–36, 104, 129, 130–34, 138–42, 144–45, 165; and Master Plan, 180; and natural reserve system, 373; and new campuses, 80, 156, 157, 169, 235, 236, 240–59, 302–3, 371; and People's Park, 128; and physical development planning, 71–72, 74–75, 82, 94, 111, 114–18, 122, 123, 146; president's report, 162; and private college and university agreements, 167; and Riverside campus, 315–16; and ROTC, 380–82; and San Francisco campus, 323–24, 325; and Santa Barbara campus, 309; Simon strategy, 202–3; southern, 19, 20, 40, 43–44, 48, 154, 162, 196, 198, 329, 331, 334–37, 386; and Sproul, 19, 20, 40, 195, 335–36; and state college system, 156–57, 175, 178; and Strong chancellorship, 349; and student housing, 94, 95, 98–99, 102–3, 237; and study abroad programs, 376, 377; and UCLA, 40, 43–44, 198, 329–37, 338; Wheeler-Sproul-Academic Senate model and, 144; and year-round operations, 392, 393–95, 397. *See also* Carter, Edward; Dickson, Edward A.

regional colleges, 308, 312

Reinhardt, William, 320–21, 324

religions, academic planning and, 86, 89

University of Illinois: cultural programs, 121; faculty salaries, 388; rankings, 57–58, 78, 368–69, 406, 407
University of Kansas, Murphy and, 208, 209, 216, 217, 218, 338, 344
University of London, School of Oriental Studies, 398
University of Michigan: autonomous regents, 227; cultural programs, 121; enrollment growth, 72; experimental undergraduate colleges, 264, 273; faculty salaries, 388; library, 365; rankings, 18, 56–59, 70, 77, 78, 405–7, 411, 412
University of Minnesota, 72, 381
University of North Carolina, rankings, 406
University of Pennsylvania (Penn), rankings, 405, 406, 407
University of Pittsburgh, Cathedral of Learning, 75
University of Southern California (USC), 108, 166–67, 237, 369
University of Texas: enrollment growth, 72; rankings, 77, 78, 369, 406
University of Virginia, faculty salaries, 388
University of Washington: Allen at, 48, 154, 330; Kerr at, 6, 14, 135; quarter system, 395; rankings, 405, 406, 407; Smith at, 159; Taylor at, 31
University of Wisconsin: enrollment growth, 72; rankings, 57–58, 77, 78, 406, 407; Van Hise and community integration, 344
Unruh, Jesse, 180
Urey, Harold, 255
USC. *See* University of Southern California
The Uses of the University (Kerr), 70

Valley Life Sciences Building, 127
veterinary medicine, Davis, 303
vice-chancellorships, 32, 53–54, 89, 222, 307, 311–12
vice presidency, 198

Vietnam War, 286, 287, 382
Virus Laboratory, 84
vocational studies, 268, 283, 290. *See also* labor
Vosper, Robert, 364, 366

Wagner, Albert R., 115
Wahlquist, John, 176, 177
Waldorf, Lynn ("Pappy"), 97, 107
Walrus Club, 134
war: Cold, 153; Vietnam, 286, 287, 382; World War I, 13, 61, 168, 377. *See also* World War II
War and Peace (Tolstoy), 37–38
War Labor Board, 14
Warren, Earl, 56, 309; and Kerr presidency, 155; and labor relations, 6, 135; and loyalty oath, 8; regent appointees, 162–63
Warren, Stafford, 330, 342
Warwick University, 264
Waterfront Employers' Association, 3, 137
Watkins, Gordon, 262, 308, 313, 315–16, 318, 330, 342
Watkins college, Riverside campus as, 158, 266, 313–14, 316, 318–19, 410
Watson, Joseph, 275
Weber, Max, 298
Webster, David S., 439–41
Welcker, William Thomas, 60
Welfare Committee, Academic Senate, 387
Wellman, Harry R., 33, 158, 240, 398; academic procession account, 215; administrative work, 158, 207, 211, 240; on Byrne report, 209, 225; on Corley, 194; and Davis campus, 304, 305, 307; and department chair appointments, 51; and faculty retirement plan, 387; and industrial arts faculty, 309; and Oswald, 159; and Riverside campus, 315–16; and San Diego campus, 256, 257, 258; and San Francisco campus, 321, 322;

Designer: Nola Burger
Compositor: Integrated Composition Systems
Text: Adobe Garamond
Display: Scala Sans, Walbaum
Printer/Binder: Friesen Corporation
Illustrations: Bill Nelson
Index: Barbara Roos